11th Conference on Lexical and Computational Semantics (*SEM 2022)

Online
14 - 15 July 2022

ISBN: 978-1-7138-5641-2

Printed from e-media with permission by:

Curran Associates, Inc.
57 Morehouse Lane
Red Hook, NY 12571

Some format issues inherent in the e-media version may also appear in this print version.

Printed with permission by Curran Associates, Inc. (2022)

For permission requests, please contact the Association for Computational Linguistics at the address below.

Association for Computational Linguistics
209 N. Eighth Street
Stroudsburg, Pennsylvania 18360

Phone: 1-570-476-8006
Fax: 1-570-476-0860

acl@aclweb.org

Additional copies of this publication are available from:

Curran Associates, Inc.
57 Morehouse Lane
Red Hook, NY 12571 USA
Phone: 845-758-0400
Fax: 845-758-2633
Email: curran@proceedings.com
Web: www.proceedings.com

*SEM 2022

The 11th Joint Conference on Lexical and Computational Semantics

Proceedings of the Conference

July 14-15, 2022

Order copies of this and other ACL proceedings from:

Association for Computational Linguistics (ACL)
209 N. Eighth Street
Stroudsburg, PA 18360
USA
Tel: +1-570-476-8006
Fax: +1-570-476-0860
acl@aclweb.org

Message from the General Chair and the Program Chairs

Welcome to ***SEM 2022**, the 11th Joint Conference on Lexical and Computational Semantics! We are pleased to present this volume containing the accepted long and short papers. *SEM 2022 was held as a hybrid conference following NAACL 2022, on July 14th-15th, 2022, due to the precautions for the COVID-19 pandemic.

Since its first edition in 2012, *SEM has become a major venue to present recent advances in all areas of lexical and computational semantics, including semantic representations, semantic processing, multilingual semantics, and others. *SEM is sponsored by SIGLEX, the ACL Special Interest Group on the Lexicon.

*SEM 2022 had a hybrid format with respect to ARR. We accepted both direct submissions through the START system and also those already reviewed through ARR. In total, we received 52 submissions in 9 areas:

- Theoretical and formal semantics
- Semantics in NLP applications
- Semantic composition and sentence-level semantics
- Resources and evaluation
- Psycholinguistics, cognitive linguistics and semantic processing
- Multilinguality
- Lexical semantics and word representations
- Commonsense reasoning and natural language understanding

We compiled an exciting program across all these areas. This year saw a particularly strong batch of submissions; finally, **30** papers were accepted – **18** long papers and **12** short papers.

The submitted papers were carefully evaluated by a program committee led by 11 area chairs, who coordinated a panel of 100 reviewers (who were assigned papers to review in the START system). Almost all submissions were reviewed by three reviewers, who were encouraged to discuss any divergence in evaluations. The papers in each area were subsequently assessed by the area chairs, who added meta-reviews to explain their accept/reject suggestions. The final selection was made by the program co-chairs after an independent check of all the reviews, meta-reviews, and discussions with the area chairs. The reviewers' recommendations were also used to shortlist a set of papers nominated for the Best Paper Award.

We are also very excited to have two excellent keynote speakers: **Allyson Ettinger** (University of Chicago) discussing controlled examinations of meaning sensitivity in pre-trained NLP models, and **Jacob Andreas** (Massachusetts Institute of Technology) discussing the extent to which language modeling induces representations of meaning.

We are deeply thankful to all area chairs and reviewers for their invaluable help in the selection of the program, for their readiness in engaging in thoughtful discussions about individual papers, and for providing valuable feedback to the authors. We are grateful to our Publicity chair, Jose Camacho-Collados (Cardiff University), who set up and regularly updated *SEM's website and publicized it through social media. We thank the Publication Chair, Alessandro Raganato (University of Milano-Bicocca), for his help with the compilation of the proceedings, and the NAACL 2022 workshop organizers for all the valuable help and support with organisational aspects of the conference. Finally, we thank all our authors and presenters for making *SEM 2022 such an exciting event. We hope you will find the content of these proceedings as well as the program of *SEM 2022 enjoyable, interesting and inspirational!

Ellie Pavlick and **Mohammad Taher Pilehvar**, Program Co-Chairs
Vivi Nastase, General Chair

Organizing Committee

General Chair

Vivi Nastase, University of Zurich

Program Chairs

Ellie Pavlick, Brown University
Mohammad Taher Pilehvar, Tehran Institute for Advanced Studies

Publicity Chair

Jose Camacho-Collados, Cardiff University

Publication Chair

Alessandro Raganato, University of Milano-Bicocca

Program Committee

Area Chairs

Marianna Apidianaki, University of Pennsylvania
Vered Shwartz, University of British Columbia
Allyson Ettinger, University of Chicago
Nafise Sadat Moosavi, TU Darmstadt
Malihe Alikhani, University of Pittsburgh
Anders Søgaard, University of Copenhagen
Najoung Kim, Johns Hopkins University
Daniel Khashabi, Allen Institute for Artificial Intelligence
Gene Kim, University of Rochester
Keisuke Sakaguchi, Allen Institute for AI
Nazneen Rajani, Salesforce Research

Program Committee

Lasha Abzianidze, Utrecht University
Rodrigo Agerri, HiTZ Center - Ixa, University of the Basque Country UPV/EHU
Md. Shad Akhtar, Indraprastha Institute of Information Technology, Delhi
Dimitris Alikaniotis, Grammarly Inc.
Forrest Sheng Bao, Iowa State Univerity
Mohamad Hardyman Barawi, University of Malaysia, Sarawak
Pierpaolo Basile, Department of Computer Science, University of Bari Aldo Moro
Tilman Beck, UKP Lab, Technical University of Darmstadt
Farah Benamara, University of toulouse
Gábor Berend, University Of Szeged
Jean-philippe Bernardy, University of Gothenburg
Eduardo Blanco, Arizona State University
Michael Bloodgood, The College of New Jersey
Marianna Bolognesi, University of Bologna
Johan Bos, University of Groningen
Paul Buitelaar, National University of Ireland Galway
Elena Cabrio, Université Côte d'Azur, Inria, CNRS, I3S
Aoife Cahill, Dataminr
Franklin Chang, Kobe City University of Foreign Studies
Aditi Chaudhary, Carnegie Mellon University
Pinzhen Chen, University of Edinburgh
Emmanuele Chersoni, Hong Kong Polytechnic University
Patricia Chiril, University of Chicago
Christos Christodoulopoulos, Amazon Research
Philipp Cimiano, Univ. Bielefeld
Robin Cooper, University of Gothenburg
Bonaventura Coppola, University of Trento
Walter Daelemans, University of Antwerp, CLiPS
Joachim Daiber, Apple
Luna De Bruyne, LT3, Language and Translation Technology Team, Ghent University
Gaël Dias, Normandie Univ, UNICAEN, ENSICAEN, CNRS, GREYC
Liviu P. Dinu, University of Bucharest

Lucia Donatelli, Saarland University
Jakub Dotlacil, Utrecht University
Luis Espinosa Anke, Cardiff University
Dan Garrette, Google Research
Debela Gemechu, Centre for Argument Technology, School of Science & Engineering,University of Dundee
Voula Giouli, ATHENA Research & Innovation Centre, Institute for Language & Speech Processing
Max Glockner, UKP, Computer Science Dpt., TU Darmstadt
Binod Gyawali, Educational Testing Service
Ivan Habernal, Technische Universität Darmstadt
Udo Hahn, Friedrich-Schiller-Universität Jena
Mareike Hartmann, University of Copenhagen
Alessandro Raganato, University of Milano-Bicocca
Dag Haug, University of Oslo
Yoshihiko Hayashi, Waseda University
Daniel Hershcovich, University of Copenhagen
Xinyu Hua, Northeastern University
Nancy Ide, Vassar College
Joseph Marvin Imperial, National University, Manila, Philippines
Sk Mainul Islam, IIT Kharagpur
Kokil Jaidka, National University of Singapore
Jenna Kanerva, University of Turku
Mladen Karan, Queen Mary University
Omid Kashefi, ETS
Roman Klinger, University of Stuttgart
Thomas Kober, NULL
Elena Kochkina, Queen Mary University
Valia Kordoni, Humboldt-Universität zu Berlin
Dan Lassiter, University of Edinburgh
Yitong Li, Huawei Technology Co. ltd
Zongxi Li, Hong Kong Metropolitan University
Nikola Ljubešić, Jožef Stefan Institute
Lorenzo Malandri, University of Milan - Bicocca
Alda Mari, http://www.institutnicod.org/
Eugenio Martínez-cámara, University of Granada
Jonathan May, USC Information Sciences Institute
Sahisnu Mazumder, Intel Labs
Nick Mckenna, University of Edinburgh, School of Informatics
Julian Michael, University of Washington
Koji Mineshima, Keio University
Amita Misra, IBM
Ali Modarressi, Iran University of Science and Technology
Andrew Moore, Lancaster University
Richard Moot, CNRS
Véronique Moriceau, IRIT, Université Toulouse 3
Gaku Morio, Research & Development Group, Hitachi, Ltd.
Larry Moss, Indiana University, Bloomington
Philippe Muller, IRIT, University of Toulouse
Nona Naderi, University of Applied Sciences HES-SO Genève, Swiss Institute of Bioinformatics (SIB)

Vivi Nastase, University of Stuttgart
Timothy Niven, Doublethink Lab
Debora Nozza, Bocconi University
Tim O'gorman, Thorn
Emerson Paraiso, Pontificia Universidade Catolica do Parana - PUCPR
Patrick Paroubek, University Paris-Saclay - CNRS - LISN
Maxime Peyrard, EPFL
Sandro Pezzelle, University of Amsterdam
Jonas Pfeiffer, TU Darmstadt
Yuval Pinter, Ben-Gurion University of the Negev
Marco Polignano, University of Bari
Sara Rajaee, Iran University of Science and Technology
Carlos Ramisch, Aix Marseille University, CNRS, LIS
Christian Retoré, University of Montpellier
Elijah Rippeth, University of Maryland
Alla Rozovskaya, Queens College, City University of New York
Irene Russo, ILC CNR
Farig Sadeque, Educational Testing Service
Mehrnoosh Sadrzadeh, University College London
Marina Santini, RISE, Research Institutes of Sweden. Division: Digital Systems
Ryohei Sasano, Nagoya University
David Schlangen, University of Potsdam
Sabine Schulte Im Walde, University of Stuttgart
Weiyan Shi, Columbia University
Melanie Siegel, Hochschule Darmstadt - University of Applied Sciences
Egon Stemle, Eurac Research
Kevin Stowe, Educational Testing Services (ETS)
Sara Stymne, Uppsala University
Yoshi Suhara, Grammarly
Alexandros Tantos, Aristotle University of Thessaloniki
Andon Tchechmedjiev, IMT Mines Alès
Gaurav Singh Tomar, Google Research
Samia Touileb, University of Bergen
Shyam Upadhyay, Google
L. Alfonso Ureña-lópez, University of Jaen
Sowmya Vajjala, National Research Council
Tim Van De Cruys, University of Leuven
Rossella Varvara, University of Fribourg
Eva Maria Vecchi, Universität Stuttgart, Institut für Maschinelle Sprachverarbeitung
Noortje Venhuizen, Saarland University
Serena Villata, Université Côte d'Azur, CNRS, Inria, I3S
Ivan Vulić, University of Cambridge
Ekaterina Vylomova, University of Melbourne
Wenbo Wang, GoDaddy Inc.
Jin Wang, Yunnan University
Zhongqing Wang, Soochow University
Jin Wang, Megagon Lab
Bonnie Webber, University of Edinburgh
Michael Wiegand, Alpen-Adria-Universitaet Klagenfurt
Adina Williams, Facebook, Inc.
Genta Winata, Bloomberg

Tak-lam Wong, Department of Computing Studies and Information Systems, Douglas College
Shijie Wu, Johns Hopkins University
Rong Xiang, The Hong Kong Polytechnic University
Ruifeng Xu, Harbin Institute of Technology, Shenzhen
Bei Yu, Syracuse University
Alessandra Zarcone, Hochschule für angewandte Wissenschaften
Chrysoula Zerva, Instituto de Telecomunicações, Instituto Superior Técnico, University of Lisbon
Lei Zhang, LinkedIn
Shuai Zhang, Amazon

Keynote Talk: "Understanding" and prediction: Controlled examinations of meaning sensitivity in pre-trained models

Allyson Ettinger
University of Chicago

Abstract: In recent years, NLP has made what appears to be incredible progress, with performance even surpassing human performance on some benchmarks. How should we interpret these advances? Have these models achieved language "understanding"? Operating on the premise that "understanding" will necessarily involve the capacity to extract and deploy meaning information, in this talk I will discuss a series of projects leveraging targeted tests to examine NLP models' ability to capture meaning in a systematic fashion. I will first discuss work probing model representations for compositional meaning, with a particular focus on disentangling compositional information from encoding of lexical properties. I'll then explore models' ability to extract and use meaning information when executing the basic pre-training task of word prediction in context. In all cases, these investigations apply tests that prioritize control of unwanted cues, so as to target the desired model capabilities with greater precision. The results of these studies suggest that although models show a good deal of sensitivity to word-level information, and to certain semantic and syntactic distinctions, when subjected to controlled tests they show little sign of representing higher-level compositional meaning, or of being able to retain and deploy such information robustly during word prediction. Instead, models show signs of heuristic predictive strategies that are unsurprising given their training, but that differ critically from systematic understanding of meaning. I will discuss potential implications of these findings with respect to the goals of achieving "understanding" with currently dominant pre-training paradigms.

Bio: Allyson Ettinger is an Assistant Professor in the Department of Linguistics at the University of Chicago. Her interdisciplinary work combines methods and insights from cognitive science, linguistics, and computer science to examine meaning extraction and predictive processes executed during language processing in artificial intelligence systems and in humans. She received her PhD in Linguistics from the University of Maryland, and spent a year as research faculty at the Toyota Technological Institute at Chicago (TTIC) before beginning her appointment at the University of Chicago. She holds an additional courtesy appointment at TTIC.

Keynote Talk: Models of meaning?

Jacob Andreas
Massachusetts Institute of Technology

Abstract: The extent to which language modeling induces representations of meaning—and the broader question of whether it is even in principle possible to learn about meaning from text alone—have remained a subject of ongoing debate across the language sciences. I'll present some evidence that transformer language models build (rudimentary) structured representations of the meaning of input sentences; that these representations support LMs' ability to reason about the entities and events described in a discourse; and that they can be modified with predictable effects on downstream language generation. Despite all this, even the largest LMs are prone to glaring semantic errors: they refer to entities that have not yet been mentioned, present contradictory facts, or describe impossible events. By understanding how (and where) LMs build models of meaning, we identify the causes of these errors, and in some cases correct them with extremely small amounts of targeted supervision.

Bio: Jacob Andreas is the X Consortium Assistant Professor at MIT. His research aims to build intelligent systems that can communicate effectively using language and learn from human guidance. Jacob earned his Ph.D. from UC Berkeley, his M.Phil. from Cambridge (where he studied as a Churchill scholar) and his B.S. from Columbia. As a researcher at Microsoft Semantic Machines, he founded the language generation team and helped develop core pieces of the technology that powers conversational interaction in Microsoft Outlook. He has been the recipient of Samsung's AI Researcher of the Year award, MIT's Kolokotrones teaching award, and paper awards at NAACL and ICML.

Table of Contents

Program

Thursday, July 14, 2022

08:30 - 10:00	*Sentence-Level Semantics*
	Compositional generalization with a broad-coverage semantic parser Pia Weißenhorn, Lucia Donatelli and Alexander Koller
	DRS Parsing as Sequence Labeling Minxing Shen and Kilian Evang
	Measuring Alignment Bias in Neural Seq2seq Semantic Parsers Davide Locatelli and Ariadna Quattoni
	Semantics-aware Attention Improves Neural Machine Translation Aviv Slobodkin, Leshem Choshen and Omri Abend
	Multilingual Extraction and Categorization of Lexical Collocations with Graph-aware Transformers Luis Espinosa Anke, Alexander Shvets, Alireza Mohammadshahi, James Henderson and Leo Wanner
	Comparison and Combination of Sentence Embeddings Derived from Different Supervision Signals Hayato Tsukagoshi, Ryohei Sasano and Koichi Takeda
10:00 - 10:30	*Break*
10:30 - 12:00	*Evaluation*
	Dyna-bAbI: unlocking bAbI's potential with dynamic synthetic benchmarking Ronen Tamari, Kyle Richardson, Noam Kahlon, Aviad Sar-shalom, Nelson F. Liu, Reut Tsarfaty and Dafna Shahaf
	A Dynamic, Interpreted CheckList for Meaning-oriented NLG Metric Evaluation – through the Lens of Semantic Similarity Rating Laura Zeidler, Juri Opitz and Anette Frank
	A Generative Approach for Mitigating Structural Biases in Natural Language Inference Dimion Asael, Zachary Ziegler and Yonatan Belinkov

Thursday, July 14, 2022 (continued)

How Does Data Corruption Affect Natural Language Understanding Models? A Study on GLUE datasets
Aarne Talman, Marianna Apidianaki, Stergios Chatzikyriakidis and Jörg Tiedemann

AnaLog: Testing Analytical and Deductive Logic Learnability in Language Models
Samuel Ryb, Mario Giulianelli, Arabella Sinclair and Raquel Fernández

Unsupervised Reinforcement Adaptation for Class-Imbalanced Text Classification
Yuexin Wu and Xiaolei Huang

12:00 - 13:30 *Break*

13:30 - 15:00 *Invited Talk: Models of meaning? - Jacobs Andreas*

15:00 - 15:30 *Break*

15:30 - 17:00 *Lexical Semantics*

Distilling Hypernymy Relations from Language Models: On the Effectiveness of Zero-Shot Taxonomy Induction
Devansh Jain and Luis Espinosa Anke

PropBank Comes of Age—Larger, Smarter, and more Diverse
Sameer Pradhan, Julia Bonn, Skatje Myers, Kathryn Conger, Tim O'gorman, James Gung, Kristin Wright-bettner and Martha Palmer

Pretraining on Interactions for Learning Grounded Affordance Representations
Jack Merullo, Dylan Ebert, Carsten Eickhoff and Ellie Pavlick

Leveraging Three Types of Embeddings from Masked Language Models in Idiom Token Classification
Ryosuke Takahashi, Ryohei Sasano and Koichi Takeda

When Polysemy Matters: Modeling Semantic Categorization with Word Embeddings
Elizabeth Soper and Jean-pierre Koenig

Thursday, July 14, 2022 (continued)

What Drives the Use of Metaphorical Language? Negative Insights from Abstractness, Affect, Discourse Coherence and Contextualized Word Representations
Prisca Piccirilli and Sabine Schulte Im Walde

Assessing the Limits of the Distributional Hypothesis in Semantic Spaces: Trait-based Relational Knowledge and the Impact of Co-occurrences
Mark Anderson and Jose Camacho-collados

Friday, July 15, 2022

08:30 - 10:00 *Discourse and Dialog*

A Simple Unsupervised Approach for Coreference Resolution using Rule-based Weak Supervision
Alessandro Stolfo, Chris Tanner, Vikram Gupta and Mrinmaya Sachan

Online Coreference Resolution for Dialogue Processing: Improving Mention-Linking on Real-Time Conversations
Liyan Xu and Jinho D. Choi

DeepA2: A Modular Framework for Deep Argument Analysis with Pretrained Neural Text2Text Language Models
Gregor Betz and Kyle Richardson

"What makes a question inquisitive?" A Study on Type-Controlled Inquisitive Question Generation
Lingyu Gao, Debanjan Ghosh and Kevin Gimpel

Speech acts and Communicative Intentions for Urgency Detection
Laurenti Enzo, Bourgon Nils, Farah Benamara, Mari Alda, Véronique Moriceau and Courgeon Camille

What do Large Language Models Learn about Scripts?
Abhilasha Sancheti and Rachel Rudinger

10:00 - 10:30 *Break*

10:30 - 12:00 *Events*

Pairwise Representation Learning for Event Coreference
Xiaodong Yu, Wenpeng Yin and Dan Roth

Event Causality Identification via Generation of Important Context Words
Hieu Man, Minh Nguyen and Thien Nguyen

Word-Label Alignment for Event Detection: A New Perspective via Optimal Transport
Amir Pouran Ben Veyseh and Thien Nguyen

Friday, July 15, 2022 (continued)

Capturing the Content of a Document through Complex Event Identification
Zheng Qi, Elior Sulem, Haoyu Wang, Xiaodong Yu and Dan Roth

Improved Induction of Narrative Chains via Cross-Document Relations
Andrew Blair-stanek and Benjamin Van Durme

12:00 - 13:30 *Break*

13:30 - 15:00 *Invited Talk: "Understanding" and prediction: Controlled examinations of meaning sensitivity in pre-trained models - Allyson Ettinger*

15:00 - 15:30 *Break*

15:30 - 17:00 *Panel discussion, Closing*

What do Large Language Models Learn about Scripts?

Abhilasha Sancheti
University of Maryland, College Park
Adobe Research
sancheti@{umd.edu,adobe.com}

Rachel Rudinger
University of Maryland, College Park
rudinger@umd.edu

Abstract

Script Knowledge (Schank and Abelson, 1975) has long been recognized as crucial for language understanding as it can help in filling in unstated information in a narrative. However, such knowledge is expensive to produce manually and difficult to induce from text due to reporting bias (Gordon and Van Durme, 2013). In this work, we are interested in the scientific question of whether explicit script knowledge is present and accessible through pre-trained generative language models (LMs). To this end, we introduce the task of generating full event sequence descriptions (ESDs) given a scenario as a natural language prompt. Through zero-shot probing, we find that generative LMs produce poor ESDs with mostly omitted, irrelevant, repeated or misordered events. To address this, we propose a pipeline-based script induction framework (SIF) which can generate good quality ESDs for unseen scenarios (e.g., bake a cake). SIF is a two-staged framework that fine-tunes LM on a small set of ESD examples in the first stage. In the second stage, ESD generated for an unseen scenario is post-processed using RoBERTa-based models to filter irrelevant events, remove repetitions, and reorder the temporally misordered events. Through automatic and manual evaluations, we demonstrate that SIF yields substantial improvements (1-3 BLEU points) over a fine-tuned LM. However, manual analysis shows that there is great room for improvement, offering a new research direction for inducing script knowledge[1].

Scenario Baking a cake

Event Sequence Description (ESD) 1. gather ingredients 2. mix cake mix, eggs and water in bowl 3. pour into pan 4. turn on oven 5. put in oven and bake at specified temperature 6.remove cake from oven to cool 7. turn off oven 8. mix frosting 9. frost cake 10. serve cake 11. refrigerate any leftovers.

Input to LM Here is a sequence of events that happen when you bake a cake :
Natural Language Prompt **Scenario**

Figure 1: Sample event sequence description (ESD) from Wanzare et al. (2016) for BAKING A CAKE scenario. We use natural language prompts (Table 2) to *generate completely ordered* ESDs for evaluating extent of script knowledge accessible through LMs.

1 Introduction

Scripts are structured commonsense knowledge in the form of event sequences that characterize commonplace scenarios, such as, eating at a restaurant (Schank and Abelson, 1975). Scripts are fundamental pieces of commonsense knowledge that humans share and assume to be tacitly understood by each other. When someone says "I went to a restaurant for lunch", our script knowledge allows us to infer that a waiter would have taken the order, the speaker would have eaten the lunch, payed for it, and tipped the waiter, even if these events are not explicitly mentioned. Knowledge of scripts, whether implicit or explicit, has been recognized as important for language understanding tasks (Miikkulainen, 1995; Mueller, 2004).

Earlier efforts to automatically induce scripts from text on a large scale include Chambers and Jurafsky (2008) who treat the problem of script induction as one of learning narrative chains using textual co-occurrence statistics. However, reporting bias (Gordon and Van Durme, 2013) remains an obstacle for script induction as many events are not mentioned explicitly in text, relying on the reader's ability to infer missing script-related events. Moreover, manual creation of such knowledge resources is challenging due to the wide coverage and complexity of relevant scenario knowledge. Although crowdsourced efforts (Singh et al., 2002; Regneri et al., 2010; Modi et al., 2017; Wanzare et al., 2016; Ostermann et al., 2018, 2019) address these issues and acquire script knowledge in the form of ESDs, the collected datasets are small, domain-specific, and crowdsourcing is not scalable.

With the success of pre-trained language mod-

[1]Code and dataset are available at https://github.com/abhilashasancheti/script-generation

Proceedings of the 11th Joint Conference on Lexical and Computational Semantics, pages 1 - 11
July 14-15, 2022

els (henceforth, PLMs) (Devlin et al., 2018; Liu et al., 2019; Radford et al., 2019) in various natural language understanding tasks, we are interested in investigating the extent and accessibility of explicit script knowledge present in PLMs. In this work, unlike cloze-based script evaluations (Chambers and Jurafsky, 2008; Mostafazadeh et al., 2016) which LMs are uniquely optimized for (Rudinger et al., 2015), we evaluate PLMs on the ability to *fully generate* event sequence descriptions (ESDs) (Regneri et al., 2010) in free-form natural language (Figure 1). This is a challenging task as scripts are complex structures with varied granularity of describing a scenario (e.g., starting from going to grocery store to buy ingredients or starting with finding a recipe for BAKING A CAKE scenario), and the requirement to produce all the scenario-*relevant* events in the correct temporal *order*.

To this end, we first probe LMs via carefully crafted prompts to analyze the quality of ESDs generated in a zero-shot setting (§3) and find that the generated ESDs are of poor quality with many scenario-irrelevant, repeated, temporally misordered, and missing events. To address this we propose a, LM-agnostic, pipeline-based script induction framework (§4), `SIF`, which can generate good quality ESDs for novel scenarios that LM has not seen during the training phase of the framework. `SIF` is a two-staged framework with fine-tuning LM on a small set of ESDs as the first stage followed by a three-stepped post-processing stage which corrects the ESDs generated from a fine-tuned LM for irrelevant, repeated, and temporally misordered events. This work makes the following **contributions**:

- We present an analysis of the extent of script knowledge accessible through LMs using probing techniques, in a zero-shot setting, via the task of generating full ESDs from natural language prompts.
- We propose script induction framework that can generate ESDs for held-out and novel scenarios drawn from a different distribution.
- We present automatic and manual evaluation of the generated ESDs, establishing the viability of our framework and paving way for future research in this direction.

2 Related Work

Narrative Chain Induction There has been a growing body of research into statistical script learning systems which can automatically infer implicit events from text. Seminal work by (Chambers and Jurafsky, 2008, 2009) describe a number of simple event co-occurrence based systems that infer (verb, dependency) pairs (known as narrative events) with partial-ordering related to one or multiple participants (Pichotta and Mooney, 2014) in discourse (known as narrative chains). As statistical co-occurrences cannot capture long-range dependencies between events, Pichotta and Mooney (2016a) represent events using LSTM leading to improved narrative cloze task performance. However, much of the information about events is usually left implicit in text. Moreover, narrative events are highly abstracted (Ostermann, 2020) and cloze task is insufficient to evaluate script knowledge (Chambers, 2017). Therefore efforts have been made to acquire crowdsourced ESDs (Singh et al., 2002; Regneri et al., 2010; Modi et al., 2017; Wanzare et al., 2016; Ostermann et al., 2018, 2019) and to learn similar events in a scenario using unsupervised (Regneri et al., 2010) and semi-supervised (Wanzare et al., 2017a) approaches.

Temporal Ordering and Relevance Previous works (Modi and Titov, 2014; Wanzare et al., 2017b; Lyu et al., 2020) have investigated induction or prediction of temporal ordering of prototypical events. Others have predicted next (Pichotta and Mooney, 2016b) or related (Lyu et al., 2020) events in natural language form. Zhou et al. (2019) acquire commonsense procedural knowledge directly from natural language source, like wikiHow, by learning representations for scenarios and events which are predictive of both relevance of event to the scenario and temporal ordering. Zhang et al. (2020) propose a non-learning based approach to predict fixed-length events given an unseen scenario and related scenarios with their events. A recent work (Sakaguchi et al., 2021) generates partially-ordered scripts using PLMs by predicting events and edges for partial-order while we are interested in completely ordered event descriptions. Lyu et al. (2021) propose the task of goal oriented script construction for multilingual wikiHow dataset and propose generation and retrieval-based approaches. However, their generation-based approach using LM only involves fine-tuning. We focus on different LMs to evaluate them on the task

Prompt Beginnings
here is a sequence of events that happen while baking a cake:
these are the things that happen when you bake a cake:
describe baking a cake in small sequences of short sentences:
here is an ordered sequence of events that occur when you bake a cake:

⊕

Continuations
None
1.
1. get a cake mix
1. get a cake mix 2. gather together other ingredients

Figure 2: Different prompt formulations for BAKING A CAKE scenario for probing. 16 prompts are created by combining a prompt beginning with a continuation.

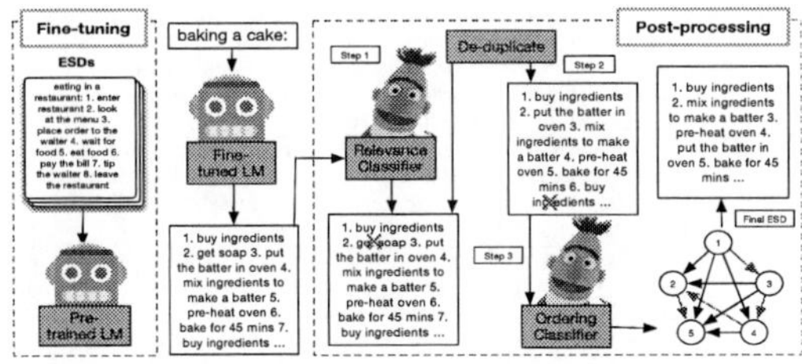

Figure 3: SIF: Pre-trained LM is fine-tuned on DeScript (Wanzare et al., 2016). Generated scripts are then post-processed with RoBERTa-based classifiers to correct for event relevance (Step 1), repetition (Step 2), and temporal ordering (Step 3).

of generating scripts both in zero-shot and fine-tuning settings. Our proposed framework is shown to outperform the fine-tuning approach.

Knowledge-acquisition from PLMs With the success of PLMs (Devlin et al., 2018; Liu et al., 2019; Radford et al., 2019) in various natural language understanding tasks, a number of works investigate how commonsense knowledge is captured in these models (Feldman et al., 2019; Petroni et al., 2020; Weir et al., 2020; Shwartz et al., 2020). Successful efforts have been made to induce relational (Bouraoui et al., 2020), numerical (Lin et al., 2020), temporal (Zhou et al., 2020) and commonsense knowledge in PLMs using fine-tuning.

Unlike prior works, we focus on investigating the extent and accessibility of explicit script knowledge from PLMs via probing techniques and inducing such knowledge in them using a pipeline-based framework to generate full ESDs for novel scenarios in free-form natural language.

3 Probing for Script Knowledge

We design a zero-shot probing experiment to evaluate PLMs' ability to generate ESDs by carefully selecting natural language prompts, which LMs are known to be sensitive to (Bouraoui et al., 2020). We experiment with 16 manually crafted prompts[2] (Table 2) with different phrasing and levels of conditioning to enquire large versions of GPT2, BART, and T5 for script knowledge. The intuition behind these prompts is similar to asking questions (prompts) to a knowledge source in various ways to get the required answer (ESD for a scenario).

BART and T5 were not able to output anything except the input prompt or start, end, and pad tokens and hence we only present qualitative outputs from GPT2, when probed with various prompts for BAKING A CAKE scenario, in Table 2. We observe that the quality of generated ESDs vary for different prompts. Although GPT2 is able to generate some scenario-relevant events with just the prompt beginnings and no continuations (e.g., 1 and 2 in Table 2), the ESDs are incomplete with many auxiliary details, and incorrect event ordering (e.g., '3. The cake is served at the table' before '6. The cake is transferred to the oven.' in 2). It sometimes outputs (e.g., 4) narrations rather than procedural descriptions. As generation from scratch is an open-ended task, we use a prompt with a number to guide GPT2 to generate a procedural script. Although 4 and 5 are more procedural, the events are still at a coarse-grained level with most of the intermediate events missing. To further guide the generation towards a fine-grained level, we condition the generation on a few events (manually curated by authors looking at sample ESDs) along with the prompt beginning. This helps us in examining whether GPT2 has temporal knowledge about the events related to a scenario. Conditioning on the events results in a better quality ESD (e.g., $6, 7, 8$). However, there is a repetition of events ('let it cool for another 10 minutes' in 6, 'add in your flour and mix by hand' in 7) in addition to wrong event ordering, irrelevant (e.g., 'is it hot?' in 8) and missing events. As GPT2 produces poor quality ESDs in this zero-shot setting with BART and T5 not even being able to output any events, we propose a script induction framework detailed in the following section.

4 SIF: Script Induction Framework

In this section, we provide details on our pipeline-based script induction framework, SIF (Figure 3), which addresses the limitations of zero-shot ESD generation. SIF is a two-staged framework which fine-tunes LM on a small set of ESDs in the first

[2] We also experiment with capitalized prompts but did not find significant change in the quality of generations.

1	**these are the things that happen when you bake a cake:** 3 tablespoons (30ml) of unsalted butter, at room temperature 2 tablespoons (30ml) of granulated sugar 2 tablespoons (30ml) of brown sugar, sifted 1 large egg, at room temperature 1 teaspoon vanilla extract 3 large egg yolks 1 cup (350ml) buttermilk To the bowl of an electric mixer fitted with a paddle attachment, add the butter, sugar, brown sugar, egg yolks, and vanilla extract and beat until light and fluffy. Add the buttermilk, then continue beating until fully incorporated. Sift the flour, baking powder, and salt into the bowl of the mixer and beat
2	**here is an ordered sequence of events that occur when you bake a cake:** 1. The cake is baked. 2. The cake is cooled. 3. The cake is served at the table. 4. The dessert is placed on the table. 5. The cake is placed in a baking pan. 6. The cake is transferred to the oven. 7. The cake is put to the middle of the oven and baked. 8. The cake is left in the oven until it is done. 9. The cake is removed from the oven and placed on a plate. 10. The cake is transferred to a cake rack. 11. The cake is placed on a cake plate.
3	**describe baking a cake in small sequences of short sentences:** "I want my cake to be soft and moist." (And, you know, don't do this: "If I use a pastry bag, I can get it back to me in less than two minutes.") You may be looking for the most simple recipe for cake, but baking requires skill and a lot of practice. You don't need to learn how to make a cake recipe. You don't even need to know the difference between the cake and the sponge. All you need is a great recipe and a couple of ovens and an oven thermometer. 2. Use a mixer. Mixers are really, really good. (A great idea is to invest in one of those mini, little, portable ones.
4	**here is a sequence of events that happen while baking a cake: 1.** The cake goes into the oven. 2. The cake cools down in the oven, because the water vapor from the oven condenses onto the top of the cake. 3. The cake is cooled and the frosting set (the sugar crystals are not allowed to fall off). 4. The frosting is set (a little more water vapor condenses onto the top of the frosting). 5. The frosting is set (more water vapor condenses onto the top of the frosting). 6. The cake cools down (the water vapor cools off). 7. The cake comes out of the oven and it is ready to eat. How is this cake not a cake? The first step is that the cake is a cake.
5	**here is an ordered sequence of events that occur when you bake a cake: 1.** You have a cake. 2. You have a batch of flour (or other ingredient, such as water, sugar or corn syrup) 3. You have your flour prepared 4. You have your flour mixture 5. You have your flour mixture pre-floured 6. You have your batter prepared 7. You have your batter made 8. You have your batter placed on a baking sheet 9. You have your batter removed from the oven 10. You have your cake cooled in the tray (you must place your cake in the tray before you take it out of the oven) 11. You take your cake out of the tray and remove it from the oven 12. You eat your cake, or leave it out to cool.
6	**here is a sequence of events that happen while baking a cake: 1. get a cake mix** 2. pour the cake mix into the pan 3. let it bake for 10 minutes 4. get out the oven lid and turn it on 5. let it bake for another 10 minutes 6. get out the oven lid and flip it on 7. let it bake for another 10 minutes 8. get out the oven lid and switch it back on 9. let it bake for another 10 minutes 10. get out the oven lid, turn it back on, and let it bake again 11. get out the oven lid and get out the knife 12. bake the cake again, and then let it cool on a rack 13. use the cake mix to make cupcakes 14. cut the cake, and then use the cupcake for serving!
7	**these are the things that happen when you bake a cake: 1. get a cake mix 2. gather together other ingredients** that you'll need for your cake (coconut oil, powdered sugar, eggs, etc.) 3. preheat oven to 350 4. pour on flour and mix by hand 5. pour in egg and mix by hand 6. add in powdered sugar and mix by hand 7. add in coconut oil and mix by hand 8. let it all sit for a minute 9. add in your flour and mix by hand 10. add in your sugar and mix by hand 11. add in your flour and mix by hand 12. add in your flour and mix by hand 13. add in your flour and mix by hand 14. add in your flour and mix by hand 15. add in your egg and mix by hand 16. add in your salt
8	**describe baking a cake in small sequences of short sentences: 1. get a cake mix 2. gather together other ingredients** 3. start to bake 4. bake a cake 5. take it to the oven 6. the cake is done 7. is it done? 8. is it still hot? 9. what is that crust? 10. what does the cake look like? If we think of a sequence of a few hundred or so words, we can take the basic idea of this example and say that we could write an equivalent, yet shorter, sentence: 1. Get a cake mix 2. Get together the ingredients 3. Bake a cake 4. Take it to the oven 5. The cake is done 6. Is it done? 7. is it hot? 8. what is that crust? 9. what does the cake look like

Table 1: Scripts generated from GPT2-L for BAKING A CAKE scenario with **bold-faced** prompts.

SEQUENCE	here is a sequence of events that happen while baking a cake: 1. e_1 2. e_2
EXPECT	these are the things that happen when you bake a cake: 1. e_1 2. e_2
ORDERED	here is an ordered sequence of events that occur when you bake a cake: 1. e_1 2. e_2
DESCRIBE	describe baking a cake in small sequences of short sentences: 1. e_1 2. e_2
DIRECT	baking a cake: 1. e_1 2. e_2
TOKENS	⟨SCR⟩ baking a cake ⟨ESCR⟩: 1. e_1 2. e_2
ALLTOKENS	⟨SCR⟩ baking a cake ⟨ESCR⟩: ⟨BEVENT⟩ e_1 ⟨EEVENT⟩ ⟨BEVENT⟩ e_2 ⟨EEVENT⟩

Table 2: Different prompt formulations for BAKING A CAKE scenario with two events (e_1 and e_2).

stage. In the second stage, ESDs generated using the fine-tuned LM are passed through a sequence of RoBERTa-based classifiers (Liu et al., 2019) to identify relevant events, remove redundant events, and predict pair-wise temporal ordering between the events. These pair-wise orderings are then used to create a full event ordering using topological sorting on a directed graph created from the predicted orderings.

4.1 Stage I: Fine-tuning PLMs

PLMs fine-tuned on commonsense datasets like ATOMIC (Sap et al., 2019) can generalize beyond the scenarios observed during fine-tuning (Bosselut et al., 2019). Hence, we investigate the learning capability of LMs when a small number of script examples are available. We fine-tune LMs on ESDs using different natural language and pseudo-natural language prompt formulations for encoding ESDs (Table 2) to study the effect of prompt formulations on this task as observed during the probing experiments. We fine-tune LMs using negative log-likelihood objective.

4.2 Stage II: Post-processing Generated ESDs

We sample ESDs for an unseen scenario using the fine-tuned LMs and employ a 3-step post-processing method to correct them for relevance, repetitions, and ordering.

4.2.1 Step 1: Irrelevant Events Removal

The first post-processing step is to remove non-scenario-relevant events from an ESD. An event is not relevant for a scenario if it is not a part of the scenario (e.g., 'tipping a waiter' is not a part of BAKING A CAKE scenario). For irrelevant events removal, we first need to identify irrelevant events for a scenario. We pose this identification problem as a binary classification task to predict if a given event belongs to a given scenario. For training purpose, a positive example is constructed by pairing a scenario with an event belonging to that scenario; negative samples are drawn from another scenario in the training data. Using this data, we train a RoBERTa-L-based (Liu et al., 2019) classifier and remove those events from an ESD which are predicted as irrelevant by this classifier.

4.2.2 Step 2: Event De-duplication

The second step involves the identification and removal of repeated events. Repetition of events can occur by an exact copy of an event or by a paraphrase of an event (e.g., '6. You have your batter prepared' and '7. You have your batter made' in 5 of Table 1). To identify such de-duplications, we train a RoBERTa-L-based paraphrase identification system using MRPC (Dolan and Brockett, 2005) dataset. However, we observe many false-positives (e.g., 'open a faucet' and 'close a faucet' were identified as paraphrases) with this system. Since false-positives can lead to unnecessary removal of events, we employ a conservative approach of only identifying repeated events. We find edit distance between each pair of events in an ESD and remove multiple occurrences of an event from the ESD, as identified by the edit distance score of 0.

4.2.3 Step 3: Temporal Order Correction

The final step is to correct the order of events in an ESD. We correct the ESDs for ordering by first obtaining pair-wise event orderings and then using a graph-based approach to get the final overall ordering. We pose the problem of pair-wise event ordering as a binary classification task to predict if the order of a given pair of events is correct with respect to the given scenario. We sample event pairs from gold ESDs to construct positive (sequence order) and negative (reverse order) examples to train a RoBERTa-L-based classifier. Topological sort is then used to get the final ESD for a scenario from the ordering predictions for all the $\binom{N}{2}$ pairs of events in an ESD. We construct a directed graph $\mathcal{G} = (\mathcal{V}, \mathcal{E})$ of events in a scenario with events as nodes ($\mathcal{V}$) of the graph and a directed edge from node $v_1 \in \mathcal{V}$ to $v_2 \in \mathcal{V}$ if event represented by v_2 is predicted to occur after the event represented by v_1. We keep the original ordering of events in case the constructed graph is cyclic[3] due to incorrect predictions from the classifiers.

4.3 Implementation Details

4.3.1 Dataset pre-proccessing

We fine-tune LMs on ESDs from DeScript (Wanzare et al., 2016) dataset which consists of 100 ESDs each for 40 scenarios, collected via crowdsourcing. The scenarios are randomly partitioned into 8 folds with each fold consisting of ESDs from 5 scenarios to perform 8-fold cross-validation of `SIF` for each of the prompt formulation. We lowercase and enclose each ESD within a begin of scenario ⟨`BOS`⟩ and an end of scenario ⟨`EOS`⟩ token for fine-tuning. The input to the relevance classifier is: `scenario` ⟨`/s`⟩ e and to the temporal classifier is `scenario name` ⟨`/s`⟩ e_1 ⟨`/s`⟩ e_2, where ⟨`/s`⟩ is a separator token and e, e_1, e_2 are events.

4.3.2 Training details

We use huggingface's transformers library (Wolf et al., 2020) to fine-tune LMs on each of the 7 prompt formulations, leading to 7 variations for each LM, for 1 epoch with a batch size of 1, gradient accumulation per 16 steps, and block size of 150. At inference time, 5 ESDs are sampled for each of the given scenarios with top 50 probable tokens, nucleus sampling (Holtzman et al., 2019) probability of 0.9, and maximum length set at 150. We use RoBERTa-L architecture from the transformers library for relevance and temporal order classifiers. Relevance (Temporal) classifier is trained for 10 (5) epochs with average validation accuracy of 84.50% (83.87%) across the folds. The model with the best accuracy on the valid split is used in the post-processing stage. We use python's *editdistance* library to compute edit distance for the de-duplication step. We use Adam optimizer with an initial learning rate of $2e^{-5}$, warm-up steps set at 0.06 of total steps, batch size of 16, and maximum input length 150 for both the classifiers. All the models are trained and tested on NVIDIA Tesla V100 SXM2 16GB GPU machine.

5 Evaluation

We use `SIF` to induce script knowledge in GPT2, BART, and T5, and evaluate full ESDs generated for a given unseen scenario using **BLEU** metric (Papineni et al., 2002), following Pichotta and Mooney (2016b) who use BLEU to score individual LM-generated events. As BLEU is a precision-based metric, we measure n-gram overlap of the sampled ESDs against multiple gold-reference ESDs[4] for each scenario in the test fold.

Additionally, for deeper analysis of the generated ESDs, two of the authors evaluate a subset of the generated ESDs (blinded to the identity of the models and prompt variants) on three levels –

[3] 66±15% (averaged across all the input variants and folds) of the complete graphs are acyclic for GPT2.

[4] We use NLTK python library to calculate BLEU score with add-1 smoothing function and n-grams upto $n = 4$. We convert the outputs of different variants & gold references into numbered form, 1. e_1 2. e_2 … n. e_n for a fair comparison.

Models	TOKENS	EXPECT	SEQUENCE	ALLTOKENS	DESCRIBE	DIRECT	ORDERED
(1) Zero-shot	03.1 (5.2)	03.6 (5.5)	05.4 (2.8)	03.1 (5.2)	03.2 (3.6)	03.9 (5.1)	06.2 (6.6)
(2) GPT2-L$_{SCRATCH}$	17.2 (3.1)	19.3 (3.7)	16.8 (2.9)	18.6 (4.5)	17.6 (2.6)	14.4 (3.9)	17.7 (3.2)
(3) BART-FT	15.5 (6.0)	20.8 (3.5)	19.6 (3.5)	19.7 (9.2)	19.2 (3.9)	18.0 (6.6)	11.7 (4.8)
(4) GPT2-FT	30.7 (5.1)	31.3 (5.5)	32.4 (6.3)	30.7 (6.6)	32.3 (5.9)	31.4 (5.8)	31.0 (4.8)
(5) BART-**SIF**	16.8 (5.1)	21.1 (4.2)	19.9 (3.7)	20.5 (11.1)	20.0 (3.8)	19.6 (7.2)	13.7 (5.0)
(6) GPT2-**SIF**	**33.6** (5.4)	**33.9** (5.6)	**35.2** (6.9)	**32.5** (6.9)	**34.2** (5.3)	**33.6** (5.7)	**33.2** (5.5)

Table 3: Automatic evaluation results: Mean BLEU scores (and std. dev.) over 8 folds of held-out scenarios are reported. (1) is pre-trained GPT2 (no fine-tuning or post-processing); (2) is randomly initialized GPT2 with fine-tuning; (3-4) are fine-tuned BART and GPT2; (5-6) are **SIF** applied to BART and GPT2.

Models	TOKENS	EXPECT	SEQUENCE	ALLTOKENS	DESCRIBE	DIRECT	ORDERED
(1) GPT2-FT	30.7 (5.1)	31.3 (5.5)	32.4 (6.3)	30.7 (6.6)	32.3 (5.9)	31.4 (5.8)	31.0 (4.8)
(2) GPT2-FT+Relevance (R)	33.1 (5.1)	33.1 (4.9)	34.7 (6.9)	31.9 (6.7)	33.7 (5.0)	32.6 (5.8)	33.2 (5.2)
(3) GPT2-FT+R+De-duplicate (D)	33.5 (5.2)	33.6 (5.2)	35.1 (6.9)	32.1 (6.7)	**34.3** (5.0)	32.9 (5.7)	**33.6** (5.5)
(4) GPT2-FT+R+D+Reorder (GPT2-SIF)	**33.6** (5.4)	**33.9** (5.6)	**35.2** (6.9)	**32.5** (6.9)	34.2 (5.3)	**33.6** (5.7)	33.2 (5.5)

Table 4: Ablation analysis of each step in the proposed pipeline for GPT2. Mean BLEU scores (and std. dev.) over 8 folds of held-out scenarios are reported. (1) fine-tuned GPT2; (2-4) are fine-tuned GPT2 with successive post-processing steps.

individual events (**Relevance (R)**), pairwise events (**Order (O)**), and the overall sequence (**Missing (M)**). **R** measures the % of generated events relevant to a scenario; **O** measures the % of consecutive event pairs correctly ordered given a scenario; and **M** measures the degree to which important events are missing on a 4-point Likert scale defined as (1) no or almost no missing events, (2) some insignificant missing events, (3) notable missing events, and (4) severe missing events. As scripts are complex structures and require an understanding of scenarios, we chose not to resort to a crowdsourcing platform for manual analysis. We manually analyze the outputs to evaluate SIF as well as perform an error analysis to identify opportunities for future research directions.

We evaluate our framework on scenarios in each of the eight folds as well as novel scenarios from Regneri et al. (2010), and day-to-day activities. As we do not have access to gold-reference ESDs for the novel scenarios, we demonstrate our framework's performance only using manual evaluation.

6 Results and Analysis

6.1 Automatic Evaluation

We present the automatic evaluation results on held-out scenarios in Table 3. As baselines, we report scores from non-fine-tuned GPT2-L (Zero-shot), a randomly-initialized GPT2-L$_{SCRATCH}$ model fine-tuned on DeScript ESDs, and BART-FT and GPT2-FT models which are fine-tuned in the first stage of SIF. We do not report any results for T5 as it was even struggling to learn the input ESD formulations during fine-tuning. We explain the findings from automatic evaluation below.

SIF significantly outperforms fine-tuning baselines. Both GPT2-SIF and BART-SIF have higher BLEU scores as compared to their corresponding fine-tuned (GPT2-FT and BART-FT) models across all the prompt variants. This clearly reflects the advantage of the post-processing stage in SIF framework. Improvement across different LMs reinforces the LM-agnostic nature of our framework. Variation in the extent of induction across prompt variants indicates the sensitivity of LMs to prompt formulations.

Script knowledge is best accessible through GPT2 than other LMs. As previously mentioned in probing experiments, BART and T5 were not able to output anything useful in the zero-shot setting while GPT2 could produce ESDs, although erroneous and of poor quality. We observe same trends even after fine-tuning these LMs or using SIF to induce script knowledge in these LMs. Interestingly, a randomly initialized and fine-tuned GPT2 (GPT2-L$_{SCRATCH}$) is able to perform comparable to a pre-trained BART fined-tuned using DeScript (BART-FT), and even better for TOKENS and ORDERED variants. Overall, GPT2 is found to be better than BART in terms of the presence and accessibility of script knowledge through them. One possible explanation for this is that GPT2 is a generative language model while BART and T5 are encoder-decoder-based language models making it challenging to encode complete script knowledge within a scenario name.

Performance across LMs is sensitive to prompt formulation and scenario. We consistently ob-

Variants	BLEU↑	Manual Evaluation		
		R↑	O↑	M↓
TOKENS	19.2/**22.8**	77.2/**84.3**	72.3/**89.3**	**2.6/2.6**
EXPECT	22.8/**26.0**	81.9/**82.7**	74.5/**86.5**	**3.0/3.0**
SEQUENCE	27.8/**33.4**	73.3/**83.2**	74.0/**87.5**	**2.5/2.5**
ALLTOKENS	33.5/**35.0**	83.5/**85.7**	82.7/**89.5**	**2.6/2.6**
DESCRIBE	27.1/**28.6**	80.7/**86.3**	83.9/**85.9**	**2.8/2.8**
DIRECT	30.9/**34.1**	81.2/**84.2**	**88.5**/86.1	**2.6/2.6**
ORDERED	**31.9**/31.5	84.9/**86.2**	78.6/**86.8**	**2.6/2.6**

Table 5: Manual and BLEU scores on fine-tuned GPT2 (GPT2-FT) SIF applied to GPT2 (FT/SIF), computed for a stratified sample of outputs (one ESD per scenario across two folds). Mean scores across two annotators are reported. Annotator agreement is measured with Cohen's Kappa (Cohen, 1960) (κ=0.61 for **O**, κ=0.56 for **R**) and Spearman's correlation (ρ=0.64 for **M**). Underline and **bold** denotes the best across variants, and between FT and Ours, respectively. O scores are calculated only when both the events are marked as relevant by the two annotators.

Scenario	R↑	O↑	M↓
Order fastfood online	81.5	84.6	2.6
Cook in a microwave	89.5	92.0	2.4
Answer telephone	65.5	91.7	2.0
Buy from vending machine	77.1	81.3	3.4
Tie shoe laces	65.8	66.7	3.6
Brush teeth	75.9	71.4	2.6
Make ginger paste	41.5	85.7	3.4
Attend a wedding	71.9	100.0	2.4
Wash a car	85.7	90.0	3.0
Take out trash	88.5	92.3	2.2
Take a taxi	85.7	76.2	2.0
Surf the internet	73.3	62.5	2.8
Watch television	77.4	73.7	3.0
Go to a club to dance	100.0	93.5	1.4
Average Score	77.1	83.0	2.6

Table 6: Manual evaluation of ESDs for novel scenarios. Averaged across 5 sampled ESDs per scenario generated using the best performing SEQUENCE variant of GPT2-SIF as per automatic measure.

serve variation in performance across prompt variants. Moreover, this variation is also observed across LMs. For BART, EXPECT outperforms other prompt variants while SEQUENCE performs the best for GPT2. High variance across folds also shows that different prompts perform differently depending upon a scenario. This indicates the sensitivity of LMs to prompt formulations and thus justifies our experiments with different prompt formulations to study the extent of script knowledge that can be accessed through PLMs.

6.2 Ablation Analysis of SIF

We next analyze the contribution of each the stage of SIF and each step of stage II leading to improvement in the performance via an ablation study, on GPT2, in Table 4. As expected stage I contributes maximum to the performance boost. and There is a consistent improvement in BLEU after each of the post-processing steps except in the case of DESCRIBE and ORDERED wherein, reordering leads to a slight decrease in BLEU as the trained classifiers are not perfectly accurate. We present qualitative outputs when SIF is used to induce script knowledge in GPT2 in Table 7.

6.3 Manual Evaluation and Error Analysis

We manually evaluate a total of 140 ESDs (for M) comprising 652 individual events (for R) and 582 consecutive pair of events (for O) generated from GPT2-FT and GPT2 SIF across all the prompt variants (Table 5). BLEU scores are also reported for the same set of ESDs to study the correlation between manual and automatic metrics. We find that outputs from SIF have higher BLEU, R, and O scores than FT across all prompt variants (except O for DIRECT and BLEU for ORDERED). M scores do not change, which shows that significantly important events are not dropped during the irrelevant events removal step. Different prompts perform well in different aspects. DESCRIBE generates most relevant events, ALLTOKENS has the best temporal ordering knowledge, and SEQUENCE leads to least severe missing events after Stage II of SIF. To our surprise, we find no statistically significant correlation between BLEU and any of the manual evaluation metrics (pearson correlation between BLEU and R, O and M was $r = 0.23, -0.06, -0.49$ with p$>$ 0.1, respectively), emphasizing a need for more sophisticated automatic metrics than BLEU for evaluating full ESDs, having a complex structure. The best performing variant as per BLEU score differs from the best one in Table 3 due to variance in performance across scenarios as well as different sampled ESDs of the same scenario in Table 5.

Manual evaluation revealed that a model can miss significant events, even though it can generate many relevant ones. As we only de-duplicate multiple occurrences of exactly the same events in a scenario, we observe repeated paraphrases (4.6% across all prompt variants) of the same event, such as 'pour some milk in the pot' and 'pour the milk into the coffee pot' (MAKING COFFEE scenario). 23.9% of the irrelevant events (13.5% across all prompt variants) are incoherent ('take the flat to the bathroom' for CLEANING A FLAT), 11.4% mixed ('sit in front of coffee shop' for MAKING COF-

		Good quality generations
GOING ON A TRAIN	FT	1. get dressed 2. go to station 3. buy ticket 4. get on train 5. wait for train 6. get on train 7. sit in seat 8. read newspaper 9. wait for train 10. get off train 11. get dressed 12. leave station
	SIF	1. go to station 2. buy ticket 3. wait for train 4. get on train 5. sit in seat 6. get off train 7. leave station
FLYING IN AN AIRPLANE	FT	1. go to airport 2. get boarding pass 3. go to the airline counter 4. present boarding pass and boarding pass id to attendant 5. present ticket and id to attendant 6. sit down in seat 7. make sure you are in seat 8. board airplane
	SIF	1. go to airport 2. go to the airline counter 3. present ticket and id to attendant 4. present boarding pass and boarding pass id to attendant 5. get boarding pass 6. board airplane 7. make sure you are in seat 8. sit down in seat
		Poor quality generations
CLEANING UP A FLAT	FT	1. get the flat 2. take the flat to the bathroom 3. take some water 4. take the flat to the sink 5. turn on the water 6. let it wash the flat 7. then put in some dryer sheet 8. get a sponge 9. scrub the flat 10. put the flat in the dryer 11. when done dry the flat with a towel 12. put away the flat
	SIF	1. get the flat 2. take the flat to the bathroom 3. take some water 4. take the flat to the sink 5. turn on the water 6. let it wash the flat 7. then put in some dryer sheet 8. get a sponge 9. scrub the flat 10. put the flat in the dryer 11. when done dry the flat with a towel 12. put away the flat
TAKING THE UNDER-GROUND	FT	1. arrive at the designated location 2. get in car 3. park in car 4. walk into the designated area 5. enter the room 6. find a chair 7. sit on a chair 8. watch movie
	SIF	1. walk into the designated area

Table 7: Scripts generated using SEQUENCE variant of GPT2 for held-out scenarios. FT denotes output from the fine-tuned model and `SIF` refers to outputs from our framework applied to GPT2.

		Good quality generations
BRUSHING TEETH	FT	1. go into bathroom 2. turn on faucet 3. remove any dirt or debris 4. grab a brush 5. scrub and floss the teeth 6. leave the bathroom
	SIF	1. go into bathroom 2. grab a brush 3. scrub and floss the teeth 4. leave the bathroom
GOING TO A CLUB TO DANCE	FT	1. choose which club to attend. 2. drive or park your car. 3. get in your car. 4. go to the club. 5. enter the club. 6. get up and dance.
	SIF	1. choose which club to attend. 2. get in your car. 3. go to the club. 4. drive or park your car. 5. enter the club. 6. get up and dance.
TAKING A TAXI	FT	1. get in car 2. get into car 3. wait for taxi 4. enter the car 5. pay the fare 6. get out the driver 7. get out the door 8. exit car
	SIF	1. get into car 2. get in car 3. wait for taxi 4. enter the car 5. pay the fare 6. get out the driver 7. exit car 8. get out the door
		Poor quality generations
MAKING GINGER PASTE	FT	1. get your hot water 2. get your bowl 3. turn on the hot water 4. whisk a bowl of sugar into a paste 5. put the bowl on the stove 6. turn on the hot water 7. boil the paste 8. add salt to the paste 9. turn off the water 10. put the bowl on a rack 11. pour the hot water into a saucepan 12. put some salt and sugar in the saucepan 13. turn the heat on 14. pour the sauce on to the bowl 15. eat the paste
	SIF	1. get your hot water 2. get your bowl 3. turn on the hot water 4. whisk a bowl of sugar into a paste 5. put the bowl on the stove 6. boil the paste 7. add salt to the paste 8. put the bowl on a rack 9. pour the hot water into a saucepan 10. put some salt and sugar in the saucepan 11. turn the heat on 12. pour the sauce on to the bowl 13. eat the paste
SURFING THE INTERNET	FT	1. get in the car. 2. drive to the beach. 3. rent a surfboard. 4. go to the beach. 5. put on my sunglasses. 6. get in my car. 7. drive to my beach. 8. go to the surfing.
	SIF	1. 1. rent a surfboard. 2. get in the car. 3. go to the surfing.
ATTENDING A WEDDING	FT	1. schedule an appointment for the reception 2. drive to the venue 3. show your guest information 4. present your wedding ceremony/ reception to the guests 5. invite the friends/ family/ coworkers/ etc. to the wedding 7. present your wedding present to the guests 8. make the guest list 9. take the invitation 10. go to the reception 11. pay the fee/ gratuity 12. give your guest his/her ticket 13. leave the venue
	SIF	1. schedule an appointment for the reception 2. drive to the venue 3. show your guest information 4. present your wedding ceremony/ reception to the guests 5. invite the friends/ family/ coworkers/ etc. to the wedding 6. present your wedding present to the guests 7. make the guest list 8. take the invitation 9. go to the reception 10. leave the venue
BUYING FROM A VENDING MACHINE	FT	1. enter the shop 2. look for the item you wish to purchase 3. go into the register to purchase the item 4. pay for the item 5. take your item to your car 6. take the item to the car and remove the card 7. leave the shop 8. return the card 9. leave the shop
	SIF	1. enter the shop 2. look for the item you wish to purchase 3. go into the register to purchase the item 4. pay for the item 5. take your item to your car 6. take the item to the car and remove the card 7. leave the shop 8. return the card

Table 8: Scripts generated using SEQUENCE variant of GPT2 for novel scenarios. FT denotes output from the fine-tuned model and `SIF` refers to outputs from our framework applied to GPT2[5].

FEE), 61.4% unrelated ('add shampoo' for WASHING DISHES), and rest ungrammatical.

We present a manual evaluation of novel scenarios to gauge the generalizability of our framework in Table 6. The framework generalizes to most of the novel scenarios except for those which involve very granular events like MAKING GINGER PASTE or TYING SHOE LACES. Although GPT2 is a contextualized model, it confuses BUYING FROM VENDING MACHINE with buying from a store, SURFING THE INTERNET with the 'surfing' activity, or ATTENDING A WEDDING with 'getting married'. Additionally, we provide a few good and bad quality outputs from GPT2 models for held-out (Table 7) and novel (Table 8) scenarios to identify the avenues for improving script induction in LMs.

7 Limitations

De-duplication of Events. As mentioned previously, `SIF` cannot de-deuplicate paraphrased version of an event. Therefore, more sophisticated paraphrase identification systems could be used to de-duplicate such events. There could be scenarios where multiple occurrence of same event is required. For instance, WASHING DISHES wherein faucet needs to be opened and closed once at the starting before applying soap and secondly after applying soap (when washed by hands). Hence, it is required to differentiate between desirable and undesirable repetition of events.

Full vs Partial Temporal Ordering. While we consider the task of generating full event sequence descriptions for a scenario, we acknowledge that many scenarios may not have strict ordering of events (e.g., either wet ingredients can be mixed first or dry ones in a BAKING A CAKE scenario) or there can be overlapping events (e.g., while oven is pre-heating, batter can be prepared). Instead of considering partial ordering of events (Sakaguchi et al., 2021), we focus on generating multiple possible full sequence of events for a scenario and report the averaged scores.

8 Conclusion and Future Work

We investigate whether pre-trained language models are capable of generating full event sequence descriptions with minimal prompting and find that pre-trained GPT2 has an incomplete understanding of scripts, while BART and T5 did not even produce anything useful through zero-shot probing experiments. We propose `SIF`, an LM-agnostic script induction framework, that is shown to produce meaningful ESDs for unseen scenarios and mitigate errors (such as scenario-irrelevant, repeated, and misordered events) that were observed during probing experiments, as measured by automatic and manual evaluation. We also provide evidence for the generalization capability of our framework to novel scenarios. However, there is great room for improvement which is evident from manual error analysis and qualitative outputs. Future work may focus on developing more sophisticated automatic metrics as well as an end-to-end system for script induction which might help in mitigating cascading of errors, due to each component, common to any pipeline-based approaches.

Acknowledgements

We would like to thank Benjamin Van Durme, Sweta Agrawal, and all the anonymous reviewers for their valuable feedback ad suggestions.

References

Antoine Bosselut, Hannah Rashkin, Maarten Sap, Chaitanya Malaviya, Asli Celikyilmaz, and Yejin Choi. 2019. COMET: Commonsense transformers for automatic knowledge graph construction. In *Proceedings of the 57th Annual Meeting of the Association for Computational Linguistics*, pages 4762–4779, Florence, Italy. Association for Computational Linguistics.

Zied Bouraoui, Jose Camacho-Collados, and Steven Schockaert. 2020. Inducing relational knowledge from BERT. In *Proceedings of the AAAI Conference on Artificial Intelligence*, volume 34, pages 7456–7463.

Nathanael Chambers. 2017. Behind the scenes of an evolving event cloze test. In *Proceedings of the 2nd Workshop on Linking Models of Lexical, Sentential and Discourse-level Semantics*, pages 41–45.

Nathanael Chambers and Dan Jurafsky. 2008. Unsupervised learning of narrative event chains. In *Proceedings of ACL-08: HLT*, pages 789–797.

Nathanael Chambers and Dan Jurafsky. 2009. Unsupervised learning of narrative schemas and their participants. In *Proceedings of the Joint Conference of the 47th Annual Meeting of the ACL and the 4th International Joint Conference on Natural Language Processing of the AFNLP*, pages 602–610.

Jacob Cohen. 1960. A coefficient of agreement for nominal scales. *Educational and psychological measurement*, 20(1):37–46.

Jacob Devlin, Ming-Wei Chang, Kenton Lee, and Kristina Toutanova. 2018. BERT: Pre-training of deep bidirectional transformers for language understanding. *arXiv preprint arXiv:1810.04805*.

William B Dolan and Chris Brockett. 2005. Automatically constructing a corpus of sentential paraphrases. In *Proceedings of the Third International Workshop on Paraphrasing (IWP2005)*.

Joshua Feldman, Joe Davison, and Alexander M Rush. 2019. Commonsense knowledge mining from pretrained models. *arXiv preprint arXiv:1909.00505*.

Jonathan Gordon and Benjamin Van Durme. 2013. Reporting bias and knowledge acquisition. In *Proceedings of the 2013 workshop on Automated knowledge base construction*, pages 25–30.

Ari Holtzman, Jan Buys, Li Du, Maxwell Forbes, and Yejin Choi. 2019. The curious case of neural text degeneration. *arXiv preprint arXiv:1904.09751*.

Bill Yuchen Lin, Seyeon Lee, Rahul Khanna, and Xiang Ren. 2020. Birds have four legs?! numersense: Probing numerical commonsense knowledge of pre-trained language models. *arXiv preprint arXiv:2005.00683*.

Yinhan Liu, Myle Ott, Naman Goyal, Jingfei Du, Mandar Joshi, Danqi Chen, Omer Levy, Mike Lewis, Luke Zettlemoyer, and Veselin Stoyanov. 2019. RoBERTa: A Robustly Optimized BERT Pretraining Approach. *arXiv preprint arXiv:1907.11692*.

Qing Lyu, Li Zhang, and Chris Callison-Burch. 2020. Reasoning about goals, steps, and temporal ordering with wikihow. In *Proceedings of The 2020 Conference on Empirical Methods In Natural Language Proceedings (EMNLP)*.

Qing Lyu, Li Zhang, and Chris Callison-Burch. 2021. Goal-oriented script construction. In *Proceedings of the 14th International Conference on Natural Language Generation*, pages 184–200, Aberdeen, Scotland, UK. Association for Computational Linguistics.

Risto Miikkulainen. 1995. Script-based inference and memory retrieval in subsymbolic story processing. *Applied Intelligence*, 5(2):137–163.

Ashutosh Modi, Tatjana Anikina, Simon Ostermann, and Manfred Pinkal. 2017. Inscript: Narrative texts annotated with script information. *arXiv preprint arXiv:1703.05260*.

Ashutosh Modi and Ivan Titov. 2014. Inducing neural models of script knowledge. In *Proceedings of the Eighteenth Conference on Computational Natural Language Learning*, pages 49–57.

Nasrin Mostafazadeh, Nathanael Chambers, Xiaodong He, Devi Parikh, Dhruv Batra, Lucy Vanderwende, Pushmeet Kohli, and James Allen. 2016. A corpus and cloze evaluation for deeper understanding of commonsense stories. In *Proceedings of the 2016 Conference of the North American Chapter of the Association for Computational Linguistics: Human Language Technologies*, pages 839–849.

Erik T Mueller. 2004. Understanding script-based stories using commonsense reasoning. *Cognitive Systems Research*, 5(4):307–340.

Simon Ostermann. 2020. Script knowledge for natural language understanding.

Simon Ostermann, Ashutosh Modi, Michael Roth, Stefan Thater, and Manfred Pinkal. 2018. Mcscript: A novel dataset for assessing machine comprehension using script knowledge. *arXiv preprint arXiv:1803.05223*.

Simon Ostermann, Michael Roth, and Manfred Pinkal. 2019. Mcscript2. 0: A machine comprehension corpus focused on script events and participants. *arXiv preprint arXiv:1905.09531*.

Kishore Papineni, Salim Roukos, Todd Ward, and Wei-Jing Zhu. 2002. Bleu: a method for automatic evaluation of machine translation. In *Proceedings of the 40th Annual Meeting of the Association for Computational Linguistics*, pages 311–318, Philadelphia, Pennsylvania, USA. Association for Computational Linguistics.

Fabio Petroni, Patrick Lewis, Aleksandra Piktus, Tim Rocktäschel, Yuxiang Wu, Alexander H Miller, and Sebastian Riedel. 2020. How context affects language models' factual predictions. *arXiv preprint arXiv:2005.04611*.

Karl Pichotta and Raymond Mooney. 2014. Statistical script learning with multi-argument events. In *Proceedings of the 14th Conference of the European Chapter of the Association for Computational Linguistics*, pages 220–229.

Karl Pichotta and Raymond J Mooney. 2016a. Learning statistical scripts with lstm recurrent neural networks. In *AAAI*, pages 2800–2806.

Karl Pichotta and Raymond J Mooney. 2016b. Using sentence-level lstm language models for script inference. *arXiv preprint arXiv:1604.02993*.

Alec Radford, Jeffrey Wu, Rewon Child, David Luan, Dario Amodei, and Ilya Sutskever. 2019. Language models are unsupervised multitask learners. *OpenAI blog*, 1(8):9.

Michaela Regneri, Alexander Koller, and Manfred Pinkal. 2010. Learning script knowledge with web experiments. In *Proceedings of the 48th Annual Meeting of the Association for Computational Linguistics*, pages 979–988, Uppsala, Sweden. Association for Computational Linguistics.

Rachel Rudinger, Pushpendre Rastogi, Francis Ferraro, and Benjamin Van Durme. 2015. Script induction as language modeling. In *Proceedings of the 2015 Conference on Empirical Methods in Natural Language Processing*, pages 1681–1686, Lisbon, Portugal. Association for Computational Linguistics.

Keisuke Sakaguchi, Chandra Bhagavatula, Ronan Le Bras, Niket Tandon, Peter Clark, and Yejin Choi. 2021. proscript: Partially ordered scripts generation via pre-trained language models. *arXiv preprint arXiv:2104.08251*.

Maarten Sap, Ronan Le Bras, Emily Allaway, Chandra Bhagavatula, Nicholas Lourie, Hannah Rashkin, Brendan Roof, Noah A Smith, and Yejin Choi. 2019. Atomic: An atlas of machine commonsense for if-then reasoning. In *Proceedings of the AAAI Conference on Artificial Intelligence*, volume 33, pages 3027–3035.

Roger C Schank and Robert P Abelson. 1975. Scripts, plans, and knowledge. In *IJCAI*, volume 75, pages 151–157.

Vered Shwartz, Peter West, Ronan Le Bras, Chandra Bhagavatula, and Yejin Choi. 2020. Unsupervised commonsense question answering with self-talk. *arXiv preprint arXiv:2004.05483*.

Push Singh, Thomas Lin, Erik T Mueller, Grace Lim, Travell Perkins, and Wan Li Zhu. 2002. Open mind common sense: Knowledge acquisition from the general public. In *OTM Confederated International Conferences" On the Move to Meaningful Internet Systems"*, pages 1223–1237. Springer.

Lilian Wanzare, Alessandra Zarcone, Stefan Thater, and Manfred Pinkal. 2017a. Inducing script structure from crowdsourced event descriptions via semi-supervised clustering.

Lilian Wanzare, Alessandra Zarcone, Stefan Thater, and Manfred Pinkal. 2017b. Inducing script structure from crowdsourced event descriptions via semi-supervised clustering. In *Proceedings of the 2nd*

Workshop on Linking Models of Lexical, Sentential and Discourse-level Semantics, pages 1–11, Valencia, Spain. Association for Computational Linguistics.

Lilian DA Wanzare, Alessandra Zarcone, Stefan Thater, and Manfred Pinkal. 2016. A crowdsourced database of event sequence descriptions for the acquisition of high-quality script knowledge.

Nathaniel Weir, Adam Poliak, and Benjamin Van Durme. 2020. Probing neural language models for human tacit assumptions. CogSci.

Thomas Wolf, Lysandre Debut, Victor Sanh, Julien Chaumond, Clement Delangue, Anthony Moi, Pierric Cistac, Tim Rault, Remi Louf, Morgan Funtowicz, Joe Davison, Sam Shleifer, Patrick von Platen, Clara Ma, Yacine Jernite, Julien Plu, Canwen Xu, Teven Le Scao, Sylvain Gugger, Mariama Drame, Quentin Lhoest, and Alexander Rush. 2020. Transformers: State-of-the-art natural language processing. In *Proceedings of the 2020 Conference on Empirical Methods in Natural Language Processing: System Demonstrations*, pages 38–45, Online. Association for Computational Linguistics.

Hongming Zhang, Muhao Chen, Haoyu Wang, Yangqiu Song, and Dan Roth. 2020. Analogous process structure induction for sub-event sequence prediction. *arXiv preprint arXiv:2010.08525*.

Ben Zhou, Qiang Ning, Daniel Khashabi, and Dan Roth. 2020. Temporal common sense acquisition with minimal supervision. *arXiv preprint arXiv:2005.04304*.

Yilun Zhou, Julie A Shah, and Steven Schockaert. 2019. Learning household task knowledge from wikihow descriptions. *arXiv preprint arXiv:1909.06414*.

DeepA2: A Modular Framework for Deep Argument Analysis with Pretrained Neural Text2Text Language Models

Gregor Betz
Karlsruhe Institute of Technology
Karlsruhe, Germany
gregor.betz@kit.edu

Kyle Richardson
Allen Institute for AI
Seattle, WA, USA
kyler@allenai.org

Abstract

In this paper, we present and implement a multi-dimensional, modular framework for performing deep argument analysis (DeepA2) using current pre-trained language models (PTLMs). ArgumentAnalyst – a T5 model (Raffel et al., 2020) set up and trained within DeepA2 – reconstructs argumentative texts, which advance an informal argumentation, as valid arguments: It inserts, e.g., missing premises and conclusions, formalizes inferences, and coherently links the logical reconstruction to the source text. We create a synthetic corpus for deep argument analysis, and evaluate ArgumentAnalyst on this new dataset as well as on existing data, specifically EntailmentBank (Dalvi et al., 2021). Our empirical findings vindicate the overall framework and highlight the advantages of a modular design, in particular its ability to emulate established heuristics (such as hermeneutic cycles), to explore the model's uncertainty, to cope with the plurality of correct solutions (underdetermination), and to exploit higher-order evidence.

[🤗 Demo] [🤗 Model] [🤗 Datasets]

1 Introduction

Argumentative text analysis is an interpretation method for clarifying arguments (Fisher, 2004). Being studied in argumentation theory, logic, or epistemology, it is widely taught and applied as a key critical thinking skill in, e.g., law (Alexy, 1989), the humanities (Bruce and Barbone, 2011), social sciences (Fairclough and Fairclough, 2012), policy advice (Hansson and Hirsch-Hadorn, 2016), or public debate (Beck et al., 2019). This paper presents a computational approach for *deep argument analysis*, i.e., for **reconstructing natural-language arguments** from a given text, as in the following example (adapted from Siegel, 2018):

source text ⇝	**reconstructed argument**
It is unethical to destroy human embryos. The most basic argument supporting this claim just stresses that it is wrong to intentionally kill innocent human beings.	(P1) It is impermissible to kill innocent human beings. (P2) The human embryo is an innocent human being. (C) THUS: It is impermissible to kill the human embryo.

The literature on argument reconstruction (cf. Feldman, 1998; Scholz, 2000; Lau, 2011; Bowell and Kemp, 2014; Brun, 2014; Brun and Betz, 2016) characterizes deep argument analysis as:

- a complex task involving a variety of **sub-tasks**, such as identifying reasons and conclusions in a text, formalizing sentences, checking validity of an inference, logical streamlining, or explicating implicit premises.
- a non-conservative, **creative task** that goes beyond mere text annotation and essentially generates a new, more transparent text.
- an **iterative process** through which reconstructions are built and revised step-by-step, and the solution space is gradually explored.
- a hermeneutical task, guided by the **principle of charity**, which urges one to come up with an interpretation (reconstruction) as strong and plausible as possible.
- assuming a **normative background theory** about what constitutes a strong and plausible argument in the first place.
- being affected by **severe underdetermination**, both in terms of the process and the final outcome; in particular, there typically exist rival, yet equally legitimate reconstructions of one and the same text.

Given these special characteristics, *deep argument analysis* poses many challenges for machine models of natural language understanding. In this paper, we introduce a novel modular modeling approach for analysing complex argumentation that builds on recent pre-trained text2text transformers (Raffel et al., 2020). Our approach – DeepA2 (illustrated in Figure 1) – works by systematically

Proceedings of the 11th Joint Conference on Lexical and Computational Semantics, pages 12 - 27
July 14-15, 2022 ©2022 Association for Computational Linguistics

decomposing a complex reconstruction problem to smaller text2text sub-tasks (see Section 3), which allows for emulating the types of interpretation strategies and heuristics studied in argument theory. Referring to the different components of a comprehensive argumentative analysis, we may also define tailor-made metrics for assessing argument reconstructions. To demonstrate the benefits of our approach, we construct a new argumentation dataset (AAAC) that exhibits several complex *interpretive dimensions*, show how to map other existing datasets into our framework (Section 4), and train and evaluate our main model, referred to as **ArgumentAnalyst**, within DeepA2 (Section 5).

Our empirical results show:

1. ArgumentAnalyst generates – out-of-domain – semantically meaningful argument reconstructions, 70% of which are logically valid. By pooling alternative reconstructions, virtually every source text in the synthetic dataset can be reconstructed as a valid argument.

2. Modular generation chains which emulate iterative reconstruction strategies are highly successful: they yield, in particular, a more coherent interpretation of an argumentative text, exploit the text more thoroughly, and generally outperform one-step generation as soon as problems become difficult.

3. ArgumentAnalyst outperforms *EntailmentWriter* (Dalvi et al., 2021) on difficult *EntailmentBank* problems with respect to telling apart relevant premises from distractors.

4. ArgumentAnalyst generates reliable higher-order evidence (Christensen, 2010) which can be used for diagnosing logical fallacies – despite the fact that ArgumentAnalyst is maximally charitable and is trained to reconstruct any input whatsoever as a logically valid argument, even if the input argument, taken at face value, *is* painstakingly fallacious.

In concluding this paper, we sum-up and interpret these findings as general vindication of DeepA2's modular, multi-angular design (Section 6).

2 Related Work

Taking **transformers as soft reasoners**, recent work, pioneered by Clark et al. (2020), has shown that pre-trained language models (PTLMs) possess basic deductive and abductive reasoning capabilities on diverse domains (Banerjee and Baral, 2020; Betz et al., 2021; Bostrom et al., 2021), but are equally prone to fallacies and biases (Kassner and Schütze, 2020; Talmor et al., 2020). Besides drawing the correct conclusion, transformers are able to generate correct reasoning chains that justify an answer, which in turn further increases answer accuracy (Saha et al., 2020; Tafjord et al., 2020; Gontier et al., 2020; Saha et al., 2021; Dalvi et al., 2021).

Neural semantic parsing uses sequence models to *formalize* natural language sentences (Kamath and Das, 2019). Shin et al. (2021) show that PTLMs are zero-shot parsers, and that intermediate steps which rephrase and streamline the original input before parsing it to a formal language improve accuracy.

Argument mining is an active research field that studies computational methods for retrieving argumentative components from a text corpus (Wachsmuth et al., 2017; Moens, 2018; Potthast et al., 2019; Lawrence and Reed, 2020). Recently, work in this field has started to use PTLMs: Ein-Dor et al. (2020) and Gretz et al. (2020) succeed in retrieving relevant pro- or con-arguments for a given topic from a large corpus with a fine-tuned BERT model (Devlin et al., 2019). Using BERT, Bar-Haim et al. (2020) map argumentative texts to key points that succinctly summarize the argument's gist. Akiki and Potthast (2020) explore abstractive argument retrieval by means of text generation with GPT2 (Radford et al., 2019). Similarly, Syed et al. (2021) deploy BART (Lewis et al., 2019) to generate conclusions of argumentative texts on a challenging corpus compiled from Reddit and various online debate corpora. Rodrigues et al. (2020), revisiting the argument comprehension task (Habernal et al., 2014, 2018), demonstrate that identifying implicit premises – and deep argument analysis *a fortiori* – remains a hard, unsolved task. Recently, Chakrabarty et al. (2021) have shown that augmenting training data with discourse-aware commonsense knowledge improves the plausibility of automatically identified implicit premises. Such a knowledge-driven perspective is orthogonal to, and may eventually complement the logical approach adopted in this paper.

3 Framework

3.1 Problem Definition

Deep argument analysis of a given text seeks to answer the following **central question**: Can we

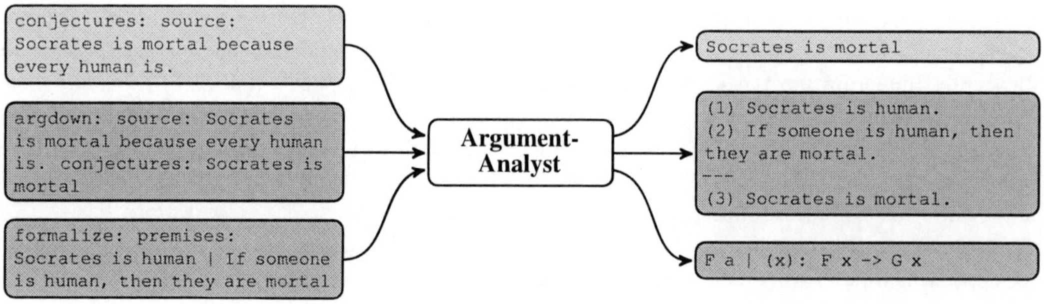

Figure 1: Example text-to-text tasks for deep argument analysis, defined by DeepA2.

make sense of the text as a presentation of a rational argument? And if so, what exactly is the argument; and how precisely is it related to the text?

In carrying out a deep argument analysis, one explicates, rephrases and rebuilds – even repairs – the text's argument in one's own words. That is why deep argument analysis is also referred to as *rational reconstruction* (cf. Leitgeb and Carus, 2021). The reconstructed argument forms, together with details about its logical properties and about its relation to the source text, a *comprehensive argumentative analysis* of a text. The latter can be seen as an interpretative hypothesis that is abductively inferred from a source text by means of an inference to the best explanation. Here is another example that illustrates how far a reconstruction may deviate from the original text that presents the argument (adapted from Brun and Betz, 2016):

source text	$\rightsquigarrow$ **reconstructed argument**
So, the researcher's central dilemma exists in an especially acute form in psychology: either the animal is not like us, in which case there is no reason for performing the experiment; or else the animal is like us, in which case we ought not to perform on the animal an experiment that would be considered outrageous if performed on one of us.	(P1) If the animal is not like us, it is wrong to perform the experiment. (P2) If the animal is like us, it is wrong to perform the experiment. (C) THUS (with *classical dilemma*): It is wrong to perform the experiment.

A compelling argumentative analysis yields (i) a rational argument that is (ii) closely related to the source text. Deep argument analysis is, accordingly, guided by a **dual goal** (cf. Brun and Betz, 2016). An argument reconstruction should both be

(i) **systematically correct**, i.e., the reconstructed argument itself is, e.g., transparent, deductively valid, non-circular, or doesn't contain irrelevant premises; and

(ii) **exegetically adequate**, i.e., the reconstructed argument accounts for the original text, because, e.g., its premises merely reformulate parts of the text, or because its overall inferential structure can be traced within the source text.

The fact that there typically exists – regarding a specific text – a trade-off between these two goals is one major reason for the underdetermination of deep argument analysis and the plurality of legitimate reconstructions of a given text (cf. Brun and Betz, 2016).

Against this background, we may finally define the problem of

Deep artificial argument analysis: Describe, analyse and implement an effective computational system for deep argument analysis!

3.2 Multi-angular Data

The DeepA2 framework is built upon a *multi-angular* data structure (Tafjord and Clark, 2021) whose dimensions represent the essential components of a comprehensive argumentative analysis (see Section 3.1). Structured argumentative data is rendered as plain text (cf. Voigt, 2014). The different data dimensions, which are related as shown in Figure 2, are (with an illustrating example):

argument source text (S)
It is unethical to destroy human embryos. The basic argument supporting this claim just stresses that it is wrong to intentionally kill innocent human beings.

verbatim reason statements in source text (R)
it is wrong to intentionally kill innocent human beings (ref: (1))

verbatim conjectures in the source text (J)
It is unethical to destroy human embryos (ref: (3))

argument reconstruction (A)
(1) It is impermissible to kill innocent human beings.
(2) The human embryo is an innocent human being.
– with hypothetical syllogism from (1) (2) –
(3) It is impermissible to kill the human embryo.

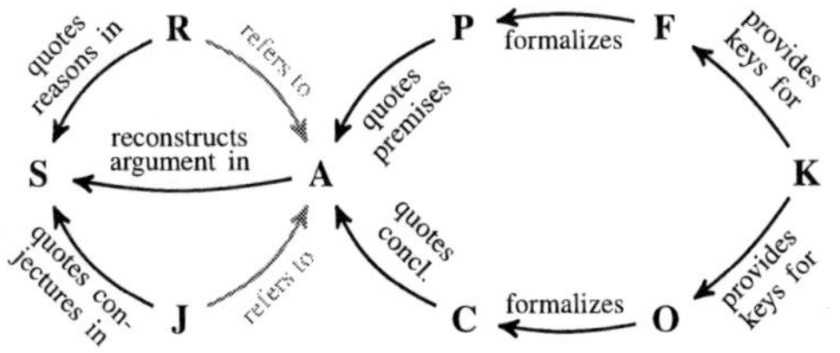

Figure 2: Relationships between dimensions of the multi-angular argumentative data.

premises of the reconstructed argument (P)
It is impermissible to kill innocent human beings | The human embryo is an innocent human being
final conclusion of reconstr. argument (C)
It is impermissible to kill the human embryo
formalizations of premises (F)
(x): F x → G x | (x): H x → F x
formalization of conclusion (O)
(x): H x → G x
keys for the formalizations' constants (K)
F: innocent human being | G: must not be killed | H: human embryo

Each record in a DeepA2 dataset contains a source text plus a legitimate comprehensive argumentative analysis, which is, given underdetermination, not necessarily the only compelling reconstruction of the text; moreover, a dataset *may* contain different records with one and the same source text analysed in several ways. So, for example, an alternative, equally legitimate argument reconstruction of the above source text (**S**) may read:

argument reconstruction (A)
(1) If it is wrong to kill innocent human beings, then it is wrong to kill a human embryo.
(2) It is wrong to kill innocent human beings.
– with modus ponens from (1) (2) –
(3) It is wrong to kill a human embryo.

Beyond this structural and functional characterization, DeepA2 is agnostic about the nature and origin of the argumentative data. Synthetically generated, automatically retrieved, manually created datasets as well as translations of other databases are all compatible with the framework and can be used side by side.

3.3 Generative Modes and Chains

Given DeepA2's multi-dimensional data structure described in the previous section, a **generative mode** maps data from some input dimensions to a target dimension. For example, the mode S⇝A takes a source text (**S**) as input and outputs an argument reconstruction (**A**), the mode RJ⇝A reconstructs the argument (**A**) given the verbatim reasons (**R**) and conjectures (**J**). All in all, we define and investigate 21 different generative modes (see Appendix B). Every mode represents a task on which a text-to-text model can be trained.

By taking some mode's output as another mode's input, modes can be concatenated into **generative chains**. For example, the output of modes S⇝R and S⇝J (reasons and conjectures from source) can be fed into mode RJ⇝A to reconstruct an argument. Such generative chains allow us to emulate different strategies (heuristics) for analysing a given argumentative text (see Appendix C for technical details).

Three generative chains which model distinct interpretative strategies, taking a source text (**S**) as sole input, are:

straight
S⇝A S⇝R S⇝J
hermeneutic cycle
S⇝A SA⇝R SA⇝J RJ⇝A
logical streamlining
S⇝A A⇝P A⇝C C⇝O CO⇝K OK⇝C PC⇝A SA⇝R SA⇝J

While the chain *straight*, where no output ever serves as input to another mode, represents a simple baseline, *hermeneutic cycle* and *logical streamlining* mimic prominent, equally-named methods in argument analysis (cf. Bowell and Kemp, 2014; Brun and Betz, 2016). One goes through a hermeneutic cycle, generally speaking, if one revisits a text in view of its previous interpretation, as, for example, in steps SA⇝R SA⇝J, where the source text (**S**) is re-interpreted (identifying reason statements and conjectures) given the previously reconstructed argument (**A**), so as to subsequently re-reconstruct the argument itself (step RJ⇝A). To logically streamline a reconstruction means to rephrase its conclusion or premises in order to make their logico-semantic structure more transparent. Such semantic clarification can be emulated by (i) formalizing a statement (e.g., A⇝C C⇝O CO⇝K) and (ii) using the keys (**K**) to retrieve the original statement from the generated logical formulas (such as in OK⇝C), from which the argument can be re-built (step PC⇝A).

For evaluation, we append to each generative chain the following sub-chain that formalizes the reconstructed argument:

formalization
A⇝P A⇝C P⇝F CPF⇝O PFCO⇝K

A generative chain can be construed as hypergraph on the dimensions of DeepA2's multi-angular datasets, with each of its modes representing a directed hyper-edge. Summing up the number of input dimensions (except **S**) over all modes yields a simple graph centrality measure, which gauges a chain's sophistication. Thus, *straight*, *hermeneutic cycle* and *logical streamlining* display a sophistication of 0, 4, and 11, respectively.

3.4 Metrics

As discussed in Section 3.1, an argument reconstruction should both be sound and make sense of the text to-be-interpreted. In line with the dual goal of argument analysis, we propose metrics both for the systematic correctness and for the exegetic adequacy of a given analysis. The following metrics measure the degree to which a given generated argument is *systematically correct*:

- **SYS-PP** 1 if the argument is not a *petitio principii* (i.e., if no premise is identical with its final conclusion), 0 otherwise;
- **SYS-RP** 1 if the argument has no *redundant premises* (i.e., if no premise occurs more than once), 0 otherwise;
- **SYS-RC** 1 if the argument has no *redundant conclusions* (i.e., if no conclusion – intermediary or final – occurs more than once), 0 otherwise;
- **SYS-US** 1 if all statements in the argument other than the final conclusion are explicitly *used in an inference*, 0 otherwise;
- **SYS-SCH** ratio of sub-arguments which correctly instantiate the explicitly stated *inference scheme* (e.g., hypothetical syllogism);
- **SYS-VAL** 1 if the argument is *globally valid* (i.e., if the final conclusion deductively follows from the premises), 0 otherwise;

All six systematic metrics can be computed automatically (SYS-SCH tries to parse the argument based on the inference schemes and templates used to construct the synthetic dataset in the first place; SYS-VAL passes the model-generated formalizations of premises and conclusion to a symbolic theorem prover (De Moura and Bjørner, 2008); and the remaining metrics check for string identity).

Whereas systematic metrics apply primarily to the generated argument (**A**), a reconstruction's interpretative adequacy will also depend on how reasons (**R**) and conjectures (**J**) coherently link the argument's components to the original text. As a first set of *exegetic metrics*, we thus propose

- **EXE-MEQ** 1 if the reasons and conjectures are *mutually exclusive verbatim quotes* from the source text, 0 otherwise;
- **EXE-RSS** semantic similiarity (BLEURT, see Sellam et al., 2020) of each reason statement and its counterpart premise in the reconstructed argument (if such exists, -1 otherwise);
- **EXE-JSS** semantic similiarity (see EXE-RSS) of each conjecture statement and its counterpart in the reconstructed argument (if such exists, -1 otherwise).

Each source text presents (more or less faithfully) an underlying target argument, which in turn marks some of the text's statements as 'target' reasons, others as 'target' conjectures. The following two metrics assess the degree to which a comprehensive argumentative analysis correctly predicts (**R**, **J**) those target reasons and conjectures.

- **EXE-PPR** predictive performance (F1-score) for identifying (target) reason statements in the source text;
- **EXE-PPJ** predictive performance (F1-score) for identifying (target) conjecture statements in the source text.

An argument's final conclusion may be implicit or explicit in a given text. The ability to fully exploit a text can be measured by verifying whether the reconstructed argument's final conclusion is implicit (= prediction) if and only if the target argument's one is.

- **EXE-TE** text exploitation, as measured by ability (F1-score) to reconstruct arguments with explicit final conclusions (prediction) if and only if the target final conclusions are explicit.

3.5 Models

Any text-to-text language model is compatible with the proposed DeepA2 framework. We refer to models used within the framework as **ArgumentAnalyst**. In this study, we train and evaluate the transformer model T5 (Raffel et al., 2020) with 770M parameters as implemented by (Wolf et al., 2020).

3.6 Limitations

In the DeepA2 framework, arguments are reconstructed from relatively short and isolated texts, disregarding both the broader context of the argument and domain-specific background knowledge. This limits the framework, as presented here, in important ways: Implicit premises that are explicated in an argument reconstruction can neither be checked for plausibility nor for agreement with the author's broader convictions. In addition, the framework cannot assess an argument's dialectic function in a wider debate. It seems worthwhile to explore according extensions of the framework in future research.

4 Datasets

For the experiments reported below, we synthetically create two artificial argument analysis corpora that comply with the DeepA2 framework (see also Appendix A): **AAAC01** and **AAAC02**. In addition, we translate the synthetic *RuleTaker* (Clark et al., 2020) and the manually compiled *EntailmentBank* (Dalvi et al., 2021) datasets into our framework.

In argument analysis, one proceeds *from* a source text *to* its reconstruction. Creating the synthetic corpora, we reverse-engineer this process:

Step 1. We sample, first of all, a possibly complex argument (**A**) from a set of valid inference schemes. In doing so, we use a multi-step templating strategy (inspired by Betz et al., 2021) to translate symbolic forms into natural language schemes (which were generated by local domain experts) and to substitute natural language terms for placeholders. Premises (**P**), conclusion (**C**) and their formalization (**F, O, K**) are side-products of such a construction of an argument.

Step 2. Given the fully explicit argument (**A**), we compose a text (**S**) that presents the argument in a more or less transparent and faithful way. Such text creation involves: rendering the argument tree as a linear story, leaving out premises or conclusions (implicit premises and conclusions), inserting irrelevant material (distractors), using templates that obfuscate the logical form of a sentence, limiting the use of premise and conclusion indicators (such as "therefore"), applying rule-based and automatic paraphrasing. In composing the argumentative text (**S**), we may record its reasons (**R**) and conjectures (**J**).

Given the synthetic and controlled nature of our dataset, which involved eliciting rule templates from a group of local domain experts, all data is assumed to be correct by *construction*. As an additional check of correctness on the logic of our examples, we ran a symbolic theorem prover (De Moura and Bjørner, 2008) over the argument formalizations to verify their validity. To ensure the fluency of the underlying language templates, all templates were hand verified by the authors.

Our two datasets AAAC01 and AAAC02 differ in the following ways:

1. predicates and names are sampled from different, disjunct domains (texts are about, e.g., allergies and family relations versus, e.g., badminton and cooking) to test a model's robustness to lexical diversity (Rozen et al., 2019);
2. similarly, AAAC01 applies automatic paraphrasing (Alisetti, 2021) to the final source text whereas AAAC02 doesn't;
3. AAAC02 allows for imprecise renditions of logical formulas, while AAAC01 sticks to plain formulations to test robustness to variations in description of rules.

Each dataset contains diverse texts and arguments. Broadly speaking, data records may differ in terms of properties of the argument (step 1 above) and properties of the argument's presentation (step 2). Along these two dimensions, we define five homogeneous subsets of the data:

simple inference: arguments with a single inference step that neither involves negation nor compositional predicates;

complex inference: arguments with four inference steps that heavily rely on syntactically intricate schemes (e.g., transposition, or de Morgan);

plain presentation: all premises and conclusions are explicit in the source text which, in addition, contains no distractors;

mutilated presentation: at least two premises and one conclusion are implicit, while the text contains two distractors and explicitly states the final conclusion;

C&M: the argument's inference is complex, plus the text contains at least two distractors.

The *RuleTaker* and *EntailmentBank* datasets contain multi-hop inference trees (**A**). To import these into the DeepA2 framework, we create source texts (**S**) for the given arguments by means of simple templates (such as "{*theory*} All this entails: {*hypothesis*}") and record reasons (**R**) and conjectures (**J**) on the fly. Unlike AAAC and *EntailmentBank*, *RuleTaker* (as updated in Tafjord et al., 2020) contains an equal share of arguments for which (i) the conclusion follows from the premises, (ii) the conclusion contradicts the premises, (iii) the conclusion is independent of the premises.

5 Experiments and Results

As first and main experiment we train our base model (see Section 3.5) on the AAAC01 corpus, and evaluate the resulting ArgumentAnalyst model out-of-domain on AAAC02. ArgumentAnalyst undergoes multi-task training on 21 generative modes, which are interpreted as sequence-to-sequence tasks (the training set-up is further described in Appendix B).

The evaluation of ArgumentAnalyst on AAAC02 proceeds in two steps: (1.) prediction: produces output in accordance with 16 different generative chains (Appendix C); (2.) metrics application: assesses the quality of the generated output by means of the systematic and exegetic metrics of the DeepA2 framework (see Section 3.4).

Table 1 reports the ability of ArgumentAnalyst to generate systematically correct and exegetically adequate argument reconstructions. We obtain similar global results with the three chains *straight*, *hermeneutic cycle*, and *logical streamlining*, whose generated reconstructions mainly differ in terms of internal coherence (EXE-RSS, EXE-JSS) and text exploitation (EXE-TE). However, the different generative chains complement each other, as shown by *pooling*, which does not only outperform individual chains, but nearly attains oracle performance.

Moreover, ArgumentAnalyst produces much better reconstructions of simple inferences and plain presentations – compared to complex inferences and mutilated presentations, i.e., difficult problems (cf. Table 5 in App. D). In addition, within one and the same subset, substantial differences show up between the three generative chains. Globally speaking, *hermeneutic cycle* outperforms the other two chains for difficult problems.

Is ArgumentAnalyst capable of reliable self-evaluation? We have **validated the logic metric** (SYS-VAL), which passes on a self-generated formalization of the reconstructed argument to a theorem prover, in three ways: First of all, ArgumentAnalyst correctly recognizes *target* arguments as valid (with accuracy 92.7%), which has been verified by running the formalization subchain on target data. Secondly, virtually every generated argument with all-correct scheme instantiations (i.e., SYS-SCH = 1) is also – and correctly – recognized as logically valid. Thirdly, a manual analysis (**human-in-the-loop**) of 100 generated arguments with incorrect scheme instantiation (i.e., SYS-SCH $<$ 1) reveals a high rate of false negatives: roughly one half of all inferences that are not automatically identified as an instantiation of the given scheme actually do correctly instantiate it. The accordingly *adjusted* global ratio of correct scheme instantiations (Table 1) equals roughly 0.65 (rather than 0.31–0.33), which is consistent with the ratio of logically valid arguments being 0.72–0.73.

Do reconstructed arguments exhibit basic semantic flaws? Regarding the full dataset, ArgumentAnalyst produces nearly **flawless argument reconstructions**, committing basic errors (petitio, redundancy, unused statements) only very rarely (Table 1). And even for very difficult problems, two thirds of all generated arguments display no basic flaw whatsoever (Table 5, SYS-PP & SYS-RP & SYS-RC & SYS-US).

Are reconstructed arguments logically valid? Roughly 70% of all arguments generated by one of the three chains are logically valid (Table 1). More importantly, though, for virtually every source text in the dataset, there is at least one chain (out of 16) which reconstructs the text as a valid argument (*pooling*). Given that logical validity can be automatically assessed, the *pooled* system may thus **guarantee to yield a valid reconstruction**. Concerning different problem types (Table 5), *hermeneutic cycle* clearly outperforms the other chains as soon as the problem gets difficult. Additional analysis shows that ArgumentAnalyst can also **cope with underdetermination**, as 68% of all generated arguments whose final conclusion differs (BLEU $\leq$ .8) from the target argument's one – i.e., arguments that are not reconstructed as expected given the target data – are still logically valid.

Are the generated interpretations internally coherent? The generative chain *hermeneutic cycle* yields comprehensive argument reconstructions where premises (**P**) and conclusions (**C**) fit much better to detected reasons (**R**) and conjectures (**J**) than *straight* or *logical streamlining* (EXE-RSS, EXE-JSS). This holds globally (Table 1), as well as for easy, and for difficult problems (Table 5). Note that the *oracle* baseline for metrics EXE-RSS, EXE-JSS is well below 1, which reflects the fact that source texts may present arguments in highly mutilated ways; it is nearly attained by *pooling* the 16 different generative chains (Table 1).

Can ArgumentAnalyst detect reasons and conjectures, and fully exploit the text? The evaluation demonstrates that reason/conjecture detection on AAAC02 is a relatively easy task (EXE-PPR, EXE-PPJ).

	systematic metrics (SYS-*)						*exegetic metrics* (EXE-*)					
chain	**PP**	**RP**	**RC**	**US**	**SCH**	**VAL**	**MEQ**	**RSS**	**JSS**	**PPR**	**PPJ**	**TE**
straight	.95	.97	.96	.96	.33	.73	.80	-.08	-.10	.93	.93	.63
herm. cy.	.95	.98	.95	.93	.31	.72	.82	.16	.12	.93	.92	.71
logic. str.	.95	.97	.96	.95	.32	.72	.82	.11	.00	.93	.92	.69
pooling	1.0	1.0	1.0	1.0	.73	1.0	1.0	.26	.29	.96	.96	.97
oracle	*1.0*	*1.0*	*1.0*	*1.0*	*1.0*	*1.0*	*1.0*	*.30*	*.37*	*1.0*	*1.0*	*1.0*

Table 1: Performance of ArgumentAnalyst on the AAAC02 data as measured by systematic and exegetic metrics. Rows display results for three illustrative generative chains (*straight, hermeneutic cycle, logical streamlining*), for the item-wise best performing generative chain out of all 16 chains (*pooling*), and for oracle performance (*oracle*), which one obtains by applying the metrics to the target data itself.

	ArgAn$_{EB}$		*ArgAn*$_{AAAC,EB}$		*EntWr*
steps	straight	herm. cycle	straight	herm. cycle	
1	.863	.866	.816	.871	.951
2	.798	.815	.813	.826	.886
3	.812	.815	.826	.806	.858
4	.757	.791	.820	.822	.838
≥ 5	.795	.811	.786	.773	.742
any	.819	.830	.816	.834	.879

Table 2: Predictive performance of ArgumentAnalyst (*ArgAn*$_{EB}$, *ArgAn*$_{AAAC,EB}$) and EntailmentWriter (*EntWr*) for identifying reason statements in an input text (metric SYS-PPR) on the *EntailmentBank task2* dataset.

In contrast, fully exploiting a text (i.e., generating an argument with implicit final conclusion if and only if the underlying target argument has an implicit final conclusion, EXE-TE) is seemingly more challenging (Table 1). Again, *hermeneutic cycle* achieves best text exploitation, performing, however, clearly below *oracle* baseline – which may simply reflect the degree of underdetermination in the AAAC02 corpus.

In a second experiment we train two models on the imported *EntailmentBank* (*task1* and *task2*) dataset (see Section 4), namely: (1.) our base model (T5), which yields ArgumentAnalyst$_{EB}$; (2.) the ArgumentAnalyst model pretrained on AAAC02 (resulting in an intermediary pre-training set-up similar to Phang et al., 2018; Geva et al., 2020), which yields ArgumentAnalyst$_{AAAC,EB}$.

Since the *EntailmentBank* data doesn't contain formalizations, we can only train on 14 modes, which are interpreted as sequence-to-sequence tasks (see Appendix B). We evaluate the models on *task2* of *EntailmentBank* only, which contains problems with a relatively large number of distractors, and proceed in two steps as before: prediction (with 11 different generative chains) and metrics application. Dalvi et al. (2021) report the ability of *EntailmentWriter* (a fine-tuned T5-11b model) to correctly distinguish relevant premises of an argument from distractors in terms of a F1-score, which corresponds to our metric EXE-PPR. That's why the sole focus in this second experiment is on EXE-PPR.

Table 2 describes the ability of ArgumentAnalyst models to correctly tell apart relevant premises from mere distractors in the *EntailmentBank task2* dataset for two generative chains (*straight*, which directly outputs reason statements, and *hermeneutic cycle*, which tries to reconstruct the argument first and uses both source text and argument to identify reasons), and compares this with the performance of *EntailmentWriter* (scores from Dalvi et al., 2021). The results, shown separately for arguments with a specific number of inference steps, let us draw three conclusions:

First, *ArgumentAnalyst* outperforms *EntailmentWriter* on difficult problems with more than 4 inference steps / sub-arguments.

Second, using the sophisticated chain *hermeneutic cycle* improves predictive performance compared to the simple *straight* chain.

Third, the chain *hermeneutic cycle* (unlike *straight*) generally benefits from intermediary pre-training on AAAC – caveat: not so for arguments with more than 4 steps. This latter observation might be due to the fact that the AAAC02 corpus, by construction, doesn't contain arguments with more than 4 steps, so that pre-training biases the model towards shorter arguments.

In a third experiment we explore the following hypothesis:

Informative higher-order evidence. The degree to which ArgumentAnalyst struggles in reconstructing a given argument (presented in the source text) as logically valid is a reliable indicator for whether the original argument is fallacious or not.

To test this hypothesis, we apply ArgumentAnalyst (trained on AAAC02, see above) to the *RuleTaker* data as imported into the DeepA2 framework (see Section 4): ArgumentAnalyst produces – by means of 13 generative chains – comprehensive reconstructions, to which the systematic and exegetic metrics are applied. *RuleTaker* contains an equal share of arguments whose conclusions follow from (label=valid), contradict (label=contradiction), or are independent of (label=neutral) the corresponding premises. Now, informative higher-order evidence would allow us to correctly predict these labels. And this is exactly what we observe: First, if reconstructions of one and the same source text which are independently generated with different chains agree (disagree), then the original argument tends to be valid (invalid). Second, by training simple classifiers on our argumentative metrics and further properties of the reconstructions, we robustly achieve a predictive accuracy 10% above the random baseline. While this is far below the SOTA results of tailor-made RuleTaker (Clark et al., 2020) and ProofWriter (Tafjord et al., 2020) models on this data, our findings nonetheless confirm the above hypothesis.

6 Conclusion

In this paper, we have presented and implemented a multi-angular, modular framework for deep argument analysis (DeepA2). It allows for defining a large variety of generative modes by combining different dimensions of the data. These modes, in turn, can be concatenated into complex generative chains. ArgumentAnalyst – a text-to-text model set up and trained within the DeepA2 framework – yields plausible reconstructions of argumentative texts. Our empirical findings vindicate the overall framework and highlight the following **advantages of a multi-angular, modular design** in general: First of all, modular chains may emulate established, well-proven, typically piece-meal, scholarly techniques for text analysis (heuristics), which hence may provide **normative, methodological guidance** in setting up NLP systems. Secondly, by defining and implementing different modular chains, and investigating the plurality of generated solutions, one can systematically **explore the system's uncertainty as well as the tasks's underdetermination**. Thirdly, monitoring the system during modular computation yields diagnostically useful information (e.g., intermediary results) which not only describes the model's performance on the given problem, but which additionally allows us – as **higher-order evidence** – to characterize (e.g., classify) the original problem in the first place. Fourthly, breaking down a complex task into sub-tasks with intermediary results that can be further processed and re-combined helps to **overcome input size limitations** of neural language models. Fifthly, modular generation with meaningful modes allows users to follow the system, comprehend generated solutions, verify sub-steps and detect errors – the NLP system becomes a **transparent, explainable AI** (Miller, 2019). Finally, modular NLP systems as described by DeepA2 may be connected to a user-interface which promises **fine-grained interactive control** of modular generations and seamless cognitive cooperation of AI and human experts in analysing texts.

Acknowledgments

We're indebted to Christian Voigt for his critical and constructive feedback throughout the DeepA2 project.

References

Christopher Akiki and Martin Potthast. 2020. Exploring argument retrieval with transformers notebook for the touche lab on argument retrieval at clef 2020.

Robert Alexy. 1989. *A theory of legal argumentation: the theory of rational discourse as theory of legal justification.* Clarendon Press, Oxford.

Sai Vamsi Alisetti. 2021. Paraphrase generator with t5. https://github.com/Vamsi995/Paraphrase-Generator.

Pratyay Banerjee and Chitta Baral. 2020. Self-supervised knowledge triplet learning for zero-shot question answering. In *Proceedings of the 2020 Conference on Empirical Methods in Natural Language Processing (EMNLP)*, pages 151–162.

Roy Bar-Haim, Lilach Eden, Roni Friedman, Yoav Kantor, Dan Lahav, and N. Slonim. 2020. From arguments to key points: Towards automatic argument summarization. In *ACL*.

Jordan Beck, Bikalpa Neupane, and John M. Carroll. 2019. Managing conflict in online debate communities. *First Monday*, 24(7).

Gregor Betz, Christian Voigt, and Kyle Richardson. 2021. Critical thinking for language models. In *Proceedings of the 14th International Conference on Computational Semantics (IWCS)*. Association for Computational Linguistics.

Kaj Bostrom, Xinyu Zhao, Swarat Chaudhuri, and Greg Durrett. 2021. Flexible operations for natural language deduction. *ArXiv*, abs/2104.08825.

Tracey Bowell and Gary Kemp. 2014. *Critical Thinking: A Concise Guide*, 4th edition edition. Routledge, London.

Michael Bruce and Steven Barbone. 2011. *Just the arguments: 100 of the most important arguments in Western philosophy*. Wiley-Blackwell, Chichester, West Sussex, U.K.

Georg Brun. 2014. Reconstructing arguments: Formalization and reflective equilibrium. *Logical Analysis and History of Philosophy*, 17:94–129.

Georg Brun and Gregor Betz. 2016. Analysing practical argumentation. In Sven Ove Hansson and Gertrude Hirsch-Hadorn, editors, *The Argumentative Turn in Policy Analysis. Reasoning about Uncertainty*, pages 39–77. Springer, Cham.

Tuhin Chakrabarty, Aadit Trivedi, and Smaranda Muresan. 2021. Implicit premise generation with discourse-aware commonsense knowledge models. In *EMNLP*.

David Christensen. 2010. Higher-order evidence. *Philosophy and Phenomenological Research*, 81(1):185–215.

Peter Clark, Oyvind Tafjord, and Kyle Richardson. 2020. Transformers as soft reasoners over language. In *Proceedings of the Twenty-Ninth International Joint Conference on Artificial Intelligence (IJCAI-20)*, pages 3882–3890.

Bhavana Dalvi, Peter Jansen, Oyvind Tafjord, Zhengnan Xie, Hannah Smith, Leighanna Pipatanangkura, and Peter Clark. 2021. Explaining answers with entailment trees. *arXiv preprint arXiv:2104.08661*.

Leonardo De Moura and Nikolaj Bjørner. 2008. Z3: An efficient smt solver. In *International conference on Tools and Algorithms for the Construction and Analysis of Systems*, pages 337–340. Springer.

J. Devlin, Ming-Wei Chang, Kenton Lee, and Kristina Toutanova. 2019. Bert: Pre-training of deep bidirectional transformers for language understanding. In *NAACL-HLT*.

L. Ein-Dor, Eyal Shnarch, Lena Dankin, Alon Halfon, Benjamin Sznajder, Ariel Gera, Carlos Alzate, Martin Gleize, Leshem Choshen, Yufang Hou, Yonatan Bilu, R. Aharonov, and N. Slonim. 2020. Corpus wide argument mining - a working solution. *ArXiv*, abs/1911.10763.

Isabela Fairclough and Norman Fairclough. 2012. *Political Discourse Analysis*. Routledge, London.

Richard Feldman. 1998. *Reason and Argument*, 2nd edition. Pearson, Prentice hall.

Alec Fisher. 2004. *The Logic of Real Arguments*, 2nd ed edition. Cambridge University Press, New York.

Mor Geva, Ankit Gupta, and Jonathan Berant. 2020. Injecting numerical reasoning skills into language models. In *ACL*.

Nicolas Gontier, Koustuv Sinha, Siva Reddy, and Christopher Pal. 2020. Measuring systematic generalization in neural proof generation with transformers.

Shai Gretz, Roni Friedman, Edo Cohen-Karlik, Assaf Toledo, Dan Lahav, R. Aharonov, and N. Slonim. 2020. A large-scale dataset for argument quality ranking: Construction and analysis. *ArXiv*, abs/1911.11408.

Ivan Habernal, Judith Eckle-Kohler, and Iryna Gurevych. 2014. Argumentation mining on the web from information seeking perspective. In Elena Cabrio, Serena Villata, and Adam Wyner, editors, *ArgNLP 2014. Frontiers and Connections between Argumentation Theory and Natural Language Processing. Proceedings of the Workshop on Frontiers and Connections between Argumentation Theory and Natural Language Processing*. CEUR-WS.org.

Ivan Habernal, Henning Wachsmuth, Iryna Gurevych, and Benno Stein. 2018. The argument reasoning comprehension task: Identification and reconstruction of implicit warrants. In *NAACL-HLT*.

Sven Ove Hansson and Gertrude Hirsch-Hadorn, editors. 2016. *The Argumentative Turn in Policy Analysis. Reasoning about Uncertainty*. Springer, Cham.

Aishwarya Kamath and R. Das. 2019. A survey on semantic parsing. *ArXiv*, abs/1812.00978.

Nora Kassner and Hinrich Schütze. 2020. Negated and misprimed probes for pretrained language models: Birds can talk, but cannot fly. In *Proceedings of the 58th Annual Meeting of the Association for Computational Linguistics*, pages 7811–7818, Online. Association for Computational Linguistics.

Joe Y. F. Lau. 2011. *An Introduction to Critical Thinking and Creativity: Think More, Think Better*. Wiley, Hoboken, N.J.

John Lawrence and Chris Reed. 2020. Argument Mining: A Survey. *Computational Linguistics*, 45(4):765–818.

Hannes Leitgeb and André Carus. 2021. Rudolf Carnap. Supplement D: Methodology. In Edward N. Zalta, editor, *The Stanford Encyclopedia of Philosophy*, Summer 2021 edition. Metaphysics Research Lab, Stanford University.

Mike Lewis, Yinhan Liu, Naman Goyal, Marjan Ghazvininejad, Abdelrahman Mohamed, Omer Levy, Ves Stoyanov, and Luke Zettlemoyer. 2019. Bart: Denoising sequence-to-sequence pre-training for natural language generation, translation, and comprehension.

Tim Miller. 2019. Explanation in artificial intelligence: Insights from the social sciences. *Artif. Intell.*, 267:1–38.

Marie-Francine Moens. 2018. Argumentation mining: How can a machine acquire common sense and world knowledge? *Argument & Computation*, 9:1–14.

Jason Phang, Thibault Févry, and Samuel R. Bowman. 2018. Sentence encoders on stilts: Supplementary training on intermediate labeled-data tasks. *CoRR*, abs/1811.01088.

Martin Potthast, Lukas Gienapp, F. Euchner, Nick Heilenkötter, Nicolas Weidmann, Henning Wachsmuth, Benno Stein, and Matthias Hagen. 2019. Argument search: Assessing argument relevance. *Proceedings of the 42nd International ACM SIGIR Conference on Research and Development in Information Retrieval.*

Alec Radford, Jeffrey Wu, Rewon Child, David Luan, Dario Amodei, and Ilya Sutskever. 2019. Language models are unsupervised multitask learners. *Preprint.*

Colin Raffel, Noam Shazeer, Adam Roberts, Katherine Lee, Sharan Narang, Michael Matena, Yanqi Zhou, Wei Li, and Peter J Liu. 2020. Exploring the limits of transfer learning with a unified text-to-text transformer. *Journal of Machine Learning Research*, 21:1–67.

J. Rodrigues, Ruben Branco, J. Silva, and A. Branco. 2020. Reproduction and revival of the argument reasoning comprehension task. In *LREC*.

Ohad Rozen, Vered Shwartz, Roee Aharoni, and Ido Dagan. 2019. Diversify your datasets: Analyzing generalization via controlled variance in adversarial datasets.

Swarnadeep Saha, Sayan Ghosh, Shashank Srivastava, and Mohit Bansal. 2020. Prover: Proof generation for interpretable reasoning over rules. In *Proceedings of the 2020 Conference on Empirical Methods in Natural Language Processing, EMNLP 2020, Online, November 16-20, 2020*, pages 122–136. Association for Computational Linguistics.

Swarnadeep Saha, Prateek Yadav, and M. Bansal. 2021. multiprover: Generating multiple proofs for improved interpretability in rule reasoning. *ArXiv*, abs/2106.01354.

Oliver R. Scholz. 2000. Was es heißt, eine argumentation zu verstehen? - zur konstitutiven rolle von präsumtionen. In Geert-Lueke Lueken, editor, *Formen der Argumentation*, pages 161–176. Leipziger Universitätsverlag, Leipzig.

Thibault Sellam, Dipanjan Das, and Ankur P Parikh. 2020. Bleurt: Learning robust metrics for text generation. *arXiv preprint arXiv:2004.04696*.

Richard Shin, C. H. Lin, Sam Thomson, Charles Chen, Subhro Roy, Emmanouil Antonios Platanios, Adam Pauls, D. Klein, J. Eisner, and Benjamin Van Durme. 2021. Constrained language models yield few-shot semantic parsers. *ArXiv*, abs/2104.08768.

Andrew Siegel. 2018. Ethics of Stem Cell Research. In Edward N. Zalta, editor, *The Stanford Encyclopedia of Philosophy*, Winter 2018 edition. Metaphysics Research Lab, Stanford University.

Shahbaz Syed, Khalid Al-Khatib, Milad Alshomary, Henning Wachsmuth, and Martin Potthast. 2021. Generating informative conclusions for argumentative texts. In *FINDINGS*.

Oyvind Tafjord and Peter Clark. 2021. General-purpose question-answering with macaw.

Oyvind Tafjord, Bhavana Dalvi Mishra, and Peter Clark. 2020. Proofwriter: Generating implications, proofs, and abductive statements over natural language. *arXiv preprint arXiv:2012.13048*.

Alon Talmor, Yanai Elazar, Yoav Goldberg, and Jonathan Berant. 2020. olmpics - on what language model pre-training captures. *Trans. Assoc. Comput. Linguistics*, 8:743–758.

Christian Voigt. 2014. Argdown and the stacked masonry layout: Two user interfaces for non-expert users. In *Computational Models of Argument*, pages 483–484, Amsterdam et al. IOS Press.

Henning Wachsmuth, Martin Potthast, Khalid Al Khatib, Yamen Ajjour, Jana Puschmann, Jiani Qu, Jonas Dorsch, Viorel Morari, Janek Bevendorff, and Benno Stein. 2017. Building an argument search engine for the web. In *ArgMining@EMNLP*.

Thomas Wolf, Lysandre Debut, Victor Sanh, Julien Chaumond, Clement Delangue, Anthony Moi, Pierric Cistac, Tim Rault, Rémi Louf, Morgan Funtowicz, Joe Davison, Sam Shleifer, Patrick von Platen, Clara Ma, Yacine Jernite, Julien Plu, Canwen Xu, Teven Le Scao, Sylvain Gugger, Mariama Drame, Quentin Lhoest, and Alexander M. Rush. 2020. Transformers: State-of-the-art natural language processing. In *Proceedings of the 2020 Conference on Empirical Methods in Natural Language Processing: System Demonstrations*, pages 38–45, Online. Association for Computational Linguistics.

A Synthetic Argument Data

The AAAC datasets used in this study are publicly available via Huggingface's Hub – `https://huggingface.co/datasets/debatelab/aaac` – where the construction of the datasets is documented meticulously.

A synthetically generated AAAC record, which nicely illustrates the underdetermination of argument reconstruction, with two implicit premises, one distracting statement and a simple (one-step) argument (formatted as presented to the model):

```
source: It is not the case that Tracy
is not an admirer of Fullerton and Tracy
has seen La Habra. Plus, if someone
loves Chico, then they haven't visited
Monterey, owing to the fact that loving
Laguna Beach is sufficient for not
having visited Monterey.
reasons: loving Laguna Beach is
sufficient for not having visited
Monterey (ref: (2))
conjectures: if someone loves Chico,
then they haven't visited Monterey (ref:
(4))
argdown:
(1) If someone is an admirer of Chico,
then they are an admirer of Laguna Beach
or a visitor of Stockton.
(2) If someone admires Laguna Beach,
then they haven't visited Monterey.
(3) If someone has visited Stockton,
then they haven't visited Monterey.
-
with generalized dilemma (neg variant)
from (1) (2) (3)
-
(4) If someone admires Chico, then they
haven't visited Monterey.
premises: If someone is an admirer
of Chico, then they are an admirer of
Laguna Beach or a visitor of Stockton.
(ref: (1)) | If someone admires Laguna
Beach, then they haven't visited
Monterey. (ref: (2)) | If someone
has visited Stockton, then they haven't
visited Monterey. (ref: (3))
conclusion: If someone admires Chico,
then they haven't visited Monterey.
(ref: (4))
premises_form: (x): Fx -> (G x v H x)
(ref: (1)) | (x): G x -> not I x (ref:
(2)) | (x): H x -> not I x (ref: (3))
conclusion_form: (x): F x -> not I x
(ref: (4))
keys: F: admirer of Chico | G: admirer
of Laguna Beach | H: visitor of Stockton
| I: visitor of Monterey
```

B Training Set-up

By interpreting a generative mode as a sequence-to-sequence task, we may translate a multi-angular DeepA2 dataset (e.g., AAAC01) into a multi-task sequence-to-sequence format, on which a sequence-to-sequence model can be trained. For each record in the multi-angular DeepA2 dataset, we randomly sample 14 modes in accordance with the weights provided in Table 3 and add, for each mode, a corresponding sequence-to-sequence record to the training data. This results, for AAAC01, in a sequence-to-sequence training dataset with 14×16.000 records.

Our models (base model T5-large with 770M parameters, and pretrained ArgumentAnalyst) are trained with batch-size 2 and learning rate 0.00001. For AAAC01, eval loss starts to increase at epoch 8; with *EntailmentBank* data, eval loss increases from epoch 2 onwards.

mode	w_1	w_2	mode	w_1	w_2	mode	w_1	w_2
S⇝A	1.	1.	S⇝R	1.	1.	P⇝F	.7	–
SR⇝A	1.	1.	SJ⇝R	1.	1.	PCO⇝F	.7	–
SJ⇝A	1.	1.	SA⇝R	1.	1.	C⇝O	.7	–
SRJ⇝A	1.	1.	S⇝J	1.	1.	CPF⇝O	.7	–
RJ⇝A	1.	1.	SR⇝J	1.	1.	PF⇝K	.7	–
PC⇝A	1.	1.	SA⇝J	1.	1.	CO⇝K	.7	–
A⇝P	.2	.2	A⇝C	.2	.2	PFCO⇝K	.7	–
FK⇝P	.7	–	OK⇝C	.7	–			

Table 3: 21 generative modes with corresponding weights in AAAC (w_1) and *EntailmentBank* (w_2) training data.

C Iterative Prediction with Generative Chains

Generative chains are implemented with a dynamic dictionary (9 keys, corresp. to the dimensions of DeepA2 data), which is initialized with the source text, provides input for the generative modes, and is updated after each generative step with the mode's generated output. Output is generated with beam search decoding and beam width 2.

Table 4 displays all generative chains we resort to in this study, all of which are used in the *first experiment*. The *second experiment* makes use of chains 1–11. The *third experiment* deploys chains 1–13.

D Additional Results

Table 5 assesses ArgumentAnalyst's reconstructions on specific subsets of the AAAC02 dataset (defined in Section 4) for three representative generative chains.

Table 6 details the performance of ArgumentAnalyst on the entire AAAC02 dataset as measured by tailor-made argumentative metrics. Table 7 shows the corresponding performance on out-of -sample eval data AAAC01.

Distinguishing four mutually exclusive subsets of AAAC02, Tables 8–11 detail the the quality of ArgumentAnalyst's reconstruction for easy and difficult problems. Tables 12–15 present the corresponding out-of-sample performance on the equally partitioned AAAC01 dataset (eval split).

#	mode sequence	len.	soph.
1	S⇝A S⇝R S⇝J	3	0
2	S⇝J S⇝R SJ⇝A	3	1
3	S⇝J S⇝R SR⇝A	3	1
4	S⇝J S⇝R RJ⇝A	3	2
5	S⇝J SJ⇝R RJ⇝A	3	3
6	S⇝J SJ⇝R SRJ⇝A	3	3
7	S⇝R SR⇝J RJ⇝A	3	3
8	S⇝R SR⇝J SRJ⇝A	3	3
9	S⇝A SA⇝R SA⇝J RJ⇝A	4	4
10	S⇝A SA⇝R SA⇝J SRJ⇝A	4	4
11	S⇝A SA⇝R SA⇝J SRJ⇝A SA⇝R SA⇝J SRJ⇝A	7	8
12	S⇝A A⇝P A⇝C P⇝F PF⇝K FK⇝P PC⇝A SA⇝R SA⇝J	9	11
13	S⇝A A⇝P A⇝C C⇝O CO⇝K OK⇝C PC⇝A SA⇝R SA⇝J	9	11
14	S⇝A A⇝P A⇝C C⇝O CO⇝K OK⇝C PC⇝A A⇝P A⇝C P⇝F PF⇝K FK⇝P PC⇝A SA⇝R SA⇝J	15	20
15	S⇝A A⇝P A⇝C P⇝F CPF⇝O PFCO⇝K FK⇝P OK⇝C PC⇝A SA⇝R SA⇝J	11	18
16	S⇝A A⇝P A⇝C P⇝F CPF⇝O PCO⇝F PFCO⇝K FK⇝P OK⇝C PC⇝A SA⇝R SA⇝J	12	21

Table 4: 16 generative chains (without final formalization sub-sequences) evaluated in this study. The illustrative chains highlighted in the main paper are #1 (straight), #9 (hermeneutic cycle), and #13 (logical streamlining).

	inference		*presentation*		
chain	simple N=1274	compl. N=180	plain N=330	mutil. N=114	C&M N=70
SYS-PP & SYS-RP & SYS-RC & SYS-US					
straight	.95	.72	.98	.61	.69
herm. c.	.94	.68	.96	.67	.61
log. str.	.95	.68	.98	.64	.61
SYS-VAL					
straight	.84	.48	.88	.40	.34
herm. c.	.83	.56	.84	.49	.50
log. str.	.82	.47	.86	.46	.37
EXE-RSS					
straight	.03	-.25	.05	-.31	-.30
herm. c.	.20	.08	.15	.08	.11
log. str.	.17	-.01	.13	.01	-.06
EXE-JSS					
straight	.06	-.32	.10	-.37	-.37
herm. c.	.23	-.06	.21	-.03	-.21
log. str.	.13	-.26	.07	-.26	-.40

Table 5: Performance of ArgumentAnalyst on specific subsets (columns) of the AAAC02 data as measured by selected systematic and exegetic metrics (sub-tables). Rows display results for three illustrative generative chains (*straight*, *hermeneutic cycle*, *logical streamlining*).

	systematic metrics (SYS-*)						exegetic metrics (EXE-*)					
chain	**PP**	**RP**	**RC**	**US**	**SCH**	**VAL**	**MEQ**	**RSS**	**JSS**	**PPR**	**PPJ**	**TE**
#1	0.95	0.97	0.96	0.96	0.33	0.73	0.80	-0.08	-0.10	0.93	0.93	0.63
#2	0.95	0.97	0.94	0.94	0.33	0.71	0.80	-0.09	0.04	0.93	0.93	0.67
#3	0.95	0.98	0.95	0.93	0.31	0.70	0.80	0.10	-0.11	0.93	0.93	0.62
#4	0.94	0.97	0.94	0.92	0.30	0.70	0.80	0.12	-0.00	0.93	0.93	0.66
#5	0.94	0.97	0.95	0.91	0.30	0.70	0.83	0.13	0.05	0.94	0.93	0.69
#6	0.94	0.97	0.95	0.93	0.31	0.70	0.83	0.10	0.03	0.94	0.93	0.67
#7	0.93	0.97	0.95	0.92	0.29	0.70	0.83	0.13	0.05	0.93	0.92	0.68
#8	0.94	0.97	0.95	0.93	0.30	0.69	0.83	0.10	0.02	0.93	0.92	0.67
#9	0.95	0.98	0.95	0.93	0.31	0.72	0.82	0.16	0.12	0.93	0.92	0.71
#10	0.96	0.98	0.96	0.94	0.32	0.71	0.82	0.14	0.09	0.93	0.92	0.69
#11	0.96	0.98	0.96	0.93	0.32	0.71	0.82	0.15	0.11	0.93	0.92	0.71
#12	0.93	0.95	0.94	0.94	0.32	0.71	0.81	-0.17	-0.08	0.93	0.92	0.68
#13	0.95	0.97	0.96	0.95	0.32	0.72	0.82	0.11	-0.00	0.93	0.92	0.69
#14	0.93	0.95	0.94	0.94	0.32	0.70	0.81	-0.18	-0.14	0.93	0.92	0.66
#15	0.92	0.96	0.94	0.95	0.33	0.71	0.81	-0.20	-0.19	0.93	0.92	0.65
#16	0.92	0.96	0.94	0.94	0.33	0.72	0.81	-0.20	-0.19	0.93	0.92	0.65

Table 6: Performance of ArgumentAnalyst for systematic and exegetic metrics on the entire OOD eval data (AAAC02). Rows display mean results for each of the 16 generative chains.

	systematic metrics (SYS-*)						exegetic metrics (EXE-*)					
chain	**PP**	**RP**	**RC**	**US**	**SCH**	**VAL**	**MEQ**	**RSS**	**JSS**	**PPR**	**PPJ**	**TE**
#1	0.97	0.98	0.97	0.98	0.61	0.87	0.78	0.08	0.13	0.95	0.95	0.64
#2	0.97	0.98	0.96	0.97	0.60	0.87	0.78	0.09	0.24	0.95	0.95	0.68
#3	0.96	0.98	0.96	0.97	0.58	0.86	0.78	0.26	0.12	0.95	0.95	0.64
#4	0.95	0.98	0.95	0.96	0.57	0.85	0.78	0.26	0.20	0.95	0.95	0.67
#5	0.96	0.98	0.95	0.96	0.57	0.84	0.80	0.27	0.27	0.96	0.95	0.70
#6	0.97	0.98	0.96	0.96	0.58	0.84	0.80	0.26	0.24	0.96	0.95	0.69
#7	0.95	0.98	0.96	0.96	0.57	0.86	0.79	0.27	0.26	0.95	0.94	0.71
#8	0.96	0.98	0.96	0.96	0.57	0.85	0.79	0.26	0.25	0.95	0.94	0.70
#9	0.97	0.99	0.97	0.97	0.59	0.88	0.79	0.31	0.36	0.96	0.95	0.78
#10	0.97	0.99	0.97	0.97	0.60	0.87	0.79	0.30	0.34	0.96	0.95	0.77
#11	0.97	0.99	0.97	0.97	0.60	0.87	0.79	0.31	0.35	0.96	0.95	0.77
#12	0.95	0.97	0.95	0.96	0.54	0.84	0.79	0.17	0.25	0.96	0.94	0.75
#13	0.97	0.99	0.97	0.97	0.61	0.87	0.79	0.29	0.32	0.96	0.95	0.76
#14	0.95	0.97	0.95	0.96	0.54	0.84	0.79	0.16	0.24	0.96	0.94	0.74
#15	0.94	0.97	0.95	0.96	0.54	0.85	0.79	0.15	0.18	0.96	0.95	0.73
#16	0.94	0.97	0.95	0.95	0.54	0.85	0.79	0.15	0.19	0.96	0.95	0.73

Table 7: Performance of ArgumentAnalyst for systematic and exegetic metrics on the entire OOS eval data (AAAC01). Rows display mean results for each of the 16 generative chains.

chain	*inference* simple	complex	*presentation* plain	mutilat.	C&M
		SYS-PP & SYS-RP & SYS-RC & SYS-US			
#1	0.95	0.72	0.98	0.61	0.69
#2	0.93	0.66	0.96	0.59	0.60
#3	0.92	0.69	0.96	0.68	0.73
#4	0.92	0.66	0.95	0.69	0.60
#5	0.92	0.68	0.95	0.59	0.61
#6	0.93	0.66	0.97	0.68	0.59
#7	0.92	0.67	0.96	0.62	0.64
#8	0.92	0.66	0.95	0.64	0.66
#9	0.94	0.68	0.96	0.67	0.61
#10	0.94	0.73	0.98	0.68	0.77
#11	0.94	0.69	0.98	0.66	0.73
#12	0.93	0.60	0.95	0.57	0.50
#13	0.95	0.68	0.98	0.64	0.61
#14	0.92	0.57	0.93	0.58	0.49
#15	0.92	0.66	0.95	0.59	0.56
#16	0.92	0.64	0.95	0.56	0.60

Table 8: Performance of ArgumentAnalyst for selected systematic metric (SYS-PP & SYS-RP & SYS-RC & SYS-US) on specific subsets (columns) of the OOD eval data.

chain	*inference* simple	complex	*presentation* plain	mutilat.	C&M
		SYS-VAL			
#1	0.84	0.48	0.88	0.40	0.34
#2	0.82	0.54	0.84	0.47	0.46
#3	0.82	0.44	0.87	0.39	0.36
#4	0.81	0.48	0.83	0.44	0.43
#5	0.82	0.44	0.85	0.45	0.37
#6	0.81	0.46	0.85	0.42	0.41
#7	0.83	0.44	0.82	0.46	0.49
#8	0.80	0.44	0.83	0.40	0.40
#9	0.83	0.56	0.84	0.49	0.50
#10	0.82	0.50	0.85	0.46	0.43
#11	0.82	0.48	0.84	0.46	0.41
#12	0.81	0.47	0.84	0.42	0.37
#13	0.82	0.47	0.86	0.46	0.37
#14	0.80	0.48	0.82	0.41	0.40
#15	0.82	0.45	0.84	0.50	0.33
#16	0.83	0.52	0.85	0.46	0.43

Table 9: Performance of ArgumentAnalyst for selected systematic metric (SYS-VAL) on specific subsets (columns) of the OOD eval data.

chain	*inference* simple	complex	*presentation* plain	mutilat.	C&M
		EXE-RSS			
#1	0.03	-0.25	0.05	-0.31	-0.30
#2	0.02	-0.27	0.07	-0.33	-0.31
#3	0.15	-0.03	0.12	-0.01	-0.06
#4	0.16	0.01	0.12	-0.01	0.04
#5	0.18	0.04	0.13	0.04	0.06
#6	0.17	-0.04	0.12	-0.02	-0.09
#7	0.18	0.05	0.14	0.03	0.08
#8	0.16	-0.02	0.12	-0.02	-0.07
#9	0.20	0.08	0.15	0.08	0.11
#10	0.19	0.04	0.15	0.05	-0.01
#11	0.21	0.04	0.15	0.07	-0.03
#12	-0.14	-0.20	-0.12	-0.23	-0.25
#13	0.17	-0.01	0.13	0.01	-0.06
#14	-0.17	-0.22	-0.16	-0.23	-0.26
#15	-0.19	-0.23	-0.24	-0.24	-0.23
#16	-0.19	-0.23	-0.24	-0.25	-0.24

Table 10: Performance of ArgumentAnalyst for selected exegetic metrics (EXE-RSS) on specific subsets (columns) of the OOD eval data.

chain	*inference* simple	complex	*presentation* plain	mutilat.	C&M
		EXE-JSS			
#1	0.06	-0.32	0.10	-0.37	-0.37
#2	0.16	-0.17	0.19	-0.12	-0.26
#3	0.02	-0.32	0.03	-0.42	-0.33
#4	0.12	-0.17	0.13	-0.14	-0.19
#5	0.15	-0.11	0.15	-0.08	-0.18
#6	0.16	-0.14	0.15	-0.22	-0.22
#7	0.16	-0.11	0.16	-0.10	-0.18
#8	0.15	-0.18	0.14	-0.19	-0.27
#9	0.23	-0.06	0.21	-0.03	-0.21
#10	0.23	-0.12	0.21	-0.15	-0.27
#11	0.25	-0.13	0.20	-0.11	-0.27
#12	0.06	-0.36	0.04	-0.28	-0.47
#13	0.13	-0.26	0.07	-0.26	-0.40
#14	-0.02	-0.39	-0.07	-0.31	-0.48
#15	-0.08	-0.41	-0.16	-0.36	-0.49
#16	-0.08	-0.37	-0.15	-0.35	-0.45

Table 11: Performance of ArgumentAnalyst for selected exegetic metric (EXE-JSS) on specific subsets (columns) of the OOD eval data.

chain	*inference* simple	*inference* complex	*presentation* plain	*presentation* mutilat.	C&M
			SYS-PP & SYS-RP & SYS-RC & SYS-US		
#1	0.98	0.78	1.00	0.75	0.76
#2	0.97	0.77	0.99	0.70	0.73
#3	0.95	0.79	0.96	0.77	0.74
#4	0.95	0.76	0.96	0.69	0.73
#5	0.97	0.75	0.98	0.66	0.74
#6	0.96	0.77	0.98	0.73	0.78
#7	0.96	0.73	0.96	0.71	0.72
#8	0.97	0.75	0.97	0.73	0.74
#9	0.98	0.80	0.99	0.80	0.70
#10	0.98	0.78	0.99	0.80	0.73
#11	0.98	0.78	0.99	0.80	0.71
#12	0.97	0.71	0.97	0.70	0.67
#13	0.98	0.81	0.99	0.76	0.78
#14	0.96	0.73	0.96	0.70	0.69
#15	0.97	0.72	0.96	0.70	0.68
#16	0.97	0.72	0.96	0.68	0.68

Table 12: Performance of ArgumentAnalyst for selected systematic metric (SYS-PP & SYS-RP & SYS-RC & SYS-US) on specific subsets (columns) of the OOS eval data.

chain	*inference* simple	*inference* complex	*presentation* plain	*presentation* mutilat.	C&M
			SYS-VAL		
#1	0.97	0.68	0.96	0.74	0.74
#2	0.97	0.68	0.97	0.73	0.71
#3	0.94	0.70	0.94	0.72	0.71
#4	0.95	0.65	0.94	0.68	0.71
#5	0.96	0.59	0.95	0.65	0.62
#6	0.95	0.62	0.96	0.69	0.63
#7	0.94	0.66	0.94	0.66	0.71
#8	0.95	0.67	0.95	0.69	0.69
#9	0.97	0.65	0.97	0.72	0.69
#10	0.97	0.67	0.97	0.68	0.72
#11	0.97	0.70	0.97	0.68	0.74
#12	0.95	0.63	0.95	0.72	0.70
#13	0.97	0.68	0.95	0.73	0.73
#14	0.95	0.63	0.94	0.72	0.69
#15	0.95	0.65	0.94	0.75	0.71
#16	0.95	0.65	0.95	0.73	0.71

Table 13: Performance of ArgumentAnalyst for selected systematic metric (SYS-VAL) on specific subsets (columns) of the OOS eval data.

chain	*inference* simple	*inference* complex	*presentation* plain	*presentation* mutilat.	C&M
			EXE-RSS		
#1	0.19	-0.16	0.11	-0.07	-0.18
#2	0.21	-0.13	0.10	-0.05	-0.15
#3	0.30	0.11	0.17	0.22	0.06
#4	0.29	0.16	0.16	0.24	0.16
#5	0.32	0.18	0.19	0.23	0.18
#6	0.31	0.11	0.18	0.19	0.07
#7	0.30	0.15	0.17	0.25	0.16
#8	0.30	0.12	0.17	0.24	0.08
#9	0.33	0.23	0.19	0.30	0.23
#10	0.33	0.20	0.19	0.27	0.16
#11	0.33	0.21	0.19	0.28	0.16
#12	0.20	0.06	0.11	0.16	0.04
#13	0.33	0.12	0.19	0.26	0.07
#14	0.20	0.06	0.10	0.16	0.03
#15	0.18	0.04	0.07	0.14	0.00
#16	0.18	0.04	0.07	0.11	0.02

Table 14: Performance of ArgumentAnalyst for selected exegetic metrics (EXE-RSS) on specific subsets (columns) of the OOS eval data.

chain	*inference* simple	*inference* complex	*presentation* plain	*presentation* mutilat.	C&M
			EXE-JSS		
#1	0.35	-0.14	0.36	-0.09	-0.13
#2	0.40	0.02	0.39	0.10	0.02
#3	0.30	-0.15	0.29	-0.08	-0.15
#4	0.36	0.03	0.33	0.08	-0.02
#5	0.41	0.15	0.39	0.17	0.11
#6	0.40	0.04	0.38	0.10	-0.01
#7	0.39	0.12	0.37	0.15	0.06
#8	0.39	0.08	0.38	0.10	-0.02
#9	0.47	0.16	0.42	0.31	0.13
#10	0.47	0.11	0.42	0.26	0.02
#11	0.47	0.11	0.42	0.26	0.02
#12	0.40	-0.01	0.35	0.14	-0.08
#13	0.45	0.03	0.36	0.21	-0.01
#14	0.38	-0.00	0.30	0.15	-0.05
#15	0.30	-0.04	0.22	0.07	-0.07
#16	0.30	-0.03	0.22	0.11	-0.06

Table 15: Performance of ArgumentAnalyst for selected exegetic metric (EXE-JSS) on specific subsets (columns) of the OOS eval data.

Semantics-aware Attention Improves Neural Machine Translation

Aviv Slobodkin **Leshem Choshen** **Omri Abend**
School of Computer Science and Engineering
The Hebrew University of Jerusalem
{aviv.slobodkin,leshem.choshen,omri.abend}@mail.huji.ac.il

Abstract

The integration of syntactic structures into Transformer machine translation has shown positive results, but to our knowledge, no work has attempted to do so with semantic structures. In this work we propose two novel parameter-free methods for injecting semantic information into Transformers, both rely on semantics-aware masking of (some of) the attention heads. One such method operates on the encoder, through a Scene-Aware Self-Attention (SASA) head. Another on the decoder, through a Scene-Aware Cross-Attention (SACrA) head. We show a consistent improvement over the vanilla Transformer and syntax-aware models for four language pairs. We further show an additional gain when using both semantic and syntactic structures in some language pairs.

1 Introduction

It has long been argued that semantic representation can benefit machine translation (Weaver, 1955; Bar-Hillel, 1960). Moreover, RNN-based neural machine translation (NMT) has been shown to benefit from the injection of semantic structure (Song et al., 2019; Marcheggiani et al., 2018). Despite these gains, to our knowledge, there have been no attempts to incorporate semantic structure into NMT Transformers (Vaswani et al., 2017). We address this gap, focusing on the main events in the text, as represented by UCCA (Universal Cognitive Conceptual Annotation; Abend and Rappoport, 2013), namely *scenes*.

UCCA is a semantic framework originating from typological and cognitive-linguistic theories (Dixon, 2009, 2010, 2012). Its principal goal is to represent some of the main elements of the semantic structure of the sentence while disregarding its syntax. Formally, a UCCA representation of a passage is a directed acyclic graph where leaves correspond to the words of the sentence and nodes correspond to semantic units. The edges are labeled by the role of their endpoint in the relation corresponding to their starting point (see Fig. 1). One of the motivations for using UCCA is its capability to separate the sentence into *"Scenes"*, which are analogous to events (see Fig. 1). Every such Scene consists of one main relation, which can be either a Process (i.e., an action), denoted by P, or a State (i.e., continuous state), denoted by S. Scenes also contain at least one Participant (i.e., entity), denoted by A. For example, the sentence in Fig. 1a comprises two scenes: the first one has the Process "saw" and two Participants – "I" and "the dog"; the second one has the Process "barked" and a single Participant – "dog".

So far, to the best of our knowledge, the only structure-aware work that integrated linguistic knowledge and graph structures into Transformers used syntactic structures (Strubell et al., 2018; Bugliarello and Okazaki, 2020; Akoury et al., 2019; Sundararaman et al., 2019; Choshen and Abend, 2021, *inter alia)*. The presented method builds on the method proposed by Bugliarello and Okazaki (2020), which utilized a Universal Dependencies graph (UD; Nivre et al., 2016) of the source sentence to focus the encoder's attention on each token's parent, namely the token's immediate ancestor in the UD graph. Similarly, we use the UCCA graph of the source sentence to generate a scene-aware mask for the self-attention heads of the encoder. We call this method *SASA* (see §2.1).

We test our model (§2) on translating English into four languages. Two that are more syntactically similar to English (Nikolaev et al., 2020; Dryer and Haspelmath, 2013): German (En-De), Russian (En-Ru), and two that are much less so: Turkish (En-Tr) and Finnish (En-Fi). We selected these language pairs for their varied grammatical properties and the availability of reliable parallel datasets for each of them in the WMT benchmark. We find consistent improvements across multiple test sets for all four cases.

In addition, we create a syntactic variant of

Proceedings of the 11th Joint Conference on Lexical and Computational Semantics, pages 28 - 43
July 14-15, 2022

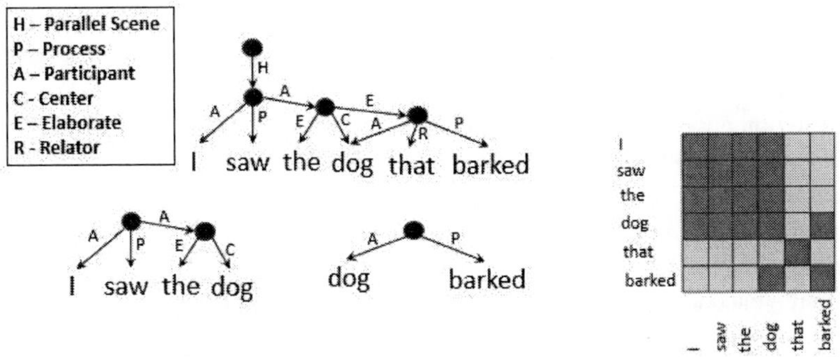

(a) I saw the dog that barked.

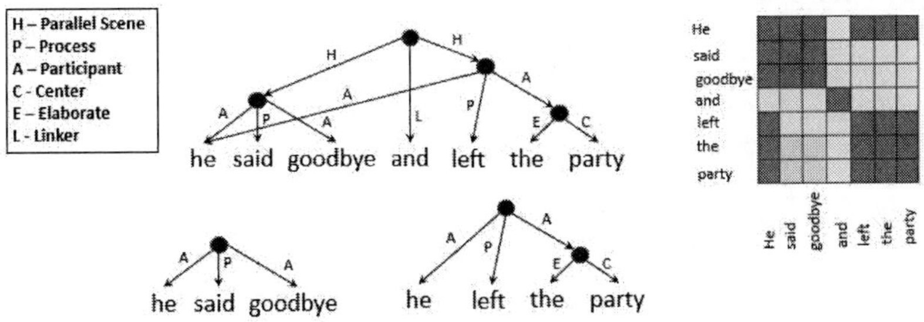

(b) He said goodbye and left the party.

Figure 1: Examples of UCCA parse graphs of the sentences "I saw the dog that barked" (1a) and "He said goodbye and left the party" (1b), accompanied by their segmentation into scenes (+ corresponding UCCA sub-graphs) and equivalent Scene-Aware masks. The dark-green color in the masks represents the value '1', and the light-green color to the value '0'.

our semantic model for better comparability. We observe that on average, our semantically aware model outperforms the syntactic models. Moreover, for the two languages less similar to English (En-Tr and En-Fi), combining both the semantic and the syntactic data results in a further gain. While improvements are often small, at times the combined version outperforms SASA and UDISCAL (our syntactic variant, see §3) by 0.52 and 0.69 BLEU points (or 0.46 and 0.43 chrF), respectively.

We also propose a novel method for introducing the source graph information during the decoding phase, namely through the cross-attention layer in the decoder (see §2.2). We find that it improves over the baseline and syntactic models, although SASA is generally better. Interestingly, for En-Fi, this model also outperforms SASA, suggesting that some language pairs may benefit more from semantic injection into the decoder.

Overall, through a series of experiments (see §4), we show the potential of semantics as an aid for NMT. We experiment with a large set of variants of our method, to see where and in what incorporation method they best help. Finally, we show that semantic models outperform UD baselines and can be complementary to them in distant languages, showing improvement when combined.

2 Models

Transformers have been shown to struggle when translating some types of long-distance dependencies (Choshen and Abend, 2019; Bisazza et al., 2021a), and when facing atypical word order (Bisazza et al., 2021b). Sulem et al. (2018a) proposed UCCA based preprocessing at inference time, splitting sentences into different scenes. They hypothesized that models need to decompose the input into scenes implicitly, and provide them with such a decomposition, as well as with the original sentence. They show that this may facilitate machine translation (Sulem et al., 2020) and sentence simplification (Sulem et al., 2018b) in some cases.

Motivated by these advances, we integrate UCCA to split the source into scenes. However, unlike Sulem et al., we do not alter the sentence length in pre-processing, as this method allows less flexibility in the way information is passed, and as preliminary results in reimplementing this method yielded inferior results (see §A.5). Instead, we investigate ways to integrate the split into the attention architecture.

We follow previous work (Bugliarello and Okazaki, 2020) in the way we incorporate our semantic information. In their paper, Bugliarello and Okazaki (2020) introduced syntax in the form of a parent-aware mask, which was applied before the softmax layer in the encoder's self-attention. We mask in a similar method to introduce semantics. However, *parent* in the UCCA framework is an elusive concept, given that nodes may have multiple parents. Hence, we use a different way to express the semantic information in our mask, i.e., we make it *scene-aware*, rather than *parent-aware*.

Following Sulem et al. (2018b), we divide the source sentence into scenes, using the sentence's UCCA parse. We then define our Scene-Aware mask:

$$M_C[i,j] = \begin{cases} 1, & \text{if i,j in the same scene} \\ 0, & \text{otherwise} \end{cases} \quad (1)$$

Intuitively, an attention head masked this way is allowed to attend to other tokens, as long as they share a scene with the current one.[1] Figure 1 demonstrates two examples of such masks, accompanied by their UCCA parse graphs and the segmentation into Scenes from which these masks were generated.

Our base model is the Transformer (Vaswani et al., 2017), which we enhance by making the attention layers more scene-aware. We force one[2] of the heads to attend to words in the same scene which we assume are more likely to be related than words from different scenes. As we replace regular self-attention heads with our scene-aware ones, we maintain the same number of heads and layers as in the baseline.

2.1 Scene-Aware Self-Attention (SASA)

Figure 2 presents the model's architecture. For a source sentence of length L, we obtain the keys, queries, and values matrices denoted by $K^i, Q^i, V^i \in \mathbb{R}^{L\times d}$, respectively. Then, to get the output matrix $O^i \in \mathbb{R}^{L\times d}$, we perform the following calculations:

[1]In case a token belongs to more than one scene, as is the case with the word "dog" in Fig. 1a, we allow it to attend to tokens of all the scenes it belongs to.

[2]Initial trials with more than one head did not show further benefit for UCCA based models.

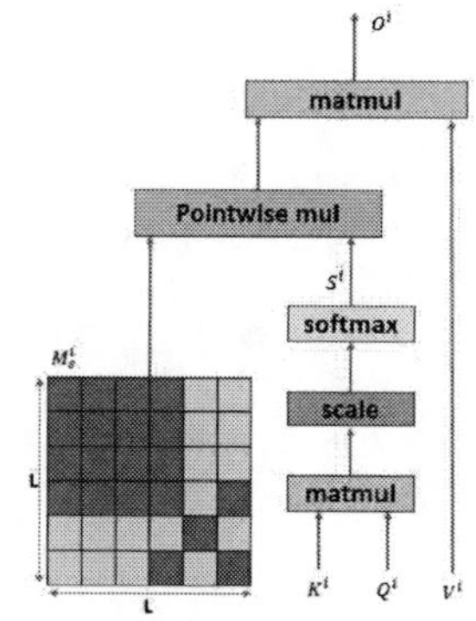

Figure 2: Scene-aware self-attention head for the input sentence "I saw the dog that barked", consisting of two scenes: "I saw the dog" and "dog barked".

$$S^i = Softmax\left(Q^i \times (K^i)^T \cdot \frac{1}{\sqrt{d_k}}\right) \quad (2)$$

$$O^i = S^i \odot M_S^i \times V^i \quad (3)$$

Where $\frac{1}{\sqrt{d_k}}$ is a scaling factor, the softmax in equation 2 is performed element-wise, $M_S^i \in 0, 1^{L\times L}$ is our pre-generated scene-aware mask and the $\odot$ in equation 3 denotes an element-wise multiplication. The difference between our method and a vanilla Transformer (Vaswani et al., 2017) lies in equation 3, with the element-wise multiplication between M_S^i and S^i, which is absent from the vanilla Transformer (the rest is the same).

2.2 Scene-Aware Cross-Attention (SACrA)

Next, we design a model in which we integrate information about the scene structure through the cross-attention layer in the decoder (see Fig. 3). Thus, instead of affecting the overall encoding of the source, we bring forward the splits to aid in selecting the next token.

Formally, for a source sentence of length L_{src} and target sentence of length L_{trg}, we compute for each head the queries and values matrices, denoted by $Q^i \in \mathbb{R}^{L_{trg}\times d_{model}}$ and $V^i \in \mathbb{R}^{L_{src}\times d}$, accordingly. Regarding key values, denoted by $\tilde{K}^i \in \mathbb{R}^{L_{src}\times L_{trg}}$, we calculate them as follows:

$$\tilde{K}^i = ((X_{enc}^i)^T \times M_S^i) \cdot \frac{1}{L_{src}} \quad (4)$$

where $X_{enc}^i \in \mathbb{R}^{L_{src}\times d_{model}}$ is the encoder's output and $M_S \in \{0,1\}^{L_{src}\times L_{src}}$ is our pre-generated mask.

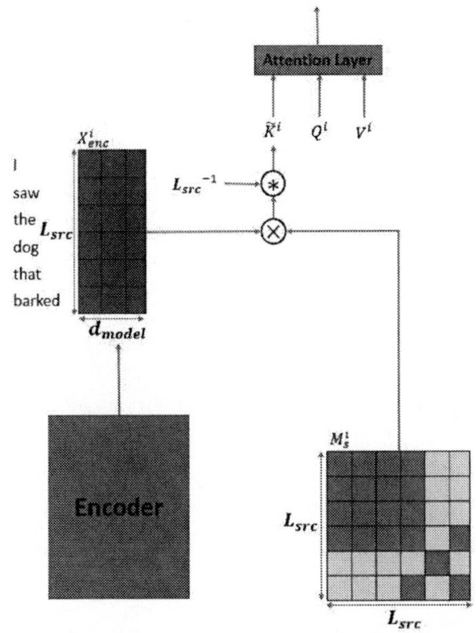

Figure 3: Scene-aware cross-attention head for the source sentence "I saw the dog that barked."

Finally, we pass V^i, Q^i and $\tilde{K}^i$ through a regular attention layer, as with the standard Transformer architecture.

Scene-Aware Key Matrix. The rationale behind the way we compute our scene-aware keys matrix lies in the role of the keys matrix in an attention layer. In the cross-attention layer, the queries come from the decoder. Source-side contextual information is encoded in the keys, which come from the encoder. Therefore, when we assign the same scene masks to all the words that are included in the same set of scenes, the key values for these words will be the same, and they will thus be treated similarly by the query. As a result, the query will give the same weight to source tokens that share the same set of scenes. Therefore, a complete scene (or a few scenes), rather than specific tokens (as with the vanilla Transformer), will influence what the next generated token will be, which will in turn yield a more scene-aware decoding process.

3 Experimental Setting

Data Preparation. First, we unescaped HTML characters and tokenized all our parallel corpora (Koehn et al., 2007). Next, we removed empty sentences, sentences longer than 100 tokens (either on the source or the target side), sentences with a source-target ratio larger than 1.5, sentences that do not match the corpus's language as determined by langid Lui and Baldwin, 2012, and sentences that *fast align* (Dyer et al., 2013) considers unlikely to align (minimum alignment score of -180). Then, for languages with capitalization, we trained true-casing models on the train set (Koehn et al., 2007) and applied them to all inputs to the network. Finally, we trained a BPE model (Sennrich et al., 2016), jointly for language pairs with a similar writing system (e.g., Latin, Cyrillic, etc.) and separately otherwise, and then applied them accordingly.

We trained our model on the full WMT16 dataset for the English→German (En-De) task, using the WMT *newstest2013* as development set. We also trained our models on a train set consisting of Yandex Corpus, News Commentary v15, and Wikititles v2 for the English→Russian (En-Ru) task. In addition, we trained our models on the full WMT19 dataset (excluding ParaCrawl, in order to avoid noisiness in the data) for the English→Finnish (En-Fi). Finally, we trained on the full WMT18 dataset for the English→Turkish (En-Tr) task. For the test sets, we used all the newstests available for every language pair since 2012, excluding the one designated for development.

Models. Hyperparameters shared by all models are described in §3. We tune the number of heads that we apply the mask to ($\#heads$) and the layers of the encoder we apply SASA to ($layer$), using the En-De development set. We start with tuning the layers for SASA, which we find is $layer = 4$, and then we tune the $\#heads$ (while fixing $layer = 4$), and get $\#head = 1$. We also use the En-De development set to tune the $\#heads$ and the layers of the SACrA model in a similar fashion, namely first the layers and then the $\#heads$ (with the tuned layers fixed). We find the best hyperparameters are $\#heads = 1$ and $layers = 2\&3$. For both models, we apply the tuned hyperparameters to all other language pairs. Interestingly, while it is common practice to change all the layers of the model, we find it suboptimal. Moreover, the fact that semantic information is more beneficial in higher layers, in contrast to the syntactic information that is most helpful when introduced in lower layers (see §3) may suggest that semantics is relevant for more complex generalization, which is reminiscent of findings by previous work (Tenney et al., 2019a; Belinkov, 2018; Tenney et al., 2019b; Peters et al., 2018; Blevins et al., 2018; Slobodkin et al., 2021).

UCCA parses are extracted using a pretrained

BERT-based TUPA model, that was trained on sentences in English, German and French (Hershcovich et al., 2017).

Binary Mask. For the SASA model, we experiment with two types of masks: a binary mask, as described in §2, and scaled masks, i.e.,

$$M_C[i,j] = \begin{cases} 1, & \text{if i,j in the same scene} \\ C, & \text{otherwise} \end{cases} \quad (5)$$

where $C \in (0,1)$. By doing so, we allow some out-of-scene information to pass through, while still emphasizing the in-scene information (by keeping the value of M for same-scene tokens at 1). In order to tune C, we performed a small grid search over $C \in \{0.05, 0.1, 0.15, 0.2, 0.3, 0.5\}$.

Additionally, similarly to Bugliarello and Okazaki (2020), we test a normally-distributed mask, according to the following equation:

$$M_{i,j} = f_{norm}(x = C \cdot dist(i,j)) \quad (6)$$

where f_{norm} is the density function of the normal distribution:

$$f_{norm}(x) = \frac{1}{\sqrt{2\pi\sigma^2}} e^{-\frac{x^2}{2\sigma^2}} \quad (7)$$

We define a scene-graph where nodes are scenes and edges are drawn between scenes with overlapping words. $dist(i,j)$ is the shortest distance between tokens i and j. $\sigma = \frac{1}{\sqrt{2\pi}}$, to ensure the value of M is 1 for words that share a scene ($dist(i,j)$=0), and C is a hyperparameter, which is determined through a grid search over $C \in \{0.1, 0.2, 0.5, \sqrt{0.5}\}$. For each of those two scaled versions of the mask, we choose the mask which has the best performance and compare it to the binary mask (see 1). We find that neither outperforms the binary mask. Therefore, we report the rest of our experiments with the binary mask.

Baselines. We compared our model to a few other models:

- **Transformer.** Standard Transformer-based NMT model, using the standard hyperparameters, as described in §3.

- **PASCAL.** Following Bugliarello and Okazaki (2020), we generate a syntactic mask for the self-attention layer in the encoder. We extract a UD-graph (Nivre et al., 2016) with udpipe (Straka and Straková, 2017). The value of the entries of the masks equal (see equation 7):

$$M_{p_t,j} = f_{norm}(x = (j - p_t)) \quad (8)$$

with $\sigma = 1$ and p_t being the middle position of the t-th token's parent in the UD graph of the sentence.

We use the same general hyperparameters as in the Transformer baseline. In addition, following the tuning of Bugliarello and Okazaki (2020), we apply the PASCAL mask to five heads of the first attention layer of the encoder, but unlike the original paper, we apply it after the layer's softmax, as it yields better results and also resembles our model's course of action.

- **UDISCAL.** In an attempt to improve the PASCAL model, we generate a mask that instead of only being sensitive to the dependency parent, is sensitive to all the UD relations in the sentences. We denote it UD-Distance-Scaled mask (UDISCAL). Namely, in order to compute the mask, we use a similar equation to that of PASCAL, with a minor alteration:

$$M_{i,j} = f_{norm}(x = dist(i,j)) \quad (9)$$

Where $\sigma = 1$, and $dist(i,j)$ is defined to be the distance between the token i and the token j in the UD graph of the sentence while treating the graph as undirectional. As with the PASCAL layer, we apply the UD-scaled mask after the softmax layer. But, unlike the PASCAL head, we tuned the architecture's hyperparameters to be just one head of the first layer, after performing a small grid search, namely testing with all layers $l \in [1,4]$, and then with $\#head \in [1,5]$.

Training Details. All our models are based on the standard Transformer-based NMT model (Vaswani et al., 2017), with 4000 warmup steps. In addition, we use an internal token representation of size 256, per-token cross-entropy loss function, label smoothing with $\epsilon_{l_s} = 0.1$ (Szegedy et al., 2016), Adam optimizer, Adam coefficients $\beta_1 = 0.9$ and $\beta_2 = 0.98$, and Adam $\epsilon = e^{-1}$. Furthermore, we incorporate 4 layers in the encoder and 4 in the decoder, and we employ a beam-search during inference, with beam size 4 and normalization coefficient $\alpha = 0.6$. In addition, we use a

models	2012	2013	2014	2015	2016	2017	2018	2019	2020	2020B
Transformer	17.60	20.49	20.55	22.17	25.46	19.70	28.01	26.84	17.71	16.94
+ binary mask (#h=1, l= 4)	**17.64**	20.37	**20.84**	**22.48**	25.32	19.76	**28.36**	26.80	17.74	16.98
+ scaled mask (#h=2, l=4, C=0.1)	17.41	20.21	20.53	22.43	24.95	**19.81**	28.25	**27.21**	**18.03**	**17.01**
+ normally distributed mask (#h=2, l=4, C=$\sqrt{0.5}$)	17.39	**20.52**	20.57	22.24	25.44	19.63	28.35	26.6	17.14	16.77

Table 1: BLEU scores for the top versions of our binary mask, scaled mask, and normally-distributed mask methods across all the WMT En-De newstests. Each column contains the BLEU scores over the WMT newstest corresponding to the year the column is labeled with (e.g., the scores under column *2015* are for En-De newstest2015). For newstest2020, there was more than one version on WMT, each translated by a different person. Both versions were included, with the second version denoted with a "B". The best score for each test set is boldfaced, unless none is better than the baseline Transformer.

batch size of 128 sentences for the training. We use *chrF++.py* with 1 word and beta of 3 to obtain chrF+ (Popovic, 2017) score as in WMT19 (Ma et al., 2019) and detokenized BLEU (Papineni et al., 2002) as implemented in Moses. We use the Nematus toolkit (Sennrich et al., 2017), and we train all our models on 4 NVIDIA GPUs for 150K steps. The average training time for the vanilla Transformer is 21.8 hours, and the average training time for the SASA model is 26.5 hours.

4 Experiments

We hypothesize that NMT models may benefit from the introduction of semantic structure, and present a set of experiments that support this hypothesis using the above-presented methods.

4.1 Scene-Aware Self-Attention

We find that on average, SASA outperforms the Transformer for all four language pairs (see 3), at times having gains larger than 1 BLEU point. Moreover, we assess the consistency of SASA's gains, using the sign-test, and get a p-value smaller than 0.01, thus exhibiting a statistically significant improvement (see §A.4). We see a similar trend when evaluating the performance using the chrF metric (see §A.2), which further highlights our model's consistent gains.

We also evaluate our model's performance on sentences with long dependencies (see A.3), which were found to pose a challenge for Transformers (Choshen and Abend, 2019). We assume that such cases could benefit greatly from the semantic introduction. In contrast to our hypothesis, we find the gain to be only slightly larger than in the general case, which leads us to conclude the improvements we see do not specifically originate from the syntactic challenge. Nevertheless, we still observe a consistent improvement, with gains of up to 1.41 BLEU points, which further underscores our model's superiority over the baseline model.

Qualitative Analysis. Table 2 presents a few examples in which the baseline Transformer errs, whereas our model translates correctly (see §A.6 for the UCCA parsings of the examples). In the first example, the Transformer translates the word "show" as a verb, i.e. *to show*, rather than as a noun. In the second example, the baseline model makes two errors: it misinterprets the word "look forward to" as "look at", and it also translates it as a present-tense verb rather than past-tense. The third example is particularly interesting, as it highlights our model's strength. In this example, the Transformer makes two mistakes: first, it translates the part "play with (someone) in the yard" as "play with the yard". Next, it attributes the descriptive clause "which never got out" to the yard, rather than the children. It seems then that introducing information about the *scene* structure into the model facilitates the translation, since it both groups the word "kids" with the phrase "I used to play with in the yard", and it also separates "never got out" from the word "yard". Instead, it clusters the latter with "kids", thus highlighting the relations between words in the sentence. In general, all these examples are cases where the network succeeds in disambiguating a word in its context.

	Source sentences and Translations	Literal Translations into English
SRC	I promised a show ?	
BASE	Я обещал показать?	I promised to show?
SASA	Я обещал шоу?	I promised a show?
SRC	Students said they looked forward to his class .	
BASE	Студенты сказали, что они смотрят на свой класс.	Students said, that they look at one's classroom.
SASA	Студенты сказали, что они с нетерпением ждали своего класса.	Students said, that they impatiently waited one's classroom.
SRC	I remember those kids I used to play with in the yard who never got out .	
BASE	Я помню тех детей, которые я играл с двором, который никогда не выходил.	I remember those kids, that I played with yard, that never got out ("that" and "got out" refer to yard).
SASA	Я помню тех детей, с которыми я играл на дворе, которые никогда не вышли.	I remember those kids, with which I played in yard, that never got out ("that" and "got out" refer to kids).

Table 2: Examples of correct translations generated by SASA, compared to the baseline Transformer.

4.2 Comparison to Syntactic Masks

Next, we wish to compare our model to other baselines. Given that this is the first work to incorporate semantic information into the Transformer-based NMT model, we compare our work to syntactically-infused models (as described in §3): one is the PASCAL model (Bugliarello and Okazaki, 2020), and the other is our adaptation of PASCAL, the UD-Distance-Scaled (UDISCAL) model, which resembles better our SASA mask. We find (Table 3) that on average, SASA outperforms both PASCAL and UDISCAL. We also compare SASA with each of the syntactic models, finding that it is significantly (sign-test $p < 0.01$; see §A.4) better. This suggests that semantics might be more beneficial for Transformers than syntax.

4.3 Combining Syntax and Semantics

Naturally, our next question is whether combining both semantic and syntactic heads will further improve the model's performance. Therefore, we test the combination of SASA with either PASCAL or UDISCAL, retaining the hyperparameters used for the separate models. We find that combining with UDISCAL outperforms the former, and so we continue with it. Interestingly, En-De and En-Ru hardly benefit from the combination compared just to the SASA model. We hypothesize that this might be due to the fact that the syntax of each language pair is already quite similar, and therefore the model mainly relies on it to separate the sentence that UCCA gives it as well. On the other hand, En-Fi and En-Tr do benefit from the combination, both on average and in most of the test sets. Evaluating the performance using the chrF metric (see §A.2) yields a similar behavior, which further confirms its validity. It leads us to hypothesize that language pairs that are more typologically distant from one another can benefit more from both semantics and syntax; we defer a more complete discussion of this point to future work. In order to confirm that the combined version persistently outperforms each of the separate versions for typologically distant languages, we compare each of the pairs using the sign-test (only on the test sets of En-Fi and En-Tr). We get a p-value of 0.02 for the comparison with SASA and 0.0008 for the comparison with UDISCAL. This suggests that for these language pairs, there is indeed a significant benefit, albeit small, from the infusion of both semantics and syntax.

4.4 Scene-Aware Cross-Attention

Following the analysis on the scene-aware *self*-attention, we wish to examine whether Transformers could also benefit from injecting source-side semantics into the decoder. For that, we develop the Scene-Aware Cross-Attention (SACrA) model, as described in §2.2. Table 3 presents the results of SACrA, compared to the Transformer baseline and SASA. We find that in general SASA outperforms

En-De

models	2012	2014	2015	2016	2017	2018	2019	2020	2020B	average
Transformer	17.6	20.55	22.17	**25.46**	19.7	28.01	26.84	17.71	16.94	21.66
PASCAL	17.34	20.59	**22.62**	25.1	19.92	28.09	26.61	17.5	16.81	21.62
UDISCAL	17.42	20.86	22.53	25.23	**19.95**	27.87	26.8	17.06	16.39	21.57
SASA	**17.64**$^{\uparrow}$	20.84	22.48	25.32	19.76	**28.36**$^{\uparrow}$	26.8	**17.74**$^{\uparrow}$	**16.98**$^{\uparrow}$	**21.77**$^{\uparrow}$
SASA + UDISCAL	17.51	20.42	22.1	24.9	19.72	28.35	**27.14***	17.59	16.68	21.60
SACrA	17.11	20.9$^{\uparrow}$	22.59	24.64	19.79	27.88	26.28	16.8	16.25	21.36
SACrA + UDISCAL	17.07	**21.09***	22.26	24.85	19.56	28.1*	26.49	16.66	15.93	21.33

En-Ru

models	2012	2013	2014	2015	2016	2017	2018	2019	2020	2020B	average
Transformer	24.32	18.11	25.35	21.1	19.77	22.34	19	20.14	15.64	22.33	20.81
PASCAL	23.78	18.37	24.87	20.97	19.81	21.83	18.81	19.93	15.42	21.48	20.53
UDISCAL	23.88	18.31	25.23	20.82	**20.31**	22.15	19.27	20.32	15.7	22.19	20.82
SASA	24.17	**18.43**$^{\uparrow}$	**25.53**$^{\uparrow}$	**21.59**$^{\uparrow}$	20.11	**22.69**$^{\uparrow}$	**19.53**$^{\uparrow}$	20.2	15.76$^{\uparrow}$	**23.36**$^{\uparrow}$	**21.14**$^{\uparrow}$
SASA + UDISCAL	**24.36***	18.29	25.43	21.01	19.79	22.49	19.25	**20.4***	**15.97***	22.42	20.94
SACrA	24.12	18.24	25.43$^{\uparrow}$	21	20.07	22.49$^{\uparrow}$	19.3$^{\uparrow}$	20.18	15.79$^{\uparrow}$	22.15	20.88$^{\uparrow}$
SACrA + UDISCAL	23.54	17.99	24.91	20.62	19.67	21.55	18.63	19.89	15.64	20.79	20.32

En-Fi

models	2015	2016	2016B	2017	2017B	2018	2019	average
Transformer	11.22	12.76	10.2	13.35	11.37	9.32	12.21	11.49
PASCAL	11.2	12.67	10.13	13.54	11.24	9.62	12.23	11.52
UDISCAL	10.87	12.78	10.23	13.51	11.43	9.2	11.99	11.43
SASA	11.37$^{\uparrow}$	**12.88**$^{\uparrow}$	**10.52**$^{\uparrow}$	13.74$^{\uparrow}$	11.5$^{\uparrow}$	9.56	12.12	11.67$^{\uparrow}$
SASA + UDISCAL	**11.56***	12.8	10.28	**13.91***	**11.52***	**9.75***	**12.64***	**11.78***
SACrA	11.48$^{\uparrow}$	12.86$^{\uparrow}$	10.41$^{\uparrow}$	13.66$^{\uparrow}$	11.49$^{\uparrow}$	9.62	12.51$^{\uparrow}$	11.72$^{\uparrow}$
SACrA + UDISCAL	11.06	12.6	10.13	13.43	11.26	9.23	12.05	11.39

En-Tr

models	2016	2017	2018	average
Transformer	8.43	8.55	8.1	8.36
PASCAL	8.5	8.76	7.98	8.41
UDISCAL	8.33	8.66	8.03	8.34
SASA	8.59$^{\uparrow}$	8.86$^{\uparrow}$	8.16$^{\uparrow}$	8.54$^{\uparrow}$
SASA + UDISCAL	**8.64***	**8.87***	**8.2***	**8.57***
SACrA	8.64$^{\uparrow}$	8.81$^{\uparrow}$	7.96	8.47$^{\uparrow}$
SACrA + UDISCAL	8.23	8.54	7.95	8.24

Table 3: BLEU scores for the baseline Transformer model, previous work that used syntactically infused models – PASCAL and UDISCAL, our SASA and SACrA models, and models incorporating UDISCAL with SASA or SACrA, across all WMT's newstests. For every language pair, each column contains the BLEU scores over the WMT newstest corresponding to the year the column is labeled with (e.g., for En-Ru, the scores under column *2015* are for En-Ru newstest2015). For some newstests, there was more than one version on WMT, each translated by a different person. For those test sets, we included both versions, denoting the second one with a "B". In addition, for every language pair, the right-most column represents the average BLEU scores over all the pair's reported newstests. For every test set (and for the average score), the best score is boldfaced. For each of the semantic models (i.e., SASA and SACrA), improvements over all the baselines (syntactic and Transformer) are marked with an arrow facing upwards. For models with both syntactic and semantic masks, improvements over each mask individually are marked with an asterisk.

SACrA, suggesting that semantics is more beneficial during encoding. With that said, for three out of the four language pairs, SACrA does yield gains over the Transformer, albeit small, and for one language pair (En-Fi) it even outperforms SASA on average. Moreover, comparing SACrA to the Transformer using the sign-test (see §A.4) shows significant improvement ($p = 0.047$).

Surprisingly, unlike its self-attention counterpart, combining the SACrA model with UDISCAL does not seem to be beneficial at all, and in most cases is even outperformed by the baseline Transformer. We hypothesize that this occurs because appointing too many heads for our linguistic injection is inefficient when those heads cannot interact with each other directly, as the information from the UDISCAL head reaches the SACrA head only after the encoding is done. One possible direction for future work would be to find ways to syntactically enrich the decoder, and then to combine it with our SACrA model.

5 Conclusion

In this work, we suggest two novel methods for injecting semantic information into an NMT Transformer model – one through the encoder (i.e. SASA) and one through the decoder (i.e. SACrA). The strength of both methods is that they both do not introduce more parameters to the model, and only rely on UCCA-parses of the source sentences, which are generated in advance using an off-the-shelf parser, and thus do not increase the complexity of the model. We compare our methods to previously developed methods of syntax injection, and to our adaptation to these methods, and find that semantic information tends to be significantly more beneficial than syntactic information, mostly when injected into the encoder (SASA), but at times also during decoding (SACrA). Moreover, we find that for sufficiently different languages, such as English and Finnish or English and Turkish, incorporating both syntactic and semantic structures further improves the performance of the translation models. Future work will further investigate the benefits of semantic structure in Transformers, alone and in unison with syntactic structure.

Acknowledgments

This work was supported in part by the Israel Science Foundation (grant no. 2424/21), and by the Applied Research in Academia Program of the Israel Innovation Authority.

References

Omri Abend and Ari Rappoport. 2013. Universal Conceptual Cognitive Annotation (UCCA). In *Proc. of ACL*, pages 228–238.

Nader Akoury, Kalpesh Krishna, and Mohit Iyyer. 2019. Syntactically supervised transformers for faster neural machine translation. In *Proceedings of the 57th Annual Meeting of the Association for Computational Linguistics*, pages 1269–1281, Florence, Italy. Association for Computational Linguistics.

Y. Bar-Hillel. 1960. The present status of automatic translation of languages. *Adv. Comput.*, 1:91–163.

Yonatan Belinkov. 2018. On internal language representations in deep learning: an analysis of machine translation and speech recognition.

Arianna Bisazza, Ahmet Üstün, and Stephan Sportel. 2021a. On the difficulty of translating free-order case-marking languages. *CoRR*, abs/2107.06055.

Arianna Bisazza, Ahmet Üstün, and Stephan Sportel. 2021b. On the difficulty of translating free-order case-marking languages. *arXiv preprint arXiv:2107.06055*.

Terra Blevins, Omer Levy, and Luke Zettlemoyer. 2018. Deep RNNs encode soft hierarchical syntax. In *Proceedings of the 56th Annual Meeting of the Association for Computational Linguistics (Volume 2: Short Papers)*, pages 14–19, Melbourne, Australia. Association for Computational Linguistics.

Emanuele Bugliarello and Naoaki Okazaki. 2020. Enhancing machine translation with dependency-aware self-attention. In *Proceedings of the 58th Annual Meeting of the Association for Computational Linguistics*, pages 1618–1627, Online. Association for Computational Linguistics.

Leshem Choshen and Omri Abend. 2019. Automatically extracting challenge sets for non-local phenomena in neural machine translation. In *Proceedings of the 23rd Conference on Computational Natural Language Learning (CoNLL)*, pages 291–303, Hong Kong, China. Association for Computational Linguistics.

Leshem Choshen and Omri Abend. 2021. Transition based graph decoder for neural machine translation. *arXiv preprint arXiv:2101.12640*.

Christos Christodoulopoulos and Mark Steedman. 2015. A massively parallel corpus: the bible in 100 languages. *Lang. Resour. Evaluation*, 49(2):375–395.

R.M.W. Dixon. 2009. *Basic Linguistic Theory Volume 1: Methodology*. Basic Linguistic Theory. OUP Oxford.

R.M.W. Dixon. 2010. *Basic Linguistic Theory Volume 2: Grammatical Topics*. Basic Linguistic Theory. OUP Oxford.

R.M.W. Dixon. 2012. *Basic Linguistic Theory Volume 3: Further Grammatical Topics*. Basic Linguistic Theory. OUP Oxford.

Matthew S Dryer and Martin Haspelmath. 2013. The world atlas of language structures online.

Chris Dyer, Victor Chahuneau, and Noah A. Smith. 2013. A simple, fast, and effective reparameterization of IBM model 2. In *Proceedings of the 2013 Conference of the North American Chapter of the Association for Computational Linguistics: Human Language Technologies*, pages 644–648, Atlanta, Georgia. Association for Computational Linguistics.

Daniel Hershcovich, Omri Abend, and Ari Rappoport. 2017. A transition-based directed acyclic graph parser for UCCA. In *Proc. of ACL*, pages 1127–1138.

Philipp Koehn, Hieu Hoang, Alexandra Birch, Chris Callison-Burch, Marcello Federico, Nicola Bertoldi, Brooke Cowan, Wade Shen, Christine Moran, Richard Zens, Chris Dyer, Ondřej Bojar, Alexandra Constantin, and Evan Herbst. 2007. Moses: Open source toolkit for statistical machine translation. In *Proceedings of the 45th Annual Meeting of the Association for Computational Linguistics Companion Volume Proceedings of the Demo and Poster Sessions*, pages 177–180, Prague, Czech Republic. Association for Computational Linguistics.

Marco Lui and Timothy Baldwin. 2012. langid.py: An off-the-shelf language identification tool. In *Proceedings of the ACL 2012 System Demonstrations*, pages 25–30, Jeju Island, Korea. Association for Computational Linguistics.

Qingsong Ma, Johnny Wei, Ondřej Bojar, and Yvette Graham. 2019. Results of the WMT19 metrics shared task: Segment-level and strong MT systems pose big challenges. In *Proceedings of the Fourth Conference on Machine Translation (Volume 2: Shared Task Papers, Day 1)*, pages 62–90, Florence, Italy. Association for Computational Linguistics.

Diego Marcheggiani, Jasmijn Bastings, and Ivan Titov. 2018. Exploiting semantics in neural machine translation with graph convolutional networks. In *Proceedings of the 2018 Conference of the North American Chapter of the Association for Computational Linguistics: Human Language Technologies, Volume 2 (Short Papers)*, pages 486–492, New Orleans, Louisiana. Association for Computational Linguistics.

Dmitry Nikolaev, Ofir Arviv, Taelin Karidi, Neta Kenneth, Veronika Mitnik, Lilja Maria Saeboe, and Omri Abend. 2020. Fine-grained analysis of cross-linguistic syntactic divergences.

Joakim Nivre, Marie-Catherine de Marneffe, Filip Ginter, Yoav Goldberg, Jan Hajic, Christopher D Manning, Ryan T McDonald, Slav Petrov, Sampo Pyysalo, Natalia Silveira, et al. 2016. Universal dependencies v1: A multilingual treebank collection. In *Proc. of LREC*.

Kishore Papineni, S. Roukos, T. Ward, and Wei-Jing Zhu. 2002. Bleu: a method for automatic evaluation of machine translation. In *ACL*.

Matthew E. Peters, Mark Neumann, Luke Zettlemoyer, and Wen-tau Yih. 2018. Dissecting contextual word embeddings: Architecture and representation. In *Proceedings of the 2018 Conference on Empirical Methods in Natural Language Processing*, pages 1499–1509, Brussels, Belgium. Association for Computational Linguistics.

Maja Popovic. 2017. chrf++: words helping character n-grams. In *WMT*.

Rico Sennrich, Orhan Firat, Kyunghyun Cho, Alexandra Birch, Barry Haddow, Julian Hitschler, Marcin Junczys-Dowmunt, Samuel Läubli, Antonio Valerio Miceli Barone, Jozef Mokry, and Maria Nadejde. 2017. Nematus: a toolkit for neural machine translation. In *Proceedings of the Software Demonstrations of the 15th Conference of the European Chapter of the Association for Computational Linguistics*, pages 65–68, Valencia, Spain. Association for Computational Linguistics.

Rico Sennrich, Barry Haddow, and Alexandra Birch. 2016. Neural machine translation of rare words with subword units. In *Proceedings of the 54th Annual Meeting of the Association for Computational Linguistics (Volume 1: Long Papers)*, pages 1715–1725, Berlin, Germany. Association for Computational Linguistics.

Aviv Slobodkin, Leshem Choshen, and Omri Abend. 2021. Mediators in determining what processing BERT performs first. In *Proceedings of the 2021 Conference of the North American Chapter of the Association for Computational Linguistics: Human Language Technologies*, pages 86–93, Online. Association for Computational Linguistics.

Linfeng Song, Daniel Gildea, Yue Zhang, Zhiguo Wang, and Jinsong Su. 2019. Semantic neural machine translation using AMR. *Transactions of the Association for Computational Linguistics*, 7:19–31.

Milan Straka and Jana Straková. 2017. Tokenizing, pos tagging, lemmatizing and parsing ud 2.0 with udpipe. In *Proceedings of the CoNLL 2017 Shared Task: Multilingual Parsing from Raw Text to Universal Dependencies*, pages 88–99, Vancouver, Canada. Association for Computational Linguistics.

Emma Strubell, Patrick Verga, Daniel Andor, David Weiss, and Andrew McCallum. 2018. Linguistically-informed self-attention for semantic role labeling. In *Proceedings of the 2018 Conference on Empirical Methods in Natural Language Processing*, pages

5027–5038, Brussels, Belgium. Association for Computational Linguistics.

Elior Sulem, Omri Abend, and Ari Rappoport. 2018a. Semantic structural evaluation for text simplification. In *Proceedings of the 2018 Conference of the North American Chapter of the Association for Computational Linguistics: Human Language Technologies, Volume 1 (Long Papers)*, pages 685–696, New Orleans, Louisiana. Association for Computational Linguistics.

Elior Sulem, Omri Abend, and Ari Rappoport. 2018b. Simple and effective text simplification using semantic and neural methods. In *Proceedings of the 56th Annual Meeting of the Association for Computational Linguistics (Volume 1: Long Papers)*, pages 162–173, Melbourne, Australia. Association for Computational Linguistics.

Elior Sulem, Omri Abend, and Ari Rappoport. 2020. Semantic structural decomposition for neural machine translation. In *Proceedings of the Ninth Joint Conference on Lexical and Computational Semantics*, pages 50–57, Barcelona, Spain (Online). Association for Computational Linguistics.

Dhanasekar Sundararaman, Vivek Subramanian, Guoyin Wang, Shijing Si, Dinghan Shen, Dong Wang, and Lawrence Carin. 2019. Syntax-infused transformer and bert models for machine translation and natural language understanding.

Christian Szegedy, Vincent Vanhoucke, Sergey Ioffe, Jon Shlens, and Zbigniew Wojna. 2016. Rethinking the inception architecture for computer vision. In *Proceedings of the IEEE Conference on Computer Vision and Pattern Recognition (CVPR)*.

Ian Tenney, Dipanjan Das, and Ellie Pavlick. 2019a. BERT rediscovers the classical NLP pipeline. In *Proceedings of the 57th Annual Meeting of the Association for Computational Linguistics*, pages 4593–4601, Florence, Italy. Association for Computational Linguistics.

Ian Tenney, Patrick Xia, Berlin Chen, Alex Wang, Adam Poliak, R Thomas McCoy, Najoung Kim, Benjamin Van Durme, Sam Bowman, Dipanjan Das, and Ellie Pavlick. 2019b. What do you learn from context? probing for sentence structure in contextualized word representations. In *International Conference on Learning Representations*.

Jörg Tiedemann. 2012. Parallel data, tools and interfaces in opus. In *Proceedings of the Eight International Conference on Language Resources and Evaluation (LREC'12)*, Istanbul, Turkey. European Language Resources Association (ELRA).

Ashish Vaswani, Noam Shazeer, Niki Parmar, Jakob Uszkoreit, Llion Jones, Aidan N Gomez, Łukasz Kaiser, and Illia Polosukhin. 2017. Attention is all you need. In *Advances in neural information processing systems*, pages 5998–6008.

Warren Weaver. 1955. Translation. *Machine translation of languages*, 14:15–23.

Krzysztof Wołk and Krzysztof Marasek. 2014. Building subject-aligned comparable corpora and mining it for truly parallel sentence pairs. *Procedia Technology*, 18:126–132. International workshop on Innovations in Information and Communication Science and Technology, IICST 2014, 3-5 September 2014, Warsaw, Poland.

A Appendix

A.1 Layer Hyperparameter-tuning for SASA

In order to optimize the contribution of the SASA model, we tuned the hyperparameter of the best layers in the encoder to incorporate our model, using the En-De newstest2013 as our development set. Table 4 presents the results.

Layers	Bleu
1	20.3
2	20.33
3	20.1
4	20.37
1,2	20.2
2,3	20.17
3,4	20.3

Table 4: Validation Bleu as a function of layers incorporating SASA (for En-De).

A.2 ChrF Results

In order to reaffirm our results, we also evaluate the performance of all the models using the chrF metric (see 7). Indeed, all the different behaviors and trends we observed when evaluating using the Bleu metric (see §4) seem to be preserved when under the chrF metric. This further validates our results.

A.3 Challenge Sets

In addition to testing on the full newstests sets, we also experiment with sentences characterized by long dependencies, which were shown to present a challenge for Transformers (Choshen and Abend, 2019). In order to acquire those challenge sets, we use the methodology described by Choshen and Abend (2019), which we apply on each of the newstest sets. In addition, for the En-Tr task, which has a limited number of newstests, we generate additional challenge sets, extracted from corpora downloaded from the Opus Corpus engine (Tiedemann, 2012): the Wikipedia parallel corpus (Wołk and Marasek, 2014), the Mozilla and EUbookshop parallel corpora (Tiedemann, 2012), and the bible parallel corpus (Christodoulopoulos and Steedman, 2015). We observe (see 8) a similar trend to the general case, which reaffirms our results. In fact, there seem to be bigger gains over the Transformer, albeit not drastically, compared to the general case.

A.4 Sign-Test

In order to assess the consistency of the improvements of our models, we perform the Sign-Test on every two models (see 5). Evidently, SASA persistently outperforms the Transformer baseline and the syntactic models, as does the combined model of SASA and UDISCAL.

BETTER / BASELINE	PASCAL	UDISCAL	SASA	SASA + UDISCAL	SACrA	SACrA + UDISCAL
Transformer	>0.5	>0.5	<0.01	<0.01	0.047	>0.5
PASCAL		0.17	<0.01	<0.01	0.06	>0.5
UDISCAL			<0.01	<0.01	0.06	>0.5
SASA				0.17	>0.5	>0.5
SASA + UDISCAL					>0.5	>0.5
SACrA						>0.5

Table 5: We perform a significance test over all test sets across all languages for every cell, where the null hypothesis is $H_0 \ : \ Bleu(model_{row}) \geq Bleu(model_{column})$

A.5 SemSplit

Following Sulem et al. (2020), we implement the SemSplit pipeline. First, we train a Transformer-based Neural Machine Translation model. Then, during inference time, we use the Direct Semantic Splitting algorithm (DSS; Sulem et al., 2018b) to split the sentences, and then translate each separated sentence separately. Finally, we concatenate the translation, using a period (".") as a delimiter. Table 6 presents the results, using the Bleu and chrF metrics. We find that the architecture does not have gains over the baseline Transformer. These results can be accounted for by the fact that in their work, Sulem et al. (2020) assessed the pipeline's performance using Human Evaluation and manual analysis, rather than the Bleu and chrF metrics, which punish for sentence separation in translation. In addition, they tested their pipeline in a pseudo-low resource scenario, and not in normal NMT settings.

A.6 Qualitative Analysis - UCCA Parsings

figure 4 presents the UCCA parsings of the examples featured in table 2.

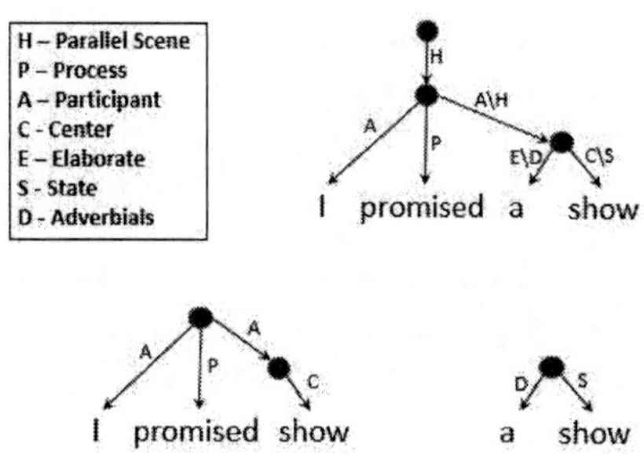

(a) I promised a show?

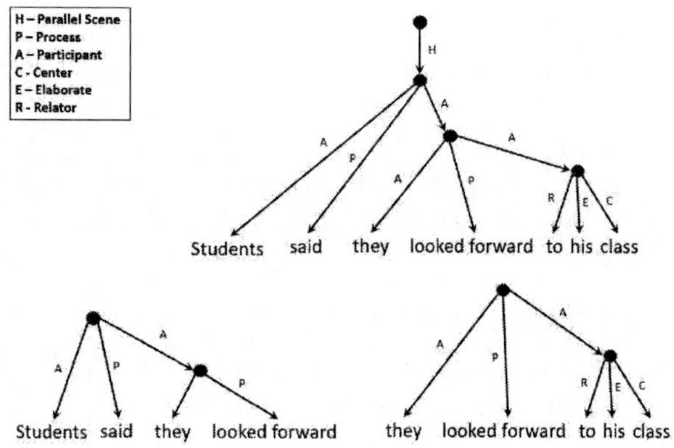

(b) Students said they looked forward to his class.

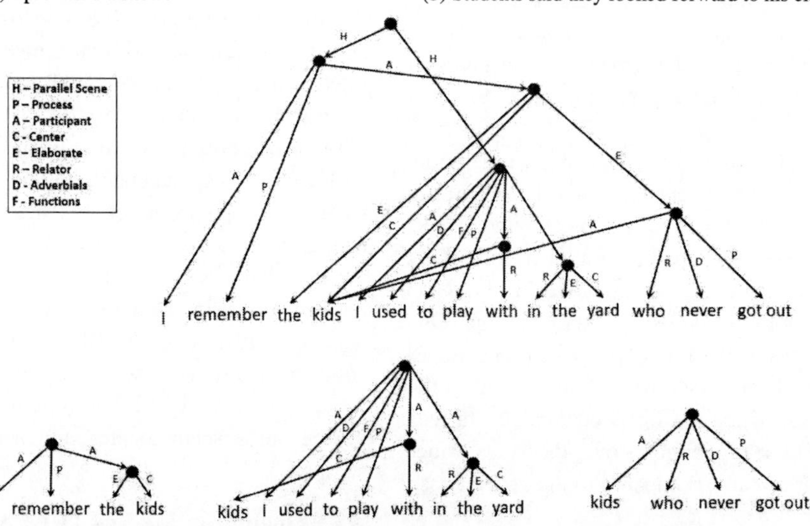

(c) I remember those kids I used to play with in the yard who never got out.

Figure 4: UCCA parse graphs of the Qualitative Analysis examples, with the equivalent UCCA sub-graphs representing the segmentation into scenes.

En-De

Metric	Models	2012	2014	2015	2016	2017	2018	2019	2020	2020B	average
Bleu	Transformer	17.6	20.55	22.17	25.46	19.7	28.01	26.84	17.71	16.94	21.66
	SemSplit	12.16	14.25	14.46	17.53	13.18	19.39	18.46	15.12	14.93	15.50
chrF	Transformer	47.37	51.85	52.52	55.06	50.87	57.81	55.48	45.19	44.18	51.15
	SemSplit	43.42	47.19	47.05	49.86	45.87	51.50	50.24	47.71	46.93	47.75

En-Ru

Metric	Models	2012	2013	2014	2015	2016	2017	2018	2019	2020	2020B	average
Bleu	Transformer	24.32	18.11	25.35	21.1	19.77	22.34	19	20.14	15.64	22.33	20.81
	SemSplit	15.29	10.9	16.43	13.28	12.79	14.61	11.95	12.56	9.92	15.25	13.30
chrF	Transformer	51.39	45.69	53.31	50.16	48.10	50.54	48.01	45.78	42.51	53.07	48.86
	SemSplit	46.10	40.50	47.66	44.58	43.16	45.34	43.38	40.97	38.93	47.84	43.85

En-Fi

Metric	Models	2015	2016	2016B	2017	2017B	2018	2019	average
Bleu	Transformer	11.22	12.76	10.2	13.35	11.37	9.32	12.21	11.49
	SemSplit	6.97	7.72	6.55	8.75	7.54	6.18	7.73	7.35
chrF	Transformer	43.79	45.48	43.43	46.39	43.96	42.06	43.10	44.03
	SemSplit	40.18	41.42	39.94	42.18	40.20	38.76	40.12	40.40

En-Tr

Metric	Models	2016	2017	2018	average
Bleu	Transformer	8.43	8.55	8.1	8.36
	SemSplit	6.15	6.07	5.37	5.86
chrF	Transformer	40.24	40.37	39.75	40.12
	SemSplit	39.04	39.00	38.85	38.97

Table 6: Bleu and ChrF scores of the baseline Transformer and the SemSplit model.

En-De

models	2012	2014	2015	2016	2017	2018	2019	2020	2020B	average
Transformer	47.37	51.85	52.52	**55.06**	50.87	57.81	55.48	**45.19**	**44.18**	51.15
PASCAL	47.27	51.87	**52.82**	54.73	50.83	57.65	55.28	44.80	43.78	51.00
UDISCAL	47.26	51.95	52.45	54.99	50.78	57.40	55.30	44.48	43.43	50.89
SASA	**47.48**$^{\uparrow}$	**52.03**$^{\uparrow}$	52.74	54.99	**51.23**$^{\uparrow}$	**57.88**$^{\uparrow}$	**55.69**$^{\uparrow}$	45.03	43.99	**51.23**$^{\uparrow}$
SASA + UDISCAL	47.42	51.94	52.50	55.00*	50.86	57.74	55.62	44.72	43.62	51.05
SACrA	47.02	51.66	52.48	54.49	50.55	57.16	55.05	44.08	43.15	50.63
SACrA + UDISCAL	46.71	51.63	52.18	54.37	50.22	57.20	54.96	43.42	42.40	50.34

En-Ru

models	2012	2013	2014	2015	2016	2017	2018	2019	2020	2020B	average
Transformer	51.39	45.69	53.31	50.16	48.10	50.54	48.01	45.78	42.51	53.07	48.86
PASCAL	51.03	45.66	53.04	49.87	48.05	50.32	47.98	45.86	42.35	52.42	48.66
UDISCAL	51.26	45.73	53.45	50.01	48.57	50.50	48.27	46.03	42.60	52.89	48.93
SASA	51.34	**45.81**$^{\uparrow}$	53.49$^{\uparrow}$	**50.32**$^{\uparrow}$	**48.60**$^{\uparrow}$	50.67$^{\uparrow}$	**48.45**$^{\uparrow}$	45.81	42.76$^{\uparrow}$	**53.62**$^{\uparrow}$	**49.09**$^{\uparrow}$
SASA + UDISCAL	**51.43***	45.67	**53.56***	50.03	48.29	50.67	48.25	**46.08***	**42.81***	53.14	48.99
SACrA	51.28	45.57	53.50$^{\uparrow}$	49.81	48.42	**50.82**$^{\uparrow}$	48.28$^{\uparrow}$	45.92	42.68$^{\uparrow}$	52.76	48.90
SACrA + UDISCAL	50.58	45.31	52.90	49.40	47.77	50.03	47.49	45.26	42.33	51.93	48.30

En-Fi

models	2015	2016	2016B	2017	2017B	2018	2019	average
Transformer	43.79	45.48	43.43	46.39	43.96	42.06	43.10	44.03
PASCAL	**43.91**	44.93	42.99	46.02	43.57	41.88	42.60	43.70
UDISCAL	43.42	45.37	43.42	46.51	44.07	42.03	43.03	43.98
SASA	43.76	45.33	43.38	46.40	43.89	42.10$^{\uparrow}$	43.02	43.98
SASA + UDISCAL	43.77*	45.20	43.17	**46.74***	44.15*	**42.34***	43.08*	44.07*
SACrA	43.88	45.20	43.15	46.62$^{\uparrow}$	44.02$^{\uparrow}$	42.25$^{\uparrow}$	43.23$^{\uparrow}$	44.05$^{\uparrow}$
SACrA + UDISCAL	43.80	**45.53***	**43.52***	46.71*	**44.19***	42.16	**43.28***	**44.17***

En-Tr

models	2016	2017	2018	average
Transformer	40.24	40.37	39.75	40.12
PASCAL	40.59	40.64	39.89	40.37
UDISCAL	40.27	40.49	40.01	40.26
SASA	40.27	40.46	39.98	40.24
SASA + UDISCAL	**40.61***	**40.92***	**40.12***	**40.55***
SACrA	40.44	40.68$^{\uparrow}$	39.85	40.33
SACrA + UDISCAL	40.23	40.48	39.96	40.22

Table 7: ChrF scores for the baseline Transformer model, the baseline Syntactically infused models PASCAL and UDISCAL, our SASA and SACrA models, and models incorporating UDISCAL with each of SASA and SACrA, across all WMT's newstests. For every language pair, each column contains the Bleu scores over the WMT newstest equivalent to the column's year (e.g., for En-Ru, the scores under column *2015* are for En-Ru newstest2015). For some newstests, there was more than one version on WMT, each translated by a different person. For those test sets, we included both versions, denoting the second one with a "B". In addition, for every language pair, the right-most column represents the average Bleu scores over all the pair's reported newstests. For every test set (and for the average score), the best score is boldfaced. For each of the semantic models (i.e., SASA and SACrA), improvements over all the baselines (syntactic and Transformer) are marked by an arrow facing upwards. For models with both syntactic and semantic masks, improvements over each mask individually are marked by an asterisk.

En-De

models	2012	2014	2015	2016	2017	2018	2019	2020	2020B	average
Transformer	15.08	16.94	17.36	21.11	14.84	23.43	22.42	16.79	15.75	18.19
PASCAL	14.96	17.45	17.85	20.22	14.66	23.76	21.28	**16.9**	**16.22**	18.14
UDISCAL	14.46	**17.84**	17.7	**21.26**	**15.48**	23.75	22.36	16.37	15.37	18.29
SASA	14.67	17.68	**18.04**†	20.89	15.09	**24.8**†	22.86†	16.85	15.76	**18.52**†
SASA + UDISCAL	**15.39***	17.07	17.38	20.42	15.35	23.53	**22.87***	16.79	15.98*	18.31
SACrA	14.67	17.03	16.89	19.69	14.45	22.21	22.08	16.64	15.6	17.70
SACrA + UDISCAL	15.07*	17.23	16.52	20.82	14.6	22.38	22.61*	16.53	15.81*	17.95

En-Ru

models	2012	2013	2014	2015	2016	2017	2018	2019	2020	2020B	average
Transformer	23.4	14.67	**24**	16.82	17.52	19.74	17.78	17.12	13.39	19.47	18.39
PASCAL	22.6	**15.67**	23.56	17.08	17.79	19.46	17.9	16.13	13.7	19.44	18.33
UDISCAL	23.19	14.75	23.46	17.06	18.17	19.67	18.32	15.7	13.44	**21.14**	18.49
SASA	23.53†	15.38	23.9	17.77†	**18.37**†	**20.12**†	18.33†	16.55	13.37	20.88	**18.82**†
SASA + UDISCAL	23.77*	14.67	23.65	16.96	18.21	19.8	18.06	**17.15***	13.57*	20.02	18.59
SACrA	**23.83**†	15.15	22.86	**18.09**†	18.13	19.98†	**18.7**†	17.1	**13.83**†	19.41	18.71†
SACrA + UDISCAL	22.98	14.58	23.16	16.76	17.37	18.89	17.4	16.07	13.18	18.53	17.89

En-Fi

models	2015	2016	2016B	2017	2017B	2018	2019	average
Transformer	9.57	**11.05**	8.8	11.45	9.99	7.78	10.22	9.84
PASCAL	9.75	10.77	8.72	11.43	10.11	8.06	10.24	9.87
UDISCAL	9.04	10.85	8.63	11.46	10.1	7.7	9.85	9.66
SASA	9.65	10.87	**9.03**†	11.62†	10.1	7.99	10.53†	9.97†
SASA + UDISCAL	9.45	10.96*	8.91	**11.88***	**10.33***	**8.42***	10.62*	10.08*
SACrA	**10.26**†	10.95	8.89†	11.57†	10.13†	8.17†	**10.76**†	**10.10**†
SACrA + UDISCAL	9.42	10.84	8.83	11.51	9.9	7.71	10.7	9.84

En-Tr

models	2016	2017	2018	wikipedia	Eubookshop	mozilla	bible	average
Transformer	7.99	8.15	8.06	7.55	4.87	3.34	0.36	5.76
PASCAL	7.81	7.83	7.69	7.52	5.04	3.41	**0.54**	5.69
UDISCAL	7.68	7.83	7.4	7.63	4.92	3.34	0.49	5.61
SASA	8.2†	8.31†	**8.12**†	7.63	5.21†	3.09	0.52	5.87†
SASA + UDISCAL	7.81	7.92	8.1	7.58	**5.28***	3.36*	0.35	5.77
SACrA	7.75	8.33†	7.51	**7.68**†	5.11†	**3.59**†	0.5	5.78†
SACrA + UDISCAL	**8.23***	**8.54***	7.95*	7.51	5.22*	3.45	0.52*	**5.92***

Table 8: Bleu scores of challenge sentences for the baseline Transformer model, the baseline Syntactically infused models PASCAL and UDISCAL, our SASA and SACrA models, and models incorporating UDISCAL with each of SASA and SACrA, across all WMT's newstests. For every language pair, each column contains the Bleu scores over the WMT newstest equivalent to the column's year (e.g., for En-Ru, the scores under column *2015* are for En-Ru newstest2015). For some newstests, there was more than one version on WMT, each translated by a different person. For those test sets, we included both versions, denoting the second one with a "B". In addition, for every language pair, the right-most column represents the average Bleu scores over all the pair's reported newstests. For every test set (and for the average score), the best score is boldfaced. For each of the semantic models (i.e., SASA and SACrA), improvements over all the baselines (syntactic and Transformer) are marked by an arrow facing upwards. For models with both syntactic and semantic masks, improvements over each mask individually are marked by an asterisk.

Compositional generalization with a broad-coverage semantic parser

Pia Weißenhorn and **Lucia Donatelli** and **Alexander Koller**
Department of Language Science and Technology
Saarland Informatics Campus
Saarland University, Germany
{piaw, donatelli, koller}@coli.uni-saarland.de

Abstract

We show how the AM parser, a compositional semantic parser (Groschwitz et al., 2018), can solve compositional generalization on the COGS dataset. It is the first semantic parser that achieves high accuracy on both naturally occurring language and the synthetic COGS dataset. We discuss implications for corpus and model design for learning human-like generalization. Our results suggest that compositional generalization can be best achieved by building compositionality into semantic parsers.

1 Introduction

A growing body of recent research investigates *compositional generalization*, the ability of a semantic parser to predict the meaning of unseen sentences by recombining training instances in novel ways. Such generalization is thought to mimic the Principle of Compositionality (Partee, 1984), essential for human language learning and use. For example, COGS (Kim and Linzen, 2020), a dataset based on fragments of English, contains training instances with sentences semantically annotated with up to two recursive PPs; a semantic parser must then predict meaning representations for sentences with three or more recursive PPs (Table 1).

Previous work has shown that compositional generalization on COGS is a difficult and complex task. Intricate sequence-to-sequence (seq2seq) models, which achieve very high accuracy on broad-coverage semantic parsing tasks on naturally occurring language (Bevilacqua et al., 2021), achieve overall accuracy of 88% or less on COGS (Akyürek and Andreas, 2021; Csordás et al., 2021; Zheng and Lapata, 2021). Much of this accuracy is due to *lexical generalization*, tasks that test for generalization to new words in known structures (Sec. 2); when evaluated only on *structural generalization* cases that test novel structures such as the PP example above, the accuracy of most of these models drops to 10% or less.

In contrast, models that achieve high accuracy on synthetic compositional generalization datasets may not be able to generalize to naturally occurring language. For instance, Shaw et al. (2021) describe a synchronous grammar induction approach that achieves perfect accuracy on SCAN (Lake and Baroni, 2018), but has very low accuracy on corpora of naturally occurring text such as GeoQuery (Zelle and Mooney, 1996) and Spider (Yu et al., 2018). Similarly, the compositional LeAR parser (Liu et al., 2021) solves COGS with near-perfect accuracy and performs very well on other synthetic datasets, but has not been evaluated on corpora of naturally occurring text. This points to a fundamental tension between broad-coverage semantic parsing on natural text and the ability to generalize compositionally from structurally limited synthetic training sets (see also Shaw et al., 2021). To our knowledge, the only parser that does well on both is the CSL-T5 system of Qiu et al. (2022), which fine-tunes T5 using a complex data augmentation (DA) method involving synchronous grammars.

In this paper, we show that the AM parser (Groschwitz et al., 2018), a compositional semantic parser that achieves high accuracy across a range of different broad-coverage graphbanks (Lindemann et al., 2019; Donatelli et al., 2019), can also solve COGS at near-perfect accuracy. This high performance is due in large part to handling cases of structural generalization much better than the seq2seq models. The AM parser is thus the first semantic parser shown to perform accurately both on naturally occurring language and on COGS without requiring DA. Given that all semantic parsers that do well on COGS are either compositional (LeAR, AM parser) or perform compositionality-based DA (CSL-T5), we conjecture that building a semantic parser on the Principle of Compositionality is beneficial to solving compositional generalization. We

Proceedings of the 11th Joint Conference on Lexical and Computational Semantics, pages 44 - 54
July 14-15, 2022 ©2022 Association for Computational Linguistics

discuss the challenge of structural, as opposed to lexical, generalization for future work on this task.

2 Compositional Generalization in COGS

Compositional generalization is the ability to determine the meaning of unseen sentences using compositional principles. Humans can understand and produce a potentially infinite number of novel linguistic expressions by dynamically recombining known elements (Chomsky, 1957; Fodor and Pylyshyn, 1988; Fodor and Lepore, 2002). For semantic parsers, compositional generalization requires systems to recombine parts of multiple training instances to predict the meaning of a single test instance by learning correct generalizations. Several synthetic datasets for evaluating compositional generalization now exist, notably SCAN (Lake and Baroni, 2018) and CFQ (Keysers et al., 2020).

COGS (Kim and Linzen, 2020) is a synthetic semantic parsing dataset in which English sentences must be mapped to logic-based meaning representations. It distinguishes 21 *generalization types*, each of which requires generalizing from training instances to test instances in a particular systematic and linguistically-informed way.

Lexical generalization cases (18 types) test how known grammatical structures are recombined with words that were not observed in these particular structures during training. For instance, the common noun "hedgehog" is only exposed to the model as subject at training time as part of an 'exposure example' sentence, but generalization requires object usage of the same word based on forming analogies to other common nouns seen in both positions. This is illustrated in Table 1.

Structural generalization cases (3 types) involve generalizing to linguistic structures that were not observed in training. The PP recursion example above is of this type: the COGS training set contains sentences and logic-based semantic representations with up two nested prepositional phrases. In-domain development and test sets also consist of sentences with PP nesting depth up to two, but the *generalization set* contains sentences with 3–12 nested PPs. Additional structural generalization includes CP recursion (predict deeply nested CPs when trained on shallow examples, similar to PPs) and "object PP to subject PP", where PPs modify only objects in training (e.g. "Noah ate *the cake on the plate*.") and only subjects at test time ("*The cake on the table* burned.").

Kim and Linzen themselves show that seq2seq models based on LSTMs and Transformers do not perform well on COGS, achieving exact-match accuracies below 35%. Intensive subsequent work has tailored a wide range of seq2seq models to the COGS task (Tay et al., 2021; Akyürek and Andreas, 2021; Conklin et al., 2021; Csordás et al., 2021; Orhan, 2021; Zheng and Lapata, 2021), but none of these have reached an overall accuracy of 90% on the overall generalization set. On structural generalization in particular, the accuracy of all these models is below 10%, with the exception of Zheng and Lapata (2021), who achieve 39% on PP recursion. By contrast, the compositional model of Liu et al. (2021) and the model of Qiu et al. (2022), which uses compositional data augmentation, achieve accuracies upwards of 98% on the full generalization set.

3 Parsing COGS with the AM parser

3.1 The AM parser

We adapt the broad-coverage AM parser to COGS. The AM parser (Groschwitz et al., 2018) is a compositional semantic parser that learns to map sentences to graphs. It was the first semantic parser to perform with high accuracy across all major graphbanks (Lindemann et al., 2019) and can achieve very high parsing speeds (Lindemann et al., 2020).

Instead of predicting the graph directly, the AM parser first predicts a graph fragment for each token in the sentence and a dependency tree that connects them (Fig. 1a). This dependency tree is then evaluated deterministically into a graph (Fig. 1b) using the operations of the *AM algebra*. The "Apply" (APP) operation fills an argument slot of a graph (drawn in red) by inserting the root node (drawn with a bold outline) of another graph into this slot; for instance, the APP_s operation inserts the "boy" node into the ARG0 of "want". The "Modify" (MOD) operation attaches a modifier to a node; MOD_m attaches the "manner-sound" graph to the "sleep" node. The dependency tree captures how the meaning of the sentence can be compositionally obtained from the meanings of the words.

AM parsing is done by combining a neural dependency parser with a neural tagger for predicting the graph fragments. We follow Lindemann et al. (2019) and rely on the dependency parsing model of Kiperwasser and Goldberg (2016), which scores each dependency edge by feeding neural represen-

Class : Type	Training	Generalization
Lexical: *Subj→Obj (common noun)*	A hedgehog ate the cake. `*cake (`x_4`); hedgehog (`x_1`) ∧ eat.agent (`x_2, x_1`) ∧ eat.theme (`x_2, x_4`)`	The baby liked the hedgehog. `*baby (`x_1`); *hedgehog (`x_4`); like.agent (`x_2, x_1`) ∧ like.theme (`x_2, x_4`)`
Structural: *PP recursion*	Ava saw a ball in a bowl on the table. `*table (`x_9`); see.agent (`x_1`,Ava) ∧ see.theme (`x_1, x_3`) ∧ ball (`x_3`) ∧ ball.nmod.in (`x_3, x_6`) ∧ bowl (`x_6`) ∧ bowl.nmod.on (`x_6, x_9`)`	Ava saw a ball in a bowl on the table on the floor. `*table (`x_9`); *floor (`x_{12}`); see.agent (`x_1`, Ava) ∧ see.theme (`x_1, x_3`) ∧ ball (`x_3`) ∧ ball.nmod.in (`x_3, x_6`) ∧ bowl (`x_6`) ∧ bowl.nmod.on (`x_6, x_9`) ∧ table.nmod.on (`x_9, x_{12}`)`

Table 1: One example of a lexical and a structural generalization type from the COGS dataset.

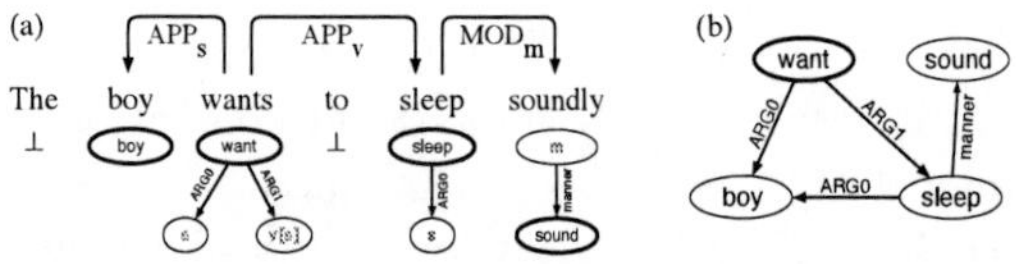

Figure 1: (a) AM dependency tree with (b) its value.

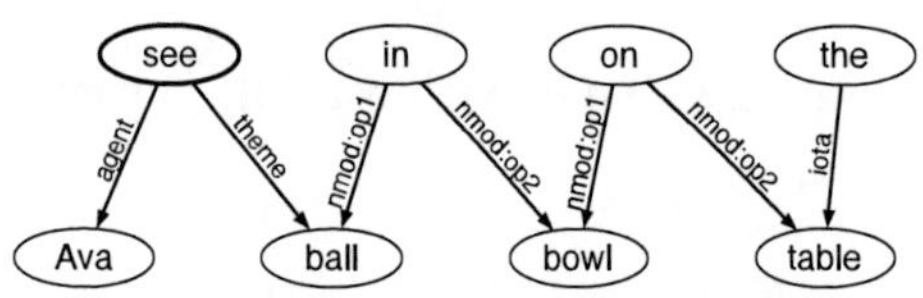

Figure 2: Logical form to graph conversion for "Ava saw a ball in a bowl on the table" (cf. Table 1).

tations for the two tokens to an MLP. We train the parser using the setup of Groschwitz et al. (2021), which does not require explicit annotations with AM dependency trees.

3.2 AM parsing for COGS

We apply the AM parser to COGS by converting the semantic representations in COGS to graphs. The conversion is illustrated in Fig. 2.

Given a logical form of COGS, we create a graph that has one node for each variable x_i and each constant (e.g. `Ava`). If a variable appears as the first argument of an atom of the form `pred.arg`(x, y), we assign it the node label `pred` in the graph. We also add an edge from x to y with label `arg`. E.g. `see.agent (`x_1`, Ava)` turns into an 'agent' edge from 'see' to 'Ava'. Each *iota term* `*noun (`x_{noun}`)` is treated as an edge from a node for the preceeding "the" token to the respective noun node. Preposition meaning `bowl.nmod.on (`x_6, x_9`)` is represented as a node (labeled 'on') with outgoing edges to the two arguments/nouns ('nmod.op1' to "bowl", 'nmod.op2' to "table"). By encoding the logical form as a graph, we lose the ordering of the conjuncts. The 'correct' order is restored in postprocessing. More details and graph conversion examples are in Appendix C.

4 Experiments on COGS

4.1 Experimental setup

We evaluate the AM parser on COGS and compare its accuracy against a number of strong baselines. We follow standard COGS practice and evaluate on both the (in-distribution) test set and the generalization set. We report exact match accuracies averaged across 5 training runs with their standard deviations.

Training regime. In addition to the regular COGS training set ('train') of 24,155 training instances, we also report numbers for models trained on the extended training set 'train100' of 39,500 instances (Kim and Linzen, 2020, Appendix E.2). These training sets allow to test 1-shot (train) or 100-shot (train100) lexical generalization. For instance, for the "hedgehog" example in Table 1, train contains *exactly one* sentence with this noun, whereas there are 100 different sentences with "hedgehog" in train100 (all in subject position). As this change can only be done for lexical generalization (tied to specific lexical items), structural generalization is not directly modulated by a training set change.

Compositional models. We train the AM parser on the COGS graph corpus (cf. Section 3.2). Most hyperparameter values come from Groschwitz et al. (2021)'s training setup for AMR to make overfitting to COGS less likely; see Appendix A for details.

The AM parser either receives pretrained word embeddings from BERT (Devlin et al., 2019) ('AM+B') or learns embeddings from the COGS

		train		train100	
		Test	Gen	Test	Gen
seq2seq	Kim and Linzen 2020	96	35	94	63
	Csordás et al. 2021	100	81	-	75.4
	Akyürek and Andreas 2021	-	83	99	84.5
	Zheng and Lapata 2021 †	-	89	-	-
compositional	Qiu et al. 2022	-	**99.5**	-	-
	Liu et al. 2021: LeAR[1]	-	98.9±0.9	-	-
	AM	100	59.9± 2.7	100	91.1±2.3
	AM+dist	100	62.6±10.8	100	88.6±4.9
	AM+B †	100	79.6± 6.4	100	93.6±1.4
	AM+B+dist †	100	78.3±22.9	100	**98.4**±0.9

Table 2: COGS exact match scores. †) models use pre-training.

data only ('AM'). We run the training algorithm with up to three argument slots to enable the analysis of ditransitive verbs. For evaluation, we reverse graph conversion to reconstruct the logical forms.

To handle PP recursion, we hypothesize that explicit distance information between tokens could help the AM parser: COGS eliminates potential PP attachment ambiguities and assumes that each PP modifies the noun immediately to its left. Instead of passing only the representations of the potential parent and child node to the edge-scoring model, we also pass an encoding of their relative distance in the string (Vaswani et al., 2017), yielding the AM parser models with the "+dist" suffix. Distance information is then available as an explicit feature for *any* dependency edge decision, and the neural model learns how to weight this feature for different edges.

Finally, we report evaluation results for LeAR, the compositional COGS parser of Liu et al. (2021). LeAR learns to predict trees of corpus-specific algebraic operations using reinforcement learning with an intricate training setup.

4.2 Results

The results are summarized in Table 2. Gray numbers are taken from original papers; black numbers we reproduced in separate experiments. Table 3 shows results by structural and lexical generalization type. See Appendix B for details.

Compositional models solve COGS. We find that when trained on 'train100', the modified AM parser solves COGS with near-perfect accuracy. The evaluation results in Table 2 suggest a clear split between compositional and seq2seq models, with both compositional models outperforming all seq2seq models. This split becomes even clearer when we distinguish different generalization types. On the three structural generalization types, no seq2seq model has an accuracy above 40%, whereas both LeAR and AM+B+dist still achieve near-perfect accuracy.

PP vs. CP recursion. A closer error analysis on PP recursion reveals (as hypothesized) that the accuracy of the AM+B parser degrades with increasing PP depth. The AM+B+dist parser maintains a high accuracy across all embedding depths.

There is an interesting asymmetry between the behavior of the AM parser on PP recursion and CP recursion: The accuracy of AM+B is stable across recursion depths for CP recursion, and the distance feature is only needed for PPs. This can be explained by the way in which the AM parser learns to incorporate PPs and CPs into the dependency tree: it uses APP edges to combine verbs with CPs, which ensures that only a single CP can be combined with each sentence-embedding verb. By contrast, each NP can be modified by an arbitrary number of PPs using MOD edges. Thus a confusion over attachment is only possible for PPs.

Effect of training regime. Parsers on COGS are traditionally not allowed any pretraining (Kim and Linzen, 2020), in order to judge their ability to generalize from limited observations. We see in the experiments above that the use of pretrained word embeddings helps the AM parser achieve accuracy parity with LeAR, but is not needed to outperform all seq2seq models on 'train100'.

Training on 'train100' helps the AM parser more than any other model in Table 2. The difference between its accuracy on 'train' and 'train100' is due to lexical issues: we found that when trained on 'train', the AM parser typically predicts the correct delexicalized formulas and then inserts an incorrect but related constant or predicate symbol.

For example, when tested on common nouns, "kennel" may be used instead of "hedgehog"; when tested on unaccusative to transitive generalization, the model may choose another verb seen commonly in that pattern instead of the target verb (e.g. "value" instead of "shatter").

We ablate the different model components (pre-trained BERT embeddings, +dist) and training setups (train100 vs. train) in Table 3. Trained on

[1]All LeAR numbers are based on our reproduction of their COGS evaluation; they report an accuracy of 97.7.

		Class / Gen. type	STRUCTURAL Obj to Subj PP	CP recursion	PP recursion	LEXICAL mean of 18 other types	Overall
compositional	AM+B+dist	train100	78	100	99	99	98
	AM+B	train100	49	100	41	99	94
	AM+B+dist	train	72	100	97	76	78
	AM+B	train	59	100	36	82	80
	AM+dist	train	26	100	98	61	63
	AM	train	38	100	61	59	60
	LeAR	train	93	100	99	99	99
seq2seq	Kim and Linzen 2020	train	0	0	0	42	35
	Akyürek and Andreas 2021	train	0	0	1	96	82
	Zheng and Lapata 2021	train	0	12	39	99	89
	Kim and Linzen 2020	train100	0	0	0	73	63
	Csordás et al. 2021	train100	0	0	0	88	75

Table 3: Exact match accuracies on the individual generalization types.

'train', AM+B+dist achieves a mean accuracy on structural generalization cases of 89.6 (compared to 92.1 for 'train100'), whereas the mean accuracy on lexical generalization cases drops to 76. This again illustrates that the larger training set compensates for a lexical weakness in the AM parser rather than a structural one. Even without BERT and trained on 'train', AM+dist gets 74.6 on structural cases, drastically outperforming the seq2seq models.

5 Conclusion

The AM parser is the first compositional semantic parser to solve COGS and achieve high accuracy on naturally occurring language.[2] Particularly on complex structural generalization cases, compositionality-based parsers seem to outperform seq2seq models systematically. By contrast, lexical generalization cases are solved easily by most models and do not require a compositionality bias. We suggest that future corpus design and evaluation focus on model accuracy for structural generalization types; an extension to COGS that incorporates a greater variety of these types would allow more insight on the overall task.

Though synthetic datasets like COGS allow focused probing parser performance on specific linguistic phenomena, it remains unclear exactly how accurate performance on such datasets transfers to naturally occurring language, and vice-versa. Another strand of future work is thus extending the broad-coverage AM parser to more compositional generalization datasets. While COGS offers a good starting point to test multiple types of both lexical and structural generalization similar to what is attested for humans, other datasets offer insight into generalization less clearly connected to human linguistic abilities (e.g. CFQ; Keysers et al., 2020) but important for generalization abilities more generally. Additional assessment of models' generalization performance ought to combine broad-coverage parsing and focused evaluation with hand-crafted datasets in a systematic way, yet to be defined.

[2]Our code is available at `https://github.com/coli-saar/am-parser`.

Acknowledgments

We thank Yuekun Yao for his insights from related experiments on COGS and Jonas Groschwitz and Matthias Lindemann for their advice on adapting the AM parser to COGS. We also thank the reviewers for their helpful comments. This research was funded in part by the Deutsche Forschungsgemeinschaft (DFG, German Research Foundation), project KO 2916/2-2.

References

Ekin Akyürek and Jacob Andreas. 2021. Lexicon learning for few shot sequence modeling. In *Proceedings of the 59th Annual Meeting of the Association for Computational Linguistics and the 11th International Joint Conference on Natural Language Processing (Volume 1: Long Papers)*, pages 4934–4946, Online. Association for Computational Linguistics.

Michele Bevilacqua, Rexhina Blloshmi, and Roberto Navigli. 2021. One SPRING to rule them both: Symmetric AMR semantic parsing and generation without a complex pipeline. In *Proceedings of the AAAI Conference on Artificial Intelligence (AAAI-21)*, volume 35, pages 12564–12573. AAAI Press.

Noam Chomsky. 1957. *Syntactic Structures*. De Gruyter Mouton.

Henry Conklin, Bailin Wang, Kenny Smith, and Ivan Titov. 2021. Meta-learning to compositionally generalize. In *Proceedings of the 59th Annual Meeting of the Association for Computational Linguistics and the 11th International Joint Conference on Natural Language Processing (Volume 1: Long Papers)*, pages 3322–3335, Online. Association for Computational Linguistics.

Róbert Csordás, Kazuki Irie, and Juergen Schmidhuber. 2021. The devil is in the detail: Simple tricks improve systematic generalization of transformers. In *Proceedings of the 2021 Conference on Empirical Methods in Natural Language Processing*, pages 619–634, Online and Punta Cana, Dominican Republic. Association for Computational Linguistics.

Jacob Devlin, Ming-Wei Chang, Kenton Lee, and Kristina Toutanova. 2019. BERT: Pre-training of deep bidirectional transformers for language understanding. In *Proceedings of the 2019 Conference of the North American Chapter of the Association for Computational Linguistics: Human Language Technologies, Volume 1 (Long and Short Papers)*, pages 4171–4186, Minneapolis, Minnesota. Association for Computational Linguistics.

Lucia Donatelli, Meaghan Fowlie, Jonas Groschwitz, Alexander Koller, Matthias Lindemann, Mario Mina, and Pia Weißenhorn. 2019. Saarland at MRP 2019: Compositional parsing across all graphbanks. In *Proceedings of the Shared Task on Cross-Framework Meaning Representation Parsing at the 2019 Conference on Natural Language Learning*, pages 66–75, Hong Kong. Association for Computational Linguistics.

Jerry A. Fodor and Ernest Lepore. 2002. *The Compositionality Papers*. Oxford University Press.

Jerry A. Fodor and Zenon W. Pylyshyn. 1988. Connectionism and cognitive architecture: A critical analysis. *Cognition*, 28(1):3–71.

Jonas Groschwitz, Meaghan Fowlie, and Alexander Koller. 2021. Learning compositional structures for semantic graph parsing. In *Proceedings of the 5th Workshop on Structured Prediction for NLP (SPNLP 2021)*, pages 22–36, Online. Association for Computational Linguistics.

Jonas Groschwitz, Matthias Lindemann, Meaghan Fowlie, Mark Johnson, and Alexander Koller. 2018. AMR dependency parsing with a typed semantic algebra. In *Proceedings of the 56th Annual Meeting of the Association for Computational Linguistics (Volume 1: Long Papers)*, pages 1831–1841, Melbourne, Australia. Association for Computational Linguistics.

Daniel Keysers, Nathanael Schärli, Nathan Scales, Hylke Buisman, Daniel Furrer, Sergii Kashubin, Nikola Momchev, Danila Sinopalnikov, Lukasz Stafiniak, Tibor Tihon, Dmitry Tsarkov, Xiao Wang, Marc van Zee, and Olivier Bousquet. 2020. Measuring compositional generalization: A comprehensive method on realistic data. In *International Conference on Learning Representations (ICLR)*.

Najoung Kim and Tal Linzen. 2020. COGS: A compositional generalization challenge based on semantic interpretation. In *Proceedings of the 2020 Conference on Empirical Methods in Natural Language Processing*, pages 9087–9105, Online. Association for Computational Linguistics.

Eliyahu Kiperwasser and Yoav Goldberg. 2016. Simple and accurate dependency parsing using bidirectional LSTM feature representations. *Transactions of the Association for Computational Linguistics*, 4:313–327.

Brenden Lake and Marco Baroni. 2018. Generalization without systematicity: On the compositional skills of sequence-to-sequence recurrent networks. In *Proceedings of the 35th International Conference on Machine Learning*, volume 80 of *Proceedings of Machine Learning Research*, pages 2873–2882, Stockholmsmässan, Stockholm Sweden. PMLR.

Matthias Lindemann, Jonas Groschwitz, and Alexander Koller. 2019. Compositional semantic parsing across graphbanks. In *Proceedings of the 57th Annual Meeting of the Association for Computational Linguistics*, pages 4576–4585, Florence, Italy. Association for Computational Linguistics.

Matthias Lindemann, Jonas Groschwitz, and Alexander Koller. 2020. Fast semantic parsing with welltypedness guarantees. In *Proceedings of the 2020 Conference on Empirical Methods in Natural Language Processing (EMNLP)*, pages 3929–3951, Online. Association for Computational Linguistics.

Chenyao Liu, Shengnan An, Zeqi Lin, Qian Liu, Bei Chen, Jian-Guang Lou, Lijie Wen, Nanning Zheng, and Dongmei Zhang. 2021. Learning algebraic recombination for compositional generalization. In *Findings of the Association for Computational Linguistics: ACL-IJCNLP 2021*, pages 1129–1144, Online. Association for Computational Linguistics.

A. Emin Orhan. 2021. Compositional generalization in semantic parsing with pretrained transformers. *Computing Research Repository (CoRR)*, arXiv: 2109.15101.

Barbara H. Partee. 1984. Compositionality. In *Varieties of Formal Semantics: Proceedings of the 4th Amsterdam Colloquium, September 1982*, volume 3, pages 281–311. Foris Publications, Dordrecht.

Linlu Qiu, Peter Shaw, Panupong Pasupat, Paweł Krzysztof Nowak, Tal Linzen, Fei Sha, and Kristina Toutanova. 2022. Improving compositional generalization with latent structure and data augmentation. In *Proceedings of NAACL*.

Peter Shaw, Ming-Wei Chang, Panupong Pasupat, and Kristina Toutanova. 2021. Compositional generalization and natural language variation: Can a semantic parsing approach handle both? In *Proceedings of the 59th Annual Meeting of the Association for Computational Linguistics and the 11th International Joint Conference on Natural Language Processing (Volume 1: Long Papers)*, pages 922–938, Online. Association for Computational Linguistics.

Yi Tay, Mostafa Dehghani, Jai Prakash Gupta, Vamsi Aribandi, Dara Bahri, Zhen Qin, and Donald Metzler. 2021. Are pretrained convolutions better than pretrained transformers? In *Proceedings of the 59th Annual Meeting of the Association for Computational Linguistics and the 11th International Joint Conference on Natural Language Processing (Volume 1: Long Papers)*, pages 4349–4359, Online. Association for Computational Linguistics.

Ashish Vaswani, Noam Shazeer, Niki Parmar, Jakob Uszkoreit, Llion Jones, Aidan N. Gomez, Łukasz Kaiser, and Illia Polosukhin. 2017. Attention is all you need. In *Advances in Neural Information Processing Systems 30 (NIPS 2017)*. Curran Associates, Inc.

Tao Yu, Rui Zhang, Kai Yang, Michihiro Yasunaga, Dongxu Wang, Zifan Li, James Ma, Irene Li, Qingning Yao, Shanelle Roman, Zilin Zhang, and Dragomir Radev. 2018. Spider: A large-scale human-labeled dataset for complex and cross-domain semantic parsing and text-to-SQL task. In *Proceedings of the 2018 Conference on Empirical Methods in Natural Language Processing*, pages 3911–3921, Brussels, Belgium. Association for Computational Linguistics.

John M. Zelle and Raymond J. Mooney. 1996. Learning to parse database queries using inductive logic programming. In *Proceedings of the Thirteenth National Conference on Artificial Intelligence - Volume 2*, AAAI'96, page 1050–1055. AAAI Press.

Hao Zheng and Mirella Lapata. 2021. Disentangled sequence to sequence learning for compositional generalization. *Computing Research Repository (CoRR)*, arXiv: 2110.04655. To appear at ACL2022.

A Training details of the AM parser

Hyperparameters. For the AM parser, we primarily copy hyperparameter values from the AMR experiments of Groschwitz et al. (2021). This helps prevent overfitting on COGS, but we also note that hyperparameter tuning for compositional generalization datasets can be difficult anyways since one can typically easily achieve perfect scores on an in-doman dev set. Copied values include for instance the number of epochs (60 due to supervised loss for edge existence and lexical labels), the batch size, the number and dimensionality of neural network layers and not using early stopping (but selecting best model based on per epoch evaluation metric on the dev set). Choosing 3 sources has worked well on other datasets (Groschwitz et al., 2021) and we adopt this hyperparameter choice. We note that with ditransitive verbs (i.e. verbs requiring NPs filling agent, theme, and recipient roles) present in COGS we need at least three sources anyway to account for these.

Deviations from Groschwitz et al. (2021)'s settings. For training on train (but not train100), we set the vocabulary threshold from 7 down to 1 to account for the fact that the lexical generalizations rely on a single occurrence of a word in the training data; on train100 we keep 7 as a threshold since trigger words (e.g. "hedgehog") occur 100 times. For word embeddings, we either use BERT-Large-uncased (Devlin et al., 2019) like Groschwitz et al. (2021) or learn embeddings from the dataset only (embedding dimension 1024, same as for the BERT model). We decrease the learning rate from 0.001 to 0.0001: we observed that the learning curves are still converging very quickly and hypothesize that COGS training set might also be easier than the AMR one used in Groschwitz et al. (2021).

We use the projective A* decoder (Lindemann et al., 2020, §4.2): in pre-experiments this showed better results. In addition, it makes comparison to related work (such as LeAR by Liu et al. (2021)) easier which uses only projective latent trees. We use supervised loss for edge existence and lexical labels.

Relative distance encoding. For the relative distance encodings we use sine-cosine interleaved encoding function introduced by Vaswani et al. (2017, §3.5) and as input to it use the relative distance $dist(i, j) = i - j$ between sentence positions i and j. We use a dimensionality of 64 for the distance encodings (d_{model} in Vaswani et al. (2017) is 512). These distance encodings are then concatenated together with the BiLSTM representations for possible heads and dependents used in the standard Kiperwasser and Goldberg (2016) edge scoring model. This constitutes the input to the MLP emitting a score for each token pair. These models have the suffix 'dist' in the tables.

Runtimes. Training the AM parser took 5 to 7 hours on train with 60 epochs and 6 to 9.5 hours on train100. In general, training with BERT took longer than without, same holds for adding relative distance encodings. Inference with a trained model on the full 21k generalization samples took about 15 minutes using the Astar decoder with the 'ignore aware' heuristic. All AM parser experiments were performed using Intel Xeon E5-2687W v3 10-core processors at 3.10Ghz and 256GB RAM, and MSI Nvidia Titan-X (2015) GPU cards (12GB).

Number of parameters. For their models, Kim and Linzen (2020) tried to keep the number of parameters comparable (9.5 to 11 million) and therefore rule out model capacity as a confound. The number of trainable parameters of the AM parser model used is 10.7 to 11.5 million (lower one is with BERT, higher without. Impact of relative distance encoding is rather minimal: < 17k), so the improved performance is not just due to a higher number of parameters.

Dev set performance. For compositional generalization datasets, it is relatively easy to get (near) perfect results on the (in domain) dev/test sets. We observe this too: all AM parser models had an exact match score of at least 99.9 on the dev set and at least 99.8 on the (in distribution) test set.

Evaluation procedure. Kim and Linzen (2020) do not provide a separate evaluation script but use (string) exact match accuracy on the logical forms as the main evaluation metric. This metric requires models to learn the 'correct' order of conjuncts: even if a logically equivalent form with a different order of conjuncts would be predicted, string exact match would count it as a failure. In lack of an official evaluation script we implemented our own evaluation script to compute exact match.

B Evaluation details

For descriptions of the generalization types we refer to Kim and Linzen (2020, §3 and Fig. 1).

AM parser. Full results for the 8 AM parser configurations (two types of embeddings, two training sets, presence/absence of distance encodings) are displayed in Table 4. Averages and standard deviations were computed across 5 runs for each configuration. For the AM+B+dist configuration trained on the smaller train set, one outlier run was observed with 39.9% overall generalization accuracy, and the other four runs ranging from 76.4% to 96.6%. This outlier therefore greatly contributed to the high variance for this configuration.

LeAR. Due to our reproduction experiment, we can report a breakdown by generalization type for Liu et al.'s LeAR model, displayed in Table 5. We observed that the LeAR model skips 22 sentences in the generalization set due to out-of-vocabulary tokens.[3] We include these sentences in the accuracy computation (as failures) for the generalization set. The published LeAR code does not convert its internally used representation back to logical forms, therefore we evaluate on the logical forms like it is done for other models, but have to rely on accuracy computation done in the LeAR code for the internal representation. From inspecting the published code,[4] LeAR makes the preprocessing choice to ignore the contribution of the definite determiner, treating indefinite and definite NPs equally, resulting in a big conjunction without any iota ('$\star$') prefixes.

Model numbers copied from other papers. Kim and Linzen (2020) provide three baseline models, among which the Transformer model reached the best performance on train and train100. Per generalization type results can be found in their Appendix F (Table 5 on page 9105) from which we report the Transformer model numbers.

The strongest model of Akyürek and Andreas (2021) is 'Lex:Simple:Soft' (cf. their Table 5) with a generalization accuracy of 83% (also reported in our Table 2), whereas their Lex:Simple model lags 1 point behind. For the latter, the authors provide per generalization type output: link. Numbers in Table 3 are for Lex:Simple, not Lex:Simple:Soft.

For Zheng and Lapata (2021), our reported number was provided directly by the authors after publication of their paper.

[3]The words "gardener" and "monastery" occur zero times in the train set, but in total in 22 sentences of the generalization set. The majority (15) of these appear in PP recursion samples.

[4]https://github.com/thousfeet/LEAR

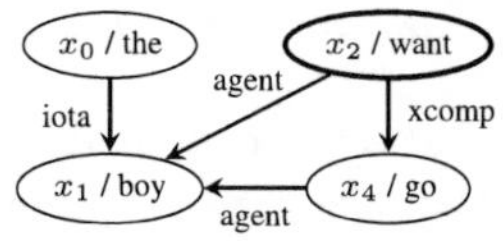

$\star$ boy(x_1) ; want.agent(x_2,x_1) $\wedge$ want.xcomp(x_2,x_4) $\wedge$ go.agent(x_4,x_1)

Figure 3: Logical form to graph conversion for "The boy wanted to go" (cf. (1)). For illustration only we use node names (the part before the '/') to outline the token alignment.

Lexical vs. structural generalization. As said above, structural generalization is underrepresented in COGS (3 out of 21 generalization types), and lexical generalization (the remaining 18 types) is therefore dominating the evaluation. As a consequence, an overall generalization accuracy above 80% can be achieved without even touching upon structural generalization. In Table 6 we report the average accuracy of both classes (by averaging over all types of the respective class), along with the overall generalization accuracy. Some models do not report standard deviations.

C Additional information on COGS to graph conversions

This is a more detailed explanation of the COGS logical form to graph conversion described in Section 3.2 based on four additional example sentences:

(1) The boy wanted to go.
$\star$boy(x_1); want.agent(x_2,x_1) $\wedge$ want.xcomp(x_2,x_4) $\wedge$ go.agent(x_4,x_1)

(2) Ava was lended a cookie in a bottle.
lend.recipient(x_2, Ava) $\wedge$ lend.theme(x_2,x_4) $\wedge$ cookie(x_4) $\wedge$ cookie.nmod.in(x_4,x_7) $\wedge$ bottle(x_7)

(3) Ava said that Ben declared that Claire slept.
say.agent(x_1, Ava) $\wedge$ say.ccomp(x_1,x_4) $\wedge$ declare.agent(x_4, Ben) $\wedge$ declare.ccomp(x_4,x_7) $\wedge$ sleep.agent(x_7, Claire)

(4) touch
$\lambda a.\lambda b.\lambda e.$ touch.agent(e,b) $\wedge$ touch.theme(e,a)

The first of these is used as the main example for now. Its graph conversion can be found in Fig. 3.

Basic ideas. *Arguments* of predicates (variables like x_i or proper names like Ava) are translated

Type	train AM	train AM+dist	train AM+B	train AM+B+dist	train100 AM	train100 AM+dist	train100 AM+B	train100 AM+B+dist
Subj to Obj (common noun)	65.8±43.4	88.3±10.9	99.7± 0.1	96.5± 6.8	99.9± 0.1	99.9± 0.1	100.0± 0.1	99.9± 0.2
Subj to Obj (proper noun)	69.9± 9.8	48.1±32.0	66.3±38.8	61.8±47.3	98.9± 1.7	100.0± 0.0	89.6± 8.1	95.8± 9.3
Obj to Subj (common noun)	53.1±45.0	97.9± 4.4	99.9± 0.2	88.0±26.7	99.9± 0.1	99.8± 0.2	100.0± 0.1	99.9± 0.1
Obj to Subj (proper noun)	90.0±21.4	88.3±25.9	88.9±11.2	78.8±42.9	99.8± 0.0	99.8± 0.1	99.9± 0.0	99.9± 0.0
Prim to Subj (common noun)	3.4± 7.6	0.0± 0.0	76.2±42.2	80.3±42.2	98.0± 4.5	59.9±54.7	100.0± 0.0	100.0± 0.0
Prim to Subj (proper noun)	4.7±10.6	1.0± 2.3	99.9± 0.1	100.0± 0.0	99.8± 0.3	99.9± 0.1	100.0± 0.0	100.0± 0.1
Prim to Obj (common noun)	0.2± 0.4	0.0± 0.0	74.5±32.5	80.1±40.7	95.9± 8.9	59.9±54.7	100.0± 0.0	100.0± 0.0
Prim to Obj (proper noun)	10.4± 9.1	22.0±15.6	90.5± 9.9	94.9± 3.7	98.8± 2.4	99.8± 0.4	84.9± 9.1	94.4± 9.0
Prim verb to Infin. arg	59.7±54.2	55.2±50.5	100.0± 0.0	82.9±38.2	17.6±30.8	1.0± 2.2	100.0± 0.0	100.0± 0.0
ObjmodPP to SubjmodPP	38.1±23.1	26.1±15.1	59.0±40.8	71.5±24.0	48.0±17.3	44.8±23.9	49.1±27.5	77.7± 7.1
CP recursion	100.0± 0.0	100.0± 0.1	100.0± 0.0	100.0± 0.0	99.9± 0.1	100.0± 0.0	100.0± 0.0	100.0± 0.0
PP recursion	60.5± 4.2	97.6± 0.9	36.3± 8.0	97.3± 2.0	57.2± 8.3	97.0± 1.1	41.5±11.2	98.6± 0.5
Active to Passive	69.3±42.2	41.7±52.3	83.0±24.8	78.8±31.3	100.0± 0.0	100.0± 0.0	100.0± 0.0	100.0± 0.0
Passive to Active	51.6±45.2	46.6±50.2	45.5±27.2	52.0±43.6	99.6± 0.7	99.9± 0.1	100.0± 0.0	100.0± 0.0
ObjOTrans. to trans.	79.6±33.6	77.8±28.2	22.3±24.0	35.6±33.4	99.9± 0.1	100.0± 0.1	100.0± 0.0	100.0± 0.0
Unacc to transitive	33.2±36.1	51.2±47.2	48.2±35.8	48.9±41.5	99.6± 0.7	100.0± 0.1	100.0± 0.0	100.0± 0.0
Dobj dative to PP dative	99.3± 0.8	98.8± 2.0	99.8± 0.1	95.0±11.0	99.9± 0.1	99.9± 0.1	100.0± 0.0	100.0± 0.0
PP dative to Dobj dative	90.4±11.9	79.5±44.5	85.6±21.7	89.5±11.5	99.7± 0.1	99.8± 0.1	100.0± 0.0	100.0± 0.0
Agent NP to Unacc Subj	78.5±43.4	99.7± 0.6	95.3± 6.4	78.2±43.9	100.0± 0.0	100.0± 0.0	100.0± 0.0	100.0± 0.0
Theme NP to ObjOTrans. Subj	99.9± 0.1	99.2± 1.7	99.9± 0.1	70.5±41.9	100.0± 0.0	100.0± 0.0	100.0± 0.0	100.0± 0.0
Theme NP to Unergative Subj	100.0± 0.1	96.6± 7.6	99.9± 0.1	64.4±49.0	100.0± 0.0	100.0± 0.0	100.0± 0.0	100.0± 0.0
Total	59.9±21.1	62.7±18.7	79.6±15.4	78.3±27.7	91.1± 3.6	88.6± 6.6	93.6± 2.7	98.4± 1.3

Table 4: Exact match accuracy on the generalization set by generalization type for all AM parser models.

Type	train LeAR
Subj to Obj (common noun)	99.8± 0.0
Subj to Obj (proper noun)	93.1±10.2
Obj to Subj (common noun)	100.0± 0.0
Obj to Subj (proper noun)	99.9± 0.0
Prim to Subj (common noun)	100.0± 0.0
Prim to Subj (proper noun)	100.0± 0.0
Prim to Obj (common noun)	99.8± 0.0
Prim to Obj (proper noun)	93.1±10.2
Prim verb to Infin. arg	100.0± 0.0
ObjmodPP to SubjmodPP	92.5± 9.4
CP recursion	100.0± 0.0
PP recursion	98.5± 0.0
Active to Passive	100.0± 0.0
Passive to Active	100.0± 0.0
ObjOTrans. to trans.	100.0± 0.0
Unacc to transitive	100.0± 0.0
Dobj dative to PP dative	99.9± 0.0
PP dative to Dobj dative	90.9± 0.0
Agent NP to Unacc Subj	100.0± 0.0
Theme NP to ObjOTrans. Subj	100.0± 0.0
Theme NP to Unergative Subj	100.0± 0.0
Total	98.9± 0.9

Table 5: Exact match accuracy on the generalization set by generalization type for the LeAR reproduction runs on train.

Model	trained on	Lexical	Structural	Overall
AM	train	58.8± 2.7	66.2± 8.2	59.9± 2.7
AM+dist	train	60.7±12.4	74.5± 5.2	62.7±10.8
AM+B	train	82.0± 7.3	65.1±11.6	79.6± 6.4
AM+B+dist	train	76.5±25.4	89.6± 8.7	78.3±22.9
AM	train100	94.9± 2.1	68.4± 6.7	91.1± 2.3
AM+dist	train100	90.0± 6.0	80.6± 8.2	88.6± 4.9
AM+B	train100	98.6± 0.9	63.5± 9.2	93.6± 1.4
AM+B+dist	train100	99.4± 1.0	92.1± 2.3	98.4± 0.9
LeAR	train	99.2± 1.1	97 ± 3.1	98.9± 0.9
Kim and Linzen 2020	train	41.2±	0 ±	35 ±
Akyürek and Andreas 2021	train	75.7± 1.1	0.5± 0.6	82.1± 0.6
Zheng and Lapata 2021	train	99.8±	16.8±	87.9±
Kim and Linzen 2020	train100	73 ±	0 ±	63 ±
Csordás et al. 2021	train100	88 ±	0 ±	75 ±

Table 6: Lexical vs structural generalization for seq2seq and compositional models

to nodes. The first part of each predicate name (e.g. `boy`, `want`, `go`) is the lemma of the token pointed to by the first argument (e.g. x_1, x_2, x_4), we strip this lemma ('delexicalize') from the predicate and insert it as the node label of the first argument (post-processing reverses this).

Binary predicates (i.e. terms with 2 arguments) are translated into edges, pointing from their first to their second argument, e.g. `want.agent` (x_2, x_1) is converted to an 'agent' edge from node x_2 (the 'want' node) to node x_1.

For *unary predicates* like `boy` (x_1) the delexicalization already suffices, so we don't add any edge (in lack of a proper target node). We restore unary predicates during postprocessing for nodes with no outgoing edges.

For a definite NP covering input token positions $i-1$ and i (i.e. "the$_{i-1}$ noun$_i$"), COGS includes a *iota term* `*noun` (x_i) `;` in the output. This definite NP meaning is treated as if it was a conjunction of the noun meaning (i.e. `noun` (x_i)) and 'definite determiner meaning' binary predicate `the.iota` (x_{i-1}, x_i).
The AM parser further requires one node to be the *root node*. For non-primitives we select it heuristically as the node with no incoming edges (excluding preposition and determiner nodes).

Prepositions. We 'reify' prepositions so each becomes a node of the graph with outgoing 'nmod' edges to the modified NP and the argument NP.

Alignments. For training the AM parser additionally needs *alignments* of the nodes to the input tokens. Luckily all x_i nodes naturally provide alignments (alignment to ith input token). For proper names we simply align them to the first occurrence in the sentence. The determiner node is aligned to the token preceding the corresponding x_{noun}. Edges are implicitly aligned by the blob heuristics, which are pretty simple here; every edge belongs to the blob of the node it originates from.

Primitives. For primitive examples (e.g. "touch" (4)) we mostly follow the same procedure. Unlike non-primitives, however, their resulting graph *can* have open sources beyond the root node, e.g. "touch" would have sources at the nodes b and a (incoming 'agent' or 'theme' edge respectively). These nodes can receive any source out of the three available (S0,S1,S2)[5], so the tree automaton build as part of Groschwitz et al. (2021)'s method would allow any combination of source names for the unfilled 'arguments'. Because there is only one input token, alignment is trivial. Primitives quite closely resemble the 'supertags' of the AM parser.

The graph conversion for (1) was already presented in Fig. 3. For the other three examples (2)–(4), we present the graph conversions in Fig. 4.

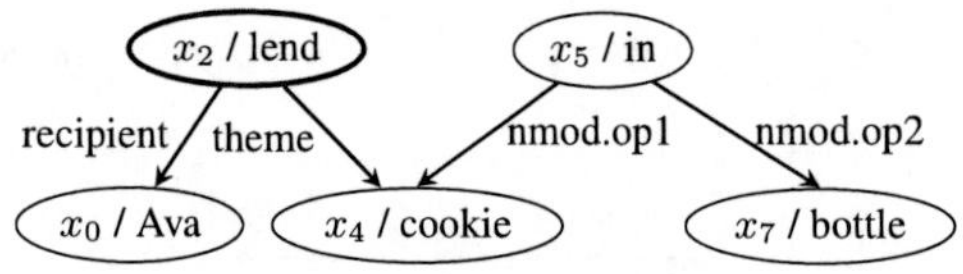

(a) See also (2).

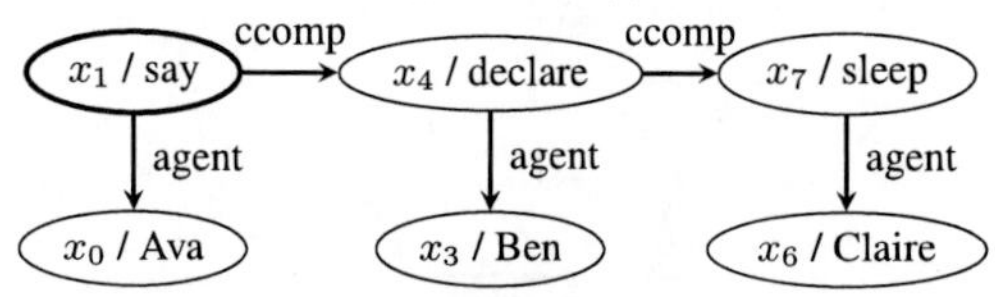

(b) See also (3).

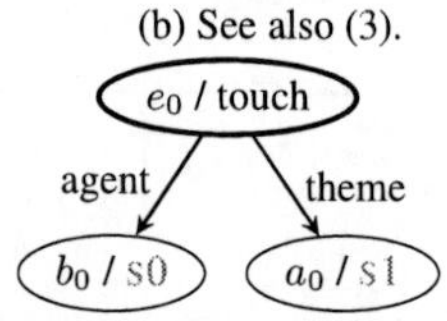

(c) See also (4).

Figure 4: Results of the logical form to graph conversion for (2)–(4). Actually for (c) the tree automaton contained all possible source name combinations for nodes a and b, not just ⟨S0,S1⟩.

[5]With the restriction that different nodes should have different sources to prevent the nodes from being merged. We don't consider non-empty type requests for these nodes here.

AnaLog: Testing Analytical and Deductive Logic Learnability in Language Models

Samuel Ryb
Tufts University
samuel.ryb@tufts.edu

Mario Giulianelli
University of Amsterdam
m.giulianelli@uva.nl

Arabella Sinclair
University of Aberdeen
arabella.sinclair@abdn.ac.uk

Raquel Fernández
University of Amsterdam
raquel.fernandez@uva.nl

Abstract

We investigate the extent to which pre-trained language models acquire analytical and deductive logical reasoning capabilities as a side effect of learning word prediction. We present AnaLog, a natural language inference task designed to probe models for these capabilities, controlling for different invalid heuristics the models may adopt instead of learning the desired generalisations. We test four language models on AnaLog, finding that they have all learned, to a different extent, to encode information that is predictive of entailment beyond shallow heuristics such as lexical overlap and grammaticality. We closely analyse the best performing language model and show that while it performs more consistently than other language models across logical connectives and reasoning domains, it still is sensitive to lexical and syntactic variations in the realisation of logical statements.

1 Introduction

Logical reasoning (Lakoff, 1970; MacCartney and Manning, 2007; Smith, 2020) is at the core of many downstream NLP tasks, such as dialogue and story generation (Fan et al., 2018; Welleck et al., 2019); narrative understanding and summarisation (Mostafazadeh et al., 2016; Vashishtha et al., 2020); question answering (Weber et al., 2019; Shi et al., 2021); relation extraction (Massey et al., 2015; Kassner et al., 2020; Yanaka et al., 2021); and visual comprehension (Suhr et al., 2017, 2019; Sethuraman et al., 2021). Because most of the current approaches to these tasks rely on pre-trained language models (LMs), it is essential to understand whether LMs can perform logical reasoning.

One way of verifying LMs' reasoning abilities is using a natural language inference (NLI) task (Dagan et al., 2005; Giampiccolo et al., 2007; Bowman et al., 2015; Bhagavatula et al., 2020; Rudinger et al., 2020). In NLI, an LM is given a premise and a hypothesis, and its task is to predict the logical relation between the two. Yet, LMs typically learn to solve NLI by using invalid heuristics, for example by extracting overlapping patterns between premises and hypotheses (McCoy et al., 2019), or by using specific lexical items and sentence grammaticality as simplistic predictors of entailment (Poliak et al., 2018).

In this paper, we examine whether pre-trained LMs rely solely on shallow heuristics, or whether they can use relevant reasoning abilities to make inferences. To do so, we develop a new NLI task, **AnaLog**,[1] that requires LMs to encode different logical reasoning patterns and we probe the behaviour of four masked and autoregressive LMs on this new dataset. Using interpretability measures, we find that, as a side effect of learning word prediction, all LMs under scrutiny have—to some extent—learned to encode information that is predictive of entailment relations.

We analyse the behaviour of the best performing model, BERT (Devlin et al., 2019), across the various inference categories present in AnaLog, finding that its reasoning abilities go beyond shallow heuristics and yield relatively consistent performance on deductive and analytical reasoning, as well as across reasoning domains (spatial and comparative) and logical connectives. Nevertheless, the model's behaviour within connectives varies, pointing out its sensitivity to lexical and syntactic variations in the realisation of logical statements.

2 Related Work

2.1 Learning Logic from Text

Recent work has explored which aspects of logical reasoning are statistically learnable from text. Examining how well LMs encode the semantics of

[1] The dataset is available at https://github.com/dmg-illc/analog

Proceedings of the 11th Joint Conference on Lexical and Computational Semantics, pages 55 - 68
July 14-15, 2022 ©2022 Association for Computational Linguistics

logical connectives can give us insight into their reasoning capabilities, i.e., their ability to reach a conclusion from one or more statements.

Kim et al. (2019b) showed that BERT (Devlin et al., 2019) achieves 10% higher accuracy than humans on tasks that involve conjunctions. However, it has also been shown that LMs fail to encode the semantics of logical formulas (Traylor et al., 2021b) and struggle to differentiate between conjunction and disjunction (Traylor et al., 2021a), particularly in instances where the operands are noun phrases (Talmor et al., 2020), suggesting that the models find it difficult to understand the scope of the logical operator. It is also known that neural LMs have difficulty understanding argument order (Kassner et al., 2020), which is arguably a pre-requisite for any logical reasoning. Clark et al. (2020) and Tian et al. (2021) showed that RoBERTa (Liu et al., 2019), in contrast to BERT, performs well at encoding instructional texts that involve conditionals. Good performance on conditionals in LMs is surprising, since humans typically find reasoning about conditionals challenging due to the fact that it requires accommodating degrees of belief (Politzer, 2007). Finally, regarding universal quantification, which implicitly involves encoding a hidden conditional statement (e.g. $\forall x.P(x) \rightarrow Q(x)$), BERT's performance has been shown to vary substantially (Kim et al., 2019b; Tian et al., 2021).

Besides different logical connectives, some recent work has studied different types of reasoning domains. Kassner et al. (2020) showed that models such as BERT and RoBERTa struggle to encode the semantics of comparative reasoning phrases. Yet, Kim et al. (2019b) showed that BERT's performance is only 11% less than human performance on comparative reasoning tasks, and 10% less than human performance on spatial reasoning tasks.

Overall, there is a lot of variation in LMs' abilities to interpret different aspects of logical reasoning. We suspect that low performance stems from the fact that LMs are struggling to encode world knowledge, which is often required in NLI and logic datasets (Clark et al., 2007; Wang et al., 2018; Lauscher et al., 2020; Kassner et al., 2020; Ryb and Van Schijndel, 2021), while high performance may be due to extracting overlapping heuristics (Beall et al., 2019; McCoy et al., 2019), or to attending to shallow predictors such as the presence of specific words or sentence grammaticality (Poliak et al., 2018). We control for these factors in AnaLog.

2.2 Diagnostic Probing

A well established way of investigating what type of linguistic information is tracked by neural LMs is *diagnostic probing* (Ettinger et al., 2016; Adi et al., 2017; Belinkov et al., 2017; Conneau et al., 2018; Hupkes et al., 2018). Probing typically consists of extracting model representations, feeding them as input to a supervised classifier trained to predict a hypothesised linguistic property (e.g., the grammatical number agreement of the main verb of a sentence), and testing the probing classifier on a set of unseen representations. Good probing performance cannot directly be taken to indicate that the hypothesised linguistic property is tracked by the LM (Belinkov, 2021). It is thus common practice to compare the true probing performance of classifiers with performance on control representations (Zhang and Bowman, 2018; Tenney et al., 2018; Chrupała et al., 2020), tasks (Hewitt and Liang, 2019a), or datasets (Ravichander et al., 2021).

In this paper, we set up a careful evaluation procedure to interpret the performance of our probing classifier, by training it on increasingly small portions of training data, and comparing its performance in relation to two baselines.

3 Dataset Design and Construction

We extend the LAKNLI dataset (Ryb and Van Schijndel, 2021) and present AnaLog, an NLI dataset that explicitly targets different types of logical reasoning. The dataset contains a total of 24,000 items (see Table 2), where each item consists of a premise, a hypothesis, and their logical relation: *entailment* or *non-entailment*. Premises and hypotheses are generated from templates, using a restricted and carefully selected vocabulary. The templates and the vocabulary can be found in Appendices A.1 and A.2. The dataset is designed to contain a balanced distribution of logical connectives and reasoning categories. Examples are provided in Table 1.

3.1 Premises

Sentences in AnaLog are constructed from templates designed for specific logical connectives. For example:

(1) N_1 P_1 N_2 ***and*** N_3

A premise is constructed through filling a tem-

	Premise	Hypothesis	
		OVERLAP	NO-OVERLAP
AND	*Jennifer is in front of Elizabeth* ***and*** *Jennifer is to the north of Linda.*	→ *Jennifer is in front of Elizabeth.* ↛ *Elizabeth is to the north of Linda.*	→ *A person is behind some woman.* ↛ *A person is behind some man.*
OR	*Jennifer is to the north of Linda* ***or*** *is below Robert. Jennifer is not below Robert.*	→ *Jennifer is to the north of Linda.* ↛ *Robert is below Jennifer.*	→ *Some person is to the south of some woman.* ↛ *Some boy is to the east of a man.*
CON	***If*** *Elizabeth is older than Jennifer* ***then*** *Linda is smaller than Jennifer. Elizabeth is older than Jennifer.*	→ *Linda is smaller than Jennifer.* ↛ *Jennifer is smaller than Linda.*	→ *A person is larger than some woman.* ↛ *A woman is arriving later than some boy.*
UNI	***Every*** *director is to the west of Patricia. James is a director.*	→ *James is to the west of Patricia.* ↛ *Patricia is to the west of James.*	→ *Some woman is to the east of some man.* ↛ *Some woman is to the right of some man.*

Table 1: Examples of premises and hypotheses for each of the logical connectives. Within the premises, connectives are **bolded** and spatial and comparative reasoning predicates are highlighted in blue and orange, respectively.

plate's slots with nouns and predicates. For instance, N_1 = *Patricia*, N_2 = *James*, N_3 = *Mary*, and P_1 = *is to the left of* would result in:

(2) *Patricia is to the left of James* ***and*** *Mary*

Logical Connectives AnaLog systematically distinguishes between the following four types of logical connectives in the premise:

- AND: conjunction (*and*)
- OR: disjunction (*or*)
- CON: conditionals (*unless, if, if then, only if*)
- UNI: universal quantification (*every, all*)

This is in contrast to both SuperGLUE (Wang et al., 2020) where the logical connectives vary between being positioned in the premise or hypothesis, and LogicNLI (Tian et al., 2021), where premises consist of multiple facts and rules and do not isolate logical connectives. LogicNLI premises may also feature negation, existential quantification, and equivalence. Since negation is often used as a heuristic to predict non-entailment in NLI tasks (McCoy and Linzen, 2019), we only include it within premises when absolutely necessary to asses LMs' understanding of a specific reasoning schema (such as disjunction and certain forms of conditionals). Existential quantification and equivalence are implicitly present in our hypotheses construction, as explained in Section 3.2.

Nouns The noun slots in our premise templates are filled with proper names, as this avoids possible confounding factors carried over by the semantics of common nouns. We choose the eight most frequent male and female first names according to the 1990 U.S. Census Bureau's Population Division. For the restrictor noun in universal quantification premises (e.g., *director* in the UNI premise in Table 1), we use the four most common nouns in COCA (Davies, 2010) which correspond to the category NOUN.PERSON in Wordnet (Fellbaum, 1998), do not begin with a vowel,[2] and are semantically compatible with our predicates. Selecting high frequency nouns ensures that LMs are not thrown off by infrequent occurrences, nor heavily influenced by specific lexical material. This enables LMs to output representations that are as stable as possible.

Predicates The predicates in our templates are also instantiated with a restricted vocabulary that limits interference with additional sorts of knowledge. We focus on two reasoning domains: *spatial* (3) and *comparative* (4) reasoning. We select pairs of spatial reasoning predicates from Kim et al. (2019a), such as *left-right* and *above-below*. To collect comparative reasoning predicates, we select pairs from the FraCaS project (Cooper et al., 1996), such as *smaller-larger* and *weaker-stronger*. Reasoning about these two types of predicates requires models to encode truth equivalent relationships, such as:

(3) N_1 **is above** $N_2 \iff N_2$ **is below** N_1

(4) N_1 **is stronger than** $N_2 \iff N_2$ **is weaker than** N_1

3.2 Hypotheses

Assessing whether a given hypothesis is entailed by a premise may require different kinds of reasoning. For example, some hypotheses follow purely on the basis of structural aspects, i.e., they can be derived by direct deduction on surface form: e.g., '*A* ***and***

[2]So that they are all compatible with the article *a*.

B' logically entails 'A' as well as 'B', as in (5-a).[3] Such hypotheses require *deductive reasoning*. In contrast, other cases of entailment go beyond manipulations at the level of surface form and instead rely on additional semantic knowledge, as in (5-c). Such hypotheses require *analytical reasoning*.

To test both types of reasoning, we generate entailment and non-entailment hypotheses for each type. For the example premise in (5), this results in the following four hypotheses, where $\rightarrow$ denotes an entailment, and $\nrightarrow$ a non-entailment relation:

(5) *Patricia is to the left of James* **and** *Mary*

  a. $\rightarrow$ *Patricia is to the left of James*

  b. $\nrightarrow$ *Mary is to the left of James*

  c. $\rightarrow$ *Some man is to the right of some other person*

  d. $\nrightarrow$ *Some man is older than some woman*

For AND, we randomly select one of the conjuncts to construct the entailed direct logical deduction hypotheses. That is, (5-a) could have also been *Patricia is to the left of Mary*. Details of the other connectives can be found in Appendix A.2 (Table 7).

AnaLog clearly distinguishes between deductive and analytical reasoning, which gives rise to a systematic distinction between hypotheses that exhibit lexical overlap and those that do not exhibit any overlap of content words (see examples in Table 1). Hence, in addition to isolating LMs' abilities to both deductively and analytically reason, this offers a way to control LMs' potential use of overlap-related heuristics, which have been shown to artificially inflate previous results on the NLI task (McCoy et al., 2019). We explain this distinction in more detail next.

Overlapping Hypotheses Overlapping hypotheses only consist of words reiterated from the premise. *Overlapping entailment* ($O^{\rightarrow}$) hypotheses are a direct logical deduction (5-a), which corresponds to the strictest case of premise overlap considered by McCoy et al. (2019). *Overlapping non-entailment* ($O^{\nrightarrow}$) hypotheses, in contrast, do not logically follow from the premise (5-b). We generate two types of $O^{\nrightarrow}$ hypotheses: grammatical instances $O^{\nrightarrow}_{G}$ such as (5-b) and ungrammatical instances $O^{\nrightarrow}_{UG}$, which correspond to an ungrammatical bag-of-words subset of the premise (e.g. '*and to left the of Patricia*').

While it may not be realistic to expect that LMs have had exposure to ungrammatical sentences during training—and hence that they will have learned to properly reason with them (i.e., to systematically classify them as non-entailment)—including ungrammatical instances allows us to test the strength of possible overlap-based heuristics: if LMs more frequently incorrectly assign the label *entailment* to ungrammatical cases that exhibit lexical overlap, then we can consider lexical overlap as a stronger heuristic than grammaticality.

Non-Overlapping Hypotheses Non-overlapping hypotheses are generated by replacing proper names with person-related hypernyms and replacing the predicate with its counterpart (e.g., *James* $\rightsquigarrow$ *some man, left* $\rightsquigarrow$ *right*).[4] We generate both *Non-Overlap entailment* ($NO^{\rightarrow}$) hypotheses (i.e., proper instances of analytical reasoning, such as (5-c)) and *Non-Overlap non-entailment* ($NO^{\nrightarrow}$) hypotheses, such as (5-d).

	O	E	G	AND	OR	CON	UNI
$O^{\rightarrow}$	✓	✓	✓	1,500	1,500	1,500	1,500
$O^{\nrightarrow}_{G}$	✓	✗	✓	750	750	750	750
$O^{\nrightarrow}_{UG}$	✓	✗	✗	750	750	750	750
$NO^{\rightarrow}$	✗	✓	✓	1,500	1,500	1,500	1,500
$NO^{\nrightarrow}$	✗	✗	✓	1,500	1,500	1,500	1,500
				6,000	6,000	6,000	6,000

Table 2: AnaLog dataset statistics. The dataset contains 24,000 items in total. Overlap (O), Entailment (E), and Grammaticality (G) are marked. For each category (numerical cell), half of the items are constructed with spatial, and half with comparative reasoning predicates.

4 Experimental Setup

4.1 Models

We probe four pre-trained Transformer (Vaswani et al., 2017) language models using AnaLog. To ensure a fair comparison, we use the `large` architecture size for all models, as available in the HuggingFace library (Wolf et al., 2020). We compare the following architectures:

BERT (Devlin et al., 2019) A Transformer-based LM pre-trained on masked language modeling and

[3] In this example, 'B' is the implicit proposition *'Patricia is to the left of Mary'*.

[4] We minimize the risk of the probe memorizing facts in the dataset by choosing to not have 1-to-1 mappings of proper names to person-related hypernyms.

next sentence prediction, known for its high performance at sentence and token classification tasks, including NLI (Talman and Chatzikyriakidis, 2019).

LUKE (Yamada et al., 2020) A masked LM with an entity-aware self-attention mechanism, that builds upon the RoBERTa architecture (Liu et al., 2019). Using LUKE enables us to investigate the degree to which entity tracking can assist in solving logic-based NLI.

StructBERT (Wang et al., 2019) A masked LM based on BERT with additional word and sentence order training objectives. We expect StructBERT to provide insight on whether structural cues are useful in solving logic-based NLI.

GPT-2 (Radford et al., 2019) An autoregressive Transformer-based LM which is known for its high performance across text-generation tasks, yet has not been frequently tested on NLI datasets. We are interested in how abstract representations built by an autoregressive LM compare to those built by masked LMs.

4.2 Probing Procedure

For each premise-hypothesis pair in AnaLog, we concatenate the text of the premise with that of the hypothesis and with the special sentence token from each LM's vocabulary.[5] We feed this text to the LM and extract the last layer's hidden activations corresponding to the special token; we take the activations to be the abstract representation of a premise-hypothesis pair. Repeating this procedure for all the items in AnaLog, we collect a dataset of representations, which we split into a training and a test set (see Section 4.3). We fit a binary logistic regression classifier[6]—as more powerful classifiers have been shown to produce unreliable results (Hewitt and Liang, 2019a)—to the training set, obtain predictions for the test set, and compute accuracy and baselined probing scores, as described in the next section.

4.3 Controlled Evaluation

Diagnostic probes are known for achieving high accuracy on linguistic tasks despite representations not necessarily encoding relevant linguistic information (Hewitt and Liang, 2019b; Belinkov, 2021). To address this issue, following the approach taken by Zhang and Bowman (2018), we measure probing performance as the difference between the classification accuracy of the probing classifier trained on the original dataset, and the accuracy of a baseline. We call this *baselined probing performance* (BPP), adopting the terminology proposed by Hewitt et al. (2021). To select the strictest baseline setup, we consider two aspects: 1) the amount of data, and 2) the type of data—i.e., controlled baseline representations obtained from the AnaLog dataset, on which the probe is trained.

Partial Training Sets We split AnaLog into a main training and testing set using an 80-20 split. To prevent overfitting of the probing classifier, we evaluate it by varying the quantity of data it is exposed to: we create partial training sets by sampling increasingly larger fractions of our main training set (1%, 2%, 4%, 6%, 8%, 10%, 12.5%, 25%, 50%, 100%), using an approach similar to that of Zhang and Bowman (2018). The testing set remains fixed, so that regardless of the split and baseline probe, we evaluate on a consistent set of sentences. All the resulting training sets and the testing set are balanced with respect to the two classification labels (entailment and non-entailment), logical connectives, reasoning predicates, and overlap vs. non-overlap.

Baselines We train the probing classifier on two baseline settings. For the *Scrambled* baseline, we scramble words in the premises and hypotheses separately, and train the probing classifier on their concatenation. Humans should achieve 50% accuracy on this version of the dataset because random word order impedes logical reasoning. For the *Random* baseline, we train the probing classifier on randomly initialised vector representations.

We consider these baselines as sufficient to ensure that entailment relations can only be predicted by using logical reasoning and not by exploiting dataset artifacts. For example, if the probes were solely learning associations between proper names and person-related hypernyms, the scrambled probe could suffice to achieve the same performance as the probe optimised on the original AnaLog testing set.

We train the probing classifier from scratch for each LM, training split, and baseline. As shown in

[5] For BERT and StructBERT, we prepend the `[CLS]` token; for GPT-2, we append the `<|endoftext|>` token; for LUKE, we append the `</s>` token.

[6] We use the scikit-learn implementation with default hyperparameters. We do not tune the hyperparameters to reduce the risk of overfitting to the collected representations, which would inflate the probing results. All logistic regression classifiers are trained until convergence.

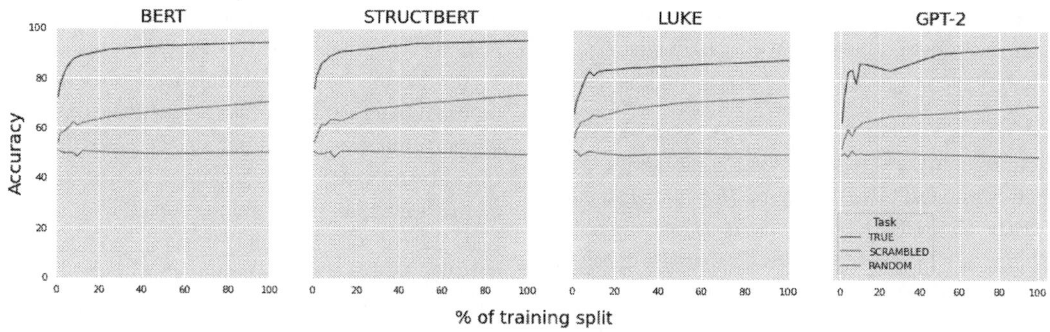

Figure 1: Accuracies of the original (*true*) vs. baseline (*scrambled, random*) probes for different training splits.

Figure 1, the *Scrambled* baseline achieves the highest accuracy (around 60%) across all LMs and training splits. The *Random* baseline achieves chance-level accuracy across LMs and training splits, confirming that the complexity of our probing classifier is appropriate for this task.[7] We therefore use *Scrambled* to compute BPP scores, as it yields the strictest (or most *selective*; Hewitt and Liang, 2019a) baseline setup.

5 Results across Models

All four LMs achieve positive average BPP scores: the average accuracy is above baseline by ca. 20 percentage points (see Figure 2). These overall results indicate that the LMs encode information that is predictive of entailment relations above and beyond simple heuristics which can be captured by a baseline. We also observe that the highest BPP scores are obtained at a relatively small training split size. This suggests training probes on more data can decrease their ability to extract the targeted linguistic features, and cause them to overfit on the dataset instead.

BERT and StructBERT are the best performing models with BPP scores ranging roughly between 15 and 40 (except for the smallest training split sizes). Their similar performance across all splits shows that StructBERT's explicit modelling of sentence and discourse structure does not produce more informative representations for our AnaLog task than BERT's simpler next word and next sentence prediction training objectives.

GPT-2's high standard deviation across splits (on average, 20.82) indicates a severe instability in its capacity to correctly encode logical reasoning cues. A closer look at GPT-2's performance shows that its representations are predictive of entailment relations when there is lexical overlap between premises and hypotheses, and of non-entailment relations when there is no lexical overlap. While GPT-2 is an autoregressive LM, as opposed to the other masked LMs, we are not certain that this factor is what causes this learning pattern. We leave exploring this further to future work.

Lastly, LUKE's performance, with an average score of 15.05, is significantly lower than that of the other three models (t-tests against BERT, StructBERT and GPT-2 yield p-values approaching zero), suggesting that its ability to track entities does not significantly help in solving logical deductions.

For the detailed results presented in the next sections, we focus on the model that achieves the highest BPP score with the lowest standard deviation. As can be seen in Figure 2, this model is BERT, probed with a classifier trained on 12.5% of the full training split.

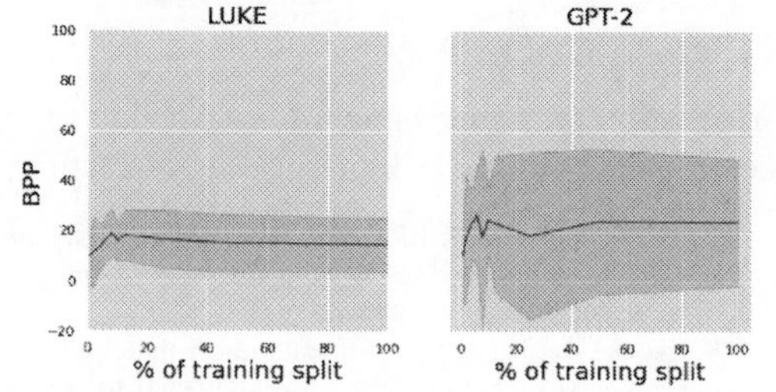

Figure 2: BPP scores for different training splits.

[7]We would have seen an accuracy greater than 50% for *Random* if the complexity of the classifier had been excessive.

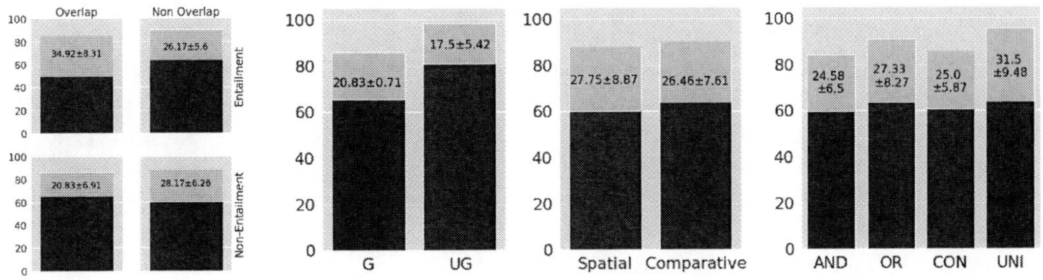

(a) Overlap (all grammatical) (b) Grammaticality ($O^{\nrightarrow}$) (c) Reasoning domains (d) Logical connectives

Figure 3: BERT probing results across dataset categories. Overall bar height indicates accuracy, broken down by baseline accuracy (dark blue) and BPP score (light blue with superimposed average score and standard deviation).

6 Detailed Results with BERT

6.1 Solving Inference without Heuristics

We start by analysing the extent to which the performance of the best model, BERT, may be the result of exploiting heuristics unrelated to logical reasoning.

Overlap If lexical overlap were used as a heuristic to predict entailment, we would expect lower performance for *overlap-non-entailment* $O^{\nrightarrow}$ and *no-overlap-entailment* $NO^{\rightarrow}$ instances, where using the overlap heuristic yields incorrect predictions. This is not the pattern we observe. As shown in Figure 3a, accuracy is highest in these two cases. We see that $O^{\nrightarrow}$ items yield the lowest BPP scores and $NO^{\rightarrow}$ the highest (this difference is statistically significant and in principle compatible with the heuristics). However, there is no significant difference between no-overlap items with entailment vs. non-entailment labels. This indicates a lexical overlap heuristic is not prominently at play.

As pointed out in Section 3.2, the overlap vs. non-overlap distinction also corresponds to the contrast between direct deduction and analytical reasoning. We do not observe any significant differences in performance across these two reasoning types. More generally, the fact that BPP scores are positive across the board for overlapping and non-overlapping cases shows that the model is solving our logic-based NLI task by using information that goes beyond simple heuristic cues.

Grammaticality If a model were to judge entailment relations purely on the basis of grammaticality, we would expect it to wrongly predict *entailment* for $O_G^{\nrightarrow}$ (*overlap-non-entailment grammatical*) instances and correctly predict non-entailment for $O_{UG}^{\nrightarrow}$ (*overlap-non-entailment ungrammatical*). This is not what we observe: BPP scores are positive and not significantly different between $O_G^{\nrightarrow}$ and $O_{UG}^{\nrightarrow}$, which indicates grammaticality is not being used as a heuristic to predict entailment.

Finally, we find that performance on ungrammatical sentences is more unstable (standard deviation is almost 8 times higher than for $O_G^{\nrightarrow}$); this may be due to BERT producing noisier representations for out of distribution, partially ungrammatical, strings.

6.2 Consistency across Reasoning Domains

Having established that two plausible heuristics are not behind our probing results, we now turn to comparing reasoning domains. We have already seen that BERT's representations seem to be amenable to both deductive and analytical reasoning. We next hypothesize that if LMs can indeed reason logically, their performance should not be significantly affected by the specific choice of lexical items. We therefore compare the probes' performance on spatial vs. comparative reasoning predicates in AnaLog (see Figure 3c). We find no significant difference ($t = 0.442, p = 0.662$) in BPP scores across predicate types. This indicates that BERT's encoding of lexical semantic relations (in particular, antonymy) is stable across reasoning domains. This result is in line with the findings of Kim et al. (2019b), who show no substantial differences between spatial and comparative reasoning for BERT and humans.

6.3 Logical Connectives

Finally, we break down the results per logical connective. As can be seen in Figure 3d, BPP scores are positive and similar across operators, suggesting that BERT representations encode the semantics of logical connectives in a relatively stable way.

We observe the lowest BPP scores with conjunction and conditionals (in both cases significantly lower than UNI, $p < 0.05$). This is somewhat surprising, particularly for conjunction, given the previous results by Kim et al. (2019b) mentioned in Section 2.1. In the next section, we conduct two case studies to further examine whether there are specific linguistic phenomena linked to conjunction and conditionals that may be confusing BERT.

7 Analysis

7.1 Case Study 1: Parsing Conjunction

In AnaLog, the arguments of a conjunction can be sentences (S), noun phrases (NP), or verb phrases (VP).[8] For example, the AND premise in Table 1 includes sentential conjuncts, while the one in example (5) features conjuncts that are NPs. We test two related hypotheses regarding aspects that may lead to lower performance in some of these conditions: (i) We conjecture that, when the conjuncts are NPs or VPs, deducing information to the right of the conjunct may be more difficult because this involves parsing long-range dependencies. For example, in instances such as *David is to the left of John and Linda* $\rightarrow$ *Some girl is to the right of a boy*, predicting the entailment relation requires encoding syntactic and semantic information to both the left and right of the logical connective. (ii) Consequently, we hypothesise that identifying the arguments of a conjunction may be easier for the model when these arguments are sentential rather than phrasal, since the former does not require parsing long-range dependencies; this would be compatible with the results by Talmor et al. (2020), who found that models struggle at making correct predictions when the conjunction is positioned between NPs.

Our two hypotheses, however, are not confirmed. On the one hand, we find no significant difference between left and right for any conjunct type (S, NP, and VP). This suggests that BERT's representations consistently encode information regardless of its position relative to the conjunction operator, which could be due to BERT's bidirectional training. On the other hand, as can be seen in Figure 4a, we observe that when the conjunction is positioned between sentences, the results are in fact significantly *worse* than when it is positioned between NPs or VPs.[9] Why this may be the case remains an open question that we leave for future work.

[8]These three types appear with equal frequency.

[9]All relevant t-tests yielded $p > 0.05$.

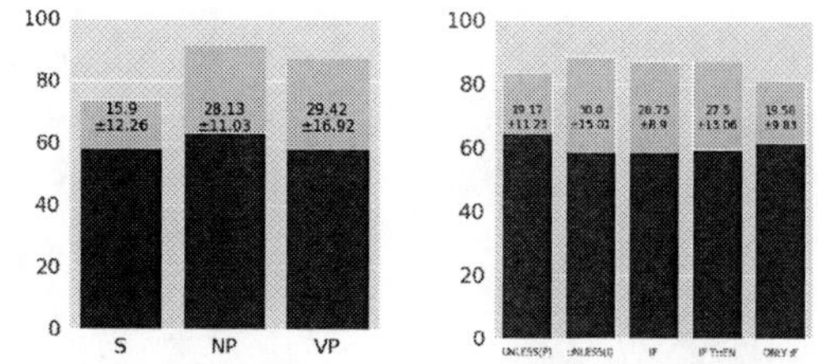

(a) Conjunction (b) Conditionals

Figure 4: BERT results within logical connectives.

7.2 Case Study 2: Types of Conditional

In this second case study, we investigate whether BERT's representations struggle to encode some types of conditionals more than others.[10] We expect to observe the highest performance for *if then* sentences, as BERT and RoBERTA reason well about modus-ponens (Clark et al., 2020). However, as shown in Figure 4b there is no significant differences between *if then*, *if*, and *unless(infix)*. The most challenging types are *only if* and *unless(prefix)*. We find that *unless(prefix)* is significantly outperformed by *unless(infix)*. This again shows that BERT is able to successfully encode relevant information to both the left and right of a connective.

8 Conclusions

We present a new NLI dataset, AnaLog, designed to test LMs' abilities to deductively and analytically reason. We choose diagnostic probing as an interpretability technique, and probe using AnaLog to inspect whether LMs acquire such logical reasoning abilities from text-based pre-training. We find that masked LMs, in particular BERT and StructBERT, can solve the inference task through encoding properties of both deductive and analytic logic, rather than solely relying on shallow heuristics such as lexical overlap and sentence grammaticality.

One main benefit of AnaLog is that it isolates different reasoning types, domains, and logical connectives, in order to gain a better understanding of which of these factors makes inference more challenging for an LM. We choose high frequency lexical items to ensure that the LMs' representations are as stable as possible, and not thrown off by surprising low frequency occurrences. We also use a fine-grained probing setup consisting of different

[10]The conditionals present in AnaLog are: *if*, *if then*, *only if*, *unless(prefix)*, *unless(infix)*; see Appendix A.2.

training splits and multiple baselines to ensure that probes are using relevant linguistic and logical information, rather than learning the dataset artifacts, to solve the task.

We perform an in-depth analysis of BERT's behaviour. Its overall stable performance is promising, though our case studies show some variance at the level of different natural language formulations of the same logical connective or their arguments as opposed to at higher reasoning levels. Overall, we think that BERT learns to encode approximations of the types of logical reasoning information necessary to solve AnaLog, although its sensitivity to surface forms can make these approximations inconsistent. While extending the AnaLog test set to also include lower frequency items may be helpful to ensure generalizability over noun and predicate relations (which we leave for future work), we hope that as it currently stands, AnaLog can be used as a benchmark to check whether LMs reason correctly by using elementary linguistic knowledge and logical semantics, as opposed to surface heuristics.

Acknowledgements

We would like to thank the anonymous ARR and *SEM 2022 reviewers for their feedback and suggestions, as well as Ece Takmaz for her comments. Samuel Ryb and Arabella Sinclair worked on this project while affiliated with the University of Amsterdam. The project has received funding from the European Research Council (ERC) under the European Union's Horizon 2020 research and innovation programme (grant agreement No. 819455).

References

Yossi Adi, Einat Kermany, Yonatan Belinkov, Ofer Lavi, and Yoav Goldberg. 2017. Fine-grained analysis of sentence embeddings using auxiliary prediction tasks. In *5th International Conference on Learning Representations, ICLR 2017, Toulon, France, April 24-26, 2017, Conference Track Proceedings*. OpenReview.net.

Jc Beall, Greg Restall, and Gil Sagi. 2019. Logical Consequence. In Edward N. Zalta, editor, *The Stanford Encyclopedia of Philosophy*, Spring 2019 edition. Metaphysics Research Lab, Stanford University.

Yonatan Belinkov. 2021. Probing Classifiers: Promises, Shortcomings, and Advances. *Computational Linguistics*, pages 1–13.

Yonatan Belinkov, Nadir Durrani, Fahim Dalvi, Hassan Sajjad, and James Glass. 2017. What do neural machine translation models learn about morphology? In *Proceedings of the 55th Annual Meeting of the Association for Computational Linguistics (Volume 1: Long Papers)*, pages 861–872.

Chandra Bhagavatula, Ronan Le Bras, Chaitanya Malaviya, Keisuke Sakaguchi, Ari Holtzman, Hannah Rashkin, Doug Downey, Wen tau Yih, and Yejin Choi. 2020. Abductive commonsense reasoning. In *International Conference on Learning Representations*.

Samuel R. Bowman, Christopher Potts, and Christopher D. Manning. 2015. Recursive neural networks can learn logical semantics. In *Proceedings of the 3rd Workshop on Continuous Vector Space Models and their Compositionality*, pages 12–21, Beijing, China. Association for Computational Linguistics.

Grzegorz Chrupała, Bertrand Higy, and Afra Alishahi. 2020. Analyzing analytical methods: The case of phonology in neural models of spoken language. In *Proceedings of the 58th Annual Meeting of the Association for Computational Linguistics*, pages 4146–4156.

Peter Clark, Phil Harrison, John Thompson, William Murray, Jerry Hobbs, and Christiane Fellbaum. 2007. On the role of lexical and world knowledge in RTE3. In *Proceedings of the ACL-PASCAL Workshop on Textual Entailment and Paraphrasing*, pages 54–59, Prague. Association for Computational Linguistics.

Peter Clark, Oyvind Tafjord, and Kyle Richardson. 2020. Transformers as soft reasoners over language. In *Proceedings of the Twenty-Ninth International Joint Conference on Artificial Intelligence, IJCAI-20*, pages 3882–3890. International Joint Conferences on Artificial Intelligence Organization. Main track.

Alexis Conneau, German Kruszewski, Guillaume Lample, Loïc Barrault, and Marco Baroni. 2018. What you can cram into a single $&!#* vector: Probing sentence embeddings for linguistic properties. In *Proceedings of the 56th Annual Meeting of the Association for Computational Linguistics (Volume 1: Long Papers)*, pages 2126–2136, Melbourne, Australia. Association for Computational Linguistics.

Robin Cooper, Richard Crouch, Jan van Eijck, Chris Fox, Josef Genabith, Jan Jaspars, Hans Kamp, David Milward, Manfred Pinkal, Massimo Poesio, Steve Pulman, Ted Briscoe, Holger Maier, and Karsten Konrad. 1996. Using the Framework: The FraCaS Consortium. Technical report, FraCaS deliverable D-16.

Ido Dagan, Oren Glickman, and Bernardo Magnini. 2005. The PASCAL recognising textual entailment challenge. In *Proceedings of the Machine Learning Challenges Workshop*, pages 177–190.

Mark Davies. 2010. The Corpus of Contemporary American English as the first reliable monitor corpus of English. *Literary and Linguistic Computing*, 25(4).

Jacob Devlin, Ming-Wei Chang, Kenton Lee, and Kristina Toutanova. 2019. BERT: Pre-training of deep bidirectional transformers for language understanding. In *Proceedings of the 2019 Conference of the North American Chapter of the Association for Computational Linguistics: Human Language Technologies, Volume 1 (Long and Short Papers)*, pages 4171–4186, Minneapolis, Minnesota. Association for Computational Linguistics.

Allyson Ettinger, Ahmed Elgohary, and Philip Resnik. 2016. Probing for semantic evidence of composition by means of simple classification tasks. In *Proceedings of the 1st Workshop on Evaluating Vector-Space Representations for NLP*, pages 134–139.

Angela Fan, Mike Lewis, and Yann Dauphin. 2018. Hierarchical neural story generation. In *Proceedings of the 56th Annual Meeting of the Association for Computational Linguistics (Volume 1: Long Papers)*, pages 889–898, Melbourne, Australia. Association for Computational Linguistics.

Christiane Fellbaum. 1998. *WordNet: An Electronic Lexical Database*. Bradford Books.

Danilo Giampiccolo, Bernardo Magnini, Ido Dagan, and Bill Dolan. 2007. The third PASCAL recognizing textual entailment challenge. In *Proceedings of the ACL-PASCAL Workshop on Textual Entailment and Paraphrasing*, pages 1–9, Prague. Association for Computational Linguistics.

John Hewitt, Kawin Ethayarajh, Percy Liang, and Christopher D. Manning. 2021. Conditional probing: measuring usable information beyond a baseline.

John Hewitt and Percy Liang. 2019a. Designing and interpreting probes with control tasks. In *Proceedings of the 2019 Conference on Empirical Methods in Natural Language Processing and the 9th International Joint Conference on Natural Language Processing (EMNLP-IJCNLP)*, pages 2733–2743.

John Hewitt and Percy Liang. 2019b. Designing and interpreting probes with control tasks. In *Proceedings of the 2019 Conference on Empirical Methods in Natural Language Processing and the 9th International Joint Conference on Natural Language Processing (EMNLP-IJCNLP)*, pages 2733–2743, Hong Kong, China. Association for Computational Linguistics.

Dieuwke Hupkes, Sara Veldhoen, and Willem Zuidema. 2018. Visualisation and'diagnostic classifiers' reveal how recurrent and recursive neural networks process hierarchical structure. *Journal of Artificial Intelligence Research*, 61:907–926.

Nora Kassner, Benno Krojer, and Hinrich Schütze. 2020. Are pretrained language models symbolic reasoners over knowledge? In *Proceedings of the 24th Conference on Computational Natural Language Learning*, pages 552–564, Online. Association for Computational Linguistics.

Najoung Kim, Roma Patel, Adam Poliak, Alex Wang, Patrick Xia, R. Thomas McCoy, Ian Tenney, Alexis Ross, Tal Linzen, Benjamin Van Durme, Samuel R. Bowman, and Ellie Pavlick. 2019a. Probing what different NLP tasks teach machines about function word comprehension. In **SEMEVAL*.

Najoung Kim, Roma Patel, Adam Poliak, Patrick Xia, Alex Wang, Tom McCoy, Ian Tenney, Alexis Ross, Tal Linzen, Benjamin Van Durme, Samuel R. Bowman, and Ellie Pavlick. 2019b. Probing what different NLP tasks teach machines about function word comprehension. In *Proceedings of the Eighth Joint Conference on Lexical and Computational Semantics (*SEM 2019)*, pages 235–249, Minneapolis, Minnesota. Association for Computational Linguistics.

George Lakoff. 1970. Linguistics and natural logic. *Synthese*, 22(1/2):151–271.

Anne Lauscher, Olga Majewska, Leonardo F. R. Ribeiro, Iryna Gurevych, Nikolai Rozanov, and Goran Glavaš. 2020. Common sense or world knowledge? investigating adapter-based knowledge injection into pretrained transformers. In *Proceedings of Deep Learning Inside Out (DeeLIO): The First Workshop on Knowledge Extraction and Integration for Deep Learning Architectures*, pages 43–49, Online. Association for Computational Linguistics.

Yinhan Liu, Myle Ott, Naman Goyal, Jingfei Du, Mandar Joshi, Danqi Chen, Omer Levy, Mike Lewis, Luke Zettlemoyer, and Veselin Stoyanov. 2019. Roberta: A robustly optimized bert pretraining approach.

Bill MacCartney and Christopher D. Manning. 2007. Natural logic for textual inference. In *Proceedings of the ACL-PASCAL Workshop on Textual Entailment and Paraphrasing*, pages 193–200, Prague. Association for Computational Linguistics.

Philip Massey, Patrick Xia, David Bamman, and Noah Smith. 2015. Annotating character relationships in literary texts. arXiv:1512.00728.

Richard T McCoy and Tal Linzen. 2019. Non-entailed subsequences as a challenge for natural language inference. *Proceedings of the Society for Computation in Linguistics*, 2(1):358–360.

Tom McCoy, Ellie Pavlick, and Tal Linzen. 2019. Right for the wrong reasons: Diagnosing syntactic heuristics in natural language inference. In *Proceedings of the 57th Annual Meeting of the Association for Computational Linguistics*, pages 3428–3448,

Florence, Italy. Association for Computational Linguistics.

Nasrin Mostafazadeh, Nathanael Chambers, Xiaodong He, Devi Parikh, Dhruv Batra, Lucy Vanderwende, Pushmeet Kohli, and James Allen. 2016. A corpus and cloze evaluation for deeper understanding of commonsense stories. In *Proceedings of the 2016 Conference of the North American Chapter of the Association for Computational Linguistics: Human Language Technologies*, pages 839–849, San Diego, California. Association for Computational Linguistics.

Adam Poliak, Jason Naradowsky, Aparajita Haldar, Rachel Rudinger, and Benjamin Van Durme. 2018. Hypothesis only baselines in natural language inference. In *Proceedings of the Seventh Joint Conference on Lexical and Computational Semantics*, pages 180–191, New Orleans, Louisiana. Association for Computational Linguistics.

Guy Politzer. 2007. Reasoning with conditionals. *Topoi*, 26:79–95.

Alec Radford, Jeff Wu, R. Child, David Luan, Dario Amodei, and Ilya Sutskever. 2019. Language models are unsupervised multitask learners. Technical report, OpenAI blog.

Abhilasha Ravichander, Yonatan Belinkov, and Eduard Hovy. 2021. Probing the probing paradigm: Does probing accuracy entail task relevance? In *Proceedings of the 16th Conference of the European Chapter of the Association for Computational Linguistics: Main Volume*, pages 3363–3377.

Rachel Rudinger, Vered Shwartz, Jena D. Hwang, Chandra Bhagavatula, Maxwell Forbes, Ronan Le Bras, Noah A. Smith, and Yejin Choi. 2020. Thinking like a skeptic: Defeasible inference in natural language. In *Findings of the Association for Computational Linguistics: EMNLP 2020*, pages 4661–4675, Online. Association for Computational Linguistics.

Samuel Ryb and Marten Van Schijndel. 2021. Analytical, symbolic and first-order reasoning within neural architectures. In *Proceedings of the 2021 Workshop on Computing Semantics with Types, Frames and Related Structures*.

Muralikrishnna Sethuraman, Ali Payani, Faramarz Fekri, and James Kerce. 2021. Visual question answering based on formal logic. In *Proceedings of the 20th IEEE International Conference on Machine Learning and Applications (ICMLA)*, pages 952–957.

Jihao Shi, Xiao Ding, Li Du, Ting Liu, and Bing Qin. 2021. Neural natural logic inference for interpretable question answering. In *Proceedings of the 2021 Conference on Empirical Methods in Natural Language Processing*, pages 3673–3684, Online and Punta Cana, Dominican Republic. Association for Computational Linguistics.

Robin Smith. 2020. Aristotle's Logic. In Edward N. Zalta, editor, *The Stanford Encyclopedia of Philosophy*, Fall 2020 edition. Metaphysics Research Lab, Stanford University.

Alane Suhr, Mike Lewis, James Yeh, and Yoav Artzi. 2017. A corpus of natural language for visual reasoning. In *Proceedings of the 55th Annual Meeting of the Association for Computational Linguistics (Volume 2: Short Papers)*, pages 217–223, Vancouver, Canada. Association for Computational Linguistics.

Alane Suhr, Stephanie Zhou, Ally Zhang, Iris Zhang, Huajun Bai, and Yoav Artzi. 2019. A corpus for reasoning about natural language grounded in photographs. In *Proceedings of the 57th Annual Meeting of the Association for Computational Linguistics*, pages 6418–6428, Florence, Italy. Association for Computational Linguistics.

Aarne Talman and Stergios Chatzikyriakidis. 2019. Testing the generalization power of neural network models across NLI benchmarks. In *Proceedings of the 2019 ACL Workshop BlackboxNLP: Analyzing and Interpreting Neural Networks for NLP*, pages 85–94, Florence, Italy. Association for Computational Linguistics.

Alon Talmor, Yanai Elazar, Yoav Goldberg, and Jonathan Berant. 2020. oLMpics-on what language model pre-training captures. *Transactions of the Association for Computational Linguistics*, 8:743–758.

Ian Tenney, Patrick Xia, Berlin Chen, Alex Wang, Adam Poliak, R Thomas McCoy, Najoung Kim, Benjamin Van Durme, Samuel R Bowman, Dipanjan Das, et al. 2018. What do you learn from context? Probing for sentence structure in contextualized word representations. In *International Conference on Learning Representations*.

Jidong Tian, Yitian Li, Wenqing Chen, Liqiang Xiao, Hao He, and Yaohui Jin. 2021. Diagnosing the first-order logical reasoning ability through LogicNLI. In *Proceedings of the 2021 Conference on Empirical Methods in Natural Language Processing*, pages 3738–3747, Online and Punta Cana, Dominican Republic. Association for Computational Linguistics.

Aaron Traylor, Roman Feiman, and Ellie Pavlick. 2021a. AND does not mean OR: Using formal languages to study language models' representations. In *Proceedings of the 59th Annual Meeting of the Association for Computational Linguistics and the 11th International Joint Conference on Natural Language Processing (Volume 2: Short Papers)*, pages 158–167, Online. Association for Computational Linguistics.

Aaron Traylor, Ellie Pavlick, and Roman Feiman. 2021b. Transferring representations of logical connectives. In *Proceedings of the 1st and 2nd Workshops on Natural Logic Meets Machine Learning*

(NALOMA), pages 22–25, Groningen, the Netherlands (online). Association for Computational Linguistics.

Siddharth Vashishtha, Adam Poliak, Yash Kumar Lal, Benjamin Van Durme, and Aaron Steven White. 2020. Temporal reasoning in natural language inference. In *Findings of the Association for Computational Linguistics: EMNLP 2020*, pages 4070–4078, Online. Association for Computational Linguistics.

Ashish Vaswani, Noam Shazeer, Niki Parmar, Jakob Uszkoreit, Llion Jones, Aidan N. Gomez, Lukasz Kaiser, and Illia Polosukhin. 2017. Attention is all you need. *CoRR*, abs/1706.03762.

Alex Wang, Yada Pruksachatkun, Nikita Nangia, Amanpreet Singh, Julian Michael, Felix Hill, Omer Levy, and Samuel R. Bowman. 2020. Superglue: A stickier benchmark for general-purpose language understanding systems.

Alex Wang, Amanpreet Singh, Julian Michael, Felix Hill, Omer Levy, and Samuel Bowman. 2018. GLUE: A multi-task benchmark and analysis platform for natural language understanding. In *Proceedings of the 2018 EMNLP Workshop BlackboxNLP: Analyzing and Interpreting Neural Networks for NLP*, pages 353–355, Brussels, Belgium. Association for Computational Linguistics.

Wei Wang, Bin Bi, Ming Yan, Chen Wu, Zuyi Bao, Jiangnan Xia, Liwei Peng, and Luo Si. 2019. Structbert: Incorporating language structures into pre-training for deep language understanding.

Leon Weber, Pasquale Minervini, Jannes Münchmeyer, Ulf Leser, and Tim Rocktäschel. 2019. NLProlog: Reasoning with weak unification for question answering in natural language. In *Proceedings of the 57th Annual Meeting of the Association for Computational Linguistics*, pages 6151–6161, Florence, Italy. Association for Computational Linguistics.

Sean Welleck, Jason Weston, Arthur Szlam, and Kyunghyun Cho. 2019. Dialogue natural language inference. In *Proceedings of the 57th Annual Meeting of the Association for Computational Linguistics*, pages 3731–3741, Florence, Italy. Association for Computational Linguistics.

Thomas Wolf, Lysandre Debut, Victor Sanh, Julien Chaumond, Clement Delangue, Anthony Moi, Pierric Cistac, Tim Rault, Remi Louf, Morgan Funtowicz, Joe Davison, Sam Shleifer, Patrick von Platen, Clara Ma, Yacine Jernite, Julien Plu, Canwen Xu, Teven Le Scao, Sylvain Gugger, Mariama Drame, Quentin Lhoest, and Alexander Rush. 2020. Transformers: State-of-the-art natural language processing. In *Proceedings of the 2020 Conference on Empirical Methods in Natural Language Processing: System Demonstrations*, pages 38–45, Online. Association for Computational Linguistics.

Ikuya Yamada, Akari Asai, Hiroyuki Shindo, Hideaki Takeda, and Yuji Matsumoto. 2020. LUKE: Deep contextualized entity representations with entity-aware self-attention. In *Proceedings of the 2020 Conference on Empirical Methods in Natural Language Processing (EMNLP)*, pages 6442–6454, Online. Association for Computational Linguistics.

Hitomi Yanaka, Koji Mineshima, and Kentaro Inui. 2021. Exploring transitivity in neural NLI models through veridicality. In *Proceedings of the 16th Conference of the European Chapter of the Association for Computational Linguistics: Main Volume*, pages 920–934, Online. Association for Computational Linguistics.

Kelly Zhang and Samuel Bowman. 2018. Language modeling teaches you more than translation does: Lessons learned through auxiliary syntactic task analysis. In *Proceedings of the 2018 EMNLP Workshop BlackboxNLP: Analyzing and Interpreting Neural Networks for NLP*, pages 359–361.

Appendix

A Dataset Construction Details

A.1 Lexical Items

Tables 3 and 6 respectively, show the noun, spatial and comparative analytic reasoning phrases used in AnaLog.

Name	Gender	% Freq.	Count
James	M	3.318	4,840,833
John	M	3.271	4,772,262
Robert	M	3.143	4,585,515
Michael	M	2.629	3,835,609
William	M	2.451	3,575,914
David	M	2.363	3,447,525
Richard	M	1.703	2,484,611
Charles	M	1.523	2,221,998
Mary	F	2.629	3,991,060
Patricia	F	1.073	1,628,911
Linda	F	1.035	1,571,224
Barbara	F	0.98	1,487,729
Elizabeth	F	0.937	1,422,451
Jennifer	F	0.932	1,414,861
Maria	F	0.828	1,256,979
Susan	F	0.794	1,205,364

Table 3: Noun phrases. Source: 1990 U.S. Census Bureau's Population Division.

As mentioned in Section 3.1, for the restrictors of the universal quantification premises (i.e., the UNI_N slot in the Table 7 template), we used the four most common nouns in COCA (Davies, 2010) which do not begin with a vowel, and that correspond to the category NOUN.PERSON in Wordnet (Fellbaum, 1998), ensuring grammaticality when used within our templates (see Table 4).

Restrictor Noun	POS	Frequency
model	n	191,448
director	n	158,028
participant	n	81,371
soldier	n	78,276

Table 4: UNI_N restrictor noun entries. Source: Corpus of Contemporary American English. POS stands for Part of Speech.

We replace the nouns from Table 3 with lexical entries from Table 5 within *non-overlapping entailment* ($NO^{\rightarrow}$) and *non-overlapping non-entailment* ($NO^{\nrightarrow}$) sentences, to ensure that models (and probes) are not using non-linguistic heuristics when solving the inference task.

Gender	Hypernyms
Female	a girl, some girl, some other girl, a woman, some woman, some person, a person
Male	a boy, some boy, some other boy, a man, some man, some person, a person

Table 5: Noun hypernyms used within AnaLog.

A.2 Premise Constructions

Premises are constructed according to different templates (see Table 7). Let N be some noun (e.g. Patricia, David ...) and P be some spatial or comparative reasoning predicate (e.g. *is to the right of, is younger than ...*). We use the $\neg$ symbol to denote negation. See Table 8 for information pertaining to the Specificity.

B Computing Infrastructure and Budget

Our experiments were carried out using a single GPU on a computer cluster with Debian Linux OS. The GPU nodes on the cluster are GPU GeForce 1080Ti, 11GB GDDR5X, with NVIDIA driver version 418.56 and CUDA version 10.1. The total computational budget required to perform all our experiments amounts to 15 hours.

Spatial Reasoning	Comparative Reasoning
N_1 is to the left of N_2 $\iff$ N_2 is to the right of N_1	**N_1 is smaller than N_2 $\iff$ N_2 is larger than N_1**
N_1 is on top of N_2 $\iff$ N_2 is below N_1	**N_1 is faster than N_2 $\iff$ N_2 is slower than N_1**
N_1 is to the north of N_2 $\iff$ N_2 is to the south of N_1	**N_1 is arriving earlier than N_2 $\iff$ N_2 is arriving later than N_1**
N_1 is in front of N_2 $\iff$ N_2 is behind N_1	**N_1 is stronger than N_2 $\iff$ N_2 is weaker than N_1**
N_1 is to the east of N_2 $\iff$ N_2 is to the west of N_1	**N_1 is younger than N_2 $\iff$ N_2 is older than N_1**

Table 6: Predicates and their reasoning categories.

LC	Specificity	Premise	Overlap Entailment
AND	S	N_1 P_1 N_2 **and** N_3 P_2 N_4.	Random[N_1 P_1 N_2, N_3 P_2 N_4].
AND	NP	N_1 P_1 N_2 **and** N_3.	Random[N_1 P_1 N_2, N_1 P_1 N_3].
AND	VP	N_1 P_1 N_2 **and** P_2 N_3.	Random[N_1 P_1 N_2, N_1 P_2 N_3].
OR	S	N_1 P_1 N_2 **or** N_3 P_2 N_4. Random[N_1 $\neg$ P_1 N_2, N_3 $\neg$ P_2 N_4].	The non-negated non-selected random sentence.
OR	NP	P: N_1 P_1 N_2 **or** N_3. Random[N_1 $\neg$ P_1 N_2, N_1 $\neg$ P_1 N_3].	The non-negated non-selected random sentence.
OR	VP	N_1 P_1 N_2 **or** P_2 N_3. Random[N_1 $\neg$ P_1 N_2, N_1 $\neg$ P_2 N_3].	The non-negated non-selected random sentence.
CON	UNLESS Prefix	**Unless** N_1 P_1 N_2, N_3 P_2 N_4. N_1 $\neg$ P_1 N_2.	N_3 P_2 N_4.
CON	UNLESS Infix	N_1 P_1 N_2 **unless** N_3 P_2 N_4. N_3 $\neg$ P_2 N_4.	N_1 P_1 N_2.
CON	IF	N_1 P_1 N_2 Random[**if, when, even though**] N_3 P_2 N_4. N_3 P_2 N_4.	N_1 P_1 N_2.
CON	IF THEN	**If** N_1 P_1 N_2 **then** N_3 P_2 N_4. N_1 P_1 N_2.	N_3 P_2 N_4.
CON	ONLY IF	N_1 P_1 N_2 **only if** N_3 P_2 N_4. N_1 P_1 N_2.	N_3 P_2 N_4.
UNI	Each	**Each** UNI_N P_1 N_1. N_2 is a UNI_N.	N_2 P_1 N_1.
UNI	Every	**Every** UNI_N P_1 N_1. N_2 is a UNI_N.	N_2 P_1 N_1.

Table 7: Syntactic templates for premises and their corresponding overlapping entailment hypotheses. The logical connectives (LC) are **bolded** within each premise. Specificity indicates the lexical representation and/or the position in which the LCs are used within premises.

Specificity	Definition
S	Conjunction/disjunction is positioned between sentences.
NP	Conjunction/disjunction is positioned between between noun phrases.
VP	Conjunction/disjunction is positioned between verb phrases.
UNLESS Prefix	The logical conditional connective is denoted by the word *unless* prefixed to the premise.
UNLESS Infix	The logical conditional connective is denoted by the word *unless* within the premise.
IF	The logical conditional connective is denoted by the word *if*.
IF THEN	The logical conditional connective is denoted by the phrase *if ... then ....*
ONLY IF	The logical conditional connective is denoted by the phrase *only if*.
Each	The universal quantifier is denoted by the word *each*.
Every	The universal quantifier is denoted by the word *every*.

Table 8: Specificity definitions.

Pairwise Representation Learning for Event Coreference

Xiaodong Yu[1] **Wenpeng Yin**[2] **Dan Roth**[1]
[1]University of Pennsylvania [2]Temple University
{xdyu, danroth}@seas.upenn.edu wenpeng.yin@temple.edu

Abstract

Natural Language Processing tasks such as resolving the coreference of events require understanding the relations between two text snippets. These tasks are typically formulated as (binary) classification problems over independently induced representations of the text snippets. In this work, we develop a Pairwise Representation Learning (PAIRWISERL) scheme for the event mention pairs, in which we jointly encode a pair of text snippets so that the representation of each mention in the pair is induced in the context of the other one. Furthermore, our representation supports a finer, structured representation of the text snippet to facilitate encoding events and their arguments. We show that PAIRWISERL, despite its simplicity, outperforms the prior state-of-the-art event coreference systems on both cross-document and within-document event coreference benchmarks. We also conduct in-depth analysis in terms of the improvement and the limitation of pairwise representation so as to provide insights for future work. [1]

1 Introduction

In this work, we study the event coreference resolution problem. Event coreference resolution is commonly modeled as a binary classification problem over independently induced representations on the text snippets of each event mention (Lee et al., 2012; Barhom et al., 2019).[2] Understanding the relations between two text snippets is the essential part in the tasks. In this work, we argue that the representations of prior work are not expressive enough to learn the pairwise relations due to the following two reasons:

(i) *Counterpart Unawareness.* The relationship between two mentions can be different in different contexts. To address different scenarios, it is better for each mention to ensure that its representation is aware of what its counterpart's representation. However, most early work induces mention representations independently by extracting features only from the sentence that contains the mention, without using the context of the other mention (Barhom et al., 2019; Huang et al., 2019). Some more recent work attempts to encode the whole document to represent each mention (Lee et al., 2017; Cattan et al., 2020). This is beneficial for short documents, since the representation of each mention will also include information from the context of the other candidate mention. However, this is not sufficient for cross-document settings, when the comparison is, for example, between two event mentions that appear in separate documents. In this case even encoding large pieces of text leave the candidate mention representations independent of each other.

(ii) *Unstructured representation learning.* An event mention consists of multiple arguments that describe the event: who, when, where, etc. When determining the relationship of two event mentions, the mismatch of some arguments could be decisive. Consider the following two sentences s_1 and s_2 (event trigger is **underlined**; argument #0 is in blue, location is in purple)

> s_1: "Over 69,000 people **lost** their lives in the quake, including 68,636 in Sichuan."
> s_2: "Up to 6,434 people **lost** their lives in Kobe earthquake and about 4,600 of them were from Kobe."

These two events "lost" are not the same events because the earthquake in Sichuan and the earthquake in Kobe are two different earthquakes, and Sichuan and Kobe do not have any geographic overlap. The mismatch of the locations "Sichuan" and "Kobe" may be enough to determine that the two events are different from each other without even considering the rest of the sentence. Most prior

[1]Our code is available at http://cogcomp.org/page/publication_view/979

[2]Some work maps the two mentions into a single matching score, e.g., (Barhom et al., 2019); this can be treated as a special case of binary classification.

Proceedings of the 11th Joint Conference on Lexical and Computational Semantics, pages 69 - 78
July 14-15, 2022 ©2022 Association for Computational Linguistics

work encodes all of the arguments into a single distributed representation vector and just compares the overall vector representations of two mention triggers. Although contextual representation could encode all of the arguments' information, this is less optimal than explicitly representing all of the arguments, thus making it easier for the model to conduct fine-grained reasoning over each of the argument.

To address the drawbacks of prior representations, we propose *pairwise representation learning* (PAIRWISERL). PAIRWISERL alleviates the aforementioned two limitations with two designs:

Pairwise representation learning. We suggest treating a mention pair, rather than a single mention, as the object for the representation learning. We encode the two mentions' sentences as a whole sequence so that one sentence's token representation is able to interact with the other sentence's from the very beginning. This is advantageous over learning two separate and independent representations because it allows for learning how compatible one mention is with the other mention's context.

Structured representation learning. The observation that mismatching arguments are critical to making the coreference decision indicates that using a single combined representation for all of the arguments could be less informative for cross-mention comparison. In this work, we explicitly represent all the arguments, and compare each argument separately.

To our knowledge, this is the first work that applies pairwise representation learning to event coreference problems. We report our performance on both within-document and cross-document event coreference benchmarks. We show that PAIRWISERL, despite its simplicity, clearly surpasses more complex state-of-the-art event coreference systems on two most popular benchmarks ECB+ (Cybulska and Vossen, 2014) and KBP17 (Getman et al., 2015). We also conduct in-depth analysis in terms of the improvement and the limitation of pairwise representation so as to provide insights for future work.

2 Related Work

In this section, we discuss prior representation learning approaches for event coreference and how pairwise representation learning has been used in other NLP problems.

Event Coreference. Earlier work uses hand-engineered event features to represent events (Chen et al., 2009; Bejan and Harabagiu, 2010).

Most recent neural models use contextual embedding and character-based embedding of event triggers with some pairwise features to represent events (Kenyon-Dean et al., 2018; Huang et al., 2019; Cattan et al., 2020). These works do not use argument information, and expect the contextual embedding includes all the necessary information.

Argument information has been integrated into event representations either by encoding some string-level features (Peng et al., 2016; Choubey and Huang, 2017) or by entity-level coreference co-training (Lee et al., 2012; Barhom et al., 2019).

In contrast, our representation learning of events has a unified system to encode the event triggers and the argument entities, which avoids the costly co-training while learning more advanced features that express the arguments on their own and their interactions with the event triggers.

Pairwise Representation Learning in Other NLP Tasks. Pairwise representation learning has been widely adopted to model the relationships of two pieces of text. The main goal is to learn contextualized sentence representations. Earlier systems commonly implement with attention mechanisms in recurrent (Hermann et al., 2015), convolutional (Yin and Schütze, 2018) or Transformer-style (Vaswani et al., 2017) neural networks to deal with text generation, such as neural machine translation (Bahdanau et al., 2015), document reconstruction (Li et al., 2015), and document summarization (Nallapati et al., 2016); machine comprehension (Hermann et al., 2015), textual entailment (Rocktäschel et al., 2016; Devlin et al., 2019), etc.

In this work, we develop the pairwise representation learning for modeling the relationship of two mentions within two separate sentences rather than the relationship of the two sentences themselves. To the best of our knowledge, we are the first to (i) study pairwise representation for event pairs by letting two mentions learn from each other's context from the beginning [3] , and (ii) build structured representation between events by fine-grained argument reasoning, without any hand-engineered features.

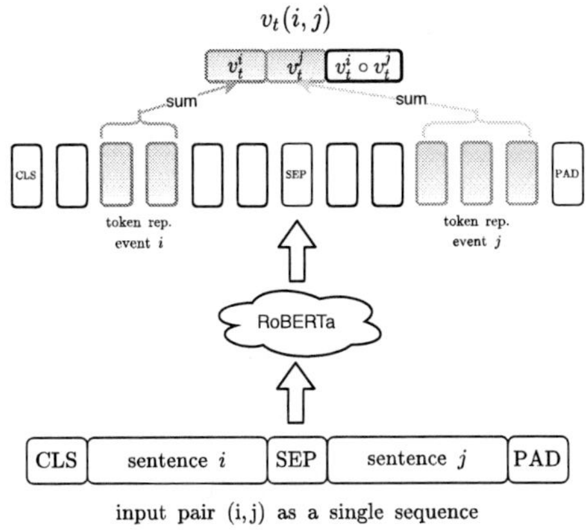

Figure 1: PAIRWISERL learns the trigger-only pairwise representation. v_t^i (resp. v_t^j) is the contextualized representation vector for the trigger in event i (resp. j). The whole trigger-based event pair (i, j) is denoted by $v_t(i, j)$ which is the concatenation: $[v_t^i, v_t^j, v_t^i \circ v_t^j]$.

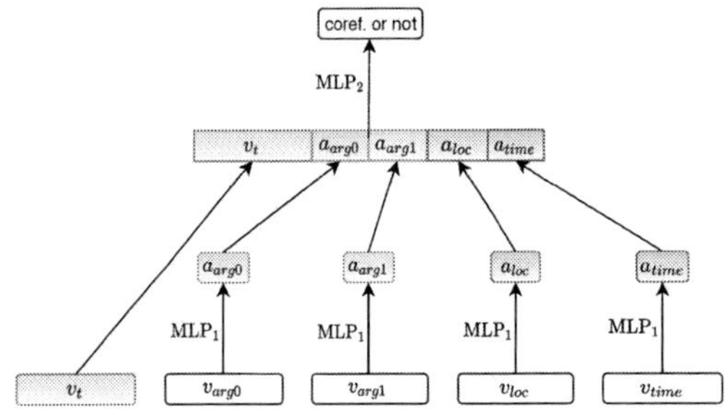

Figure 2: The full reasoning process in PAIRWISERL. The final PAIRWISERL representation is the concatenation of the trigger's representation and four feature values, each coming from a mention argument.

3 PAIRWISERL for Coreference

PAIRWISERL takes two sentences containing each mention as the input and outputs a score indicating how likely the two mentions refer to the same event. Given the mention pair e_i and e_j with their arguments [arg0; arg1; loc; time], as shown in Fig 1, we concatenate the sentences of e_i and e_j, and encode the concatenated sentence using RoBERTa (Liu et al., 2019). After encoding each token of the sequence to a representation vector, we sum up the token representations of the mention span as the representations for event trigger and event arguments respectively: v_{t} for event trigger, $v_{\mathrm{arg0}}/v_{\mathrm{arg1}}$ for argument #0 or #1, v_{loc} for location and v_{time} for time.

Next, we conduct fine-grained coreference reasoning, as Figure 2 shows. The goal is to let each role of event arguments learn its contribution to the final task. For each role, where role $\in$ {t, arg0, arg1, loc, time}, we first build the following role-wise representation:

$$v_{\mathrm{role}}(i,j) = [v^i_{\mathrm{role}}, v^j_{\mathrm{role}}, v^i_{\mathrm{role}} \circ v^j_{\mathrm{role}}] \quad (1)$$

where $\circ$ is element-wise multiplication. Because these four arguments may not always exist in the local context, if one of the role is missing, then the corresponding v^i_{role} will be a zero vector.

We keep the v_{t} as the main representation in PAIRWISERL, and let each of the remaining four arguments contribute a feature value indicating their own decisiveness. The feature value is learnt with a multi-layer perceptron (MLP) as follows:

$$a_{\mathrm{role}}(i,j) = \mathrm{MLP}_1(v_{\mathrm{role}}(i,j)) \quad (2)$$

where "role" refers to mention arguments other than the trigger, MLP_1 has four layers and the output of MLP_1 is a single scalar as the argument feature value. As a result, the final representation PAIRWISERL for event coreference is:

$$v(i,j) = [v_t(i,j), a_{\mathrm{arg0}}, a_{\mathrm{arg1}}, a_{\mathrm{loc}}, a_{\mathrm{time}}] \quad (3)$$

Since entities do not have arguments, the final representation PAIRWISERL for entity coreference is:

$$v(i,j) = v_t(i,j) \quad (4)$$

Once obtaining the pairwise representation $v(i, j)$, another four-layer MLP, as shown in Figure 2, will act as a binary classifier (i.e., is coreferential or not)

$$p(i,j) = \mathrm{Softmax}(\mathrm{MLP}_2(v(i,j))) \quad (5)$$

where $p(i, j)[0]$ is the probability that the two mentions i and j are coreferential.

4 Experiments

We apply PAIRWISERL to cross-document and within-document event coreference problems.

4.1 Cross-document Event Coreference

Dataset We use the ECB+ (Cybulska and Vossen, 2014) corpus to train and test our model. ECB+ is the largest and most popular dataset for cross-document Event Coreference, which is extended from ECB (Bejan and Harabagiu, 2010). For each topic in ECB, Cybulska and Vossen (2014) add different but similar events as subtopics. We follow

[3](Zeng et al., 2020) uses a similar method, and is a contemporary work with ours.

	Train	Dev	Test
Topics	25	8	10
Documents	574	196	206
Sentences	1,037	346	457
Event mentions	3,808	1,245	1,780
Event Singletons	1,116	280	623
Event Clusters	1,527	409	805
Entity mentions	4,758	1,476	2055
Entity Singletons	472	125	196
Entity Clusters	1,286	330	608

Table 1: ECB+ statistics. We follow the data split by Cybulska and Vossen (2015): *train*: 1, 3, 4, 6-11, 13-17, 19-20, 22, 24-33; *dev*: 2, 5, 12, 18, 21, 23, 34, 35; *test*: 36-45. Event/Entity Clusters include singletons.

the same setup as previous work (Cybulska and Vossen, 2015; Kenyon-Dean et al., 2018; Barhom et al., 2019). The detailed statistics are shown in Table 1. For both training and evaluation, we use gold event mentions. ECB+ also annotates coreference between entities that are arguments of events. We also use gold entity mentions to evaluate Entity Coreference on ECB+.

Preprocessing:

Argument generation. ECB+ annotates arguments of each event in the same sentence, but does not annotate the role of the arguments and the event that the arguments belong to. To predict arguments for each event mention, we use AI2 SRL system ,[4] which is a reimplementation of Shi and Lin (2019), and then we map the predicted arguments to the gold arguments. If any gold argument span overlaps with a predicted argument span, we assign the predicted role to it.

Topic Clustering. Topic clustering is a common componet of cross-document coreference because it is computationally inefficient to calculate similarity of the mention pairs in all the documents. People prefer to only collect mention pairs within documents that are related. Barhom et al. (2019) implements a strong topic clustering model that uses the K-Means algorithm on the documents represented by TF-IDF scores of unigrams, bi-grams, and trigrams. They choose the K value based on the Silhouette Coefficient method (Rousseeuw, 1987), and perfectly get the number of gold topics. Though there still exist wrong documents in each topic cluster, their nearly perfect clustering allows very simple baseline models to achieve very good results (Barhom et al., 2019). Since we focus on the improvement that the pairwise representation can bring, we use exactly the same topic clustering model they implemented. We use gold topics for training, and predicted topics for inference.

Postprocessing: Mention Clustering. After training the pairwise coreference scorer, following previous work (Choubey and Huang, 2017; Kenyon-Dean et al., 2018; Barhom et al., 2019; Cattan et al., 2020), we apply agglomerative clustering to the event pairs by the score from the trained scorer in Equation 5. Agglomerative clustering merges event clusters until no cluster pairs have a similarity score higher than a threshold. We define the cluster pair similarity score as the average score of all the event pairs across two clusters, and tune the threshold on development data.

Results: We compare with two state-of-the-art cross-document Event Coreference models using different methods: Barhom et al. (2019), which jointly trains Entity Coreference and Event Coreference, and Cattan et al. (2020), which jointly learns mention detection and coreference. We also compare with the same head lemma baseline implemented by Barhom et al. (2019), which simply clusters events with same head lemma.

To reveal the true merit of PAIRWISERL, in Table 2, we separately show the effectiveness of the structured and pairwise representations as proposed in PAIRWISERL. In "Unstructured", our system only uses the trigger representation, Equation 4, to denote the representation of a pair of mention; in "Structured", the structured representation depicted in Equation 3 is used; in "Unpaired", the representations of trigger and arguments are generated with their own sentence only instead of the concatenated two sentences; in "Pairwise", the representations are generated by the two concatenated sentences as described in Sec 3. We see that using only structured representations improves F1 by 1.6 (from 81.3 to 82.9) from the baseline unpaired+unstructured setting, and using only pairwise representation improves F1 by 2.7 (from 81.3 to 84.0). Both 82.9 and 84.0 already outperform the state-of-the-art model Cattan et al. (2020) on all of the evaluation metrics with large margins, particularly when using pairwise representation, 84.0 vs. 81.0 by CoNLL F1 score. When incorporating

[4]`https://demo.allennlp.org/semantic-role-labeling`

Model	MUC R	MUC P	MUC F1	B^3 R	B^3 P	B^3 F1	$CEAF_e$ R	$CEAF_e$ P	$CEAF_e$ F1	CoNLL F1
same head lemma	76.5	79.9	78.1	71.7	85	77.8	75.5	71.7	73.6	76.5
Barhom et al. (2019)	77.6	84.5	80.9	76.1	85.1	80.3	81	73.8	77.3	79.5
Cattan et al. (2020)	85.1	81.9	83.5	82.1	82.7	82.4	75.2	78.9	77.0	81.0
Unpaired										
Unstructured	81.7	84.4	83.1	79.8	86.3	82.9	79.6	76.7	78.1	81.3
Structured	84.6	84.6	84.6	83.6	84.2	83.9	80.2	80.2	80.2	82.9
Pairwise										
Unstructured	91.6	83.1	**87.2**	89.4	81.1	85.1	75.0	85.5	79.9	84.0
Structured	88.1	85.1	86.6	86.1	84.7	**85.4**	79.6	83.1	**81.3**	**84.4**
$Structured_{BERT}$	87.4	81.4	84.3	85.7	80.2	82.9	73.7	80.9	77.1	81.4

Table 2: Cross-document event coreference performance on ECB+. All the models use gold mentions and predicted topics. "Unstructured" means the model only uses the representation of the event trigger. "Structured" means the model uses the structured representation of arguments. "Unpaired" is the baseline model without pairwise representation. "Pairwise" is the model using pairwise representation. $Structured_{BERT}$ means this baseline model uses BERT (Devlin et al., 2019) as contextual embeddings instead of RoBERTa. Details in Sec 4.1.

Model	MUC R	MUC P	MUC F1	B^3 R	B^3 P	B^3 F1	$CEAF_e$ R	$CEAF_e$ P	$CEAF_e$ F1	CoNLL F1
Barhom et al. (2019)	78.6	80.9	79.7	65.5	76.4	70.5	65.4	61.3	63.3	71.2
Cattan et al. (2020)	85.7	81.7	83.6	70.7	74.8	72.7	59.3	67.4	63.1	73.1
PAIRWISERL	92.3	86.8	**89.5**	82.1	81.0	**81.5**	68.0	80.2	**73.6**	**81.5**

Table 3: Cross-document Entity coreference performance on ECB+. All the models evaluate on gold mentions and predicted topics.

structured representation into pairwise representation, the system obtains further improvement (from 82.9 to 84.4 CoNLL F1). Please note that both Barhom et al. (2019) and Cattan et al. (2020) have relatively complex systems to learn event features as well as entity features. Our system only models the trigger and arguments representations given the context of two involved mentions. It clearly demonstrates the superiority of our model in learning the event-pair representation.

ECB+ also annotates coreference between entities that are arguments of events. Because entities do not have arguments, we just use PAIRWISERL to learn the pairwise representation as Equation 4. We compare with the same two baselines: Barhom et al. (2019) and Cattan et al. (2020). Both of these two baselines train their model on gold mentions, so the comparison is fair. As shown in Table 3, our system PAIRWISERL significantly outperforms the two baselines: 81.5 vs. 73.1.

	Train	Dev	Test
Documents	360	169	167
Event mentions	12,976	4,155	4,375
Event Singletons	5,256	2,709	2,358
Event Clusters	7,460	3,191	2,963

Table 4: KBP statistics. We use KBP2015 for *train*, KBP 2016 for *dev* and KBP 2017 for *test*. Event Clusters include singletons.

4.2 Within-document Event Coreference

Within-document event coreference focuses on event pairs in the same document, so topic clustering of documents is not needed. We use the same pairwise scorer and mention clustering algorithm described in Section 4.1.

We evaluate on the most widely used KBP benchmark. Similar to Huang et al. (2019) and Lu et al. (2020), we use the KBP 2015 dataset (Ellis et al., 2015) as training data, the KBP 2016 dataset (Ellis et al., 2016) as dev data, and the KBP 2017 (Get-

Model	MUC	B^3	$CEAF_e$	BLANC	AVG-F
Huang et al. (2019)					
Predicted Mentions	35.66	43.20	40.02	32.43	36.75
Lu et al. (2020)					
Predicted Mentions	39.06	47.77	45.97	30.60	40.85
Gold Mentions	-	-	-	-	53.72
Unpaired (Gold Mentions)	60.23	52.34	47.44	45.32	51.33
PAIRWISERL (Gold Mentions)	63.67	58.41	54.66	51.72	**57.12**
$\text{PAIRWISERL}_{\text{BERT}}$ (Gold Mentions)	59.11	53.11	50.6	45.81	52.16

Table 5: Within-document event coreference performance on KBP17. Please note that the KBP15 corpus (training data) only provides trigger annotation, so we only evaluate the performance of trigger representation. "Unpaired" is the baseline model without pairwise representation. $\text{PAIRWISERL}_{\text{BERT}}$ means this baseline model uses BERT as contextual embeddings instead of RoBERTa.

man et al., 2015) as test data. The detailed statistics are shown in Table 4. Because the training data KBP 2015 dataset does not have the annotation of arguments, we evaluate the performance of the representation with trigger only.

We compare with two state-of-the-art systems on the KBP benchmark: Huang et al. (2019), which exploits unlabeled data to learn argument compatibility in order to improve coreference performance, and Lu et al. (2020), which jointly learns event detection and event coreference. Lu et al. (2020) claims the state-of-the-art performance when predicting event coreference given predicted events, and they also report numbers using gold event mentions. Our model does not conduct mention detection, so we report our performance on gold mentions only (this is still fair since the prior SOTA system Lu et al. (2020) reports on gold mentions too) and leave our numbers on predicted mentions as future work. As shown in Table 5, PAIRWISERL outperforms the unpaired baseline model with a big margin: 57.12 vs. 51.33 (on "AVG-F"). This further verifies the effectiveness of the pairwise representation in modeling event coreference regardless of whether it is within-document or cross-document. We also need to give credit to RoBERTa that helps our simple model easily outperform the state-of-the-art model (57.12 vs. 53.72), which is a much more complicated model than ours.

4.3 Implementation Details

For both ECB+ and KBP models, we use $\text{RoBERTa}_{\text{Large}}$ as the encoder. The sizes of four layers of MLP_1 are: 3076/1024/1024/1. The sizes of four layers of MLP_2 are: 3072/1024/1024/1. We set the learning rate as 1e-06, the batch size as 32, and we run 10 epochs for training. All hyperparameters are tuned based on development data, including the threshold of agglomerative clustering.

5 Analysis

To further understand why pairwise representation performs much better than unpaired representation, and what limitations pairwise representation still has, we do a quantitative analysis on the errors of PAIRWISERL and the errors of the unpaired baseline model on ECB+. For each model, we randomly sample 100 errors: 50 false negatives and 50 false positives. False negative means that the gold label of the event pair is "coref", but the model predicts "not coref". False positives mean that the gold label of the event pair is "not coref", but the model predicts "coref". We manually classify these errors into different types, and study the difference between the error distributions of the two models.

5.1 False Negatives

Given event mention pairs with the two sentences, as listed on the bottom of Figure 3, we classify these false negatives into these 7 types: "No direct evidence", "Different contexts". "Similar contexts", "Require argument matches", "Annotation mistakes", "Require commonsense knowledge", and "Other".

"No direct evidence" means that, just by reading the two sentences, there is no evidence in them to decide that these two mentions must be the same event. For example:

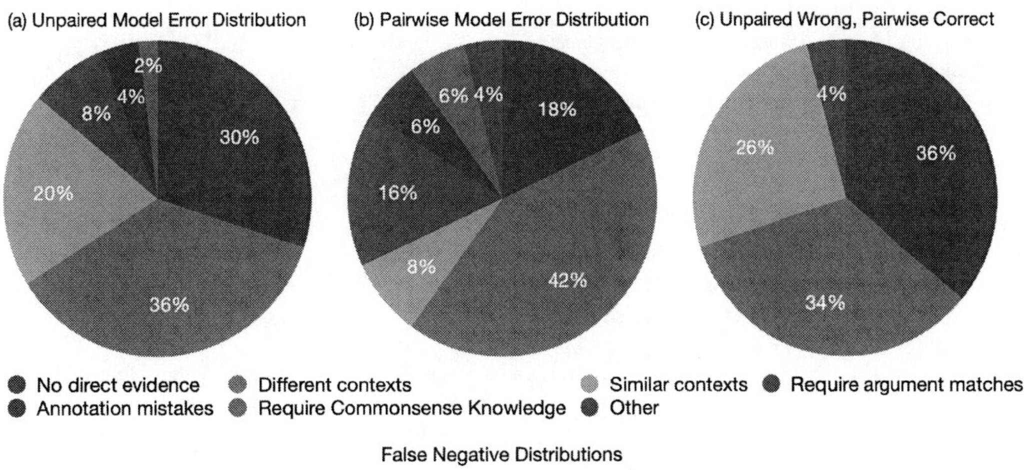

Figure 3: False Negative distributions of unpaired model, and pairwise model. False negative refers to gold coreferential event pairs that the model predicts "not coref". More details in Sec 5.1

> s_1: Smith, 26, who played a young political researcher in the show, will become the biggest star of all after **winning** the role of the 11th Doctor.
> s_2: The guy is relatively unknown and the skeptics wondered if the right person was **chosen**.

Just by reading these two sentences, we really do not know whether the event "winning" and the event "chosen" are same event or not. To make the correct prediction, more contexts are needed. Most prior work encoded events within only a single sentence; in this work, we use a single sentence as event context for fair comparison. As shown in Figure 3, the unpaired model has 30% mistakes belong to "No direct evidence", while the pairwise model only has 18.4%. This indicates that pairwise model may be more capable to learn the similarity between the context in order to make a "guess" that is more likely to be correct. However, 18.4% is also high. This indicates that sentence-level representation is not enough to represent an event. Event arguments usually appear in multiple sentences. Representing events in a multi-sentence level could be interesting to future work.

"Different contexts" means that the two sentences are too hard for the model to understand and there is no obvious textual similarity for the model to rely on. However, if the model understands the contexts completely, it should make the correct prediction. For example:

> s_1: Scott Peterson has been found guilty of first-degree murder, a verdict that means he could be **executed** if these same jurors vote as the "conscience of their community" that he deserves to die for his crimes.
> s_2: Laci Peterson's loved ones have "a hole in their hearts that will never be repaired," a prosecutor told jurors today as he asked them to send convicted double-murderer Scott Peterson to his **death** for killing his wife and unborn son.

In this example, sentences are both complicated and sharing limited vocabulary, but by understanding the sentences, we can say that two event mentions are the same event. We regard this error type as hard cases, and the pairwise model suffers from these hard cases. 40.2% mistakes of the pairwise model belong to hard cases "Different contexts". Please note that a higher ratio (40.2% vs. 36%) doesn't mean our pairwise model is worse than the unpaired competitor; this is because our system has resolved most of the simpler cases so the hard cases occupied the majority proportion of remaining errors. Improving the performance on complicated sentences still acts as the main challenge.

"Similar contexts" means that the two sentences are very similar, which should be easy for the model to make the correct prediction. For example:

s_1: A strong **earthquake** struck Indonesia's Aceh province on Tuesday, killing at least one person and leaving two others missing.

s_2: A powerful **6.1 magnitude earthquake** hit Indonesia's Aceh province, on the island of Sumatra .

These two sentences have similar context and similar structure, which should be easy to predict two mentions as the same events. We regard this error type as easy cases. Our pairwise model reduces the error rate dramatically from 20% to 8% in this category, which indicates that the pairwise model is very effective to solve these simple cases.

"Require argument matches" means that to make the correct prediction, systems need to use more context or external knowledge to conduct non-trivial argument matching. For example:

s_1: An earthquake with a preliminary magnitude of 4.4 **struck** in Sonoma County this morning near The Geysers, according to the U.S. Geological Survey.

s_2: The temblor **occurred** at 9:27 a.m. , 13 miles east of Cloverdale and 2 miles southeast of The Geysers , where geothermal forces by more than 20 power plants are harnessed to provide energy for several North Bay counties.

In order to make the correct prediction of these two sentences, the model need to realize the match between "9:27 a.m." and "this morning", and know that "Sonoma County" is "13 miles east of Cloverdale", which requires more context or external knowledge.

We also sample 50 errors of unpaired model where the pairwise model could predict correctly. As shown in Figure 3(c), the improvement of the pairwise representation mainly comes from better performance on "No direct evidence", "Different contexts" and "Similar contexts". We find that the sentences are usually very long for these errors, which suggests that the pairwise representation is better at understanding the meaning of long sentences than the unpaired representation is.

5.2 False Positives

For the sampled false positives, we also manually classify them into 7 types same as the types of false negatives. The only difference is that, now "Similar contexts" become hard cases, and "Different contexts" become easy cases. As shown in Figure 4, for both the unpaired model and the pairwise model, most of the precision errors

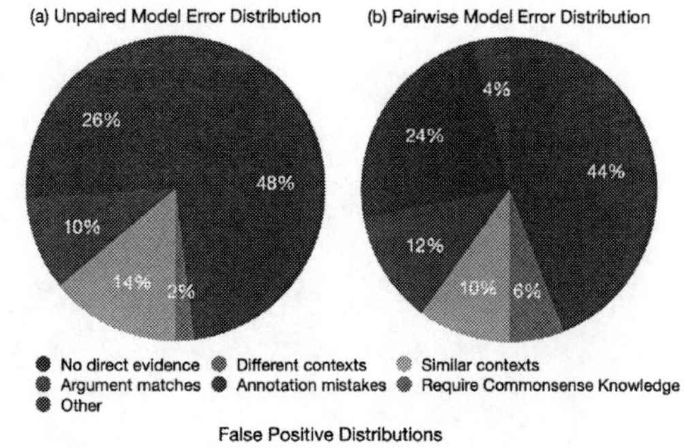

Figure 4: False positive distributions of unpaired model, and pairwise model. False positive refers to gold event pairs that are not coreferential, but the model predicts "coref". More details in Sec 5.2

belong to "No direct evidence" and "Annotation mistakes". After carefully studying these errors, we find that it is actually very hard to determine that two mentions are not the same event. For example:

s_1: Four bombs were dropped within just a few moments - two **landed** inside the camp itself, while the other two bombs were dropped near the airstrip where a UN helicopter was delivering much needed food aid.

s_2: "Two of the bombs **fell** within the Yida camp , including one close to the school," said UNHCR spokesman Adrian Edwards .

By understanding these two sentences, we think, without knowing whether "the camp itself" in the first sentence is the same camp as "Yida camp" in the second sentence, it is impossible to make the correct prediction. The gold label for this pair is "not coref", so we can only classify it to "No direct evidence". We think that these errors again emphasize that the representation of events should be multi-sentences level instead of sentence level. We only use SRL to find event arguments, which limits arguments to be in the same sentences. We think that it may be essential to find events across sentences in future works.

We also find that there exist some errors that we think are *annotation mistakes*. For example:

s_1: Smith, 26, who played a young political researcher in the show, will become the biggest star of all after **winning** the role of the 11th Doctor .

s_2: The BBC says little-known actor Matt Smith will **take over** the title role in the long-running sci-fi series "Doctor Who."

We do not see any reasons that these two mentions are not the same event, but if there are other contexts indicating that they are not the same event, this error would be classified to "No direct evidence". So in conclusion, to further improve the performance on false positives, longer-range context will be needed.

6 Conclusion

In this work, we propose a simple representation learning scheme, PAIRWISERL, for event coreference. PAIRWISERL learns a mention-pair representation by forwarding concatenated sentences into RoBERTa, where sentences provide the context of mentions. This representation is applied to both within-document and cross-document event coreference benchmarks and obtains state-of-the-art performance. In addition, we augment this pairwise representation with structured argument features to further improve its performance.

Acknowledgments

This work was supported by Contract FA8750-19-2-1004 with the US Defense Advanced Research Projects Agency (DARPA), the Office of the Director of National Intelligence (ODNI), Intelligence Advanced Research Projects Activity (IARPA), via IARPA Contract No. 2019-19051600006 under the BETTER Program, and a Focused Award from Google. Approved for Public Release, Distribution Unlimited. The views and conclusions contained herein are those of the authors and should not be interpreted as necessarily representing the official policies, either expressed or implied, of ODNI, IARPA, the Department of Defense, or the U.S. Government. The U.S. Government is authorized to reproduce and distribute reprints for governmental purposes notwithstanding any copyright annotation therein.

References

Dzmitry Bahdanau, Kyunghyun Cho, and Yoshua Bengio. 2015. Neural machine translation by jointly learning to align and translate. In *ICLR*.

Shany Barhom, Vered Shwartz, Alon Eirew, Michael Bugert, Nils Reimers, and Ido Dagan. 2019. Revisiting joint modeling of cross-document entity and event coreference resolution. In *Proceedings of the 57th Annual Meeting of the Association for Computational Linguistics*, pages 4179–4189, Florence, Italy. Association for Computational Linguistics.

Cosmin Bejan and Sanda Harabagiu. 2010. Unsupervised event coreference resolution with rich linguistic features. In *Proceedings of the 48th Annual Meeting of the Association for Computational Linguistics*, pages 1412–1422, Uppsala, Sweden. Association for Computational Linguistics.

Arie Cattan, Alon Eirew, Gabriel Stanovsky, Mandar Joshi, and Ido Dagan. 2020. Streamlining cross-document coreference resolution: Evaluation and modeling. *arXiv preprint arXiv:2009.11032*.

Zheng Chen, Heng Ji, and R Haralick. 2009. Event coreference resolution: Algorithm, feature impact and evaluation. In *Proceedings of Events in Emerging Text Types (eETTs) Workshop, in conjunction with RANLP, Bulgaria*.

Prafulla Kumar Choubey and Ruihong Huang. 2017. Event coreference resolution by iteratively unfolding inter-dependencies among events. In *Proceedings of the 2017 Conference on Empirical Methods in Natural Language Processing*, pages 2124–2133, Copenhagen, Denmark. Association for Computational Linguistics.

Agata Cybulska and Piek Vossen. 2014. Using a sledgehammer to crack a nut? lexical diversity and event coreference resolution. In *LREC*, pages 4545–4552.

Agata Cybulska and Piek Vossen. 2015. " bag of events" approach to event coreference resolution. supervised classification of event templates. *Int. J. Comput. Linguistics Appl.*, 6(2):11–27.

J. Devlin, Ming-Wei Chang, Kenton Lee, and Kristina Toutanova. 2019. Bert: Pre-training of deep bidirectional transformers for language understanding. In *NAACL-HLT*.

Joe Ellis, Jeremy Getman, Dana Fore, Neil Kuster, Zhiyi Song, Ann Bies, and Stephanie M Strassel. 2015. Overview of linguistic resources for the tac kbp 2016 evaluations: Methodologies and results. In *TAC*.

Joe Ellis, Jeremy Getman, Neil Kuster, Zhiyi Song, Ann Bies, and Stephanie M Strassel. 2016. Overview of linguistic resources for the tac kbp 2015 evaluations: Methodologies and results. In *TAC*.

Jeremy Getman, J. Ellis, Zhiyi Song, Jennifer Tracey, and S. Strassel. 2015. Overview of linguistic resources for the tac kbp 2017 evaluations: Methodologies and results. *Theory and Applications of Categories*.

Karl Moritz Hermann, Tomás Kociský, Edward Grefenstette, Lasse Espeholt, Will Kay, Mustafa Suleyman, and Phil Blunsom. 2015. Teaching machines to read and comprehend. In *NeurIPS*, pages 1693–1701.

Yin Jou Huang, Jing Lu, Sadao Kurohashi, and Vincent Ng. 2019. Improving event coreference resolution by learning argument compatibility from unlabeled data. In *Proceedings of the 2019 Conference of the North*

American Chapter of the Association for Computational Linguistics: Human Language Technologies, Volume 1 (Long and Short Papers), pages 785–795.

Kian Kenyon-Dean, Jackie Chi Kit Cheung, and Doina Precup. 2018. Resolving event coreference with supervised representation learning and clustering-oriented regularization. In *Proceedings of the Seventh Joint Conference on Lexical and Computational Semantics*, pages 1–10, New Orleans, Louisiana. Association for Computational Linguistics.

Heeyoung Lee, Marta Recasens, Angel Chang, Mihai Surdeanu, and Dan Jurafsky. 2012. Joint entity and event coreference resolution across documents. In *Proceedings of the 2012 Joint Conference on Empirical Methods in Natural Language Processing and Computational Natural Language Learning*, pages 489–500.

Kenton Lee, Luheng He, Mike Lewis, and Luke Zettlemoyer. 2017. End-to-end neural coreference resolution. In *Proceedings of the 2017 Conference on Empirical Methods in Natural Language Processing*, pages 188–197, Copenhagen, Denmark. Association for Computational Linguistics.

Jiwei Li, Minh-Thang Luong, and Dan Jurafsky. 2015. A hierarchical neural autoencoder for paragraphs and documents. In *ACL*, pages 1106–1115.

Yinhan Liu, Myle Ott, Naman Goyal, Jingfei Du, Mandar Joshi, Danqi Chen, Omer Levy, Mike Lewis, Luke Zettlemoyer, and Veselin Stoyanov. 2019. Roberta: A robustly optimized bert pretraining approach. *arXiv preprint arXiv:1907.11692*.

Yaojie Lu, Hongyu Lin, Jialong Tang, Xianpei Han, and Le Sun. 2020. End-to-end neural event coreference resolution. *arXiv preprint arXiv:2009.08153*.

Ramesh Nallapati, Bowen Zhou, Cícero Nogueira dos Santos, Çaglar Gülçehre, and Bing Xiang. 2016. Abstractive text summarization using sequence-to-sequence rnns and beyond. In *CoNLL*, pages 280–290. ACL.

Haoruo Peng, Yangqiu Song, and Dan Roth. 2016. Event detection and co-reference with minimal supervision. In *Proceedings of the 2016 Conference on Empirical Methods in Natural Language Processing*, pages 392–402, Austin, Texas. Association for Computational Linguistics.

Tim Rocktäschel, Edward Grefenstette, Karl Moritz Hermann, Tomás Kociský, and Phil Blunsom. 2016. Reasoning about entailment with neural attention. In *ICLR*.

Peter J Rousseeuw. 1987. Silhouettes: a graphical aid to the interpretation and validation of cluster analysis. *Journal of computational and applied mathematics*, 20:53–65.

Peng Shi and Jimmy Lin. 2019. Simple bert models for relation extraction and semantic role labeling. *arXiv preprint arXiv:1904.05255*.

Ashish Vaswani, Noam Shazeer, Niki Parmar, Jakob Uszkoreit, Llion Jones, Aidan N. Gomez, Lukasz Kaiser, and Illia Polosukhin. 2017. Attention is all you need. In *NeurIPS*, pages 5998–6008.

Wenpeng Yin and Hinrich Schütze. 2018. Attentive convolution: Equipping cnns with rnn-style attention mechanisms. *TACL*, 6:687–702.

Yutao Zeng, Xiaolong Jin, Saiping Guan, Jiafeng Guo, and Xueqi Cheng. 2020. Event coreference resolution with their paraphrases and argument-aware embeddings. In *Proceedings of COLING*, pages 3084–3094.

A Simple Unsupervised Approach for Coreference Resolution using Rule-based Weak Supervision

Alessandro Stolfo[1] **Chris Tanner**[2] **Vikram Gupta**[3] **Mrinmaya Sachan**[1]
[1]ETH Zürich [2]Harvard University [3]Sharechat
{alessandro.stolfo, mrinmaya.sachan}@inf.ethz.ch
christanner@g.harvard.edu
vikramgupta@sharechat.co

Abstract

Labeled data for the task of Coreference Resolution is a scarce resource, requiring significant human effort. While state-of-the-art coreference models rely on such data, we propose an approach that leverages an end-to-end neural model in settings where labeled data is unavailable. Specifically, using weak supervision, we transfer the linguistic knowledge encoded by Stanford's rule-based coreference system to the end-to-end model, which jointly learns rich, contextualized span representations and coreference chains. Our experiments on the English OntoNotes corpus demonstrate that our approach effectively benefits from the noisy coreference supervision, producing an improvement over Stanford's rule-based system (+3.7 F_1) and outperforming the previous best unsupervised model (+0.9 F_1). Additionally, we validate the efficacy of our method on two other datasets: PreCo and Litbank (+2.5 and +5 F_1 on Stanford's system, respectively).

1 Introduction

Coreference resolution is an important problem in language understanding. In the recent years, significant progress has been made on this task with coreference annotated corpora (Hovy et al., 2006) and deep neural network architectures (Wiseman et al., 2015; Clark and Manning, 2016a,b; Lee et al., 2017). Further gains have been obtained by leveraging contextualized text encoders like ELMo (Lee et al., 2018), BERT, SpanBERT, and Longformer (Kantor and Globerson, 2019; Joshi et al., 2019, 2020; Wu et al., 2020; Kirstain et al., 2021).

The progress in supervised coreference resolution has not been accompanied by analogous improvements in unsupervised methods. The best performing work in this domain is the unsupervised mention-ranking systems proposed by Ma et al. (2016). Approaches that do not rely on gold annotation are highly desirable for this task, as coreference corpora are expensive to create. Addressing this issue, weak supervision has been used for multilingual coreference resolution to automatically obtain labels for languages with no annotated datasets (Wallin and Nugues, 2017).

In this paper, we introduce a simple yet effective approach for unsupervised coreference resolution, which leverages an end-to-end span-ranking coreference model (Lee et al., 2018) and contextualized span representations. The end-to-end model is trained with weak supervision from Stanford's coreference system (Lee et al., 2011), which, in turn uses a set of linguistic rules for coreference. Previous works have used Stanford system's rules as feature extractors (Fernandes et al., 2012; Wiseman et al., 2015; Ma et al., 2016). However, our approach uses Stanford's rule-based sieves to produce noisy labels that are subsequently used to train the neural end-to-end resolver.

The rationale behind the use of Stanford's resolver for producing noisy labels lies in its ease of use and its modular structure, which allows us to interpret the value of the linguistic knowledge encoded in the system. Linguists building a coreference resolver in a new domain can encode their prior knowledge via rules and improve the Stanford system. Our approach would further boost the resolver by incorporating pre-trained representations. Nevertheless, our framework can be applied in combination with any method able to produce informative coreference labels.

We assess our approach on three coreference corpora: English OntoNotes (Pradhan et al., 2012), PreCo (Chen et al., 2018), and Litbank (Bamman et al., 2020). Our experiments show that the imperfect information contained in the noisy labels can be effectively used to train the end-to-end model, producing an improvement over Stanford's system. Experimenting with different pre-trained language models, we observe that using BERT boosts the performance of the end-to-end resolver. Results

Proceedings of the 11th Joint Conference on Lexical and Computational Semantics, pages 79 - 88
July 14-15, 2022

further improve by using SpanBERT (Joshi et al., 2020), which outperforms previous unsupervised models (Ma et al., 2016) on the English OntoNotes benchmark. We also evaluate the approach on two other coreference datasets: PreCo and Litbank, and show strong gains over the Stanford system. Finally, we present a set of analyses that examine the information incorporated by weakly supervised training.

2 Method

Our approach relies on the *c2f-coref* end-to-end architecture proposed by Lee et al. (2018), and on the classic rule-based Stanford coreference system (Lee et al., 2011, 2013) for the CoNLL 2011 shared task (Pradhan et al., 2011).

Overview of c2f-coref The end-to-end coreference resolution system (Lee et al., 2017) uses a span-based neural model that learns a distribution $P(\cdot)$ over antecedents y for each span i. Spans are represented using fixed-length embeddings obtained via bidirectional LSTMs (Hochreiter and Schmidhuber, 1997) and taken as input by a pairwise scoring function.

Subsequent models revisited this approach: Lee et al. (2018) proposed the c2f-coref method, introducing coarse-to-fine antecedent pruning and embedding representations from ELMo (Peters et al., 2018) at the input to the LSTMs. Later, Joshi et al. (2019) used BERT to represent spans, demonstrating the power of pre-trained language models for coreference resolution. Most recently, Joshi et al. (2020) introduced SpanBERT and further improved the state of the art.

Stanford's Rule-based System Stanford's system is a deterministic coreference resolver consisting of a set of sieves applied in a cascade fashion. Initially, the *Mention Detection* considers all noun phrases, pronouns, and named entity mentions as candidate mentions, then filters them according to a set of exclusion rules. Specifically, each identified mention is considered as a singleton cluster. Then, akin to agglomerative clustering, the clusters are sequentially processed by the sieves. Each sieve embodies a specific linguistic rule and builds on the result of the previous sieve by merging a mention into a partially-formed entity cluster, depending on whether it satisfies a set of constraints. The architecture guarantees that high-precision constraints are given high priority (e.g., exact string match, head match), while rules with lower precision but higher recall are applied later (e.g., the Pronominal Coreference Sieve). We provide a description of the most important sieves in Appendix A.

Weak Supervision using Linguistic Rules Although Stanford's sieve-based system is unsupervised, it captures rich, task-specific coreference information in English, and we hypothesize that it could effectively serve as supervision for training the neural span-ranking model. By exploiting contextualized span representations within the end-to-end learning framework, the neural model can exhibit stronger generalization capabilities.

Specifically, we employ Stanford's system to obtain cluster labels, representing a *noisy* (i.e., non-gold) signal for both mention identification and coreference. As in the supervised case, only clustering information is observed. The training is carried out by optimizing the marginal log-likelihood of the antecedents $\tilde{y}$ implied by the noisy cluster assignment:

$$\log \prod_{i=1}^{N} \sum_{\tilde{y} \in \mathcal{C}(i)} P(\tilde{y})$$

where N is the total number of mentions in the document and $\mathcal{C}(i)$ is the set of antecedents of span i that are coreferent to i according to the cluster assignment produced by Stanford's system.

3 Experiments

We assess the proposed approach on three datasets: the English OntoNotes v5.0 data from the CoNLL-2012 shared task (Pradhan et al., 2012), PreCo (Chen et al., 2018), and Litbank (Bamman et al., 2020). We evaluate the c2f-coref model combined with different pre-trained language models (ELMo, BERT, and SpanBERT). These results are compared to the ones produced by Stanford's system, in order to show the efficacy of the noisy supervision. Moreover, we examine the performance of our weakly-supervised approach in contrast to two previous unsupervised models: Multigraph (Martschat, 2013) and the EM-based ranking model by Ma et al. (2016).

3.1 Experimental Setup

We use the original implementations of the ELMo-based c2f-coref[1] (Lee et al., 2018) and of the BERT/SpanBERT-based models[2] (Joshi et al.,

[1] https://github.com/kentonl/e2e-coref

[2] https://github.com/mandarjoshi90/coref

	MUC			B^3			$CEAF_{\phi_4}$			CoNLL
	P	R	F_1	P	R	F_1	P	R	F_1	F_1
Stanford (Lee et al., 2011)	64.3	65.2	64.7	49.2	56.8	52.7	52.5	46.6	49.4	55.6
Multigraph (Martschat, 2013)	-	-	65.4	-	-	54.4	-	-	50.2	56.7
Unsup. Ranking (Ma et al., 2016)	-	-	67.7	-	-	55.9	-	-	51.8	58.4
c2f-coref	65.7	68.0	66.9	50.9	59.4	54.8	52.9	49.1	50.9	57.5
BERT-base + c2f-coref	66.8	69.2	68.0	51.5	60.6	55.7	53.1	50.3	51.7	58.5
SpanBERT-base + c2f-coref	67.6	68.5	68.1	53.1	60.1	56.4	54.8	50.4	52.5	59.0
BERT-large + c2f-coref	67.2	69.7	68.5	52.3	61.2	56.4	54.0	51.0	52.5	59.1
SpanBERT-large + c2f-coref	67.4	69.8	**68.6**	52.4	61.8	**56.7**	54.1	51.4	**52.7**	**59.3**

Table 1: Results on the test set of the English CoNLL-2012 shared task[3]. The c2f-coref models were trained via weak supervision. Scores for Multigraph and the Unsupervised Ranking model are reported in Ma et al. (2016).

2019), while using their original, respective hyperparameters. We use the implementation of Stanford's system provided with the Stanford CoreNLP suite (Manning et al., 2014). Further training details are provided in Appendix B.

We report precision, recall, and F_1 for the standard MUC (Vilain et al., 1995), B^3 (Bagga and Baldwin, 1998), and $CEAF_{\phi_4}$ (Luo, 2005) metrics. We use the CoNLL F_1 score (average F_1 of the three metrics) as the main evaluation measure, which is common practice in coreference[3].

3.2 Results on OntoNotes

Table 1 shows that the c2f-coref model trained with noisy supervision is able to produce a gain over Stanford's system. The incremental improvement produced by the pre-trained language models highlights the importance of the representation of spans for this task, and suggests that the end-to-end model learns how to effectively exploit it from the noisy supervision. The version of the c2f-coref model augmented with SpanBERT-large achieves 59.3 CoNLL F_1, improving on the Unsupervised Ranking model (Ma et al., 2016) by 0.9 F_1. In contrast with what was observed in the supervised realm (Joshi et al., 2019), the score increase produced by BERT-base over ELMo (+1.0 F_1) is larger than the gain yielded by the large versions of BERT and SpanBERT over their base counterparts (+0.6 and +0.3 F_1, respectively). This might be explained as an effect of the weak supervision, which is likely to reduce the marginal improvement produced by an increase in model complexity. Table 3 illustrates the mention detection performance of Staford's system and the c2f-coref models based on SpanBERT-Base and SpanBERT-Large.

	Dataset	MUC	B^3	$CEAF_{\phi_4}$	CoNLL
Stanford	PC	59.7	49.7	45.2	51.5
SB-B + c2f	PC	62.0	52.3	47.6	**54.0**
Stanford	LB	65.8	41.6	26.8	44.7
SB-B + c2f	LB	71.4	46.5	31.2	**49.7**

Table 2: F_1 sccore comparison between Stanford's system and the c2f-coref model based on SpanBERT-base (SB-B) on PreCo (PC) and Litbank (LB).

3.3 Results on PreCo and Litbank

An important feature of PreCo and Litbank is that they contain annotations for singleton mentions, unlike OntoNotes. However, both Stanford's system and the c2f-coref model present a recall-oriented mention detection strategy, which tends to overestimate the number of proposed mentions, as singletons typically would be filtered out from the response. Moreover, the training process of the c2f-coref model does not take singleton mentions into account. For this reasons, we adapt the evaluation on Litbank and PreCo to the OntoNotes guidelines, which assert that predicted singleton mentions should be ignored and non-coreferent spans should be removed from the response. Table 2 shows performance gains consistent with the results on OntoNotes, with the weakly-supervised c2f-coref model improving by 2.5 and 5 CoNLL F_1 on PreCo and Litbank, respectively.

4 Analysis

Performance on Different Types of Coreference
We investigate the capabilities of the weakly super-

[3]The metrics are computed using the most recent version of the official CoNLL scorer (Pradhan et al., 2014)

[3]We observed a small discrepancy between the results relative to Stanford's system reported by Ma et al. (2016) and the ones we obtained (~0.2 F_1). Here we report the scores we produce, which are the higher ones.

	P	R	F_1
Stanford	88.7	40.2	55.4
SpanBERT-base + c2f-coref	76.2	77.1	76.6
SpanBERT-large + c2f-coref	75.3	77.8	76.5

Table 3: Comparison of mention detection precision (P), recall (R) and F_1 score on the development set of the CoNLL-2012 shared task.

Link Type	Stanford	SB-L + c2f	Δ (%)
Nominal - Pronominal	35.7	38.9	+9.0
Nominal - Nominal	54.1	58.6	+8.3
Nominal - Proper	15.1	17.1	+13.2
Pronominal - Proper	60.2	60.4	+0.3
Pronominal - Pronominal	70.9	73.1	+3.1
Proper - Proper	80.8	82.8	+3.5

Table 4: Performance (F_1 scores) on CoNLL-2012 development set in terms of identification of coreference links between different kinds of mentions.

vised end-to-end model in identifying the different kinds of coreference links given by the combination of three mention categories: proper, nominal, and pronominal. We study the performance of the c2f-coref model based on SpanBERT-large in comparison to Stanford's system. The results are illustrated in Table 4. We observe a global improvement in all the considered types of links, with the most significant gains from links involving nominal mentions. This improvement is coherent with the observations of Durrett and Klein (2013): coreference decisions involving nominal mentions usually require richer semantic inference, which in our setting is provided by the contextualized span representations

Impact of Document Length We compare the c2f-coref model to Stanford's system on documents of different lengths. As reported in Table 5, Stanford's resolver performs better than the span-ranking system on particularly short documents. However, for all groups of documents longer than 64 tokens, we observe a consistent improvement provided by the c2f-coref model. This could be explained by the contextualized span representations, which were shown to be more informative when larger context is available (Beltagy et al., 2020).

Varying the Amount of Training Data We assess the performance of the model on PreCo when the training is carried out on subsets of different sizes (Fig. 1). We observe that the c2f-coref model requires only 100 weakly-annotated documents to outperform Stanford's system, indicating that the noisy signal is quickly incorporated by the model.

Doc Length	# of Docs	Stanford	SB-L + c2f	Δ (%)
0 - 64	17	52.1	49.6	-4.8
64 - 128	39	57.2	58.6	+2.4
128 - 256	74	56.2	60.9	+8.4
256 - 512	76	58.9	62.3	+5.8
512 - 768	73	56.5	59.6	+5.5
768 - 1152	52	53.3	56.3	+5.6
1152+	12	47.0	50.7	+7.9

Table 5: Average CoNLL F_1 on the OntoNotes development split for sets of documents with different lengths (expressed as number of tokens).

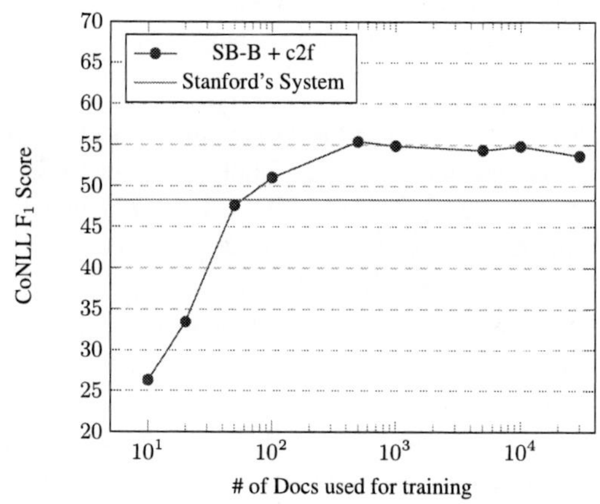

Figure 1: Performance on a held-out set of 1000 PreCo documents using the c2f-coref model as the number of documents used for training varies.

Using more than 1000 documents does not seem to boost the score further. We suspect that this behavior might be caused by the homogeneity and the small vocabulary size of the documents of the PreCo dataset.

Using Different Linguistic Priors We study how the performance of our approach is impacted as we vary the complexity of the linguistic rules used for the weak supervision. We do this by training the c2f-coref model on the noisy labels obtained using three different implementations of Stanford's system: (1) `1-sieve`, which considers only the Exact String Match rule; (2) `3-sieve`, which consists of the three most effective sieves: Exact String Match, Strict Head Match, and the Pronominal Coreference sieve; and (3) `complete`, which implements all ten sieves. Results in Table 6 show that the improvement provided by the end-to-end model increases as the noisy signal for the training becomes more accurate, suggesting that better supervision helps the model benefit from the knowledge-rich span representations.

Rule Implementation	Stanford	SB-B + c2f	Δ (%)
`1-sieve`	27.9	27.6	-1.1
`3-sieve`	53.5	56.2	+5.0
`complete`	57.0	60.0	+5.3

Table 6: CoNLL F_1 scores on the OntoNotes development set using different combinations of sieves.

1	*Directly facing* [***him***]$_1$ *was* [*the box of old*]$_2$ *Mrs. Manson Mingott, whose monstrous obesity had long since made* [*it*]$_2$ *impossible for* [*her*]$_3$ *to attend the Opera...*
	Directly facing [***him***]$_1$ *was the box of* [*old Mrs. Manson Mingott*]$_2$*, whose monstrous obesity had long since made it impossible for* [*her*]$_2$ *to attend the Opera...*
2	*I persuaded* [***two***]$_1$ *young neighbors to stop playing basketball and to help us get the tree into the house and set* [***it***]$_1$ *correctly in the stand.*
	I persuaded two young neighbors to stop playing basketball and to help us get [***the tree***]$_1$ *into the house and set* [***it***]$_1$ *correctly in the stand.*

Table 7: Example predictions by Stanford's system (upper sub-row) and c2f-coref (lower sub-row) on Litbank (sentence 1) and PreCo Dev (sentence 2). $[\cdot]_x$ represents a mention assigned to cluster x.

Qualitative Analysis In order to better illustrate how the end-to-end system profits from modeling choices unavailable to Stanford's resolver (e.g., contextualized representations), in Table 7 we provide instances of coreference clusters predicted by the two models. In the first example, the c2f-coref model, unlike Stanford's system, correctly identifies the valid mention *Mrs. Manson Mingott*, links it to the appropriate pronoun (*her*), and correctly neglects the expletive pronoun *it*. This is perhaps because pre-trained models are known to strongly encode syntax (Goldberg, 2019). A similar improvement is observed in the second sentence, where the response produced by our weakly-supervised model correctly identifies the noun phrase *the tree* and correctly links it to the pronoun *it*. We present additional examples of predicted chains in Appendix C.

5 Conclusion

We presented an approach for coreference resolution that, while being simple, effectively leverages the end-to-end span-ranking model in settings where labeled data is unavailable. Experimental results highlight the efficacy of the weak supervision that the method is based upon, and showed performance gains over previous unsupervised systems.

6 Ethical Considerations

Since our approach is unsupervised and based on the coreference signal produced by Stanford's deterministic coreference system (Lee et al., 2011, 2013), it is prone to echoing biases present in the linguistic rules embodied by Stanford's resolver. Moreover, as most coreference resolvers, the approach we presented is not designed for a particular use case, but it is rather expected to be employed within more complex NLP systems. Specific domains in which these systems are applied (e.g., biomedical data, legal documents) might reveal potential fairness shortcomings in the underlying Stanford's sieve-based system. Depending on the setting of application (e.g., voice assistants or search engines), these possible defects could produce undesirable outcomes. For instance, wrongly classifying two people as the same person is possible to affect information extraction results (e.g., search engines). Further studies on alternative domains are needed to assess these aspects.

Contextual word embedding models such as ELMo (Peters et al., 2018), BERT (Devlin et al., 2019), and SpanBERT (Joshi et al., 2020) are pretrained with self-supervised procedures on large portions of unlabeled text. These models are optimized to capture statistical dependencies and might retain and amplify prejudices and stereotypes present in the training data (Kurita et al., 2019). Since the method we propose relies on such pretrained models, it inevitably inherits possible biases that might affect its fairness.

Acknowledgements

This research is supported by armasuisse Science and Technology through a CYD Doctoral Fellowship to Alessandro Stolfo.

References

Amit Bagga and Breck Baldwin. 1998. Algorithms for scoring coreference chains. In *The first international conference on language resources and evaluation workshop on linguistics coreference*, volume 1, pages 563–566. Citeseer.

David Bamman, Olivia Lewke, and Anya Mansoor. 2020. An annotated dataset of coreference in English literature. In *Proceedings of the 12th Language Resources and Evaluation Conference*, pages 44–54, Marseille, France. European Language Resources Association.

Iz Beltagy, Matthew E Peters, and Arman Cohan. 2020. Longformer: The long-document transformer. *arXiv preprint arXiv:2004.05150*.

Hong Chen, Zhenhua Fan, Hao Lu, Alan Yuille, and Shu Rong. 2018. PreCo: A large-scale dataset in preschool vocabulary for coreference resolution. In *Proceedings of the 2018 Conference on Empirical Methods in Natural Language Processing*, pages 172–181, Brussels, Belgium. Association for Computational Linguistics.

Kevin Clark and Christopher D. Manning. 2016a. Deep reinforcement learning for mention-ranking coreference models. In *Proceedings of the 2016 Conference on Empirical Methods in Natural Language Processing*, pages 2256–2262, Austin, Texas. Association for Computational Linguistics.

Kevin Clark and Christopher D. Manning. 2016b. Improving coreference resolution by learning entity-level distributed representations. In *Proceedings of the 54th Annual Meeting of the Association for Computational Linguistics (Volume 1: Long Papers)*, pages 643–653, Berlin, Germany. Association for Computational Linguistics.

Jacob Devlin, Ming-Wei Chang, Kenton Lee, and Kristina Toutanova. 2019. BERT: Pre-training of deep bidirectional transformers for language understanding. In *Proceedings of the 2019 Conference of the North American Chapter of the Association for Computational Linguistics: Human Language Technologies, Volume 1 (Long and Short Papers)*, pages 4171–4186, Minneapolis, Minnesota. Association for Computational Linguistics.

Greg Durrett and Dan Klein. 2013. Easy victories and uphill battles in coreference resolution. In *Proceedings of the 2013 Conference on Empirical Methods in Natural Language Processing*, pages 1971–1982, Seattle, Washington, USA. Association for Computational Linguistics.

Eraldo Fernandes, Cícero dos Santos, and Ruy Milidiú. 2012. Latent structure perceptron with feature induction for unrestricted coreference resolution. In *Joint Conference on EMNLP and CoNLL - Shared Task*, pages 41–48, Jeju Island, Korea. Association for Computational Linguistics.

Yoav Goldberg. 2019. Assessing bert's syntactic abilities. *CoRR*, abs/1901.05287.

Sepp Hochreiter and Jürgen Schmidhuber. 1997. Long short-term memory. *Neural computation*, 9(8):1735–1780.

Eduard Hovy, Mitchell Marcus, Martha Palmer, Lance Ramshaw, and Ralph Weischedel. 2006. OntoNotes: The 90% solution. In *Proceedings of the Human Language Technology Conference of the NAACL, Companion Volume: Short Papers*, pages 57–60, New York City, USA. Association for Computational Linguistics.

Mandar Joshi, Danqi Chen, Yinhan Liu, Daniel S. Weld, Luke Zettlemoyer, and Omer Levy. 2020. SpanBERT: Improving pre-training by representing and predicting spans. *Transactions of the Association for Computational Linguistics*, 8:64–77.

Mandar Joshi, Omer Levy, Luke Zettlemoyer, and Daniel Weld. 2019. BERT for coreference resolution: Baselines and analysis. In *Proceedings of the 2019 Conference on Empirical Methods in Natural Language Processing and the 9th International Joint Conference on Natural Language Processing (EMNLP-IJCNLP)*, pages 5803–5808, Hong Kong, China. Association for Computational Linguistics.

Ben Kantor and Amir Globerson. 2019. Coreference resolution with entity equalization. In *Proceedings of the 57th Annual Meeting of the Association for Computational Linguistics*, pages 673–677, Florence, Italy. Association for Computational Linguistics.

Yuval Kirstain, Ori Ram, and Omer Levy. 2021. Coreference resolution without span representations. *arXiv preprint arXiv:2101.00434*.

Keita Kurita, Nidhi Vyas, Ayush Pareek, Alan W Black, and Yulia Tsvetkov. 2019. Measuring bias in contextualized word representations. In *Proceedings of the First Workshop on Gender Bias in Natural Language Processing*, pages 166–172, Florence, Italy. Association for Computational Linguistics.

Heeyoung Lee, Angel Chang, Yves Peirsman, Nathanael Chambers, Mihai Surdeanu, and Dan Jurafsky. 2013. Deterministic coreference resolution based on entity-centric, precision-ranked rules. *Computational Linguistics*, 39(4):885–916.

Heeyoung Lee, Yves Peirsman, Angel Chang, Nathanael Chambers, Mihai Surdeanu, and Dan Jurafsky. 2011. Stanford's multi-pass sieve coreference resolution system at the CoNLL-2011 shared task. In *Proceedings of the Fifteenth Conference on Computational Natural Language Learning: Shared Task*, pages 28–34, Portland, Oregon, USA. Association for Computational Linguistics.

Kenton Lee, Luheng He, Mike Lewis, and Luke Zettlemoyer. 2017. End-to-end neural coreference resolution. In *Proceedings of the 2017 Conference on Empirical Methods in Natural Language Processing*, pages 188–197, Copenhagen, Denmark. Association for Computational Linguistics.

Kenton Lee, Luheng He, and Luke Zettlemoyer. 2018. Higher-order coreference resolution with coarse-to-fine inference. In *Proceedings of the 2018 Conference of the North American Chapter of the Association for Computational Linguistics: Human Language Technologies, Volume 2 (Short Papers)*, pages 687–692, New Orleans, Louisiana. Association for Computational Linguistics.

Xiaoqiang Luo. 2005. On coreference resolution performance metrics. In *Proceedings of Human Language Technology Conference and Conference on Empirical Methods in Natural Language Processing*, pages 25–32, Vancouver, British Columbia, Canada. Association for Computational Linguistics.

Xuezhe Ma, Zhengzhong Liu, and Eduard Hovy. 2016. Unsupervised ranking model for entity coreference resolution. In *Proceedings of the 2016 Conference of the North American Chapter of the Association for Computational Linguistics: Human Language Technologies*, pages 1012–1018, San Diego, California. Association for Computational Linguistics.

Christopher Manning, Mihai Surdeanu, John Bauer, Jenny Finkel, Steven Bethard, and David McClosky. 2014. The Stanford CoreNLP natural language processing toolkit. In *Proceedings of 52nd Annual Meeting of the Association for Computational Linguistics: System Demonstrations*, pages 55–60, Baltimore, Maryland. Association for Computational Linguistics.

Sebastian Martschat. 2013. Multigraph clustering for unsupervised coreference resolution. In *51st Annual Meeting of the Association for Computational Linguistics Proceedings of the Student Research Workshop*, pages 81–88, Sofia, Bulgaria. Association for Computational Linguistics.

Matthew Peters, Mark Neumann, Mohit Iyyer, Matt Gardner, Christopher Clark, Kenton Lee, and Luke Zettlemoyer. 2018. Deep contextualized word representations. In *Proceedings of the 2018 Conference of the North American Chapter of the Association for Computational Linguistics: Human Language Technologies, Volume 1 (Long Papers)*, pages 2227–2237, New Orleans, Louisiana. Association for Computational Linguistics.

Sameer Pradhan, Xiaoqiang Luo, Marta Recasens, Eduard Hovy, Vincent Ng, and Michael Strube. 2014. Scoring coreference partitions of predicted mentions: A reference implementation. In *Proceedings of the 52nd Annual Meeting of the Association for Computational Linguistics (Volume 2: Short Papers)*, pages 30–35, Baltimore, Maryland. Association for Computational Linguistics.

Sameer Pradhan, Alessandro Moschitti, Nianwen Xue, Olga Uryupina, and Yuchen Zhang. 2012. CoNLL-2012 shared task: Modeling multilingual unrestricted coreference in OntoNotes. In *Joint Conference on EMNLP and CoNLL - Shared Task*, pages 1–40, Jeju Island, Korea. Association for Computational Linguistics.

Sameer Pradhan, Lance Ramshaw, Mitchell Marcus, Martha Palmer, Ralph Weischedel, and Nianwen Xue. 2011. CoNLL-2011 shared task: Modeling unrestricted coreference in OntoNotes. In *Proceedings of the Fifteenth Conference on Computational Natural Language Learning: Shared Task*, pages 1–27, Portland, Oregon, USA. Association for Computational Linguistics.

Shubham Toshniwal, Sam Wiseman, Allyson Ettinger, Karen Livescu, and Kevin Gimpel. 2020. Learning to Ignore: Long Document Coreference with Bounded Memory Neural Networks. In *Proceedings of the 2020 Conference on Empirical Methods in Natural Language Processing (EMNLP)*, pages 8519–8526, Online. Association for Computational Linguistics.

Marc Vilain, John Burger, John Aberdeen, Dennis Connolly, and Lynette Hirschman. 1995. A model-theoretic coreference scoring scheme. In *Sixth Message Understanding Conference (MUC-6): Proceedings of a Conference Held in Columbia, Maryland, November 6-8, 1995.*

Alexander Wallin and Pierre Nugues. 2017. Coreference resolution for Swedish and German using distant supervision. In *Proceedings of the 21st Nordic Conference on Computational Linguistics*, pages 46–55, Gothenburg, Sweden. Association for Computational Linguistics.

Sam Wiseman, Alexander M. Rush, Stuart Shieber, and Jason Weston. 2015. Learning anaphoricity and antecedent ranking features for coreference resolution. In *Proceedings of the 53rd Annual Meeting of the Association for Computational Linguistics and the 7th International Joint Conference on Natural Language Processing (Volume 1: Long Papers)*, pages 1416–1426, Beijing, China. Association for Computational Linguistics.

Wei Wu, Fei Wang, Arianna Yuan, Fei Wu, and Jiwei Li. 2020. CorefQA: Coreference resolution as query-based span prediction. In *Proceedings of the 58th Annual Meeting of the Association for Computational Linguistics*, pages 6953–6963, Online. Association for Computational Linguistics.

	CoNLL F_1
Stanford	57.0
c2f-coref	58.3
BERT-base + c2f-coref	59.1
SpanBERT-base + c2f-coref	60.0
BERT-large + c2f-coref	**60.1**
SpanBERT-large + c2f-coref	**60.1**

Table 8: CoNLL F_1 scores computed on the development set of the CoNLL-2012 shared task.

A Stanford's System

The coreference method proposed by Stanford University at the CoNLL 2011 shared task (Pradhan et al., 2011) is based on a succession of ten independent coreference models (or *sieves*), applied from highest to lowest precision. Here we report a short description of the three most effective sieves, according to Lee et al. (2013).

Exact String Match: links two mentions only if they consist of the exact same text string;

Strict Head Match: implements multiple constraints that must all be matched in order to yield a link. First, the mention head word matches any head word of mentions in the antecedent cluster. Then, all the non-stop words[4] in the cluster of the current mention to be solved are included in the set of non-stop words of the antecedent entity cluster. Moreover, the mention's modifiers (e.g., possessive and personal pronouns) must be all included in the modifiers of the antecedent candidate. Eventually, the two mentions cannot be in an i-within-i construct, (i.e., one must not be a child NP in the other's NP constituent);

Pronominal Coreference Sieve: links pronouns to their compatible antecedents enforcing agreement constraints on a set of attributes, such as gender, number, and animacy.

B Implementation and Training Details

As in previous unsupervised work (Ma et al., 2016), we use the version of the OntoNotes corpus in which the supplementary layers of annotation (e.g., parse trees) were provided automatically using off-the-shelf tools. Using Stanford's system, we obtained the noisy labels for the training and development sets of the CoNLL-2012 shared task data (2802 and 343 documents, respectively), for the PreCo training split (36620 documents), and for Litbank (100 documents). As common practice (Toshniwal et al., 2020), on Litbank we perform 10-fold cross-validation, using sets of 80/10/10 documents for train/development/test.

We trained the models using a batch size of 1 document. On the OntoNotes corpus, the ELMo-based c2f-coref model is trained for a maximum of 150 epochs and the BERT and SpanBERT-based models for 20 epochs. On PreCo and Litbank, the SpanBERT-based c2f-coref model is trained for a maximum of 2 and 400 epochs, respectively. During training, BERT and SpanBERT are fine-tuned. The validation sets used to monitor the training are the development set of OntoNotes and Litbank and a held-out portion of 500 documents from the PreCo corpus. For all datasets, the validation metrics were computed with respect to the Stanford's system-produced noisy labels (i.e., no gold coreference information was used in this process).

We keep the hyperparameter configurations as in Lee et al. (2018) and in Joshi et al. (2020). In particular, for each version of BERT and SpanBERT, we use the combination of `max_segment_len` and learning rates illustrated in table 9.

Training the c2f-coref model based on ELMo, BERT-base and SpanBERT-base took ~6 hours on a 24GB Nvidia TITAN RTX, while the training of the models based on the large versions of BERT and SpanBERT required ~12 hours on a 32GB Nvidia Tesla V100.

C Qualitative Examples

Table 10 displays additional examples of coreference chain predictions. In the first example, the weakly-supervised c2f-coref model shows an improved response in terms of both mention identification and cluster assignment, correctly establishing the chains relative to *Alice* and *book*. In example 2, Stanford's system incorrectly links the pronoun *her* to *Mother*, while the neural model rightly associates it with the speaker (*Beth*). Similar improvements are illustrated in sentence 3. Finally, we report an example of an error propagated from the noisy supervision (sentence 4). Note that singleton mentions were removed from the response cluster,

[4] Stop words are, for instance, *there*, *ltd.*, *etc.*, *'s*.

Model	`max_segment_len`	`bert_learning_rate`	`task_learning_rate`
BERT-base + c2f-coref	128	10^{-5}	$2 \cdot 10^{-4}$
SpanBERT-base + c2f-coref	384	$2 \cdot 10^{-5}$	10^{-4}
BERT-large + c2f-coref	384	10^{-5}	$2 \cdot 10^{-4}$
SpanBERT-large + c2f-coref	512	10^{-5}	$3 \cdot 10^{-4}$

Table 9: Hyperparameters used for the BERT/SpanBERT-based cef-coref models.

Ex.	Prediction
1	[***CHAPTER I. Down*** [***the Rabbit-Hole Alice***]$_2$]$_1$ *was beginning to get very tired of sitting by* [[***her***]$_2$ ***sister***]$_3$ *on the bank, and of having nothing to do: once or twice* [***she***]$_2$ *had peeped into the book* [[***her***]$_2$ ***sister***]$_3$ *was reading, but* [***it***]$_1$ *had* [***no pictures or conversations in*** [***it***]$_1$]$_4$, *'and what is the use of a book,' thought Alice 'without* [***pictures or conversations***]$_4$*?'*
	CHAPTER [***I.***]$_1$ *Down the Rabbit-Hole* [***Alice***]$_2$ *was beginning to get very tired of sitting by* [[***her***]$_2$ ***sister***]$_3$ *on the bank, and of having nothing to do: once or twice* [***she***]$_2$ *had peeped into the* [***book***]$_4$ [[***her***]$_2$ ***sister***]$_3$ *was reading, but* [***it***]$_4$ *had no pictures or conversations in* [***it***]$_4$, *'and what is the use of a book,' thought* [***Alice***]$_2$ *'without pictures or conversations?'*
2	*"*[***We***]$_1$*'ve got* [***Father***]$_2$ *and* [***Mother***]$_3$, *and each other," said* [***Beth***]$_4$ *contentedly from* [***her***]$_3$ *corner.*
	"[***We***]$_1$*'ve got* [***Father***]$_2$ *and* [***Mother***]$_3$, *and each other," said* [***Beth***]$_4$ *contentedly from* [***her***]$_4$ *corner.*
3	*At* [***most terrestrial men***]$_1$ *fancied there might be other men upon* [***Mars***]$_2$, *perhaps inferior to* [***themselves***]$_3$ *and ready to welcome a missionary enterprise.*
	At [***most terrestrial men***]$_1$ *fancied there might be other men upon* [***Mars***]$_2$, *perhaps inferior to* [***themselves***]$_1$ *and ready to welcome a missionary enterprise.*
4	*To prevent* [***this***]$_1$, *humans on* [***Mars***]$_2$ *have to wear special shoes to make* [***themselves***]$_1$ *heavier.*
	To prevent [***this***]$_1$, *humans on* [***Mars***]$_2$ *have to wear special shoes to make* [***themselves***]$_1$ *heavier.*

Table 10: Example predictions by Stanford's system (upper sub-row) and c2f-coref (lower sub-row) on Litbank (examples 1-3) and PreCo Dev (example 4). $[\cdot]_x$ represents a mention assigned to cluster x.

and the mentions that appear as singletons in the reported examples are predicted as coreferent to mentions present in other portions of the text.

D Results on the OntoNotes Development Set

We additionally report in Table 8 the results obtained on the development set of the OntoNotes corpus for the five c2f-models.

Multilingual Extraction and Categorization of Lexical Collocations with Graph-aware Transformers

Luis Espinosa-Anke[†] **Alexander Shvets**[♡] **Alireza Mohammadshahi**[◇♠]
James Henderson[◇] **Leo Wanner**[♣♡]
[†]CardiffNLP (Cardiff University) - AMPLYFI [♡]TALN Group, Universitat Pompeu Fabra
[◇]Idiap Research Institute [♠]EPFL [♣]ICREA
espinosa-ankel@cardiff.ac.uk
{alexander.shvets,leo.wanner}@upf.edu
{alireza.mohammadshahi,james.henderson}@idiap.ch

Abstract

Recognizing and categorizing lexical collocations in context is useful for language learning, dictionary compilation and downstream NLP. However, it is a challenging task due to the varying degrees of frozenness lexical collocations exhibit. In this paper, we put forward a sequence tagging BERT-based model enhanced with a graph-aware transformer architecture, which we evaluate on the task of collocation recognition in context. Our results suggest that explicitly encoding syntactic dependencies in the model architecture is helpful, and provide insights on differences in collocation typification in English, Spanish and French.[1]

1 Introduction

Native speech is idiosyncratic. Of special prominence are syntactically-bound restricted binary co-occurrences of lexical items, in which one of the items conditions the selection of the other item. Consider a CNN sports headline from 02/15/2021:

> Rafael Nadal eases into Australian Open quarterfinals, remains on course for record-breaking grand slam (cnn.com).

In this short headline, we see already three of such co-occurrences: *ease* [*into*] *quarterfinals*, *remain* [*on*] *course*, and *record-breaking grand slam*. *Quarterfinals* conditions the selection of [*to*] *ease* [*into*], *course* of *remain* [*on*], and *grand slam* of *record-breaking*. The idiosyncrasy of these co-occurrences becomes obvious when we look at them from a multilingual angle. Thus, in French, instead of the literal translation of *ease* [*into*], we would use *se qualifier* 'qualify [oneself]', in Spanish, *remain* [*on*] will be translated as *seguir* [*en*] 'continue in', and in Italian *record-breaking* will be *da record*, lit. 'of record' – while the translation of *quarterfinals*, *course*, and *grand slam* will be literal. In lexicology, such binary co-occurrences are referred to as *collocations* (Hausmann, 1985; Cowie, 1994; Mel'čuk, 1995; Kilgarriff, 2006), with the conditioning item called the *base* and the conditioned item the *collocate*. Collocations in this sense are of high relevance to second language learning, lexicography and NLP alike, and constitute a challenge for computational models because of their heterogeneity in terms of idiosyncrasy and degree of semantic composition (Mel'čuk, 1995).

Research in NLP has already addressed a number of collocation-related tasks, in particular: **(1)** collocation error detection, categorization, and correction in writings of second language learners (Ferraro et al., 2011; Wanner et al., 2013; Ferraro et al., 2014; Rodríguez-Fernández et al., 2015); **(2)** creation of collocation-enriched lexical resources (Espinosa-Anke et al., 2016; Maru et al., 2019; Di Fabio et al., 2019); **(3)** use of knowledge on collocations in downstream NLP tasks, among them, e.g., machine translation (Seretan, 2014), word sense disambiguation (Maru et al., 2019), natural language generation (Wanner and Bateman, 1990), or semantic role labeling (Scozzafava et al., 2020); **(4)** probes involving collocations for understanding to which extent language models are able to identify non-compositional meanings (Shwartz and Dagan, 2019; Garcia et al., 2021); and **(5)** detection and categorization of collocations with respect to their semantics (Wanner et al., 2006; Espinosa Anke et al., 2019; Levine et al., 2020; Espinosa-Anke et al., 2021). It is this last task which is the focus of this paper.

In general, collocation identification and categorization tend to be treated as two disjoint tasks. Most of the research deals only with collocation identification (Smadja, 1993; Lin, 1999; Pecina and Schlesinger, 2006; Bouma, 2009; Dinu et al., 2014; Levine et al., 2020). Some works deal with the categorization of manually precompiled lists

[1]Data and code are available at https://github.com/TalnUPF/graph-aware-collocation-recognition.

Proceedings of the 11th Joint Conference on Lexical and Computational Semantics, pages 89 - 100
July 14-15, 2022

of collocations, either in isolation (Wanner, 2004; Wanner et al., 2006; Espinosa Anke et al., 2019) or with their original sentence-level contextual information (Wanner et al., 2017). Only a few works in the early phase of the neural network era of NLP address the problem of collocation identification and semantic categorization as a joint task in monolingual settings (Rodríguez-Fernández et al., 2015; Espinosa-Anke et al., 2016). Accordingly, the performance of the models put forward in these works is still rather low. In this paper, we propose a sequence tagging framework for simultaneous collocation identification and categorization, with respect to the taxonomy of *lexical functions* (LFs) (Mel'čuk, 1996). The proposed framework is based on mono- and multilingual BERT-based sequence taggers, which are enhanced by a Graph-aware Transformer (Mohammadshahi and Henderson, 2020, 2021a) in order to ensure that the specific syntactic dependencies between the base and the collocate are taken into account. The sequence taggers are executed as part of a multitask learning setup, which is complemented by a sentence classification task, which predicts the occurrence of an instance of a specific LF instance in the sentence under consideration. Our results for English, French and Spanish show the flexibility of our framework and shed light on the multilingual idiosyncrasies of collocations.

2 Background on Collocations

Although widely used in lexicology in the sense defined above, the term *collocation* is ambiguous in linguistics. As introduced by Firth (1957), it refers to common word co-occurrences in discourse in general. Thus, *cast* and *vote*, *strong* and *tea*, but also *public* and *sector*, *night* and *porter*, *supermarket* and *price* form collocations in English in Firth's sense. In computational linguistics, Firth's definition has been taken up, e.g., by (Church and Hanks, 1989; Lin, 1999; Evert, 2007; Pecina, 2008; Bouma, 2009; Dinu et al., 2014; Levine et al., 2020). To avoid confusion between the two different senses, Krenn (2000) proposed to use the narrower term *lexical collocation* to refer to restricted binary lexical item co-occurrences. In what follows, we will use this term to refer to the definition underlying our work.

Lexical collocations can be typified with respect to the meaning of the collocate and the syntactic structure formed by the base and the collocate.

relation	example	LF label
intense	*heavy*$_C$ ~ *smoker*$_B$	Magn
minor	*occasional*$_C$ ~ *smoker*$_B$	AntiMagn
genuine	*legitimate*$_C$ ~ *demand*$_B$	Ver
non-genuine	*illegitimate*$_C$ ~ *demand*$_B$	AntiVer
Increase.existence	*temperature*$_B$ ~ *rise*$_C$	IncepPredPlus
End.existence	*fire*$_B$ ~ *go out*$_C$	FinFunc0
A0.Come.to.effect	*avalanche*$_B$ ~ *strike*$_C$	Fact0
A0/A1.Cause.existence	*raise*$_C$ ~ *hope*$_B$	CausFunc0
A0/A1.Cause.function	*start*$_C$ ~ *engine*$_B$	CausFact0
Cause.decrease	*relieve*$_C$ ~ *tension*$_B$	CausPredMinus
A0/A1.Cause.involvement	*raise*$_C$ *hope*$_B$ [*in*]	CausFunc1
Emit.sound	*elephant*$_B$ ~ *trumpet*$_C$	Son
A0/A1.act	*lend*$_C$ ~ *support*$_B$	Oper1
A0/A1.begin.act	*gain*$_C$ ~ *impression*$_B$	IncepOper1
A0.end.act	*withdraw*$_C$ ~ *support*$_B$	FinOper1
A0/A1.Act.acc.expectation	*prove*$_C$ ~ *accusation*$_B$	Real1
A2.Act.acc.expectation	*enjoy*$_C$ ~ *support*$_B$	Real2
A2.Act.x.expectation	*betray*$_C$ ~ *trust*$_B$	AntiReal2

Table 1: LF relations used in this paper. 'A_i' refer to AMR argument labels (Banarescu et al., 2013).

Practical collocations dictionaries such as, e.g., the *Oxford Collocations Dictionary*[2] or the *McMillan Collocations Dictionary*[3], already offer a coarse-grained semantic typification. However, their typification still does not make a distinction between, e.g., *control* and *cut* in co-occurrence with *expenditure* or between *cavernous* and *palatial* in co-occurrence with *room* — distinctions which are essential in the context of both second language learning and NLP. To the best of our knowledge, *lexical Functions* (LFs) (Mel'čuk, 1996) are the most fine-grained taxonomy of lexical collocations.

A lexical function (LF) is defined as a function $f(B)$ that delivers for a base B a set of synonymous collocates that express the meaning of f. LFs are assigned Latin abbreviations as labels; cf., e.g., "Oper1" ("operare" 'perform'): Oper1(*condolences*) = {*convey, express, extend*}; "Magn" ("magnum" 'big'/'intense'): Magn(*grief*) = {*deep, inconsolable, great, ...* }. Each LF can also be considered as a specific lexico-semantic relation between the base and the collocate of a collocation in question (Evens, 1988). Table 1 displays the subset of the relations we experiment with, along with their corresponding LF names and illustrative examples.

As seen in Table 1, where pertinent, an LF label also encodes the subcategorization structure of the base+collocate combination; cf., e.g., FinFunc0, Oper1, Real2, etc. Thus, the index '1' in Oper1 encodes the information that the first argument of the base (A0/A1) is realized as grammatical subject and the base itself as object; the '2' in Real2

[2]https://www.freecollocation.com/

[3]https://www.macmillandictionary.com/collocations

encodes the realization of the second argument of the base (A2) as grammatical subject and the base as object; etc. This generic structure translates into a number of *Universal Dependency* (UD) patterns.

3 Related Work

Previous works that consider collocations in a Firthian sense look at word adjacency in terms of n-grams (Smadja, 1993), although most often, statistical measures of co-occurrence are used; cf. Pearce et al. (2002); Pecina and Schlesinger (2006); Pecina (2010); Garcia et al. (2019). Some complement statistical measures by morphological (Krenn and Evert, 2001; Evert and Krenn, 2001) and/or syntactic (Heid and Raab, 1989; Lin, 1999; Seretan and Wehrli, 2006) patterns. In view of the *asymmetrical* nature of the relation between the base and the collocate, e.g., Gries (2013) proposes to investigate "directional measures" as an addition to association measures; Carlini et al. (2014) explicitly encode this asymmetry in terms of NPMI (Bouma, 2009), which is a normalized version of PMI; see also (Garcia et al., 2019). In the collocation classification task, substantial research focused on the identification of *Light Verb Constructions*, which are captured by the Oper- (and partially by the Real-) families of LFs; cf., e.g., (Dras, 1995; Vincze et al., 2013; Kettnerová et al., 2013; Chen et al., 2016; Cordeiro and Candito, 2019; Shwartz and Dagan, 2019), whereas Huang et al. (2009) and Wanner et al. (2017) focus on broad semantic collocation categories. Several works also use LFs as a collocation taxonomy. Thus, Wanner et al. (2006) leverage a vector-based similarity metric on a subset of LFs, whereas Gelbukh and Kolesnikova (2012) explore a suite of classical supervised ML algorithms.

More recently, word embeddings have been successfully applied in unsupervised setups, e.g., Rodríguez Fernández et al. (2016a) use simple vector arithmetic. In supervised setups, we find, first, the "collocate retrieval" approach proposed by Rodríguez Fernández et al. (2016b), who train a linear transformation to go from a "base" to a "collocate" vector space, exploiting regularities in multilingual word embeddings (Mikolov et al., 2013), and second, Espinosa Anke et al. (2019), who train an SVM on a dedicated relation vector space for base and collocate. Embeddings have also been used in multilingual English/Spanish (Rodríguez Fernández et al., 2016b) and English/Portuguese/Spanish

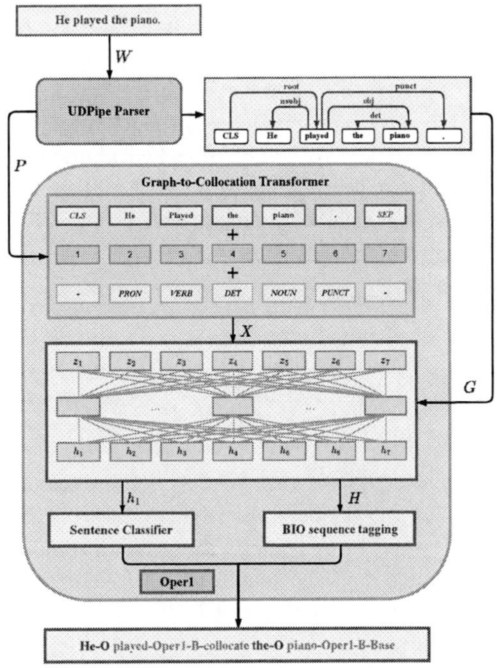

Figure 1: Graph-to-Collocation Transformer, which generates a BIO-tagged sequence given a sentence with, optionally, its parsed tree.

(Garcia et al., 2017) LF classification. While successful, none of these approaches explicitly leveraged in the language model the crucial syntactic dependency information between base and collocate, or considered how sentence-level information could benefit the extraction task – as we do.

4 Graph-to-Collocation Transformer

We propose a Graph-to-Collocation Transformer (G2C-Tr) to: (1) cast collocation identification and classification as a **sequence tagging** problem: as pointed out above, lexical collocations are lexico-semantic relations, and relation extraction has been recently successfully addressed as sequence tagging (Ji et al., 2021); (2) **boost performance** by enabling multitask learning via joint sentence classification and LF-instance BIO tagging; and (3) capture the asymmetric **semantic and syntactic dependency** between the base and the collocate by the use of a modified attention mechanism.

The G2C-Tr is implemented as a suite of BERT-based models for joint sentence classification and sequence tagging. The syntactic dependency graph of the sentence is input to a G2C-Tr model through its attention mechanism. Figure 1 illustrates the framework of our model. Given the input sentence $W = (\mathbf{w}_1, \mathbf{w}_2, ..., \mathbf{w}_N)$, we first use a pre-trained dependency parser $\mathrm{DP}()$ to build the dependency graph G, and Part-of-Speech (PoS) tags $P = (\mathbf{p}_1, \mathbf{p}_2, ..., \mathbf{p}_N)$. Due to the fact that each LF is characterized by the PoS of its lexical items and the syntactic dependency between them, this information is of significant importance. Then, G2C-Tr predicts the tagged sequence $Y = (\mathbf{y}_1, \mathbf{y}_2, ..., \mathbf{y}_N)$ as follows:

$$\begin{cases} P, G = \mathrm{DP}(W) \\ H = \mathrm{Enc}(W, P, G) \\ Y = \mathrm{Dec}(H) \end{cases} \tag{1}$$

where $\mathrm{Enc}()$, $\mathrm{Dec}()$ are the encoder and decoder parts of our model, described below. $H = [\mathbf{h}_1, \ldots, \mathbf{h}_T]$ is the contextualised vector representation, and T is the length of the tokenized sequence. The parameters of $\mathrm{DP}()$ are frozen for training.

4.1 Encoder

To compute the contextualised vector embeddings H, we use a modified version of the Graph-to-Graph Transformer model proposed by Mohammadshahi and Henderson (2021a) to encode both PoS tags (P) and the dependency graph (G). Let us first introduce the encoding mechanism.

4.1.1 Input Embeddings

Given an input sentence (W) with its associated PoS tags (P), the G2C-Tr model first computes the input embeddings ($X = (\mathbf{x}_1, \mathbf{x}_2, ..., \mathbf{x}_T)$). To make it compatible with BERT (Devlin et al., 2019), we append two special tokens, `CLS`, and `SEP` to the start and end of the tokenized sequence, respectively. The input embeddings are calculated as the summation of pre-trained token embeddings of BERT, position embeddings, and PoS tag embeddings (as shown in the green part of Figure 1).

4.1.2 Self-attention Mechanism

Given the input embeddings (X), and a dependency graph (G), we compute the contextualised vector representations (H) using a modified version of the Transformer architecture. The original Transformer model (Vaswani et al., 2017) is composed of several Transformer layers. Each Transformer layer includes a self-attention module and a position-wise feed-forward network. Previous work (Ying et al., 2021; Mohammadshahi and Henderson, 2020, 2021a,b) modified the attention mechanism by adding scalar biases to the attention scores (Ying et al., 2021), or multiplying the query representation with relation vectors (Mohammadshahi and Henderson, 2021a, 2020) to encode graph structures.

Algorithm 1: Build Relation Matrix R

Input: Graph $G = \{(i, j, l)\}, j = 1, .., T$
`/* i,j,l are parent node id, dependent id and label */`
`/* CLS is the root node */`
Output: Relation Matrix R
R = $\mathrm{zeros}(T, T)$
for $(i, j, l) \in G$ **do**
  $r_{i,j} = k_l$
  $r_{j,i} = k_l + |G|$
`/* `k_l` is the index of label `l` */`

Since in collocations, base and collocate are syntactically related and LFs are characterized by specific dependency relations, we modify the attention mechanism of the base transformer model to inject syntactic information. In each Transformer layer, given $Z_n = (\mathbf{z}_1, \mathbf{z}_2, ..., \mathbf{z}_T)$ as the output representations of the previous layer, the attention weights are calculated as a Softmax over the attention scores α_{ij}, defined as:

$$\alpha_{ij} = \frac{1}{\sqrt{3d}} \Big[\mathbf{z}_i \boldsymbol{W^Q} (\mathbf{z}_j \boldsymbol{W^K})^T + \mathbf{z}_i \boldsymbol{W^Q} (\mathbf{r}_{ij} \boldsymbol{W^R_A})^T + \mathbf{r}_{ij} \boldsymbol{W^R_A} (\mathbf{z}_j \boldsymbol{W^K})^T \Big] \tag{2}$$

where $\boldsymbol{W^Q}, \boldsymbol{W^K} \in \mathbb{R}^{d_h \times d}$ are learned query and key parameters. $\boldsymbol{W^R_A} \in \mathbb{R}^{2|G|+1 \times d}$ is the graph relation embedding matrix, learned during training, d_h is the dimension of hidden vectors, d is the head dimension of self-attention module, and $|G|$ is the overal number of dependency labels. $\mathbf{r}_{ij}$ is the one-hot vector representing both the relation and direction of syntactic relation between token $\mathbf{x}_i$ and $\mathbf{x}_j$, so $\mathbf{r}_{ij} \boldsymbol{W^R_A}$ selects the embedding vector for the appropriate syntactic relation. Algorithm 1 shows the procedure of building relation matrix R. Finally, we also add the graph information to the value computation of the Transformer as:

$$\mathbf{v}_i = \sum_j \frac{\exp(\alpha_{ij})}{\sum_j \exp(\alpha_{ij})} (\mathbf{z}_j \boldsymbol{W^V} + \mathbf{r}_{ij} \boldsymbol{W^R_V}) \tag{3}$$

where $\frac{\exp(\alpha_{ij})}{\sum_j \exp(\alpha_{ij})}$ is the Softmax for the attention weights, $\boldsymbol{W^V} \in \mathbb{R}^{d_h \times d}$ is the learned value matrix, $\boldsymbol{W^R_V} \in \mathbb{R}^{2|G|+1 \times d}$ is the graph embedding parameter, and v_i is the output representation of the self-attention mechanism for the token i. To find the output representations (H), we use the same mechanism for position-wise feed-forward layer, and layer normalisation as proposed in Vaswani et al. (2017).

Intuitively, additional terms in Equation 2 (second and third multiplications), and Equation 3 (second addition) add a soft bias toward the syntactic information. The model can still decide to use the injected syntactic information, or just rely on the context information (first terms in both Equation 2 and 3).

4.2 Decoder

BERT-based joint sentence classification and sequence tagging has already been used, e.g., for natural language understanding in the context of question answering and goal-oriented dialogue systems, where it serves for *speaker intent* identification and *semantic frame slot filling* (Chen et al., 2019; Castellucci et al., 2019). In the context of sentence classification, we can specify such a model as:

$$y^i = \text{softmax}\left(\mathbf{W}^i \mathbf{h}_1 + \mathbf{b}^i\right), \quad (4)$$

with i as the index of the sentence that is to be classified, and $\mathbf{h}_1$ as the hidden state of the first pooled special token (CLS in the case of BERT). For sequence tagging, this equation is extended such that the sequence $[\mathbf{h}_2, \ldots, \mathbf{h}_T]$ is fed to word-level softmax layers:

$$y^s_n = \text{softmax}\left(\mathbf{W}^i \mathbf{h}_n + \mathbf{b}_n\right), n \in 1 \ldots |W| \quad (5)$$

where $\mathbf{h}_n$ is the hidden state corresponding to w_n. Finally, the joint model combines both architectures and is trained, end-to-end, by minimizing the cross-entropy loss for both tasks.

$$p\left(y^i, y^s|W\right) = p\left(y^i|H\right) \prod_{n=1}^{N} p\left(y^s_n|H\right) \quad (6)$$

5 Experimental setup

5.1 Dataset Construction

We carry out experiments on English, French, and Spanish datasets constructed from manually compiled instances of LFs. For English and French, we start from Fisas et al. (2020). For English, Fisas et al.'s list is enriched by 500 instances of low-resourced LFs in order to obtain a more balanced distribution of samples across different LFs; for French, we work with their original list. To obtain the LF instances for Spanish, we use the English list: for each English LF instance, we retrieve from the web via the multilingual search index *Reverso-Context*[4] its translation equivalents, which are then examined and filtered manually.

In all three lists, the bases and collocates are annotated with PoS and lemmas. As corpora, we use the 2019 Wikipedia dumps. First, we preprocess (removing metadata and markups) and parse the dumps with the UDPipe2.5 parsers.[5] Then, we extract from the parsed dumps sentences that contain LF instances from any of our collocation lists, observing the PoS of the base and collocate and the dependency relation between them. To further filter the remaining erroneous samples in which the base and the collocate items do not form a collocation, an additional manual check is performed.

The validated sentences and the collocations they contain are labeled. As sentence label, the sentence's most frequent LF or the first one in case of a draw is chosen. In practice, this most often means that the label of the only LF instance in the sentence is chosen. For instance, in the case of CausFunc0, in the French dataset, only in 1.63% of the cases its instances appear together with instances of other LFs in a sentence, in the Spanish dataset these are 1.85% and in the English dataset 3.42%. However, it should be noted that this varies from LF to LF and for some of the LFs our labeling strategy might be an oversimplification. The highest percentage of "cohabitation" with instances of other LFs can be observed for Oper1: in the French dataset in 7.19% of the cases, in the Spanish dataset in 14.32% and in the English dataset in 25.61%. A more detailed study is necessary to identify potential correlations between different LFs.[6]

To annotate collocations, we use the BI labels of the BIO sequence annotation schema ('B-<LF>$_b$' and 'I-<LF>$_b$' for the base, 'B-<LF>$_c$', 'I-<LF>$_c$' for the collocate, and 'O' for other tokens) (Figure 1). The BIO annotation facilitates a convenient labeling of multi-word elements, and the separate annotation of the base and collocate

[4] https://context.reverso.net/

[5] https://ufal.mff.cuni.cz/udpipe

[6] We would like to thank an anonymous reviewer for pointing out the relevance of the correlation between LFs.

allows for flawless annotation of cases where they are not adjacent.

For the experiments, the annotated datasets are split into training, development, and test subsets in proportion 80–10–10 in terms of LF-wise unique instances, such that all occurrences of a specific instance, i.e., a specific lexical collocation, appear only in one of the subsets. Sentences with several collocations that belong to different splits are dropped. The distribution of samples per LF and language is shown in Figure 2.

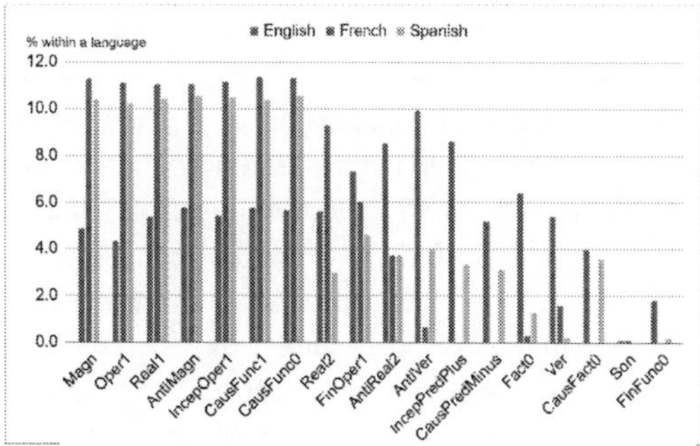

Figure 2: Distribution of examples across lexical functions within a language.

5.2 Experiments

In our experiments, we compare the following architectures:[7]

- Baseline BERT (or similar)-based models (denoted as – in the results tables), specifically BERT-base and large (Devlin et al., 2019), RoBERTa-base and large (Liu et al., 2019); CamemBERT (Martin et al., 2019) and RoBERTa-BNE (Gutiérrez-Fandiño et al., 2021) as monolingual French and Spanish models; and XLM-R for cross-lingual experiments (Conneau et al., 2019).

- Enhanced architectures with the G2C architecture, but without access to the PoS embeddings (G2C (wo) PoS).

- The full model, as depicted in Figure 1, which we refer to as 'G2C'.

In terms of hyperparameter tuning, we fine-tune learning rate and warmup independently for the baseline, G2C(wo)PoS and G2C English models, and fix these values for both French and Spanish. We also use early stopping on the validation set for selecting the best performing models in each configuration.

[7]In all cases, we report only results for the joint architecture, as initial experiments showed a consistent improvement with respect to a sequence tagging-only setup.

6 Results

In what follows, we first present the outcome of the sentence classification and collocation extraction and categorization experiments for the three datasets and then analyze the performance with respect to the individual LFs.

6.1 Sentence classification and collocation extraction results

Tables 2–4 show the performance of various joint models in their original form (marked by '–'), as well as of their G2C(wo)PoS and G2C enhanced variants. We display results on the development ('Dev*') and test sets ('Test*') for the tasks of both sentence classification ('*SentClf') and collocation extraction ('*CollExt'). Sentence classification results are reported in terms of accuracy (there are 18 distinct LF labels), whereas for the collocation extraction task, we report macro F1 over correctly predicted spans. For all experiments, we report average score and standard deviation after three independent runs.

		DevSentClf	DevCollExt	TestSentClf	TestCollExt
	–	66.86+-5.08	63.21+-1.41	66.04+-1.13	62.95+-3.51
BERT_b	G2C(wo)PoS	61.72+-2.92	59.90+-1.50	65.18+-1.61	63.61+-1.25
	G2C	64.23+-1.34	62.48+-0.94	**67.25+-0.82**	64.44+-1.12
	–	66.79+-1.89	65.69+-1.66	63.05+-1.23	61.61+-1.15
BERT_l	G2C(wo)PoS	67.58+-1.19	66.13+-1.48	66.24+-3.30	64.38+-3.36
	G2C	**70.30+-1.89**	**68.82+-0.86**	64.57+-3.60	62.70+-3.74
	–	58.09+-0.49	55.93+-1.52	60.96+-1.72	59.20+-3.31
RoBERTa_b	G2C(wo)PoS	59.89+-1.06	58.05+-0.40	62.51+-0.37	62.17+-0.74
	G2C	59.76+-0.78	58.00+-0.35	62.17+-0.67	61.90+-0.97
	–	67.47+-2.77	66.97+-1.14	65.55+-0.83	64.79+-3.12
RoBERTa_l	G2C(wo)PoS	67.40+-3.49	67.97+-4.77	65.95+-2.44	64.84+-1.29
	G2C	61.71+-2.57	59.85+-2.95	65.10+-3.24	**64.98+-2.85**

Table 2: Main results for the English dataset, comparing BERT and RoBERTa, in their base ($_b$) and large ($_l$) variants, and in vanilla (–) and G2C versions.

The results let us conclude, firstly, that the proposed model is considerably more competitive for the task of the compilation of LF-classified collocation resources than competitive baselines. Secondly, incorporating the G2C architecture contributes to an improvement in performance across the board, for all three languages and for most of the models. Thus, for English we see that BERT base sees an improvement of 1 and 2 points in the sentence classification and sequence labeling results on both the development and test sets, with the improvement on BERT large and RoBERTa base being even more pronounced. RoBERTa large seems to be the model that benefits least from G2C architectures in relative terms, although comparatively, this model is the best performing one on the collocation extraction task on the test set.

With respect to the experiments on French, we can observe that the French camemBERT model does not profit from an enhancement with G2C(wo)PoS; just on the contrary, for the collocation extraction task, performance drops significantly when expanded with either of the G2C variants. This is not the case for XLM-R with its different training variants; its performance is largely maintained in collocation extraction with G2C regimes. The best performance is achieved when XLM-R is enhanced with G2C and trained on both French and English. This also true for the sentence classification task. It is interesting to observe that when trained on English, XLM shows on the development set a higher performance than its extensions for both tasks.

		DevSentClf	DevCollExt	TestSentClf	TestCollExt
camembert Tr: FR	–	66.69+-2.37	62.18+-3.32	54.52+-3.10	51.96+-2.78
	G2C(wo)PoS	64.38+-1.79	38.99+-2.45	50.43+-3.09	30.63+-3.50
	G2C	63.60+-1.33	39.36+-6.38	50.16+-0.46	30.62+-5.24
XLM-r Tr: FR	–	62.22+-2.40	59.30+-5.04	56.38+-3.47	55.23+-3.33
	G2C(wo)PoS	67.08+-4.07	64.32+-6.20	58.41+-3.51	56.97+-2.24
	G2C	64.63+-5.93	61.05+-5.57	56.99+-1.54	55.92+-1.78
XLM-r Tr: EN	–	**67.18+-1.99**	**64.54+-5.65**	54.60+-0.69	52.84+-0.04
	G2C(wo)PoS	65.86+-1.83	64.42+-6.84	54.23+-3.12	50.96+-1.05
	G2C	65.46+-1.49	64.09+-1.03	55.20+-3.62	52.43+-3.77
XLM-r Tr: FR+EN	–	63.07+-2.46	61.59+-1.88	63.35+-2.15	61.32+-1.27
	G2C(wo)PoS	64.40+-0.34	63.88+-1.27	64.95+-0.85	63.55+-0.84
	G2C	62.02+-1.53	61.03+-3.72	**66.48+-1.55**	**64.96+-2.02**

Table 3: Main results for French, comparing the monolingual model CamemBERT with XLM-R variants trained on different slices of the dataset, and G2C(wo)PoS-based extensions.

For Spanish, the performance of the monolingual RoBERTa is in clear contrast to its performance on English. Although it somewhat profits from the G2C enhancement, it seems to underperform compared to XLM-R (which is not the case for English). The reason might be the corpus on which it has been pre-trained (the National Library of Spain corpus) or under-tuning of the set of hyperparameters, which we optimized on the English dataset. We also experiment with XLM-R, trained also only on the Spanish monolingual data (Tr: ES), as well as on the English training set (Tr: EN), and both combined (Tr: ES+EN). Surprisingly enough, XLM-R (stand-alone and G2C+POS-enhanced) performs somewhat better on the test set for both sentence classification and LF-classification when trained on English than when trained on Spanish. In general, the increase in performance provided by the multilingual setting becomes apparent[8], with the G2C model yielding the best results in 3 out of 4 metrics. The best test results of a non-G2C-enhanced model on the collocation extraction task are almost 10 points below the G2Cs models. Moreover, combining both EN and ES training sets into a multilingual language model results in an increase of 6% F1 score. Finally, the differences in the performance of sentence classification and collocation extraction for all three datasets suggest that the predicted sentence label does not always match the label predicted by the BIO-tagger. However, since our primary intention was to use the sentence classifier as an auxiliary task that boosts the performance of the BIO-tagger in a multitask learning setup, we did not analyze the behavior of the sentence classifier and these mismatches in detail.

		DevSentClf	DevCollExt	TestSentClf	TestCollExt
RoBERTa$_{es}$ Tr: ES	–	34.42+-0.65	26.65+-1.20	37.90+-0.67	27.94+-0.16
	G2C(wo)PoS	35.62+-1.90	28.42+-2.20	38.60+-1.33	29.73+-2.05
	G2C	37.60+-3.14	31.20+-1.63	40.49+-0.84	31.20+-5.47
XLM-r Tr: ES	–	66.44+-1.02	62.77+-0.01	52.99+-0.29	51.57+-0.12
	G2C(wo)PoS	68.69+-1.96	66.08+-1.95	54.96+-0.35	53.74+-0.42
	G2C	63.96+-5.06	65.32+-2.20	56.42+-0.84	55.07+-0.71
XLM-r Tr: EN	–	65.02+-1.61	63.16+-1.93	60.56+-0.52	56.95+-2.48
	G2C(wo)PoS	63.00+-0.72	62.21+-0.67	58.82+-1.41	57.90+-0.62
	G2C	62.54+-0.45	61.37+-0.48	57.65+-1.81	54.50+-1.57
XLM-r Tr: ES+EN	–	65.91+-0.13	62.73+-0.59	64.26+-1.97	63.37+-0.72
	G2C(wo)PoS	74.18+-1.01	71.20+-0.88	75.42+-0.02	**72.89+-0.07**
	G2C	**74.52+-0.18**	**71.64+-0.01**	**75.55+-0.18**	72.18+-0.92

Table 4: Main results for Spanish, comparing the monolingual model RoBERTa-bne with XLM-R variants trained on different slices of the dataset, and G2C(wo)PoS-based extensions.

6.2 Lexical Function analysis

To obtain a more detailed picture, we report in Table 5 the results of a run for the best performing models for each language and LF, for both of its collocation elements, the base (_b) and the collocate (_c). While there is certain consistency across LFs and languages, there are also notable cases of discrepancies. For instance, we see that Real2 (as, e.g., *enjoy support*), Ver (as, e.g., *legitimate*

[8]We leave for future work an analysis of whether these results can be fully attributed to multilingual transfer, to having access to more training data, or to a combination of the two.

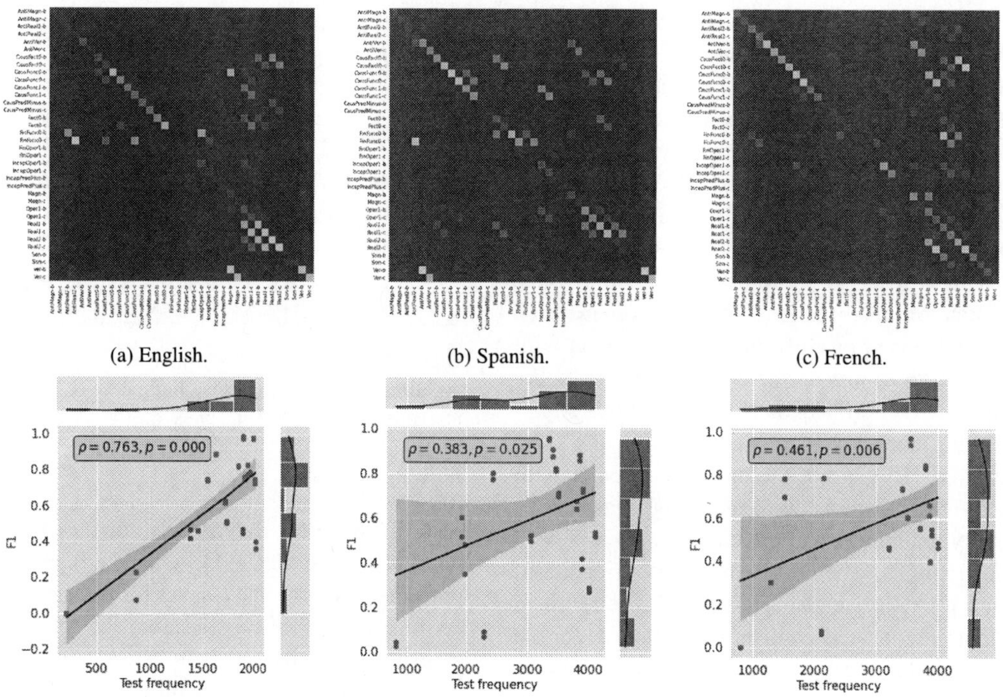

(a) English. (b) Spanish. (c) French.

(d) English. (e) Spanish. (f) French.

Figure 3: LF analysis visualization. Top row shows confusion matrices for the three languages under study, for all LFs and their corresponding base and collocate label. Bottom row shows scatter plot where we show frequency in the x axis, and F1 score in the y axis, again, for each LF.

demand) and Magn (as, e.g., *heavy smoker*) have been better captured in Spanish than in English and French. This can probably be explained by the number of unique instances of the LFs in our training / test data. For instance, in the case of Magn, the ratio between the total number of instances and the number of the unique number of instances in the English test set is 16.8, while in the Spanish test set it is 31.8. In other words, our Spanish dataset contains less variety to express the meaning of intensification than English and French, and is thus easier to capture. Conversely, the performance on Fact0 (as, e.g., *an avalanche strike(s)*) is much better for English, which is likely due to the limitations of the training dataset: out of the 2,112 occurrences of Fact0 instances in total, [*el*] *avión vuela* 'the airplane flies' is counted 602 times.

Note the overall high figures of the recognition of the Magn and AntiMagn instances, and thus a clear distinction between these antonymic LFs, which is a well-known challenge (Rodríguez Fernández et al., 2016b; Wanner et al., 2017). In the case of AntiVer (as, e.g., *illegitimate demand*), the figures are lower in the case of Spanish, which may again hint at the limitations of the Spanish dataset. For the prediction of the individual collocation items, in general, similar results are obtained for the base and collocate. However, some interesting outliers emerge. For instance, for the Spanish CausFact0 (as, e.g., *start an engine*), the performance for the base elements (in our example, *engine*) is more than twice as high as for the collocate elements (in our example, *start*). We hypothesize that this is because most of the CausFact0 base elements in the Spanish dataset denote artefacts and the model learns to recognize them well. Finally, note that only the Spanish model is able to correctly identify a few FinFunc0 collocations (as, e.g., *fire going out*), possibly due to the fact that Spanish contains less multiword expressions and certainly less phrasal verbs associated with this LF.

To understand whether there are obvious sources of confusion across LFs, and whether we can attribute performance to frequency in the datasets, we plot in Figure 3 confusion matrices, as well as the relationship between results and frequency. In English and French, Oper1 and Real1 are great sources of confusion for Real2, especially when it

	EN			ES			FR		
	P	R	F1	P	R	F1	P	R	F1
AntiMagn_b	90.99	93.15	92.06	85.92	89.46	87.65	86.55	81.78	84.10
AntiMagn_c	90.16	94.39	92.23	82.11	91.72	86.65	85.60	83.55	84.56
AntiReal2_b	77.13	83.19	80.05	66.47	86.39	75.14	83.69	65.71	73.62
AntiReal2_c	83.83	93.19	88.26	70.81	92.10	80.07	79.57	68.40	73.62
AntiVer_b	96.05	83.81	89.51	78.53	46.53	58.44	89.57	45.78	60.59
AntiVer_c	93.52	88.88	91.14	78.81	44.95	57.25	86.90	46.12	60.26
CausFact0_b	25.81	08.26	12.51	62.79	16.39	25.99	66.93	19.47	30.17
CausFact0_c	18.33	06.31	09.39	28.36	7.79	12.22	67.20	19.55	30.29
CausFunc0_b	76.94	30.66	43.85	66.27	38.24	48.49	50.02	32.86	39.66
CausFunc0_c	72.05	34.67	46.81	71.04	42.84	53.44	52.19	32.27	39.88
CausFunc1_b	91.15	75.79	82.76	78.37	70.94	72.05	89.00	79.40	83.93
CausFunc1_c	89.40	77.52	83.04	78.37	71.84	74.96	87.63	78.48	82.80
CausPredMinus_b	88.44	68.09	76.94	82.31	91.81	86.80	78.34	62.86	69.75
CausPredMinus_c	86.97	69.70	77.38	82.57	95.26	88.46	86.97	71.05	78.21
Fact0_b	80.10	45.82	58.30	10.28	6.65	8.07	19.40	3.64	6.13
Fact0_c	73.89	49.14	59.02	10.59	7.26	8.61	26.78	4.63	7.90
FinFunc0_b	0.00	0.00	0.00	10.28	6.65	8.07	0.00	0.00	0.00
FinFunc0_c	0.00	0.00	0.00	36.69	12.36	18.50	0.00	0.00	0.00
FinOper1_b	98.44	99.53	98.98	93.83	99.16	96.42	92.20	95.96	94.04
FinOper1_c	97.44	99.69	98.55	64.52	99.46	96.93	92.20	95.96	94.04
IncepOper1_b	78.54	74.91	76.68	60.40	62.15	61.26	96.30	97.25	96.77
IncepOper1_c	82.10	85.59	83.81	58.47	66.09	62.04	71.41	53.95	61.46
IncepPredPlus_b	95.53	99.10	97.28	87.12	90.50	88.78	71.41	53.95	61.46
IncepPredPlus_c	93.75	98.85	96.24	88.21	92.87	90.48	95.42	90.34	92.81
Magn_b	40.35	85.01	54.72	58.21	82.08	68.05	49.24	63.03	55.27
Magn_c	36.94	97.22	51.90	64.44	83.91	70.94	48.63	63.92	55.23
Oper1_b	38.11	79.47	51.90	41.61	59.48	48.97	34.81	68.95	46.26
Oper1_c	37.11	82.24	51.14	39.06	72.75	50.83	32.85	74.13	45.52
Real1_b	41.22	46.48	43.69	29.13	25.30	27.08	37.55	60.57	46.36
Real1_c	37.11	82.24	51.14	29.16	30.07	29.61	39.02	63.45	48.32
Real2_b	50.82	42.43	46.25	59.61	95.56	73.42	54.64	54.53	54.59
Real2_c	50.66	42.53	46.24	59.86	94.65	73.34	55.67	48.91	52.07
Ver_b	80.97	31.99	45.86	84.16	85.30	84.73	89.17	70.31	78.62
Ver_c	78.52	32.74	46.21	84.16	85.30	84.73	88.72	70.17	78.36

Table 5: Results breakdown per language and per LF, where, for each LF, we list individual results for base and collocate categorization.

comes to categorizing Real2 collocates. However, this is not the case for Spanish. In this context, we need to keep in mind that Real1 and Real2 differ only with respect to their subcategorization pattern (in Real1, it is A0/A1, which is realized grammatical subject, and in Real2, it is A2) and that the semantic difference betweeen Oper and Real is rather fine. Still, for Spanish this difference is captured, while for English and French it is not. This is similar for the distinction between CausFact_i / Oper_i and Real_i. Why the confusions are minor for Spanish requires a deeper analysis. We can also see that Magn and Oper bases are often confused in French, but not in English and Spanish. This might be due to parsing and PoS tagging errors. Finally, in the lower part of Figure 3, we see that for English, there is a clear correlation between results and LF frequencies (ρ=0.76), followed by French (ρ=0.46) and, finally, Spanish (ρ=0.38), where we also find highest dispersion across all F1 bins.

7 Conclusions and Future Work

We have proposed an architecture for joint collocation extraction and lexical function typification by explicitly encoding syntactic dependencies in the attention mechanism. Our experiments show that our proposed architecture drastically improves over its language model-only counterparts, and that joint multilingual training is a promising direction for less resourced languages. For the future, we would like to extend these experiments to other languages and explore zero or few-shot prompt-based methods.

Acknowledgements

Many thanks to Beatriz Fisas, Alba Táboas, and Inmaculada López for their help with the datasets. We would also like to thank the anonymous reviewers for their very helpful comments. The work by Alexander Shvets and Leo Wanner has been supported by the European Commission in the context of the Horizon 2020 Research Program under the grant numbers 825079 and 870930. Alireza Mohammadshahi is supported by the Swiss National Science Foundation (grant number CRSII5-180320).

References

Laura Banarescu, Claire Bonial, Shu Cai, Madalina Georgescu, Kira Griffitt, Ulf Hermjakob, Kevin Knight, Philipp Koehn, Martha Palmer, and Nathan Schneider. 2013. Abstract meaning representation for sembanking. In *Proceedings of the 7th Linguistic Annotation Workshop and Interoperability with Discourse*, pages 178–186.

Gerlof Bouma. 2009. Normalized (pointwise) mutual information in collocation extraction. *Proceedings of GSCL*, 30:31–40.

Roberto Carlini, Joan Codina-Filba, and Leo Wanner. 2014. Improving collocation correction by ranking suggestions using linguistic knowledge. In *Proceedings of the third workshop on NLP for computer-assisted language learning*, pages 1–12.

Giuseppe Castellucci, Valentina Bellomaria, Andrea Favalli, and Raniero Romagnoli. 2019. Multi-lingual intent detection and slot filling in a joint bert-based model. *arXiv preprint arXiv:1907.02884*.

Qian Chen, Zhu Zhuo, and Wen Wang. 2019. Bert for joint intent classification and slot filling. *arXiv preprint arXiv:1902.10909*.

Wei-Te Chen, Claire Bonial, and Martha Palmer. 2016. English light verb construction identification using lexical knowledge. In *Proceedings of the Twenty-Ninth AAAI Conference on Artificial Intelligence*, pages 2375–2381.

Kenneth W. Church and Patrick Hanks. 1989. Word Association Norms, Mutual Information, and Lexicography. In *Proceedings of the 27th Annual Meeting of the Association for Computational Linguistics (ACL)*, pages 76–83, Vancouver, Canada.

Alexis Conneau, Kartikay Khandelwal, Naman Goyal, Vishrav Chaudhary, Guillaume Wenzek, Francisco Guzmán, Edouard Grave, Myle Ott, Luke Zettlemoyer, and Veselin Stoyanov. 2019. Unsupervised cross-lingual representation learning at scale. *arXiv preprint arXiv:1911.02116*.

Silvio Ricardo Cordeiro and Marie Candito. 2019. Syntax-based identification of light-verb constructions. In *Proceedings of the 22nd Nordic Conference on Computational Linguistics*, pages 97–104, Turku, Finland. Linköping University Electronic Press.

Anthony P. Cowie. 1994. Phraseology. In R.E. Asher and J.M.Y. Simpson, editors, *The Encyclopedia of Language and Linguistics, Vol. 6*, pages 3168–3171. Pergamon, Oxford.

Jacob Devlin, Ming-Wei Chang, Kenton Lee, and Kristina Toutanova. 2019. BERT: Pre-training of deep bidirectional transformers for language understanding. In *Proceedings of the 2019 Conference of the North American Chapter of the Association for Computational Linguistics: Human Language Technologies, Volume 1 (Long and Short Papers)*, pages 4171–4186, Minneapolis, Minnesota. Association for Computational Linguistics.

Andrea Di Fabio, Simone Conia, and Roberto Navigli. 2019. Verbatlas: a novel large-scale verbal semantic resource and its application to semantic role labeling. In *Proceedings of the 2019 Conference on Empirical Methods in Natural Language Processing and the 9th International Joint Conference on Natural Language Processing (EMNLP-IJCNLP)*, pages 627–637.

A. Dinu, L.P. Dinu, and I.T. Sorodoc. 2014. Aggregation methods for efficient collocation detection. In *Proceedings of LREC*, pages 4041–4045.

Mark Dras. 1995. Automatic identification of support verbs: A step towards a definition of semantic weight. In *Proceedings of the Eighth Australian Joint Conference on Artificial Intelligence*, pages 451–458.

Luis Espinosa-Anke, Jose Camacho-Collados, Sara Rodríguez Fernández, Horacio Saggion, and Leo Wanner. 2016. Extending wordnet with fine-grained collocational information via supervised distributional learning. In *Proceedings of COLING 2016: Technical Papers. The 26th International Conference on Computational Linguistics; 2016 Dec. 11-16; Osaka (Japan): COLING; 2016. p. 900-10.* COLING.

Luis Espinosa-Anke, Joan Codina-Filbá, and Leo Wanner. 2021. Evaluating language models for the retrieval and categorization of lexical collocations. In *Proceedings of the 16th Conference of the European Chapter of the Association for Computational Linguistics: Main Volume*, pages 1406–1417.

Luis Espinosa Anke, Steven Schockaert, and Leo Wanner. 2019. Collocation classification with unsupervised relation vectors. In *Proceedings of the 57th Annual Meeting of the Association for Computational Linguistics*, pages 5765–5772, Florence, Italy. Association for Computational Linguistics.

Martha W. Evens. 1988. *Relational Models of the Lexicon: Representing Knowledge in Semantic Networks.* Cambridge University Press, Cambridge, UK.

Stefan Evert. 2007. Corpora and Collocations. In A. Lüdeling and M. Kytö, editors, *Corpus Linguistics. An International Handbook.* Mouton de Gruyter, Berlin.

Stefan Evert and Brigitte Krenn. 2001. Methods for the qualitative evaluation of lexical association measures. In *Proceedings of the 39th annual meeting of the association for computational linguistics*, pages 188–195.

Gabriela Ferraro, Rogelio Nazar, Margarita Alonso Ramos, and Leo Wanner. 2014. Towards advanced collocation error correction in spanish learner corpora. *Language resources and evaluation*, 48(1):45–64.

Gabriela Ferraro, Rogelio Nazar, and Leo Wanner. 2011. Collocations: A challenge in computer assisted language learning.

John R. Firth. 1957. Modes of Meaning. In J.R. Firth, editor, *Papers in Linguistics, 1934-1951*, pages 190–215. Oxford University Press, Oxford.

Beatriz Fisas, Luis Espinosa Anke, Joan Codina-Filbá, and Leo Wanner. 2020. CollFrEn: Rich bilingual English–French collocation resource. In *Proceedings of the Joint Workshop on Multiword Expressions and Electronic Lexicons*, pages 1–12, online. Association for Computational Linguistics.

Marcos Garcia, Marcos García Salido, and Margarita Alonso Ramos. 2017. Using bilingual word-embeddings for multilingual collocation extraction. In *Proceedings of the 13th Workshop on Multiword Expressions (MWE 2017)*, pages 21–30.

Marcos Garcia, Marcos García Salido, and Margarita Alonso Ramos. 2019. A comparison of statistical association measures for identifying dependency-based collocations in various languages. In *Proceedings of the Joint Workshop on Multiword Expressions and WordNet (MWE-WN 2019)*, pages 49–59.

Marcos Garcia, Tiago Kramer Vieira, Carolina Scarton, Marco Idiart, and Aline Villavicencio. 2021. Probing for idiomaticity in vector space models. In *Proceedings of the 16th Conference of the European Chapter of the Association for Computational Linguistics: Main Volume*, pages 3551–3564.

Alexander Gelbukh and Olga Kolesnikova. 2012. *Semantic analysis of verbal collocations with lexical functions*, volume 414. Springer.

Stefan Th Gries. 2013. 50-something years of work on collocations: What is or should be next.... *International Journal of Corpus Linguistics*, 18(1):137–166.

Asier Gutiérrez-Fandiño, Jordi Armengol-Estapé, Marc Pàmies, Joan Llop-Palao, Joaquín Silveira-Ocampo, Casimiro Pio Carrino, Aitor Gonzalez-Agirre, Carme Armentano-Oller, Carlos Rodriguez-Penagos, and Marta Villegas. 2021. Spanish language models. *arXiv preprint arXiv:2107.07253*.

Franz Josef Hausmann. 1985. Kollokationen im Deutschen Woerterbuch: ein Beitrag zur Theorie des lexicographischen Biespiels. *Lexikographie und Grammatik*.

Ulrich Heid and Sybille Raab. 1989. Collocations in multilingual generation. In *Fourth Conference of the European Chapter of the Association for Computational Linguistics*.

Chung-Chi Huang, Kate H. Kao, Chiung-Hui Tseng, and Jason S. Chang. 2009. A thesaurus-based semantic classification of english collocations. *Computational Linguistics and Chinese Language Processing*, 14(3):257–280.

Bin Ji, Shasha Li, Jie Yu, Jun Ma, and Huijun Liu. 2021. Boosting span-based joint entity and relation extraction via squence tagging mechanism. *https://arxiv.org/abs/2105.10080*.

Václava Kettnerová, Markéta Lopatková, Eduard Bejček, Anna Vernerová, and Marie Podobová. 2013. Corpus based identification of czech light verbs. In *Proceedings of the Seventh International Conference Slovko, Natural Language Processing, Corpus Linguistics, E-Learning*, pages 118–128, Lüdenscheid, Germany. RAM Verlag.

Adam Kilgarriff. 2006. Collocationality (And How to Measure it). In *Proceedings of the 12th Euralex International Congress on Lexicography (EURALEX)*, pages 997–1004, Turin, Italy. Springer-Verlag.

Brigitte Krenn. 2000. *The Usual Suspects: Data-Oriented Models for the Identification and Representation of Lexical Collocations*, volume 7 of *Saarbrücken Dissertations in Computational Linguistics and Language Technology*. DFKI and Universität des Saarlandes.

Brigitte Krenn and Stefan Evert. 2001. Can we do better than frequency? a case study on extracting pp-verb collocations. In *Proceedings of the ACL Workshop on Collocations*, pages 39–46.

Yoav Levine, Barak Lenz, Opher Lieber, Omri Abend, Kevin Leyton-Brown, Moshe Tennenholtz, and Yoav Shoham. 2020. Pmi-masking: Principled masking of correlated spans. *arXiv preprint arxiv:2010.01825*.

Dekang Lin. 1999. Automatic identification of non-compositional phrases. In *Proceedings of the 37th Annual of the Association for Computational Linguistics (ACL)*, pages 317–324.

Hairong Liu, Mingbo Ma, Liang Huang, Hao Xiong, and Zhongjun He. 2019. Robust neural machine translation with joint textual and phonetic embedding. In *Proceedings of the 57th Annual Meeting of the Association for Computational Linguistics*, pages 3044–3049, Florence, Italy. Association for Computational Linguistics.

Louis Martin, Benjamin Muller, Pedro Javier Ortiz Suárez, Yoann Dupont, Laurent Romary, Éric Villemonte de La Clergerie, Djamé Seddah, and Benoît Sagot. 2019. Camembert: a tasty french language model. *arXiv preprint arXiv:1911.03894*.

Marco Maru, Federico Scozzafava, Federico Martelli, and Roberto Navigli. 2019. Syntagnet: challenging supervised word sense disambiguation with lexical-semantic combinations. In *Proceedings of the 2019 Conference on Empirical Methods in Natural Language Processing and the 9th International Joint Conference on Natural Language Processing (EMNLP-IJCNLP)*, pages 3525–3531.

Igor A. Mel'čuk. 1995. Phrasemes in Language and Phraseology in Linguistics. In M. Everaert, E.-J. van der Linden, A. Schenk, and R. Schreuder, editors, *Idioms: Structural and Psychological Perspectives*, pages 167–232. Lawrence Erlbaum Associates, Hillsdale.

Igor A. Mel'čuk. 1996. Lexical functions: A tool for the description of lexical relations in the lexicon. In Leo Wanner, editor, *Lexical Functions in Lexicography and Natural Language Processing*, pages 37–102. Benjamins Academic Publishers, Amsterdam.

Tomas Mikolov, Quoc V Le, and Ilya Sutskever. 2013. Exploiting similarities among languages for machine translation. *arXiv preprint arXiv:1309.4168*.

Alireza Mohammadshahi and James Henderson. 2020. Graph-to-graph transformer for transition-based dependency parsing. In *Findings of the Association for Computational Linguistics: EMNLP 2020*, pages 3278–3289, Online. Association for Computational Linguistics.

Alireza Mohammadshahi and James Henderson. 2021a. Recursive Non-Autoregressive Graph-to-Graph Transformer for Dependency Parsing with Iterative Refinement. *Transactions of the Association for Computational Linguistics*, 9:120–138.

Alireza Mohammadshahi and James Henderson. 2021b. Syntax-aware graph-to-graph transformer for semantic role labelling.

Darren Pearce et al. 2002. A comparative evaluation of collocation extraction techniques. In *LREC*.

Pavel Pecina. 2008. A Machine Learning Approach to Multiword Expression Extraction. In *Proceedings of the LREC 2008 Workshop Towards a Shared Task for Multiword Expressions)*, pages 54–57, Marrakech, Morocco.

Pavel Pecina. 2010. Lexical association measures and collocation extraction. *Language resources and evaluation*, 44(1):137–158.

Pavel Pecina and Pavel Schlesinger. 2006. Combining association measures for collocation extraction. In *Proceedings of the COLING/ACL 2006 main conference poster sessions*, pages 651–658.

Sara Rodríguez Fernández, Roberto Carlini, Luis Espinosa-Anke, and Leo Wanner. 2016a. Example-based acquisition of fine-grained collocational resources. In *Calzolari N, Choukri K, Declerck T, Goggi S, Grobelnik M, Maegaard B, Mariani J, Mazo H, Moreno A, Odijk J, Piperidis S, editors. LREC 2016, Tenth International Conference on Language Resources and Evaluation; 2016 May 23-28; Portorož (Slovenia).[Sl]: European Language Resources Association (ELRA); 2016. Session P28, Multiword expressions; p. 2317-22.* ELRA (European Language Resources Association).

Sara Rodríguez-Fernández, Roberto Carlini, and Leo Wanner. 2015. Classification of grammatical collocation errors in the writings of learners of spanish. *Procesamiento del Lenguaje Natural*, 55.

Sara Rodríguez Fernández, Luis Espinosa-Anke, Roberto Carlini, and Leo Wanner. 2016b. Semantics-driven recognition of collocations using word embeddings. In *Proceedings of the 54th Annual Meeting of the Association for Computational Linguistics; 2016 Aug. 7-12; Berlin (Germany).[place unknown]: ACL; 2016. Vol. 2, Short Papers; p. 499-505.* ACL (Association for Computational Linguistics).

Federico Scozzafava, Marco Maru, Fabrizio Brignone, Giovanni Torrisi, and Roberto Navigli. 2020. Personalized pagerank with syntagmatic information for multilingual word sense disambiguation. In *Proceedings of the 58th Annual Meeting of the Association for Computational Linguistics: System Demonstrations*, pages 37–46.

Violeta Seretan. 2014. On collocations and their interaction with parsing and translation. *Informatics*, 1(1):11–31.

Violeta Seretan and Eric Wehrli. 2006. Accurate collocation extraction using a multilingual parser. In *Proceedings of the 21st international conference on computational linguistics and 44th annual meeting of the Association for Computational Linguistics*, pages 953–960.

Vered Shwartz and Ido Dagan. 2019. Still a pain in the neck: Evaluating text representations on lexical composition. *Transactions of the Association for Computational Linguistics*, 7:403–419.

Frank Smadja. 1993. Retrieving collocations from text: Xtract. *Computational linguistics*, 19(1):143–178.

Ashish Vaswani, Noam Shazeer, Niki Parmar, Jakob Uszkoreit, Llion Jones, Aidan N Gomez, Ł ukasz Kaiser, and Illia Polosukhin. 2017. Attention is all you need. In *Advances in Neural Information Processing Systems*, volume 30. Curran Associates, Inc.

Veronika Vincze, István Nagy, and János Zsibrita. 2013. Learning to detect English and Hungarian light verb constructions. *ACM Transactions on Speech and Language Processeing*, 10(2):1–25.

Leo Wanner. 2004. Towards automatic fine-grained semantic classification of verb-noun collocations. *Natural Language Engineering*, 10(2):95–143.

Leo Wanner and John A. Bateman. 1990. A collocational based approach to salience sensitive lexical selection. In *Proceedings of the 5th International Workshop on Natural Language Generation*, Dawson, PA.

Leo Wanner, Bernd Bohnet, and Mark Giereth. 2006. Making sense of collocations. *Computer Speech & Language*, 20(4):609–624.

Leo Wanner, Gabriela Ferraro, and Pol Moreno. 2017. Towards distributional semantics-based classification of collocations for collocation dictionaries. *International Journal of Lexicography*, 30(2):167–186.

Leo Wanner, M Alonso Ramos, Orsolya Vincze, Rogelio Nazar, Gabriela Ferraro, Estela Mosqueira, and Sabela Prieto. 2013. Annotation of collocations in a learner corpus for building a learning environment. *Twenty years of learner corpus research. Looking back, moving ahead*, pages 493–503.

Chengxuan Ying, Tianle Cai, Shengjie Luo, Shuxin Zheng, Guolin Ke, Di He, Yanming Shen, and Tie-Yan Liu. 2021. Do transformers really perform bad for graph representation?

Dyna-bAbI: unlocking bAbI's potential with dynamic synthetic benchmarking

Ronen Tamari[†*] **Kyle Richardson**[*] **Noam Kahlon**[†] **Aviad Sar-Shalom**[△]
Nelson F. Liu[◇] **Reut Tsarfaty**[*‡] **Dafna Shahaf**[†]
[†]The Hebrew University of Jerusalem [*]Allen Institute for AI
[‡]Bar-Ilan University [△]Tel-Aviv University [◇]Stanford University
{ronent,dshahaf}@cs.huji.ac.il, {reutt,kyler}@allenai.org

Abstract

While neural language models often perform surprisingly well on natural language understanding (NLU) tasks, their strengths and limitations remain poorly understood. Controlled synthetic tasks are thus an increasingly important resource for diagnosing model behavior. In this work we focus on story understanding, a core competency for NLU systems. However, the main synthetic resource for story understanding, the bAbI benchmark, lacks such a systematic mechanism for controllable task generation. We develop Dyna-bAbI, a dynamic framework providing fine-grained control over task generation in bAbI. We demonstrate our ideas by constructing three new tasks requiring compositional generalization, an important evaluation setting absent from the original benchmark. We tested both special-purpose models developed for bAbI as well as state-of-the-art pre-trained methods, and found that while both approaches solve the original tasks (>99% accuracy), neither approach succeeded in the compositional generalization setting, indicating the limitations of the original training data. We explored ways to augment the original data, and found that though diversifying training data was far more useful than simply increasing dataset size, it was still insufficient for driving robust compositional generalization (with <70% accuracy for complex compositions). Our results underscore the importance of highly controllable task generators for creating robust NLU systems through a virtuous cycle of model and data development.[1]

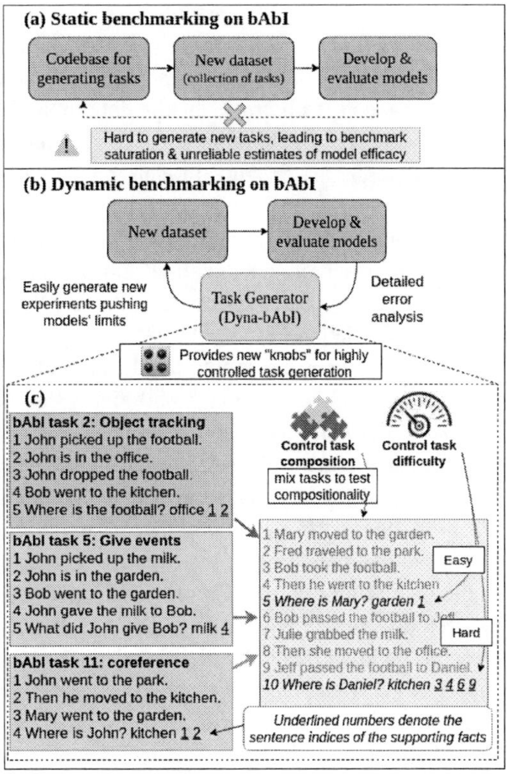

Figure 1: (a) Low task configurability leads to static datasets, benchmark saturation & unreliable model development. (b) We propose a dynamic benchmarking approach; developing models and tasks in a tight feedback loop using (c) Dyna-bAbI task generator. Dyna-bAbI provides fine-grained control over task structure, composition and difficulty, yielding challenging new test sets exposing limitations of state-of-the-art models.

1 Introduction

Considerable progress has been made recently in natural language understanding (NLU), driven largely by advances in model pre-training (Devlin et al., 2019; Raffel et al., 2020) and the development of large-scale NLU benchmarks across a wide range of tasks (Wang et al., 2018, 2019; Liang et al., 2020). Such successes, however, have coincided with the discovery of various shortcomings in existing human curated datasets, largely related to *annotation artifacts* (Gururangan

* Work begun during an internship at the Allen Institute.
[1] Data and code available at https://dyna-babi-project.github.io/.

Proceedings of the 11th Joint Conference on Lexical and Computational Semantics, pages 101 - 122
July 14-15, 2022 ©2022 Association for Computational Linguistics

et al., 2018), or systematic biases that create shortcuts that can inflate model performance and harm generalization.

In order to overcome these issues, two avenues of research have recently gained traction: 1) development of *dynamic benchmarks* (Potts et al., 2021; Kiela et al., 2021) where, in contrast to conventional *static* benchmarks, evaluation and data collection are conducted interactively with humans and models in a rapidly evolving feedback loop and; 2) renewed interest in *synthetic benchmarks* (Lake and Baroni, 2018; Sinha et al., 2019; Clark et al., 2020; Ruis et al., 2020) that allow for absolute control over the data creation process in order to help understand the strengths and weaknesses of existing models on targeted tasks and language phenomena.

Story understanding is a particularly important domain for research on dynamic and synthetic benchmarks; it is a core competency for NLU systems (McClelland et al., 2020; Dunietz et al., 2020), but the scale and annotation detail required make human data collection prohibitively costly. However, the main synthetic resource for story understanding remains the bAbI task suite (Weston et al., 2016), which is saturated by models reaching near-perfect performance (Liu et al., 2021), and further limited by exploitable biases in the data (Kaushik and Lipton, 2018). Despite its creators' initial intentions, bAbI has largely remained a static benchmark limited to a small subset of the tasks potentially possible to generate within the bAbI "micro-world". Accordingly, two natural questions arise: **(Q1)** *is near-perfect model performance on the original bAbI tasks a reliable indicator of story understanding competence?*; **(Q2)** *are there still interesting challenges to discover inside the broader bAbI task space that help identify weaknesses in current models and drive modelling innovation?*

To answer these questions, we employ a *dynamic synthetic benchmarking* approach on bAbI, combining the benefits of the agile approach of recent dynamic benchmarks with the scale and control provided by synthetic datasets. As illustrated in Figure 1, in dynamic synthetic benchmarks the data generator itself is designed for agile development, enabling experimentation with increasingly complex tasks and a wider range of linguistic phenomena.[2] Constructing challenging tasks is a challenge in and of itself, requiring precise control over the reasoning patterns underlying each question. To meet these requirements, we developed a new task generator for bAbI called Dyna-bAbI[3].

Using Dyna-bAbI, we first devise new splits that systematically test *compositional generalization* across tasks; as shown in Fig. 1c, we test models on novel combinations (right side, line 10) of concepts seen at training, like co-reference and object tracking (left). We find that training on the original bAbI tasks (hereafter: bAbI 1.0) is not sufficient for models to attain good compositional generalization. Though general purpose pre-trained models far outperform special-purpose (non-pre-trained) architectures developed for bAbI, they still suffer a 20-50% drop in accuracy compared to the non-pre-trained models which suffer a 50-80% drop. Both types attain near perfect performance on the original tasks, suggesting that bAbI 1.0 is not challenging enough to differentiate between the two classes of models **(Q1)**.

We next investigate how different enhancements of training data affect compositional generalization: (a) injecting more questions into bAbI 1.0, and (b) generating new, more diverse training samples. Compared to question injection, we find that diverse training data better facilitates compositional generalization, as well as being more data efficient. However, neither approach drives *reliable* compositional generalization; a representative state-of-the-art (SOTA) model, T5 (Raffel et al., 2020), demonstrates a lack of robustness to novel combinations and also exhibits knowledge inconsistency, for example, by correctly answering certain types of questions but systematically failing to answer equivalent paraphrases. These results suggest that there remain many important challenges within the broader bAbI task space **(Q2)** which can be discovered through more careful control of task generation.

To sanity-check the quality of our new tests compared with bAbI 1.0, we employ the notion of *concurrence* proposed by Liu et al. (2021);

[2] While our framework does not enable *automatic* collection of new data based on model errors as in other dynamic benchmarks, we still chose the term "dynamic" to highlight their important common function: data generation frameworks that enable easily "moving the goalposts" in meaningful directions (in our case, for probing models' systematic generalization capacities).

[3] Implemented in Python for improved accessibility compared with the original Lua implementation (`https://github.com/facebookarchive/bAbI-tasks`).

concurrence is a measure of correlation between models' performance on a synthetic task and their performance on an existing, non-synthetic NLU benchmark. We find high concurrence between our new challenge tasks and the widely used SQuAD dataset (Rajpurkar et al., 2016), in contrast to bAbI 1.0, which achieved low concurrence.

Giving the continued interest in using bAbI 1.0 to evaluate new modelling approaches (Banino et al., 2020, 2021; Schlag et al., 2021), our new challenge splits and the Dyna-bAbI task generator contribute to more reliably guiding future efforts. While we focused on bAbI, our results apply more generally, telling a cautionary tale about the limits of static synthetic datasets, and motivating the development of controllable task generators for dynamic synthetic benchmarking.

2 Related Work

Our work brings together two promising areas of current research: dynamic benchmarking such as Dynabench (Kiela et al., 2021) that address many existing issues with static benchmarks (Bowman and Dahl, 2021), and synthetic benchmarking, which is widely used for high-precision and data-intensive problems such as relational and logical reasoning (Sinha et al., 2019; Clark et al., 2020; Betz et al., 2021; Richardson and Sabharwal, 2022), robot planning (Banerjee et al., 2020), instruction following and language grounding (Long et al., 2016; Lake and Baroni, 2018) among many others (Richardson et al., 2020; Khot et al., 2021). Most approaches to synthetic benchmarking focus on model development on a static benchmark, and are not designed to facilitate agile and highly controlled task space exploration, which is our focus here.

The recent gSCAN dataset (Ruis et al., 2020) and later extensions (Qiu et al., 2021; Wu et al., 2021) can be seen as an example of a synthetic benchmark "going dynamic". Our work differs in terms of target domain (story understanding as opposed to multi-modal language grounding), and we further focus attention on a more general research direction of intentional, a-priori design of NLU benchmarks for agile development. In this regard, our work can be seen as part of a trend towards *data-centric* research efforts in response to prevailing *model-centric* research, which generally focuses heavily on architectural design and novelty (Kaushik and Lipton, 2018), at the expense of work on the data side (Sambasivan et al., 2021; Rogers, 2021).

We address the domain of story understanding as a particularly core (and data-intensive) capacity underlying language use (McClelland et al., 2020), thought to require constructing and manipulating situation models of entities and their relations as they unfold throughout discourse (Zwaan, 2016; Tamari et al., 2020). Procedural text datasets (Dalvi et al., 2018; Tandon et al., 2020) are closely related in that they provide detailed annotation of entities and state changes, and have mostly focused on relatively small and static benchmarks using human collected data. Overall, recent works identify a lack of benchmarks which systematically probe the situation models constructed by systems processing discourse-level texts (Sugawara et al., 2021).

The bAbI benchmark (Weston et al., 2016) is seen as highly relevant in terms of objective (targeting situation modelling) (Dunietz et al., 2020), but has been viewed critically due to its constrained nature and exploitable artifacts (Kaushik and Lipton, 2018). Our work focuses on improving the evaluation in bAbI through compositional generalization, widely used across NLP to more rigorously probe model robustness (Finegan-Dollak et al., 2018; Keysers et al., 2020; Gontier et al., 2020; Yanaka et al., 2021), but to our knowledge still not applied to story understanding or bAbI.

3 Synthetic Dynamic Benchmarking on bAbI

3.1 Dyna-bAbI

What makes a synthetic benchmark *dynamic*? We think of a dynamic synthetic benchmark as a highly controllable task generator, enabling rapid exploration of interesting areas of a task space. The original bAbI 1.0 simulator code does not readily facilitate such exploration; each of the bAbI 1.0 tasks is generated by a hard-coded script which does not enable parametric manipulation of interesting generation aspects such as question difficulty or compositionality.

Accordingly, we developed Dyna-bAbI, a Python-based version of the original simulator. Dyna-bAbI facilitates control of task generation through a configuration file, effectively abstracting away much of the underlying implementation complexity. The configuration file allows users to specify high-level task parameters such as the set of target concepts, passage length, and filtering conditions to mine for harder/rarer examples. We also modularized the code to facilitate adding new questions and other concepts more easily.

In this next sections we describe the underlying structure of the bAbI 1.0 tasks, and how we combine them using Dyna-bAbI to create more complex compositional generalization tasks.

3.2 bAbI task structure

A task in bAbI 1.0 is a set of train, validation and test splits. Each split is a set of instances, where an instance is a tuple (p, q, a)=(*passage, question, answer*). Passages are generated using a micro-world simulator by sampling a valid sequence of world events from an event set $\mathcal{E}$ and generating a linguistic description of them. By default, linguistic descriptions are generated by a simple sentence-level mapping from an event to a natural language sentence. For example, the event `move(john,park)` could be translated to "John moved to the park."

Some tasks also incorporate more complex linguistic mappings between events and sentences, such as co-reference: the event sequence (`move(john,park)`, `move(john,kitchen)`) could be mapped to "John moved to the park. Then he went to the kitchen." We denote the set of possible linguistic mappings by $\mathcal{L}$.

Finally, a valid question-answer pair (q,a) over p is sampled from question set $\mathcal{Q}$. In bAbI, each split is generated using some particular subset of all possible events, linguistic constructs and questions (§3.3); for a given split we can then define its *concept set*, $\mathcal{C} = \mathcal{E} \cup \mathcal{L} \cup \mathcal{Q}$. Instances also include a set of supporting facts (f), or the relevant lines from which a can be derived (see Fig. 1). The support composition (f_c) is the set of events and linguistic constructs contained in f (see examples in §4.2.1), and is useful for characterizing compositionality performance (§3.4).

3.3 Original bAbI 1.0 tasks

Our focus here is on a particular subset of 12 bAbI 1.0 tasks evaluating aspects of story understanding. Table 1 summarizes them, detailing $\mathcal{E}$,$\mathcal{L}$,$\mathcal{Q}$ for each task. For $\mathcal{L}$, we list only complex constructs beyond the default event-sentence mapping (which is present in every task). See appendix A.1 for additional details on task construction. Not all of the story understanding tasks are considered. For example, tasks 14 and 20 address time reasoning and agent motivations, and we leave their integration for future work.

Task	Events ($\mathcal{E}$)	Linguistic Constructs ($\mathcal{L}$)	Questions ($\mathcal{Q}$)	Avg. sents. & supp. facts per story
1	MOVE	-	where-P	6, 1
2	MOVE, POSS	-	where-O	15.52, 2
3	MOVE, POSS	-	where-was-O	51.9, 3
5	MOVE, GIVE, POSS	-	give-qs	20.1, 1
6	MOVE	-	yes-no	6.27, 1
7	MOVE, GIVE, POSS	-	counting	8.67, 2.33
8	MOVE, POSS	-	list	8.75, 1.94
9	MOVE	NEGATE	yes-no	6, 1
10	MOVE	INDEF	yes-no	6, 1
11	MOVE	CO-REF	where-P	6, 2
12	MOVE	CONJ.	where-P	6, 1
13	MOVE	CONJ., CO-REF	where-P	6, 2

Table 1: Subset of 12 bAbI 1.0 tasks considered here. Each task is characterized by the possible events, linguistic constructs and questions that can occur in instances. POSS (possession) is short for GRAB and DROP events. Statistics based on training sets. A large space of task configurations remains unexplored.

3.4 Compositional generalization on bAbI

As can be seen in Table 1, many possible task configurations are not covered by the original benchmark; which directions should be explored? We focus on out-of-distribution (OOD) robustness, which is increasingly seen as a vital evaluation criteria across AI/NLP research (Shanahan et al., 2020; Hendrycks et al., 2020). We target *compositional generalization*, a particularly important class of OOD problems (Lake et al., 2017; Lake and Baroni, 2018). Compositional generalization refers to the ability to systematically generalize to test inputs containing novel combinations of more basic elements seen at training time (Partee et al., 1995). For example, a model that has learned basic object tracking and co-reference *separately* (tasks 2 and 11, see Fig. 1c) could be expected to solve tasks requiring a *mixture* of both object tracking and co-reference (Fig. 1c, line 10 question on right side). Compositional tasks are absent from bAbI 1.0 which features only IID test sets (independent, identically distributed).[4]

Compositional task generation. To create compositional generalization tasks in practice, we create training (and validation) splits composed of M sub-tasks with concept sets $\{\mathcal{C}^i_{\text{train}}\}^M_{i=1}$, and a test set $\mathcal{C}_{\text{test}}$ such that $\mathcal{C}_{\text{test}} \neq \mathcal{C}^i_{\text{train}} \forall i$, but $\mathcal{C}_{\text{test}} = \bigcup^M_{i=1} \mathcal{C}^i_{\text{train}}$. In other words, each training sub-task can be thought of focusing on a particular subset of test concepts, so models are exposed to all test concepts at training time, but not to all combinations of them (Yanaka et al., 2021).

Task difficulty. We hypothesize that support composition (f_c) and supporting fact set size ($|f|$) are main factors underlying a particular instance's difficulty, and especially *novel* support compositions not seen at training time. Additionally, the difference between train and test splits results in potentially harder distractors, as test-time distractors appear in novel contexts.

Our notions of concepts and support composition resemble atoms and compounds in DBCA, a related study on compositionality (Keysers et al., 2020). While DBCA enables automatic creation of compositional train and test splits, we opt here for a more human-interpretable representation that allows more precise manual control of the combinations of concepts a model is exposed to at train and test time.

Quality comparison vs. bAbI 1.0 tasks. Intuitively, good synthetic datasets help drive the development of better modelling approaches. Our new compositional tasks might be harder than bAbI 1.0, but how do we know whether they are a more useful target? To provide a preliminary answer to this question, we adopt the notion of *concurrence* as a quality measure (Liu et al., 2021). Two benchmarks are said to have high concurrence when they rank a set of modelling approaches similarly. Concurrence offers a way to formalize the intuition above, as high concurrence between a synthetic and natural language benchmark suggests that the synthetic benchmark could have driven similar innovations. We follow the setup of Liu et al. (2021) using SQuAD for the natural language benchmark.[5] Notably, bAbI 1.0 achieved very low concurrence with SQuAD; for example, pre-training consistently yields large gains on SQuAD, but on bAbI 1.0, both pre-trained and non-pre-trained models achieve perfect performance on many tasks. The low concurrence thus suggests that bAbI 1.0 may be an unreliable benchmark for model development, and highlights the importance of improving its quality.

Split	Type	Avg. length	Size	Avg. supp. fact set size
concat(T2)	Train	10.76	18,000	2
concat(T7)	Train	13.5	63,000	1.68
inject(T7)	Train	23.25	190,158	1.42
diverse(T7)	Train	20	17,000	2.17
concat(T12)	Train	10.8	108,000	1.42
inject(T12)	Train	15.97	368,831	1.28
diverse(T12)	Train	20	24,772	2.45
mix(T2)	Test	13.25	1,000	2.05
mix(T7)	Test	20	3,000	2.50
mix(T12)	Test	20	6,000	3.70

Table 2: Splits used for our experiments. All except the original data (*concat*) are created with Dyna-bAbI.

4 Experiments

With the controllable task generation afforded by Dyna-bAbI, we can now create datasets probing deeper story understanding capabilities of models.

We present two main experiments targeting the following questions:

- Exp. 1: (q1.a) What role does model architecture play in the capacity for compositional generalization? (q1.b) What is the concurrence of our compositional tasks with real datasets, compared with bAbI 1.0?
- Exp. 2: (q2) How do training data quantity and diversity affect compositional generalization?

Data

For our experiments we created 4 kinds of splits over three subsets of bAbI 1.0 tasks, summarized in Table 2. We denote a subset of tasks T, and consider $T_2 = \{2, 11\}$, $T_7 = \{1, 2, 3, 5, 11, 12, 13\}$, and $T_{12} = \{1, 2, 3, 5, ..., 13\}$.

- ***concat*** splits are simply concatenations of the official data for the tasks T. We considered the larger version where each task consists of 9,000/1,000 training/development examples; e.g., *concat(T_2)* consists of 18,000 training examples and 2,000 development examples.
- ***inject*** splits enrich the *concat* data as follows:

[4] Weston et al. (2016) noted that transfer learning was an important goal out of the original work's scope.

[5] Liu et al. (2021) consider a set of 20 modelling approaches used on SQuAD, including 10 pre-trained and 10 non-pre-trained methods.

for each question in the original data, we supplement it with all possible additional questions of the specified types. In this work, the supplement question types were *where-P* and *where-O* (to provide location information of objects and agents).
- ***diverse*** splits use rejection sampling to generate more diverse samples, such that the number of supporting facts per question is roughly uniform across all sub-task instances for a given question type. Without rejection sampling, most generated questions would be trivial (e.g., 1-2 supporting facts). Compositionality is retained by holding out certain combinations. In particular, at training time, complex linguistic constructs (e.g., co-reference) are only seen with MOVE events.
- ***mix*** are test splits generated using rejection sampling like *diverse*, and consist of instances which may feature elements from any of the considered tasks. As a result, questions in *mix* splits require novel/more complex reasoning patterns compared to those seen during training.

See appendix A.1 for examples and extended details on task generation.

4.1 Exp. 1: Can training on bAbI 1.0 facilitate compositional generalization?

For this experiment, we compared models on T_2 and T_7, since they allow for a direct conversion to an extractive QA format,[6] enabling us to use the same concurrence framework of Liu et al. (2021).

Models. We considered 3 classes of models:
- Non-pre-trained specialized architectures for bAbI 1.0 including EntNet (Henaff et al., 2017) and STM (Le et al., 2020), the latter being current SOTA on bAbI 1.0[7].
- Non-pretrained general-purpose QA methods, such as BiDAF (Seo et al., 2017).
- General purpose pre-trained approaches including RoBERTa (Liu et al., 2020) and T5 (base) (Raffel et al., 2020).

The last two categories are comprised of the 20 models evaluated in Liu et al. (2021), with the addition of T5 to the last group. For implementation details, see appendix A.2.

[6] Tasks 6-10 require generative QA, for answering *yes-no*, *count* and *list* questions.

[7] As of March 10, 2022.

Results & Analysis

Experiment results are summarized in Table 3. All models perform well in IID settings, but performance drops considerably in OOD settings

Architecture alone is not a significant compositionality driver (q1.a). The large OOD performance gap between pre-trained and non-pre-trained models indicates that pre-training plays a much greater role than specialized architectures for QA performance, adding to similar findings in other NLP domains (Hendrycks et al., 2020). These results raise questions about special purpose relational reasoning architectures that continue to be developed today: the poor OOD performance suggests that such models may not be fulfilling their intended design. Either way, these results underscore the importance of rigorous evaluation to verify that modelling motivations are borne out in practice (Aina et al., 2019).

Compositionality increases concurrence (q1.b). As can be seen in the Fig. 2 plots[8], increasing compositionality is correlated with increased concurrence. In contrast to the original bAbI 1.0 tasks which exhibited virtually no correlation with SQuAD, our compositional task *mix*(T_7) exhibits high concurrence of $r = 0.92, \tau = 0.78$ (Pearson and Kendall correlation functions, resp.). These results are comparable to other *natural* language as well as purpose-built synthetic datasets considered in Liu et al. (2021), which feature r, τ in the ranges $[0.87, 0.99]$ and $[0.77, 0.94]$, respectively. Our results thus extend the findings of Liu et al. (2021); they demonstrated the *existence* of high concurrence synthetic benchmarks, we additionally suggest a guiding principle for how to *create* them (incorporate compositionality evaluation).

4.2 Exp. 2: enriching bAbI 1.0 training data

The results above suggest that the bAbI data in their current form may not be rich enough to drive compositional generalization.[9] In this experiment we probe this question, enriching the training data to better understand its impact on compositional generalization. In particular, we investigate two approaches to enriching the training data while maintaining the compositionality evaluation, corresponding to the *inject* and *diverse* splits.

[8] See appendix A.4 for full numeric results.

[9] An alternate hypothesis is that certain patterns may be too hard for models to learn; we confirm this is not the case by using the inoculation methodology of Liu et al. (2019), see details in Appendix A.3.

Name	Train	Test	Evaluation accuracy					SQuAD Concurrence	
			EntNet	STM	BiDAF	Roberta	T5	ρ	τ
2-task IID	concat(T2)	concat(T2)	98.95	99.85	100	100	99.85	[-0.35,0.08]	[-0.35,-0.19]
2-task OOD	concat(T2)	mix(T2)	72.0	67.6	97.2	98.7	98.1	0.48	0.51
7-task IID	concat(T7)	concat(T7)	96.8	99.4	99.98	99.98	99.8	[-0.4,0.08]	[-0.35,0.03]
7-task OOD	concat(T7)	mix(T7)	22.2	26.7	30.5	57.7	49.57	0.92	0.78
12-task IID	concat(T12)	concat(T12)	96.19	99.34	–	–	99.54	–	–
12-task OOD	concat(T12)	mix(T12)	31.97	35.65	–	–	67.4	–	–

Table 3: Experiment 1. OOD evaluation exposes large differences between pre-trained and non-pre-trained models, and also achieves high concurrence with the SQuAD benchmark. We report [min,max] concurrence for bAbI 1.0.

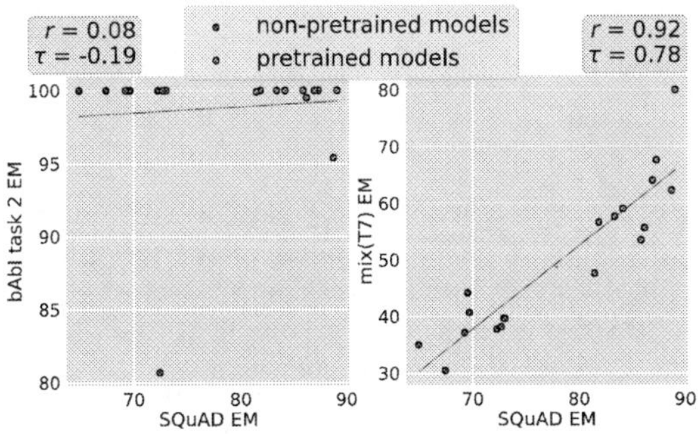

Figure 2: SQuAD concurrence plots for bAbI 1.0 task 2 (left; reproduced from Liu et al. (2021) with permission) and *mix(T_7)* (right). bAbI task 2 has the highest concurrence of all T_7 tasks, yet exhibits virtually no correlation with SQuAD. *mix(T_7)* exhibits high concurrence, highlighting the relevance of compositional evaluation.

Train	Test	Evaluation accuracy / # supporting facts			
		1	2	3+	Total
inject(T7)	concat(T7)	99.83	100	93.35	99.05
inject(T7)	mix(T7)	89.82	80.55	64.16	71.57
diverse(T7)	concat(T7)	99.58	100	78.36	96.94
diverse(T7)	mix(T7)	100	98.44	93.84	95.8
inject(T12)	concat(T12)	99.94	99.97	91.91	99.35
inject(T12)	mix(T12)	92.45	85.29	67.67	72.2
diverse(T12)	concat(T12)	99.75	98.73	76.81	97.73
diverse(T12)	mix(T12)	99.01	96.29	81.24	84.82

Table 4: Enriching the training data. Injecting knowledge to the original bAbI tasks doesn't substantially improve compositionality. Sampling more structurally diverse instances yields more significant improvements, though is still limited, especially for more complex compositions.

Notably, Exp. 2 can be seen as a first iteration of the dynamic benchmarking loop depicted in Fig. 1: based on the error analysis of Exp. 1, we leverage Dyna-bAbI for targeted creation of new tasks, which allow us to systematically test our hypotheses.

In this experiment we focus on pre-trained models, as they significantly out-performed non-pre-trained methods. We use T5 as a representative since its generative abilities make it straightforward to apply also to T_{12} (unlike the extractive methods which were applicable only to T_7).

Injecting supplementary questions. One hypothesis for the poor performance of models on the *mix* splits could be that the original bAbI tasks do not provide enough supervision for models to learn the basic event semantics. For example, tasks 5 and 7 are the only bAbI 1.0 tasks featuring the GIVE event, and neither includes any questions about the location of participants. However, test-time compositional questions may require models to infer that the participants in a GIVE event share the same location (e.g., line 10 question in Fig. 1c). Error analysis shows that such implicit inferences are indeed challenging for models trained on the *concat* splits (see details in appendix A.5). Perhaps the *inject* splits supplementing the original tasks with relevant information will improve compositionality performance? Table 4 displays the result of this experiment; performance on *mix* is improved only marginally, despite a 3-fold increase in training data (Table 2).

Sampling structurally diverse training data. As shown in Table 2, though *inject* splits significantly increase dataset size, their diversity remains low: most questions require only one or two supporting facts. Therefore, we next enrich training data through sampling more structurally diverse samples. This method is known to improve data efficiency for both compositional generalization as well as IID settings (Oren et al., 2021). As can be seen in Table 4, training on the *diverse* splits yields a more significant improvement; similar to the findings of Oren et al. (2021), sampling more diverse training data leads to greater

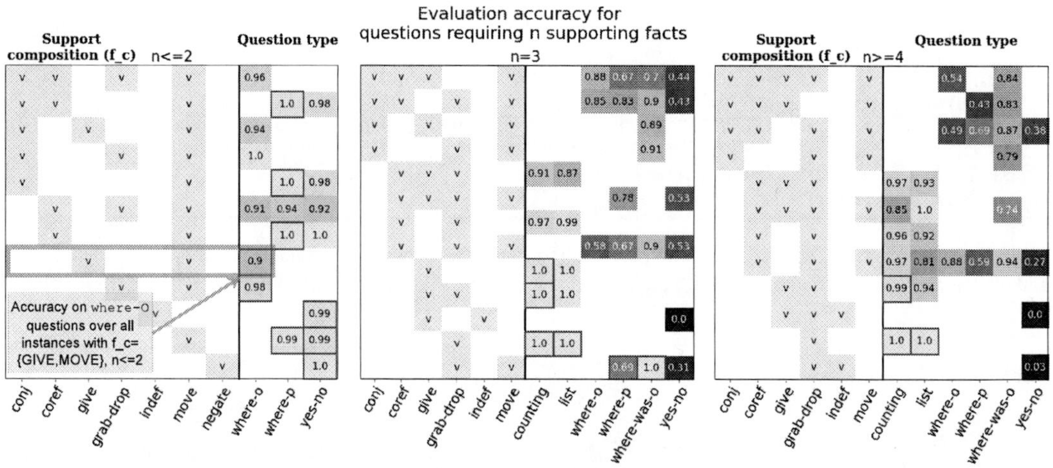

Figure 3: Error analysis on *mix(T_{12})* for T5 trained on *diverse(T_{12})* data. The sub-plots break down performance on questions requiring $\{\leq 2, 3, \geq 4\}$ supporting facts. For each sub-plot, the left side of each row corresponds to a particular support composition (f_c), and the right side displays accuracy over inputs sharing f_c, across various question types. Performance on f_c seen at training time (blue frames) is generally high, but overall generalization is not systematic, as evidenced by high variance across different f_c, especially for higher complexity ($n = 3, n \geq 4$) and more novel compositions.

generalization as well as much improved data efficiency.[10] However, as the error analysis of the next section shows, performance on compositional generalization is still fundamentally limited.

4.2.1 Discussion and error analysis

Figure 3 breaks down the performance of T5 on *mix(T_{12})* after training on *diverse(T_{12})*. The heatmaps plot performance across various support compositions (f_c) occurring in the test data, subdivided by the number of required supporting facts n per question. Performance on support compositions seen at training time (blue frames) is generally high, indicating the importance of training pattern diversity for better generalization. The plots indicate that T5 shows some ability to generalize to new support compositions, especially for lower n. Furthermore, certain question types appear to be more learned more robustly; for *list* and *count* questions, performance remains relatively high even for larger n and across novel f_c. We hypothesize that such questions may be easier as simple counting rules suffice to reach an answer, and these are "close to the surface"; unlike other events that may implicitly convey information, in our stories, changes of possession are always explicit in the text.

```
1 Bill and Jeff moved to the park.
2 Following that they journeyed to the bathroom.
3 Bill is either in the hallway or the office.
4 Jeff picked up the apple.
5 Following that he dropped the apple.
6 John is in the school.
7 Fred is either in the garden or the office.
8 Mary is in the bedroom.
9 Bill grabbed the milk.
10 Afterwards he grabbed the football.
11 Julie and John travelled to the bedroom.
12 Bill is either in the kitchen or the bathroom.
13 Daniel is in the hallway.
14 Sandra is in the school.
15 Bill got the apple.
16 Jeff travelled to the garden.
17 After that he travelled to the bathroom.
18 Daniel is either in the garden or the school.
19 Bill dropped the apple.
20 Bill handed the milk to Jeff.
21 Is Bill in the bathroom? yes    1 2 4 5 15 T5: maybe
22 Where is Bill?bathroom    1 2 4 5 15 T5: bathroom
```

Figure 4: Example *mix(T_{12})* instance demonstrating the question phrasing sensitivity failure mode in T5: the model correctly answers the question in *where-P* form (line 22), and incorrectly in *yes-no* form (line 21).

In general however, the plots indicate that T5 is far from robust compositional generalization:

Performance deteriorates with increased complexity. Performance is near perfect for simple compositions ($n \leq 2$) but deteriorates significantly for more complex cases ($n \geq 3$).

[10]The relatively low performance of *diverse* trained models in the "3+" column for *concat* splits is predominantly due to length discrepancies at train and test time: *concat* contains some very long stories which are challenging for the model trained on the uniform length and shorter *diverse* stories.

Question phrasing sensitivity. The discrepancy between the relatively high performance on *where-P* questions compared with very low performance on *yes-no* questions suggests that models are learning highly question-dependent story representations. E.g., if a model answers y correctly to some "Where is p?" question, we would expect it to answer "yes" correctly for the same question in *yes-no* format, "Is p at y?". Figure 4 shows a characteristic example: T5 answers correctly in the *where-P* format, but incorrectly answers "maybe" for the *yes-no* format, likely thrown off by the distractor indefinite phrase in sentence 3.

We present further empirical support for question phrasing sensitivity in appendix A.6. These results suggest models may be learning shortcuts that work well for the story/question pairs seen at training time, but not more robust rules that also generalize to novel test instances. Such highly question-dependent story representation stands in contrast to more human-like narrative comprehension, which is thought to involve the construction of *situation models*, or structured representations of entities and their relations as depicted by the text. Situation models are less dependent on a-priori knowledge of a question (or its phrasing), and are often generated on-line during the course of comprehension (Graesser et al., 1994).

Performance below chance for certain question types. The heatmaps expose a particularly challenging class of *yes-no* questions involving disjunctions over indefinites (center and right plots, bottom right); accuracy for such questions is close to zero. See appendix A.7 for an example instance.

5 Future work & conclusions

Our work opens up multiple new directions for future research. Our new tool, Dyna-bAbI is readily extendable for systematic probing of more diverse linguistic phenomena. A beneficial first step could include integration of additional bAbI tasks. That said, our experience suggests that the design of truly scalable synthetic and dynamic benchmarks poses significant theoretical and engineering challenges, warranting deeper research on their own right.

Our results raise new questions about the viability of learning robust situation models using standard question-answering training, and our datasets present new challenges for future efforts.

Additionally, Dyna-bAbI can naturally complement parallel work probing the the situation representations constructed by neural language models (Li et al., 2021) by facilitating tailored data generation for specific questions, thus broadening and deepening the scope of possible research.

In conclusion, we introduced Dyna-bAbI, a new framework for highly controllable bAbI task generation. We used it to create compositional generalization datasets providing new modelling challenges for state-of-the-art neural language models. More broadly, our results underscore the importance in development of benchmarks themselves, beyond only the models solving them.

Broader Impact

While large, neural language models are increasingly seen as foundations for a wide array of NLP tasks, we still lack a clear understanding of their capabilities and failure modes. Our work joins many recent efforts using carefully controlled synthetic tasks to more rigorously evaluate models' language comprehension abilities.

While our choice of a synthetic language benchmark allows more precise control over evaluation, the synthetic nature of the data is an obvious limitation. Similar to the original bAbI benchmark, our tasks are not a substitute for real natural language datasets, but should rather complement them. Even if a method works well on our data, it should be shown to perform well on real data as well. Rather, our tasks are better thought of as comprehension "unit-tests", where poor performance on our tasks serves as a warning sign suggesting the model may exhibit limited systematicity and robustness on more difficult, naturalistic inputs.

Acknowledgements

We thank the Aristo team at the Allen Institute for AI for valuable support and feedback. Ronen Tamari was supported by the Center for Interdisciplinary Data-science Research at HUJI. This work was supported by the European Research Council (ERC) under the European Union's Horizon 2020 research and innovation programme (grant no. 852686, SIAM, Shahaf). Part of this research is also supported by the European Research Council, ERC-StG grant no. 677352 (Tsarfaty), which we gratefully acknowledge.

References

Laura Aina, Carina Silberer, Ionut-Teodor Sorodoc, Matthijs Westera, and Gemma Boleda. 2019. What do entity-centric models learn? insights from entity linking in multi-party dialogue. In *Proceedings of the 2019 Conference of the North American Chapter of the Association for Computational Linguistics: Human Language Technologies, Volume 1 (Long and Short Papers)*, pages 3772–3783, Minneapolis, Minnesota. Association for Computational Linguistics.

Pratyay Banerjee, Chitta Baral, Man Luo, Arindam Mitra, Kuntal Pal, Tran C. Son, and Neeraj Varshney. 2020. Can transformers reason about effects of actions? *Computing Research Repository*, arXiv:2012.09938.

Andrea Banino, Adrià Puigdomènech Badia, Raphael Köster, Martin J. Chadwick, Vinicius Zambaldi, Demis Hassabis, Caswell Barry, Matthew Botvinick, Dharshan Kumaran, and Charles Blundell. 2020. Memo: A deep network for flexible combination of episodic memories. In *International Conference on Learning Representations*.

Andrea Banino, Jan Balaguer, and Charles Blundell. 2021. Pondernet: Learning to ponder. In *8th ICML Workshop on Automated Machine Learning (AutoML)*.

Gregor Betz, Christian Voigt, and Kyle Richardson. 2021. Critical thinking for language models. *Proceedings of IWCS*.

Lukas Biewald. 2020. Experiment tracking with weights and biases. Software available from wandb.com.

Samuel R. Bowman and George Dahl. 2021. What will it take to fix benchmarking in natural language understanding? In *Proceedings of the 2021 Conference of the North American Chapter of the Association for Computational Linguistics: Human Language Technologies*, pages 4843–4855, Online. Association for Computational Linguistics.

Peter Clark, Oyvind Tafjord, and Kyle Richardson. 2020. Transformers as soft reasoners over language. In *Proceedings of the Twenty-Ninth International Joint Conference on Artificial Intelligence, IJCAI-20*, pages 3882–3890. International Joint Conferences on Artificial Intelligence Organization. Main track.

Bhavana Dalvi, Lifu Huang, Niket Tandon, Wen-tau Yih, and Peter Clark. 2018. Tracking state changes in procedural text: a challenge dataset and models for process paragraph comprehension. In *Proceedings of the 2018 Conference of the North American Chapter of the Association for Computational Linguistics: Human Language Technologies, Volume 1 (Long Papers)*, pages 1595–1604, New Orleans, Louisiana. Association for Computational Linguistics.

Jacob Devlin, Ming-Wei Chang, Kenton Lee, and Kristina Toutanova. 2019. BERT: Pre-training of deep bidirectional transformers for language understanding. In *Proceedings of the 2019 Conference of the North American Chapter of the Association for Computational Linguistics: Human Language Technologies, Volume 1 (Long and Short Papers)*, pages 4171–4186, Minneapolis, Minnesota. Association for Computational Linguistics.

Jesse Dunietz, Greg Burnham, Akash Bharadwaj, Owen Rambow, Jennifer Chu-Carroll, and Dave Ferrucci. 2020. To test machine comprehension, start by defining comprehension. In *Proceedings of the 58th Annual Meeting of the Association for Computational Linguistics*, pages 7839–7859, Online. Association for Computational Linguistics.

William Falcon et al. 2019. Pytorch lightning. *GitHub. Note: https://github.com/PyTorchLightning/pytorch-lightning*, 3.

Catherine Finegan-Dollak, Jonathan K. Kummerfeld, Li Zhang, Karthik Ramanathan, Sesh Sadasivam, Rui Zhang, and Dragomir Radev. 2018. Improving text-to-SQL evaluation methodology. In *Proceedings of the 56th Annual Meeting of the Association for Computational Linguistics (Volume 1: Long Papers)*, pages 351–360, Melbourne, Australia. Association for Computational Linguistics.

Nicolas Gontier, Koustuv Sinha, Siva Reddy, and Christopher Pal. 2020. Measuring systematic generalization in neural proof generation with transformers. In *Advances in Neural Information Processing Systems 33*. Curran Associates, Inc.

Arthur C. Graesser, Murray Singer, and Tom Trabasso. 1994. Constructing Inferences During Narrative Text Comprehension. *Psychological Review*, 101(3):371–395.

Suchin Gururangan, Swabha Swayamdipta, Omer Levy, Roy Schwartz, Samuel Bowman, and Noah A. Smith. 2018. Annotation artifacts in natural language inference data. In *Proceedings of the 2018 Conference of the North American Chapter of the Association for Computational Linguistics: Human Language Technologies, Volume 2 (Short Papers)*, pages 107–112, New Orleans, Louisiana. Association for Computational Linguistics.

Mikael Henaff, Jason Weston, Arthur Szlam, Antoine Bordes, and Yann LeCun. 2017. Tracking the world state with recurrent entity networks. 5th International Conference on Learning Representations, ICLR 2017 ; Conference date: 24-04-2017 Through 26-04-2017.

Dan Hendrycks, Xiaoyuan Liu, Eric Wallace, Adam Dziedzic, Rishabh Krishnan, and Dawn Song. 2020. Pretrained transformers improve out-of-distribution robustness. In *Proceedings of the 58th Annual Meeting of the Association for Computational Linguistics*, pages 2744–2751, Online. Association for Computational Linguistics.

Divyansh Kaushik and Zachary C. Lipton. 2018. How much reading does reading comprehension require? a critical investigation of popular benchmarks. In *Proceedings of the 2018 Conference on Empirical Methods in Natural Language Processing*, pages 5010–5015, Brussels, Belgium. Association for Computational Linguistics.

Daniel Keysers, Nathanael Schärli, Nathan Scales, Hylke Buisman, Daniel Furrer, Sergii Kashubin, Nikola Momchev, Danila Sinopalnikov, Lukasz Stafiniak, Tibor Tihon, Dmitry Tsarkov, Xiao Wang, Marc van Zee, and Olivier Bousquet. 2020. Measuring compositional generalization: A comprehensive method on realistic data. In *International Conference on Learning Representations*.

Tushar Khot, Kyle Richardson, Daniel Khashabi, and Ashish Sabharwal. 2021. Learning to Solve Complex Tasks by Talking to Agents. *arXiv preprint arXiv:2110.08542*.

Douwe Kiela, Max Bartolo, Yixin Nie, Divyansh Kaushik, Atticus Geiger, Zhengxuan Wu, Bertie Vidgen, Grusha Prasad, Amanpreet Singh, Pratik Ringshia, Zhiyi Ma, Tristan Thrush, Sebastian Riedel, Zeerak Waseem, Pontus Stenetorp, Robin Jia, Mohit Bansal, Christopher Potts, and Adina Williams. 2021. Dynabench: Rethinking benchmarking in nlp.

Diederik P. Kingma and Jimmy Ba. 2017. Adam: A method for stochastic optimization.

Brenden Lake and Marco Baroni. 2018. Generalization without systematicity: On the compositional skills of sequence-to-sequence recurrent networks. In *International conference on machine learning*, pages 2873–2882. PMLR.

Brenden M Lake, Tomer D Ullman, Joshua B Tenenbaum, and Samuel J Gershman. 2017. Building machines that learn and think like people. *Behavioral and brain sciences*, 40.

Hung Le, Truyen Tran, and Svetha Venkatesh. 2020. Self-attentive associative memory. In *International Conference on Machine Learning*, pages 5682–5691. PMLR.

Belinda Z. Li, Maxwell Nye, and Jacob Andreas. 2021. Implicit representations of meaning in neural language models. In *Proceedings of the 59th Annual Meeting of the Association for Computational Linguistics and the 11th International Joint Conference on Natural Language Processing (Volume 1: Long Papers)*, pages 1813–1827, Online. Association for Computational Linguistics.

Yaobo Liang, Nan Duan, Yeyun Gong, Ning Wu, Fenfei Guo, Weizhen Qi, Ming Gong, Linjun Shou, Daxin Jiang, Guihong Cao, Xiaodong Fan, Ruofei Zhang, Rahul Agrawal, Edward Cui, Sining Wei, Taroon Bharti, Ying Qiao, Jiun-Hung Chen, Winnie Wu, Shuguang Liu, Fan Yang, Daniel Campos, Rangan Majumder, and Ming Zhou. 2020. XGLUE: A new benchmark datasetfor cross-lingual pre-training, understanding and generation. In *Proceedings of the 2020 Conference on Empirical Methods in Natural Language Processing (EMNLP)*, pages 6008–6018, Online. Association for Computational Linguistics.

Nelson F. Liu, Tony Lee, Robin Jia, and Percy Liang. 2021. Can small and synthetic benchmarks drive modeling innovation? a retrospective study of question answering modeling approaches. *Computing Research Repository*, arXiv:2102.01065.

Nelson F. Liu, Roy Schwartz, and Noah A. Smith. 2019. Inoculation by fine-tuning: A method for analyzing challenge datasets. In *Proceedings of the 2019 Conference of the North American Chapter of the Association for Computational Linguistics: Human Language Technologies, Volume 1 (Long and Short Papers)*, pages 2171–2179, Minneapolis, Minnesota. Association for Computational Linguistics.

Yinhan Liu, Myle Ott, Naman Goyal, Jingfei Du, Mandar Joshi, Danqi Chen, Omer Levy, Mike Lewis, Luke Zettlemoyer, and Veselin Stoyanov. 2020. Ro{bert}a: A robustly optimized {bert} pretraining approach.

Reginald Long, Panupong Pasupat, and Percy Liang. 2016. Simpler context-dependent logical forms via model projections. In *Proceedings of the 54th Annual Meeting of the Association for Computational Linguistics (Volume 1: Long Papers)*, pages 1456–1465, Berlin, Germany. Association for Computational Linguistics.

James L. McClelland, Felix Hill, Maja Rudolph, Jason Baldridge, and Hinrich Schütze. 2020. Placing language in an integrated understanding system: Next steps toward human-level performance in neural language models. *Proceedings of the National Academy of Sciences*, arXiv:1707(Xx):201910416.

Inbar Oren, Jonathan Herzig, and Jonathan Berant. 2021. Finding needles in a haystack: Sampling structurally-diverse training sets from synthetic data for compositional generalization.

Barbara Partee et al. 1995. Lexical semantics and compositionality. *An invitation to cognitive science: Language*, 1:311–360.

Christopher Potts, Zhengxuan Wu, Atticus Geiger, and Douwe Kiela. 2021. DynaSent: A dynamic benchmark for sentiment analysis. In *Proceedings of the 59th Annual Meeting of the Association for Computational Linguistics and the 11th International Joint Conference on Natural Language Processing (Volume 1: Long Papers)*, pages 2388–2404, Online. Association for Computational Linguistics.

Linlu Qiu, Hexiang Hu, Bowen Zhang, Peter Shaw, and Fei Sha. 2021. Systematic generalization on gscan: What is nearly solved and what is next? *Computing Research Repository*, arXiv:2109.12243.

Colin Raffel, Noam Shazeer, Adam Roberts, Katherine Lee, Sharan Narang, Michael Matena, Yanqi Zhou, Wei Li, and Peter J. Liu. 2020. Exploring the limits of transfer learning with a unified text-to-text transformer. *Journal of Machine Learning Research*, 21(140):1–67.

Pranav Rajpurkar, Jian Zhang, Konstantin Lopyrev, and Percy Liang. 2016. SQuAD: 100,000+ questions for machine comprehension of text. In *Proceedings of the 2016 Conference on Empirical Methods in Natural Language Processing*, pages 2383–2392, Austin, Texas. Association for Computational Linguistics.

Kyle Richardson, Hai Hu, Lawrence Moss, and Ashish Sabharwal. 2020. Probing natural language inference models through semantic fragments. In *Proceedings of AAAI*.

Kyle Richardson and Ashish Sabharwal. 2022. Pushing the limits of rule reasoning in transformers through natural language satisfiability. *Proceedings of AAAI*.

Anna Rogers. 2021. Changing the world by changing the data. In *Proceedings of the 59th Annual Meeting of the Association for Computational Linguistics and the 11th International Joint Conference on Natural Language Processing (Volume 1: Long Papers)*, pages 2182–2194, Online. Association for Computational Linguistics.

Laura Ruis, Jacob Andreas, Marco Baroni, Diane Bouchacourt, and Brenden M Lake. 2020. A benchmark for systematic generalization in grounded language understanding. In *Advances in Neural Information Processing Systems*, volume 33, pages 19861–19872. Curran Associates, Inc.

Nithya Sambasivan, Shivani Kapania, Hannah Highfill, Diana Akrong, Praveen Paritosh, and Lora M Aroyo. 2021. "everyone wants to do the model work, not the data work": Data cascades in high-stakes ai. In *Proceedings of the 2021 CHI Conference on Human Factors in Computing Systems*, CHI '21, New York, NY, USA. Association for Computing Machinery.

Imanol Schlag, Tsendsuren Munkhdalai, and Jürgen Schmidhuber. 2021. Learning associative inference using fast weight memory. In *International Conference on Learning Representations*.

Minjoon Seo, Aniruddha Kembhavi, Ali Farhadi, and Hannaneh Hajishirzi. 2017. Bidirectional attention flow for machine comprehension. In *International Conference on Learning Representations*.

Murray Shanahan, Matthew Crosby, Benjamin Beyret, and Lucy Cheke. 2020. Artificial intelligence and the common sense of animals. *Trends in Cognitive Sciences*, 24(11):862–872.

Koustuv Sinha, Shagun Sodhani, Jin Dong, Joelle Pineau, and William L. Hamilton. 2019. CLUTRR: A diagnostic benchmark for inductive reasoning from text. In *Proceedings of the 2019 Conference on Empirical Methods in Natural Language Processing and the 9th International Joint Conference on Natural Language Processing (EMNLP-IJCNLP)*, pages 4506–4515, Hong Kong, China. Association for Computational Linguistics.

Saku Sugawara, Pontus Stenetorp, and Akiko Aizawa. 2021. Benchmarking machine reading comprehension: A psychological perspective. In *Proceedings of the 16th Conference of the European Chapter of the Association for Computational Linguistics: Main Volume*, pages 1592–1612, Online. Association for Computational Linguistics.

Ronen Tamari, Chen Shani, Tom Hope, Miriam R L Petruck, Omri Abend, and Dafna Shahaf. 2020. Language (re)modelling: Towards embodied language understanding. In *Proceedings of the 58th Annual Meeting of the Association for Computational Linguistics*, pages 6268–6281, Online. Association for Computational Linguistics.

Niket Tandon, Keisuke Sakaguchi, Bhavana Dalvi, Dheeraj Rajagopal, Peter Clark, Michal Guerquin, Kyle Richardson, and Eduard Hovy. 2020. A dataset for tracking entities in open domain procedural text. In *Proceedings of the 2020 Conference on Empirical Methods in Natural Language Processing (EMNLP)*, pages 6408–6417, Online. Association for Computational Linguistics.

Alex Wang, Yada Pruksachatkun, Nikita Nangia, Amanpreet Singh, Julian Michael, Felix Hill, Omer Levy, and Samuel Bowman. 2019. Superglue: A stickier benchmark for general-purpose language understanding systems. In *Advances in Neural Information Processing Systems*, volume 32. Curran Associates, Inc.

Alex Wang, Amanpreet Singh, Julian Michael, Felix Hill, Omer Levy, and Samuel Bowman. 2018. GLUE: A multi-task benchmark and analysis platform for natural language understanding. In *Proceedings of the 2018 EMNLP Workshop BlackboxNLP: Analyzing and Interpreting Neural Networks for NLP*, pages 353–355, Brussels, Belgium. Association for Computational Linguistics.

Jason Weston, Antoine Bordes, Sumit Chopra, and Tomás Mikolov. 2016. Towards ai-complete question answering: A set of prerequisite toy tasks. In *4th International Conference on Learning Representations, ICLR 2016, San Juan, Puerto Rico, May 2-4, 2016, Conference Track Proceedings*.

Thomas Wolf, Lysandre Debut, Victor Sanh, Julien Chaumond, Clement Delangue, Anthony Moi, Pierric Cistac, Tim Rault, Remi Louf, Morgan Funtowicz, Joe Davison, Sam Shleifer, Patrick von Platen, Clara Ma, Yacine Jernite, Julien Plu, Canwen Xu, Teven Le Scao, Sylvain Gugger, Mariama Drame, Quentin Lhoest, and Alexander Rush. 2020. Transformers: State-of-the-art natural language processing. In *Proceedings of the 2020 Conference on Empirical Methods in Natural Language Processing: System*

Demonstrations, pages 38–45, Online. Association for Computational Linguistics.

Zhengxuan Wu, Elisa Kreiss, Desmond C. Ong, and Christopher Potts. 2021. ReaSCAN: Compositional reasoning in language grounding. *NeurIPS 2021 Datasets and Benchmarks Track.*

Hitomi Yanaka, Koji Mineshima, and Kentaro Inui. 2021. SyGNS: A systematic generalization testbed based on natural language semantics. In *Findings of the Association for Computational Linguistics: ACL-IJCNLP 2021*, pages 103–119, Online. Association for Computational Linguistics.

Rolf A. Zwaan. 2016. Situation models, mental simulations, and abstract concepts in discourse comprehension. *Psychonomic Bulletin and Review*, 23(4):1028–1034.

A Appendix

A.1 Extended task construction details

This section provides further details of the training and test splits used for our experiments.

Table 5 enumerates the basic "building blocks", or concepts underlying the tasks, as presented in §3.2.

Tables 6 and 7 detail the concept sets for each of the sub-tasks comprising the training and test sets, for the T_2, T_7 and T_{12} groups of tasks.

As can be seen from the tables, the main sources of compositionality are:

- Following the bAbI 1.0 task structure, at training time, all of the more complex linguistic constructs are seen only with MOVE events (and none of the other event types).
- Similarly, at training time, *yes-no* questions are always seen only with MOVE events (and none of the other event types), and with the INDEF or NEGATE linguistic constructs (but not others, such as COREF).
- *where-was-O* questions are never seen in stories with GIVE events.

Language templates. For our new generated tasks we use the same language templates as used in the original bAbI 1.0 benchmark (e.g., the same entity names, verb synonyms). The only modification to the language generation engine was that we completely omit the use of "there"; in the original benchmark, "there" could be used in confusing contexts, as shown in Fig. 5.

A.1.1 Example instances

Figure 6 shows examples from each of the 4 types of splits used in our experiments. The *concat* instance is from the original bAbI 1.0 task 5. The *inject* data contains the same passages as *concat*, but adds supplementary questions on agent and object locations. *diverse* instances contain more diverse support compositions (f_c), but certain combinations are held out. In particular, *diverse* instances only feature non-default linguistic mappings with MOVE events, never with POSS (GRAB or DROP) or GIVE. In the *mix* instances, all combinations of support compositions are possible, as shown in the example which features possession (POSS) events along with co-reference.

1 Mary journeyed to the bathroom.
2 Sandra went to the garden.
3 Daniel went back to the garden.
4 Daniel went to the office.
5 Sandra grabbed the milk there.
6 Sandra put down the milk there.
7 Where is the milk? garden 6 2

Figure 5: Example from original bAbI 1.0 benchmark with confusing usage of "there". In Dyna-bAbI we do not include "there", to avoid this confusion.

A.1.2 Long instances in the bAbI 1.0 tasks

For the T5 experiments, we used a slightly modified version of the bAbI 1.0 tasks, where we trimmed all training and validation examples that didn't fit into the 512-token input window. This resulted in trimming 1,585 training instances and 175 validation instances from T_7 and T_12 (common to both sets). These data points are not consequential as our analysis focuses on the effects of compositionality and not story length; all instances in *diverse* and *mix* are substantially shorter than the 512-token maximum input window size.

A.2 Implementation details

T5. We use the publicly available HuggingFace pre-trained T5-base implementation (Wolf et al., 2020) which has 220M parameters. We similarly use the HuggingFace tokenization pipeline. We fine-tune T5 for 12 epochs on our bAbI data, using the Adam optimizer (Kingma and Ba, 2017), an initial learning rate of $5 * 10^{-5}$ and training batch size of 8.

STM. We used the official STM implementation[11], with the only change being a batch size of 32 instead of 128, due to technical constraints.

EntNet. We re-implemented the model in PyTorch, similarly using a batch-size of 32. Following the official Lua reference implementation[12], we used 20 memory units each with dimension 100. We used the SGD optimizer.

For both the EntNet and STM, we trained models for 200 epochs, and took the best of 10 tries, following Henaff et al. (2017).

For the 20-model concurrence benchmark, refer to Liu et al. (2021) for model details, as we used the same experimental setup.

[11] `https://github.com/thaihungle/SAM`

[12] `https://github.com/facebookarchive/MemNN/tree/master/EntNet-babi`

Events	Template	Example	Notes
MOVE	P {moved} to the L.	John traveled to the park.	
GRAB	P {grabbed} the O.	Mary picked up the apple.	
DROP	P {dropped} the O.	Daniel dropped the milk.	
GIVE	P1 {gave} P2 the O.	John handed Mary the apple.	
Linguistic Constructs			
COREF	P (MOVE|GRAB|DROP) Following that, {he} (MOVE|GRAB|DROP).	John went to the garden. Following that, he moved to the store	Co-reference
CONJ	P1 and P2 {moved} to the L1.	Jeff and Fred went to the cinema.	Conjunction
COMPOUND	P1 and P2 {moved} to the L1. Then they {moved} to the L2.	Jeff and Fred went to the cinema. Then they traveled to the school.	Compound co-reference
NEGATE	P is not at the L.	Julie is not in the park.	Negation
INDEF	P is either at the L1 or the L2.	John is either in the park or the school.	Indefinite expression
Questions			
where-P	Where is P?	Where is John?	
where-O	Where is the O?	Where is the football?	
where-was-O	Where was the O before the L?	Where was the football before the hallway?	
yes-no	Is P at the L?	Is John at the park?	
list	What is P carrying?	What is John carrying?	
counting	How many objects is P carrying?	How many objects is John carrying?	
give-qs	Who gave the O to P2? Who gave the O? Who received the O? Who did P1 give the P2 to? What did P1 give to P2?	Who gave the football to John? ...	Constitutes multiple question types over GIVE events.

Table 5: Details of the events, linguistic constructs and questions constituting the bAbI tasks covered in this work. Words in {brackets} are drawn from a small set of synonyms.

concat(T12) + inject(T12)
1 Bill travelled to the office.
2 Bill picked up the football there.
3 Bill went to the bedroom.
4 Bill gave the football to Fred.
5 What did Bill give to Fred? football {4}
6 Where is the football? bedroom {3, 4}
7 Where is Bill? bedroom {3}
8 Where is Fred? bedroom {3, 4}

diverse(T12)
1 Fred went back to the garden.
2 Sandra travelled to the cinema.
3 Fred went to the bathroom.
4 Fred got the football.
5 Fred travelled to the garden.
6 Bill journeyed to the garden.
7 Fred passed the football to Bill.
8 Bill discarded the football.
9 Jeff got the football.
10 Jeff discarded the football.
11 Sandra journeyed to the office.
12 Fred journeyed to the kitchen.
13 Bill got the football.
14 Bill travelled to the office.
15 Bill passed the football to Julie.
16 Julie passed the football to Daniel.
17 Daniel left the football.
18 Mary journeyed to the bedroom.
19 Bill picked up the football.
20 Bill left the football.
21 Where is Jeff? garden
f = {6, 8, 9}
f_c = {MOVE, POSS}

mix(T12)
1 John is no longer in the bedroom.
2 Bill is in the bedroom.
3 Bill took the apple.
4 Afterwards he discarded the apple.
5 Bill is no longer in the bedroom.
6 Daniel is either in the kitchen or the bathroom.
7 Fred and Bill journeyed to the kitchen.
8 Jeff is either in the park or the office.
9 Daniel is either in the garden or the kitchen.
10 Sandra is in the school.
11 Bill is either in the bathroom or the school.
12 Mary is not in the office.
13 Sandra journeyed to the hallway.
14 After that she grabbed the milk.
15 Julie is either in the bedroom or the office.
16 Daniel is no longer in the garden.
17 Jeff moved to the bathroom.
18 Julie picked up the apple.
19 Following that she got the football.
20 Jeff is in the hallway.
21 Where is the football? bedroom
f = {2, 3, 4, 18, 19}
f_c = {MOVE, POSS, COREF}

Figure 6: Example instances from each of the 4 types of splits used in our experiments.

		Events				Linguistic Constructs			Questions			
Sub-task	Type	Move	Grab	Drop	Give	Co-reference	Conjunction	Compound co-ref.	where-P	where-O	where-was-O	give
1	Train	✓							✓			
2	Train	✓	✓	✓					I/D	✓		
3	Train	✓	✓	✓					I	I	✓	
5	Train	✓	✓	✓	✓				I/D	I/D		✓
11	Train	✓				✓			✓			
12	Train	✓					✓		✓			
13	Train	✓						✓	✓			
mix(T_2)	Test	✓	✓	✓		✓				✓		
mix(T_7)	Test	✓	✓	✓	✓	✓	✓	✓	✓	✓	✓	

Table 6: Concept sets for the T_2 and T_7 sub-set of the original bAbI tasks, and the new tasks generated with Dyna-bAbI. Train sub-task numbering follows the original bAbI numbering. The *inject* and *diverse* tasks inherit the same concept set from the original tasks, and additionally "I", "D" denote question types included only in the *inject* or *diverse* tasks, respectively. "I/D" denotes question types included in both.

		Events				Linguistic Constructs					Questions						
Task	Type	Move	Grab	Drop	Give	Co-reference	Conjunction	Compound co-ref.	Negation	Indefinite	where-P	where-O	where-was-O	yes-no	counting	list	give
1	Train	✓									✓						
2	Train	✓	✓	✓							I/D	✓					
3	Train	✓	✓	✓							I	I	✓				
5	Train	✓	✓	✓	✓						I/D	I/D					✓
6	Train	✓									I/D			✓			
7	Train	✓	✓	✓	✓						I	I			✓		
8	Train	✓	✓	✓							I	I				✓	
9	Train	✓							✓		I/D			✓			
10	Train	✓								✓	I/D			✓			
11	Train	✓				✓					✓						
12	Train	✓					✓				✓						
13	Train	✓						✓			✓						
mix(T_{12})	Test	✓	✓	✓	✓	✓	✓	✓	✓	✓	✓	✓	✓	✓	✓	✓	

Table 7: Concept sets for the T_{12} sub-set of the original bAbI tasks, and the new tasks generated with Dyna-bAbI. Train sub-task numbering follows the original bAbI numbering. The *inject* and *diverse* tasks inherit the same concept set from the original tasks, and additionally "I", "D" denote question types included only in the *inject* or *diverse* tasks, respectively. "I/D" denotes question types included in both.

For the T5 experiments, we used the PyTorch Lightning (Falcon et al., 2019) trainer implementation, and Weights & Biases (Biewald, 2020) for experiment tracking and artifacts management.

We used standard hyper-parameter settings for all models, with slight changes in the case of memory issues as described above.

Experimental infrastructure details. Our experiments were performed using an RTX-8000 GPU, with a total computational budget of roughly 1,000 GPU hours.

A.3 Inoculation experiment results

To rule out the hypothesis that certain patterns may be too hard for models to learn, we follow the inoculation methodology presented in Liu et al. (2019): after training on the original tasks, we fine-tune the T5 on small amounts of OOD data (disjoint from the test data), and evaluate performance as a function of "inoculation dose". As can be seen in Fig. 7, we find that performance quickly (with only 500 additional inoculation samples per question type) reaches over 90% accuracy on both the *mix*(T_7) and *mix*(T_{12}) challenge sets. These results support the hypothesis that the training data is not rich enough, indicating clearly that the model is capable of quickly learning to solve the challenge tasks, given exposure to training samples with similar enough patterns.

A.4 Concurrence experiments

Table 8 presents the full results for the concurrence experiments of §4.1. SQuAD and bAbI task 2 results are reproduced from Liu et al. (2021), see there also for implementation details of the models used.

A.5 Extended error analysis: GIVE events

We analyze the performance of models on the *mix*(T_7) split after being trained on *concat*(T_7), and in particular we focus on GIVE events. As noted in §4.2, compositions involving GIVE are intuitively challenging as they entail multiple inferences which are not explicit in the text: the actors share the same location, and the possession of the object being given is transferred from the giver to the recipient. The only task in *concat*(T_7) featuring GIVE events is task 5, which never asks about the locations of actors or objects, but only about the participant roles in the event (e.g., who was the giver or recipient; see Fig. 1 example from task 5).

Model	Evaluation accuracy			
	SQuAD	mix(T2)	mix(T7)	babi task 2
rasor	64.86	88.20	35.03	100.00
bidaf	67.39	97.20	30.50	100.00
documentreader	69.66	90.20	40.70	100.00
documentreader (no_features)	69.21	82.50	37.17	100.00
bidafplusplus	69.49	99.50	44.20	80.70
mnemonicreader	73.02	98.20	39.63	100.00
mnemonicreader (no_features)	72.67	97.50	38.20	100.00
qanet	72.41	67.70	-	100.00
fusionnet	72.90	99.50	39.73	100.00
fusionnet (no_features)	72.24	88.10	37.80	100.00
bert	81.46	95.50	47.63	100.00
bert_large	84.17	98.30	59.10	100.00
bert_large_wwm	87.33	98.70	67.63	99.90
albert	81.86	98.20	56.70	100.00
albert_xxlarge	89.07	99.80	80.00	100.00
roberta	83.37	98.70	57.70	100.00
roberta_large	86.96	99.80	64.07	100.00
electra	85.88	98.70	53.47	100.00
spanbert	86.20	98.40	55.70	99.50
spanbert_large	88.74	98.60	62.27	95.40

Table 8: Full results of concurrence experiments presented in §4.1.

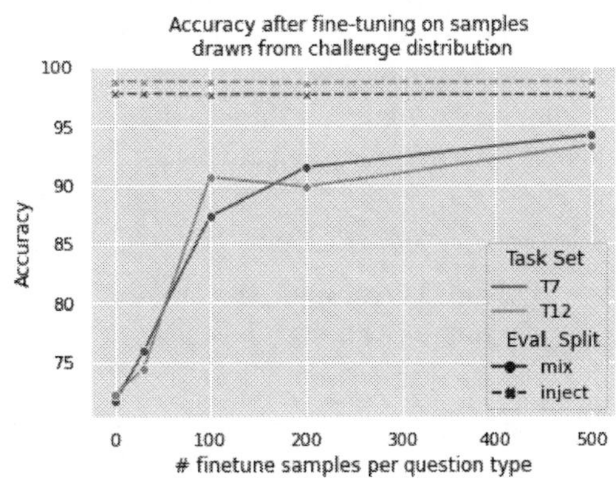

Figure 7: Inoculation experiment results.

Num. supporting facts	Num. samples	Evaluation accuracy		
		BiDAF	RoBERTa	T5
1	334	53.3	93.4	86.8
2 (w/o GIVE)	734	51.50	82.3	71.8
2 (with GIVE)	99	3.03	7.07	5.05
3 (w/o GIVE)	1365	24.6	47.2	44.3
3 (with GIVE)	468	4.27	7.05	15.2

Table 9: Breakdown of model performance on *mix*(T_7) for questions including (or not) GIVE events in the supporting fact set. The poor performance on questions including GIVE indicates that training on the bAbI 1.0 data does not facilitate generalization to novel compositions of GIVE.

where-P (→) *yes-no* (↓)	correct	incorrect
correct	209	4
incorrect	145	88

Table 10: Confusion matrix displaying question phrasing sensitivities in T5. We pose a question in two formats: (1) *yes-no*: "Is X at L? yes" vs (2) *where-P*: "Where is X? L". We find performance is considerably higher for questions posed in the *where-P* format, indicating the model isn't learning the equivalence of both forms.

To measure this intuition empirically, we analyze a subset of 567 questions including GIVE events in the supporting facts set. As shown in Table 9, performance for all models on questions including GIVE is extremely low, far below performance for questions without it. Qualitative analysis indicates many failure cases follow the pattern shown in the right-side example of Fig. 1c, question on line 10: the location of an entity (e.g., Daniel) must be inferred via the known (co-)location of a second participant in the GIVE event (e.g., Jeff). These results strengthen the hypothesis that standard QA training on the original bAbI data does not drive strong event comprehension in models.

A.6 Extended error analysis: question phrasing sensitivity

This section presents further empirical analysis of the question phrasing sensitivities discussed in §4.2.1, relating to the performance of the T5 model trained on the *diverse*(T_{12}) data and evaluated on the challenge set *mix*(T_{12}).

We collected all *yes-no* questions from *mix*(T_{12}) for which the answer was "yes", yielding 446 questions in total. For each such (question, answer) pair, of the form ("Is `person` at the `location`?", "yes"), we created an equivalent pair in the format of a *where-P* question, ("Where is `person`?", `location`). Figure 4 shows a characteristic example. Ideally, we would expect a model to be agnostic to equivalent phrasings of a question. However, as displayed in Table 10, we find that T5 is considerably more accurate for questions posed in the *where-P* format, likely due to exposure to a larger variety of such questions at training time.

1 Bill grabbed the milk.
2 Bill put down the milk.
3 John is either in the bedroom or the kitchen.
4 Fred journeyed to the kitchen.
5 John grabbed the football.
6 Following that he put down the football.
7 Bill picked up the milk.
8 Following that he went to the bedroom.
9 Bill is in the office.
10 Bill is in the cinema.
11 Bill passed the milk to Julie.
12 Julie handed the milk to Bill.
13 Jeff is not in the school.
14 John took the football.
15 Fred and Jeff moved to the school.
16 Afterwards they journeyed to the bathroom.
17 Bill handed the milk to Julie.
18 John dropped the football.
19 Daniel is either in the school or the bedroom.
20 Daniel took the football.
21 Is John in the bedroom? yes 3 18 19 20

Figure 8: Double disjunction example from *mix*(T_{12}).

A.7 Extended error analysis: double disjunctions

As the shown in the §4.2.1 error analysis, a particularly difficult class of questions are double disjunctions over indefinite expressions. Figure 8 displays a typical example from *mix*(T_{12}), where the locations of two actors are given in indefinite form (sentences 3 and 19), and are also known to be co-located, since they share the location of the object "football", as inferred from sentences 18 and 20. Hence it is possible to infer their location as the intersection of the two indefinite expressions (here "bedroom"). Rather than answering "yes" to the question "Is John in the bedroom?", T5 invariably answers "maybe" for such cases. This pattern is likely due to the fact that in the training data "maybe" is a typical answer for *yes-no* questions about actors mentioned by indefinite expressions (task 10 in bAbI 1.0).

B Datasheet for datasets

Motivation

For what purpose was the dataset created? Was there a specific task in mind? Was there a specific gap that needed to be filled? Please provide a description.

Few synthetic resources for probing NLP models' performance on discourse-level narrative understanding texts. Existing resources lack customizability (control over data created + amenable to extension).

Who created this dataset (e.g., which team, research group) and on behalf of which entity (e.g., company, institution, organization)?

Joint team of researchers at Hebrew University of Jerusalem (Israel) and the Allen Institute for Artifical Intelligence.

Who funded the creation of the dataset? If there is an associated grant, please provide the name of the grantor and the grant name and number.

Work was supported by the Center for Interdisciplinary Data-science Research (CIDR) at HUJI. This work was also supported by the European Research Council (ERC) under the European Union's Horizon 2020 research and innovation programme (grant no. 852686, SIAM) and NSF-BSF grant no. 2017741 (Shahaf). Part of this research is also supported by the European Research Council, ERC-StG grant no. 677352 (Tsarfaty).

Any other comments?

Composition

What do the instances that comprise the dataset represent (e.g., documents, photos, people, countries)? Are there multiple types of instances (e.g., movies, users, and ratings; people and interactions between them; nodes and edges)? Please provide a description.

Instances represent variable length stories.

How many instances are there in total (of each type, if appropriate)?

Any size dataset can be created (programmatic generation).

Does the dataset contain all possible instances or is it a sample (not necessarily random) of instances from a larger set? If the dataset is a sample, then what is the larger set? Is the sample representative of the larger set (e.g., geographic coverage)? If so, please describe how this representativeness was validated/verified. If it is not representative of the larger set, please describe why not (e.g., to cover a more diverse range of instances, because instances were withheld or unavailable).

Used rejection sampling for some datasets to cover more diverse instances.

What data does each instance consist of? "Raw" data (e.g., unprocessed text or images) or features? In either case, please provide a description.

Simple textual stories generated using templates ("John went to the kitchen. He grabbed the apple.").

Is there a label or target associated with each instance? If so, please provide a description.

Each instance is accompanied by a (question, answer) pair, both in natural language.

Is any information missing from individual instances? If so, please provide a description, explaining why this information is missing (e.g., because it was unavailable). This does not include intentionally removed information, but might include, e.g., redacted text.

N/A

Are there recommended data splits (e.g., training, development/validation, testing)? If so, please provide a description of these splits, explaining the rationale behind them.

The data is organized in splits, which are explained in section 4 of the paper.

Are there any errors, sources of noise, or redundancies in the dataset? If so, please provide a description.

Template based language generation may result in somewhat unnatural texts.

Is the dataset self-contained, or does it link to or otherwise rely on external resources (e.g., websites, tweets, other datasets)? If it links to or relies on external resources, a) are there guarantees that they will exist, and remain constant, over time; b) are there official archival versions of the complete dataset

(i.e., including the external resources as they existed at the time the dataset was created); c) are there any restrictions (e.g., licenses, fees) associated with any of the external resources that might apply to a future user? Please provide descriptions of all external resources and any restrictions associated with them, as well as links or other access points, as appropriate.
Self contained.

Does the dataset contain data that, if viewed directly, might be offensive, insulting, threatening, or might otherwise cause anxiety? If so, please describe why.
No.

Does the dataset relate to people? If not, you may skip the remaining questions in this section.
No.

Any other comments?

Collection Process

How was the data associated with each instance acquired? Was the data directly observable (e.g., raw text, movie ratings), reported by subjects (e.g., survey responses), or indirectly inferred/derived from other data (e.g., part-of-speech tags, model-based guesses for age or language)? If data was reported by subjects or indirectly inferred/derived from other data, was the data validated/verified? If so, please describe how.
Programmatically generated using logical rules and templates.

If the dataset is a sample from a larger set, what was the sampling strategy (e.g., deterministic, probabilistic with specific sampling probabilities)?
Rejection sampling was used in some cases, described in Section 4.

Does the dataset relate to people? If not, you may skip the remaining questions in this section.
No.

Any other comments?

Preprocessing/cleaning/labeling

Was any preprocessing/cleaning/labeling of the data done (e.g., discretization or bucketing, tokenization, part-of-speech tagging, SIFT feature extraction, removal of instances, processing of missing values)? If so, please provide a description. If not, you may skip the remainder of the questions in this section.
No.

Was the "raw" data saved in addition to the preprocessed/cleaned/labeled data (e.g., to support unanticipated future uses)? If so, please provide a link or other access point to the "raw" data.
N/A

Is the software used to preprocess/clean/label the instances available? If so, please provide a link or other access point.
N/A

Any other comments?

Uses

Has the dataset been used for any tasks already? If so, please provide a description.
Benchmark to guide model development for reading comprehension and textual reasoning tasks.

Is there a repository that links to any or all papers or systems that use the dataset? If so, please provide a link or other access point.
Not currently, we will use the `https://paperswithcode.com/` integration to track results.

What (other) tasks could the dataset be used for?
N/A

Is there anything about the composition of the dataset or the way it was collected and preprocessed/cleaned/labeled that might impact future uses? For example, is there anything that a future user might need to know to avoid uses that could result in unfair treatment of individuals or groups (e.g., stereotyping, quality of service issues) or other undesirable harms (e.g., financial harms, legal risks) If so, please provide a description. Is there anything a future user could do to mitigate these undesirable harms?

N/A

Are there tasks for which the dataset should not be used? If so, please provide a description.

Similar to the original bAbI benchmark, our tasks are not a substitute for real natural language datasets, but should rather complement them. Even if a method works well on our data, it should be shown to perform well on real data as well. Rather, our tasks are better thought of as comprehension "unit-tests", where poor performance on our tasks serves as a warning sign suggesting the model may exhibit limited systematicity and robustness on more difficult, naturalistic inputs.

Any other comments?

Distribution

Will the dataset be distributed to third parties outside of the entity (e.g., company, institution, organization) on behalf of which the dataset was created? If so, please provide a description.

N/A

How will the dataset will be distributed (e.g., tarball on website, API, GitHub) Does the dataset have a digital object identifier (DOI)?

Github + Weights and Biases. No DOI currently.

When will the dataset be distributed?

Data and code-base for task generation to be uploaded upon publication.

Will the dataset be distributed under a copyright or other intellectual property (IP) license, and/or under applicable terms of use (ToU)? If so, please describe this license and/or ToU, and provide a link or other access point to, or otherwise reproduce, any relevant licensing terms or ToU, as well as any fees associated with these restrictions.

Will be available with standard MIT license.

Have any third parties imposed IP-based or other restrictions on the data associated with the instances? If so, please describe these restrictions, and provide a link or other access point to, or otherwise reproduce, any relevant licensing terms, as well as any fees associated with these restrictions.

N/A

Do any export controls or other regulatory restrictions apply to the dataset or to individual instances? If so, please describe these restrictions, and provide a link or other access point to, or otherwise reproduce, any supporting documentation.

N/A

Any other comments?

Maintenance

Who will be supporting/hosting/maintaining the dataset?

Corresponding author of paper.

How can the owner/curator/manager of the dataset be contacted (e.g., email address)?

Via email with corresponding author, and through dedicated GitHub repository.

Is there an erratum? If so, please provide a link or other access point.

N/A

Will the dataset be updated (e.g., to correct labeling errors, add new instances, delete instances)? If so, please describe how often, by whom, and how updates will be communicated to users (e.g., mailing list, GitHub)?

Extensions will be maintained via GitHub.

If the dataset relates to people, are there applicable limits on the retention of the data associated with the instances (e.g., were individuals in question told that their data would be retained for a fixed period of time and then deleted)? If so, please describe these limits and explain how they will be enforced.

N/A

Will older versions of the dataset continue to be supported/hosted/maintained? If so, please describe how. If not, please describe how its obsolescence will be communicated to users.

Data versioning supported natively through Weights and Biases.

If others want to extend/augment/build on/contribute to the dataset, is there a mechanism for them to do so? If so, please provide a description. Will these contributions be validated/verified? If so, please describe how. If not, why not? Is there a process for communicating/distributing these contributions to other users? If so, please provide a description.

The codebase can be freely extended, we will only be responsible of course for changes to the main branch.

Any other comments?

When Polysemy Matters: Modeling Semantic Categorization with Word Embeddings

Elizabeth Soper and **Jean-Pierre Koenig**
Department of Linguistics
State University of New York at Buffalo
{esoper, jpkoenig}@buffalo.edu

Abstract

Recent work using word embeddings to model semantic categorization have indicated that static models outperform the more recent contextual class of models (Majewska et al., 2021). In this paper, we consider polysemy as a possible confounding factor, comparing sense-level embeddings with previously studied static embeddings on both coarse- and fine-grained categorization tasks. We find that the effect of polysemy depends on how one defines semantic categorization; while sense-level embeddings dramatically outperform static embeddings in predicting coarse-grained categories derived from a word sorting task, they perform approximately equally in predicting fine-grained categories derived from context-free similarity judgments. Our findings highlight the different processes underlying human behavior on different types of semantic tasks.

1 Introduction

A great deal of work has been devoted in recent years to creating computational models of meaning (Landauer and Dumais, 1997; Mikolov et al., 2013; Pennington et al., 2014; Peters et al., 2018; Devlin et al., 2019). Such models have been evaluated on a variety of semantic tasks, from word pair similarity judgments to document classification. One task that has received relatively little attention is semantic categorization. Besides making pair-wise judgments about the similarity between two words, humans can also reason about higher-order structures; we can tell not only that *robin* and *sparrow* are similar to each other, for example, but also that they belong in a group with other birds (e.g. *ostrich* and *pigeon*). Based on the impressive performance of embedding models on other semantic tasks, we expect such models to excel at identifying semantic categories as well.

Our particular interest is on the role of polysemy in semantic categorization. Because words generally have multiple distinct senses, categorization decisions will depend on which sense of a word is being considered. Representing the distinct senses of polysemous words, then, should be important to modeling how humans categorize words. For this reason, we expect contextual embeddings, which represent each instance of a word in context as a unique embedding, to model semantic categorization better than static models, which conflate every use of a word into a single representation. But, in fact, recent work evaluating different word embedding models on verb categorization suggests just the opposite; Majewska et al. (2021) found that contextual models perform poorly compared to older static models.

In the following paper, we challenge this result. First, we extend the evaluation from Majewska et al. (2021), who compare word embedding clusters to coarse-grained semantic categories generated by humans in a word sorting task, by evaluating sense-specific embeddings in addition to the static embeddings previously reported. We find that retaining sense-level information from contextual BERT embeddings more than doubles its F1 score, outperforming static embeddings by a large margin. This result suggests that the reported under-performance of BERT in Majewska et al. (2021) was due not to the irrelevance of context to categorization or an inherent weakness of contextual embedding models, but rather to the fact that information about polysemy was thrown away in generating static embeddings from contextual models.

Next, we evaluate the same set of models on fine-grained categorization, using categories derived from human similarity judgments. Contrary to the coarse-grained setting, we find that static and contextual models perform about the same in predicting fine-grained categories. We surmise that humans use different cognitive processes to perform word sorting vs similarity judgment tasks. Choosing the best word embeddings thus depends on the type of behavior one is trying to model.

Proceedings of the 11th Joint Conference on Lexical and Computational Semantics, pages 123 - 131
July 14-15, 2022 ©2022 Association for Computational Linguistics

2 Background

Since both static and contextual embeddings have been shown to model pairwise similarity between words well (Pereira et al., 2016; Chronis and Erk, 2020), and since similarity is a primary criterion for categorization, it seems intuitive that word embeddings should perform well at categorization tasks. Some previous work supports this intuition; word embeddings have excelled at word sense disambiguation (Giulianelli et al., 2020; Soler and Apidianaki, 2021; Chronis and Erk, 2020) and topic modeling (Sia et al., 2020; Aharoni and Goldberg, 2020) when cast as categorization problems.

In the present paper, we are interested in semantic category induction. Instead of grouping instances of a word into distinct senses, or documents into topics, the goal of semantic categorization is to group unique words into semantically related clusters. This more abstract type of categorization has received less attention in the word embedding literature; a few probing studies have tested whether different models encode a pre-defined set of categories (Senel et al., 2018; Yaghoobzadeh et al., 2019; Michael et al., 2020), but in all cases these categories were stipulated by the researchers and had not been experimentally validated.

Majewska et al. (2021) recently published a more empirical categorization dataset, based on judgments from non-expert native speakers, rather than stipulated by trained researchers. The dataset, SpA-Verb[1], contains data from two tasks. The first is a sorting task, where participants grouped a set of verbs into broad semantic classes. The second task involves spatial multi-arrangement, which provides finer-grained judgments about the similarity between words within a single semantic domain. SpA-Verb is valuable as an evaluation resource for modeling categorization because it allows for a more direct comparison between human categorization behavior and model behavior than previous datasets. Also, SpA-Verb contains 825 verbs in 17 semantic classes, which is much more comprehensive than other available category datasets.

Most of the verbs in SpA-Verb are polysemous. While many words belong to more than one class (corresponding to distinct senses of those words), the dataset has so far only been used to evaluate static word embeddings (either from static models or extracted static representations from contextual models). Our goal with the following study is to find out when polysemy matters in modeling natural language semantics, in particular, whether sense-specific representations are better predictors of human behavior on some semantic tasks, but not others.

[1] `https://github.com/om304/SpA-Verb`

3 Models

Below we describe the word embedding models we evaluate on SpA-Verb:

3.1 Word2vec

The first model we evaluate is a word2vec model trained on part-of-speech-tagged data (Fares et al., 2017). POS tagging allows the static model to distinguish between senses which have different parts of speech (e.g. *duck_NOUN* and *duck_VERB*), although senses which have the same POS are still conflated into a single vector (e.g. *get#ACQUIRE* and *get#UNDERSTAND*). Skip-gram with negative sampling was used to train the model on Gigaword 5th Edition (Parker et al., 2011), with a context window size 5 and 300 dimensions.

3.2 BERT

We evaluate three methods of extracting BERT embeddings: two baseline methods, which create one representation per word form, and a multi-prototype method which generates one representation per word sense. For all methods we use BERT Base Uncased from HuggingFace's transformers package (Wolf et al., 2020).

Decontextualized (Decont). First and most simply, we extract embeddings from BERT by feeding each word to the model in isolation. This creates a single, static embedding for each word. This strategy has been used previously as a way to easily extract 'context-free' representations from BERT (Liu et al., 2019; Vulić et al., 2020).

Aggregated (Aggr). Next, we create static embeddings from BERT by averaging a word's embeddings across 100 unique contexts. This aggregated approach still reduces a word to a single representation, but has been shown to produce higher quality representations than the decontextualized strategy (Bommasani et al., 2020).

Multiprototype (MPro). Finally, to test whether sense-specific information is important to semantic categorization, we distill token-level BERT embeddings into multiple prototype embeddings. We use the method of Chronis and Erk (2020) to generate representations which corre-

Model	F1-optimal	F1-gold
Random baseline	0.204	0.161
Majewska word2vec	0.355	0.326
Majewska best BERT	0.340	0.322
POS-tagged word2vec	0.442	0.433
Decont. BERT	0.309	0.191
Aggr. BERT	0.398	0.346
MPro BERT	**0.743**	**0.687**

Table 1: Average F1 across models on coarse-grained categories. 'Gold' is for k=17, as in the ground truth. 'Optimal' is best result for k in the range (5, 50).

spond to different senses of a word, without collapsing every token into a single representation (see Appendix A).

3.3 Random Baseline

Finally, we generate random vectors and evaluate them in order establish a baseline for random chance performance.

4 Evaluation

To evaluate the performance of each model on the ground truth classes, k-means clustering is used to group verbs into predicted classes. We use the same metrics as Majewska et al. (2021): modified purity and weighted class accuracy are combined in an F1 score, calculated as their balanced harmonic mean. Modified purity is the mean precision of predicted clusters, while weighted class accuracy targets recall (see Appendix B).

Because MPro BERT has multiple representations for a single word, the same word form may show up more than once within a single cluster. To prevent artificially inflating the recall in evaluating MPro BERT, we eliminate duplicates within each cluster before evaluation.

5 Coarse-grained Categorization

Next we describe our evaluation of each model on coarse-grained categorization.

5.1 Dataset

The Phase 1 data of SpA-Verb contains 825 verbs in 17 broad classes (see Appendix C). 116 verbs belong to more than one class. No words were assigned to more than 3 classes.

5.2 Results

Table 1 shows the results of each embedding type, compared to results reported in Majewska et al. (2021). The baseline models (Decont. and Aggr. BERT) perform comparably to previously reported results. POS-sensitive word2vec model scores about 10 points higher than reported for a similar model architecture without POS information. MPro BERT performs dramatically better than other embeddings, achieving more than double the F1 score of the best previously reported BERT results. This suggests that polysemy does play an important role in modeling semantic categorization.

When we look more closely at MPro BERT, we find that embeddings from later layers are better predictors of the ground truth categories than earlier layers (see Appendix D). Interestingly, layer 0 performance is about on par with the static BERT baselines. Earlier layers of BERT have been shown to contain less contextual information than later layers (Ethayarajh, 2019), so this result further supports the idea that contextual information is important to semantic categorization, and that averaging over all contexts or feeding a word in isolation essentially neutralizes the benefit of contextual models over static models for this task.

The benefit of sense-specific embeddings for this task is clear in the example of *freeze*. In the ground truth data, *freeze* belongs to just one class, related to cooking (along with words like *bake, fry, melt,* and *thaw*). *Freeze* has another figurative sense, meaning to stop or suspend. Because the word is polysemous, static embedding clusters struggle to categorize it appropriately. In the aggregated BERT clusters, *freeze* appears in a cluster predominated by verbs related to violence (*whip, shoot, choke, crush, smash*). Decontextualized BERT puts *freeze* in a heterogeneous cluster with a few cooking words (*melt, stew, fry*) but also many seemingly unrelated words (*knit, greet, disturb, wander*). It appears that the different senses of the word skew its static representation and prevent accurate classification. MPro BERT, by contrast, puts *freeze* in two clusters: one related to cooking (as in the ground truth) and another cluster with words like *stop, delay, arrest* and *restrict*, which seems to correspond to the figurative sense of *freeze*. Thus factoring out different senses allows MPro BERT to give a more accurate and reasonable categorization.

MPro BERT tends to capture more distinct senses per word than human participants did, as they generally focused on a single sense when categorizing. On average, each word form appeared in

3.02 MPro BERT clusters, but only in 1.14 ground truth classes. For example, the word form *jump* occurs in one MPro BERT cluster corresponding to violence (*jump#ATTACK*), another cluster corresponding to physical movement (*jump#HOP*), and a third one related to change (*jump#INCREASE*). In the ground truth data, *jump* only occurs once, in a class related to physical movement. Perhaps this is the most salient sense of the word *jump*, and therefore participants were more likely to be thinking of this sense during the word sorting task and ignore its other possible senses. But although the other two senses of *jump* counted against MPro BERT in our evaluation, the fact that embeddings for *jump* were assigned three separate clusters is not necessarily a weakness: the MPro BERT clusters are more thorough as they represent each sense of the word separately and appropriately assign them to separate clusters.

This example demonstrates that F1 scores do not give a full picture of the quality or reasonableness of the word embedding clusters. Categorization is a relatively flexible task; there may be many possible criteria for sorting a group of words, especially when given such a large set of words to sort (Tversky, 1977; Barsalou, 1982). This might explain the low inter-annotator agreement between two initial test participants on Majewska et al. (2021)'s verb sorting task (0.400 B-Cubed score), suggesting that humans don't perform very consistently in creating broad semantic categories from a large group of words. As a result, it's possible for induced categories from word embeddings to be reasonable, but still correlate poorly with our ground truth data.

6 Fine-grained Categorization

Next, we examine how word embeddings fare on finer-grained categories. We speculated that given a smaller, more focused set of words, there is less ambiguity about the relevant criteria for categorizing words, and so evaluating word embeddings on fine-grained categorization may be a better test of model quality than coarse-grained categorization. This section describes how we created a benchmark for fine-grained categorization from the SpA-Verb Phase 2 data, and evaluated the same models on this new benchmark.

6.1 Dataset

In addition to the broad semantic classes created in Phase 1, SpA-Verb also contains Phase 2: a set of fine-grained similarity data from a spatial multi-arrangement task, where participants arranged all words within a single Phase 1 class on a screen according to their relative similarity. The result is a complete matrix of semantic distances for all words within each Phase 1 class. While the original authors use this as resource for evaluating models on standard pair-wise similarity, it can also serve indirectly as a resource for evaluating category structure. In order to use this similarity data to evaluate embedding clusters, we take each row of a class' distance matrix as the vector representation for that word. We run k-means clustering on these representations, and use these clusters as the ground truth to compare with word embedding clusters.

In the fine-grained categorization setting, we assume that only one sense is relevant for each word; the other words in the class implicitly disambiguate between possible senses of a polysemous word, since they were all assigned to a single semantic class in Phase 1. For example, when *stew* occurs in a class with other words related to cooking, the sense of *stew* meaning to worry or fret is not relevant. Since there is only one relevant sense per word for the fine-grained categorization task, in order to evaluate our MPro BERT embeddings in this setting, we need to automatically decide which of a word's sense embeddings is the most relevant given a particular class. To do this, we apply the MAXSIM method used by Chronis and Erk (2020): for each pair of words in a given class, we find the MPro embeddings that yield the highest similarity between the two words. Then, for each word, the prototype that produced the MAXSIM for the most other class members is selected as its most relevant sense, and all other sense embeddings are discarded.

6.2 Results

Table 2 shows the average F1 scores across all 17 classes for each type of embedding. Unlike in the coarse-grained setting, there is not a significant difference between models. Aggregated BERT has a slight advantage with an average F1 of 0.643. All three types of static embeddings do significantly better on fine-grained than coarse-grained categorization. By contrast, F1 for BERT MPro embeddings is 15 points lower in the fine-grained compared to the coarse-grained setting. Furthermore, the opposite pattern appears across BERT layers, with earlier layers performing better and later lay-

Model	Average F1
Random baseline	0.033
word2vec	0.626
BERT decontext.	0.586
BERT aggregated	**0.643**
MPro BERT	0.582

Table 2: Average F1 across all classes for each embedding type on fine-grained categorization.

ers performing worse. It seems that accounting for polysemy makes little difference in the ability of embeddings to identify fine-grained categories.

The ground truth classes with the highest F1 across models were related to sound (*buzz, boom, chirp, rattle*) and physiological processes (*sweat, cough, breathe, yawn*). The classes with the lowest F1 across models were transitive verbs related to physical movement (*drag, fling, tow, throw, lift*) and verbs of communication (*announce, discuss, explain, tell*). In general, smaller and more specific classes were easier to categorize than larger, broader classes (see Appendix E for detailed breakdown of model performance by category).

This stark difference in the relative performance of static and contextual embeddings on two different levels of category granularity is surprising. One possible explanation for this result is that the ground truth for fine-grained categorization was derived from similarity judgment data, and thus may reflect a fundamentally different cognitive process than the coarse-grained ground truth, which came from a sorting task. Phase 2 data was obtained by asking participants to make similarity judgments among a group of words. Our assumption was that since similarity is the primary criteria for categorizing words, similarity data would yield the same categories as a sorting task. However, in the absence of any disambiguating context, participants may have made decisions about similarity based on all exemplars of a word, rather than focusing on one particular sense. By contrast, participants in the Phase 1 sorting task were asked to make explicit category judgments. Categorizing words forces participants to select criteria or features for membership in a particular category. Because of this, participants in the sorting task may have singled out a particular sense of a word in making their decision. Evidence from psycholinguistics supports the idea that human performance on different semantic tasks may derive from very different cognitive processes (Kumar, 2021).

If context-free similarity judgments activate all exemplars of a word, this would explain why static embeddings (in particular the aggregated BERT embeddings, which average over many exemplars) would better fit the Phase 2 data. On the other hand, if semantic categorization activates specific criteria and forces participants to focus on a particular sense of words in making a decision, this would explain why MPro BERT better predicts the Phase 1 data. In order to make a more direct comparison between coarse- and fine-grained categorization, we plan to replicate the Phase 1 sorting task for each individual semantic class.

7 Conclusion

Majewska et al. (2021) found that contextual BERT embeddings performed more poorly than static word2vec on the SpA-Verb semantic categorization benchmark. In this paper, we challenged their analysis, testing the effect of sense-specific contextual information on model performance on two different levels of category granularity, and find that the rich sense-specific information contained in BERT, if properly exploited, allows BERT to excel in predicting coarse-grained human semantic categories. Our results suggest that polysemy affects coarse-grained categorization, and that accounting for polysemy can significantly improve the predictions of embedding models.

On the other hand, contextual information seems to be less relevant in modeling finer-grained categories derived from similarity judgments. It seems that humans rely on different underlying processes in making context-free similarity judgments between words than when making decisions about category membership. While similarity is judged based on a summary of all of a word's exemplars, categorization requires choosing specific criteria for membership and thus focuses attention on a particular sense of a word.

While using sense-specific embeddings seems best for performing category induction, static representations are still desirable for some applications. For example, in making a cross-linguistic or historical comparison of word meanings, clustering average representations may be more appropriate than many sense-specific ones. Ultimately, both types of behavior are of interest within NLP, but it's important to choose an approach carefully, by considering exactly what type of behavior one is trying to model.

References

Roee Aharoni and Yoav Goldberg. 2020. Unsupervised domain clusters in pretrained language models. In *Proceedings of the 58th Annual Meeting of the Association for Computational Linguistics*, pages 7747–7763.

Lawrence W Barsalou. 1982. Context-independent and context-dependent information in concepts. *Memory & cognition*, 10(1):82–93.

BNC Consortium. 2007. British national corpus. *Oxford Text Archive Core Collection*.

Rishi Bommasani, Kelly Davis, and Claire Cardie. 2020. Interpreting pretrained contextualized representations via reductions to static embeddings. In *Proceedings of the 58th Annual Meeting of the Association for Computational Linguistics*, pages 4758–4781.

Gabriella Chronis and Katrin Erk. 2020. When is a bishop not like a rook? when it's like a rabbi! multi-prototype BERT embeddings for estimating semantic relationships. In *Proceedings of the 24th Conference on Computational Natural Language Learning*, pages 227–244, Online. Association for Computational Linguistics.

Jacob Devlin, Ming-Wei Chang, Kenton Lee, and Kristina Toutanova. 2019. BERT: Pre-training of deep bidirectional transformers for language understanding. In *Proceedings of the 2019 Conference of the North American Chapter of the Association for Computational Linguistics: Human Language Technologies, Volume 1 (Long and Short Papers)*, pages 4171–4186, Minneapolis, Minnesota. Association for Computational Linguistics.

Kawin Ethayarajh. 2019. How contextual are contextualized word representations? comparing the geometry of bert, elmo, and gpt-2 embeddings. In *Proceedings of the 2019 Conference on Empirical Methods in Natural Language Processing and the 9th International Joint Conference on Natural Language Processing (EMNLP-IJCNLP)*, pages 55–65.

Murhaf Fares, Andrey Kutuzov, Stephan Oepen, and Erik Velldal. 2017. Word vectors, reuse, and replicability: Towards a community repository of large-text resources. *Proceedings of the 21st Nordic Conference on Computational Linguistics, NoDaLiDa, 22-24 May 2017, Gothenburg, Sweden*, 131:271–276.

Mario Giulianelli, Marco Del Tredici, and Raquel Fernández. 2020. Analysing lexical semantic change with contextualised word representations. In *Proceedings of the 58th Annual Meeting of the Association for Computational Linguistics*, pages 3960–3973, Online. Association for Computational Linguistics.

Abhilasha A Kumar. 2021. Semantic memory: A review of methods, models, and current challenges. *Psychonomic Bulletin & Review*, 28(1):40–80.

Thomas K Landauer and Susan T Dumais. 1997. A solution to plato's problem: The latent semantic analysis theory of acquisition, induction, and representation of knowledge. *Psychological review*, 104(2):211.

Qianchu Liu, Diana McCarthy, Ivan Vulić, and Anna Korhonen. 2019. Investigating cross-lingual alignment methods for contextualized embeddings with token-level evaluation. In *Proceedings of the 23rd Conference on Computational Natural Language Learning (CoNLL)*, pages 33–43.

Olga Majewska, Diana McCarthy, Jasper JF van den Bosch, Nikolaus Kriegeskorte, Ivan Vulić, and Anna Korhonen. 2021. Semantic data set construction from human clustering and spatial arrangement. *Computational Linguistics*, 47(1):69–116.

Julian Michael, Jan A Botha, and Ian Tenney. 2020. Asking without telling: Exploring latent ontologies in contextual representations. In *Proceedings of the 2020 Conference on Empirical Methods in Natural Language Processing (EMNLP)*, pages 6792–6812.

Tomas Mikolov, Kai Chen, Greg Corrado, and Jeffrey Dean. 2013. Efficient estimation of word representations in vector space. *1st International Conference on Learning Representations, ICLR 2013 - Workshop Track Proceedings*, pages 1–12.

George A Miller. 1995. Wordnet: a lexical database for english. *Communications of the ACM*, 38(11):39–41.

Robert Parker, David Graff, Junbo Kong, Ke Chen, and Kazuaki Maeda. 2011. *English Gigaword Fifth Edition*. Linguistic Data Consortium.

Jeffrey Pennington, Richard Socher, and Christopher D Manning. 2014. Glove: Global vectors for word representation. In *Proceedings of the 2014 conference on empirical methods in natural language processing (EMNLP)*, pages 1532–1543.

Francisco Pereira, Samuel Gershman, Samuel Ritter, and Matthew Botvinick. 2016. A comparative evaluation of off-the-shelf distributed semantic representations for modelling behavioural data. *Cognitive Neuropsychology*, 33(3-4):175–190.

Matthew E. Peters, Mark Neumann, Mohit Iyyer, Matt Gardner, Christopher Clark, Kenton Lee, and Luke Zettlemoyer. 2018. Deep contextualized word representations. In *Proceedings of the 2018 Conference of the North American Chapter of the Association for Computational Linguistics: Human Language Technologies, Volume 1 (Long Papers)*, pages 2227–2237, New Orleans, Louisiana. Association for Computational Linguistics.

Lutfi Kerem Senel, Ihsan Utlu, Veysel Yucesoy, Aykut Koc, and Tolga Cukur. 2018. Semantic structure and interpretability of word embeddings. *IEEE/ACM Transactions on Audio Speech and Language Processing*, 26(10):1769–1779.

Suzanna Sia, Ayush Dalmia, and Sabrina J Mielke. 2020. Tired of topic models? clusters of pretrained word embeddings make for fast and good topics too! In *Proceedings of the 2020 Conference on Empirical Methods in Natural Language Processing (EMNLP)*, pages 1728–1736.

Aina Gari Soler and Marianna Apidianaki. 2021. Let's play mono-poly: Bert can reveal words' polysemy level and partitionability into senses. *arXiv preprint arXiv:2104.14694*.

Amos Tversky. 1977. Features of similarity. *Psychological Review*, 84(4):327–352.

Ivan Vulić, Simon Baker, Edoardo Maria Ponti, Ulla Petti, Ira Leviant, Kelly Wing, Olga Majewska, Eden Bar, Matt Malone, Thierry Poibeau, et al. 2020. Multi-simlex: A large-scale evaluation of multilingual and crosslingual lexical semantic similarity. *Computational Linguistics*, 46(4):847–897.

Thomas Wolf, Lysandre Debut, Victor Sanh, Julien Chaumond, Clement Delangue, Anthony Moi, Pierric Cistac, Tim Rault, Rémi Louf, Morgan Funtowicz, et al. 2020. Transformers: State-of-the-art natural language processing. In *Proceedings of the 2020 conference on empirical methods in natural language processing: system demonstrations*, pages 38–45.

Yadollah Yaghoobzadeh, Katharina Kann, Timothy J Hazen, Eneko Agirre, and Hinrich Schütze. 2019. Probing for semantic classes: Diagnosing the meaning content of word embeddings. In *Proceedings of the 57th Annual Meeting of the Association for Computational Linguistics*, pages 5740–5753.

A Multi-Prototype BERT embeddings

Multi-prototype embeddings were generated as follows:

1. For each verb in the dataset, we sampled up to 100 sentences from the British National Corpus (BNC Consortium, 2007), excluding non-verbal uses of the target word. A few words in the set occurred in BNC fewer than 100 times. Four words (*broil*, *corrupt*, *exhale*, and *misspend*) did not occur as verbs at all in the BNC and were excluded from our analysis. The average number of occurrences sampled for a word was 95.6.

2. We extract BERT token embeddings for each collected occurrence of a word. For words which BERT tokenizes into multiple word pieces, we average over all component pieces.

3. We cluster the token embeddings for each verb. Like Chronis and Erk (2020), we use *k*-means clustering to group tokens into 'sense' clusters. We use the number of verb senses listed in WordNet (Miller, 1995) to determine the appropriate *k* for each word. Verbs in the dataset had on average 5.9 senses. (min: 1, max: 59, for *buzz*).

4. After identifying clusters, we take the *k* cluster centroids for each word. These are the embeddings we evaluate against the SpA-Verb categorization data.

B Evaluation metrics

As in Majewska et al. (2021), we evaluate performance of word embeddings on semantic categorization using modified purity and weighted class accuracy, which are combined in an F1 score, calculated as their balanced harmonic mean. Modified purity is the mean precision of automatically induced verb clusters:

$$\text{MPUR} = \frac{\sum_{C \in Clust, n_{prev(C)}>1} n_{prev(C)}}{\#test\_verbs} \quad (1)$$

where each cluster C from the set of all K_{Clust} induced clusters *Clust* is associated with its prevalent gold class, and $n_{prev(C)}$ is the number of verbs in an induced cluster C taking that prevalent class, with all other verbs considered errors. $\#test\_verbs$ is the total number of verbs in the dataset. While modified purity is a measure of precision, weighted class accuracy targets recall:

$$\text{WACC} = \frac{\sum_{C \in Gold} n_{dom(C)}}{\#test\_verbs} \quad (2)$$

where for each class C from the set of gold standard classes *Gold*, we identify the dominant cluster from the set of induced clusters having most verbs in common with C ($n_{dom(C)}$).

C Ground truth coarse-grained categories

The ground truth categories used for evaluating models on coarse-grained categorization come from Phase 1 of SpA-Verb. 825 verbs are grouped into 17 broad semantic classes. Table 3 gives an overview of the classes.

D MPro BERT Cross Layer Analysis

The MPro BERT embeddings from later layers of BERT are better predictors of the ground truth categories than earlier layers. As shown in Figure 1, F1

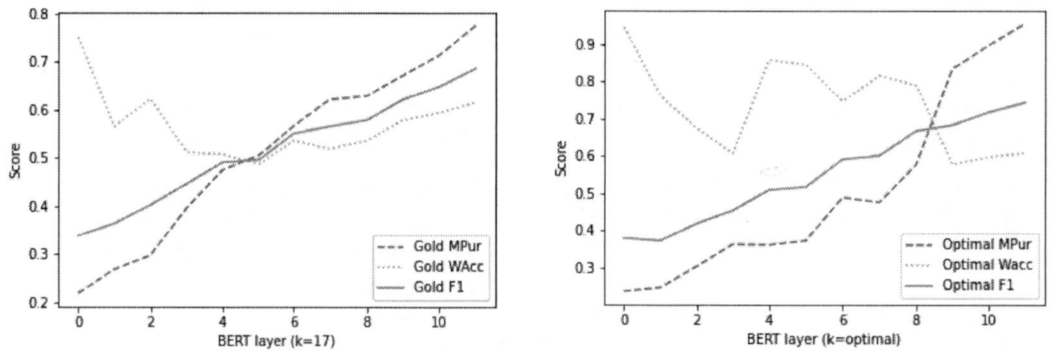

Figure 1: Performance of multi-prototype BERT embeddings from each layer. Left: gold case (k=17), right: optimal case

Cluster label	Example verbs
movement	*wander, fly, glide, roam*
communication	*persuade, command, tell*
crime & law	*beat, abduct, abuse, shoot*
negative emotion	*offend, aggravate, enrage*
positive emotion	*admire, respect, adore, like*
cognitive process	*suppose, assume, realize*
cooking	*cook, slice, stew, boil*
possession	*belong, obtain, acquire*

Table 3: A sample of the 17 gold classes in SpA-Verb dataset (labels are given for descriptive purposes only)

scores increase virtually monotonically from the first to last layer of BERT. Layer 0 performance is about on par with the static BERT baselines.

In general, recall (WACC) decreases from earlier to later layers of BERT, while the precision measure (MPUR) increases. The increase in precision is steeper than the decrease in recall, leading the F1 scores to trend up in later layers. The optimal k value for the middle layers is very low (5-10) but much higher for early and later layers (20-30). As can be seen in Figure 1, there is a spike in recall in the middle layers, likely due to the lower k values. Having a few large clusters means that clusters are more likely to overlap with gold classes, even if they contain extra irrelevant members.

E Fine-Grained Categorization Results

Table 4 shows a breakdown of the F1 scores for each model by class. The classes which all models did best at categorizing were Class 13 (which contains words describing sounds like *boom, buzz, crunch, rattle, squeak*), Class 3 (related to change: *accelerate, diminish, grow*) and Class 12 (physiological processes: *sweat, cough, breathe, yawn*). The classes which models struggled most with were Class 15 (physical movement: *catch, grab, fling, jerk*), Class 7 (communication: *announce, discuss, explain, tell*), and Class 9 (cognitive processes: *analyze, describe, ponder, think*).

Class	word2vec	BERT decontext.	BERT aggreg.	MPro BERT	Average
1	0.624	0.521	0.547	0.541	0.558
2	0.563	0.606	0.619	0.563	0.588
3	0.679	0.660	0.685	0.629	0.663
4	0.535	0.498	0.654	0.545	0.558
5	0.610	0.676	0.673	0.671	0.657
6	0.600	0.589	0.697	0.61	0.625
7	0.498	0.532	0.605	0.556	0.548
8	0.649	0.542	0.649	0.586	0.606
9	0.579	0.521	0.578	0.539	0.554
10	0.504	0.59	0.587	0.598	0.570
11	0.788	0.624	0.60	0.585	0.651
12	0.722	0.581	0.727	0.616	0.661
13	0.742	0.647	0.764	0.573	0.682
14	0.603	0.499	0.653	0.58	0.584
15	0.508	0.572	0.531	0.561	0.543
16	0.740	0.629	0.672	0.545	0.646
17	0.694	0.658	0.682	0.595	0.657
Average	0.626	0.586	0.643	0.582	0.609

Table 4: F1 for each class and embedding type on fine-grained categorization.

Word-Label Alignment for Event Detection: A New Perspective via Optimal Transport

Amir Pouran Ben Veyseh
Department of Computer and Information Science
University of Oregon
Eugene, Oregon, USA
apouranb@cs.uoregon.edu

Thien Huu Nguyen
Department of Computer and Information Science
University of Oregon
Eugene, Oregon, USA
thien@cs.uoregon.edu

Abstract

Event Detection (ED) aims to identify mentions/triggers of real world events in text. In the literature, this task is modeled as a sequence-labeling or word-prediction problem. In this work, we present a novel formulation in which ED is modeled as a word-label alignment task. In particular, given the words in a sentence and possible event types, the objective is to infer an alignment matrix in which event trigger words are aligned with the most likely event types. Moreover, we show that this new perspective facilitates the incorporation of word-label alignment biases to improve alignment matrix for ED. Novel alignment biases and Optimal Transport are introduced to solve our alignment problem for ED. We conduct experiments on a benchmark dataset to demonstrate the effectiveness of the proposed model for ED.

1 Introduction

Event Detection (ED) is one of the critical tasks in Information Extraction. Its goal is to identify and classify event triggers, i.e., the words/phrases that most clearly refer to the occurrence of an event of some predefined types in text. For example, in the sentence "*Joe Biden was born on November 20, 1942*", an ED system should recognize the word "*born*" as a trigger word of an event of type *Birth*.

A major challenge for ED is to assign an appropriate event type label for each word in a given sentence. In this work, we introduce a new perspective to solve ED as a word-label alignment problem that aims to align the set of words in the input sentence with the set of possible event type labels to represent correct label assignment for words. A key requirement for ED models in this new perspective involve inferring an alignment matrix to capture an alignment likelihood score between each pair of words and label types. The models can then be trained by enforcing the similarity between the predicted alignment matrix and the golden alignment matrix (computed from training data). In this way, previous ED models can be seen as a way to achieve the alignment matrix between words and labels where label distributions computed by the models serve as the alignment likelihood scores (Nguyen and Grishman, 2015; Chen et al., 2015; Wang et al., 2019; Cui et al., 2020; Ngo et al., 2021). However, given the word-label alignment perspective, previous ED models are suboptimal in at least two ways. First, the alignment likelihood scores in prior models are only used locally for each word (i.e., to compute the cross-entropy loss for each word to train models). The global uses of alignment matrix (e.g., to compute an overall distance between words and labels for training signals) are thus not yet explored in previous ED models. Second, current ED models mainly obtain alignment likelihood scores based on representation vectors for words and types, thus unable to exploit assignment biases to improve quality of the alignment matrix to train ED models. In particular, we propose two types of alignment biases that can be helpful for ED: (1) Word Preference: words with high likelihoods to be event triggers should be more aligned with event type labels (i.e., not the *Other* type for non-trigger words), and (2) Type Preference: event types that have higher chance to be appear in the input sentence should be associated with greater alignment scores. In all, we expect that global application and alignment biases can provide complementary information to boost current ED models in the new perspective.

To implement this idea, we propose to encode event trigger likelihoods for words and appearance likelihoods for event types as two distributions over words and event type labels (respectively) that will be induced from a deep learning architecture. Next, to inject the alignment biases into our ED model, we propose to feed the two distributions into Optimal Transport (OT) (Peyre and Cuturi, 2019) to induce an alignment matrix between words and event type labels. OT is an established framework

Proceedings of the 11th Joint Conference on Lexical and Computational Semantics, pages 132 - 138
July 14-15, 2022

to find the optimal alignment between two distributions, thus providing a decent solution to incorporate alignment biases to compute alignment matrix in our ED problem. Finally, the induced alignment matrix will be leveraged to obtain a distance between words and event type labels, serving as a global application of the alignment matrix to introduce new training signals for ED. We conduct extensive experiments on a benchmark dataset to deliver state-of-the-art performance for ED. In summary, our contributions include:

- A new perspective based on word-label alignment for event detection.
- Introduction of optimal transport to incorporate novel alignment biases for event detection.
- State-of-the-art performance for sequence-labeling event detection.

2 Model

Given an input sentence $S = [w_1, w_2, \ldots, w_n]$, the goal of ED is to predict the label sequence $L = [l_1, l_2, \ldots, l_n]$ where $l_i \in \mathcal{T}$ is the label for the word $w_i \in S$. Here, the label set $\mathcal{T}$ involves the BIO encoding tags for the event types in a given event ontology (e.g., *B_Birth*, *I_Birth*, and *Other*). In this work, we propose to model ED as a word-label alignment problem where an alignment matrix is formed to capture the assignment likelihood for every pair of words in S and labels in $\mathcal{T}$. We will first discuss word/label representations, and alignment matrix computation for training afterward.

Word & Label Representation: To represent the words in S, following prior work (Wang et al., 2019), we employ the pre-trained BERT model (Devlin et al., 2019). Concretely, the input sentence $[[CLS], w_1, w_2, \ldots, w_n]$ is fed into BERT to compute the contextualized embedding vectors $E = [e_{cls}, e_1, e_2, \ldots, e_n]$. We employ the average of vectors in the last layer of BERT to produce E. For the words with multiple word-pieces, we take the average of their word-piece representations.

To represent the event type labels l_i, we employ a randomly initialized embedding table T in which every label is represented by a vector t_i. The representations of the labels are updated during training.

Alignment: To predict the label sequence L with our alignment idea, for every word w_i, an alignment likelihood score $a_{i,j}$ between w_i and each label l_j is required (i.e., forming an alignment matrix A). Using the scores $a_{i,j}$, the label $\bar{l}_i$ can be predicted by $\bar{l}_i = \text{argmax}_j a_{i,j}$. Note that in prior ED models, the alignment scores $a_{i,j}$ are directly computed using the final task-specific feed-forward networks (Wang et al., 2019; Veyseh et al., 2021b). This approach is equivalent to computing the similarity between the representation vectors w_i and t_j, e.g., via dot-product. We call this approach "*Vanilla Alignment*". However, as discussed in the introduction, vanilla alignment scores $a_{i,j}$ are solely dependent on the learned representations e_i and t_j. As such, they cannot incorporate the alignment biases into the alignment matrix for ED.

To this end, we introduce two alignment biases that can be exploited to improve the word-label alignment for ED. In particular, for an effective ED model, we expect the words that are more likely to be event triggers to have higher alignment scores with event types. In contrast, the other words should be better aligned with the special label *Other*. i.e., non-trigger. We call this bias "*Word Preference*" for ED. In addition, among all event types, it is expected that the event types that have higher chance to be mentioned in the input sentence to be associated with greater scores in the alignment matrix A. We name this bias as "*Type Preference*". In this work, we aim to modify the vanilla alignment approach such that the two aforementioned preferences are observed. The quantification of Word and Type Preference and their incorporation into alignment matrix will be discussed in the following.

Word & Type Preference: To compute the word preference and type preference in the input sentence S, we consider two simpler versions of the ED problem. Specifically, for word preference, we utilize the Trigger Identification (TI) task that seeks to recognize the event trigger words without classifying them by event types. The event trigger probability computed for TI can be used to quantify the event trigger likelihood for each word $w_i \in S$. Concretely, the representation e_i of w_i is fed into a feed-forward network with sigmoid activation function to compute the trigger likelihood p_i^w for w_i: $p_i^w = \sigma(FF_w(e_i))$, where σ and FF_w are sigmoid and feed-forward layer, respectively. To supervise the trigger likelihood scores, we include the binary cross-entropy loss function for TI into the overall loss for training: $\mathcal{L}_{TI} = -\frac{1}{n}\sum_{i=1}^{n}(y_i^w * \log(p_i^w) + (1-y_i^w) * \log(1-p_i^w))$, where y_i^w is a binary number to indicate whether if w_i is a trigger in S. The likelihood scores p_i^w are employed to represent the word preference.

Next, for the type preference, we exploit the task of Type Prediction (TP) for ED. In this task, the objective is to predict which event types are mentioned in the sentence S (i.e., without predicting the trigger words). For an event type label t_j, we predict the likelihood for t_j to be mentioned in S by concatenating the type representation t_j with the sentence representation e_{cls} and feeding the result into a separate feed-forward network FF_t with sigmoid activation to obtain the appearance likelihood for t_j: $p_j^t = \sigma(FF_t([t_j, e_{cls}]))$. To supervise the appearance likelihoods, the binary cross-entropy loss function for TP is employed: $\mathcal{L}_{TP} = -\frac{1}{|\mathcal{T}|}\sum_{j=1}^{|\mathcal{T}|}(y_j^t * \log(p_j^t) + (1 - y_j^t) * \log(1 - p_j^t)$, where y_j^t is a binary number to indicate the appearance of the event type t_j in S. The likelihood scores p_j^t are utilized to represent the type preference.

Alignment Computation: Given the word and type preference scores p_i^w and p_j^t, how can we compute an alignment matrix A between the words in S and the event type labels in $\mathcal{T}$ that can incorporate both word-label representation similarity (as in vanilla alignment) and designed preference scores for ED? Note that the preference scores can be modeled as two distributions over words and event type labels by applying a softmax function over the word and type likelihoods: $D^{WP} = softmax(p_1^w, p_2^w, \ldots, p_n^w)$ and $D^{TP} = softmax(p_1^t, p_2^t, \ldots, p_T^t)$. As such, we propose to employ Optimal Transport (OT) to elegantly combine the information to produce the alignment matrix A between S and $\mathcal{T}$ for ED.

Formally, given the probability distributions $p(x)$ and $q(y)$ over the domains $\mathcal{X}$ and $\mathcal{Y}$, and the cost/distance function $C(x, y) : \mathcal{X} \times \mathcal{Y} \to \mathbb{R}_+$ for mapping $\mathcal{X}$ to $\mathcal{Y}$, OT finds the optimal joint alignment/distribution $\pi^*(x, y)$ with marginals $p(x)$ and $q(y)$ that converts $p(x)$ to $q(y)$ (i.e., the cheapest plan), by solving the following problem:

$$\pi^*(x,y) = \min_{\pi \in \Pi(x,y)} \sum_{\mathcal{Y}} \sum_{\mathcal{X}} \pi(x,y) C(x,y) \quad \text{s.t. } x \sim p(x) \text{ and } y \sim q(y), \tag{1}$$

Here, $\Pi(x, y)$ involves all joint distributions with marginals $p(x)$ and $q(y)$. As such, the joint distribution $\pi^*(x, y)$ is a matrix whose entry (x, y) ($x \in \mathcal{X}, y \in \mathcal{Y}$) represents the probability of transforming x to y in the optimal transport. We use the Sinkhorn algorithm to approximately solve OT (Peyre and Cuturi, 2019). Finally, given $\pi^*(x, y)$, one approach to employ its global information is to compute the cost of optimal conversion $Dist(\pi^*) = \Sigma_{x\in\mathcal{X}}\Sigma_{y\in\mathcal{Y}}\pi^*(x, y)C(x, y)$ to measure the distance between $\mathcal{X}$ and $\mathcal{Y}$ (i.e., the Wasserstein distance).

To apply OT in our model, the domains $\mathcal{X}$ and $\mathcal{Y}$ are defined as the words $w_i \in S$ and types $t_j \in \mathcal{T}$; the distributions $p(x)$ and $q(y)$ are set to the preference distributions D^{WP} and D^{TP}; and the cost function $C(w_i, t_j)$ is computed using the Euclidean distance between the representations e_i and t_j. As such, solving the OT equation leads to the optimal alignment $\pi^*(w_i, t_j)$, serving as our predicted alignment matrix (i.e., $a_{i,j} = \pi^*(w_i, t_j)$).

To train the ED model with word-label alignment, we propose two training signals obtained from the predicted alignment $\pi^*(e_i, t_j)$. First, by treating the alignment score $\pi^*(e_i, t_j)$ as the probability for w_i to be assigned with label t_j, we employ the negative log-likelihood loss to train our model: $\mathcal{L}_{task} = -\frac{1}{n}\sum_{i=1}^{n}\log(\pi^*(w_i, l_i))$, where l_i is the golden label for w_i in S. Second, we propose to globally enforce the similarity between the predicted alignment matrix $\pi^*(w_i, t_j)$ from OT and the golden binary alignment matrix $\pi^g(w_i, t_j)$ (i.e., $\pi^g(w_i, t_j) = 1$ if only if w_i has the golden label t_j). As such, to aggregate the information in the alignment matrices, we first compute the Wasserstein distances $Dist(\pi^*)$ and $Dist(\pi^g)$ based on the predicted and golden alignments π^* and π^g. Afterward, we seek to minimize the difference between $Dist(\pi^*)$ and $Dist(\pi^g)$ to achieve alignment matrix similarity to train our ED models, leading to the loss: $\mathcal{L}_{OT} = |Dist(\pi^*) - Dist(\pi^g)|$. Finally, the overall loss function for the entire model is $\mathcal{L} = \alpha_{task}\mathcal{L}_{task} + \alpha_{OT}\mathcal{L}_{OT} + \alpha_{TI}\mathcal{L}_{TI} + \alpha_{TP}\mathcal{L}_{TP}$.

3 Experiments

Datasets & Baselines: We evaluate the performance of the proposed model (called **OTED**) on the ACE 2005 dataset (Walker et al., 2006) that annotates 599 documents for 33 event types in English. We use the same data split and preprocessing as prior work (Wang et al., 2019; Veyseh et al., 2021b) for this dataset. The numbers of documents for the training/development/test data are 529/30/40 respectively. Following (Wang et al., 2020a; Veyseh et al., 2021b), we use the sequence-labeling setting for the ED task in ACE 2005 that adheres to the original annotation to allow event

Model	ACE		
	P	R	F1
BiLSTM	77.20	74.90	75.40
DMBERT	71.49	76.95	74.12
BERT+CRF	71.30	77.10	74.10
ED3C	80.31	76.04	78.12
OTED (ours)	79.28	79.48	**79.38**

Table 1: Model performance on the test sets. OTED is significantly better than the baselines with $p < 0.05$.

Line	Model	P	R	F1
1	OTED (full)	79.12	79.94	**79.53**
2	OTED - WP	75.14	81.39	78.14
3	OTED - TP	77.32	78.55	77.93
4	OTED - WP- TP	76.90	76.92	76.91
5	OTED - $\mathcal{L}_{task}$	75.24	77.02	76.12
6	OTED - $\mathcal{L}_{OT}$	75.92	80.28	78.04
7	OTED - $\mathcal{L}_{TI}$	78.91	75.60	77.22
8	OTED - $\mathcal{L}_{TP}$	78.21	76.05	77.12
9	Distance	76.66	78.03	77.34
10	Alignment	77.98	78.93	78.45

Table 2: Model performance on the ACE 2005 dev set.

triggers to span multiple words.

As the baselines, we compare with the typical sequence labeling models for ED, i.e., **BiLSTM**, **DMBERT** (BERT with dynamic multi-pooling), and **BERT+CRF** in (Wang et al., 2020a), and the prior state-of-the-art (SOTA) model reported for ACE 2005, i.e., **ED3C** (Veyseh et al., 2021b). For all the models, we use the same version of pre-trained BERT$_{base}$ to achieve a fair comparison. Following prior work (Wang et al., 2020b; Veyseh et al., 2021b), we use span-based precision, recall and F1 scores for correctly predicting the boundaries and types of event triggers as the performance metrics. Finally, we fine-tune the hyper-parameters for OTED using the development data of ACE 2005. In our model we use the BERT$_{base}$ model to encode data; 2 layers for all the feed-forward neural networks with 200 hidden dimensions in the layers. The trade-off parameters α_{task}, α_{OT}, α_{TI} and α_{TP} are set to 1.0, 0.01, 0.05, and 0.01 respectively. The learning rate is set to 3e-5 for the Adam optimizer and the batch size of 8 is employed during training.

Results: The model performance is presented in Table 1. This table shows that OTED significantly outperforms the baseline models on ACE 2005. We attribute the superiority of OTED to its capability to incorporate alignment biases, i.e., word and type preference, into alignment-based ED. The better performance of OTED over ED3C is important as unlike this baseline OTED does not require additional document context or supervision from other related tasks.

Ablation Study: We conduct an ablation study for the components of OTED over the ACE 2005 development set. Table 2 presents the performance of three groups of ablated models for OTED. In the first group (lines 2-4), we exclude one or both alignment biases, i.e., WP and TP, from OTED. Concretely, to remove a preference, its corresponding distribution in the OT (i.e., D^{WP} and D^{TP}) is replaced with the uniform distribution in the OT computation for OTED. It is clear from the table that both alignment biases are beneficial for OTED as removing any of them would hurt the performance significantly. Next, the second group (lines 5-8), we exclude each loss component (i.e., $\mathcal{L}_{task}$, $\mathcal{L}_{OT}$, $\mathcal{L}_{TP}$, and $\mathcal{L}_{TI}$) from the overall loss $\mathcal{L}$ to train OTED. As can be seen, all the designed losses contribute significantly to the performance of OTED, thus testifying to their effectiveness in alignment-based ED. Also, in the third group (lines 9-10), we explore two variants of OTED to justify the design of the loss $\mathcal{L}_{OT}$ to incorporate OT into the model. In one variant (called **Distance** in line 9), instead of minimizing the difference $\mathcal{L}_{OT}$ between the Wasserstein distances based on predicted and golden alignments, we directly minimize the predicted Wasserstein distance $Dist(\pi^*)$ between words and labels. Moreover, in the **Alignment** variant in line 10, instead of employing the Wasserstein distance, we directly minimize the distance between the predicted and golden alignment $\pi^*(w_i, t_j)$ and $\pi^g(w_i, t_j)$ (i.e., evaluated by $\sum_{i,j} |\pi^*(w_i, t_j) - \pi^g(w_i, t_j)|/(n|\mathcal{T}|)$). As can be seen, both **Distance** and **Alignment** lead to inferior performance for OTED, thereby showing the effectiveness of $\mathcal{L}_{OT}$ for ED. As such, we attribute the poor performance of **Distance** to the lack of supervision from the golden alignment-based distance $\pi^g(w_i, t_j)$, and the worse performance of **Alignment** to the missing of contextual similarity (i.e., the cost $C(w_i, t_j)$) in the distance computation.

Analysis: In this section, we present a qualitative analysis to shed more light on the superiority of the proposed model OTED to the prior sequence labeling methods. Specifically, we compare our model with the **BERT+CRF** baseline by analyzing the examples in which **BERT+CRF** fails to recog-

ID	Example	BERT+CRF Prediction	OTED Prediction	Gold Event Trigger & Type
1	These are the reasons that none of these mothereffers should ever see the light of day ... they need to be all lined up and **shot**.	Trigger: "*shot*", Event Type: ***Contact:Meet***	Trigger: "*shot*", Event Type: *Justice:Execute*	Trigger: "*shot*", Event Type: *Justice:Execute*
2	Well , John, given all that you've said, we know that there's an American **retired** general **waiting** in Kuwait.	Trigger: "***waiting***", Event Type: *Personnel:End-Position*	Trigger: "*retired*", Event Type: *Personnel:End-Position*	Trigger: "*retired*", Event Type: *Personnel:End-Position*

Table 3: Case study on the development set of the ACE 2005 dataset. The golden trigger words are underlined.

nize the event types and triggers, but OTED can successfully perform the predictions. A major findings in our analysis is that OTED can exploit the introduced alignment bias (i.e., word and type preference) to avoid unlikely event triggers and types (i..e, the ones that should be obviously eliminated based on overall sentence context). This leads to correct predictions for examples that **BERT+CRF** make mistakes. Table 3 shows two examples from the development set of the ACE 2005 dataset to illustrate our findings. In the first example, the baseline can recognize the event trigger "*shot*", but fails to predict the event type. Given the context of the sentence, the predicted event type *Contact:Meet* by **BERT+CRF** should be considered as unlikely to be mentioned in the sentence. As the proposed model OTED employs type preference knowledge, it successfully avoids unlikely event types for this sentence. In addition, in the second example, the baseline incorrectly predicts a non-trigger word (i.e., "*waiting*") as a trigger. In contrast, since OTED employs word preference knowledge, it can effectively avoid unlikely event triggers.

4 Related Work

Early methods for ED employed feature engineering models (Ahn, 2006; Ji and Grishman, 2008; Liao and Grishman, 2010; Hong et al., 2011; Li et al., 2013; Miwa et al., 2014; Yang and Mitchell, 2016). Recently, deep learning was adopted as the SOTA approach for ED (Chen et al., 2015; Nguyen et al., 2016; Sha et al., 2018; Nguyen and Grishman, 2018; Yang et al., 2019; Wang et al., 2019; Lai et al., 2020; Cui et al., 2020; Tong et al., 2020; Nguyen et al., 2021). Unlike such prior work, we introduce a new word-label alignment perspective using OT for ED. Finally, some recent work has utilized OT for character/word/example alignment problems (Dou and Neubig, 2021; Xu et al., 2021; Veyseh et al., 2021a, 2022; Guzman-Nateras et al., 2022). However, none of them explores OT for word-label alignment in ED.

5 Conclusion

We present a general word-label alignment formulation for ED in which each pair of words and types is associated with an alignment score for label assignment likelihood. Moreover, we introduce two alignment biases based on type and word preference to improve the word-label alignment matrix computation with OT. Extensive analysis on a benchmark dataset demonstrates the benefits of the proposed technique for ED. In the future, we plan to evaluate our method on more datasets for ED (Wang et al., 2020a; Man et al., 2020; Lai et al., 2021) to better understand its operation.

Acknowledgement

This research has been supported by the Army Research Office (ARO) grant W911NF-21-1-0112 and the NSF grant CNS-1747798 to the IUCRC Center for Big Learning. This research is also based upon work supported by the Office of the Director of National Intelligence (ODNI), Intelligence Advanced Research Projects Activity (IARPA), via IARPA Contract No. 2019-19051600006 under the Better Extraction from Text Towards Enhanced Retrieval (BETTER) Program. The views and conclusions contained herein are those of the authors and should not be interpreted as necessarily representing the official policies, either expressed or implied, of ARO, ODNI, IARPA, the Department of Defense, or the U.S. Government. The U.S. Government is authorized to reproduce and distribute reprints for governmental purposes notwithstanding any copyright annotation therein. This document does not contain technology or technical data controlled under either the U.S. International Traffic in Arms Regulations or the U.S. Export Administration Regulations.

References

David Ahn. 2006. The stages of event extraction. In *Proceedings of the Workshop on Annotating and Reasoning about Time and Events*.

Yubo Chen, Liheng Xu, Kang Liu, Daojian Zeng, and Jun Zhao. 2015. Event extraction via dynamic multi-pooling convolutional neural networks. In *Proceedings of the Annual Meeting of the Association for Computational Linguistics (ACL)*.

Shiyao Cui, Bowen Yu, Tingwen Liu, Zhenyu Zhang, Xuebin Wang, and Jinqiao Shi. 2020. Edge-enhanced graph convolution networks for event detection with syntactic relation. In *Findings of the Association for Computational Linguistics: EMNLP 2020*, pages 2329–2339, Online. Association for Computational Linguistics.

Jacob Devlin, Ming-Wei Chang, Kenton Lee, and Kristina Toutanova. 2019. Bert: Pre-training of deep bidirectional transformers for language understanding. In *Proceedings of the Conference on Empirical Methods in Natural Language Processing (EMNLP)*.

Zi-Yi Dou and Graham Neubig. 2021. Word alignment by fine-tuning embeddings on parallel corpora. In *Proceedings of the 16th Conference of the European Chapter of the Association for Computational Linguistics (EACL)*.

Luis Fernando Guzman-Nateras, Minh Van Nguyen, and Thien Huu Nguyen. 2022. Cross-lingual event detection via optimized adversarial training. In *Proceedings of the Conference of the North American Chapter of the Association for Computational Linguistics: Human Language Technologies (NAACL-HLT)*.

Yu Hong, Jianfeng Zhang, Bin Ma, Jianmin Yao, Guodong Zhou, and Qiaoming Zhu. 2011. Using cross-entity inference to improve event extraction. In *Proceedings of the Annual Meeting of the Association for Computational Linguistics (ACL)*.

Heng Ji and Ralph Grishman. 2008. Refining event extraction through cross-document inference. In *Proceedings of the Annual Meeting of the Association for Computational Linguistics (ACL)*.

Viet Lai, Minh Van Nguyen, Heidi Kaufman, and Thien Huu Nguyen. 2021. Event extraction from historical texts: A new dataset for black rebellions. In *Findings of the Association for Computational Linguistics: ACL-IJCNLP 2021*, pages 2390–2400, Online. Association for Computational Linguistics.

Viet Dac Lai, Tuan Ngo Nguyen, and Thien Huu Nguyen. 2020. Event detection: Gate diversity and syntactic importance scores for graph convolution neural networks. In *Proceedings of the Conference on Empirical Methods in Natural Language Processing (EMNLP)*.

Qi Li, Heng Ji, and Liang Huang. 2013. Joint event extraction via structured prediction with global features. In *Proceedings of the Annual Meeting of the Association for Computational Linguistics (ACL)*.

Shasha Liao and Ralph Grishman. 2010. Filtered ranking for bootstrapping in event extraction. In *Proceedings of the 23rd International Conference on Computational Linguistics (Coling 2010)*.

Duc Trong Hieu Man, Duc Trong Le, Amir Pouran Ben Veyseh, Thuat Nguyen, and Thien Huu Nguyen. 2020. Introducing a new dataset for event detection in cybersecurity texts. In *Proceedings of the 2020 Conference on Empirical Methods in Natural Language Processing (EMNLP)*.

Makoto Miwa, Paul Thompson, Ioannis Korkontzelos, and Sophia Ananiadou. 2014. Comparable study of event extraction in newswire and biomedical domains. In *Proceedings of the International Conference on Computational Linguistics (COLING)*.

Nghia Trung Ngo, Duy Phung, and Thien Huu Nguyen. 2021. Unsupervised domain adaptation for event detection using domain-specific adapters. In *Findings of the Association for Computational Linguistics: ACL-IJCNLP 2021*, pages 4015–4025, Online. Association for Computational Linguistics.

Minh Van Nguyen, Viet Dac Lai, and Thien Huu Nguyen. 2021. Cross-task instance representation interactions and label dependencies for joint information extraction with graph convolutional networks. In *Proceedings of the Conference of the North American Chapter of the Association for Computational Linguistics: Human Language Technologies (NAACL-HLT)*.

Thien Huu Nguyen, Kyunghyun Cho, and Ralph Grishman. 2016. Joint event extraction via recurrent neural networks. In *Proceedings of the Conference of the North American Chapter of the Association for Computational Linguistics: Human Language Technologies (NAACL-HLT)*.

Thien Huu Nguyen and Ralph Grishman. 2015. Event detection and domain adaptation with convolutional neural networks. In *Proceedings of the Annual Meeting of the Association for Computational Linguistics (ACL)*.

Thien Huu Nguyen and Ralph Grishman. 2018. Graph convolutional networks with argument-aware pooling for event detection. In *Proceedings of the Association for the Advancement of Artificial Intelligence (AAAI)*.

Gabriel Peyre and Marco Cuturi. 2019. Computational optimal transport: With applications to data science. In *Foundations and Trends in Machine Learning*.

Lei Sha, Feng Qian, Baobao Chang, and Zhifang Sui. 2018. Jointly extracting event triggers and arguments by dependency-bridge rnn and tensor-based argument interaction. In *Proceedings of the Association for the Advancement of Artificial Intelligence (AAAI)*.

Meihan Tong, Bin Xu, Shuai Wang, Yixin Cao, Lei Hou, Juanzi Li, and Jun Xie. 2020. Improving event detection via open-domain trigger knowledge. In *Proceedings of the Annual Meeting of the Association for Computational Linguistics (ACL)*.

Amir Pouran Ben Veyseh, Viet Lai, Franck Dernoncourt, and Thien Huu Nguyen. 2021a. Unleash GPT-2 power for event detection. In *Proceedings of the 59th Annual Meeting of the Association for Computational Linguistics and the 11th International Joint Conference on Natural Language Processing (Volume 1: Long Papers)*.

Amir Pouran Ben Veyseh, Minh Van Nguyen, Franck Dernoncourt, Bonan Min, and Thien Huu Nguyen. 2022. Document-level event argument extraction via optimal transport. In *Findings of the Association for Computational Linguistics: ACL 2022*.

Amir Pouran Ben Veyseh, Minh Van Nguyen, Nghia Ngo Trung, Bonan Min, and Thien Huu Nguyen. 2021b. Modeling document-level context for event detection via important context selection. In *Proceedings of the 2021 Conference on Empirical Methods in Natural Language Processing*, pages 5403–5413, Online and Punta Cana, Dominican Republic. Association for Computational Linguistics.

Christopher Walker, Stephanie Strassel, Julie Medero, and Kazuaki Maeda. 2006. Ace 2005 multilingual training corpus. In *Technical report, Linguistic Data Consortium*.

Xiaozhi Wang, Xu Han, Zhiyuan Liu, Maosong Sun, and Peng Li. 2019. Adversarial training for weakly supervised event detection. In *Proceedings of the 2019 Conference of the North American Chapter of the Association for Computational Linguistics: Human Language Technologies, Volume 1 (Long and Short Papers)*, pages 998–1008.

Xiaozhi Wang, Ziqi Wang, Xu Han, Wangyi Jiang, Rong Han, Zhiyuan Liu, Juanzi Li, Peng Li, Yankai Lin, and Jie Zhou. 2020a. MAVEN: A Massive General Domain Event Detection Dataset. In *Proceedings of the 2020 Conference on Empirical Methods in Natural Language Processing (EMNLP)*.

Xiaozhi Wang, Ziqi Wang, Xu Han, Wangyi Jiang, Rong Han, Zhiyuan Liu, Juanzi Li, Peng Li, Yankai Lin, and Jie Zhou. 2020b. Maven: A massive general domain event detection dataset. In *Proceedings of the Annual Meeting of the Association for Computational Linguistics (ACL)*.

Jingjing Xu, Hao Zhou, Chun Gan, Zaixiang Zheng, and Lei Li. 2021. Vocabulary learning via optimal transport for neural machine translation. In *Proceedings of the 59th Annual Meeting of the Association for Computational Linguistics and the 11th International Joint Conference on Natural Language Processing (Volume 1: Long Papers)*.

Bishan Yang and Tom M. Mitchell. 2016. Joint extraction of events and entities within a document context. In *Proceedings of the Conference of the North American Chapter of the Association for Computational Linguistics: Human Language Technologies (NAACL-HLT)*.

Sen Yang, Dawei Feng, Linbo Qiao, Zhigang Kan, and Dongsheng Li. 2019. Exploring pre-trained language models for event extraction and generation. In *Proceedings of the 57th Annual Meeting of the Association for Computational Linguistics*, pages 5284–5294, Florence, Italy. Association for Computational Linguistics.

Comparison and Combination of Sentence Embeddings Derived from Different Supervision Signals

Hayato Tsukagoshi **Ryohei Sasano** **Koichi Takeda**
Graduate School of Informatics, Nagoya University
tsukagoshi.hayato.r2@s.mail.nagoya-u.ac.jp,
{sasano,takedasu}@i.nagoya-u.ac.jp

Abstract

There have been many successful applications of sentence embedding methods. However, it has not been well understood what properties are captured in the resulting sentence embeddings depending on the supervision signals. In this paper, we focus on two types of sentence embedding methods with similar architectures and tasks: one fine-tunes pre-trained language models on the natural language inference task, and the other fine-tunes pre-trained language models on word prediction task from its definition sentence, and investigate their properties. Specifically, we compare their performances on semantic textual similarity (STS) tasks using STS datasets partitioned from two perspectives: 1) sentence source and 2) superficial similarity of the sentence pairs, and compare their performances on the downstream and probing tasks. Furthermore, we attempt to combine the two methods and demonstrate that combining the two methods yields substantially better performance than the respective methods on unsupervised STS tasks and downstream tasks.

1 Introduction

Sentence embeddings are dense vector representations of a sentence. A variety of methods have been proposed to derive sentence embeddings, including those based on unsupervised learning (Kiros et al., 2015; Hill et al., 2016; Logeswaran and Lee, 2018; Cer et al., 2018; Wang et al., 2021) and supervised learning (Conneau et al., 2017). Pre-trained Transformer-based (Vaswani et al., 2017) language models, such as BERT (Devlin et al., 2019) and RoBERTa (Liu et al., 2019), have been successfully applied in a wide range of NLP tasks, and sentence embedding methods that leverage pre-trained language models have also performed well on semantic textual similarity (STS) tasks and several downstream tasks. These methods refine pre-trained language models for sophisticated sentence embeddings by unsupervised learning (Li et al., 2020; Wang and Kuo, 2020; Giorgi et al., 2021; Carlsson et al., 2021; Yan et al., 2021; Gao et al., 2021), or supervised learning (Reimers and Gurevych, 2019; Tsukagoshi et al., 2021; Gao et al., 2021).

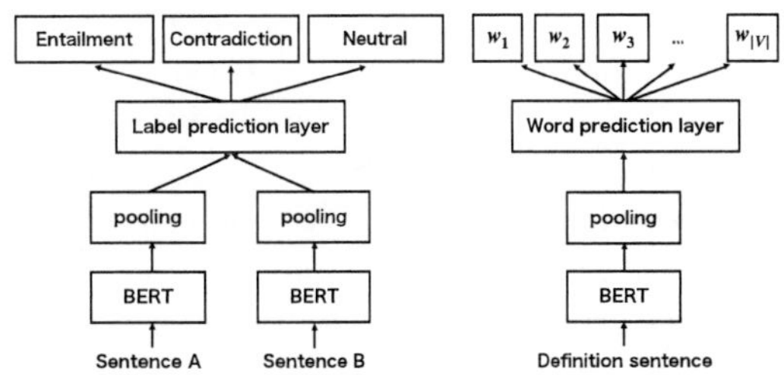

Figure 1: Overviews of SBERT (left) and DefSent (right).

Among them, Reimers and Gurevych (2019) proposed Sentence-BERT (SBERT), which fine-tunes pre-trained language models on the natural language inference (NLI) task. SBERT performed well on the STS and downstream tasks. Recently, Tsukagoshi et al. (2021) proposed DefSent, which fine-tunes pre-trained language models on the task of predicting a word from its definition sentence in a dictionary, and reported that it performed comparably to SBERT. Figure 1 shows overviews of SBERT and DefSent. Although both methods fine-tune the same pre-trained models and use the same pooling operations to derive a sentence embedding, the supervision signals for fine-tuning are different. That is, SBERT leverages NLI datasets, whereas DefSent leverages word dictionaries.

It is expected that the properties of the sentence embeddings depend on their supervision signals. However, since existing research has mainly focused on achieving better performance on benchmark tasks, it has not been revealed what property differences the resulting sentence embeddings have. Investigating the properties of sentence embeddings would give us a better understanding of existing sentence embedding methods and help develop further methods. In this paper, we empirically investigate the influence of supervision signals on

Proceedings of the 11th Joint Conference on Lexical and Computational Semantics, pages 139 - 150
July 14-15, 2022 ©2022 Association for Computational Linguistics

sentence embeddings. We focus on SBERT and DefSent because they leverage different supervision signals but have very similar architectures, as shown in Figure 1; thus, they would be appropriate for analyzing the influence of the supervision signals on sentence embeddings.

First, we partitioned the STS datasets (Agirre et al., 2012, 2013, 2014, 2015, 2016; Cer et al., 2017; Marelli et al., 2014) on the basis of two different perspectives and examine what type of meaning each type of sentence embeddings captures by analyzing the performance of each method on these partitioned STS datasets. We then apply each type of embeddings to the downstream and probing tasks of SentEval (Conneau and Kiela, 2018) and analyze what type of information is captured. Our results demonstrate that the supervision signals have a significant impact on performance on these tasks and that the properties of SBERT and DefSent would be complementary. Thus, we further explore whether combining the two methods yields better sentence embeddings to confirm their complementarity, and demonstrate that combining the two methods yields substantially better performance than the respective methods on unsupervised STS tasks and downstream tasks of SentEval.

2 Preparation

In this section, we present detailed descriptions of SBERT and DefSent, the two sentence embedding methods compared in this study, and describe the tasks and settings for the experiments.

2.1 Sentence-BERT

Sentence-BERT (SBERT) proposed by Reimers and Gurevych (2019) is a sentence embedding method that fine-tunes pre-trained language models in a Siamese network architecture on the NLI task. An overview of SBERT is given on the left side of Figure 1[1]. For fine-tuning of SBERT, NLI datasets, such as the Stanford NLI (SNLI) dataset (Bowman et al., 2015) and Multi-Genre NLI (MultiNLI) dataset (Williams et al., 2018), are used. These datasets consist of sentence pairs labeled as either entailment, contradiction, or neutral. The NLI task is a classification task to predict these labels.

SBERT first inputs each sentence of a pair into BERT and obtains sentence embeddings from the output contextualized word embeddings by a pooling operation. SBERT uses three types of pooling strategies: `CLS`, which uses the embedding of the first token of the input sequence (e.g., the [CLS] token for BERT); `Mean`, which uses the average of all word embeddings; and `Max`, which uses the max-over-time of all word embeddings. Let u and v be the sentence embeddings obtained by such pooling. SBERT composes a vector $[u; v; |u - v|]$ and inputs it into a three-way softmax classifier to predict the label of the given sentence pair.

2.2 DefSent

DefSent proposed by Tsukagoshi et al. (2021) is a sentence embedding method that fine-tunes pre-trained language models on the task of predicting a word from its definition sentence in a dictionary. An overview of DefSent is given on the right side of Figure 1. As well as SBERT, DefSent first inputs a definition sentence into BERT and obtains the sentence embedding by a pooling operation, which uses `CLS`, `Mean`, and `Max` as the pooling strategies. The derived sentence embedding is then input to the word prediction layer and fine-tunes the model to predict the corresponding word. The word prediction layer is the one that was used for masked language modeling during pre-training. Tsukagoshi et al. (2021) reported that DefSent performed comparably to SBERT.

2.3 STS tasks

We use STS tasks to investigate the properties of sentence embeddings. STS tasks evaluate how the semantic similarity between two sentences calculated with a model correlates with a human-labeled similarity score through Pearson and Spearman correlations. There are two types of settings: supervised and unsupervised. In the supervised setting, a model learns a regression function that maps a pair of sentences to a similarity score using some of the STS datasets. In the unsupervised setting, no training is performed on STS datasets, and we compute the similarity between two sentence embeddings, with a similarity score such as cosine similarity.

For the evaluation of the STS tasks, STS12–STS16 (Agirre et al., 2012, 2013, 2014, 2015, 2016), STS Benchmark (Cer et al., 2017), and SICK-R (Marelli et al., 2014) are often used. Each dataset contains sentence pairs with their semantic similarity scores as gold labels given by real numbers ranging from 0 to 5. Each of the STS12–STS16 datasets consists of sentence pairs from multiple sources. For example, STS12 consists of sen-

[1]Actually, it is possible to use RoBERTa and others instead of BERT, but for simplicity we refer to it as BERT here.

Sources		#	Origin
STS12	*MSRpar*	750	newswire
	MSRvid	750	videos
	SMTeuroparl	459	WMT eval.
	OnWN	750	glosses
	SMTnews	399	WMT eval.
STS13	*FNWN*	189	glosses
	headlines	750	newswire
	OnWN	561	glosses
STS14	*deft-forum*	450	forum posts
	deft-news	300	news summary
	headlines	750	newswire headlines
	images	750	image descriptions
	OnWN	750	glosses
	tweet-news	750	tweet-news pairs
STS15	*answers-forums*	375	Q&A forum answers
	answers-students	750	student answers
	belief	375	committed belief
	headlines	750	newswire headlines
	images	750	image descriptions
STS16	*answer-answer*	254	Q&A forum answers
	headlines	249	newswire headlines
	plagiarism	230	short-answer plag.
	postediting	244	MT postedits
	question-question	209	Q&A forum questions

Table 1: Statistics of STS datasets partitioned by source. "#" denotes number of sentence pairs, and "Origin" denotes origin of dataset.

tence pairs from five sources: *MSRpar*, *MSRvid*, *SMTeuroparl*, *OnWN*, and *SMTnews*. Table 1 lists the sources of each dataset in STS12–STS16.

2.4 SentEval

We also compare SBERT and DefSent on SentEval (Conneau and Kiela, 2018) tasks. SentEval is a widely used toolkit to evaluate the quality of sentence embeddings by measuring the performance on classification tasks. Since SentEval provides various classification tasks, it is suitable for investigating the properties of sentence embeddings. SentEval consists of two types of tasks: downstream tasks and probing tasks. Downstream tasks are binary or multi-class classification tasks, such as sentiment classification in movie reviews and question-type classification. Probing tasks are classification tasks for linguistic information, such as sentence length and tense classification.

2.5 Experimental settings

In the experiments reported in Sections 3 and 4, we use BERT-base (bert-base-uncased), BERT-large (bert-large-uncased), RoBERTa-base (roberta-base), and RoBERTa-large (roberta-large) from Transformers (Wolf et al., 2020) as the pre-trained language models and adopt `Mean` as the pooling strategy. We use the same settings as Reimers and Gurevych (2019) and Tsukagoshi et al. (2021) for fine-tuning. We provide further training details in Appendix A, and report the fine-tuning time and computing infrastructure in Appendix B.

3 Comparison of Sentence Embeddings

The supervision signal used for fine-tuning sentence embeddings might affect their properties. For example, since it is crucial to capture the differences in meaning even when the given sentence pair is superficially similar in the NLI task, SBERT is considered suitable for determining the semantic similarity between superficially similar sentence pairs. In this section, we attempt to reveal such properties of each type of sentence embeddings. First, we partition the STS datasets on the basis of the source of the sentence pairs and the superficial similarity of the sentence pair. We then apply each type of embeddings to the downstream and probing tasks of SentEval.

3.1 STS partitioned by source

We assume that each sentence embedding method might better capture the meaning of sentences similar to those in the dataset used for fine-tuning, i.e., NLI datasets for SBERT and word dictionaries for DefSent. Thus, we partition STS12–STS16 datasets in accordance with the source of the sentences and measure the performance for each subset. We adopt the unsupervised setting. We calculate Spearman's rank correlation coefficient (ρ) between semantic similarity scores and each type of sentence embeddings. For comparison, we conduct evaluations on the concatenation of all subsets, i.e., the STS datasets without partitioning. We fine-tune and evaluate SBERT and DefSent 10 times with different seed values and report the average. We also evaluate the model without fine-tuning (w/o FT) for comparison.

Figure 2 shows the Spearman's ρ for the subsets of the STS12–STS16 datasets. It is worth noting that since we use correlations, the evaluation score on the concatenation of all subsets is not the average of the other scores, and in extreme cases it can be smaller than the minimum of the other scores. We can see that both SBERT and DefSent achieve higher scores than w/oFT on most subsets. Although DefSent consistently performs better than w/oFT in all subsets, SBERT performs worse than w/oFT in some subsets. Comparing SBERT and DefSent, when we focus on individual subsets, we can find that there are cases in

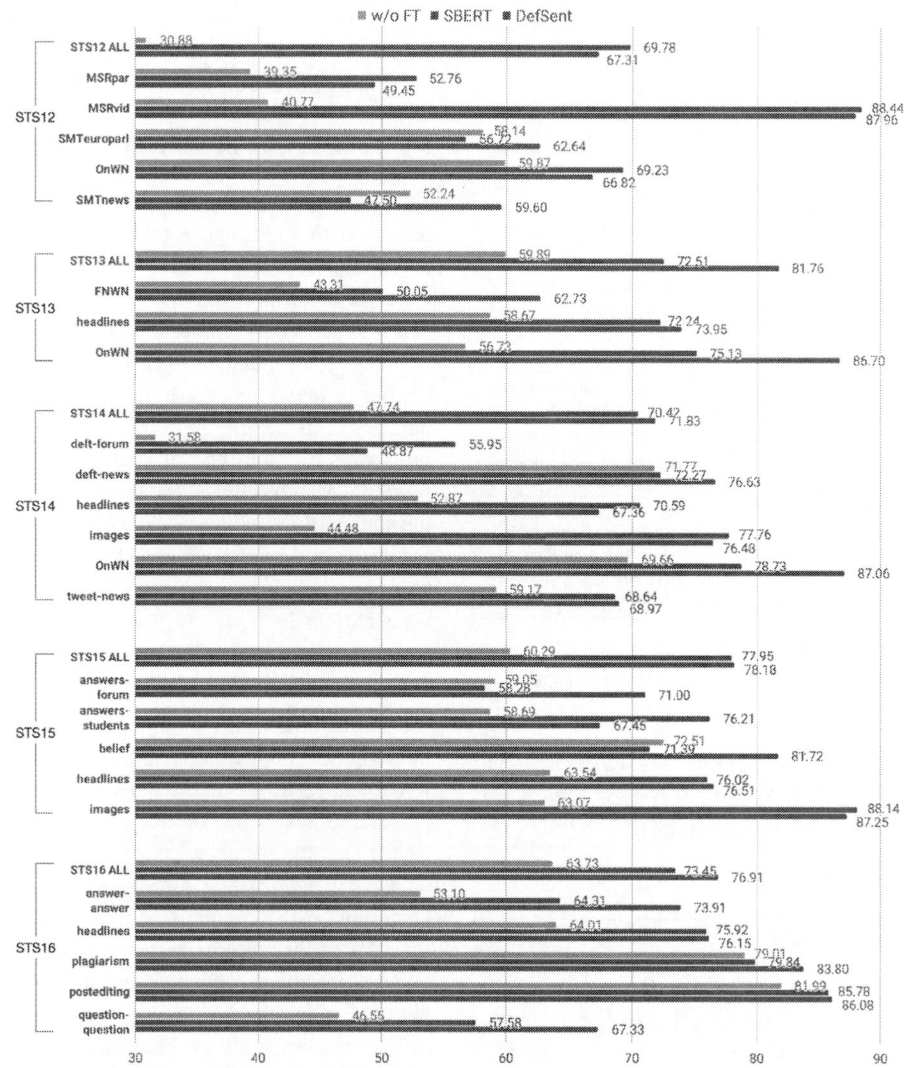

Figure 2: Spearman's $\rho \times 100$ for STS12–STS16 datasets partitioned by source. "STS# ALL" denotes the concatenation of all subsets for each STS dataset.

which SBERT achieves higher scores than DefSent, but we can say that DefSent achieves slightly higher scores as a whole. DefSent achieves noticeably higher scores than SBERT on *OnWN* and *FNWN* of STS13 and *OnWN* of STS14. *OnWN* and *FNWN* of STS13 are datasets created using definition sentences in OntoNotes, FrameNet, and WordNet. These results, as expected, indicate that DefSent is capable of adequately representing the meaning of definition sentences. However, SBERT achieves higher scores than DefSent on *deft-forum* and *headlines* of STS14 and *answer-students* of STS15. Regarding *answer-students*, since it is built from a dataset that has a similar format to the NLI datasets (Agirre et al., 2015), it is considered a score such as the one observed is as expected for SBERT, which is trained on the NLI datasets.

3.2 STS partitioned by Dice coefficient

We then explore how the similarity of sentence embeddings is affected by the superficial similarity of the sentences. Generally speaking, it is considered difficult to correctly order the similarity of a dataset consisting of pairs with high superficial similarity. However, since the NLI datasets contain a relatively large number of superficially similar sentences, SBERT built on such a dataset is expected to be relatively robust to sentence pairs with high superficial similarity. To verify whether there is such a tendency, we partition STS Benchmark datasets in accordance with the superficial similarity of the sentences and investigate the per-

sentence 1	sentence 2	Human	Dice	w/oFT	SBERT	DefSent
A man is playing a guitar.	The man is playing the guitar.	4.909	0.800	0.906	0.985	0.978
A man is playing a guitar.	A guy is playing an instrument.	3.800	0.545	0.945	**0.646**	0.895
A man is playing a guitar.	A man is playing a guitar and singing.	3.200	0.833	0.979	0.874	**0.977**
A man is playing a guitar.	The girl is playing the guitar.	2.250	0.600	0.900	0.747	0.831
A man is playing a guitar.	A woman is cutting vegetable.	0.000	0.400	0.890	0.290	0.595

Table 2: Example sentence pairs in STS Benchmark datasets and their scores. "Human" denotes human-labeled similarity scores, "Dice" denotes Dice coefficients, and "w/oFT", "SBERT", and "DefSent" denote cosine similarities between each sentence embedding computed with BERT without fine-tuning, SBERT, and DefSent, respectively. The average cosine similarity for w/oFT is 0.816, for SBERT is 0.678, and for DefSent is 0.809.

formance of each embedding method on the partitioned datasets. Specifically, we use Dice coefficients between the sets of words in a sentence pair as the superficial similarity, which is defined as

$$\text{Dice}(S_1, S_2) = \frac{2|W_1 \cap W_2|}{|W_1| + |W_2|},$$

where S_1 and S_2 are the sentence pair, and W_1 and W_2 are the sets of words in $S1$ and $S2$, respectively. We sort the sentence pairs in all STS Benchmark datasets including training, development, and test sets in accordance with the Dice coefficient, and partition them into five subsets, that is, grouping 20% of the sentences from bottom to top.

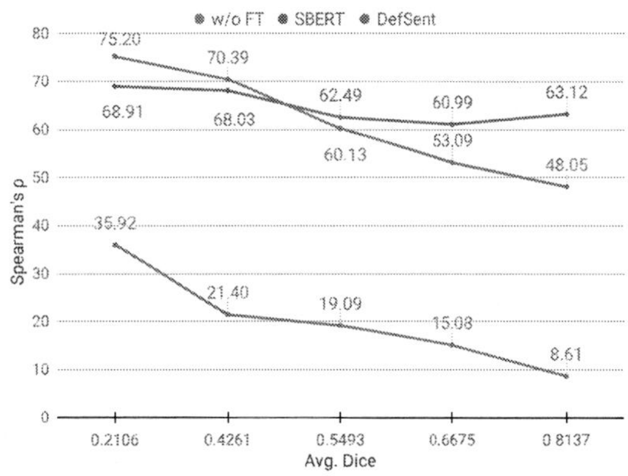

Figure 3: Spearman's $\rho \times 100$ for STS Benchmark partitioned in accordance with the ratio of shared words. Sentence pairs are more superficially similar to right.

Figure 3 shows the Spearman's ρ for each subsets. We can confirm that the subsets with larger Dice coefficients, that is, a higher superficial similarity, tend to be more difficult to rank the semantic similarities. However, as expected, SBERT is more robust to the subsets with higher superficial similarity, and consequently, SBERT achieves a higher score than DefSent for these subsets, whereas DefSent achieved a higher score than SBERT for the subsets with a lower superficial similarity.

For further investigation, we conduct a qualitative analysis of how superficial similarity affects the behavior of the methods. Table 2 shows example sentence pairs from STS Benchmark datasets with their human-labeled similarity scores, Dice coefficients, and cosine similarities between each sentence embedding with the respective methods. As shown in the second row from the top, we observe that each sentence of the pair represents almost the same thing except for minor details ("guitar" or "instrument"), but SBERT assigns relatively a much lower similarity than other examples. As shown in the third row from the top, the similarity score of DefSent is very high, even though the human-labeled score is not that high. In summary, we can say that SBERT is better at capturing the semantic similarity of superficially similar sentences, while DefSent is better at capturing the similarity of sentences with low superficial similarity.

3.3 SentEval donwstream tasks

We then apply each type of embeddings to the downstream tasks of SentEval and analyze what type of information each type of embeddings captures that is useful for the downstream task. We train a logistic regression classifier with 10-fold cross-validation, a batch size of 64, an epoch size of 4, and Adam (Kingma and Ba, 2015) optimizer, the same as the default configurations of SentEval. Specifically, parameters of sentence embedding models are fixed during training of the classifier. We fine-tune and evaluate SBERT and DefSent three times with different seed values and report the average of accuracy for each downstream task. We also evaluate w/oFT for comparison.

Figure 4 shows the accuracy for downstream tasks. As a whole, SBERT and DefSent perform comparably. SBERT performs best for MR, CR, SST2, and MRPC. Since MR, CR, and SST2 are sentiment prediction tasks, it suggests that SBERT encodes the sentiment of sentences into the embedding. Also, MRPC is a paraphrase-prediction

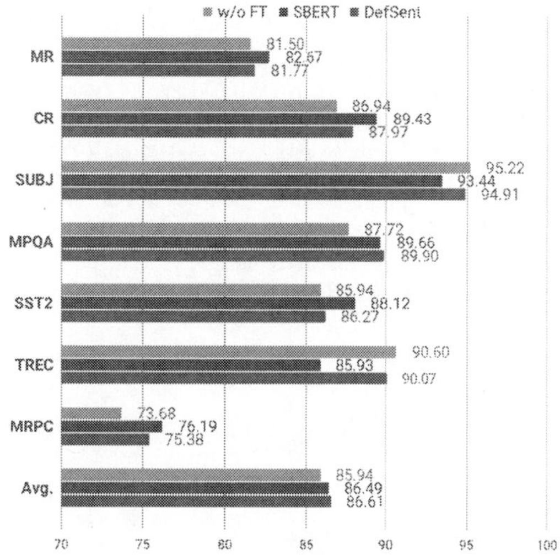

Figure 4: Experimental results on each SentEval downstream task with the accuracy (%).

task, which predicts whether two sentences have the same meaning on the basis of their embeddings. Therefore, MRPC is similar to the NLI task, and thus it is not surprising that SBERT performs better.

DefSent performs best for MPQA and is comparable to w/oFT for SUBJ and TREC. MPQA is a phrase-level opinion polarity classification task, and it is necessary to compose the meaning of phrases adequately. We conjecture that the performance of DefSent is high because DefSent successfully composes the meaning of the corresponding words from the definition sentences during fine-tuning. It is worth noting that w/oFT performs best for SUBJ and TREC, and SBERT performs much worse for them. SUBJ is a subjectivity classification task and TREC is a question-type classification task. Since information about words in sentences is particularly important for these tasks, SBERT is considered to have less information about which words are included in sentences than DefSent and w/oFT. Therefore, we can say that SBERT encodes mainly sentiment information into the sentence embedding, and the sentence embedding is suitable for determining whether the meaning is the same. Also, DefSent successfully composes the meaning of the sentence from its words and encodes information about words the sentence has.

3.4 SentEval probing tasks

Finally, we apply each type of embeddings to the probing tasks of SentEval and analyze what type of linguistic information each type of embeddings captures. We use the same setting as in Section 3.3.

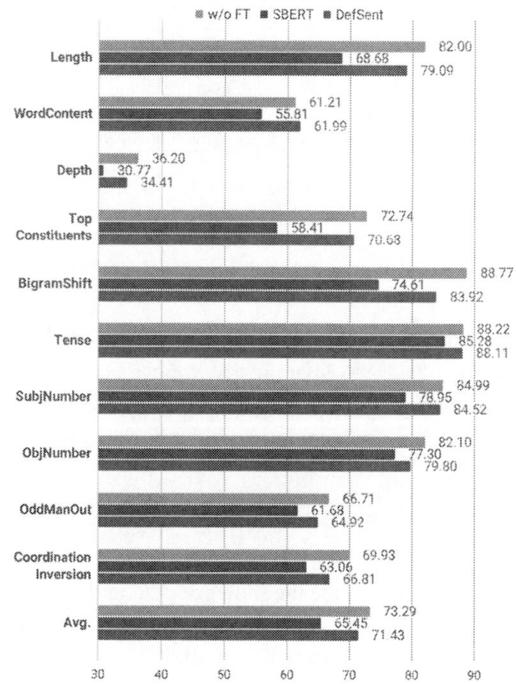

Figure 5: Experimental results on each SentEval probing task with the accuracy (%).

Figure 5 shows the accuracy for probing tasks. Overall, w/oFT performs best on average, followed by DefSent, and then SBERT. The overall performance of SBERT is relatively low. SBERT encodes the semantic information of sentences according to the results of SentEval downstream tasks. These results also indicate that SBERT encodes semantic information rather than linguistic information such as words in a sentence. DefSent is comparable to w/oFT in WordContent, Tense, and SubjNumber. This also indicates that the sentence embeddings from DefSent have information about words the sentence contains.

4 Combination of Sentence Embeddings

We have shown that SBERT and DefSent have different properties and that they may be complimentary. This suggests that combining the two methods may yield better sentence embeddings. Thus, we attempt to combine SBERT and DefSent and evaluate the resulting sentence embeddings on unsupervised STS tasks and SentEval downstream tasks. Specifically, we use the following five methods of combining SBERT and DefSent for BERT[2].

[2]The experimental results for RoBERT are given in Appendix C and D.

Model	Method	STS12	STS13	STS14	STS15	STS16	STS-B	SICK-R	Avg.
BERT-base	w/oFT	30.88	59.90	47.74	60.29	63.73	47.29	58.22	52.58
BERT-base	SBERT	69.78	72.51	70.42	77.95	73.45	75.96	72.26	73.19
BERT-base	DefSent	67.31	81.76	71.83	78.18	76.91	76.98	73.47	75.20
BERT-base	S+D	70.71	**83.48**	**76.66**	**82.00**	**78.70**	**80.76**	**76.83**	**78.45**
BERT-base	D+S	68.68	73.65	70.60	76.96	72.54	75.30	72.46	72.89
BERT-base	MULTI	63.10	74.34	70.30	77.64	74.08	77.35	73.42	72.89
BERT-base	AVERAGE	**72.40**	81.36	75.80	81.90	77.64	79.74	75.87	77.81
BERT-base	CONCAT	71.13	78.54	74.03	79.95	76.01	78.37	74.17	76.03
BERT-large	w/oFT	27.69	55.78	44.48	51.67	61.85	47.00	53.85	48.90
BERT-large	SBERT	70.76	73.68	72.56	79.00	74.61	77.11	72.47	74.31
BERT-large	DefSent	63.30	82.16	72.67	79.06	77.52	77.40	74.02	75.16
BERT-large	S+D	69.48	**83.90**	76.83	**82.61**	**80.14**	**81.72**	**78.77**	**79.06**
BERT-large	D+S	71.25	75.71	73.39	79.68	75.20	77.67	73.78	75.24
BERT-large	MULTI	70.33	81.16	75.84	80.02	76.52	78.65	74.30	76.69
BERT-large	AVERAGE	**71.85**	82.60	**77.33**	82.52	79.12	80.71	76.30	78.63
BERT-large	CONCAT	71.37	80.28	76.08	81.10	77.63	79.57	74.71	77.25

Table 3: Experimental results on unsupervised STS tasks with Spearman's $\rho \times 100$.

S+D Fine-tuning the pre-trained model with SBERT then with DefSent sequentially.

D+S Fine-tuning the pre-trained model with DefSent then with SBERT sequentially.

MULTI Multi-task learning with SBERT and DefSent. The ratio of the size of the NLI dataset to the dictionary dataset is about 19:1, so we do 19 steps with SBERT and then 1 step with DefSent for the same model.

AVERAGE Averaging embeddings of separately fine-tuned models with SBERT and DefSent.

CONCAT Concatenate embeddings of separately fine-tuned models with SBERT and DefSent.

4.1 Evaluation on unsupervised STS tasks

We first estimate the resulting sentence embeddings on unsupervised STS tasks. We use the same settings described in Section 2.5. We use STS12–STS16, STS Benchmark test set (STS-B), and SICK-Relatedness (SICK-R) for the evaluation. We compute sentence similarities by using the cosine similarity of sentence embeddings derived from the respective combinations and calculate Spearman's ρ with gold labels. We conduct fine-tuning and evaluations 10 times with different seed values and report the average.

Table 3 shows the experimental results. The combinations S+D, AVERAGE, and CONCAT always outperform SBERT and DefSent. Among them, S+D achieves the best average score for base and large models. However we cannot confirm much performance improvement with D+S and MULTI. We leave an analysis of what affects this difference in performances as future work.

4.2 Evaluation on the SentEval tasks

We then estimate the resulting sentence embeddings on the SentEval tasks. We use the same settings described in Section 3.3. We conduct fine-tuning and evaluations three times with different seed values and report the average.

Table 4 shows the results. We can see that CONCAT achieves the highest average score but it should be noted that since SentEval performed supervised learning of a logistic regression classifier, the high dimensionality of the sentence embeddings of CONCAT is advantageous. Other than CONCAT, AVERAGE performs relatively well, which always outperforms S+D, D+S, and MULTI, unlike in the STS tasks. This suggests that fine-tuning the same model with different tasks might degrade the generalization ability.

5 Related work

Sentence embedding has been studied intensively. Kiros et al. (2015) proposed SkipThought, which trains a sentence embedding model by predicting the previous and next sentence from the embedding of a given sentence. Conneau et al. (2017) proposed InferSent, which trains a sentence embedding model built on BiLSTM in a Siamese network architecture on the NLI task. Cer et al. (2018) proposed Universal Sentence Encoder (USE), which is trained on an NLI dataset, and has also shown the effectiveness of NLI datasets in obtaining sophisticated sentence embeddings.

Recently, methods that leverage pre-trained language models to acquire sentence embeddings have attracted much attention. Pre-trained language models, such as BERT (Devlin et al., 2019) and RoBERTa (Liu et al., 2019), acquire linguistic

Model	Method	MR	CR	SUBJ	MPQA	SST-2	TREC	MRPC	Avg.
BERT-base	w/oFT	81.50	86.94	**95.22**	87.72	85.94	90.60	73.68	85.94
BERT-base	SBERT	82.67	89.43	93.44	89.66	88.12	85.93	76.19	86.49
BERT-base	DefSent	81.77	87.97	94.91	89.90	86.27	90.07	75.38	86.61
BERT-base	S+D	81.29	89.10	93.99	90.09	86.69	89.33	77.08	86.80
BERT-base	D+S	82.43	89.22	93.24	90.16	**88.98**	83.33	75.27	86.09
BERT-base	MULTI	81.73	88.80	93.17	89.27	87.28	87.87	75.54	86.23
BERT-base	AVERAGE	83.17	89.50	94.67	90.35	88.50	89.67	76.41	87.47
BERT-base	CONCAT	**83.24**	**89.64**	95.18	**90.51**	88.94	**90.60**	**77.37**	**87.93**
BERT-large	w/oFT	84.30	89.16	**95.60**	86.65	89.29	**91.40**	71.65	86.86
BERT-large	SBERT	84.76	90.61	94.08	90.04	90.77	85.47	75.90	87.38
BERT-large	DefSent	84.54	89.40	95.55	90.04	89.49	88.73	74.82	87.51
BERT-large	S+D	84.01	90.49	95.07	90.50	90.35	90.20	75.61	88.03
BERT-large	D+S	84.55	90.68	93.46	90.22	90.21	84.73	75.01	86.98
BERT-large	MULTI	84.63	90.56	94.10	89.85	90.23	88.70	76.56	87.80
BERT-large	AVERAGE	85.46	**90.92**	95.20	90.53	91.27	88.27	**77.00**	88.38
BERT-large	CONCAT	**85.53**	90.83	95.27	**90.66**	**91.95**	89.60	75.88	**88.53**

Table 4: Experimental results on each SentEval task with the accuracy (%).

knowledge by training on large texts and perform well on downstream tasks. Pre-trained models are also considered helpful for sentence embedding. There are two types of methods based on pre-trained models: unsupervised and supervised.

Unsupervised methods do not require labeled text but exploit the properties of pre-trained language models or create training data artificially. Li et al. (2020) showed that the sentence embedding space of BERT is anisotropic, and proposed BERT-flow, which learns a map to an isotropic Gaussian distribution to obtain sentence embedding. Several studies have also been based on contrastive learning, and are different in the way to make positive examples: DeCLUTR (Giorgi et al., 2021) takes into account different spans of the same document as positives; ConSERT (Yan et al., 2021) takes into account a pair of an original sentence and a collapsed sentence as positives; unsupervised SimCSE (Gao et al., 2021) takes into account the corresponding embeddings of the same sentence with different dropout masks applied as positives.

Supervised methods use labeled text to encode higher-level semantic information. Supervised methods generally produce more sophisticated sentence embeddings than unsupervised methods. In addition to SBERT and DefSent, supervised SimCSE (Gao et al., 2021) is one of the supervised sentence embedding methods. Supervised SimCSE fine-tunes BERT by contrastive learning using entailment pairs in the NLI datasets as positives.

6 Conclusion

In this paper, we empirically investigated the influence of supervision signals used for obtaining sentence embeddings. We focused on two methods: SBERT, which uses NLI datasets, and DefSent, which uses word dictionaries. We showed that there is a difference in the ability to order the similarity of sentences depending on their source or superficial similarity by comparing their performances on subsets of the STS datasets and tasks of SentEval. We found that SBERT is suitable for superficially similar sentence pairs because SBERT is based on the NLI datasets that contain a relatively large number of superficially similar sentences, whereas DefSent is suitable for sentence pairs that need to represent the compositional meaning because DefSent is based on definition sentences of a dictionary.

We also showed that SBERT performed better in tasks where sentiment information was important, while DefSent performed better in tasks where information about words and the compositionality of meaning were important by comparing their performances on downstream and probing tasks of SentEval. Finally, we demonstrated that combining the two methods yielded substantially better performance than the respective methods on unsupervised STS tasks and downstream tasks of SentEval.

For future work, we will expand the scope of our analysis to other pre-trained language models and sentence embedding methods to obtain insights for better sentence embeddings. In addition, We will investigate how those combination methods affect the properties of resulting sentence embeddings and explore how to effectively combine unsupervised sentence embedding methods, which have recently achieved good performance, such as DeCLUTR (Giorgi et al., 2021) and unsupervised SimCSE (Gao et al., 2021), with supervised sentenece embedding methods. Moreover, the combination of unsupervised methods, which have recently achieved good performance, such as DeCLUTR (Giorgi et al., 2021) and unsupervised SimCSE (Gao et al., 2021), and supervised methods should also be promising.

Acknowledgements

This work was supported by JSPS KAKENHI Grant Number 21H04901.

References

Eneko Agirre, Carmen Banea, Claire Cardie, Daniel Cer, Mona Diab, Aitor Gonzalez-Agirre, Weiwei Guo, Iñigo Lopez-Gazpio, Montse Maritxalar, Rada Mihalcea, German Rigau, Larraitz Uria, and Janyce Wiebe. 2015. SemEval-2015 Task 2: Semantic Textual Similarity, English, Spanish and Pilot on Interpretability. In *Proceedings of the 9th International Workshop on Semantic Evaluation (SemEval)*, pages 252–263.

Eneko Agirre, Carmen Banea, Claire Cardie, Daniel Cer, Mona Diab, Aitor Gonzalez-Agirre, Weiwei Guo, Rada Mihalcea, German Rigau, and Janyce Wiebe. 2014. SemEval-2014 Task 10: Multilingual Semantic Textual Similarity. In *Proceedings of the 8th International Workshop on Semantic Evaluation (SemEval)*, pages 81–91.

Eneko Agirre, Carmen Banea, Daniel Cer, Mona Diab, Aitor Gonzalez-Agirre, Rada Mihalcea, German Rigau, and Janyce Wiebe. 2016. SemEval-2016 Task 1: Semantic Textual Similarity, Monolingual and Cross-Lingual Evaluation. In *Proceedings of the 10th International Workshop on Semantic Evaluation (SemEval)*, pages 497–511.

Eneko Agirre, Daniel Cer, Mona Diab, and Aitor Gonzalez-Agirre. 2012. SemEval-2012 Task 6: A Pilot on Semantic Textual Similarity. In **SEM 2012: The First Joint Conference on Lexical and Computational Semantics – Semantic Evaluation (SemEval)*, pages 385–393.

Eneko Agirre, Daniel Cer, Mona Diab, Aitor Gonzalez-Agirre, and Weiwei Guo. 2013. *SEM 2013 shared task: Semantic Textual Similarity. In *Second Joint Conference on Lexical and Computational Semantics (*SEM)*, pages 32–43.

Samuel R. Bowman, Gabor Angeli, Christopher Potts, and Christopher D. Manning. 2015. A large annotated corpus for learning natural language inference. In *Proceedings of the 2015 Conference on Empirical Methods in Natural Language Processing (EMNLP)*, pages 632–642.

Fredrik Carlsson, Amaru Cuba Gyllensten, Evangelia Gogoulou, Erik Ylipää Hellqvist, and Magnus Sahlgren. 2021. Semantic Re-tuning with Contrastive Tension. In *International Conference on Learning Representations (ICLR)*.

Daniel Cer, Mona Diab, Eneko Agirre, Iñigo Lopez-Gazpio, and Lucia Specia. 2017. SemEval-2017 task 1: Semantic textual similarity multilingual and crosslingual focused evaluation. In *Proceedings of the 11th International Workshop on Semantic Evaluation (SemEval)*, pages 1–14.

Daniel Matthew Cer, Yinfei Yang, Sheng yi Kong, Nan Hua, Nicole Limtiaco, Rhomni St. John, Noah Constant, Mario Guajardo-Cespedes, Steve Yuan, C. Tar, Yun-Hsuan Sung, B. Strope, and R. Kurzweil. 2018. Universal Sentence Encoder. *arXiv:1803.11175*.

Alexis Conneau and Douwe Kiela. 2018. SentEval: An Evaluation Toolkit for Universal Sentence Representations. In *Proceedings of the Eleventh International Conference on Language Resources and Evaluation (LREC)*, pages 1699–1704.

Alexis Conneau, Douwe Kiela, Holger Schwenk, Loïc Barrault, and Antoine Bordes. 2017. Supervised Learning of Universal Sentence Representations from Natural Language Inference Data. In *Proceedings of the 2017 Conference on Empirical Methods in Natural Language Processing (EMNLP)*, pages 670–680.

Jacob Devlin, Ming-Wei Chang, Kenton Lee, and Kristina Toutanova. 2019. BERT: Pre-training of Deep Bidirectional Transformers for Language Understanding. In *Proceedings of the 2019 Conference of the North American Chapter of the Association for Computational Linguistics: Human Language Technologies (NAACL)*, pages 4171–4186.

Tianyu Gao, Xingcheng Yao, and Danqi Chen. 2021. SimCSE: Simple Contrastive Learning of Sentence Embeddings. In *Proceedings of the 2021 Conference on Empirical Methods in Natural Language Processing (EMNLP)*, pages 6894–6910.

John Giorgi, Osvald Nitski, Bo Wang, and Gary Bader. 2021. DeCLUTR: Deep Contrastive Learning for Unsupervised Textual Representations. In *Proceedings of the 59th Annual Meeting of the Association for Computational Linguistics and the 11th International Joint Conference on Natural Language Processing (ACL-IJCNLP)*, pages 879–895.

Felix Hill, Kyunghyun Cho, and Anna Korhonen. 2016. Learning Distributed Representations of Sentences from Unlabelled Data. In *Proceedings of the 2016 Conference of the North American Chapter of the Association for Computational Linguistics: Human Language Technologies (NAACL-HLT)*, pages 1367–1377.

Diederik P. Kingma and Jimmy Ba. 2015. Adam: A Method for Stochastic Optimization. In *3rd International Conference on Learning Representations (ICLR)*.

Ryan Kiros, Yukun Zhu, Russ R Salakhutdinov, Richard Zemel, Raquel Urtasun, Antonio Torralba, and Sanja Fidler. 2015. Skip-Thought Vectors. In *Advances in Neural Information Processing Systems (NIPS)*, pages 3294–3302.

Bohan Li, Hao Zhou, Junxian He, Mingxuan Wang, Yiming Yang, and Lei Li. 2020. On the Sentence Embeddings from Pre-trained Language Models. In *Proceedings of the 2020 Conference on Empirical Methods in Natural Language Processing (EMNLP)*, pages 9119–9130.

Yinhan Liu, Myle Ott, Naman Goyal, Jingfei Du, Mandar Joshi, Danqi Chen, Omer Levy, M. Lewis, Luke Zettlemoyer, and Veselin Stoyanov. 2019. RoBERTa: A Robustly Optimized BERT Pretraining Approach. *arXiv:1907.11692*.

Lajanugen Logeswaran and Honglak Lee. 2018. An efficient framework for learning sentence representations. In *International Conference on Learning Representations (ICLR)*.

Marco Marelli, Stefano Menini, Marco Baroni, Luisa Bentivogli, Raffaella Bernardi, and Roberto Zamparelli. 2014. A SICK cure for the evaluation of compositional distributional semantic models. In *Proceedings of the Ninth International Conference on Language Resources and Evaluation (LREC)*, pages 216–223.

Nils Reimers and Iryna Gurevych. 2019. Sentence-BERT: Sentence Embeddings using Siamese BERT-Networks. In *Proceedings of the 2019 Conference on Empirical Methods in Natural Language Processing and the 9th International Joint Conference on Natural Language Processing (EMNLP-IJCNLP)*, pages 3982–3992.

Hayato Tsukagoshi, Ryohei Sasano, and Koichi Takeda. 2021. DefSent: Sentence Embeddings using Definition Sentences. In *Proceedings of the 59th Annual Meeting of the Association for Computational Linguistics and the 11th International Joint Conference on Natural Language Processing (ACL-IJCNLP)*, pages 411–418.

Ashish Vaswani, Noam Shazeer, Niki Parmar, Jakob Uszkoreit, Llion Jones, Aidan N Gomez, Łukasz Kaiser, and Illia Polosukhin. 2017. Attention is All you Need. In *Advances in Neural Information Processing Systems (NIPS)*, pages 5998–6008.

Bin Wang and C.-C. Jay Kuo. 2020. SBERT-WK: A Sentence Embedding Method by Dissecting BERT-Based Word Models. *IEEE/ACM Transactions on Audio, Speech, and Language Processing*, 28:2146–2157.

Kexin Wang, Nils Reimers, and Iryna Gurevych. 2021. TSDAE: Using Transformer-based Sequential Denoising Auto-Encoder for Unsupervised Sentence Embedding Learning. *arXiv:2104.06979*.

Adina Williams, Nikita Nangia, and Samuel Bowman. 2018. A broad-coverage challenge corpus for sentence understanding through inference. In *Proceedings of the 2018 Conference of the North American Chapter of the Association for Computational Linguistics: Human Language Technologies (NAACL)*, pages 1112–1122.

Thomas Wolf, Lysandre Debut, Victor Sanh, Julien Chaumond, Clement Delangue, Anthony Moi, Pierric Cistac, Tim Rault, Rémi Louf, Morgan Funtowicz, Joe Davison, Sam Shleifer, Patrick von Platen, Clara Ma, Yacine Jernite, Julien Plu, Canwen Xu, Teven Le Scao, Sylvain Gugger, Mariama Drame, Quentin Lhoest, and Alexander M. Rush. 2020. Transformers: State-of-the-Art Natural Language Processing. In *Proceedings of the 2020 Conference on Empirical Methods in Natural Language Processing (EMNLP): System Demonstrations*, pages 38–45.

Yuanmeng Yan, Rumei Li, Sirui Wang, Fuzheng Zhang, Wei Wu, and Weiran Xu. 2021. ConSERT: A Contrastive Framework for Self-Supervised Sentence Representation Transfer. In *Proceedings of the 59th Annual Meeting of the Association for Computational Linguistics and the 11th International Joint Conference on Natural Language Processing (ACL-IJCNLP)*, pages 5065–5075.

A Training Details

For fine-tuning of SBERT and DefSent, we use a batch size of 16, an epoch size of 1, Adam (Kingma and Ba, 2015) optimizer with $\beta_1 = 0.9$, $\beta_2 = 0.999$, and a linear learning rate warm-up over 10% of training steps for each, as the same setting as Reimers and Gurevych (2019) and Tsukagoshi et al. (2021). We choose the learning rate that achieves the highest average score on the validation set for each respective model by fine-tuning three times with different seed values at each learning rate in a range of $x \times 10^{-6}, x \in \{1, 2, 5, 10, 20, 50\}$. We also use smart batching, and the max sequence length is 128 for training efficiency.

B Average Runtime and Computing Infrastructure

Fine-tuning of SBERT with BERT-base and RoBERTa-base took about 120 minutes on a single NVIDIA GeForce GTX 1080 Ti. Fine-tuning of DefSent with BERT-base and RoBERTa-base took about 10 minutes on a single NVIDIA GeForce GTX 1080 Ti. Fine-tuning of SBERT with BERT-large and RoBERTa-large took about 130 minutes on a single Quadro GV100. Fine-tuning of DefSent with BERT-large and RoBERTa-large took about 15 minutes on a single Quadro GV100.

C The details of evaluation on unsupervised STS tasks of RoBERTa

Table 5 shows the average of Spearman's rho for RoBERTa-base and RoBERTa-large on unsupervised STS tasks.

D The details of evaluation on SentEval of RoBERTa

Table 6 shows the average of accuracy for RoBERTa-base and RoBERTa-large on SentEval.

Model	Method	STS12	STS13	STS14	STS15	STS16	STS-B	SICK-R	Avg.
RoBERTa-base	w/oFT	30.61	55.55	46.78	58.43	61.21	54.36	62.17	52.73
RoBERTa-base	SBERT	70.20	74.44	71.86	78.70	74.47	76.92	72.11	74.10
RoBERTa-base	DefSent	60.05	76.16	69.06	74.07	77.86	76.58	74.05	72.55
RoBERTa-base	S+D	73.19	83.86	77.45	83.32	78.88	80.67	76.97	79.19
RoBERTa-base	D+S	70.97	75.07	72.50	79.04	74.56	77.13	72.81	74.58
RoBERTa-base	MULTI	69.27	77.34	73.10	80.68	76.08	77.97	73.61	75.44
RoBERTa-base	AVERAGE	71.61	78.65	74.65	80.30	76.71	78.56	74.04	76.36
RoBERTa-base	CONCAT	70.69	76.03	72.92	79.08	75.34	77.50	72.73	74.90
RoBERTa-large	w/oFT	26.00	54.35	44.10	56.35	60.37	47.01	58.11	49.47
RoBERTa-large	SBERT	74.04	79.47	75.47	82.77	79.50	80.49	74.19	77.99
RoBERTa-large	DefSent	57.79	74.67	69.01	72.98	75.48	77.39	72.55	71.41
RoBERTa-large	S+D	66.62	79.60	75.81	77.91	78.45	80.46	77.45	76.61
RoBERTa-large	D+S	74.18	79.81	76.38	82.85	78.78	80.38	74.86	78.18
RoBERTa-large	MULTI	61.34	57.43	60.17	75.56	73.78	74.92	70.10	67.62
RoBERTa-large	AVERAGE	73.43	82.97	77.85	83.82	80.65	82.09	75.91	79.53
RoBERTa-large	CONCAT	74.04	80.96	76.60	83.20	80.33	81.24	74.77	78.73

Table 5: Experimental results on unsupervised STS tasks with Spearman's $\rho \times 100$.

Model	Method	MR	CR	SUBJ	MPQA	SST-2	TREC	MRPC	Avg.
RoBERTa-base	w/oFT	84.35	88.19	95.28	86.49	89.46	93.20	74.20	87.31
RoBERTa-base	SBERT	85.35	91.50	93.15	90.95	92.06	87.07	76.62	88.10
RoBERTa-base	DefSent	84.70	91.15	94.55	90.56	89.88	92.40	76.43	88.52
RoBERTa-base	S+D	85.04	91.40	94.17	90.81	90.63	92.00	77.14	88.74
RoBERTa-base	D+S	85.20	91.34	93.45	90.84	92.20	88.20	76.29	88.22
RoBERTa-base	MULTI	85.15	91.00	93.25	90.69	91.47	89.67	77.08	88.33
RoBERTa-base	AVERAGE	85.57	91.66	94.01	91.14	92.55	89.67	78.12	88.96
RoBERTa-base	CONCAT	86.04	91.68	94.70	91.02	92.40	93.93	78.24	89.72
RoBERTa-large	w/oFT	85.46	88.72	96.04	88.34	91.27	93.80	73.80	88.20
RoBERTa-large	SBERT	87.35	92.56	94.13	90.99	92.77	92.20	76.00	89.43
RoBERTa-large	DefSent	86.28	91.14	95.12	90.97	90.74	92.33	73.74	88.62
RoBERTa-large	S+D	86.77	92.28	94.68	91.22	91.98	92.60	77.51	89.58
RoBERTa-large	D+S	87.02	92.40	93.62	90.80	92.59	90.93	77.35	89.25
RoBERTa-large	MULTI	87.52	92.56	94.39	91.09	93.15	91.60	76.69	89.57
RoBERTa-large	AVERAGE	87.82	92.81	94.69	91.36	93.24	93.93	77.49	90.19
RoBERTa-large	CONCAT	87.87	92.84	95.22	91.64	93.06	94.27	76.23	90.16

Table 6: Experimental results on each SentEval task with the accuracy (%).

Distilling Hypernymy Relations from Language Models: On the Effectiveness of Zero-Shot Taxonomy Induction

Devansh Jain[♠*] **Luis Espinosa Anke**[◇]
[♠] Department of Computer Science and Information Systems, BITS Pilani, India
[◇] CardiffNLP (Cardiff University) - AMPLYFI
f20180798@pilani.bits-pilani.ac.in
espinosa-ankel@cardiff.ac.uk

Abstract

In this paper, we analyze zero-shot taxonomy learning methods which are based on distilling knowledge from language models via prompting and sentence scoring. We show that, despite their simplicity, these methods outperform some supervised strategies and are competitive with the current state-of-the-art under adequate conditions. We also show that statistical and linguistic properties of prompts dictate downstream performance[1].

1 Introduction

Taxonomy learning (TL) is the task of arranging domain terminologies into hierarchical structures where terms are nodes and edges denote *is-a* (hypernymic) relationships (Hwang et al., 2012). Domain-specific concept generalization is at the core of human cognition (Yu et al., 2015), and a key enabler in NLP tasks where inference and reasoning are important, e.g.: semantic similarity (Pilehvar et al., 2013; Yu and Dredze, 2014), WSD (Agirre et al., 2014) and, more recently, QA (Joshi et al., 2020) and NLI (Chen et al., 2020).

Earlier approaches to taxonomy learning focused on mining lexico-syntactic patterns from candidate (hyponym, hypernym) pairs (Hearst, 1992; Snow et al., 2004; Kozareva and Hovy, 2010; Boella and Di Caro, 2013; Espinosa-Anke et al., 2016), clustering (Yang and Callan, 2009), graph-based methods (Fountain and Lapata, 2012; Velardi et al., 2013) or word embeddings (Fu et al., 2014; Yu et al., 2015). These methods, which largely rely on hand-crafted features, are still relevant today, and complement modern approaches exploiting language models (LMs), either via sequence classification (Chen et al., 2021), or combining contextual, distributed, and lexico-syntactic features (Yu et al., 2020). In parallel, several works have recently focused on using LMs as zero-shot tools for solving NLP tasks, e.g., commonsense, relational and analogical reasoning (Petroni et al., 2019; Bouraoui et al., 2020; Ushio et al., 2021; Paranjape et al., 2021), multiword expression (MWE) identification (Espinosa-Anke et al., 2021; Garcia et al., 2021), QA (Shwartz et al., 2020; Banerjee and Baral, 2020), domain labeling (Sainz and Rigau, 2021), or lexical substitution and simplification (Zhou et al., 2019). Moreover, by tuning and manipulating natural language queries (often referred to as *prompts*), impressive results have been recently obtained on tasks such as semantic textual similarity, entailment, or relation classification (Shin et al., 2020; Qin and Eisner, 2021).

In this paper, we evaluate LMs on TL benchmarks using prompt-based and sentence-scoring techniques, and find not only that they are competitive with common approaches proposed in the literature (which are typically supervised and/or reliant on external resources), but that they achieve state-of-the-art results in certain domains.

2 Methodology

We follow Ushio et al. (2021) and define a prompt generation function $\tau_p(t_1, t_2)$ which maps a pair of terms and a prompt type p to a single sentence. For instance,

$$\tau_{kind}(\text{“physics”, “science”}) = \text{“physics is a kind of science”}$$

Then, given a terminology $\mathcal{T}$, the goal is to, given an input term $t \in \mathcal{T}$, retrieve its top k most likely hypernyms, (in our experiments, $k \in \{1, 3, 5\}$), using either masked language model (MLM) prompting (§2.1), or sentence-scoring (§2.2).

2.1 MLM Prompting

RestrictMLM Petroni et al. (2019) introduced a "fill-in-the-blanks" approach based on cloze state-

[*] Work done during an internship at CardiffNLP.
[1] Code available at https://github.com/devanshrj/zero-shot-taxonomy.

Proceedings of the 11th Joint Conference on Lexical and Computational Semantics, pages 151 - 156
July 14-15, 2022 ©2022 Association for Computational Linguistics

ments (or *prompts*) to extract relational knowledge from pretrained LMs. The intuition being that an LM can be considered to "know" a fact (in the form of a <*subject, relation, object*> triple) such as <*Madrid, capital-of, Spain*> if it can successfully predict the correct words when queried with prompts such as "Madrid is the capital of `[MASK]`". We extend this formulation to define a hypernym retrieval function $f_R(\cdot)$ as follows:

$$f_R(p, t, \mathbf{T}) = P(\texttt{[MASK]} | \tau_p(t, \texttt{[MASK]})) * \mathbf{T} \quad (1)$$

where p is a prompt type, and $\mathbf{T}$ is a one-hot encoding of the terms $\mathcal{T}$ in the LM's vocabulary. We follow previous works (Petroni et al., 2019; Kassner et al., 2021) and restrict the output probability distribution since this task requires the construction of a lexical taxonomy starting from a fixed vocabulary.

PromptMLM For completeness, we also report results for an unrestricted variant of *RestrictMLM*, where the LM's entire vocabulary is considered.

2.2 LMScorer

Factual (and true) information such as "Trout is a type of fish" should be scored higher by a LM than fictitious information such as "Trout is a type of mammal". The method for scoring a sentence depends on the type of LM used.

Causal Language Models Given a sentence $\mathbf{W}$, causal LMs ($\mathcal{C}$) predict token w_i using only past tokens $\mathbf{W}_{<i}$. Thus, a likelihood score can be estimated for each token w_i from the LM's next token prediction. The corresponding scores are then aggregated to yield a score for sentence $\mathbf{W}$.

$$s_{\mathcal{C}}(\mathbf{W}) = \exp\left(\sum_{i=1}^{|\mathbf{W}|} logP_{\mathcal{C}}(w_i | \mathbf{W}_{<i})\right) \quad (2)$$

Masked Language Models Given a sentence $\mathbf{W}$, masked LMs ($\mathcal{M}$) replace w_i by `[MASK]` and predict it using past and future tokens. Thus, a pseudo-likelihood score can be computed for each token w_i by iteratively masking it and using the LM's masked token prediction (Wang and Cho, 2019; Salazar et al., 2020). The corresponding scores are then aggregated to yield a score for sentence $\mathbf{W}$.

$$s_{\mathcal{M}}(\mathbf{W}) = \exp\left(\sum_{i=1}^{|\mathbf{W}|} logP_{\mathcal{M}}(w_i | \mathbf{W}_{\setminus i})\right) \quad (3)$$

Given the above, we can cast TL as a sentence-scoring problem by evaluating the natural fluency of hypernymy-eliciting sentences. Specifically, for each term t, we score the sentences generated using $\tau_p(\cdot)$ with every other term t' in the terminology. We then select the term-pair with the highest sentence score and assume that the corresponding term t' is a hypernym of t. Formally, we define a hypernym selection function $f_S(\cdot)$ as follows:

$$f_S(p, t, \mathcal{T}) = \arg\max_{t' \in \mathcal{T} \setminus t}[s(\tau_p(t, t'))] \quad (4)$$

where s refers to the scoring function determined by the LM used.

3 Experimental setup

This section covers the datasets and prompts we use in our experiments[2], as well as the different LMs we consider. Concerning evaluation metrics, we report standard precision (P), recall (R) and F-score at the *edge level* (Bordea et al., 2016).

Dataset Details We evaluate our proposed approaches on datasets belonging to two TL SemEval tasks (*TExEval-1*, Bordea et al. (2015) and *TExEval-2*, Bordea et al. (2016)). Following recent literature, we consider the *equipment* taxonomy from *TExEval-1* and the English-language *environment*, *science* and *food* taxonomies from *TExEval-2*. For the *science* taxonomy, our results are based on an *average of the 3 subsets*, which is in line with previous work. Since these datasets do not come with training data, they are well suited for unsupervised approaches.

Domain	Source	V	E
environment	Eurovoc	261	261
science	Combined	453	465
	Eurovoc	125	124
	WordNet	429	452
food	Combined	1556	1587
equipment	Combined	612	615

Table 1: Taxonomies statistics. Vertices (V) and Edges (E) are often used as structural measures.

[2]We use PyTorch and the `transformers` library (Wolf et al., 2020), as well as `mlm-scoring` (Salazar et al., 2020) (`https://github.com/awslabs/mlm-scoring`).

Prompts We use the following prompts:

- *gen.*: $[t_2]$ is more general than $[t_1]$.
- *spec.*: $[t_1]$ is more specific than $[t_2]$.
- *type*: $[t_1]$ is a type of $[t_2]$.

$gen.$ and $spec.$ prompts are hand-crafted templates to encode, in a general way, the hypernymy relationship. The choice of the $type$ prompt, however, comes from a set of experiments involving all *LPAQA* (Jiang et al., 2020) prompts under the "*is a subclass of*" category. We do not consider automatic prompt generation techniques (Shin et al., 2020) due to the absence of training data. Note that for each prompt, we replace t_1 with the input term so that the task is always to predict its hypernym.

Language Models We interrogate BERT (Devlin et al., 2019) and RoBERTa (Liu et al., 2019) among masked LMs, and GPT2 (Radford et al., 2019) among causal LMs. For each LM, we consider two variants corresponding to approximately 117M parameters and 345M parameters.

4 Results

Table 2 shows the results on *TExEval-2*'s *science* and *environment*. We compare with the current state of the art (*Graph2Taxo*) (Shang et al., 2020), as well as with other strong baselines such as *TaxoRL* (Mao et al., 2018) and *TAXI* (Panchenko et al., 2016), the highest ranked system in *TExEval-2*. We also compare with *CTP* (Chen et al., 2021) to illustrate the advantages of zero-shot methods vs finetuning. For the *environment* domain, we find that *RestrictMLM* performs similar to *CTP* and *LMScorer* outperforms it. Moreover, all 3 proposed approaches fail to outperform the other baselines. However, in *science*, all 3 of our approaches outperform *CTP*, while our best model (*RestrictMLM*) outperforms *TAXI* and is competitive with *TaxoRL* (ours has higher precison, but lower recall). Note that compared to our zero-shot approaches, these methods are either supervised, expensive to train or take advantage of external taxonomical resources such as WordNet, or lexico-syntactic patterns mined from the web using different hand-crafted heuristics.

We also show results for *TExEval-1*'s *equipment* and *TExEval-2*'s *food* (Table 3). Both datasets are considerably larger than *environment* and *science*. We compare with the corresponding highest ranked system, namely *TAXI* for *food*, and *INRIASAC* (Grefenstette, 2015) for *equipment*. For both domains, all 3 of our approaches outperform the corresponding *TExEval* best-performing systems. This suggests that zero-shot TL with LMs is robust, easily scalable and feasible on large taxonomies. However, a clear bottleneck for prompt-based methods is that only single-token terms can be predicted (using a single `[MASK]` token), making this approach a lower bound for TL.

	environment			*science*		
Model	P	R	F	P	R	F
TAXI	33.8	26.8	29.9	35.2	35.3	35.2
TaxoRL	32.3	32.3	32.3	37.9	37.9	37.9
Graph2Taxo	89.0	24.0	**37.0**	84.0	30.0	**44.0**
CTP	23.1	23.0	23.0	29.4	28.8	29.1
PromptMLM	19.2	19.2	19.2	34.4	32.0	33.1
RestrictMLM	23.0	23.0	23.0	39.3	36.7	37.9
LMScorer	26.4	26.4	26.4	33.1	30.7	31.8

Table 2: Comparison of our best performing methods with previous work (*environment* and *science*).

	food			*equipment*		
Model	P	R	F	P	R	F
TExEval	13.2	25.1	17.3	51.8	18.8	27.6
PromptMLM	23.2	22.6	22.9	29.4	29.3	29.4
RestrictMLM	25.2	24.6	**24.9**	38.4	38.2	**38.3**
LMScorer	25.2	24.6	**24.9**	37.7	37.6	37.6

Table 3: Comparison of our best configurations with the best TExEval systems on *food* and *equipment*.

5 Analysis

In this section, we provide an in-depth analysis of our approaches, including comparison of LMs and statistical and semantic properties of prompts.

LM Comparison Table 4 compares the best configuration for each LM. We can immediately see that a conservative approach (i.e., $k = 1$ with the *type* prompt) almost always yields the best F-score. Another important conclusion is that, among MLMs, BERT-Large performs best across the board, with BERT generally outperforming RoBERTa, a finding in line with previous works (Shin et al., 2020). Concerning causal LMs, GPT-2 Medium outperforms its smaller counterpart as well as both MLMs for sentence-scoring.

Sensitivity to Prompts There is interest in understanding models' sensitivity to prompts and

		environment				*science*				*food*				*equipment*			
Method	LM	(p,k)	P	R	F	(p,k)	P	R	F	(p,k)	P	R	F	(p,k)	P	R	F
PromptMLM	BERT-Base	$(t,1)$	18.8	18.8	18.8	$(t,1)$	30.2	28.1	29.1	$(t,1)$	20.9	20.4	20.6	$(t,1)$	29.4	29.3	29.4
	BERT-Large	$(t,1)$	19.2	19.2	19.2	$(t,1)$	34.4	32.0	33.1	$(t,1)$	23.2	22.6	22.9	$(t,1)$	28.4	28.3	28.4
	RoBERTa-Base	$(t,1)$	18.0	18.0	18.0	$(t,1)$	24.5	23.0	23.7	$(t,1)$	18.5	18.0	18.2	$(t,1)$	26.3	26.2	26.3
	RoBERTa-Large	$(t,1)$	18.0	18.0	18.0	$(t,1)$	28.1	26.2	27.1	$(t,1)$	20.3	19.8	20.0	$(t,1)$	28.4	28.3	28.4
RestrictMLM	BERT-Base	$(t,1)$	23.0	23.0	23.0	$(t,1)$	35.8	33.5	34.6	$(t,1)$	22.8	22.2	22.5	$(t,1)$	38.4	38.2	38.3
	BERT-Large	$(t,1)$	21.8	21.8	21.8	$(t,1)$	39.3	36.7	**37.9**	$(t,1)$	25.2	24.6	**24.9**	$(t,1)$	37.9	37.7	**37.8**
	RoBERTa-Base	$(t,1)$	5.4	5.4	5.4	$(t,1)$	11.0	10.6	10.8	$(t,1)$	9.3	9.1	9.2	$(t,1)$	0.0	0.0	0.0
	RoBERTa-Large	$(t,1)$	8.4	8.4	8.4	$(t,1)$	12.3	11.8	12.0	$(t,1)$	10.7	10.5	10.6	$(t,1)$	0.0	0.0	0.0
LMScorer	BERT-Base	$(t,1)$	20.3	20.3	20.3	$(t,1)$	15.2	14.4	14.8	$(t,3)$	6.8	19.7	10.1	$(t,3)$	7.5	22.4	11.2
	BERT-Large	$(t,3)$	13.7	41.0	20.5	$(t,1)$	13.0	12.4	12.6	$(t,1)$	13.9	13.6	13.7	$(t,1)$	15.2	15.1	15.1
	RoBERTa-Base	$(g,3)$	7.7	23.0	11.5	$(t,3)$	5.5	15.7	8.1	$(t,3)$	2.5	7.2	3.7	$(t,5)$	4.2	21.0	7.0
	RoBERTa-Large	$(t,3)$	11.1	33.3	16.7	$(t,1)$	13.6	12.8	13.2	$(t,3)$	3.6	10.6	5.4	$(t,3)$	9.2	27.5	13.8
	GPT-2 Base	$(t,1)$	24.9	24.9	24.9	$(t,1)$	29.3	27.4	28.3	$(t,1)$	21.0	20.5	20.7	$(t,1)$	36.8	36.6	36.7
	GPT-2 Medium	$(t,1)$	26.4	26.4	**26.4**	$(t,1)$	33.1	30.7	31.8	$(t,1)$	25.2	24.6	**24.9**	$(t,1)$	37.7	37.6	37.7

Table 4: Comparison of best configuration for each LM and proposed approach. (p, k) refers to the prompt and top-k combination that gives the best results for that setting, where $p = g$ for *gen.*, s for *spec.* and t for *type* prompt.

whether frequency can explain downstream performance in lexical semantics tasks (Chiang et al., 2020). In the context of prompt vs. performance correlation, we find that prompt-based downstream performance on TL can be attributed to: (1) syntactic completeness and (2) semantic correctness. For (1), we find that prompts that are syntactically more complete (e.g., "*[X] is a type of [Y]*" vs "*[X] is a type [Y]*", the difference being the prepositional phrase) perform better. For (2), we find that prompts that unambiguously encode hypernymy are also better (i.e., the *type* prompt, as opposed to other noise-inducing templates such as "*is a*" or "*is kind of*"). Finally, out of the cleanest prompts, the most frequent in pretraining corpora are the most competitive. Table 5 confirms the intuition that the *type* prompt is not only unambiguous, but also highly frequent when compared to similar (noise-free and syntactically complete) prompts.

Prompt	*avg* F	Frequency
is a type of	25.5	14,503
is the type of	24.2	809
is a kind of	23.6	2,934
is a form of	22.1	9,518
is one form of	17.9	124
is a	7.4	9,328,426
is a type	1.0	15,085

Table 5: Domain-wise average F-score of LPAQA prompts and their frequency in BERT's pretraining corpora.

Single-Token vs Multi-Token Hypernyms Table 6 compares *F-score* on original terminology vs filtered terminology, where filtered terminology contains only the terms that have single-token hypernyms. The results show that % Increase in *F-score* is inversely proportional to the % Retained. This can be explained by the fact that smaller % of terms retained implies higher % of multi-token hypernyms in the original dataset that cannot be predicted using prompting. Thus, the increase in *F-score* by removing such hypernyms should increase as the % Retained decreases.

Domain	Total Terms	% Retained	% Increase
environment	261	29.89	2.32
equipment	612	44.77	1.24
science	452	53.32	0.90
science_ev	125	52.80	0.89
food	1555	59.55	0.57
science_wn	370	69.73	0.51

Table 6: Comparison of *F-score* on original terminology vs filtered terminology. % Retained refers to the percentage of terms that have single-token hypernyms and are thus retained for the filtered dataset. % Increase shows the increase in *F-score* on filtered dataset compared to *F-score* on original dataset.

6 Conclusion and Future Work

We have presented a study of different LMs under different settings for zero-shot taxonomy learning. Compared with computationally expensive and highly heuristic methods, our zero-shot alternatives prove remarkably competitive. For the future, we could explore multilingual signals and the integration of traditional word embeddings with contextual representations.

References

Eneko Agirre, Oier Lopez de Lacalle, and Aitor Soroa. 2014. Random walks for knowledge-based word sense disambiguation. *Computational Linguistics*, 40(1):57–84.

Pratyay Banerjee and Chitta Baral. 2020. Self-supervised knowledge triplet learning for zero-shot question answering. In *Proceedings of the 2020 Conference on Empirical Methods in Natural Language Processing (EMNLP)*, pages 151–162.

Guido Boella and Luigi Di Caro. 2013. Supervised learning of syntactic contexts for uncovering definitions and extracting hypernym relations in text databases. In *Machine learning and knowledge discovery in databases*, pages 64–79. Springer.

Georgeta Bordea, Paul Buitelaar, Stefano Faralli, and Roberto Navigli. 2015. Semeval-2015 task 17: Taxonomy extraction evaluation (texeval). In *Proceedings of the 9th International Workshop on Semantic Evaluation*. Association for Computational Linguistics.

Georgeta Bordea, Els Lefever, and Paul Buitelaar. 2016. Semeval-2016 task 13: Taxonomy extraction evaluation (texeval-2). In *Proceedings of the 10th International Workshop on Semantic Evaluation*. Association for Computational Linguistics.

Zied Bouraoui, Jose Camacho-Collados, and Steven Schockaert. 2020. Inducing relational knowledge from bert. In *Proceedings of the AAAI Conference on Artificial Intelligence*, volume 34, pages 7456–7463.

Catherine Chen, Kevin Lin, and D. Klein. 2021. Constructing taxonomies from pretrained language models. In *NAACL*.

Mingda Chen, Zewei Chu, Karl Stratos, and Kevin Gimpel. 2020. Mining knowledge for natural language inference from wikipedia categories. In *Proceedings of the 2020 Conference on Empirical Methods in Natural Language Processing: Findings*, pages 3500–3511.

Hsiao-Yu Chiang, Jose Camacho-Collados, and Zachary Pardos. 2020. Understanding the source of semantic regularities in word embeddings. In *Proceedings of the 24th Conference on Computational Natural Language Learning*, pages 119–131.

J. Devlin, Ming-Wei Chang, Kenton Lee, and Kristina Toutanova. 2019. Bert: Pre-training of deep bidirectional transformers for language understanding. In *NAACL*.

Luis Espinosa-Anke, Joan Codina-Filbá, and Leo Wanner. 2021. Evaluating language models for the retrieval and categorization of lexical collocations. In *Proceedings of the 16th Conference of the European Chapter of the Association for Computational Linguistics: Main Volume*, pages 1406–1417.

Luis Espinosa-Anke, Horacio Saggion, Francesco Ronzano, and Roberto Navigli. 2016. Extasem! extending, taxonomizing and semantifying domain terminologies. In *Proceedings of AAAI*, Phoenix, USA.

Trevor Fountain and Mirella Lapata. 2012. Taxonomy induction using hierarchical random graphs. In *Proceedings of NAACL*, pages 466–476. Association for Computational Linguistics.

Ruiji Fu, Jiang Guo, Bing Qin, Wanxiang Che, Haifeng Wang, and Ting Liu. 2014. Learning semantic hierarchies via word embeddings. In *Proceedings of ACL*, volume 1.

Marcos Garcia, Tiago Kramer Vieira, Carolina Scarton, Marco Idiart, and Aline Villavicencio. 2021. Probing for idiomaticity in vector space models. In *Proceedings of the 16th Conference of the European Chapter of the Association for Computational Linguistics: Main Volume*, pages 3551–3564.

Gregory Grefenstette. 2015. Inriasac: Simple hypernym extraction methods. In *Proceedings of the 9th International Workshop on Semantic Evaluation (SemEval 2015)*, pages 911–914.

Marti A Hearst. 1992. Automatic acquisition of hyponyms from large text corpora. In *Proceedings of the 14th conference on Computational linguistics*, pages 539–545.

Sung Ju Hwang, Kristen Grauman, and Fei Sha. 2012. Semantic kernel forests from multiple taxonomies. In *Advances in Neural Information Processing Systems*, pages 1718–1726.

Zhengbao Jiang, Frank F. Xu, J. Araki, and Graham Neubig. 2020. How can we know what language models know? *Transactions of the Association for Computational Linguistics*, 8:423–438.

Mandar Joshi, Kenton Lee, Yi Luan, and Kristina Toutanova. 2020. Contextualized representations using textual encyclopedic knowledge. *arXiv preprint arXiv:2004.12006*.

Nora Kassner, Philipp Dufter, and Hinrich Schütze. 2021. Multilingual LAMA: Investigating knowledge in multilingual pretrained language models. In *Proceedings of the 16th Conference of the European Chapter of the Association for Computational Linguistics: Main Volume*, pages 3250–3258, Online. Association for Computational Linguistics.

Zornitsa Kozareva and Eduard Hovy. 2010. A semi-supervised method to learn and construct taxonomies using the web. In *Proceedings of EMNLP*, pages 1110–1118.

Yinhan Liu, Myle Ott, Naman Goyal, Jingfei Du, Mandar Joshi, Danqi Chen, Omer Levy, M. Lewis, Luke Zettlemoyer, and Veselin Stoyanov. 2019. Roberta: A robustly optimized bert pretraining approach. *ArXiv*, abs/1907.11692.

Yuning Mao, Xiang Ren, J. Shen, X. Gu, and Jiawei Han. 2018. End-to-end reinforcement learning for automatic taxonomy induction. In *ACL*.

Alexander Panchenko, Stefano Faralli, E. Ruppert, Steffen Remus, Hubert Naets, Cedric Fairon, Simone Paolo Ponzetto, and Chris Biemann. 2016. Taxi at semeval-2016 task 13: a taxonomy induction method based on lexico-syntactic patterns, substrings and focused crawling. In *SemEval@NAACL-HLT*.

Bhargavi Paranjape, Julian Michael, Marjan Ghazvininejad, Luke Zettlemoyer, and Hannaneh Hajishirzi. 2021. Prompting contrastive explanations for commonsense reasoning tasks. *arXiv preprint arXiv:2106.06823*.

Fabio Petroni, Tim Rocktäschel, Patrick Lewis, A. Bakhtin, Yuxiang Wu, Alexander H. Miller, and S. Riedel. 2019. Language models as knowledge bases? In *EMNLP*.

Mohammad Taher Pilehvar, David Jurgens, and Roberto Navigli. 2013. Align, Disambiguate and Walk: a Unified Approach for Measuring Semantic Similarity. In *Proceedings of ACL*, pages 1341–1351, Sofia, Bulgaria.

Guanghui Qin and Jason Eisner. 2021. Learning how to ask: Querying lms with mixtures of soft prompts. In *Proceedings of the 2021 Conference of the North American Chapter of the Association for Computational Linguistics: Human Language Technologies*, pages 5203–5212.

Alec Radford, Jeff Wu, Rewon Child, David Luan, Dario Amodei, and Ilya Sutskever. 2019. Language models are unsupervised multitask learners.

Oscar Sainz and German Rigau. 2021. Ask2transformers: Zero-shot domain labelling with pretrained language models. In *Proceedings of the 11th Global Wordnet Conference*, pages 44–52.

Julian Salazar, Davis Liang, Toan Q. Nguyen, and Katrin Kirchhoff. 2020. Masked language model scoring. In *ACL*.

Chao Shang, Sarthak Dash, Md. Faisal Mahbub Chowdhury, Nandana Mihindukulasooriya, and A. Gliozzo. 2020. Taxonomy construction of unseen domains via graph-based cross-domain knowledge transfer. In *ACL*.

Taylor Shin, Yasaman Razeghi, Robert L Logan IV, Eric Wallace, and Sameer Singh. 2020. Eliciting knowledge from language models using automatically generated prompts. In *Proceedings of the 2020 Conference on Empirical Methods in Natural Language Processing (EMNLP)*, pages 4222–4235.

Vered Shwartz, Peter West, Ronan Le Bras, Chandra Bhagavatula, and Yejin Choi. 2020. Unsupervised commonsense question answering with self-talk. In *Proceedings of the 2020 Conference on Empirical Methods in Natural Language Processing (EMNLP)*, pages 4615–4629.

Rion Snow, Daniel Jurafsky, and Andrew Y Ng. 2004. Learning syntactic patterns for automatic hypernym discovery. *Advances in Neural Information Processing Systems 17*.

Asahi Ushio, Luis Espinosa-Anke, Steven Schockaert, and Jose Camacho-Collados. 2021. BERT is to NLP what AlexNet is to CV: Can Pre-Trained Language Models Identify Analogies? In *Proceedings of the ACL-IJCNLP 2021 Main Conference*. Association for Computational Linguistics.

Paola Velardi, Stefano Faralli, and Roberto Navigli. 2013. OntoLearn Reloaded: A graph-based algorithm for taxonomy induction. *Computational Linguistics*, 39(3):665–707.

Alex Wang and Kyunghyun Cho. 2019. BERT has a mouth, and it must speak: BERT as a Markov random field language model. In *Proceedings of the Workshop on Methods for Optimizing and Evaluating Neural Language Generation*, pages 30–36, Minneapolis, Minnesota. Association for Computational Linguistics.

Thomas Wolf, Lysandre Debut, Victor Sanh, Julien Chaumond, Clement Delangue, Anthony Moi, Pierric Cistac, Tim Rault, Rémi Louf, Morgan Funtowicz, Joe Davison, Sam Shleifer, Patrick von Platen, Clara Ma, Yacine Jernite, Julien Plu, Canwen Xu, Teven Le Scao, Sylvain Gugger, Mariama Drame, Quentin Lhoest, and Alexander M. Rush. 2020. Transformers: State-of-the-art natural language processing. In *Proceedings of the 2020 Conference on Empirical Methods in Natural Language Processing: System Demonstrations*, pages 38–45, Online. Association for Computational Linguistics.

Hui Yang and Jamie Callan. 2009. A metric-based framework for automatic taxonomy induction. In *Proceedings of ACL/IJCNLP*, pages 271–279. Association for Computational Linguistics.

Mo Yu and Mark Dredze. 2014. Improving lexical embeddings with semantic knowledge. In *ACL (2)*, pages 545–550.

Yue Yu, Yinghao Li, Jiaming Shen, Haoyang Feng, Jimeng Sun, and Chao Zhang. 2020. Steam: Self-supervised taxonomy expansion with mini-paths. *Proceedings of the 26th ACM SIGKDD International Conference on Knowledge Discovery & Data Mining*.

Zheng Yu, Haixun Wang, Xuemin Lin, and Min Wang. 2015. Learning term embeddings for hypernymy identification. In *Proceedings of IJCAI*, pages 1390–1397.

Wangchunshu Zhou, Tao Ge, Ke Xu, Furu Wei, and Ming Zhou. 2019. Bert-based lexical substitution. In *Proceedings of the 57th Annual Meeting of the Association for Computational Linguistics*, pages 3368–3373.

A Dynamic, Interpreted *CheckList* for Meaning-oriented NLG Metric Evaluation – through the Lens of Semantic Similarity Rating

Laura Zeidler and **Juri Opitz** and **Anette Frank**
Department of Computational Linguistics
Heidelberg University, Germany
`{zeidler|opitz|frank}@cl.uni-heidelberg.de`

Abstract

Evaluating the quality of generated text is difficult, since traditional NLG evaluation metrics, focusing more on surface form than meaning, often fail to assign appropriate scores. This is especially problematic for AMR-to-text evaluation, given the abstract nature of AMR. Our work aims to support the development and improvement of NLG evaluation metrics that focus on *meaning*, by developing a *dynamic CheckList* for NLG metrics that is *interpreted* by being organized around meaning-relevant linguistic phenomena. Each test instance consists of a pair of sentences with their AMR graphs and a human-produced *textual semantic similarity* or *relatedness* score. Our *CheckList* facilitates comparative evaluation of metrics and reveals strengths and weaknesses of novel and traditional metrics. We demonstrate the usefulness of *CheckList* by designing a new metric GRACO that computes lexical cohesion graphs over AMR concepts. Our analysis suggests that GRACO presents an interesting NLG metric worth future investigation and that meaning-oriented NLG metrics can profit from graph-based metric components using AMR.

1 Introduction

Abstract Meaning Representation (AMR, Banarescu et al. (2013)) has become popular in NLP, one of the reasons being that AMR captures the essence of a sentence's meaning, while abstracting away from syntactic idiosyncrasies. Especially AMR-to-text generation (Konstas et al., 2017; Song et al., 2018; Wang et al., 2020; Blloshmi et al., 2021) has received much attention for applications that require text generation from structured content. However, the evaluation of text generated from AMR has been argued to be unsatisfactory (Manning et al., 2020). Also, Opitz and Frank (2021) show that the syntactic diversity of sentences generated from AMR is challenging for traditional NLG metrics, especially when candidates differ from the reference in surface properties.

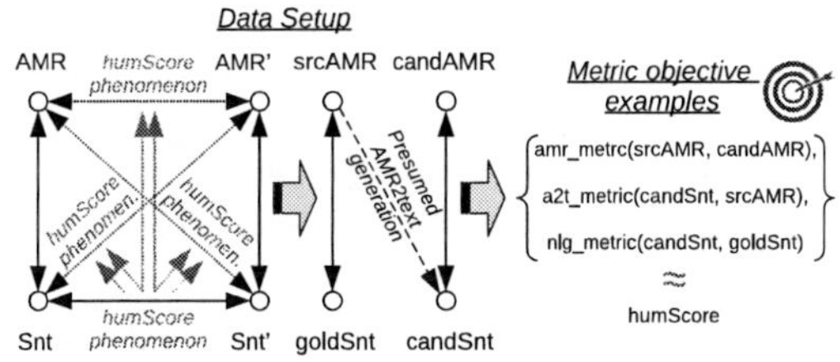

Figure 1: Our *CheckList* design for evaluating meaning-oriented NLG metrics against human semantic textual similarity and relatedness judgements – applicable to textual, meaning graph based and hybrid metrics.

Several metrics have been proposed that aim to rate the similarity of the meaning of sentences or phrases (Zhang et al. (2020); Opitz and Frank (2021); Zhao et al. (2019)). However, it is difficult to judge where exactly such a metric fails, making it hard for developers to further improve it. To address similar problems, Ribeiro et al. (2020) recently proposed a "task-agnostic methodology for testing NLP models" called *CheckList*. They argue that such a method should be used for testing NLP systems instead of solely relying on automatic metrics, which can overestimate a model's performance. Similar processes have been applied in early NLP research, e.g. with the TSNLP testsuite (Lehmann et al., 1996). Inspired by *CheckList*, in this work we aim to build a testsuite to enable systematic study and development of NLG evaluation metrics, with a focus on meaning.

Given the high variability of surface realizations that can be mapped into a single AMR graph, building reliable AMR-to-text NLG evaluation metrics is hard. Hence, it can be useful to construct a systematic *CheckList*, organized around diverse linguistic properties, to measure the performance of different metrics in an interpretable way. We frame our proposed CHECKLIST[1] and analyses derived

[1] The term *CheckList*, coined by Ribeiro et al. (2020), refers to their proposed methodology as well as concrete instantiations of such testsuites. We thus use the term *CheckList* (in

Proceedings of the 11th Joint Conference on Lexical and Computational Semantics, pages 157 - 172
July 14-15, 2022 ©2022 Association for Computational Linguistics

from it in an AMR-to-Text NLG setting, and focus especially on a metric's capability to assess how well a specific meaning component of an AMR is reflected in its textual realization. We measure this using sentence pairs that differ in single linguistic aspects and measure how well various NLG metrics are able to rate such meaning differences. We compare the metric scores to human judgments from semantic textual similarity (STS) and relatedness datasets and analyze the metrics using our interpreted *CheckList* (an outline is shown in Fig. 1). Our contributions in this work are as follows:

i) We empirically identify properties relevant for rating the quality of generated sentences based on their meaning.
ii) We design an extensible, interpreted *CheckList* for evaluating NLG metrics, which offers 939 paired sentences with human judgements, covering 11 core linguistic phenomena.
iii) We propose a new metric GRACO to assess the semantic similarity of sentence pairs through the lens of AMR graphs.
iv) To showcase the potential of our approach, we provide an extensive comparative analysis of different types of NLG metrics, measuring their capacity of rating sentence similarity and relatedness according to linguistic differences.

2 Related Work

AMR-to-text evaluation Systems generating text from AMR graphs are typically evaluated using NLG metrics that were originally designed for other NLG tasks. BLEU (Papineni et al., 2002) or the CHRF(++) (Stanojević et al., 2015; Popović, 2015, 2016; Popov, 2017) metrics, e.g., are extensively used in MT. But May and Priyadarshi (2017) have shown that BLEU does not correspond well to human ratings of generations from AMR. Confirming this result, Manning et al. (2020) argue that existing automatic metrics fail to provide nuanced views on AMR-to-text generation quality. In an attempt to mitigate such issues, Opitz and Frank (2021) introduced a metric that combines meaning ($\mathcal{M}$) and form ($\mathcal{F}$) assessment in a weighted $\mathcal{MF}$ score, finding that system performances differ considerably in these two key quality aspects.

But to date, little is known about how different metrics measure meaning differences of generated sentences with regard to specific meaning alterations that may occur between a source and a reference. Our work provides a method and resources that can be used for performing such a detailed assessment for AMR-to-text generation metrics, and NLG evaluation metrics in general.

Checklist The current practice for evaluating NLP models is to assess their performance on unseen test data. Yet, summarizing performance in a single numerical score makes it difficult to assess where a model fails and how to fix remaining errors (Wu et al., 2019). Ribeiro et al. (2020) therefore proposed CHECKLIST, a methodology and tool for evaluating NLP systems based on the idea of *behavioural testing*, often used in software engineering. It aims at assessing specific capabilities of a system by testing whether inputs that feature specific properties will produce the expected output, without requiring knowledge of system's inner workings. This procedure is well-known in NLP, where before the rise of large-scale evaluation datasets, systems were tested and evaluated on so-called *testsuites* (Lehmann et al., 1996) that focused on specific *linguistic capabilities*. Ribeiro et al. (2020) adopted this approach to make their methodology applicable to many different NLP tasks. They evaluate multiple models on Sentiment Analysis, QA or Machine Reading Comprehension, showing that their method is beneficial in NLP: complementary to broad-scale evaluations, it can reveal specific points of failure, hence giving more detailed insight into a model's performance.

Semantic Textual Similarity (STS) Judging the similarity of texts is essential in tasks such as IR, text summarization or QA. But capturing semantic ambiguity, syntactic variance and paraphrasing is difficult. Hence, research started to investigate *Semantic* Textual Similarity (STS)[2], by tasking systems to judge the semantic similarity of sentences. Besides knowledge-based and distributional methods, neural methods have recently been proposed for STS estimation (Chandrasekaran and Mago, 2021). For example, S(entence)-BERT (Reimers and Gurevych, 2019) leverages pre-trained language models to predict STS scores, building on the insight of models that compute general sentence representations using paired sentence encoders (Conneau et al., 2017). These models outperform most traditional STS metrics, but lack interpretabil-

italics), to refer to our interpreted NLG testsuite.

[2]STS is a main component of SentEval and follow-up challenges, initiated by Conneau and Kiela (2018).

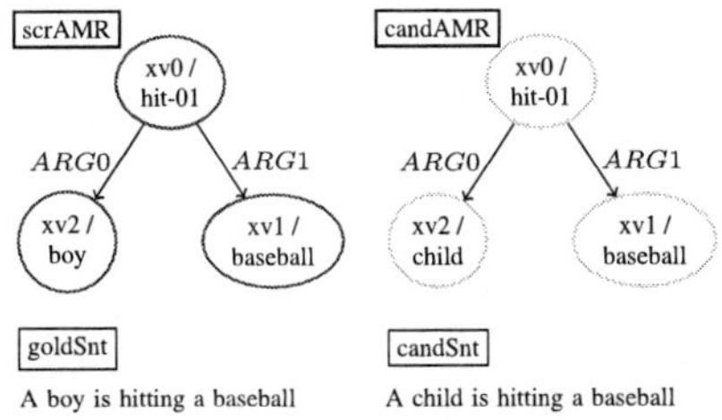

Figure 2: Example of a test case in our *CheckList* consisting of two sentence and AMR pairs. Drawn from the SICK dataset, with semantic relatedness score 4.4.

Phenomenon	Reference	AMR-to-text Generation
Antonymy	Flowers are so inconsistent !	flowers are so consistent .
Negation	My Drawing Number One .	not my picture number one .
Omission	the prince laughed , puzzled .	the prince laughed .
Passive	The wind blows them away .	they were blown away by wind .
Role Switch	The planet was inhabited by a conceited man .	the conceit man is inhabited by the planet .
more phenomena	hyponymy, co-hyponymy, partial synonymy, articles, subordinate clause types	

Table 1: (Modified) sentence pairs from AMR-to-text on the Little Prince AMR corpus.

ity. In our work we leverage STS and SentEval challenge datasets with human-rated semantic similarity (STS) and semantic relatedness (SICK) scores, to construct an interpreted *CheckList* that can be used to assess meaning-oriented NLG evaluation metrics, by evaluating them against human ratings.

3 An Interpreted Testsuite for Meaning-oriented NLG Evaluation Metrics

3.1 Aims and Method

The challenge of AMR-to-text NLG evaluation lies in the wide variability of sentences that can verbalize an abstract meaning representation. In our *CheckList*, we will consider human judgements of semantic textual similarity as a criterion for evaluating the adequacy of different NLG metrics for the AMR-to-text NLG evaluation task.

Specifically, we employ sentence pairs with human scores from the SICK and STS benchmarks[3] as test instances for our *CheckList* (cf. Fig. 2). We select pairs that *differ* by specific phenomena that can affect their semantic similarity, such as additional modifiers of a noun or verb, negation, or changes in the semantic roles of verb arguments. We parse such sentence pairs $S_{A,B}$ into pairs of AMR graphs $AMR_{A,B}$ that we manually validate.

Given such instances, we consider sentences S_A and S_B as a reference and candidate generation, and a pair of AMR and S as a sentence generated from an input AMR. For AMR_A we can take S_A as gold reference and S_B as a candidate generation; conversely, S_B can serve as a reference for AMR_B, and S_A as a candidate. We then interpret the human score for $S_{A,B}$ as a gold standard for a metric score that rates the appropriateness of S_B for AMR_A, given S_A as a reference, or S_A for AMR_B, given S_B as reference (see Fig. 1).

[3]https://github.com/facebookresearch/SentEval

Following this rationale, our *CheckList* will offer curated input AMR graphs, their underlying sentences as references, and paired sentences from STS or SICK data points as candidate generations. The human scores serve as an objective to assess and compare various NLG evaluation metrics for their suitability in (A)MR-to-text evaluation tasks.

Aims Our *CheckList* is intended as a tool for researchers to build new or assess existing NLG metrics, regarding their ability to assess specific meaning aspects by comparing them to human judgements, thereby helping users to improve metrics, or better understand differences between metrics in meaning-oriented NLG evaluation in general and AMR-to-text generation in particular.

The suite is *interpreted* in two ways: by structuring the instances according to linguistic phenomena, and by pairing each sentence with its AMR graph, so that sentences can be compared at the textual and at the meaning representation level. Finally, the *CheckList* is conceived to be *dynamic*, by inviting developers to add new linguistic phenomena, test cases, and metrics.

Method To achieve this, we proceed as follows:

i) Empirical investigation We investigated sentences generated from the 'Little Prince Corpus'[4] using the AMR-to-text system of Song et al. (2018). We studied differences between the original and the generated sentences, to determine core phenomena that may influence the semantic similarity judgement of sentences generated from AMR towards their references. We distilled a list of phenomena shown in Table 1 that we further extended with phenomena observed in the STS and SICK datasets.

ii) Selection from STS and SICK Next, we select instances from the STS and Semantic Relatedness datasets (§5.1) that exhibit the phenomena identified in **i)**, and establish a suite of sentence

[4]https://amr.isi.edu/download.html

pairs with their assigned human scores and respective AMRs. The data is structured into subsets exhibiting single phenomena, and is organized as an extensible *CheckList*.

iii) NLG metric scores & evaluation We implement scorers for various NLG metrics, and provide code to evaluate them via multiple measures to assess their strengths and weaknesses in view of phenomena captured in the CheckList. In addition, we propose a novel metric GRACO (§3.2) that constructs lexical cohesion graphs over tokens represented in the sentence's AMR, and compare it to existing metrics. The full range of functionalities to investigate NLG metrics is embedded into a CHECKLIST design (Ribeiro et al., 2020) (cf. A.1).

iv) Analysis and Interpretation We analyze the results and show how our *CheckList* enables systematic assessment of strenghts and weaknesses of NLG metrics when applied to outputs of AMR-to-text systems, taking into account the nature of different metrics in view of different phenomena.

3.2 Textual and AMR-based metrics

With our *CheckList* we aim at the evaluation of diverse metrics used in NLG and in semantic parsing, which we structure along two dimensions (cf. Table 2): metrics that evaluate candidate generations based on a) their textual (*tM*) vs. graph (*gM*) representations or both (hybrid, *hyM*), and b) whether the metric is based on symbolic as opposed to embedding representations. We don't include trained metrics, since their interpretation is difficult and would go beyond the current scope, but they can be evaluated on our *CheckList*, too. Table 6 provides an overview of characterizing traits of these metric types, which we will refer to in our analyses in §5.

Word/Char Ngram Matching Metrics Originally developed for MT evaluation, the BLEU (Papineni et al., 2002), Meteor (Lavie and Agarwal, 2007) and chrF++ (Popović, 2015) metrics have been increasingly used for evaluating NLG systems by comparing generated text to a reference on textual symbols. BLEU and Meteor compute overlap in word ngrams, while chrF++ extends the character ngram metric chrF by adding word ngrams.

Embedding-based Metrics BERTSCORE, proposed by Zhang et al. (2020), allows for reference-based evaluation using dense representations. Reference and candidate sentences are embedded with BERT to obtain contextualized representations for each token. A mapping between candidate and reference tokens is computed by greedy matching, based on cosine similarity of the encoding vectors. BERTSCORE shows a high correlation with human judgements for MT and Image Captioning tasks (Zhang et al., 2020). But while the metric is clearly meaning-based, it is focused on lexical meaning, and is not well equipped to capture word order and compositional meaning.

category	metric	gold information gldS	cndAMR	srcAMR
gM	S(^{2})match, W(W)LK	n	y	y
gM^{cndS}	S(^{2})match, W(W)LK	n	n	y
gM^{cndS}_{gldS}	S(^{2})match, W(W)LK	y	n	n
tM	BERTsc, Meteor, BLEU, chrF++	y	n	n
hyM	GRACO (this paper)	y	y	y

Table 2: Categorization of metrics into graph-based *gM*, text-based *tM* and hybrid *hyM* metrics, and their dependencies on gold information.

AMR Parse Evaluation Metrics While the previous metrics evaluate candidates against a reference at the *textual level* (tM), in our CheckList, we complement them by assessing similarity of meaning *structurally*, at the level of AMR graphs constructed from candidate and reference (gM).

We distinguish three potential setups: i) the metric is computed on manually rectified gold graphs (gM in Table 2); ii) an integrated parser component constructs an automatic candidate AMR *cndAMR* from the candidate sentence *cndSnt* to alleviate the requirement for a golden *cndAMR* (gM^{cndS} in Table 2); iii.) the parser constructs both *srcAMR* and *candAMR* from the reference and candidate sentence, i.e., we trade the dependency on a golden *srcAMR* against the dependency on a golden reference sentence (gM^{cndS}_{gldS} in Table 2). Variants ii) and iii) have also been used in the $\mathcal{M}$ ('Meaning') component of MF-score (Opitz and Frank, 2021). For simplicity, in this paper, we assume access to gold graphs and only consider gM, tM, and hyM metrics.

As AMR graph metrics, we use the canonical SMATCH (Cai and Knight, 2013), the recent S^{2}MATCH metric proposed by Opitz et al. (2020), and Weisfeiler-Leman based AMR graph similarity proposed by Opitz et al. (2021) that match contextualized AMR graphs.

SMATCH is a *binary* triple overlap metric that assesses the structural similarity of candidate and reference AMRs, where a triple is a pair of AMR nodes connected by a labeled edge. S^{2}MATCH, by contrast, computes a *graded* triple overlap score using the embedding similarity between the concept nodes of a triple pair, to reflect concept similarity in the overall AMR similarity score. Given a reference AMR for *'a kitten meows'*, S^{2}MATCH will assign a relatively high score for a candidate AMR for *'a cat meows'* that reflects high lexical similarity of *kitten* and *cat* in the overall score, while SMATCH will assign it a much lower score.

The Weisfeiler-Leman AMR metric comes in two variants: W(eisfeiler)L(eman)K(ernel) (WLK) compares contextualized AMR graphs structurally, while W(asserstein)WLK (WWLK) compares the contextualized AMR graphs in latent space, using an alignment-based Wasserstein distance. WWLK extends S^{2}MATCH beyond the lexical level, to capture *compositional* meaning similarity at the phrasal level, as between *'a young cat meows'* vs. *'a kitten meows'*.

Hybrid Metrics The above metrics take as input sentence pairs or AMR pairs. But a meaning-oriented NLG metric may profit from considering both explicit meaning structure as captured in AMR, and the textual level, to leverage knowledge from pretrained language models trained on text. We thus propose a **hybrid similarity metric** GRACO, which is based on *Lexical Cohesion Graphs* proposed by Sporleder and Li (2009). They construct an undirected graph from a text sequence where each node represents a content word, and compute edge weights between the lexical nodes using Normalized Google Distance (Cilibrasi and Vitanyi, 2007). By averaging the weights they derive a *connectivity* score for the graph. In their work they use the lexical cohesion graph of a given token sequence to predict whether it has an *idiomatic* as opposed to a *literal* meaning, depending on whether the presence of its subgraph in the overall graph raises or lowers the overall connectivity score.

We adapt Sporleder and Li (2009)'s approach to define a *hybrid metric* that measures the similarity of sentence pairs via their AMR graphs. We do this by building a lexical cohesion graph from the concept nodes present in a sentence's AMR. To do so, we align words from the sentence with concepts in the AMR graph using the JAMR (Flanigan et al., 2014a) alignment tool. The concepts are either represented using contextualized BERT embeddings or pretrained GloVe word embeddings. To compute edge weights, we follow Haagsma et al. (2018) and compute cosine similarity between nodes. We pursue two strategies. i) We follow Sporleder and Li (2009) and compute cosine similarity between all possible pairs of nodes of a single graph, creating a *fully connected* graph. Alternatively, ii) we compute a reduced graph that only takes into account edges connecting nodes that *differ* between the two sentences and their respective graphs (see Fig. 3). In case graph g_A differs from graph g_B in a single concept which is only present in g_A, the reduced graph g_B is empty, and we assign a connectivity score of 1 (consistent with anything).

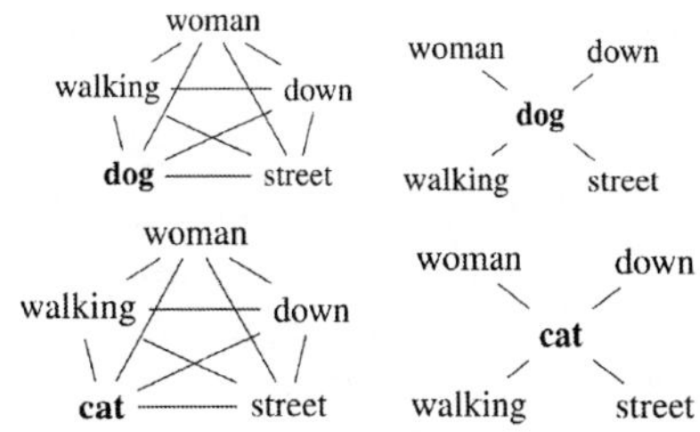

Figure 3: Two lexical cohesion graphs: fully connected (left) and reduced (right) for sentences S_A: *The woman is walking the **dog** down the street* – S_B: *The woman is walking the **cat** down the street.*

By applying this method to a pair of sentences S_A and S_B, we obtain their *connectivity scores* cs_A and cs_B, the average of their respective graphs' edge weights. From these we compute the GRACO Score (1) that rates the similarity of S_A and S_B by taking the difference between cs_A and cs_B to model their semantic difference – which we convert to a similarity score by subtracting it from 1.

$$\text{GRACO}Score = 1 - |cs_A - cs_B| \quad (1)$$

The resulting metric is hybrid by relying on the sentence's *AMR* to select text tokens for the connectivity graph – and represents nodes with *contextualized embeddings* in the BERT variant.

4 Semantic Phenomena

We consider structural and lexical phenomena that are likely to affect a sentence's meaning. Details and example AMRs are given in Appendix A.4.[5]

4.1 Structural Phenomena

Aspect Given its abstract nature, AMR does not represent aspect, hence present perfect and simple present are not distinguished in an AMR graph[6].

[5]AMR specifications follow Banarescu et al. (2019).

[6]This phenomenon was only found in the STS data.

Negation AMR represents negation with the feature `:polarity -`. Fig. 10 (A.4.1) shows sentence negation, with `polarity` attached to the matrix verb. Fig. 11 (A.4.1) shows an AMR that negates a constituent in a sentence. Both verb- and constituent negation are represented in the testsuite.

Omission or Hallucination of words or phrases is a recurring problem in NLG (Xiao and Wang, 2021) especially for AMR-to-text (Manning et al., 2020). We sampled three types involving *adjectives*, *adverbs*, *PPs*. In AMR, omission/hallucination is captured by (non-)existence of the corresponding structure (see Fig. 13, A.4.2).

Passive AMR does not distinguish active from passive voice: AMR graphs for active vs. passive sentences do not differ and do not reflect voice.

Semantic Role Switch describes cases where two verb arguments switch semantic roles. Fig. 15 (A.4.4) shows that the switch changes the `:ARG` roles of both arguments, involving two triples.

Subordinate Clauses In AMR, relative clauses can involve *inverse roles* if the relativizer is dependent on a verb. The AMR for *A boy who believes*, e.g., contains an inverse ARG0 role. Other types of relative clauses, *Noun Compound Expansions*, reveal a semantic relation between compound nouns. Such expansions can be expressed in various ways:

(1) a. *A man is playing a flute made of bamboo*
b. *A man is playing a bamboo flute*

(2) a. *A child is running in and out of the waves of the ocean*
b. *A child is running in and out of the ocean waves*

While the expansions in (1a, 2a) differ (*made of* vs. *of*), the two compound nouns in (1b) and (2b) are connected with same AMR relation `:part-of`, which reveals their semantic relation. The expansion in (1a), by contrast, emphasizes the process of the flute being *made*, which is reflected in its AMR (see Fig. 12, A.4.5). Hence, whenever we compare sentences that make use of a noun compound or an expansion of it, they may differ in their textual *and* their AMR representations, which can have implications for different types of metrics.

4.2 Lexical Phenomena

Articles AMR does not specify articles, so the sentence variants {*A*|*The*} *child is playing.* yield identical AMRs. I.e., it cannot distinguish sentences differing in definiteness of an article. Our *CheckList* includes pairs exhibiting such differences.

Antonymy denotes a relation of contrast that can apply to *adjectives*, *adverbs*, *nouns*, *prepositions* or *verbs*. In AMR, antonymy is either implicit for concept pairs or represented by negating a concept with `:polarity -` (Fig. 17 in A.4.7).

Note that human ratings in STS and SICK differ for antonymy and negation. While in STS, antonymy and negation are penalized with low similarity scores, this is different for SICK, which rates *semantic relatedness* of sentences. Pairs including a single opposing concept may yield higher scores than comparison to a random sentence. This must be observed when interpreting *CheckList* results.

Hypernymy and Hyponymy, and the derived **Co-Hyponymy** relation, while known from WordNet, are not explicitly expressed between AMR concepts. They form the basis for inferential relations between sentences and play an important role in judging NLG quality from a semantic view. Often, a candidate may differ from its reference sentence by resorting to a superordinate, less specific concept, but may combine it with a differentiating modifier, yielding an equivalent meaning. Equivalence of compositional meaning is difficult to capture for word-based and lexical NLG metrics, and is even more challenging for metrics based on structured meaning representations. **Co-Hyponymy**, however, involves contrast and interferes with **Antonymy** and **Negation**.

(Partial) Synonymy We distinguish *total* and *partial* synonymy. In the former, linguistic expressions are interchangeable without restriction, while in the latter this may hold in a context given their denotative meaning, may not hold when considering their connotative meaning (Edmonds and Hirst, 2002). Examples are *lie – untruth*, or *task – job*. While the former type is unproblematic for meaning-oriented, lexical NLG metrics, the latter is not, as it requires judging contextual conditions. Since AMR specifies abstract concepts, choosing contextually adequate synonyms is a challenge, and contextualized metrics may have an advantage.

5 Interpreted Evaluation of NLG Metrics

5.1 Datasets and Statistics

We sampled 939 sentence pairs, each differing in a single phenomenon from SICK (877) and STS (62)[7], parsed them into AMRs using the parser of Raffel et al. (2019) and manually corrected them.[8]

[7] Distributions of phenomena and human scores in A.3.2.

[8] Manual correction was performed by two of the authors.

STS (Semantic Textual Similarity). Since the first SemEval STS task (Agirre et al., 2012), a total of 15,459 sentence pairs were created in follow-up challenges. Each sentence pair is annotated for semantic similarity on a Likert scale from 5: "completely equivalent" to 0: “on different topics”.

SICK: Sentences Involving Compositional Knowledge by Marelli et al. (2014) contains 10,000 English sentence pairs, annotated for *semantic relatedness* and *entailment*. Pairs were normalized, expanded using specific linguistic phenomena, and finally paired with one another. Due to this process, pairs often differ by single linguistic phenomena, making them well suited for our aims. The sentence pairs were rated for semantic relatedness on a five-point Likert scale, from 1: “completely unrelated” to 5: “very related”.

Since the annotations on SICK and STS are not equivalent, they will be analyzed separately.

5.2 Experimental Setup

Metrics All metrics except GraCo use existing implementations. To enhance comparability between metrics, we standardize and normalize the scores of every metric and the annotated human scores (see A.3.3 for details on both).

Evaluation metrics for metric performance We compute **i) Correlations** of the metric scores with the human scores using *Spearman's rho*. **ii) Pairwise Ranking scores** for all metrics, where for each phenomenon we consider all possible combinations of pairs (x, y) and (x', y'). A metric m scores one point if the relation between the predicted scores $m(x, y)$ and $m(x', y')$ for the given pairs corresponds to the relation between their human scores $h(x, y)$ and $h(x', y')$. If for instance $h(x, y) < h(x', y')$, metric m earns one point if

$$m(x,y) < m(x',y') \quad \wedge$$
$$|m(x,y) - m(x',y')| > \tau$$

where τ is a threshold we define as the fifth percentile of all scores. We define $m(x, y) = m(x', y')$ if $|m(x, y) - m(x', y')| \leq \tau$. **iii)** Mean Average score and its **Mean Absolute Deviation** (MAD) from the human score over test cases.

5.3 Hypotheses

We state hypotheses on how various metrics are expected to perform for selected phenomena.[9]

H1: ***gM* vs. *tM*** AMR metrics are less sensitive to surface variation than textual metrics. This can be beneficial when variations have a mild impact on human judgements of similarity (*Passive*, *Articles*), but may have adverse effects when the impact is high. This may happen with *Antonymy*, if the metric cannot capture relevant differences in lexical meaning, as in SMATCH.

We expect BERTScore to compete with *gM* metrics, due to its contextualized representations. In general we expect all AMR metrics to have an advantage over textual metrics, except for BERTSCORE, in detecting *Switched Roles*, since they explicitly represent argument roles.

H2: Impact of small substrings or subgraphs Irrespective of differences in human judgement for *Antonymy, Co-hyponymy* and *Negation* between SICK vs. STS (cf. §4), metrics can differ in how strongly a contrast at token or concept level affects a pair's overall rating. In such cases only few triples may differ between sentence pairs, so we don't expect $S(^2)$MATCH to reflect strong drops in human score. W(W)LK may fare better, as its kernel can capture a wider context of a given node. BERTScore faces similar problems when small text portions cause a strong contrast, but its contextualization may reflect the impact of neighboring words, an effect that could be shared with W(W)LK.

While all prior metrics compute scores over the entire sentences, GRACO^{red} only considers local subgraphs restricted to *differing* nodes. We expect this to be beneficial for phenomena like *Negation*.

H3: Capturing (dis)similarity We expect S^2MATCH and W(W)LK to perform closer to human judgement than SMATCH for sentences that differ by semantically similar or closely related words, e.g., with *Partial Synonymy* or *Hyponymy*. The same should hold true for Meteor as opposed to BLEU and chrF++, since it accounts for synonyms and paraphrases. W(W)LK is expected to capture compositional similarity (*young cat – kitten*) better than S^2MATCH, which is purely lexical. But S^2MATCH and WWLK could perform worse for *Antonymy*, since antonyms tend to be close to each other in latent space (Samenko et al., 2020).

5.4 Results and Analyses

Results are displayed in Tables 3 and 4 for SICK.[10] Fig. 4 displays an aggregated view of correlations between the metric scores and human scores for

[9]Due to space restrictions, we only discuss a selection, which we mark with ✓Hx vs. ✗Hx if (un)supported by results.

[10]STS results are seen in Tables 7, 8 and Fig. 5, in A.2.

	Antonymy	Article	Co-Hyp.	Hyponymy	Negation	Omission	Part. Syn.ymy	Passive	Sem. Roles	Sub. Clauses	Overall
Ann. Score	0.614	0.977	0.628	0.863	0.597	0.86	0.941	0.976	0.6	0.963	0.789
BLEU	0.672 ± *0.19*	0.772 ± 0.21	0.775 ± 0.22	0.72 ± 0.18	0.582 ± 0.2	0.645 ± 0.23	0.734 ± 0.22	0.108 ± 0.87	0.298 ± 0.3	0.579 ± 0.38	0.611 ± 0.28
chrF++	0.796 ± 0.2	0.865 ± 0.11	0.794 ± 0.2	0.779 ± 0.12	0.846 ± 0.25	0.728 ± 0.14	0.798 ± 0.15	0.339 ± 0.64	0.669 ± 0.12	0.733 ± 0.23	0.75 ± 0.22
Meteor	0.421 ± 0.24	0.605 ± 0.37	0.444 ± 0.22	0.669 ± 0.26	0.46 ± *0.16*	0.466 ± 0.39	0.808 ± 0.18	0.258 ± 0.72	0.415 ± 0.19	0.408 ± 0.56	0.482 ± 0.33
BERTSCORE	0.868 ± 0.26	0.953 ± 0.04	0.854 ± 0.24	0.86 ± *0.08*	0.749 ± 0.17	0.813 ± *0.08*	0.925 ± **0.04**	0.512 ± 0.46	0.726 ± 0.16	0.783 ± 0.18	0.805 ± 0.17
SMATCH	0.793 ± 0.22	0.998 ± **0.02**	0.833 ± 0.22	0.83 ± **0.07**	0.921 ± 0.32	0.844 ± **0.06**	0.829 ± 0.12	0.995 ± **0.03**	0.647 ± *0.11*	0.917 ± 0.09	0.877 ± **0.14**
S^2MATCH	0.793 ± 0.22	0.998 ± **0.02**	0.838 ± 0.23	0.831 ± **0.07**	0.921 ± 0.32	0.844 ± **0.06**	0.829 ± 0.12	0.995 ± **0.03**	0.647 ± *0.11*	0.917 ± 0.09	0.877 ± **0.14**
WLK	0.575 ± **0.16**	0.989 ± *0.03*	0.586 ± **0.16**	0.539 ± 0.32	0.791 ± 0.2	0.782 ± 0.1	0.614 ± 0.33	0.993 ± **0.03**	0.525 ± **0.1**	0.896 ± 0.11	0.745 ± *0.16*
WWLK	0.76 ± 0.21	0.996 ± *0.03*	0.736 ± *0.19*	0.721 ± 0.16	0.644 ± **0.15**	0.685 ± 0.18	0.734 ± 0.21	0.994 ± **0.03**	0.936 ± 0.34	0.907 ± 0.1	0.774 ± **0.14**
GRACO_{gl}	0.952 ± 0.36	1.0 ± **0.02**	0.97 ± 0.34	0.963 ± 0.11	0.974 ± 0.38	0.926 ± 0.13	0.975 ± *0.05*	0.936 ± 0.06	0.998 ± 0.4	0.992 ± **0.03**	0.961 ± 0.2
GRACO_{gl}^{red}	0.883 ± 0.35	1.0 ± **0.02**	0.942 ± 0.32	0.933 ± 0.09	0.381 ± 0.23	0.277 ± 0.59	0.951 ± *0.05*	0.93 ± 0.06	1.0 ± 0.4	0.853 ± 0.16	0.711 ± 0.26
GRACO	0.952 ± 0.34	0.969 ± 0.04	0.959 ± 0.33	0.949 ± 0.11	0.942 ± 0.35	0.935 ± 0.11	0.965 ± *0.05*	0.938 ± *0.05*	0.985 ± 0.38	0.946 ± *0.04*	0.948 ± 0.19
GRACO^{red}	0.875 ± 0.32	1.0 ± **0.02**	0.91 ± 0.29	0.915 ± 0.11	0.497 ± 0.24	0.447 ± 0.43	0.937 ± 0.06	0.92 ± 0.07	0.92 ± 0.39	0.865 ± 0.14	0.755 ± 0.23

Table 3: Avg. normalized score & mean abs. deviation (most indicative, lower is better) from human score for SICK.

	Ant.my	Art.	CoHyp	Hyp	Neg	Omiss	P.Syn	Pass	SRL	Sb.Cl	Ovll
BLEU	0.492	0.34	*0.54*	0.419	0.433	0.459	0.391	*0.335*	0.469	0.321	0.424
chrF++	0.5	0.342	0.523	0.437	0.441	*0.489*	0.435	0.303	*0.562*	0.336	0.367
Meteor	**0.538**	0.35	**0.564**	**0.494**	0.441	0.435	**0.524**	0.322	0.438	0.365	0.463
BERTSC	0.483	0.36	0.505	*0.469*	0.473	**0.523**	0.435	0.31	0.406	0.355	0.47
SMATCH	0.485	0.357	0.486	0.402	0.408	0.456	0.399	**0.349**	0.406	0.364	0.579
S^2MATCH	0.484	0.357	0.474	0.395	0.408	0.456	0.399	**0.349**	0.406	0.364	0.578
WLK	*0.516*	*0.375*	0.509	0.413	0.429	0.471	0.349	**0.349**	0.469	0.363	*0.628*
WWLK	0.485	0.357	0.456	0.439	0.449	0.47	0.396	**0.349**	0.469	0.357	**0.636**
GRACO_{glo}	0.489	**0.385**	0.469	0.436	0.458	0.415	0.296	0.302	0.219	0.368	0.511
GraCo_{glo}^{red}	0.437	0.367	0.509	0.406	*0.496*	0.405	0.402	0.305	0.188	0.378	0.553
GRACO	0.473	0.292	0.497	0.411	0.428	0.46	*0.485*	0.321	**0.625**	**0.46**	0.449
GraCo^{red}	0.433	0.367	0.481	0.416	**0.505**	0.418	0.444	0.327	0.219	*0.384*	0.565

Table 4: Pairwise ranking scores for the SICK test cases.

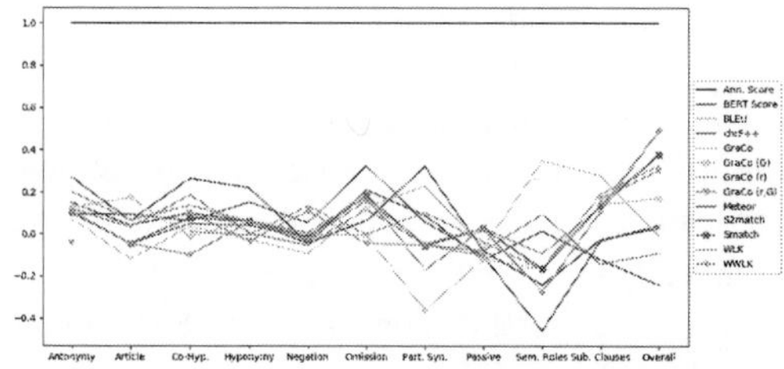

Figure 4: Spearman's rho correlation between metric and human scores for SICK. Broken lines indicate phenomena where no correlation coefficient could be computed due to identical metric scores for all instances.

individual phenomena. Finally, Table 5 presents a summary for all metrics and the phenomena they perform best or 2nd best on, according to our three evaluation metrics: ranking score, MAD and correlation to human judgement scores.

The *gM* metrics W(W)LK show best overall performance, sharing 1st place with $S(^2)$MATCH in SICK and obtaining first place in pairwise ranking, and we see top places being achieved for 4-5 phenomena (✓ H1, ✓ H3). But $S(^2)$MATCH produce very similar scores across the board (✗ H3).

Among symbolic *tM* metrics, *Meteor* performs best in ranking score, and *chrF++* for MAD. BERTSCORE performs better than symbolic *tM* metrics overall, except for ranking score for STS, where it only fails on *Aspect* (✓H1). But it falls behind *gM* and most *hyM* metrics in *overall* scores. GRACO performance varies across phenomena and its variants. It occupies 1st and 2nd places in ranking score for *Neg* in SICK in the *reduced* variant, where the drop in avg score and MAD is striking (✓H2). For other phenomena, the performance aligns with the other *gM* metrics. This suggests that the connectivity score captures most lexical phenomena well – while for *SRL* this is evidently not sufficient (✓H1).

Beyond tendencies in overall results, we now focus on observations for single phenomena.

While *gM* generally outperform *tM* metrics, this doesn't necessarily hold for Meteor: it outperforms *gM* for phenomena reflecting lexical-semantic relations for SICK (Table 4, Fig. 4). The spike in correlation for *Part. Syn.* is expected, as Meteor accounts for synonyms and paraphrases (✓H3). This may also explain its superior performance for *(Co-)Hyponymy.* But its high performance for *Antonymy* is surprising (✗H3).

S^2MATCH performing very similar to SMATCH is most likely due to a high threshold for allowing a soft match. GRACO was designed to better represent semantic contrast between sentences and their AMR graphs. We can see this reflected in a large drop of MAD for GRACO^{red} in *Negation.* In comparison, for *Antonymy* we only see a relatively small drop in MAD. This is because, for *Negation*, GRACO^{red} produces a bigger contrast between the connectivity scores as one of them is 1 for the empty graph. For *Antonymy* the scores are closer, since both graphs have neighbors. Another factor could be the proximity of antonyms in embedding space, which suggests that a threshold, similar to S^2MATCH, could be beneficial.

We also observe that GRACO using BERT outperforms GRACO_{glo} in *Part.Syn, SRL, SubCl* (Table 4, Fig. 4). This is unexpected since neither of them uses AMR relations. This could be explained by the contextualized node embeddings that see context at textual level–combined with connectivity graphs

	Best & 2nd Best Ranking Scores	**Best** & 2nd Best MAD	**Highest** & 2nd Highest Correlation w/ Human
BLEU	Passive, Co-Hyp.	Antonymy	Co-Hyp., SRL
chrF++	Omission, SRL		Omission
Meteor	**Co-Hyp.**, **Antonymy**, **Part. Synonymy**, **Hyp.**	Negation	**Part. Synonymy**, **Antonymy**, **Co-Hyp.**, **Hyp.**
BERTSc	**Omission**, Hyp.	**Part. Synonymy**, Omission, Hyp.	**Omission**, Hyp.
SMATCH	**Passive**	**Article**, **Passive**, **Omission**, **Hyp.**, SRL	**Passive**
S^2MATCH	**Passive**	**Article**, **Passive**, **Omission**, **Hyp.**, SRL	**Passive**
WLK	**Passive**, Article, Antonymy	**Passive**, **SRL**, **Antonymy**, **Co-Hyp.**, Article	**Passive**, Antonymy
WWLK	**Passive**	**Passive**, **Negation**, Article, Co-Hyp.	**Passive**
GRACO$_{glo}$	**Article**	**Article**, **Sub. Clauses**, Part. Synonymy	**Article**
GraCo$^{red}_{glo}$	Negation	**Article**, Part. Synonymy	Negation
GRACO	**SRL**, **Sub. Clause**, Part. Synonymy	Sub. Clauses, Part. Synonymy, Passive	**SRL**, **Sub. Clauses**, Part. Synonymy
GraCo^{red}	**Negation**, Sub. Clause	**Article**	**Negation**, Sub. Clauses

Table 5: **Best** & 2nd Best Metric Performances in Ranking Score, MAD, Corr. with Human Scores for SICK dataset.

		textual level					graph level				
Type	Metric	words	chars/pieces	lexicon	dense	contextual	concepts	sem. edges	sim. edges	dense	contextual
	BLEU	+	-	-	-	+					
tM	chrF++	+	+	-	-	+					
	Meteor	+	-	+	-	-					
	BERTScore	-	+	-	+	+					
	SMATCH						+	+	-	-	-
gM	S^2MATCH						+	+	-	+	-
	WLK						+	+	-	-	+
	WWLK						+	+	-	+	+
	GRACO$_{glo}$	+	-	-	-	-	+	-	+	+	-
hyM	GRACO$^{red}_{glo}$	+	-	-	-	-	+	-	+	+	-
	GRACO	+	-	-	-	-	+	-	+	+	+
	GRACO^{red}	+	-	-	-	-	+	-	+	+	+

Table 6: Characterization of the used textual (*tM*), graph-based (*gM*) and hybrid (*hyM*) metrics in terms of textual and graph-level properties. **textual level**: word/char/lexicon-based; **graph-level**: semantic vs. similarity edges; **both levels**: dense = embedding-based representation; contextual = contextualized representation.

that look at the sentence only via AMR nodes.

Overall we see surprising effects with GRACO: i) by restricting connectivity to local subgraphs for contrasting elements, it yields strong performance for *Negation*; ii) it only focuses on AMR nodes, but the contrast with GRACO$_{glo}$ suggests that the contextualization helps to assess surface differences underlying *SRL* and *SubCl*. The insights from GRACO could trigger ideas for improving a *tM* metric like BERTSCORE, by computing it under a similar AMR lens, and handling *Negation* in similar ways. It also suggests studying the use of BERT embeddings in WWLK, and seeking ways of integrating a comparable mechanism for *Negation*. As for *tM* metrics, it came as a surprise to find Meteor keep 1st rank for lexical relations ((Co-)Hyp; (Partial)Syn, Antonymy), beyond BERTSCORE.

6 Conclusion

We introduced an extensible *CheckList* for meaning-oriented NLG metrics that allows for comparison of a wide range of NLG metrics. It is interpreted by way of offering test cases grouped by linguistic phenomena. Our analyses showcase how *CheckList* can be used to compare metrics, to reveal their strengths and weaknesses. They align with a number of hypotheses, but also show surprising effects, opening avenues to further improve NLG evaluation metrics. We propose a novel, hybrid similarity metric GRACO that builds cohesion graphs over contextualized AMR concept nodes. The metric can focus on contrastive subgraphs, which yields strong correlation with human judgements for negation. With regard to current practice in AMR-to-text evaluation, we find evidence that meaning-oriented graph-based metrics present advantages over typical text-based metrics, confirming the findings of Opitz and Frank (2021); Manning et al. (2020). Therefore we recommend to include graph metrics or hybrid graph- and textual metrics into AMR-to-text evaluation protocols. Our data and code will be publicly available.[11] We welcome contributions to grow it.

Acknowledgements

We thank the anonymous reviewers for useful feedback and suggestions.

[11] https://github.com/Heidelberg-NLP/NLG-CHECKLIST

References

Eneko Agirre, Daniel Cer, Mona Diab, and Aitor Gonzalez-Agirre. 2012. SemEval-2012 task 6: A pilot on semantic textual similarity. In **SEM 2012: The First Joint Conference on Lexical and Computational Semantics – Volume 1: Proceedings of the main conference and the shared task, and Volume 2: Proceedings of the Sixth International Workshop on Semantic Evaluation (SemEval 2012)*, pages 385–393, Montréal, Canada. Association for Computational Linguistics.

Laura Banarescu, Claire Bonial, Shu Cai, Madalina Georgescu, Kira Griffitt, Ulf Hermjakob, Kevin Knight, Philipp Koehn, Martha Palmer, and Nathan Schneider. 2013. Abstract Meaning Representation for sembanking. In *Proceedings of the 7th Linguistic Annotation Workshop and Interoperability with Discourse*, pages 178–186, Sofia, Bulgaria. Association for Computational Linguistics.

Laura Banarescu, Claire Bonial, Shu Cai, Madalina Georgescu, Kira Griffitt, Ulf Hermjakob, Kevin Knight, Philipp Koehn, Martha Palmer, and Nathan Schneider. 2019. Abstract meaning representation (amr) 1.2.6 specification.

Steven Bird, Ewan Klein, and Edward Loper. 2009. *Natural language processing with Python: analyzing text with the natural language toolkit.* " O'Reilly Media, Inc.".

Rexhina Blloshmi, Michele Bevilacqua, Edoardo Fabiano, Valentina Caruso, and Roberto Navigli. 2021. SPRING Goes Online: End-to-End AMR Parsing and Generation. In *Proceedings of the 2021 Conference on Empirical Methods in Natural Language Processing: System Demonstrations*, pages 134–142, Online and Punta Cana, Dominican Republic. Association for Computational Linguistics.

Shu Cai and Kevin Knight. 2013. Smatch: an evaluation metric for semantic feature structures. In *Proceedings of the 51st Annual Meeting of the Association for Computational Linguistics (Volume 2: Short Papers)*, pages 748–752, Sofia, Bulgaria. Association for Computational Linguistics.

Dhivya Chandrasekaran and Vijay Mago. 2021. Evolution of semantic similarity—a survey. *ACM Comput. Surv.*, 54(2).

Rudi L Cilibrasi and Paul MB Vitanyi. 2007. The google similarity distance. *IEEE Transactions on knowledge and data engineering*, 19(3):370–383.

Alexis Conneau and Douwe Kiela. 2018. SentEval: An evaluation toolkit for universal sentence representations. In *Proceedings of the Eleventh International Conference on Language Resources and Evaluation (LREC 2018)*, Miyazaki, Japan. European Language Resources Association (ELRA).

Alexis Conneau, Douwe Kiela, Holger Schwenk, Loïc Barrault, and Antoine Bordes. 2017. Supervised learning of universal sentence representations from natural language inference data. In *Proceedings of the 2017 Conference on Empirical Methods in Natural Language Processing*, pages 670–680, Copenhagen, Denmark. Association for Computational Linguistics.

Michael Denkowski and Alon Lavie. 2014. Meteor universal: Language specific translation evaluation for any target language. In *Proceedings of the Ninth Workshop on Statistical Machine Translation*, pages 376–380, Baltimore, Maryland, USA. Association for Computational Linguistics.

Jacob Devlin, Ming-Wei Chang, Kenton Lee, and Kristina Toutanova. 2019. BERT: Pre-training of deep bidirectional transformers for language understanding. In *Proceedings of the 2019 Conference of the North American Chapter of the Association for Computational Linguistics: Human Language Technologies, Volume 1 (Long and Short Papers)*, pages 4171–4186, Minneapolis, Minnesota. Association for Computational Linguistics.

Philip Edmonds and Graeme Hirst. 2002. Near-synonymy and lexical choice. *Computational Linguistics*, 28(2):105–144.

Jeffrey Flanigan, Sam Thomson, Jaime Carbonell, Chris Dyer, and Noah A. Smith. 2014a. A discriminative graph-based parser for the Abstract Meaning Representation. In *Proceedings of the 52nd Annual Meeting of the Association for Computational Linguistics (Volume 1: Long Papers)*, pages 1426–1436, Baltimore, Maryland. Association for Computational Linguistics.

Jeffrey Flanigan, Sam Thomson, Jaime Carbonell, Chris Dyer, and Noah A. Smith. 2014b. A discriminative graph-based parser for the Abstract Meaning Representation. In *Proceedings of the 52nd Annual Meeting of the Association for Computational Linguistics (Volume 1: Long Papers)*, pages 1426–1436, Baltimore, Maryland. Association for Computational Linguistics.

Hessel Haagsma, Malvina Nissim, and Johan Bos. 2018. The other side of the coin: Unsupervised disambiguation of potentially idiomatic expressions by contrasting senses. In *Proceedings of the Joint Workshop on Linguistic Annotation, Multiword Expressions and Constructions (LAW-MWE-CxG-2018)*, pages 178–184, Santa Fe, New Mexico, USA. Association for Computational Linguistics.

Ioannis Konstas, Srinivasan Iyer, Mark Yatskar, Yejin Choi, and Luke Zettlemoyer. 2017. Neural AMR: Sequence-to-sequence models for parsing and generation. In *Proceedings of the 55th Annual Meeting of the Association for Computational Linguistics (Volume 1: Long Papers)*, pages 146–157, Vancouver, Canada. Association for Computational Linguistics.

Alon Lavie and Abhaya Agarwal. 2007. METEOR: An automatic metric for MT evaluation with high levels of correlation with human judgments. In *Proceedings of the Second Workshop on Statistical Machine Translation*, pages 228–231, Prague, Czech Republic. Association for Computational Linguistics.

Sabine Lehmann, Stephan Oepen, Sylvie Regnier-Prost, Klaus Netter, Veronika Lux, Judith Klein, Kirsten Falkedal, Frederik Fouvry, Dominique Estival, Eva Dauphin, Herve Compagnion, Judith Baur, Lorna Balkan, and Doug Arnold. 1996. TSNLP - test suites for natural language processing. In *COLING 1996 Volume 2: The 16th International Conference on Computational Linguistics*.

Emma Manning, Shira Wein, and Nathan Schneider. 2020. A human evaluation of AMR-to-English generation systems. In *Proceedings of the 28th International Conference on Computational Linguistics*, pages 4773–4786, Barcelona, Spain (Online). International Committee on Computational Linguistics.

Marco Marelli, Stefano Menini, Marco Baroni, Luisa Bentivogli, Raffaella Bernardi, and Roberto Zamparelli. 2014. A SICK cure for the evaluation of compositional distributional semantic models. In *Proceedings of the Ninth International Conference on Language Resources and Evaluation (LREC'14)*, pages 216–223, Reykjavik, Iceland. European Language Resources Association (ELRA).

Jonathan May and Jay Priyadarshi. 2017. SemEval-2017 task 9: Abstract Meaning Representation parsing and generation. In *Proceedings of the 11th International Workshop on Semantic Evaluation (SemEval-2017)*, pages 536–545, Vancouver, Canada. Association for Computational Linguistics.

Juri Opitz, Angel Daza, and Anette Frank. 2021. Weisfeiler-leman in the bamboo: Novel AMR graph metrics and a benchmark for AMR graph similarity. *Transactions of the Association for Computational Linguistics*, 9:1425–1441.

Juri Opitz and Anette Frank. 2021. Towards a decomposable metric for explainable evaluation of text generation from AMR. In *Proceedings of the 16th Conference of the European Chapter of the Association for Computational Linguistics: Main Volume*, pages 1504–1518, Online. Association for Computational Linguistics.

Juri Opitz, Letitia Parcalabescu, and Anette Frank. 2020. AMR similarity metrics from principles. *Transactions of the Association for Computational Linguistics*, 8:522–538.

Kishore Papineni, Salim Roukos, Todd Ward, and Wei-Jing Zhu. 2002. Bleu: a method for automatic evaluation of machine translation. In *Proceedings of the 40th Annual Meeting of the Association for Computational Linguistics*, pages 311–318, Philadelphia, Pennsylvania, USA. Association for Computational Linguistics.

Jeffrey Pennington, Richard Socher, and Christopher Manning. 2014. GloVe: Global vectors for word representation. In *Proceedings of the 2014 Conference on Empirical Methods in Natural Language Processing (EMNLP)*, pages 1532–1543, Doha, Qatar. Association for Computational Linguistics.

Alexander Popov. 2017. Word sense disambiguation with recurrent neural networks. In *Proceedings of the Student Research Workshop Associated with RANLP 2017*, pages 25–34, Varna. INCOMA Ltd.

Maja Popović. 2015. chrF: character n-gram F-score for automatic MT evaluation. In *Proceedings of the Tenth Workshop on Statistical Machine Translation*, pages 392–395, Lisbon, Portugal. Association for Computational Linguistics.

Maja Popović. 2016. chrF deconstructed: beta parameters and n-gram weights. In *Proceedings of the First Conference on Machine Translation: Volume 2, Shared Task Papers*, pages 499–504, Berlin, Germany. Association for Computational Linguistics.

Colin Raffel, Noam Shazeer, Adam Roberts, Katherine Lee, Sharan Narang, Michael Matena, Yanqi Zhou, Wei Li, and Peter J. Liu. 2019. Exploring the limits of transfer learning with a unified text-to-text transformer. *CoRR*, abs/1910.10683.

Nils Reimers and Iryna Gurevych. 2019. Sentence-BERT: Sentence embeddings using Siamese BERT-networks. In *Proceedings of the 2019 Conference on Empirical Methods in Natural Language Processing and the 9th International Joint Conference on Natural Language Processing (EMNLP-IJCNLP)*, pages 3982–3992, Hong Kong, China. Association for Computational Linguistics.

Marco Tulio Ribeiro, Tongshuang Wu, Carlos Guestrin, and Sameer Singh. 2020. Beyond accuracy: Behavioral testing of NLP models with CheckList. In *Proceedings of the 58th Annual Meeting of the Association for Computational Linguistics*, pages 4902–4912, Online. Association for Computational Linguistics.

Igor Samenko, Alexey Tikhonov, and Ivan P. Yamshchikov. 2020. Synonyms and antonyms: Embedded conflict. arXiv:2004.12835.

Linfeng Song, Yue Zhang, Zhiguo Wang, and Daniel Gildea. 2018. A graph-to-sequence model for AMR-to-text generation. In *Proceedings of the 56th Annual Meeting of the Association for Computational Linguistics (Volume 1: Long Papers)*, pages 1616–1626, Melbourne, Australia. Association for Computational Linguistics.

Caroline Sporleder and Linlin Li. 2009. Unsupervised recognition of literal and non-literal use of idiomatic expressions. In *Proceedings of the 12th Conference of the European Chapter of the ACL (EACL 2009)*, pages 754–762, Athens, Greece. Association for Computational Linguistics.

Miloš Stanojević, Amir Kamran, Philipp Koehn, and Ondřej Bojar. 2015. Results of the WMT15 metrics shared task. In *Proceedings of the Tenth Workshop on Statistical Machine Translation*, pages 256–273, Lisbon, Portugal. Association for Computational Linguistics.

Tianming Wang, Xiaojun Wan, and Hanqi Jin. 2020. AMR-to-text generation with graph transformer. *Transactions of the Association for Computational Linguistics*, 8:19–33.

Tongshuang Wu, Marco Tulio Ribeiro, Jeffrey Heer, and Daniel Weld. 2019. Errudite: Scalable, reproducible, and testable error analysis. In *Proceedings of the 57th Annual Meeting of the Association for Computational Linguistics*, pages 747–763, Florence, Italy. Association for Computational Linguistics.

Yijun Xiao and William Yang Wang. 2021. On hallucination and predictive uncertainty in conditional language generation. In *Proceedings of the 16th Conference of the European Chapter of the Association for Computational Linguistics: Main Volume*, pages 2734–2744, Online. Association for Computational Linguistics.

Tianyi Zhang, Varsha Kishore, Felix Wu, Kilian Q. Weinberger, and Yoav Artzi. 2020. BERTScore: Evaluating Text Generation with BERT. In *Proceedings of the Eighth International Conference on Learning Representations (ICLR)*.

Wei Zhao, Maxime Peyrard, Fei Liu, Yang Gao, Christian M. Meyer, and Steffen Eger. 2019. MoverScore: Text generation evaluating with contextualized embeddings and earth mover distance. In *Proceedings of the 2019 Conference on Empirical Methods in Natural Language Processing and the 9th International Joint Conference on Natural Language Processing (EMNLP-IJCNLP)*, pages 563–578, Hong Kong, China. Association for Computational Linguistics.

A Appendix

A.1 *CheckList*'s functionalities and resources

As described in §3.1, *CheckList* contains the selected sentence pairs as well as the corresponding AMR structures and their human score grouped by linguistic phenomena in `json` format. It further includes the assigned scores for the test instances as well as code to run the implementation for the following metrics:

- BLEU
- Meteor
- chrF++
- BERTSCORE
- SMATCH
- S^{2}MATCH
- WLK
- WWLK

Output. The *CheckList* can be run from the command line, printing an overview of the data used, accompanied by statistics concerning human judgement for each phenomenon. These statistics include the mean, median, standard deviation and standard error of the human scores. Finally, it will output tables displaying the overall results of the *CheckList* (hereby, we use the evaluation measures that were also applied in the paper). If a metric were to be tested, it would furthermore print the correlation of that metric with the others in decreasing order.
The results for the phenomena are summarized in individual text files. These files once more list the statistics about the human score and then display the average scores of all metrics for that very phenomenon. Finally, each test case is listed, including the sentences as well as their AMR structures and the scores assigned to it by the metrics and the annotator.

A.2 STS Results

Table 7 and 8 and Fig. 5 demonstrate the results on the test cases selected from the STS data set. Table 9 shows a summary of metrics yielding Best and 2nd Best Results.

	Article	Aspect	Co-Hyponymy	Hyponymy	Omission	Overall
Ann. Score	0.967	1.0	0.282	0.647	0.77	0.647
BLEU	0.358 ± 0.61	0.155 ± 0.84	0.674 ± 0.48	0.58 ± 0.2	0.508 ± 0.27	0.503 ± 0.45
chrF++	0.661 ± 0.31	0.521 ± 0.48	0.661 ± 0.39	0.683 ± *0.12*	0.707 ± 0.14	0.654 ± 0.29
Meteor	0.385 ± 0.58	0.557 ± 0.44	0.313 ± **0.2**	0.462 ± 0.3	0.407 ± 0.36	0.408 ± 0.33
BERTSCORE	0.863 ± 0.1	0.824 ± 0.18	0.838 ± 0.56	0.761 ± *0.12*	0.801 ± **0.07**	0.816 ± 0.26
S^{2}MATCH	1.0 ± **0.03**	1.0 ± **0.0**	0.779 ± 0.5	0.737 ± 0.13	0.785 ± *0.09*	0.83 ± 0.21
SMATCH	1.0 ± **0.03**	1.0 ± **0.0**	0.779 ± 0.5	0.737 ± 0.13	0.785 ± *0.09*	0.83 ± 0.21
WLK	1.0 ± **0.03**	1.0 ± **0.0**	0.459 ± *0.25*	0.426 ± 0.23	0.733 ± 0.11	0.659 ± **0.15**
WWLK	1.0 ± **0.03**	1.0 ± **0.0**	0.689 ± 0.41	0.587 ± **0.1**	0.612 ± 0.19	0.732 ± *0.2*
GRACO$_{gl}$	1.0 ± **0.03**	0.859 ± 0.14	0.936 ± 0.65	0.963 ± 0.32	0.957 ± 0.19	0.94 ± 0.34
GRACO$_{gl}^{reduced}$	1.0 ± **0.03**	0.875 ± 0.12	0.924 ± 0.64	0.949 ± 0.3	0.322 ± 0.45	0.782 ± 0.39
GRACO	0.978 ± *0.05*	0.876 ± 0.12	0.969 ± 0.69	0.949 ± 0.3	0.961 ± 0.19	0.949 ± 0.35
GRACO^{reduced}	1.0 ± **0.03**	0.904 ± *0.1*	0.957 ± 0.67	0.939 ± 0.29	0.51 ± 0.26	0.841 ± 0.35

Table 7: Avg. normalized score & mean abs. deviation (most indicative, lower is better) from human score for STS

	Article	Aspect	Co-Hyponymy	Hyponym	Omission	Overall
BLEU	0.389	*0.52*	0.17	0.504	0.573	0.218
chrF++	*0.611*	0.1	*0.68*	0.653	0.511	0.403
Meteor	0.556	0.22	0.35	0.636	0.52	0.625
BERTSCORE	**0.722**	0.1	**0.75**	**0.785**	**0.689**	0.537
SMATCH	0.333	**1**	0.305	0.603	*0.591*	0.682
S^{2}MATCH	0.333	**1**	0.305	0.603	*0.591*	0.682
WLK	0.333	**1**	0.32	0.603	0.582	**0.748**
WWLK	0.333	**1**	0.67	*0.769*	0.582	*0.712*
GRACO$_{gl}$	0.333	0.1	0.655	0.62	0.316	0.579
GRACO$_{gl}^{reduced}$	0.333	0.1	0.665	0.587	0.538	0.52
GRACO	0.278	0.1	0.36	0.554	0.493	0.417
GRACO^{reduced}	0.333	0.1	0.36	0.669	**0.689**	0.443

Table 8: Pairwise ranking scores for the STS test cases

	Best & <u>2nd Best</u> Ranking Scores	**Best** & <u>2nd Best</u> MAD	**Highest** & <u>2nd Highest</u> Correlation w/ Human
BLEU	<u>Aspect</u>		
chrF++	<u>Co-Hyponymy</u>, <u>Article</u>	<u>Hyponymy</u>	<u>Article</u>
Meteor		**Co-Hyponymy**	
BERTSc	**Hyponymy**, **Co-Hyponymy**, **Article**, **Omission**	**Omission**, <u>Hyponymy</u>	**Hyponymy**, **Article**, **Co-Hyponymy**, **Omission**
SMATCH	**Aspect**, <u>Omission</u>	**Aspect**, **Article**, <u>Omission</u>	<u>Omission</u>
S^2MATCH	**Aspect**, <u>Omission</u>	**Aspect**, **Article**, <u>Omission</u>	<u>Omission</u>
WLK	**Aspect**	**Aspect**, **Article**, <u>Co-Hyponymy</u>	
WWLK	**Aspect**, <u>Hyponymy</u>	**Aspect**, **Article**, **Hyponymy**	<u>Hyponymy</u>, <u>Co-Hyponymy</u>
GRACO$_{glo}$		**Article**	
GraCo$^{red}_{glo}$		**Article**	
GRACO		<u>Article</u>	
GraCo^{red}	**Omission**	**Article**, <u>Aspect</u>	

Table 9: Overview over **Best** and <u>2nd Best</u> Metric Performances in Ranking Score, MAD and Corr. to Human Scores for the STS dataset.

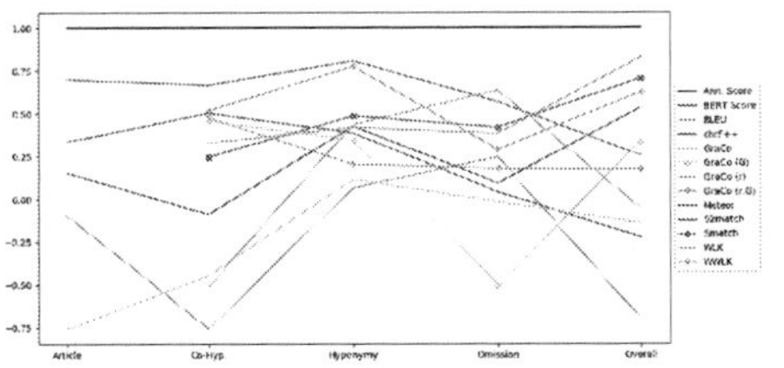

Figure 5: Spearman's rho correlation between metric and human scores for STS. *Aspect* is not included since all annotated scores are 1.

A.3 Experimental Settings

A.3.1 Generating sentences from the *Little Prince* AMR corpus.

We investigated sentences generated from AMRs from the 'Little Prince Corpus'[12] using the AMR-to-text system of Song et al. (2018). We used their pretrained *G2S_silver_2m* model and validated it on test data from Song et al. (2018), with a difference of -0.35 points BLEU score. For the 'Little Prince', consisting of 1,562 sentences, we obtained a BLEU score of 13.5.

constructional	lexical	SICK	STS	SICK	STS
Negation		156	-		
Omission		155	15		
Passive		78	-		
Aspect		-	10		
Semantic Roles		8	-		
Subordinate Clauses		69	-		
	Antonymy			157	-
	Article			77	6
	Hyponymy			116	11
	Co-Hyponymy			35	20
	Partial Synonymy			26	-
		466	25	411	37
Overall				877	62

Table 10: Number of SICK and STS test cases grouped by linguistic phenomena

[12]https://amr.isi.edu/download.html

A.3.2 Data Statistics

The following figures show the distribution of the human human scores in the *CheckList* for the individual linguistic phenomena. SICK and STS are displayed separately.
Fig. 7 further displays the sentence length distribution for SICK and STS.

A.3.3 Implementation details of metrics

Here, we list the hyperparameters and libraries employed for the metrics used in the CheckList.

For the text-based metrics, we employ NLTK's implementation for **BLEU**, where we add the method4 smoothing function (Bird et al., 2009)[13]; for **chrF++** use the sentence-level implementation by Popović (2015), and for **Meteor** the Version 1.5 implementation by Denkowski and Lavie (2014).

For Zhang et al. (2020)'s embedding-based metric **BERTSCORE**, we employ the implementation provided by Huggingface[14].

As for graph-based metrics, we made use of the implementations of **SMATCH** and the refined **S^2MATCH** provided by Opitz et al. (2020). For S^2MATCH we defined a cut-off threshold of 0.9, so that only concepts with a cosine similarity above that threshold would be granted a soft match. Further, the coefficient by which the similarity of differing senses is multiplied was set to 0.95.

For WLK and WWLK we employ the implementation by Opitz et al. (2021) without any additional hyperparameters.

For the implementation of the GRACO, we used the AMR Alignment tool from JAMR (Flanigan et al., 2014b) to align words from the sentence with concepts in the AMR structure. For concepts that have been successfully

[13]https://www.nltk.org/_modules/nltk/translate/bleu_score.html

[14]https://huggingface.co/metrics/bertscore

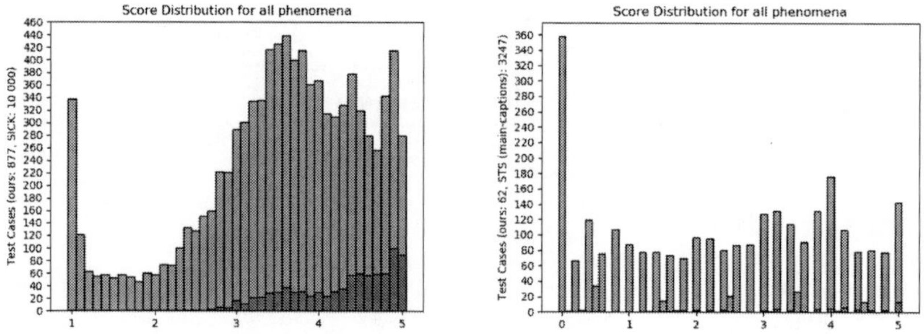

Figure 6: Score distribution for the test cases in the *CheckList* (green) grouped by SICK (left) and STS (right) test cases alongside the distribution of the whole datasets (grey)

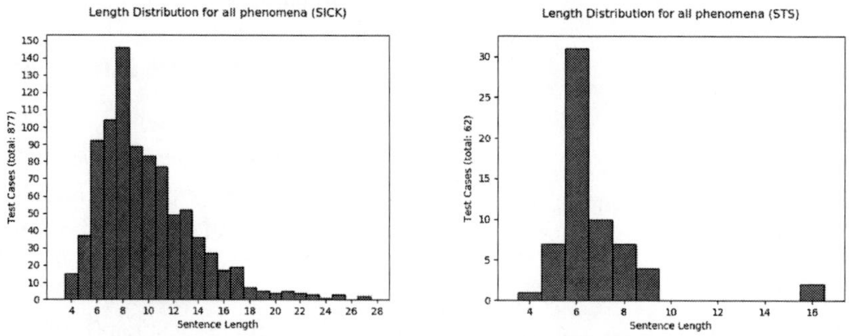

Figure 7: Sentence length distribution for the test cases in the *CheckList* grouped by SICK (left) and STS (right) test cases

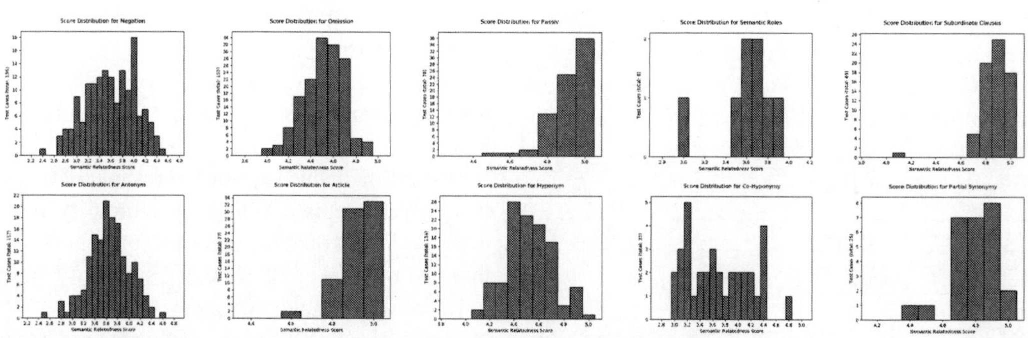

Figure 8: Score distributions for SICK per phenomenon: top: a.) Negation, b. Omission, c. Passive, d. Sem. Roles, e. subord. Clauses; bottom: f. Antonymy, g. Article, h. Hymonymy, i. Co-Hyponymy, j. Partial Synonymy.

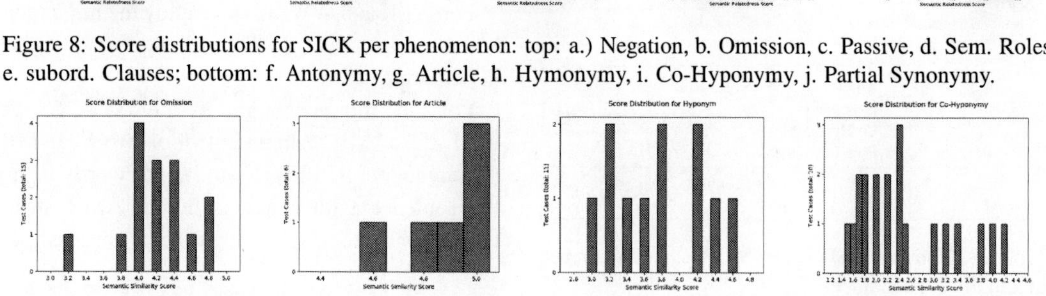

Figure 9: Score distributions for STS per phenomenon: b. Omission, g. Article, h. Hymonymy, i. Co-Hyponymy.

aligned, we experimented with contextualized BERT word embeddings, for which we use the `bert-large-uncased` model with a dimensionality of 1024 (Devlin et al., 2019), and 300 dimensional pretrained GloVe word embeddings (Pennington et al., 2014). In case GloVe may not have seen some inflected word, the embedding of its lemma will be used instead (the lemmata are obtained using the spacy lemmatizer and the `en_core_web_sm` model). If neither the token nor its lemma is contained in the vocabulary, we generate a zero vector representing an unknown token.

For standardization, given a metric predicts $s = \{s_1, ...s_n\}$, where n is the size of the data, we define the standardized score for an example i as $s'_i = \frac{s_i - mean(s)}{std(s)}$. Given s as above, the normalized score for an example i is defined as $s'_i = \frac{s_i - min(s)}{max(s) - min(s)}$.

A.4 Phenomena

A.4.1 Negation

We display two types of negation. In Fig. 10 the whole sentence is negated since `polarity` is attached to the matrix verb. Fig. 11 shows an AMR where only one constituent in a coordinated sentence is negated.

```
(xv0 / exercise-01
       :ARG0 (xv1 / man)
       :polarity - )
```

Figure 10: AMR for the sentence *The man is not doing excercises.* Semantic relatedness score: 3.8

```
(xv0 / and
       :op1 (xv1 / walk-01
              :ARG0 (xv3 / child))
       :op2 (xv2 / pull-up-07
              :ARG1 (xv5 / jeep-01)
              :polarity - )
```

Figure 11: AMR for the sentence *A child is walking and a jeep is not pulling up.* Semantic relatedness score: 3.5

A.4.2 Omission and Hallucination

Fig. 13 demonstrates the AMR of the sentence *The man is cautiously operating a stenograph.* The adverb is realized by the use of the role `:manner`. The sentence *The man is operating a stenograph* would look the same, except that the red-colored branch would not exist. Since concepts can be described in various ways, some words may be represented by more than one branch which would lead to more than two triples that don't have a counterpart. The omission of a prepositional phrase often resembles the omission of adjectives or adverbs, especially for phrases that can be realized by so-called "none-core-roles" such as `destination`, `location` or `medium`, hence, within one branch. As described in section A.3, prepositions, however, can be realized in various ways. The omission of a prepositional expression might therefore concern only one branch, but can also concern multiple branches like in Fig. 14.

A.4.3 Passive

Since AMR aims to capture the events of a sentence and not necessarily its *point of view*, AMR structures of an active-passive sentence pair do not differ at all.

A.4.4 Semantic and Syntactic Role Switch

The AMRs in Fig. 15 show that semantic and syntactic role switch is expressed by switching the `:ARG` roles. This results in the pair of AMRs differing in two triples.

A.4.5 Subordinate Clauses

In §4.1 we already discussed *inverse roles* for relative clauses when the relativizer is dependet on a verb. For attributive adjectives on the other hand, AMR structures should look the same. This is demonstrated by the AMR representations for *A black bird is sitting on a dead tree* and *A bird, which is black, is sitting on a dead tree* in Fig. 16. Fig. 12 displays a sentence pair featuring a noun compound expansion.

A.4.6 Article

Banarescu et al. (2013) specifically state that "AMR does not represent inflectional morphology for tense and number, and [...] omits articles".

A.4.7 Antonomy

In Fig. 17, we see two AMR graphs for a sentence pair exhibiting an antonymous relation between *young* and *old.* The antonymy is realized by mapping the differing concepts to the variable `xv3` respectively.

Another way of realizing antonymy between adjectives in an AMR graph is adding the feature

```
(xv0 / play-11
     :ARG0 (xv2 / man)
     :ARG1 (xv1 / flute
           :consist-of (xv3 / bamboo)))
```

```
(xv0 / play-11
     :ARG0 (xv2 / man)
     :ARG1 (xv1 / flute
           :ARG1-of (xv3 / make-01
                 :ARG2 (xv4 / bamboo))))
```

Figure 12: AMR structures for the sentence pair *A man is playing a bamboo flute – A man is playing a flute made of bamboo* Semantic relatedness score: 4.9

```
(xv0 / operate-01
     :ARG0 (xv2 / man)
     :ARG1 (xv1 / stenograph)
           :manner (xv3 / cautious-02))
```

Figure 13: Gold AMR for the sentence *A man is cautiously operating a stenograph.* Semantic relatedness score: 4.5

```
(xv0 / attack-01
     :ARG0 (xv2 / dog
          :mod (xv3 / brown))
     :ARG1 (xv1 / animal)
     :location (xv4 / in-front-of
          :op1 (xv5 / man)))
```

Figure 14: Gold AMR for the sentence *The brown dog is attacking an animal in front of the man.*

`:polarity -` to the branch of the adjective's concepts which inverts its meaning.

A.4.8 Hyperonymy, Hyponymy and Co-Hyponymy

An AMR structure of two sentences displaying a sub- or superset relation would differ merely in the concepts mapped to the corresponding variable as demonstrated in Fig. 18. This is also true for co-hyponymy.

```
(xv0 / follow-02
     :ARG0 (xv1 / turtle)
     :ARG1 (xv2 / fish))
```

```
(xv0 / follow-02
     :ARG0 (xv2 / fish)
     :ARG1 (xv1 / turtle))
```

Figure 15: AMR structures of the sentence pair *The turtle is following the fish. – The fish is following the turtle.* Semantic relatedness score: 3.8

```
(xv0 / sit-01
     :ARG1 (xv1 / bird
           :ARG1-of (xv3 / black-04) )
     :ARG2 (xv2 / tree
           :ARG1-of (xv4 / die-01)))
```

Figure 16: AMR structure for the sentence pair *A black bird is sitting on a dead tree. – A bird, which is black, is sitting on a dead tree.* Semantic relatedness score: 5.0

```
(xv0 / talk-01
     :ARG0 (xv1 / man
          :mod (xv3 / young))
     :ARG2 (xv2 / leaf))
```

```
(xv0 / talk-01
     :ARG0 (xv1 / man
          :mod (xv3 / old))
     :ARG2 (xv2 / leaf))
```

Figure 17: AMR structures for the sentence pair *A young man is talking to a leaf. – An old man is talking to the leaf.* Semantic relatedness score: 3.915

```
(xv0 / run-02
     :ARG0 (xv2 / squirrel)
     :ARG1 (xv1 / circle))
```

```
(xv0 / run-02
     :ARG0 (xv2 / animal)
     :ARG1 (xv1 / circle))
```

Figure 18: AMR structures for the sentence pair *A squirrel is running in circles. – An animal is running in circles.* Semantic relatedness score: 4.4

Assessing the Limits of the Distributional Hypothesis in Semantic Spaces: Trait-based Relational Knowledge and the Impact of Co-occurrences

Mark Anderson
PIN Caerdydd
Prifysgol Caerdydd
AndersonM8@caerdydd.ac.uk

Jose Camacho-Collados
Cardiff NLP
Cardiff University
CamachoColladosJ@cardiff.ac.uk

Abstract

The increase in performance in NLP due to the prevalence of distributional models and deep learning has brought with it a reciprocal decrease in interpretability. This has spurred a focus on *what* neural networks *learn* about natural language with less of a focus on *how*. Some work has focused on the data used to develop data-driven models, but typically this line of work aims to highlight issues with the data, e.g. highlighting and offsetting harmful biases. This work contributes to the relatively untrodden path of what is required in data for models to capture meaningful representations of natural language. This entails evaluating how well English and Spanish semantic spaces capture a particular type of relational knowledge, namely the traits associated with concepts (e.g. *bananas-yellow*), and exploring the role of co-occurrences in this context.

1 Introduction

Vector space models have been the main driving force behind progress in NLP. Most work in this area, either in the form of static or contextualised embeddings, has been based on co-occurrence statistics and largely driven by the distributional hypothesis (Harris, 1954; Firth, 1957). This has also resulted in these representations seemingly capturing certain relational knowledge, such as word analogies (Mikolov et al., 2013b; Gittens et al., 2017). In this context, Chiang et al. (2020) found that the ability of word embeddings to evaluate analogies was not greatly impaired by removing co-occurrences related to relational pairs. This suggests there are limits to how the distributional hypothesis impacts the encoding of relational knowledge. We extend this line of work by focusing on the relational knowledge of concepts and traits. We also creep beyond English by translating concept and traits used in one of our datasets into Spanish.

Contributions: (1) We show that there is no impact on the ability of semantic spaces to predict whether a pair of embeddings corresponds to a trait-concept pair or to predict what traits a given concept has when removing co-occurrences of concepts and traits. **(2)** We developed a freely available dataset that can be used for further trait-based relational knowledge analyses for English and Spanish.[1]

2 Related work

What models learn Evaluation of *neural* semantic spaces has focused on what knowledge they capture with a slew of work showing that some knowledge of analogies can be seen by applying simple transformations (Mikolov et al., 2013b; Levy and Goldberg, 2014; Arora et al., 2016; Paperno and Baroni, 2016; Gittens et al., 2017; Ethayarajh et al., 2019). Others have investigated what syntactic information neural semantic spaces seem to capture with most showing that they do capture something deeper than surface patters (Linzen et al., 2016; Gulordava et al., 2018; Giulianelli et al., 2018). However, they fail to exhaustively capture syntactic phenomena and specifically have been shown to struggle with polarity (Futrell et al., 2018; Jumelet and Hupkes, 2018) and certain *filler-gap* dependencies (Wilcox et al., 2018; Chowdhury and Zamparelli, 2018). Pretrained language models (PLMs) have been found to capture varying degrees of syntactic information (Peters et al., 2018; Tenney et al., 2019; Goldberg, 2019; Clark et al., 2019), however, they have also been shown to struggle to predict the grammaticality of sentences (Marvin and Linzen, 2018; Warstadt et al., 2019) and seem to depend on fragile heuristics rather than anything deeper (McCoy et al., 2019).

Relational knowledge More specifically with respect to relational knowledge and semantic spaces, for some time now work has shown that semantic

[1] https://github.com/cardiffnlp/trait-concept-datasets

Proceedings of the 11th Joint Conference on Lexical and Computational Semantics, pages 173 - 185
July 14-15, 2022 ©2022 Association for Computational Linguistics

spaces could encode certain relational knowledge, e.g. knowledge of the relative positioning of geographical locations (Louwerse and Zwaan, 2009). Similarly, Gupta et al. (2015) found that embeddings capture something of relational knowledge associated with countries and cities, e.g. how countries related to one another with respect to GDP. Rubinstein et al. (2015) found that word embeddings captured some taxonomic relational knowledge but fared less well with respect to trait-based relational knowledge. Often analogy completion tasks are used to investigate what sort of relational knowledge a semantic space has captured with early work showing that simple linear transformations were enough to highlight analogies (Mikolov et al., 2013a; Vylomova et al., 2016). This method has drawn some criticism and has been challenged as a robust means of evaluating what relational knowledge models capture (Drozd et al., 2016; Gladkova et al., 2016; Schluter, 2018; Bouraoui et al., 2018). Attempts to evaluate what PLMs capture of relational knowledge have also been made, highlighting that these larger, more data-hungry models capture some but not all relational knowledge (Forbes et al., 2019; Bouraoui et al., 2020).

Patterns in data However, all the work cited above focuses work focuses on *what* models learn about relational knowledge and not *how*, or rather what are the salient signals in the data used in these techniques that manifest in relational knowledge. Some work has been done in this direction, with Pardos and Nam (2020) showing co-occurrences are not necessary in their distributional model of courses to predict similar or related courses. Chiang et al. (2020) evaluated this finding in neural semantic spaces, finding that the ability of a semantic space to complete analogies isn't impacted when removing co-occurrences

It is important to understand what aspects of the data result in what models learn because without this semblance of interpretability, problematic biases can creep in, e.g. gender biases in Word2Vec (Bolukbasi et al., 2016) or in BERT (Bhardwaj et al., 2021). Attempts have been made to mitigate certain biases in contexualised word embeddings (Kaneko and Bollegala, 2021), but in order to do so, the biases have to be known. Also, Shwartz and Choi (2020) discuss the issue of reporting bias in the data typically used in NLP, where rarer occurrences are more likely to be explicitly mentioned than common ones which results in models that can generalise about under-reported phenomena but not temper the over-reported information. Therefore it is necessary to understand the nature of the data and how it impacts what models capture and how.

In this work, we aim to expand on the work of Chiang et al. (2020) in two main ways. First, we do not use analogies and analogy completion to evaluate the impact co-occurrences of concept-traits has on relational knowledge developed in neural semantic spaces, but instead use a dataset of different trait-based relations (e.g. `is-colour`, `has-component`) derived from the McRAE and NORMS feature datasets. This allows us to more directly evaluate the ability of models to predict relational knowledge by casting the evaluation as a simple classification task (both in a multi class and binary class setting). And second, we extend the analysis by looking at Spanish data as well to evaluate whether the results extend beyond English.

3 Methodology

The methodology follows five sequential steps: the development of datasets that include concepts and their traits (Section 3.1); the selection and processing of large general-domain corpora (Section 3.2); the transformation of the selected corpora based on the concept-trait datasets to test our hypothesis (Section 3.3); training of word embeddings on the original and adapted corpora (Section 3.4); and finally the evaluation of the embeddings based on the trait-based datasets (Section 3.5).

3.1 Datasets

The datasets were based on the McRAE features dataset (McRae et al., 2005). This is a collection of semantics features associated with a large set of concepts (541) generated from features given by human participants. A secondary trait-based dataset was also collated for English based on the NORMS dataset (Devereux et al., 2014). This is developed in the same way as McRAE and is partially an extension of that dataset with 638 concepts. We wanted to avoid value judgements (such as `is-feminine`) and to collate more trait-based relations, that is pairs of words related by an inherent attribute of a concept.

McRAE-EN The first step in developing the datasets used in this work was to collate certain features into subsets of similar traits. This was done in a partially manual way by splitting data into 5 subsets. Each feature in McRAE has the number

	trait type	N_C	N_T	Traits
McRAE-EN	colour	148	7	green (32), brown (32), black (24), white (21), red (16), yellow (13), orange (10)
	components	110	6	handle (39), legs (19), wheels (14), leaves (14), seeds (13), doors (11)
	materials	144	4	metal (79), wood (43), cotton (11), leather (11)
	size & shape	234	4	small (83), large (70), long (44), round (37)
	tactile	117	7	heavy (21), soft (19), furry (18), sharp (17), hard (16), juicy (16), slimy (10)
NORMS	colour	133 (78)	5	green (35), brown (32), white (30), black (22), yellow (14)
	components	35 (26)	2	handle (25), sugar (10)
	materials	94 (62)	5	metal (46), wood (16), water (11), paper (11), bones (10)
	size & shape	242 (138)	4	small (109), large (73), long (31), round (29)
	tactile	106 (70)	6	heavy (28), sharp (26), liquid (14), light (13), juicy (13), soft (12)
McRAE-ES	colour	140	7	verde (31), marrón (31), blanco (21), negro (20), rojo (16), amarillo (12), naranja (9)
	components	100	6	mango (33), piernas (18), ruedas (14), hojas (14), semillas (11), puertas (10)
	materials	131	4	métal (72), madera (38), algodón (11), cuero (10)
	size & shape	216	4	pequeño (75), grande (66), largo (41), redondo (34)
	tactile	101	6	pesado (19), suave (19), peludo (17), duro (16), afilado (16), jugoso (14)

Table 1: Dataset statistics: N_C is the number of concepts, N_T is the number of unique features, NORMS N_C includes unique count in parenthesis, and the number in parenthesis for traits is the number of concepts with that trait.

of participants who specified that feature for that concept, so initially a frequency cut of 10 was applied to the features. From this set, we observed a number of similar traits that broadly fit into trait categories. A series of simple heuristics were then applied to extract all potential concept-feature pairs for each subset. For some trait types this was trivial with the MCRAE dataset, e.g. colour relations could be found using the feature classification in MCRAE of `visual-colour`. The full details of the heuristics can be seen in Appendix A.

This process resulted in 5 trait-based subsets: **colours**, **components**, **materials**, **size & shape**, and **tactile**. From each subset, we removed duplicates (e.g. ambulance has the features `is-white`, `is-red`, and `is-orange` in the colour subset).[2] And from the remaining concept-feature pairs, we cut on 10+ concepts per trait to ensure a suitable number of instances per target in our evaluation. The resulting statistics associated with this dataset can be seen in the top section of Table 1.

MCRAE-ES The set of concepts and trait words that occur across all 5 subsets were manually translated. The translators consisted of one native English speaker with some knowledge of Spanish and one native Spanish speaker who is fluent in English.

As might be expected, issues occurred when undertaking the translation that required judgements to be made. When there was a one to many translation, we used the translation that was *Iberian* if multiple translations were due to regional variants. Otherwise we chose the most common or most canonical. However, we also chose single word alternatives to avoid multiword concepts when this wouldn't have resulted in using an obscure word. We also made some choices to avoid having duplicate/competing concepts, i.e. *boat* was translated as *barca* and *ship* as *barco*. Further, we tried to match the intended use in English, i.e. translated *sledgehammer* to *almádena* rather than more generic term in Spanish *mazo* as heavy metal version is more standard in English. Otherwise we tried to use more generic options. A variety of resources were used to aid this including bilingual dictionaries, Wikipedia, and RAE (Real Academia Española). Despite our best efforts to maintain as many concept-trait pairs as possible, certain concepts just don't work in Spanish, typically many to one translations, e.g. *dove* translates to *paloma* which also means normal mangy pigeons. A more common issue was the tendency to use multi-word expressions in Spanish for certain concepts, such as *goldfish* (*pez dorado*) and *escalator* (*escalera mecánica*) with no single-word alternatives. The statistics resulting to the trait subsets for MCRAE-ES are shown in the bottom section of Table 1.

NORMS-EN To make our experiments more robust, we also used the NORMS dataset. In order to use this dataset, we manually classified features in this dataset based on the subset from our MCRAE trait dataset. First, we cut the features in NORMS that occurred less than 10 times and then took the set of remaining features and classified them as one of the five subsets and then automatically cast each

[2] A multi-label version of these subsets are included at `https://github.com/cardiffnlp/trait-concept-datasets` for MCRAE-EN and NORMS-EN.

	Corpus	Sentences	Tokens
English	UMBC	135M	3.4B
	Wiki	114M	2.5B
	Wee-Wiki	71M	1.6B
Spanish	ES1B	62M	1.4B
	Wiki	28M	0.6B
	Wee-Wiki	19M	0.4B

Table 2: Basic statistics of corpora used.

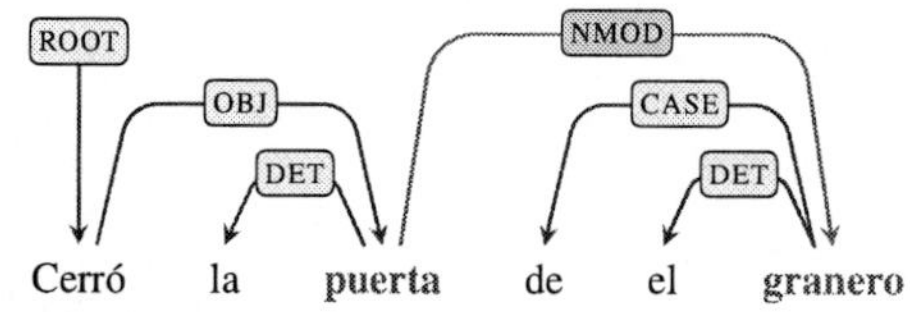

Original text: *Cerró la puerta del granero*
English: *She/he closed the barn door*

Figure 1: *granero* (highlighted in red) is a concept in McRae-ES with a component trait of *puerta* (highlighted in blue). In the example here they are linked by an *nmod* edge (highlighted in blue). For the syntactic removal method this sentence would be removed.

concept-trait pair into their respective subset. We manually checked to see if any features not used had been erroneously omitted due to annotation issues and folded those features into the relative subsets. This entailed adding `is-liquid` and `is-furry` to the tactile subset after some consideration (with `is-furry` subsequently being removed due to the minimum frequency cut after removing duplicates). The resulting subsets had duplicate concepts removed and then a minimum frequency cut on the remaining features of 10. The statistics of the resulting subsets can be seen in the middle section of Table 1 with the number of new unique concepts added to each subset shown in parenthesis in the concept count (N_C) column.

3.2 Corpora

For the statistics of the corpora used see Table 2.

UMBC The University of Maryland, Baltimore County (UMBC) webbase corpus is the resulting collection of paragraphs from a webcrawl in 2007 over millions of webpages (Han et al., 2013).

ES1B The Spanish Billion Words Corpus (ES1B) is a collection of unannotated sentences takens from the web which span difference sources from Europarl to books. It also include data from a Wikipedia dump from 2015, so has some crossover with the Spanish Wikipedia corpus (Cardellino, 2019).

Wiki We used English Wikipedia dump from 1st October 2021 and Spanish Wikipedia dump from 1st January 2022. They were extracted and cleaned using the WikiExtractor tool from Attardi (2015). This left document ID HTML tags in the data which we removed with a simple heuristic.

Wee-Wiki Similar to the standard pre-processing of the Wikipedia data, but we also cut articles with very little views as these tend to be stub articles and automatically generated articles. The idea behind this is to cultivate a *cleaner* and more natural version of the data. We used Wikipedia's official viewing statistics for 1st December 2021.[3] Articles with less than 10 views were removed.

3.3 Removing co-occurrences

We used 3 methods to remove co-occurrences with different levels of granularity to find co-occurrences. The first step in the process was to segment the corpora by sentence and to lemmatise the tokens. This was done using the spaCy library and the corresponding pre-trained models for English and Spanish (Montani et al., 2022). We used lemmas to handle gender of adjectives and nouns in Spanish and for plural forms in both languages. The segmented version of each corpus was then split into two separate corpora with 80% of the sentences in the first, which were used as the standard corpora in our experiments, and with 20%, which were used as reserves for replacing sentence with co-occurrences when creating input data without co-occurrences. When an instance was removed based on the criteria specified below, a random sentence was selected from the reserves, so as to balance the total number of sentences in each set.[4] The resulting number of instances removed is shown in Table 3 (English) and in Table 4 (Spanish).

Sentence The simplest method used was to merely remove any sentence where a concept and its corresponding trait was observed. The lemmatised version of the data was used to search for co-occurrences to be more thorough, especially with respect to the Spanish data. This entails using the lemmatised version of the concepts and traits to

[3] `https://dumps.wikimedia.org/other/pageviews/2021/2021-12/`

[4] Chiang et al. (2020) observed only a small difference when using this methodology and when using one where instances were replaced with sentences containing the relative concepts (and as is shown in §4 this holds for our work).

		UMBC			Wiki			Wee-Wiki		
		instances removed			instances removed			instances removed		
	trait type	sentence	window	syntactic	sentence	window	syntactic	sentence	window	syntactic
McRae	colour	76,800	70,159	8,974	105,614	97,728	13,397	70,194	64,594	9,083
	components	33,284	23,347	9,745	22,307	15,500	5,915	15,553	10,987	4,544
	material	28,061	19,171	6,030	29,695	20,477	5,771	21,239	14,669	4,431
	size & shape	104,478	68,697	18,213	131,165	88,453	26,612	90,280	60,516	17,452
	tactile	18,881	13,845	4,632	14,437	10,658	3,657	11,413	8,529	2,981
Norms	colour	25,106	18,737	7,422	26,378	19,824	8,360	19,561	14,777	6,581
	components	5,270	3,793	1,291	4,463	3,110	1,005	3,637	2,483	766
	material	51,898	34,484	12,150	30,916	20441	7338	21,051	13,823	4,694
	size & shape	105,895	68,162	18,372	117,210	79,041	22,812	83,329	55,933	15,814
	tactile	17,965	13,040	4,264	13,683	10,156	3,533	11,048	8,307	2,929

Table 3: Total instances removed and replaced for English Corpora (UMBC, Wiki, Wee-Wiki) for each dataset (McRae and Norms) by trait type and removal method (sentence, window, and syntactic as described in §3.3).

		ES1B			Wiki			Wee-Wiki		
		instances removed			instances removed			instances removed		
	trait type	sentence	window	syntactic	sentence	window	syntactic	sentence	window	syntactic
McRae	colour	31,267	25,121	208	19,424	15,804	2,729	12,473	10,129	1,836
	components	11,855	7,680	1,551	6,628	4,048	1,873	4,318	2,716	1,317
	material	8,473	6,087	1,344	6,704	4,698	2,200	4,353	3,091	1,501
	size & shape	34,416	19,276	248	23,224	13,513	4,001	15,584	9,157	2,798
	tactile	3,508	2,404	185	2,459	1,743	782	1,787	1,291	584

Table 4: Total instances removed and replaced for each Spanish Corpora (ES1B, Wiki, Wee-Wiki) for the McRae dataset broken down by trait type and removal method (sentence, window, and syntactic as described in §3.3).

match them in the lemmatised instances in the data. This was done independently for each trait type.

Window The second method used removed instances when the concept and its relative trait occurred within a given window, again using lemmatised forms. The window size used was 10 to match the size used during the training of the embeddings.

Syntactic Finally, used the Stanza library and the corresponding pre-trained models available for English and Spanish to parse the instances where a concept and its relative trait occurred (Qi et al., 2020). If an edge between the concept and the trait was predicted after finding a co-occurrence using the lemmas, this was removed, otherwise the instance was left. This method tests whether co-occurrences which are syntactically related are more impactful than haphazard co-occurrences. An example is shown in Figure 1.

3.4 Word embeddings

The models used to evaluate the impact of co-occurrences were trained using the Gensim library (Řehůřek and Sojka, 2010). We used CBOW Word2Vec embedding models (Mikolov et al., 2013a) as they are quicker to train than skip-gram models which was paramount considering the number of models that were required. Further, Chiang et al. (2020) found no significant differences between CBOW and Skip-gram models with respect to the differences observed in analogy completion between models trained with and without co-occurrences. We used the default hyperparameters in Gensim except for embedding size which was set to 300 and window size which was set to 10, i.e. the same settings from Chiang et al. (2020). For each trait-type and for each corpus a model was trained on the data containing co-occurrences (**with** or **w/** in tables) and the data not containing co-occurrences (**without** or **w/o** in tables). We trained multiple models for the data including co-occurrences — once per trait type — giving us a robust measurement of those models' performance. This means that results for each **with** for each trait type across the extraction methods are trained on the same data and are reported to show the variation seen training models on the same data.[5]

3.5 Classifiers

Trait-based relational knowledge was evaluated by casting it as a classification problem.

[5]Variation could also be due to slightly different datasets if **without** data doesn't contain any occurrences of a concept.

		UMBC						Wiki						Wee-Wiki					
		sentence		window		syntactic		sentence		window		syntactic		sentence		window		syntactic	
	trait type	w/	w/o	w/	w/o	w/	w/o	w/	w/o	w/	w/o	w/	w/o	w/	w/o	w/	w/o	w/	w/o
McRae	colour	0.35	0.35	0.34	0.34	**0.36**	0.35	**0.38**	0.36	**0.38**	0.30	**0.41**	0.36	**0.39**	0.38	**0.39**	0.38	**0.41**	0.35
	components	**0.82**	0.81	**0.81**	0.80	**0.82**	0.81	0.78	**0.80**	0.75	**0.77**	**0.79**	0.76	**0.75**	0.74	0.75	**0.79**	0.77	0.77
	materials	0.65	**0.69**	**0.67**	0.65	0.67	**0.68**	**0.68**	0.67	0.65	**0.69**	0.65	**0.67**	**0.71**	0.65	**0.67**	0.66	0.67	**0.68**
	size & shape	**0.57**	0.53	0.55	**0.58**	0.54	**0.58**	**0.60**	0.58	**0.58**	0.56	0.56	**0.61**	**0.58**	0.56	**0.59**	0.56	**0.57**	0.56
	tactile	0.61	**0.62**	**0.64**	0.60	**0.65**	0.64	0.54	**0.55**	0.56	**0.59**	**0.58**	0.55	0.50	**0.51**	0.50	**0.54**	0.51	**0.55**
Norms	colour	**0.40**	0.38	0.41	0.41	0.38	**0.40**	0.39	0.39	**0.41**	0.39	**0.44**	0.40	**0.43**	0.39	0.37	**0.39**	0.37	**0.41**
	components	0.89	0.89	0.89	0.89	0.89	0.89	0.91	0.91	0.89	**0.91**	0.91	0.91	0.89	**0.91**	0.89	**0.91**	0.94	0.94
	materials	**0.88**	0.87	**0.87**	0.85	0.87	**0.88**	**0.86**	0.84	0.85	0.85	0.86	0.86	0.84	0.84	**0.83**	0.82	**0.86**	0.82
	size & shape	**0.59**	0.57	0.58	**0.60**	**0.61**	0.58	0.59	0.59	**0.62**	0.57	0.59	**0.61**	**0.62**	0.59	**0.58**	0.55	**0.62**	0.57
	tactile	0.69	**0.72**	**0.68**	0.66	**0.70**	0.66	0.61	**0.65**	0.63	0.63	0.65	**0.67**	0.60	**0.61**	0.61	0.61	0.63	0.63

Table 5: Multi-class SVM results for English corpora and datasets by trait type and extraction method for models trained on data with (**w/**) and without (**w/o**) co-occurrences. Average accuracy across 3-fold cross validation is reported with best performing model between paired **w/** and **w/o** models highlighted in bold.

		ES1B						Wiki						Wee-Wiki					
		sentence		window		syntactic		sentence		window		syntactic		sentence		window		syntactic	
	trait type	w/	w/o	w/	w/o	w/	w/o	w/	w/o	w/	w/o	w/	w/o	w/	w/o	w/	w/o	w/	w/o
McRae	colour	0.29	**0.30**	**0.33**	0.31	**0.33**	0.30	**0.32**	0.29	**0.34**	0.32	**0.35**	0.33	0.31	**0.32**	0.30	**0.31**	**0.31**	0.29
	components	**0.77**	0.71	**0.81**	0.77	**0.74**	0.73	0.71	**0.75**	0.70	**0.75**	0.72	**0.74**	**0.73**	0.72	**0.71**	0.66	0.71	0.71
	materials	0.63	**0.67**	**0.67**	0.65	0.66	**0.67**	0.63	**0.64**	**0.70**	0.63	0.61	**0.66**	0.59	0.59	0.59	**0.61**	**0.63**	0.59
	size & shape	0.50	**0.52**	0.48	**0.53**	**0.46**	0.45	**0.52**	0.49	0.49	0.49	0.49	**0.50**	0.47	**0.48**	**0.49**	0.48	0.46	**0.53**
	tactile	0.54	**0.58**	**0.55**	0.53	**0.55**	0.53	**0.60**	0.58	0.60	**0.62**	**0.60**	0.59	**0.51**	0.50	**0.52**	0.51	**0.49**	0.48

Table 6: Multi-class SVM results for Spanish corpora and datasets by trait type and extraction method for models trained on data with (**w/**) and without (**w/o**) co-occurrences. Average accuracy across 3-fold cross validation is reported with best performing model between paired **w/** and **w/o** models highlighted in bold.

Multi-class First we used a multi-class evaluation. Using the datasets described in Section 3.1, given a concept (e.g. *banana*), the task consisted of selecting the most appropriate trait for a given trait type (e.g. *yellow* in the colour dataset). We used a support vector machine (SVM) as our classifier from the Scikit-learn library (Pedregosa et al., 2011) with the word embeddings learned in the previous step as the only input. For each model we used 3-fold cross-validation and report the mean score across the splits.[6] For each pair of models (i.e. with and without co-occurrences for a given trait-type and for a given corpus), we checked to see if concepts appeared in both semantic spaces. When a concept was missing in one or both, it was removed from the dataset for both, such that the comparison of results is robust between the two models we are interested in comparing, however, this was not common. It brought up an issue with *orange* and *naranja*, namely that it occurs as a concept and as trait, so that in our extraction method for sentence and window occurrences of these are always removed from the corpora and so were removed from the evaluation datasets.

Binary We also use binary classification by exploiting the earlier findings suggesting that differences between embeddings can be used as a proxy to capture semantic relations (Mikolov et al., 2013b; Vylomova et al., 2016). Again, we used SVM models, but this time the input features were the differences between concepts and their respective traits (i.e. $e_c - e_t$, where e_c is the concept embedding and e_t is the trait embedding) and the model predicted whether a pair was related or not. This required developing negative samples. This was done by randomly selecting words from the vocab space of the union of vocabs between each pair of model (i.e. with and without co-occurrences for a given trait type and a given corpus). These words then underwent a modicum of a control check by using lexical databases: WordNet (Fellbaum, 2000) for English and the Multilingual Central Repository version 3.0 for Spanish (Gonzalez-Agirre et al.,

[6]The full results for each model can be found at `https://github.com/cardiffnlp/trait-relations-and-co-occurrences`, including the number of concepts and features used for each model's evaluation and the standard deviations which are all very small.

2012) via the Natural Language Toolkit (Bird et al., 2009). Once a word was randomly selected from the vocab space (excluding the concepts in the given dataset), the respective lexical database was checked to see if it contained the word and if so whether the synonyms associated with it were at least sometimes nouns (that is the synonym set of nouns contained at least one item). This was so that the selected word could in theory be something akin to a concept and not just gobbledygook. This procedure was done so the number of concepts in the negative sample set matched the number in the positive sample set (which had instances removed that didn't appear in one or both of the paired models similar to the multi-class setup). Then each randomly extracted negative *concept* was ascribed a trait from the given trait space. Similar to the multi-class SVM setup, 3-fold cross-validation was used and the mean score across the splits is reported.[7]

4 Results

Multi-class results The results for the multi-class experiments can be seen in Table 5 for the English corpora and in Table 6 for the Spanish corpora. The highest performing model for each pair of models, i.e. with (**w/**) and without (**w/o**) co-occurrences is highlighted in bold for clarity. Across the board, it is clear that there is no consistent pattern as to whether a model trained with co-occurrences outperforms a model trained without them or vice versa. This holds for all three co-occurrence extraction techniques, for all trait types, for all datasets, and for all corpora across both languages. This is similar to the findings of Chiang et al. (2020) where little effect was observed on analogy completion whether co-occurrences were included or not, however, a systemic decrease was observed in that context despite it being small. While there are some differences between some models, the differences that would be required to make claims of one model being superior to another are much larger than what are observed here as the experimental setup isn't robust enough to verify that a difference of 0.01-0.02 is significant or not. A visualisation of the differences between each corresponding with and without model for McRae-EN by trait type can be seen in Figure 2 (equivalent visualisations

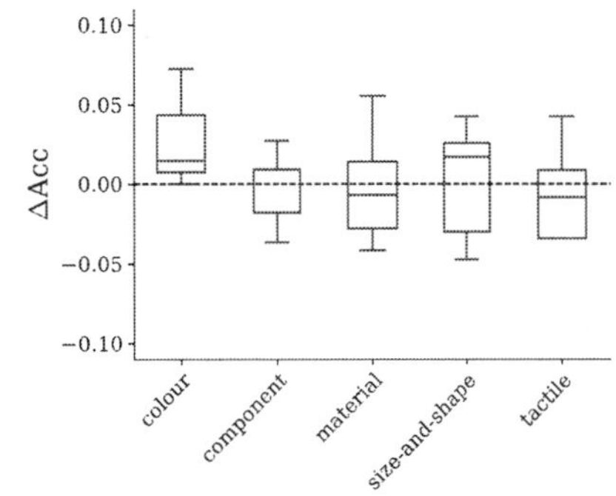

Figure 2: Distributions of delta accuracy (ΔAcc) for corresponding pairs for each trait type in McRae-EN.

for Norms-EN and McRae-ES are shown in Figure 4 and 5, respectively, in Appendix B). Figure 2 does highlight a slight difference with respect to colour traits, where a modest increase in performance is seen on average when training the models with co-occurrences, however, this isn't consisted across corpora and datasets as this increase is not observed in Figures 4 and 5 in Appendix B.

Binary results The results from the binary classification experiments substantiate these findings. They can be seen in Table 7 for English and in Table 8 for Spanish. Again, no pattern emerges across the different experimental dimensions that would suggest the removal of co-occurrences has impacted a model's ability to predict whether a pair is related or not. The overall high performance on the binary classification experiment for both English and Spanish suggests these models manage to encode meaningful information about these trait relations. But how this emerges is not clear. The simplest explanation is that suitably accurate representations are learnt due to the amount of data, but it could be for any number of other reasons not investigated here.

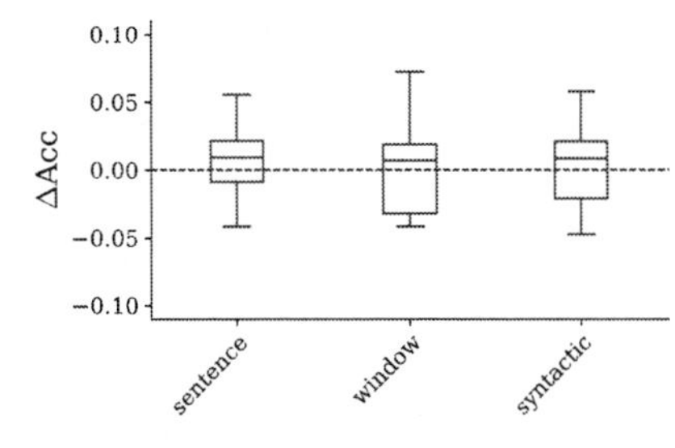

Figure 3: Distributions of delta accuracy (ΔAcc) for pairs for each extraction method in McRae-EN.

[7]Full results for the binary classifier can be found at `https://github.com/cardiffnlp/trait-relations-and-co-occurrences`, including the number of instances for each model and the standard deviations.

		UMBC						Wiki						Wee-Wiki					
		sentence		window		syntactic		sentence		window		syntactic		sentence		window		syntactic	
	trait type	w/	w/o	w/	w/o	w/	w/o	w/	w/o	w/	w/o	w/	w/o	w/	w/o	w/	w/o	w/	w/o
McRae	colour	**0.90**	0.88	**0.88**	0.86	0.86	0.86	0.84	**0.85**	**0.88**	0.86	0.88	0.88	0.89	**0.90**	0.87	0.87	0.87	0.87
	components	**0.90**	0.88	0.90	0.90	0.90	0.90	**0.88**	0.87	0.87	**0.88**	0.89	**0.90**	0.86	0.86	0.92	0.92	0.89	0.89
	materials	**0.93**	0.92	0.92	0.92	0.90	0.90	**0.90**	0.88	0.88	**0.89**	0.89	0.89	**0.86**	0.85	0.88	**0.89**	**0.90**	0.89
	size & shape	0.88	0.88	0.85	0.85	0.85	0.85	0.86	0.86	0.83	0.83	0.84	0.84	**0.88**	0.87	0.87	**0.88**	0.86	0.86
	tactile	0.89	**0.90**	0.88	0.88	0.86	**0.88**	0.88	0.88	0.82	0.82	0.87	**0.88**	**0.84**	0.82	**0.84**	0.81	**0.82**	0.81
Norms	colour	0.86	0.86	**0.84**	0.83	0.83	0.83	0.86	0.86	**0.85**	0.83	**0.84**	0.83	0.84	0.84	**0.87**	0.86	**0.86**	0.85
	components	0.80	**0.82**	**0.87**	0.77	0.80	0.80	0.90	0.90	**0.87**	0.78	**0.86**	0.84	0.86	**0.87**	**0.93**	0.90	**0.84**	0.83
	materials	0.84	**0.85**	**0.88**	0.86	0.88	**0.91**	**0.89**	0.87	0.86	**0.89**	0.85	**0.87**	0.85	**0.88**	0.85	**0.88**	0.90	**0.91**
	size & shape	0.84	**0.87**	0.88	**0.89**	**0.87**	0.86	**0.88**	0.86	0.84	0.84	0.85	0.85	0.88	0.88	**0.88**	0.87	**0.87**	0.85
	tactile	**0.87**	0.84	**0.86**	0.84	0.84	**0.86**	**0.83**	0.82	0.82	**0.84**	**0.86**	0.84	**0.78**	0.77	0.80	**0.81**	0.86	0.86

Table 7: Binary SVM results for English corpora and datasets by trait type and extraction method for models trained on data with (**w/**) and without (**w/o**) co-occurrences. Average accuracy across 3-fold cross validation is reported with best performing model between paired **w/** and **w/o** models highlighted in bold.

		ES1B						Wiki						Wee-Wiki					
		sentence		window		syntactic		sentence		window		syntactic		sentence		window		syntactic	
	trait type	w/	w/o	w/	w/o	w/	w/o	w/	w/o	w/	w/o	w/	w/o	w/	w/o	w/	w/o	w/	w/o
McRae	colour	0.81	**0.82**	**0.85**	0.83	**0.81**	0.80	**0.84**	0.81	**0.81**	0.78	**0.87**	0.84	**0.83**	0.81	**0.83**	0.80	0.79	**0.82**
	components	**0.88**	0.87	**0.83**	0.80	**0.81**	0.80	0.86	**0.89**	0.78	0.78	0.79	**0.82**	0.77	**0.78**	0.82	**0.84**	**0.76**	0.74
	materials	0.81	**0.82**	0.86	0.86	0.84	0.84	**0.78**	0.76	0.75	0.75	**0.70**	0.67	0.75	**0.80**	**0.75**	0.74	0.74	0.74
	size & shape	**0.82**	0.81	**0.75**	0.73	**0.76**	0.74	0.79	**0.80**	**0.76**	0.75	**0.79**	0.78	0.79	0.79	0.75	**0.78**	0.82	**0.83**
	tactile	**0.72**	0.71	0.75	**0.79**	**0.81**	0.78	**0.74**	0.73	0.71	**0.72**	0.74	**0.75**	**0.78**	0.72	**0.77**	0.75	0.78	**0.80**

Table 8: Binary SVM results for Spanish corpora and datasets by trait type and extraction method for models trained on data with (**w/**) and without (**w/o**) co-occurrences. Average accuracy across 3-fold cross validation is reported with best performing model between paired **w/** and **w/o** models highlighted in bold.

5 Discussion

The results highlight some tentatively interesting patterns with respect to trait types. In both English and Spanish, models perform consistently well on component traits, although for NORMS this turned out to be only over 2 traits, effectively casting it as a binary classification. Materials is the next consistently highest performing trait type across corpora and language with size & shape and tactile not far behind for English, but with a bigger gap in Spanish. The performance on colour traits is low across all settings and languages. This doesn't appear to be based on the size of the trait subset, e.g. the component subset is one of the smaller sets, yet has high performance and the performance of the other trait types don't vary with respect to the number of instance and unique features.

The number of removed sentences, as shown in Tables 3 and 4, gives a vague indication of the occurrences of the concepts in the dataset and the occurrence of their traits with colour sentence removals being the second highest for MCRAE-EN across all three English corpora, the third highest for NORMS-EN, and the highest for MCRAE-ES across all Spanish corpora. These rankings are consistent across extraction methods. Therefore, it is unlikely that the embeddings for the colours and the corresponding concepts (often concepts that occur in the other datasets) are somehow low quality due to low occurrences of these words. More likely is that the colour relation is more difficult than the other trait types as the other types are more tangible and more specific. Although this doesn't necessarily hold for size & shape traits, specifically sizes which tend to be relative, e.g. in MCRAE a *plane* can be *large* (which it is, relative to most things) but so too can a *bathtub* (which it is, relative to a mouse or other such timorous beasties, but not relative to a house). However, size & shape is consistently one of the traits that models perform worst on especially with NORMS-EN and MCRAE-ES.

As a final note, the different extraction methods yield no differences when compared to one another. This can be observed clearly in Figure 3 in the main text and Figure 6 in Appendix B. While the number of extracted instances using the syntactically related co-occurrences is very low and so difficult to draw any major conclusions, the number of sentence-based and window-based instances removed are quite high and are similar in magnitude. From this, we can deduce that the proximity of the words also doesn't have a major impact on the ability of a semantic space to encode relational knowledge. It could still be the case that if the data used to train models contained more syntactically related concept-trait pairs, they would encode *more* relational knowledge, but it is clear that their absence doesn't result in the models losing what relational knowledge they can capture. Many questions remain on how these distributional models encode relational knowledge. We have merely presented results which *do not* support the hypothesis that direct co-occurrence are the major signal for this process as related to trait-based relational knowledge.

Language models and wider impact of findings. Whether the results observed here for static embeddings would hold for PLMS isn't a given. While they are still based on the same distributional hypothesis and adopt statistical methods to encode salient features of language, they could potentially be more sensitive to the loss of co-occurrences in the training data. But this is an open research question that requires specific experimentation which has its own difficulties, i.e. prompting language models often includes lexical *clues* which cloud our ability to say with any great certainty if they have captured some phenomenon or not, see Kassner and Schütze (2020) for sensitivity of PLMs to mispriming).

The results do suggest that merely increasing the amount of data used likely won't result in any major improvements in the ability of models to encode relational knowledge or commonsense knowledge more generally, which is attested to by recent work in Li et al. (2021). Potentially, we need to look to more complex methods to augment NLP systems with commonsense knowledge potentially using multimodal systems, e.g. language models trained with visual cues as was done in Paik et al. (2021) to offset reporting bias with respect to colours. Alternatively, we can focus on the linguistic input and consider how to add stronger signals in the data used to train NLP systems.

6 Conclusion

We have contributed to the emerging interest in how neural semantic models encode linguistic information, focusing on trait-based relational knowledge. We have extended findings which showed that co-occurrences of relational pairs didn't have a major impact on a model's ability to encode knowledge of analogies by complementing this analysis with an evaluation of trait-based relational knowledge. We extended the analysis to include different extraction methods to evaluate whether a more fine-grained approach would highlight any differences in performance and found that this is not the case. The work presented here also expands beyond English and includes results in Spanish which follow the same trend. Finally, we have cultivated a set of datasets for different trait types in both English and Spanish (based on MCRAE and NORMS) which are available at `https://github.com/cardiffnlp/trait-concept-datasets`.

Acknowledgements

Mark and Jose are supported by a UKRI Future Leaders Fellowship (MR/T042001/1).

References

Sanjeev Arora, Yuanzhi Li, Yingyu Liang, Tengyu Ma, and Andrej Risteski. 2016. A latent variable model approach to pmi-based word embeddings. *Transactions of the Association for Computational Linguistics*, 4:385–399.

Giuseppe Attardi. 2015. Wikiextractor. `https://github.com/attardi/wikiextractor`.

Rishabh Bhardwaj, Navonil Majumder, and Soujanya Poria. 2021. Investigating gender bias in bert. *Cogn. Comput.*, 13:1008–1018.

Steven Bird, Ewan Klein, and Edward Loper. 2009. *Natural language processing with Python: analyzing text with the natural language toolkit.* " O'Reilly Media, Inc.".

Tolga Bolukbasi, Kai-Wei Chang, James Y Zou, Venkatesh Saligrama, and Adam T Kalai. 2016. Man is to computer programmer as woman is to homemaker? debiasing word embeddings. *Advances in Neural Information Processing Systems*, 29.

Zied Bouraoui, Jose Camacho-Collados, and Steven Schockaert. 2020. Inducing relational knowledge from bert. *Proceedings of the AAAI Conference on Artificial Intelligence*, 34(5):7456–7463.

Zied Bouraoui, Shoaib Jameel, and Steven Schockaert. 2018. Relation induction in word embeddings revisited. In *Proceedings of the 27th International Conference on Computational Linguistics*, pages 1627–1637, Santa Fe, New Mexico, USA. Association for Computational Linguistics.

Cristian Cardellino. 2019. Spanish Billion Words Corpus and Embeddings.

Hsiao-Yu Chiang, Jose Camacho-Collados, and Zachary Pardos. 2020. Understanding the source of semantic regularities in word embeddings. In *Proceedings of the 24th Conference on Computational Natural Language Learning*, pages 119–131, Online. Association for Computational Linguistics.

Shammur Absar Chowdhury and Roberto Zamparelli. 2018. Rnn simulations of grammaticality judgments on long-distance dependencies. In *Proceedings of the 27th International Conference on Computational Linguistics*, pages 133–144.

Kevin Clark, Urvashi Khandelwal, Omer Levy, and Christopher D. Manning. 2019. What does BERT look at? An analysis of BERT's attention. In *Proceedings of the 2019 ACL Workshop BlackboxNLP: Analyzing and Interpreting Neural Networks for NLP*, Florence, Italy. Association for Computational Linguistics.

Barry Devereux, Lorraine K. Tyler, Jeroen Geertzen, and Billi Randall. 2014. The centre for speech, language and the brain (cslb) concept property norms. *Behavior Research Methods*, 46:1119 – 1127.

Aleksandr Drozd, Anna Gladkova, and Satoshi Matsuoka. 2016. Word embeddings, analogies, and machine learning: Beyond king - man + woman = queen. In *Proceedings of COLING 2016, the 26th International Conference on Computational Linguistics: Technical Papers*, pages 3519–3530, Osaka, Japan. The COLING 2016 Organizing Committee.

Kawin Ethayarajh, David Duvenaud, and Graeme Hirst. 2019. Towards understanding linear word analogies. In *Proceedings of the 57th Annual Meeting of the Association for Computational Linguistics*, pages 3253–3262, Florence, Italy. Association for Computational Linguistics.

Christiane D. Fellbaum. 2000. Wordnet : an electronic lexical database. *Language*, 76:706.

John R Firth. 1957. A synopsis of linguistic theory, 1930-1955. *Studies in linguistic analysis*.

Maxwell Forbes, Ari Holtzman, and Yejin Choi. 2019. Do neural language representations learn physical commonsense? In *CogSci*.

Richard Futrell, Ethan Wilcox, Takashi Morita, and Roger Levy. 2018. Rnns as psycholinguistic subjects: Syntactic state and grammatical dependency. *arXiv preprint arXiv:1809.01329*.

Alex Gittens, Dimitris Achlioptas, and Michael W Mahoney. 2017. Skip-gram- zipf+ uniform= vector additivity. In *Proceedings of the 55th Annual Meeting of the Association for Computational Linguistics (Volume 1: Long Papers)*, pages 69–76.

Mario Giulianelli, Jack Harding, Florian Mohnert, Dieuwke Hupkes, and Willem Zuidema. 2018. Under the hood: Using diagnostic classifiers to investigate and improve how language models track agreement information. In *Proceedings of the 2018 EMNLP Workshop BlackboxNLP: Analyzing and Interpreting Neural Networks for NLP*, pages 240–248, Brussels, Belgium. Association for Computational Linguistics.

Anna Gladkova, Aleksandr Drozd, and Satoshi Matsuoka. 2016. Analogy-based detection of morphological and semantic relations with word embeddings: what works and what doesn't. In *Proceedings of the Student Research Workshop at NAACL*, pages 8–15.

Yoav Goldberg. 2019. Assessing BERT's syntactic abilities. *arXiv preprint arXiv:1901.05287*.

Aitor Gonzalez-Agirre, Egoitz Laparra, and German Rigau. 2012. Multilingual central repository version 3.0: upgrading a very large lexical knowledge base. In *Proceedings of the 6th Global WordNet Conference (GWC 2012)*, Matsue.

Kristina Gulordava, Piotr Bojanowski, Edouard Grave, Tal Linzen, and Marco Baroni. 2018. Colorless green recurrent networks dream hierarchically. In *Proceedings of the 2018 Conference of the North American Chapter of the Association for Computational Linguistics: Human Language Technologies, Volume 1 (Long Papers)*, pages 1195–1205, New Orleans, Louisiana. Association for Computational Linguistics.

Abhijeet Gupta, Gemma Boleda, Marco Baroni, and Sebastian Padó. 2015. Distributional vectors encode referential attributes. In *Proceedings of the 2015 Conference on Empirical Methods in Natural Language Processing*, pages 12–21, Lisbon, Portugal. Association for Computational Linguistics.

Lushan Han, Abhay L. Kashyap, Tim Finin, James Mayfield, and Jonathan Weese. 2013. UMBC_EBIQUITY-CORE: Semantic textual similarity systems. In *Second Joint Conference on Lexical and Computational Semantics (*SEM), Volume 1: Proceedings of the Main Conference and the Shared Task: Semantic Textual Similarity*, pages 44–52, Atlanta, Georgia, USA. Association for Computational Linguistics.

Zellig S. Harris. 1954. Distributional structure. *Word*, 10:146–162.

Jaap Jumelet and Dieuwke Hupkes. 2018. Do language models understand anything? On the ability of LSTMs to understand negative polarity items. In *Proceedings of the 2018 EMNLP Workshop BlackboxNLP: Analyzing and Interpreting Neural Networks for NLP*, pages 222–231.

Masahiro Kaneko and Danushka Bollegala. 2021. Debiasing pre-trained contextualised embeddings. *ArXiv*, abs/2101.09523.

Nora Kassner and Hinrich Schütze. 2020. Negated and misprimed probes for pretrained language models: Birds can talk, but cannot fly. In *Proceedings of the 58th Annual Meeting of the Association for Computational Linguistics*, pages 7811–7818, Online. Association for Computational Linguistics.

Omer Levy and Yoav Goldberg. 2014. Linguistic regularities in sparse and explicit word representations. In *Proceedings of the Eighteenth Conference on Computational Natural Language Learning*, pages 171–180, Ann Arbor, Michigan. Association for Computational Linguistics.

Xiang Lorraine Li, Adhiguna Kuncoro, Cyprien de Masson d'Autume, Phil Blunsom, and Aida Nematzadeh. 2021. Do language models learn commonsense knowledge? *ArXiv*.

Tal Linzen, Emmanuel Dupoux, and Yoav Goldberg. 2016. Assessing the ability of LSTMs to learn syntax-sensitive dependencies. *Transactions of the Association for Computational Linguistics*, 4(1):521–535.

Max M. Louwerse and Rolf A. Zwaan. 2009. Language encodes geographical information. *Cognitive science*, 33 1:51–73.

Rebecca Marvin and Tal Linzen. 2018. Targeted syntactic evaluation of language models. In *Proceedings of the 2018 Conference on Empirical Methods in Natural Language Processing*, pages 1192–1202.

R. Thomas McCoy, Ellie Pavlick, and Tal Linzen. 2019. Right for the wrong reasons: Diagnosing syntactic heuristics in natural language inference. In *Proceedings of the 57th Annual Meeting of the Association for Computational Linguistics*, pages 3428–3448.

Ken McRae, George S. Cree, Mark S. Seidenberg, and Chris McNorgan. 2005. Semantic feature production norms for a large set of living and nonliving things. *Behavior Research Methods*, 37:547–559.

Tomas Mikolov, Kai Chen, Gregory S. Corrado, and Jeffrey Dean. 2013a. Efficient estimation of word representations in vector space. In *ICLR*.

Tomas Mikolov, Wen tau Yih, and Geoffrey Zweig. 2013b. Linguistic regularities in continuous space word representations. In *NAACL*.

Ines Montani, Matthew Honnibal, Sofie Van Landeghem, Adriane Boyd, et al. 2022. explosion/spaCy: v3.3.0: Improved speed, new trainable lemmatizer, and pipelines for Finnish, Korean and Swedish.

Cory Paik, Stéphane Aroca-Ouellette, Alessandro Roncone, and Katharina Kann. 2021. The World of an Octopus: How Reporting Bias Influences a Language Model's Perception of Color. In *Proceedings of the 2021 Conference on Empirical Methods in Natural Language Processing*, pages 823–835, Online and Punta Cana, Dominican Republic. Association for Computational Linguistics.

Denis Paperno and Marco Baroni. 2016. When the whole is less than the sum of its parts: How composition affects pmi values in distributional semantic vectors. *Computational Linguistics*, 42:345–350.

Zachary A. Pardos and Andrew Joo Hun Nam. 2020. A university map of course knowledge. *PLoS ONE*, 15.

F. Pedregosa, G. Varoquaux, A. Gramfort, V. Michel, B. Thirion, O. Grisel, M. Blondel, P. Prettenhofer, R. Weiss, V. Dubourg, J. Vanderplas, A. Passos, D. Cournapeau, M. Brucher, M. Perrot, and E. Duchesnay. 2011. Scikit-learn: Machine learning in Python. *Journal of Machine Learning Research*, 12:2825–2830.

Matthew E. Peters, Mark Neumann, Luke Zettlemoyer, and Wen tau Yih. 2018. Dissecting contextual word embeddings: Architecture and representation. In *Proceedings of the 2018 Conference on Empirical Methods in Natural Language Processing*, pages 1499–1509.

Peng Qi, Yuhao Zhang, Yuhui Zhang, Jason Bolton, and Christopher D. Manning. 2020. Stanza: A Python natural language processing toolkit for many human languages. In *Proceedings of the 58th Annual Meeting of the Association for Computational Linguistics: System Demonstrations*.

Radim Řehůřek and Petr Sojka. 2010. Software Framework for Topic Modelling with Large Corpora. In *Proceedings of the LREC 2010 Workshop on New Challenges for NLP Frameworks*, pages 45–50, Valletta, Malta. ELRA. `http://is.muni.cz/publication/884893/en`.

Dana Rubinstein, Effi Levi, Roy Schwartz, and Ari Rappoport. 2015. How well do distributional models capture different types of semantic knowledge? In *Proceedings of the 53rd Annual Meeting of the Association for Computational Linguistics and the 7th International Joint Conference on Natural Language Processing (Volume 2: Short Papers)*, pages 726–730, Beijing, China. Association for Computational Linguistics.

Natalie Schluter. 2018. The word analogy testing caveat. In *Proceedings of the 2018 Conference of the North American Chapter of the Association for Computational Linguistics: Human Language Technologies, Volume 2 (Short Papers)*, pages 242–246.

Vered Shwartz and Yejin Choi. 2020. Do neural language models overcome reporting bias? In *Proceedings of the 28th International Conference on Computational Linguistics*, pages 6863–6870, Barcelona, Spain (Online). International Committee on Computational Linguistics.

Ian Tenney, Dipanjan Das, and Ellie Pavlick. 2019. BERT rediscovers the classical NLP pipeline. In *Proceedings of the 57th Annual Meeting of the Association for Computational Linguistics*, pages 4593–4601.

Ekaterina Vylomova, Laura Rimell, Trevor Cohn, and Timothy Baldwin. 2016. Take and took, gaggle and goose, book and read: Evaluating the utility of vector differences for lexical relation learning. In *Proceedings of the 54th Annual Meeting of the Association for Computational Linguistics (Volume 1: Long Papers)*, pages 1671–1682, Berlin, Germany. Association for Computational Linguistics.

Alex Warstadt, Amanpreet Singh, and Samuel R. Bowman. 2019. Neural network acceptability judgments. *Transactions of the Association for Computational Linguistics*, 7:625–641.

Ethan Wilcox, Roger Levy, Takashi Morita, and Richard Futrell. 2018. What do rnn language models learn about filler-gap dependencies? In *Proceedings of the 2018 EMNLP Workshop BlackboxNLP: Analyzing and Interpreting Neural Networks for NLP*, pages 211–221.

A McRae-EN trait subset extraction heuristics

Here we describe the full heuristics used to develop the trait-based subsets from McRae used in our experiments

Some traits were trivial to extract. Colour relations were the simplest as they could be found using the feature classification in McRae of visual-colour. Component relations were shortlisted cutting on the WB feature classification (this is simply a classification of trait types where W and B refer to the practitioners who classified the concept-features pairs in unpublished work) in McRae using `external_component` and `internal_component` and then by extracting features beginning with *has_*. Similarly for material relations, the WB classification of `made_of` was used. Some manual corrections were applied to the components to extend the number of instances in the dataset and to make certain traits fit our experimental setup better. This involved casting features such as `has-4-legs` and `has-4-wheels` as simply `has-legs` and `has-wheels`, respectively. The feature `made-of-material` was cut from the material subset, the feature `has-an-inside` from the components subset, and the features `is-colourful` and `different-colours` were removed from the colour subset.

We then looked at the WB label `external_surface_property` (excluding features that fit into the colour, concept, or material subset) as this fit our desired trait-based feature space. The majority of concepts in this subset tended to have features relating to their shape or to their size, so we opted to use this pair (size & shape) as another subset. This required manually removing features that didn't fit this trait-type, e.g. `is-smelly`, `is-shiny`, and so on. In this process, a final possible subset of tactile-based traits became apparent which was cut using the BR feature classification (this is simply a classification of trait types from different practitioners than WB) `tactile` and then manually removing certain features which were more value judgements than traits, such as `is-comfortable` or `is-warm`.

B Visualisations of Norms-EN and McRae-ES results

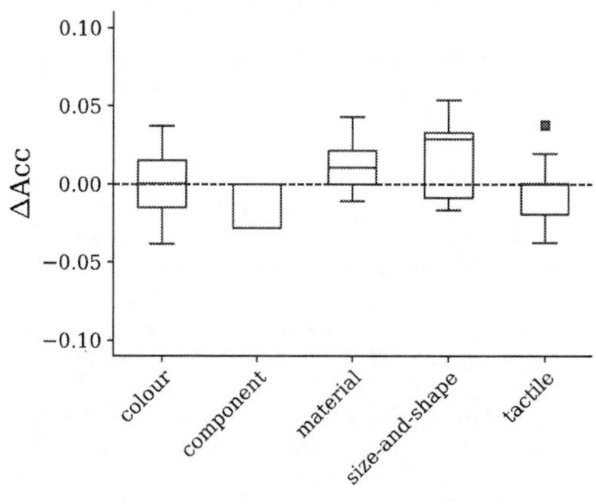

Figure 4: Distributions of delta accuracy (ΔAcc) for corresponding pairs for each trait type in Norms-EN.

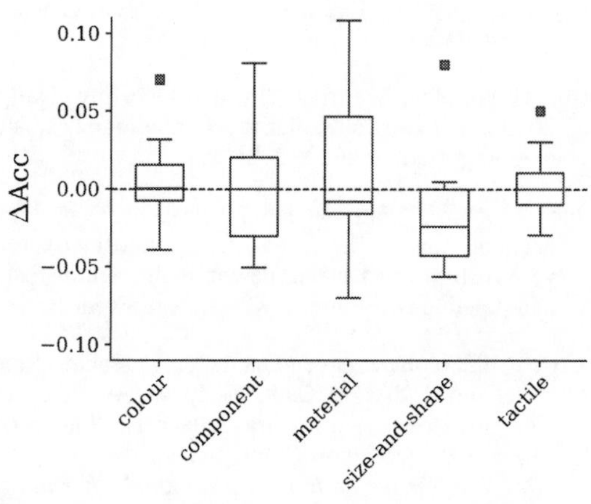

Figure 5: Distributions of delta accuracy (ΔAcc) for corresponding pairs for each trait type in McRae-ES.

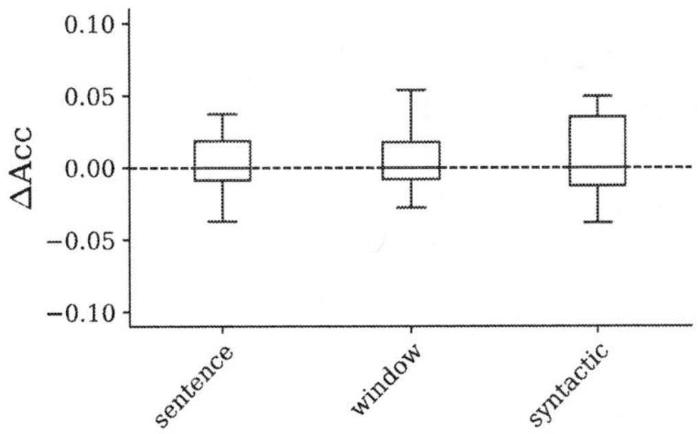

Figure 6: Distributions of delta accuracy (ΔAcc) for corresponding pairs for extraction method in NORMS-EN.

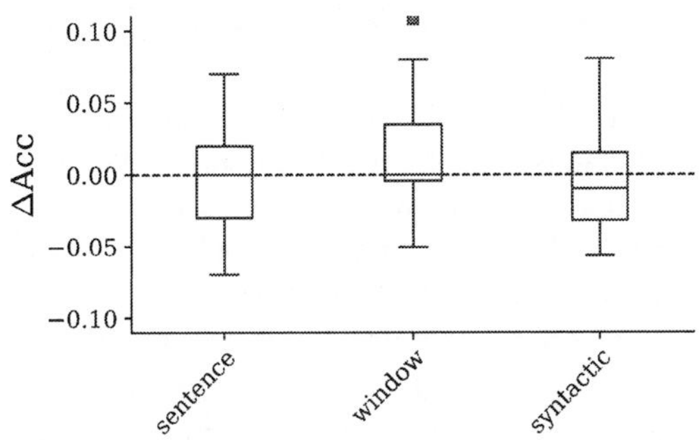

Figure 7: Distributions of delta accuracy (ΔAcc) for corresponding pairs for each extraction method in MCRAE-ES.

A Generative Approach for Mitigating Structural Biases in Natural Language Inference

Dimion Asael[†] **Zachary Ziegler**[‡] **Yonatan Belinkov**[†*]
[†]Technion – Israel Institute of Technology
{dimion@cs,belinkov@}technion.ac.il
[‡]SEAS, Harvard University
zziegler@g.harvard.edu

Abstract

Many natural language inference (NLI) datasets contain biases that allow models to perform well by only using a biased subset of the input, without considering the remainder features. For instance, models are able to classify samples by only using the hypothesis, without learning the true relationship between it and the premise. These structural biases lead discriminative models to learn unintended superficial features and generalize poorly out of the training distribution. In this work, we reformulate NLI as a generative task, where a model is conditioned on the biased subset of the input and the label and generates the remaining subset of the input. We show that by imposing a uniform prior, we obtain a provably unbiased model. Through synthetic experiments, we find this approach to be highly robust to large amounts of bias. We then demonstrate empirically on two types of natural bias that this approach leads to fully unbiased models in practice. However, we find that generative models are difficult to train and generally perform worse than discriminative baselines. We highlight the difficulty of the generative modeling task in the context of NLI as a cause for this worse performance. Finally, by fine-tuning the generative model with a discriminative objective, we reduce the performance gap between the generative model and the discriminative baseline, while allowing for a small amount of bias.[1]

1 Introduction

Natural language processing (NLP) datasets are plagued with artifacts and biases, which allow models to perform tasks without learning the desired underlying language capabilities. For instance, in natural language inference (NLI) datasets, models can predict an entailment relationship y from the hypothesis text H alone, without considering the premise P at all (Gururangan et al., 2018; Poliak et al., 2018). Another identified source of bias is lexical overlap between P and H, which is associated with an entailment prediction (McCoy et al., 2019). We refer to such biases as *structural biases*, cases where an undesired subset of the input alone incorrectly identifies the label. Relying on such biases results in poor out-of-distribution (o.o.d) generalization when models are applied to data without bias. Furthermore, models that contain such biases may make surprising predictions when the bias is present, causing problems in critical systems.

A line of work has attempted to improve the performance on o.o.d datasets by proposing different objective functions (e.g., Utama et al., 2020a; Karimi Mahabadi et al., 2020). However, these methods typically still result in a significant gap between the performance in and out of distribution, which indicates that the models are still biased. Table 1 shows this gap, which we term the o.o.d generalization gap (Δ).

In this work, we reformulate classification as a generative task, where the model's task is to generate the remainder features R conditioned on the biased features B and the label y. Using Bayes' Rule, we decompose the posterior $p(y \mid B, R)$ into the likelihood $p(R \mid y, B)$ and the prior $p(y \mid B)$. This reformulation lets us control the amount of bias present in the final model. By setting a uniform prior we can obtain a provably unbiased model. We denote this generative model as **GEN.**.

To assess the extent to which a given model is biased w.r.t a specific structural bias, we consider two metrics: the o.o.d generalization gap and the correlation between a model and a biased model $p(y \mid B)$, such as a hypothesis-only or overlap-only model. We first experiment with injecting synthetic bias into a fraction of the training set and evaluating on test sets with and without that bias. We find that the discriminative model's performance decreases as the amount of bias increases, while

* Supported by the Viterbi Fellowship in the Center for Computer Engineering at the Technion.

[1]Our code is available at https://github.com/technion-cs-nlp/Generative-NLI.

Proceedings of the 11th Joint Conference on Lexical and Computational Semantics, pages 186 - 199
July 14-15, 2022 ©2022 Association for Computational Linguistics

	SNLI			MNLI		
	Test	**Hard test**	Δ	**Test**	**Hard test**	Δ
Utama et al. (2020a)	–	–	–	82.8	79.8	+3.00
Karimi Mahabadi et al. (2020)	**89.57**	**83.01**	+6.56	**83.47**	76.83	+6.64
Sanh et al. (2021)	–	–	–	83.32	**77.63**	+5.69
Gururangan et al. (2018)	86.5	72.7	+13.8	76.5	64.4	+11.1
Stacey et al. (2020)	79.39	69.92	+9.47	–	–	–
GEN. (BERT)	65.53	66.18	**−0.65**	58.55	57.33	**+1.22**
GEN. (BART)	70.58	72.19	−1.61	64.09	65.74	−1.65

Table 1: Results on regular and hard (o.o.d) test sets of SNLI and MNLI. Prior work exhibits large o.o.d generalization gaps (Δ), while our generative approach reduces the gap significantly. The "Hard test" set refers to a subset of the regular test set that a hypothesis-only model fails on.

GEN maintains similar performance at all bias levels. Moreover, the biased-ness of the discriminative model increases, while GEN remains unbiased.

Next, we experiment with two kinds of natural bias: hypothesis-only and overlap. We demonstrate that GEN is unbiased compared to the discriminative baseline as measured by its low Δ and low absolute correlation with a biased model (ρ).

However, while our approach leads to unbiased models, it performs worse than the discriminative baseline even on o.o.d data. We then identify and quantify several causes for the poor performance of GEN. We show that generative modeling is a more challenging task than discriminative modeling, and that it requires learning a large amount of spurious signal compared to the discriminative model.

Finally, to mitigate the difficulty of the generative modeling task, we fine-tune GEN with a discriminative objective (Lewis and Fan, 2019). While this leaks some bias into the model, the final model (denoted as **GEN-FT**) matches or surpasses the discriminative baseline while maintaining a relatively small o.o.d generalization gap.

To conclude, our contributions are as follows:

- We develop a generative modeling approach, which provably eliminates structural biases in natural language understanding tasks.
- We demonstrate experimentally on two bias types and different NLI datasets that this approach leads to unbiased models.
- We analyze the strengths and weaknesses of the generative model.
- We show how discriminative fine-tuning improves the generative model, while allowing some bias to leak into the model.

2 Related Work

2.1 Biases and Artifacts

Many natural language understanding (NLU) datasets contain biases or artifacts, superficial features that are associated with a certain label. Examples include hypothesis-only biases in NLI such as negation words in the hypothesis being correlated with a contradiction label (Poliak et al., 2018; Gururangan et al., 2018). Similar one-sided biases have been found in other tasks, including visual question answering (VQA) (Agrawal et al., 2018; Manjunatha et al., 2019; Das et al., 2019), reading comprehension (Kaushik and Lipton, 2018), and fact verification (Schuster et al., 2019). Another kind of bias identified in NLI is lexical overlap, which is correlated with an entailment decision in NLI datasets (McCoy et al., 2019). We view all these cases as structural biases, cases where the input can be split into two disjoint sets, of the biased features and the remainder features.

The existence of structural biases in datasets allows models to perform unreasonably well when given access only to the biased features, such as a hypothesis-only model being able to predict entailment without access to the premise. The bias learned by the model manifests in poor o.o.d generalization when evaluated on a test set where the training set correlation between the biased features and a certain label does not hold.

2.2 Mitigation Strategies

Common approaches for improving o.o.d generalization combine the main model with a bias model, such as a hypothesis-only model. For instance, a bias model may be trained adversarially, making the main model perform worse when the bias model performs well (Belinkov et al., 2019b; Stacey et al., 2020). Others use a bias model to modulate the main model's predictions in various ways (He et al., 2019; Karimi Mahabadi et al., 2020; Utama et al., 2020b; Sanh et al., 2021; Mendelson and Belinkov, 2021). All these approaches use discriminative models to estimate $p(y \mid P, H)$. Moreover, they typically still result in a gap between in- and out-of-distribution performance.

In contrast, we propose a novel generative formulation of the NLI task, which leads to an unbiased model, in theory, and in practice. Belinkov et al. (2019a) also proposed to solve a generative problem, modeling $p(P \mid y, H)$, in order to encourage the model to consider the premise in its predictions. However, they ended up not using a generative model; rather, they approximated it with discriminative models. Lewis and Fan (2019) used a generative model for a different task, VQA, and found it improves generalization from biased training data. While our basic approach is similar, we analyze the generative model more rigorously, investigate the effect of different modeling options, and focus on quantifying the model's bias.

3 Structural Bias

Consider the general case of a classification task, for which we wish to build a model $p_\theta(y|X)$ where y is a low-dimensional label and X is an arbitrarily large set of features. The model is trained on an empirical training set $\mathcal{D} = \{(X_i, y_i)\}_{i=1}^N$. The dataset is constructed by humans, and inadvertently contains *structural biases*. We define a structural bias as a case where, if the input X is split into two disjoint sets X=$(B, R = X - B)$, the label y can be learned to be reliably predicted given only B. For most choices of B this is not a problem, but in some cases, the subset represents an externally imposed constraint that needs to be maintained or an externally imposed understanding of how the model should operate.

This formulation comprises a broad set of commonly considered biases. For example, in the NLI task, $X = (P, H)$ where P and H are the premise and hypothesis. If we choose the split $B = H$, we arrive at the hypothesis-only bias. This is an undesirable bias because as humans we know that NLI is impossible if one is only given the hypothesis.

Taking different splits corresponds to different biases. For instance, we can model the lexical overlap bias under the structural bias framework with the subset $B = P \cap H$. NLI models should perform no better than chance when given only the overlapping tokens between P and H.

Finally, this formulation extends beyond NLI and NLP to broader biases. For example, if X is a vector of information about individuals and one of the features in X is a protected characteristic s (e.g., gender or race), $B = s$.[2] Then, depending on the task, an undesirable structural bias may exist if a model can learn to predict y given s.

We denote these biases as structural biases because they are defined through the structure $B \subset X$, rather than specific known patterns in the data. For example, in the hypothesis-only case, this formulation does not require knowledge about what aspects of the hypothesis allow a hypothesis-only model to predict the label (e.g., negation words), only that somehow the hypothesis alone incorrectly gives a signal about the label. Thus, this type of bias is broader than specific known biases such as the presence of negation words, but narrower than unknown biases because it requires some knowledge of where the bias might be found.

3.1 Generative Classifiers Eliminate Structural Bias

Generative classifiers are models that make predictions according to Bayes' Rule. The generative classifier framework provides a principled way of handling structural bias:

$$\begin{aligned} p_\theta(y \mid X) &= p_\theta(y \mid B, R) \\ &= \frac{p_\theta(R \mid y, B) p_\theta(y \mid B)}{p_\theta(R \mid B)} \\ &= \frac{p_\theta(R \mid y, B) p_\theta(y \mid B)}{\sum_{y'} p_\theta(R \mid y', B) p_\theta(y' \mid B)}. \end{aligned} \quad (1)$$

We emphasize that under this framework, one may separately model $p_\theta(R \mid y, B)$ and $p_\theta(y \mid B)$, but the marginal likelihood must be constructed by marginalizing over the product of those components rather than estimated separately.

Separating the bias component gives explicit control over a given structural bias in the model. Formally, consider the ability of any model to predict the label given the bias subset, $p(y \mid B)$, defined by marginalizing out the remainder features:

$$p(y \mid B) = \int p_\theta(y \mid R, B) p_\theta(R \mid B) \mathrm{d}R. \quad (2)$$

[2]A non-trivial factorization of gender/race information from other features may be required in the NLP case.

For a discriminative model this may take any value, but for a generative classifier this becomes:

$$p(y \mid B) = \int p_\theta(y \mid R, B) p_\theta(R \mid B) \mathrm{d}R \quad (3)$$
$$= \int p_\theta(R \mid y, B) p_\theta(y \mid B) \mathrm{d}R$$
$$= p_\theta(y \mid B) \int p_\theta(R \mid y, B) \mathrm{d}R = p_\theta(y \mid B).$$

Therefore, for any given structural bias, the ability of the model to rely on the bias alone, $p(y \mid B)$, can be eliminated in a principled way by training a generative model to learn $p_\theta(R \mid y, B)$ and setting $p_\theta(y \mid B) = \text{Uniform}(\mathcal{Y})$. R and B are collections of tokens, so the actual training process amounts to training a standard encoder–decoder model. Predictions are made using Equation 1 at inference time. Unlike other methods, this approach does not require a specific model for $p_\theta(y \mid B)$; it simply requires the *desired* $p_\theta(y \mid B)$, which is often uniform.

3.2 Measuring Structural Bias

Typically, debiasing methods are evaluated by measuring the accuracy of the resulting model on a "hard" test set, a subset of the test set for which a bias-only model $p(y \mid B)$ predicts the incorrect label. While this captures overall quality, it alone does not assess the extent to which bias remains. For example, a model that scores well on the "hard" set but much better on the original test set must retain a portion of the bias, whereas a model that scores less well on the "hard" set but identically on the original test set likely does not retain any of the target bias. Thus, while the score on the "hard" test set is related to the biased-ness of a model, it alone does not tell the whole story. For some applications, the overall quality on non-biased data is a reasonable final objective, but for other applications complete removal of bias is critical.

To quantify the remaining biased-ness of a given model, we consider two metrics: the difference between the accuracy of the model on the standard test set and its accuracy on a "hard" set created with respect to the bias in question, which we term the o.o.d generalization gap (Δ), and the correlation (ρ) between the predictions of a given model and a fully biased model, i.e., $p(y \mid B)$.

A truly unbiased model will give a similar performance on the original test set and the hard test set, because it cannot rely on the predictive power of B in the original test set even when it is present. Thus low values of Δ indicate the model is unbiased.

Similarly, a model that consistently makes similar decisions to the fully biased model $p(y \mid B)$ in the original test set is likely using only the biased features B as the fully biased model. Therefore, a larger ρ gives additional evidence that a specific structural bias remains in a given model.

4 Experiments

In all experiments, we estimate $p(R \mid y, B)$ with an encoder-decoder model, with inputs (y, B) and output R. To condition on y, we prefix a label-specific token to B. We then train the model as a conditional generative model, by fine-tuning BERT (Devlin et al., 2019) or BART (Lewis et al., 2020) with the standard auto-regressive cross-entropy loss. To use BERT as an autoregressive decoder, the bidirectional self-attention mechanism of BERT is masked, and a language modeling layer, which starts generating from the "CLS" token, is added. A generative BERT model is comprised of a regular BERT model as an encoder and a BERT decoder (Rothe et al., 2020). All models are taken from the Transformers library (Wolf et al., 2019), and are fine-tuned with either the baseline discriminative objective or our proposed generative formulation. At test time, we attach all possible label tokens to each B and pick $\hat{y} = \arg\max_{y \in \mathcal{Y}} p_\theta(R|y, B)$.

4.1 Synthetic Experiment

To empirically verify the analysis in Section 3, we construct a synthetic experiment by artificially injecting a hypothesis-only bias into an NLI dataset, similarly to He et al. (2019). We use MNLI (Williams et al., 2018), an English NLI dataset, as the base dataset. For each example, we add one of three tokens to the beginning of the hypothesis, each token corresponding to a label. With probability p the token corresponds to the true label and with probability $1 - p$ the token is randomly selected from the three labels. The result is that p directly controls the amount of hypothesis-only bias present in the data[3]. We then train discriminative and generative BERT models on the resulting data.

[3] A reviewer pointed out that the generative model may rely on artifacts introduced by annotators when generating the hypothesis. However, the synthetic bias token is arguably more dominant than any such artifacts.

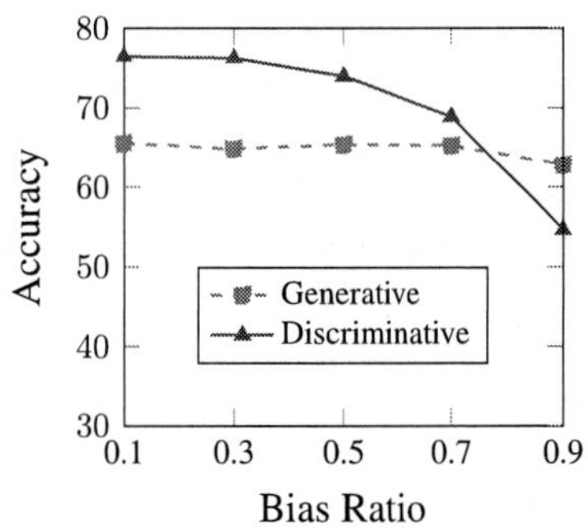

Figure 1: Results for models trained with synthetic bias and evaluated on MNLI dev hard without bias.

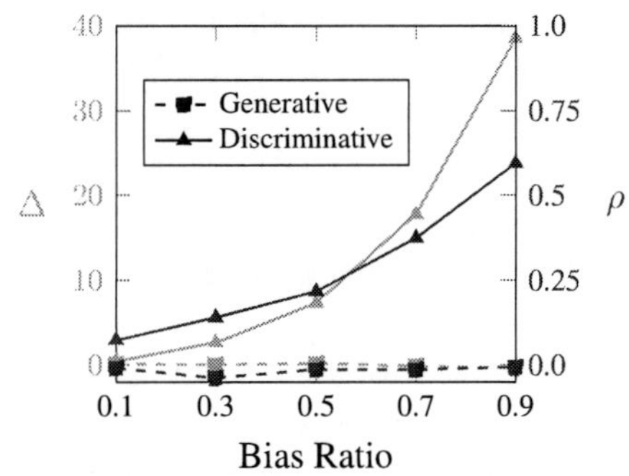

Figure 2: The o.o.d generalization gap (Δ) and the correlation to a bias model (ρ) of generative and discriminative models. ρ is calculated on an unbiased test set. Appendix A.1 shows correlations on a biased set.

4.2 Hypothesis-only Bias

We train our models on the (English) Stanford Natural Language Inference dataset (SNLI; Bowman et al. 2015) and on the MNLI dataset, two NLI datasets that are known to contain hypothesis-only biases (Poliak et al., 2018; Gururangan et al., 2018; Tsuchiya, 2018). We evaluate models on the available in-distribution test sets and on o.o.d test sets that have fewer or no hypothesis-only biases. For SNLI, we use the hard set provided by Gururangan et al. (2018). For MNLI, we use the blind evaluation test and hard test sets for MNLI matched.

4.3 Overlap Bias

Another type of bias that has been demonstrated in the MNLI dataset is lexical overlap bias. McCoy et al. (2019) demonstrate that, while somewhat uncommon, lexical overlap, subsequence overlap, and constituent overlap between the premise and hypothesis give a strong signal for entailment. Like hypothesis-only bias, this signal comes from peculiarities of the dataset creation process. For a model performing actual NLI, the overlap of words between the hypothesis and the premise should not give any indication of the label. This is emphasized by McCoy et al. (2019), as they create a separate label-balanced evaluation set where each example has a high overlap.

To treat overlap bias in the generative formulation, we set $B = P \cap H$. Specifically, we concatenate the premise and hypothesis and mask out any tokens that do not appear in both of them. The input to the encoder of GEN is then the label y followed by this partially masked concatenation. For simplicity, the output of GEN is the unmasked concatenation of P and H. In principle, we do not need to output the unmasked tokens, but this simplifies training and remains probabilistically valid.[4]

Because this setup is closely connected to the way the BART model is pretrained, we experiment solely with the BART model for this configuration.

While not traditionally studied in the overlap bias case, we perform the same analysis as in the hypothesis-only bias by constructing a hard set for overlap bias. We train a discriminative model that predicts the label from the masked concatenated premise–hypothesis input, and filter the MNLI dev set for examples where this model is incorrect.[5]

5 Results

5.1 Synthetic Experiment Results

Figure 1 shows the results when training with synthetic bias in MNLI, for different values of p, and evaluating on MNLI dev hard (without synthetic bias), a subset that a hypothesis-only model predicts incorrectly. The discriminative model's performance degrades gradually as p increases, while GEN maintains similar performance. At high levels of p, the discriminative model falls below the generative one, indicating that the presence of large amounts of bias precludes the discriminative model from learning the task effectively.

Figure 2 shows the two biased-ness metrics, calculated for the generative and discriminative models across a range of p values. For each p, Δ is calculated from the difference in accuracy for a given model between a version of the dev set with the synthetic bias included as in training, and a version of the dev set with the synthetic bias token

[4] An example for the data preparation is in Appendix A.3.

[5] As we cannot use the hidden test to filter based on labels, we use dev matched/mismatched for val./eval. respectively.

	Model	SNLI Test	SNLI Hard test	SNLI Δ	MNLI Test	MNLI Hard test	MNLI Δ
BERT	Bias-only	70.82±0.6	32.09±1.7	38.73±1.2	59.77±0.4	34.41±2.3	25.36±2.1
	Discriminative	90.49±0.2	80.55±0.3	9.94±0.1	84.08±0.4	76.27±0.3	7.81±0.2
	GEN, hyp-only	81.42±0.5	61.39±1.4	20.02±0.9	68.5±0.3	52.24±1.4	16.21±1.5
	GEN, uniform	65.86±0.3	66.74±0.5	**−0.88**±0.3	56.98±0.7	54.73±0.2	2.26±0.5
BART	Hypothesis-only	70.37±0.3	31.61±0.3	38.76±0.1	57.89±2.3	37.83±1.6	20.05±3.9
	Discriminative	**90.78**±0.3	**81.04**±0.6	9.74±0.3	**85.67**±0.1	**78.84**±0.4	6.83±0.4
	GEN, hyp-only	84.36±0.1	67.22±0.8	17.14±0.7	73.85±0.6	60.79±0.6	13.06±0.2
	GEN, uniform	70.80±0.2	73.16±0.9	−2.36±0.7	64.22±0.4	64.11±1.0	**0.11**±0.8

Table 2: Comparison between discriminative baselines and generative models, with Hyp-only or uniform prior, in the hypothesis-only bias case.

Model	Dev	Hard dev	Δ
Bias-only	56.32±0.3	9.37±8.3	46.95±8.5
Disc.	**86.44**±0.5	**79.72**±0.8	6.73±0.2
GEN	63.67±1.1	65.56±0.6	**−1.88**±0.4

Table 3: Comparison of discriminative and generative models (fine-tuned from BART) in the lexical overlap bias case. GEN was trained with a uniform prior.

Model	Lex.	Subseq.	Const.
Hypothesis-only	48.2	48.7	50.4
Discriminative	80.7	55.5	66.3
Learned-mixin	77.5	54.1	63.2
PoE	72.9	65.3	69.6
Conf. reg.	73.3	66.5	67.2
Generative	50.7	57.7	53.2

Table 4: Discriminative and generative models evaluated on the three HANS evaluation sets.

randomly chosen for each example. The fully biased model - $p(y \mid H)$ used as the reference when calculating ρ is a model that always selects the label that corresponds with the synthetic bias token prefixed to the hypothesis. According to both metrics, as the bias ratio p increases, the discriminative model quickly becomes significantly biased while GEN remains entirely unbiased.

5.2 GEN Reduces the Generalization Gap

Hypothesis-only bias Table 2 shows the results of the proposed generative model and the discriminative baseline in the case of hypothesis-only bias. For GEN, we show results with either a hypothesis-only prior for $p(y \mid H)$ or a uniform prior. The generative approach with the uniform prior leads to nearly identical accuracy on the i.i.d and o.o.d test sets, that is, unbiased models as measured by low o.o.d generalization gap (Δ between -2 and 3). In contrast, the discriminative model has much larger gaps (Δ of at least 9 on SNLI and 7 on MNLI), meaning that it is a more biased model. GEN with a hypothesis-only prior also exhibits large generalization gaps, demonstrating the bias leak in this model. Obviously, a hypothesis-only model is the most biased, with the largest gaps.

These results also show the advantage of using a pre-trained encoder-decoder (BART) compared to plugging a pre-trained encoder (BERT) and fine-tuning it as an encoder-decoder. While both generative models are unbiased, BART is more amenable to the generative fine-tuning than BERT, with overall better results. For this reason, we only report results with BART henceforth.

Overlap bias Table 3 shows similar results in the case of overlap bias on a hard set w.r.t this bias. GEN exhibits a lower generalization gap (Δ) than the discriminative baseline. As expected, the overlap bias model shows the greatest gap.

While the generative approach leads to unbiased models for both bias types, it also performs significantly worse than the discriminative model, on both in-distribution and o.o.d test sets. We return to this issue in Sections 6 and 7.

Finally, Table 4 shows the accuracies of the generative classifier and previous results from the literature, reported by Utama et al. (2020a) on the three HANS evaluation sets (McCoy et al., 2019). In general, the accuracies for the generative clas-

Label	Hypothesis	Generated premise
contradiction		a woman in a black shirt is sitting on a bench with a bag in her lap
entailment	the woman has been shot	a woman is being shot by a man in a blue shirt
neutral		a woman in a blue shirt is sitting on a bench with a bag in her lap
contradiction		a woman in a black shirt is smiling
entailment	the woman is very happy	a woman in a white shirt is smiling
neutral		a woman in a white shirt is smiling
contradiction		an elderly woman is sitting on a bench with her legs crossed and [...]
entailment	the woman is young	a young woman in a black shirt and jeans is walking down the street
neutral		a woman in a red shirt is sitting on a bench with a bag in her lap

Table 5: Generated premises by GEN from <y, H> pairs. The original premise for the hypothesis was *"A woman with a green headscarf, blue shirt and a very big grin"* and the gold label was "neutral".

Model	Hyp-SNLI	Hyp-MNLI	Overlap
Disc.	0.271	0.223	0.171
GEN	−0.025	−0.009	−0.043
Majority	0.005	0.055	0.016
Uniform	−0.018	−0.006	0.007

Table 6: Correlations of discriminative, generative, majority, and uniform models with bias models, on hyp-only (on SNLI/MNLI) and overlap bias (on MNLI).

sifier are low. We hypothesize that this is due to the fact that the examples in the HANS evaluation set are significantly out of distribution compared to the training set, w.r.t the amount of overlap between premise and hypothesis. In the training set, sentences often have 20 or 30 tokens with only 1 or 2 token overlaps. In the HANS set, sentences are shorter and all but 1 or 2 tokens overlap. This makes the input significantly more out of domain for the generative classifier only, which is used to seeing many mask tokens in the input and in the HANS set sees almost no mask tokens.

5.3 GEN is Uncorrelated with a Bias Model

Table 6 shows correlations ρ of GEN and the discriminative baseline with a bias-only model. In the hypothesis-only case, the models were trained on SNLI or MNLI and correlations were measured on predictions on SNLI test or MNLI dev mismatched, respectively. In the overlap case, the models were trained on MNLI and correlations were measured on MNLI dev mismatched.

In both bias types, the discriminative model predictions are much more correlated with the bias models than the predictions of the generative models. In fact, the correlations of the generative models are as low as those of a majority model or a uniform model, which is unbiased by construction.

6 Evaluating Generated Premises

So far, we have only used GEN to score existing examples (with teacher forcing), conditioned on the label and the biased features. In this section, we evaluate the quality of its generations when decoding without constraints. For the experiments here, we consider the hypothesis-only bias and evaluate the quality of GEN in generating premises. We use a BART model trained on SNLI and generate premises for all hypotheses in the test set.

To evaluate how well our model can generate premises, we used two metrics: BLEU (Papineni et al., 2002) of the generated premises w.r.t gold premises, to measure the generation quality (higher is better), and self-BLEU (Zhu et al., 2018) to measure the diversity of the generations (lower is more diverse). We report a BLEU value of 0.1078, indicating that the model is not very good at generating premises. We report self-BLEU of 0.8032 for the generated premises compared to 0.5875 for the original premises, suggesting that the generated premises are less diverse. Table 5 also shows examples where, given different hypotheses, the model generates very similar premises.

A possible explanation for the difficulty of the generative task may be found in the nature of NLI examples in common datasets. In many cases, the relationship is determined by a small number of words in the premise and hypothesis pair. To quantify this, we measured the number of words highlighted as explanations in the e-SNLI dataset (Camburu et al., 2018) and found that less than 21% of words in the premise are highlighted on average.[6] This pattern is reflected also in decisions made by

[6] Of the premises that were highlighted at all.

Model	SNLI				MNLI			
	Test	Hard test	Δ	ρ	Test	Hard test	Δ	ρ
Disc.	**90.78**±0.3	81.04±0.6	9.74±0.3	0.27	**85.67**±0.1	**78.84**±0.4	6.83±0.4	0.22
GEN-FT	86.30±0.4	**82.20**±0.3	**4.09**±0.1	**0.09**	79.66±1.5	76.45±0.7	**3.21**±1.3	**0.07**

Table 7: Fine-tuned model results for hypothesis-only bias. Disc. is the discriminative baseline.

NLI models. By applying gradient attributions,[7] we found that more than 70% of the premise words have low attributions values (between -0.1 to 0.1), with fewer than 6% of the words having absolute values greater than 0.3. This shows that only a small number of words had any significant effect on the model predictions. Table 12 in the appendix shows a qualitative example of this behavior. Finally, this pattern is also reflected in the generations produced by GEN, as demonstrated in Table 5.

7 Discriminative Fine-tuning

The analysis in Section 6 suggests that the central limitation of GEN is that the purely generative task for which it is trained is challenging in its own right, but unaligned with the downstream classification task. The model is rewarded at training time for devoting significant capacity to modeling the full high-dimensional distribution of R, even when large parts of that distribution are unimportant for making downstream predictions.

To help GEN in such cases, we experiment with an additional fine-tuning step in which we directly optimize for predictive performance. Specifically, for the fine-tuning step we construct the discriminative distribution using Bayes' Rule in Equation 1 and use it at *training time* by minimizing the label cross-entropy loss:

$$\mathcal{L}_{ft} = -\sum_{i=1}^{N} \log p_\theta(y_i \mid B_i, R_i) \quad (4)$$
$$= -\sum_{i=1}^{N} \log \frac{p_\theta(R_i \mid y_i, B_i) p_\theta(y_i \mid B_i)}{\sum_{y'} p_\theta(R_i \mid y', B_i) p_\theta(y' \mid B_i)}.$$

Using this objective requires a choice of $p_\theta(y \mid B)$. We explore the impact of different choices for this distribution in Appendix A.2, but found that using a pretrained and frozen $p_\theta(y \mid B)$ during the fine-tuning step works best. We hypothesize that this setup allows the generative component $p_\theta(R \mid y, B)$ to ignore as much bias as possible. At inference, as we would like to ignore the bias, we take the fine-tuned generative component $p_\theta(R \mid y, B)$ and perform inference the same way as before, using Bayes' Rule with a uniform prior.

[7] We computed attributions for a discriminative BERT model trained on SNLI, using Integrated Gradients (Sundararajan et al., 2017) with Captum (Kokhlikyan et al., 2020).

Model	Dev	Hard dev	Δ	ρ
Disc.	**86.44**	**79.72**	6.73	0.171
GEN-FT	79.87	74.98	**4.89**	**0.106**

Table 8: Fine-tuned model results for overlap bias on MNLI mismatched dev set.

The adjusted training procedure is composed of the following steps: 1) Train a discriminative prior model, $p_\theta(y \mid B)$, freeze the weights. 2) Train a generative model, $p_\theta(R \mid y, B)$, as in Section 4. 3) Fine-tune the model using Equation 4, using the pretrained $p_\theta(y \mid B)$. 4) Test the model using Equation 1 with a uniform prior.

7.1 Results

Tables 7 and 8 show the results of the fine-tuning pipeline. The fine-tuned generative models (denoted as **GEN-FT**) achieve smaller o.o.d generalization gaps (Δ) and correlations to the biased models (ρ) than the discriminative baselines. GEN-FT is also significantly better than GEN in terms of o.o.d performance, at the expense of slight bias leakage (higher ρ compared to GEN in Table 6). In the case of hypothesis-only bias, GEN-FT match or surpass the results of the discriminative baselines on the o.o.d sets. In the overlap bias case, GEN-FT does not match the discriminative model on the o.o.d set, but it narrows the gap.

The above results were obtained using a bias model prior in the fine-tuning step and a uniform prior at inference time. This was the strategy that achieved the lowest generalization gap (Δ) on the dev set while outperforming the discriminative baseline. See Appendix A.2 for an ablation study of additional options.

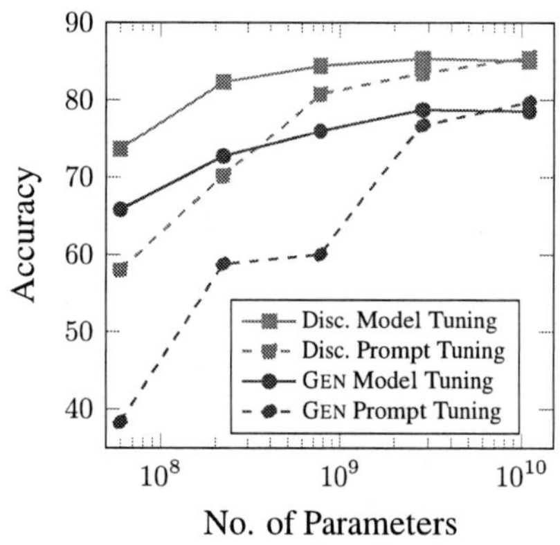

Figure 3: SNLI Hard results with different T5 models.

8 Scalability

Given that the generative approach consumes more compute than the discriminative baseline, it is natural to ask whether it can scale to larger models. To answer this, we experimented with the T5 model (Raffel et al., 2020), an encoder-decoder available in five sizes, from 60M to 11B parameters. We focus on the hypothesis-only bias case in SNLI. We train the generative and discriminative models using regular fine-tuning (also called *model-tuning*), and also experiment with *prompt-tuning* (Lester et al., 2021), a faster and cheaper approach, which adds a small number of learnable tokens to the start of the input, and trains them end-to-end, while the model's original weights stay frozen. (Memory and training statistics are found in Table 14, Appendix A.5.)

Figure 3 shows that both the generative and discriminative approaches scale with model size. Prompt-tuning is effective, matching model-tuning performance at larger sizes. In larger models, the generative approach narrows the gap from the discriminative one, but cannot close it. Table 9 shows that with the largest 11B model, the generative approach leads to unbiased models. The table also shows that discriminative fine-tuning is possible at this scale and obtains a similar performance to the discriminative model on the hard set. Prompt-tuning also allows us to hold only one model for the discriminative fine-tuning phase (compared to two models in model-tuning). We conclude that the generative approach is scalable and can be used with very large models to mitigate structural biases.

Method	Model	Test	Hard test	Δ
Model-tuning	Disc.	92.80	85.00	7.8
	GEN	76.76	78.53	−1.77
Prompt-tuning	Disc.	92.88	85.46	7.42
	GEN	79.91	79.70	0.21
	GEN-FT	89.68	85.22	4.46

Table 9: Results on SNLI with T5-XXL (11B) model.

9 Conclusion

Structural biases are common in various NLI datasets and are a major obstacle when trying to create robust systems for this task. We proposed a generative approach for NLI, which leads to unbiased models. We demonstrated that our generative models are robust to large amounts of bias and perform equally well in and out of distribution. This comes, however, with a trade-off, where the generative models perform worse than discriminative baselines. We investigated reasons for the difficulty of training generative NLI models, highlighting the large output space of generating sentences, as opposed to identifying a small subset of words that are often sufficient for solving the task. We showed how to mitigate this problem by fine-tuning GEN with a discriminative objective. Finally, we demonstrated that the method scales efficiently to large language models.

Our work lays down a novel formulation for the NLI task, which may be applied to many other natural language understanding tasks. Future work can examine other kinds of bias and different tasks. For instance, if the bias variables are constructed according to protected attributes like race or gender, our approach leads to unbiased models w.r.t the protected attributes.

Acknowledgements

We thank Alexander Rush for helpful discussions, Brian Lester for answering questions about the prompt-tuning approach, and the anonymous reviewers for their useful suggestions. This research was supported by the ISRAEL SCIENCE FOUNDATION (grant No. 448/20) and by an Azrieli Foundation Early Career Faculty Fellowship.

References

Aishwarya Agrawal, Dhruv Batra, Devi Parikh, and Aniruddha Kembhavi. 2018. Don't just assume; look and answer: Overcoming priors for visual question answering. In *2018 IEEE Conference on Computer Vision and Pattern Recognition, CVPR 2018, Salt Lake City, UT, USA, June 18-22, 2018*, pages 4971–4980. IEEE Computer Society.

Yonatan Belinkov, Adam Poliak, Stuart Shieber, Benjamin Van Durme, and Alexander Rush. 2019a. Don't take the premise for granted: Mitigating artifacts in natural language inference. In *Proceedings of the 57th Annual Meeting of the Association for Computational Linguistics*, pages 877–891, Florence, Italy. Association for Computational Linguistics.

Yonatan Belinkov, Adam Poliak, Stuart Shieber, Benjamin Van Durme, and Alexander Rush. 2019b. On adversarial removal of hypothesis-only bias in natural language inference. In *Proceedings of the Eighth Joint Conference on Lexical and Computational Semantics (*SEM 2019)*, pages 256–262, Minneapolis, Minnesota. Association for Computational Linguistics.

Samuel R. Bowman, Gabor Angeli, Christopher Potts, and Christopher D. Manning. 2015. A large annotated corpus for learning natural language inference. In *Proceedings of the 2015 Conference on Empirical Methods in Natural Language Processing*, pages 632–642, Lisbon, Portugal. Association for Computational Linguistics.

Oana-Maria Camburu, Tim Rocktäschel, Thomas Lukasiewicz, and Phil Blunsom. 2018. e-SNLI: Natural language inference with natural language explanations. In *Advances in Neural Information Processing Systems 31: Annual Conference on Neural Information Processing Systems 2018, NeurIPS 2018, December 3-8, 2018, Montréal, Canada*, pages 9560–9572.

Anubrata Das, Samreen Anjum, and Danna Gurari. 2019. Dataset bias: A case study for visual question answering. *Proceedings of the Association for Information Science and Technology*, 56(1):58–67.

Jacob Devlin, Ming-Wei Chang, Kenton Lee, and Kristina Toutanova. 2019. BERT: Pre-training of deep bidirectional transformers for language understanding. In *Proceedings of the 2019 Conference of the North American Chapter of the Association for Computational Linguistics: Human Language Technologies, Volume 1 (Long and Short Papers)*, pages 4171–4186, Minneapolis, Minnesota. Association for Computational Linguistics.

Suchin Gururangan, Swabha Swayamdipta, Omer Levy, Roy Schwartz, Samuel Bowman, and Noah A. Smith. 2018. Annotation artifacts in natural language inference data. In *Proceedings of the 2018 Conference of the North American Chapter of the Association for Computational Linguistics: Human Language Technologies, Volume 2 (Short Papers)*, pages 107–112, New Orleans, Louisiana. Association for Computational Linguistics.

He He, Sheng Zha, and Haohan Wang. 2019. Unlearn dataset bias in natural language inference by fitting the residual. In *Proceedings of the 2nd Workshop on Deep Learning Approaches for Low-Resource NLP (DeepLo 2019)*, pages 132–142, Hong Kong, China. Association for Computational Linguistics.

Rabeeh Karimi Mahabadi, Yonatan Belinkov, and James Henderson. 2020. End-to-end bias mitigation by modelling biases in corpora. In *Proceedings of the 58th Annual Meeting of the Association for Computational Linguistics*, pages 8706–8716, Online. Association for Computational Linguistics.

Divyansh Kaushik and Zachary C. Lipton. 2018. How much reading does reading comprehension require? a critical investigation of popular benchmarks. In *Proceedings of the 2018 Conference on Empirical Methods in Natural Language Processing*, pages 5010–5015, Brussels, Belgium. Association for Computational Linguistics.

Narine Kokhlikyan, Vivek Miglani, Miguel Martin, Edward Wang, Bilal Alsallakh, Jonathan Reynolds, Alexander Melnikov, Natalia Kliushkina, Carlos Araya, Siqi Yan, et al. 2020. Captum: A unified and generic model interpretability library for pytorch. *arXiv preprint arXiv:2009.07896*.

Brian Lester, Rami Al-Rfou, and Noah Constant. 2021. The power of scale for parameter-efficient prompt tuning. *arXiv preprint arXiv:2104.08691*.

Mike Lewis and Angela Fan. 2019. Generative question answering: Learning to answer the whole question. In *7th International Conference on Learning Representations, ICLR 2019, New Orleans, LA, USA, May 6-9, 2019*. OpenReview.net.

Mike Lewis, Yinhan Liu, Naman Goyal, Marjan Ghazvininejad, Abdelrahman Mohamed, Omer Levy, Veselin Stoyanov, and Luke Zettlemoyer. 2020. BART: Denoising sequence-to-sequence pre-training for natural language generation, translation, and comprehension. In *Proceedings of the 58th Annual Meeting of the Association for Computational Linguistics*, pages 7871–7880, Online. Association for Computational Linguistics.

Varun Manjunatha, Nirat Saini, and Larry S. Davis. 2019. Explicit bias discovery in visual question answering models. In *IEEE Conference on Computer Vision and Pattern Recognition, CVPR 2019, Long Beach, CA, USA, June 16-20, 2019*, pages 9562–9571. Computer Vision Foundation / IEEE.

Tom McCoy, Ellie Pavlick, and Tal Linzen. 2019. Right for the wrong reasons: Diagnosing syntactic heuristics in natural language inference. In *Proceedings of the 57th Annual Meeting of the Association for Computational Linguistics*, pages 3428–3448, Florence, Italy. Association for Computational Linguistics.

Michael Mendelson and Yonatan Belinkov. 2021. Debiasing methods in natural language understanding make bias more accessible. In *Proceedings of the 2021 Conference on Empirical Methods in Natural Language Processing*, pages 1545–1557, Online and Punta Cana, Dominican Republic. Association for Computational Linguistics.

Kishore Papineni, Salim Roukos, Todd Ward, and Wei-Jing Zhu. 2002. BLEU: a method for automatic evaluation of machine translation. In *Proceedings of the 40th Annual Meeting of the Association for Computational Linguistics*, pages 311–318, Philadelphia, Pennsylvania, USA. Association for Computational Linguistics.

Adam Poliak, Jason Naradowsky, Aparajita Haldar, Rachel Rudinger, and Benjamin Van Durme. 2018. Hypothesis only baselines in natural language inference. In *Proceedings of the Seventh Joint Conference on Lexical and Computational Semantics*, pages 180–191, New Orleans, Louisiana. Association for Computational Linguistics.

Colin Raffel, Noam Shazeer, Adam Roberts, Katherine Lee, Sharan Narang, Michael Matena, Yanqi Zhou, Wei Li, and Peter J Liu. 2020. Exploring the limits of transfer learning with a unified text-to-text transformer. *Journal of Machine Learning Research*, 21:1–67.

Sascha Rothe, Shashi Narayan, and Aliaksei Severyn. 2020. Leveraging pre-trained checkpoints for sequence generation tasks. *Transactions of the Association for Computational Linguistics*, 8:264–280.

Victor Sanh, Thomas Wolf, Yonatan Belinkov, and Alexander M Rush. 2021. Learning from others' mistakes: Avoiding dataset biases without modeling them. In *International Conference on Learning Representations*.

Tal Schuster, Darsh Shah, Yun Jie Serene Yeo, Daniel Roberto Filizzola Ortiz, Enrico Santus, and Regina Barzilay. 2019. Towards debiasing fact verification models. In *Proceedings of the 2019 Conference on Empirical Methods in Natural Language Processing and the 9th International Joint Conference on Natural Language Processing (EMNLP-IJCNLP)*, pages 3419–3425, Hong Kong, China. Association for Computational Linguistics.

Joe Stacey, Pasquale Minervini, Haim Dubossarsky, Sebastian Riedel, and Tim Rocktäschel. 2020. Avoiding the Hypothesis-Only Bias in Natural Language Inference via Ensemble Adversarial Training. In *Proceedings of the 2020 Conference on Empirical Methods in Natural Language Processing (EMNLP)*, pages 8281–8291, Online. Association for Computational Linguistics.

Mukund Sundararajan, Ankur Taly, and Qiqi Yan. 2017. Axiomatic attribution for deep networks. In *Proceedings of the 34th International Conference on Machine Learning, ICML 2017, Sydney, NSW, Australia, 6-11 August 2017*, volume 70 of *Proceedings of Machine Learning Research*, pages 3319–3328. PMLR.

Masatoshi Tsuchiya. 2018. Performance impact caused by hidden bias of training data for recognizing textual entailment. In *Proceedings of the Eleventh International Conference on Language Resources and Evaluation (LREC 2018)*, Miyazaki, Japan. European Language Resources Association (ELRA).

Prasetya Ajie Utama, Nafise Sadat Moosavi, and Iryna Gurevych. 2020a. Mind the trade-off: Debiasing NLU models without degrading the in-distribution performance. In *Proceedings of the 58th Annual Meeting of the Association for Computational Linguistics*, pages 8717–8729, Online. Association for Computational Linguistics.

Prasetya Ajie Utama, Nafise Sadat Moosavi, and Iryna Gurevych. 2020b. Towards debiasing NLU models from unknown biases. In *Proceedings of the 2020 Conference on Empirical Methods in Natural Language Processing (EMNLP)*, pages 7597–7610, Online. Association for Computational Linguistics.

Adina Williams, Nikita Nangia, and Samuel Bowman. 2018. A broad-coverage challenge corpus for sentence understanding through inference. In *Proceedings of the 2018 Conference of the North American Chapter of the Association for Computational Linguistics: Human Language Technologies, Volume 1 (Long Papers)*, pages 1112–1122, New Orleans, Louisiana. Association for Computational Linguistics.

Thomas Wolf, Lysandre Debut, Victor Sanh, Julien Chaumond, Clement Delangue, Anthony Moi, Pierric Cistac, Tim Rault, Rémi Louf, Morgan Funtowicz, et al. 2019. Huggingface's transformers: State-of-the-art natural language processing. *ArXiv*, pages arXiv–1910.

Yaoming Zhu, Sidi Lu, Lei Zheng, Jiaxian Guo, Weinan Zhang, Jun Wang, and Yong Yu. 2018. Texygen: A benchmarking platform for text generation models. In *The 41st International ACM SIGIR Conference on Research & Development in Information Retrieval, SIGIR 2018, Ann Arbor, MI, USA, July 08-12, 2018*, pages 1097–1100. ACM.

A Appendix

A.1 Correlations

Figure 4 shows the correlations of generative and discriminative models to a bias model under different bias ratios in the synthetic bias case. Here the correlations are calculated on a biased test set, while in Section 5.3 they were calculated on an unbiased test set. The pattern is the same: the discriminative model is become more biased (higher ρ) as the bias ratio increases, while GEN remains unbiased (small ρ).

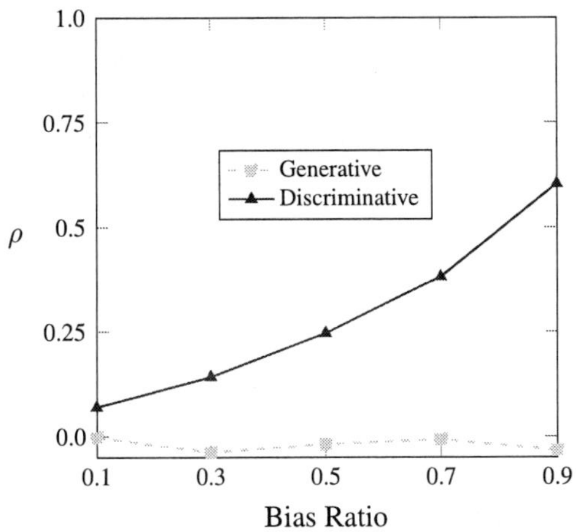

Figure 4: The correlation to a bias model (ρ) of generative and discriminative models under different bias ratios. ρ is calculated on a biased test set, so that each model used the same bias ratio at training and inference time.

A.2 Ablation study of fine-tuning pipeline

Our fine-tuning pipeline allows different ways to combine the steps, such as choosing a prior or whether to use another step of fine-tuning. Table 10 presents an ablation study of the different possible combinations, using BART on SNLI with hypothesis-only bias. (The table shows means and standard deviations of 3 runs with different random seeds.) Row 1 shows the results of GEN, without any fine-tuning; the same model from Section 3. Fine-tuning with a hypothesis-only prior leads to a smaller gap than fine-tuning with a uniform prior (compare rows 3 and 5). We can explain these apparently surprising results by the hypothesis-only prior capturing some of the bias, such that removing it during inference allows the predictions to be less biased. Fine-tuning with a uniform prior does not allow such a decomposition, resulting in a large gap (row 3). In contrast, using a hypothesis-only prior at inference leads to biased predictions (large generalization gaps; rows 2, 4 and 6). These models perform well on the test set (relative to using uniform prior at inference; rows 3, 5, 7), but relatively poorly on the o.o.d set. In fact, maintaining the same kind of prior throughout the pipeline (rows 3 and 6) leads to results similar to the discriminative baseline (row 11).

The fine-tuning step allows a balancing of bias and performance. Fine-tuning with a hypothesis-only prior and using a uniform prior at test time results in good o.o.d performance and relatively small generalization gaps (row 5). This setting achieve the smallest generalization gap that still beats the discriminative baseline (row 11).

Another consideration is the additional training time incurred by two phases of training. If we skip the generative training phase and directly train with the discriminative objective, we lose a bit in terms of test performance but maintain a good o.o.d performance, resulting in a medium-size generalization gap (row 9).

The model on row 9 shows comparable performance to the one in row 5, with a slight performance drop and a larger standard derivation. In practice, that model demonstrated slight instability and performed worse on the test and hard test sets than the model on row 6, showing that the initial generative training phase may allow the model to generalize better.

A.3 Data preparation for overlap bias

Table 11 shows an example for how a P, H pair is transformed to R, B which are used as an input to the model in Section 4.3.

A.4 Gradient Attributions Example

Table 12 gives qualitative examples for the phenomenon in Section 6.

A.5 Hyperparameters and Training Details

Table 13 shows the hyperparameters for the models used throughout the paper. We experimented with word dropout values of: $0.01, 0.1, 0.3, 0.5$, weight decay values of: $0.001, 0.01, 0.1, 1$, learning rate values in the range: $[10^{-6}, 10^{-4}]$, and maximum number of $5, 10, 20$ and 100 epochs. The values that achieved the best accuracy on the validation set appear in the table. All other hyperparameters are the default ones in Wolf et al. (2019). Where mean and standard deviation is specified, we calculate

	Training	Prior		Dev	Hard Dev	Δ
		Fine-tuning	Inference			
1	GEN	–	Uniform	71.14±0.4	72.68±0.2	**−1.54**±0.3
2		–	Hypothesis-only	84.99±0.3	64.29±0.7	20.69±0.9
3		Uniform	Uniform	**90.32**±0.1	77.17±0.8	13.15±0.7
4		Uniform	Hypothesis-only	89.31±0.5	70.33±1.9	18.98±1.4
5		Hypothesis-only	Uniform	87.12±0.5	**80.55**±0.1	6.57±0.5*
6		Hypothesis-only	Hypothesis-only	90.06±0.0	75.53±0.8	14.53±0.8
7	–	Uniform	Uniform	90.05±0.1	76.54±0.4	13.51±0.3
8		Uniform	Hypothesis-only	89.66±0.4	71.71±1.5	17.95±1.2
9		Hypothesis-only	Uniform	87.11±0.9	80.53±1.2	6.58±0.6
10		Hypothesis-only	Hypothesis-only	90.04±0.2	76.13±0.6	13.91±0.4
11		Discriminative baseline		91.49±0.0	79.59±0.5	11.90±0.5

Table 10: Ablations on SNLI validation set (Dev) with BART-base. Hard Dev was created similarly to SNLI hard (Gururangan et al., 2018). Fine-tuning is done with a discriminative objective, while inference is always using the generative objective. Uniform/Hypothesis-only refers to the kind of prior that was used during this phase. "*" marks the model with the smallest o.o.d generalization gap (Δ) that is better than the discriminative baseline.

Premise	Hypothesis
A smiling costumed **woman** is holding **an umbrella**	**A** happy **woman** in **a** fairy costume holds **an umbrella**
Remainder	**Bias**
A smiling costumed **woman** is holding **an umbrella** <SEP> **A** happy **woman** in **a** fairy costume holds **an umbrella**	**A** <mask> <mask> **woman** <mask> <mask> **an umbrella** <SEP> **A** <mask> **woman** <mask> **a** <mask> <mask> <mask> **an umbrella**

Table 11: Example for the data preparation for the overlap bias case.

those values over 3 runs, each with a different seed. Otherwise, those are the results of only one run.

Each experiment was performed on one or two NVIDIA RTX 2080 Ti GPUs. Training takes about 6–7 hours for discriminative models, 7–8 hours for generative models, and 15–20 hours for the discriminative fine-tuning step. Discriminative BERT/BART models have 109M/140M parameters, while generative BERT/BART models have 247M/139M parameters.

The experiment in Section 8 were preformed using NVIDIA A100s cards. The statistics for those experiments are presented in Table 14. All experiments used a batch size of 32, except for the model-tuned T5-XL and T5-XXL, which were trained with batch sizes of 16 and 8 respectively . For a fair comparison, we used T5.1.1 "LM Adapted" checkpoints, which are compatible with both model-tuning and prompt-tuning.[8] For prompt-tuning, we used 20 additional tokens, resulting in <100K trainable parameters even for the largest 11B model.

[8] https://github.com/google-research/text-to-text-transfer-transformer/blob/main/released_checkpoints.md#lm-adapted-t511lm100k

Premise	Hypothesis	Label
a woman in a black shirt looking at a bicycle .	a woman dressed in black shops for a bicycle .	entailment
a black man in a white uniform makes a spectacular reverse slam dunk to the crowd ' s amazement.	the man is asian	contradiction

Table 12: Gradient attributions example. Green/red show positive/negative attributions.

Model	Learning rate	No. of epochs	Word dropout	Weight decay
Discriminative / Hypothesis-only	10^{-5}	20	–	–
Generative	10^{-5}	20	–	–
Fine-tuning	$5 \cdot 10^{-6}$	5	0.1	0.1

Table 13: Hyperparameters for models. All of the models used early stooping of 3 epochs without improvement.

	Model	Number of Parameters (approx.)	Training Time (hours)	Number of GPUs For Training
Model-Tuning	Small	60M	2	1
	Base	220M	5	2
	Large	770M	10	2
	XL	2.8B	24	4
	XXL	11B	48	8
Prompt-Tuning	Small	60M + 10K	2	1
	Base	220M + 15K	4	1
	Large	770M + 20K	6	1
	XL	2.8B + 40K	15	2
	XXL	11B + 80K	20	4

Table 14: T5 model statistics. For the number of parameters for prompt-tuning, $X + Y$ means that the model has X frozen parameters, and additional Y learnable parameters are used for prompt-tuning.

Measuring Alignment Bias in Neural Seq2Seq Semantic Parsers

Davide Locatelli
Universitat Politècnica de Catalunya
Campus Nord, Barcelona
davide.locatelli@upc.edu

Ariadna Quattoni
Universitat Politècnica de Catalunya
Campus Nord, Barcelona
aquattoni@cs.upc.edu

Abstract

Prior to deep learning the semantic parsing community has been interested in understanding and modeling the range of possible word alignments between natural language sentences and their corresponding meaning representations. Sequence-to-sequence models changed the research landscape suggesting that we no longer need to worry about alignments since they can be learned automatically by means of an attention mechanism. More recently, researchers have started to question such premise. In this work we investigate whether seq2seq models can handle both simple and complex alignments. To answer this question we augment the popular GEO semantic parsing dataset with alignment annotations and create GEO-ALIGNED. We then study the performance of standard seq2seq models on the examples that can be aligned monotonically versus examples that require more complex alignments. Our empirical study shows that performance is significantly better over monotonic alignments. [1]

1 Introduction

In semantic parsing, the goal is to map natural language (NL) sentences into machine-readable meaning representations (MR) which allow for automated reasoning. For example, consider the following pair:

NL : *What is the population of Georgia ?*
MR : *answer (population (state (georgia)))*

Prior to deep learning models, a popular approach was to learn a grammar-based parser that explicitly models alignments between the NL and MR sequences (Wong and Mooney, 2006; Zettlemoyer and Collins, 2005, 2007; Lu et al., 2008; Kwiatkowksi et al., 2010; Kwiatkowski et al., 2011). The emergence of sequence-to-sequence (seq2seq) semantic parsers with attention mechanisms changed the research landscape: one of the initial premises of seq2seq models is that alignments no longer need to be explicitly modeled because the attention mechanisms will automatically learn them (Bahdanau et al., 2015). More recently, researchers started to question such premise, having observed that seq2seq models fail to make proper generalizations on out-of-distribution test sets on which traditional grammar-based models excel (Liu et al., 2020, 2021; Wang et al., 2021).

In this paper we follow this line of research and ask the questions: Can standard seq2seq models handle arbitrary alignments? And if not, what kind of alignment bias do they have? To answer these questions, we augment the GEO semantic parsing benchmark (Zelle and Mooney, 1996) with alignment annotations and create GEO-ALIGNED. We then compare the performance of seq2seq models on examples that can be easily aligned with simple monotonic alignments to the performance of these models on examples that require word reordering. Our empirical study shows that seq2seq parsers perform significantly better over examples that can be monotonically aligned. In other words, the flexibility of not having to explicitly model alignments comes at a cost: seq2seq models have difficulties in learning complex alignments.

The main contributions of this paper are:

1. We introduce a new dataset: GEO-ALIGNED that augments the GEO semantic benchmark with alignment annotations. We used the English and German versions of the original dataset, and we additionally introduce a new Italian version.

2. Using GEO-ALIGNED we define new evaluation splits to distinguish parsing performance

[1] The code and data is publicly available at https://github.com/interact-erc/geo-aligned

Proceedings of the 11th Joint Conference on Lexical and Computational Semantics, pages 200 - 207
July 14-15, 2022 ©2022 Association for Computational Linguistics

over easier and harder examples.

3. Our empirical study shows that seq2seq parsers are significantly better in handling monotonic alignments, and quantifies the impact of using attention.

4. As a side contribution we offer a measure of the complexity of the GEO dataset, showing that more than half of the examples involve monotonic alignments.

2 The GEO-ALIGNED Benchmark

In this section we describe the GEO-ALIGNED dataset, an augmentation of the popular GEO semantic parsing benchmark first introduced by Zelle and Mooney (1996). We start by providing a brief formal definition of word alignments following standard notation from the statistical machine translation literature, and we define monotonic and non-monotonic alignments (Wu, 2010). We then detail how we augment the GEO dataset and provide statistics that measure the complexity of the dataset.

2.1 Bi-text alignments

Given an input sequence of N words $\mathbf{x} = x_1, \ldots, x_N$, and a target sequence of M words $\mathbf{y} = y_1, \ldots, y_M$, a bi-text is defined as the tuple $(\mathbf{x}, \mathbf{y})$. A bi-text word alignment is a set of bi-symbols $\mathcal{A}$, where each bi-symbol (x_i, y_j) couples a word x_i in the input sequence at position i to a word y_j in the target sequence at position j.

If a word x_i from the input sequence does not need an alignment to a word in the target, we introduce an ε in $\mathbf{y}$ at position i. This bi-symbol (x_i, ε_i) amounts to a deletion, i.e. mapping from input to target involves deleting a word from the input. Conversely, if a word y_j from the target does not require an alignment to a word in the input, we introduce an ε in $\mathbf{x}$ at position j. This bi-symbol (ε_j, y_j) amounts to an insertion, i.e. mapping from input to target involves inserting an extra word in the target. We refer to the number of insertions and deletions in an alignment as the gap length. Figure 1 shows examples of alignments from the GEO-ALIGNED dataset.

2.2 Monotonic and non-monotonic alignments

Monotonic alignments are bi-text alignments where $\mathcal{A}$ contains bi-symbols of the forms (x_i, y_j), (x_i, ε_j) or (ε_i, y_j) where $i = j$. In other words, a monotonic alignment does not involve any reordering of the words. Conversely, non-monotonic alignments also include bi-symbols of the form (x_i, y_j) where $i \neq j$. Figure 1 shows an example of a monotonic alignment versus a non-monotonic one.

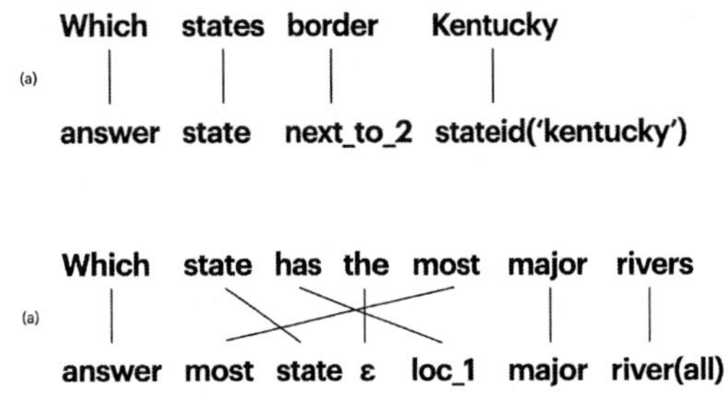

Figure 1: Examples alignments from the GEO-ALIGNED benchmark. Each bi-symbol is represented as a vertical line coupling words in the NL with words in the corresponding MR. The monotonic alignment (a) does not involve crossings of bi-symbols, while the non-monotonic alignment (b) involves considerable reordering.

2.3 Alignment annotation

The original GEO dataset contains 880 English questions about US geography, paired with a meaning representation. Several MR formalisms have been introduced for this dataset, including a first-order logic as in Zelle and Mooney (1996), a variable-free functional language introduced by Kate et al. (2005) and SQL (Popescu et al., 2003; Giordani and Moschitti, 2013; Iyer et al., 2017). In GEO-ALIGNED, we use the variable-free functional language formalism. Similarly to Wang et al. (2021), we further simplify the MR by removing the brackets. This is done to avoid introducing numerous ε in the alignments, and also to better reveal the structural similarity between the NL and MR sequences. Similarly to Dong and Lapata (2016), we remove constants used to identify states, rivers, cities, places and countries by substituting them with their type.

Alignments were provided by four expert annotators. For each pair, the annotators were first asked to decide whether there was a monotonic or non-monotonic alignment. Secondly, annotators were asked to provide the actual alignment from NL to MR words. More specifically, two annotators aligned the entire dataset, while the other two each annotated fifty disjoint examples. Inter-annotation agreement was calculated by comparing the alignments provided. A first agreement metric is Cohen's Kappa statistic (Cohen, 1960) to measure the agreement of monotonic versus non-monotonic labels: the average score obtained is 0.803, which corresponds to substantial agreement. We then calculated the average percentage of exact matches between the alignments of the two main annotators and each of the other three, which resulted in a 90% average match. Disagreements were resolved by keeping the annotation that best matched the alignment strategy taken by the majority.

Bi-text word alignments vary depending on the order in which the words appear both in the natural language and the meaning representation (Steedman, 2020). If we keep the MR fixed, a sentence in one language might be monotonically aligned, while the same sentence in another language might not be. To better understand the range of alignments between natural language utterances and meaning representations one should ideally consider multiple languages. With this objective in mind, we additionally annotated the German version (Jones et al., 2012) of GEO, and a new Italian version that we introduce, obtained by translations of the English sentences provided by an Italian native speaker.

The resulting dataset contains the NL and MR data pairs, augmented with

- a label indicating whether there is a monotonic alignment;
- the alignment that maps NL and MR words.

Table 1 reports annotation statistics for GEO-ALIGNED. In general, it can be observed that across all languages the majority of the alignments are monotonic and the average gap length is less than three. For non-monotonic alignments the average number of reordered words is below three.

With respect to differences between the three languages, Figure 2 shows a histogram of the gap lengths of monotonic alignments. As we can see the distributions are quite similar, but slightly shifted towards longer gaps for German and Italian. In particular, there are significantly more alignments with no gap in English. The proportion of monotonic alignments reflects the structural similarity between the variable-free MRs and the NL sequences. It is highest in the case of English, after which the MR formalism was modeled. German

Lang	Len	MP	MG	M0	NMR
EN	7.67	0.75	2.52	8.2	2.14
DE	7.72	0.65	2.91	0.55	2.52
IT	7.92	0.52	2.54	1.5	2.23

Table 1: Alignment annotation statistics for different languages. Len is the mean length of input NL sentences, MP is the percentage of monotonic alignments, MG is the average gap in monotonic alignments, M0 is the percentage of monotonic alignments with no gap, and NMR is the average number of words reordered in the non-monotonic alignments.

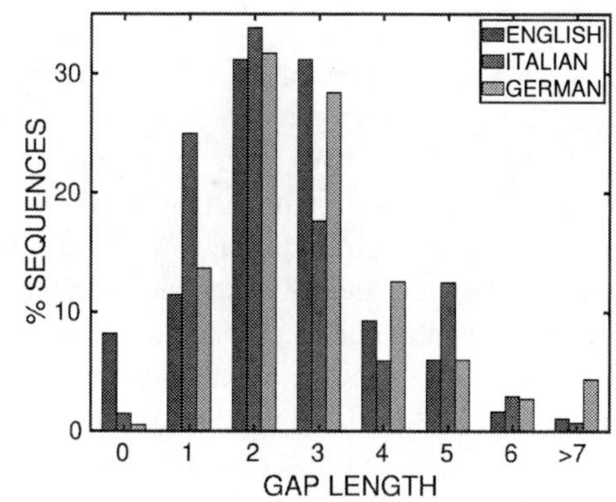

Figure 2: Distribution of gap lengths for the monotonic alignments.

is syntactically more similar to English than Italian and as a result it can be more easily aligned with the MR sequences. An exemplary syntactic difference is adjective placement: in English and German adjectives come before nouns, whilst in Italian they are usually placed after. When a superlative is used in the NL sentence, the MR, being modeled after English, places it before the noun. This creates a monotonic alignment with English and German sentences and a non-monotonic one with Italian ones. For example, if the question is *What is the largest state ?* the corresponding MR will be *answer(largest(state(all)))*. Because *largest* comes before *state* in both English and German as well as in the MR, the alignment will be monotonic. In Italian, *largest* comes after *state* and the alignment will require reordering.

3 Measuring Alignment Bias

3.1 Models and Experiments

The goal of our study is to compare the performance of neural seq2seq models over monotonic and non-monotonic alignments. Our hypothesis is that seq2seq models can implicitly learn monotonic alignments more easily than non-monotonic alignments. To evaluate this hypothesis we compared the performance of two seq2seq architectures on GEO-ALIGNED.

LSTM SEQ2SEQ A standard seq2seq model based on a bidirectional-LSTM encoder (Hochreiter and Schmidhuber, 1997; Schuster and Paliwal, 1997), and a unidirectional LSTM decoder that uses attention (Bahdanau et al., 2015). We then ablate the decoder of the attention layer to investigate its impact on the performance for the different alignments.

BART A pre-trained seq2seq model based on a bidirectional encoder and a left-to-right decoder (Lewis et al., 2020). Since it was pre-trained on English corpora, we only used this model on the English version of the dataset.

For our experiment we use exact-match accuracy as the evaluation metric, i.e. the percentage of exact matches between the predicted and ground-truth MRs. The alignment labels in GEO-ALIGNED allow us to break down the accuracy score for the two classes of alignments and observe whether the seq2seq framework has an implicit bias towards monotonic alignments. Further implementation and experimental setup details can be found in Appendix A.

3.2 Results

Table 2 shows the performance for the different models and languages. As we can observe accuracy for all models is significantly lower over non-monotonic alignments and this is true for all languages. The difference in performance between monotonic and non-monotonic alignments is more pronounced for models with no attention, but it holds true for all of them.

The performance follows the same pattern across languages and models: accuracies are higher for monotonic sequences than for non-monotonic ones. For English and Italian the differences are quite similar: models with attention score 0.13 point higher for monotonic sequences; without attention the difference is 0.19 for English and 0.17 for Italian. German has a lower accuracy overall. One possible explanation (as shown in Figure 2) is that the monotonic gap distribution for these two languages has a slight shift towards shorter gaps and in particular the sequences with no gap could help the models to implicitly induce better alignments. Moreover, the difference between monotonic and non-monotonic performance is starker: the model scored 0.19 and 0.23 better on monotonic examples with and without attention respectively. This might be due to the fact that more words are reordered on average for German than for the other two languages (see Table 1). Figure 3 shows accuracy for monotonic sequences binned by gap length. We observe that for all languages there is a negative correlation between accuracy and gap length.

We performed a qualitative analysis of the predictions by categorizing errors based on how many steps are needed to correct the mistake. Simpler errors are those where the correct MR can be recovered by inserting, deleting or changing at

Lang	Model	Acc	MAcc	NMAcc
EN	LSTM	0.83	0.87	0.74
	LSTM-attn	0.75	0.80	0.61
	BART	0.85	0.87	0.80
DE	LSTM	0.63	0.73	0.54
	LSTM-attn	0.57	0.69	0.46
IT	LSTM	0.77	0.84	0.71
	LSTM-attn	0.71	0.80	0.63

Table 2: Summary of results for the different models and languages: LSTM is the seq2seq model based on a bidirectional LSTM encoder and an LSTM decoder with attention. LSTM-attn ablates the attention layer in the decoder. Acc reports the overall accuracy for each model, MAcc and NMAcc are the accuracy over sequences with monotonic and non-monotonic alignments respectively.

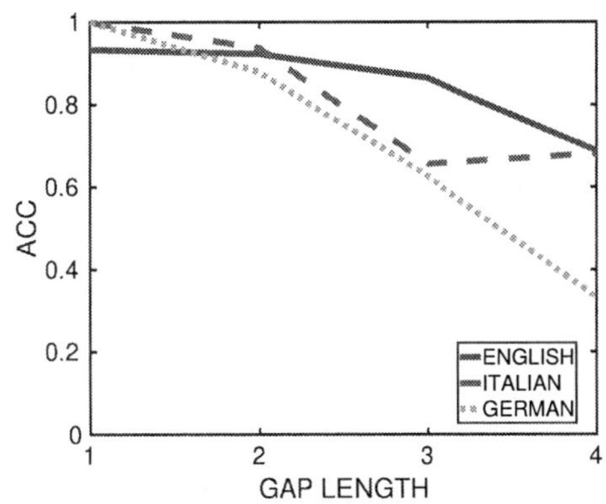

Figure 3: Accuracy for monotonic examples as a function of gap length.

Lang	Align	Model	1T	2T	Other
EN	M	LSTM	0.46	0.19	0.32
	NM	LSTM	0.24	0.15	0.61
	M	BART	0.67	0.25	0.08
	NM	BART	0.29	0.17	0.54
DE	M	LSTM	0.72	0.08	0.20
	NM	LSTM	0.32	0.27	0.41
IT	M	LSTM	0.72	0.05	0.23
	NM	LSTM	0.43	0.18	0.39

Table 3: Statistics of qualitative analysis on prediction errors. Align indicates the type of alignment: M stands for monotonic, NM for non-monotonic. 1T is the proportion of examples requiring a one-token correction without reordering. Similarly, 2T is for two-token corrections without reordering. Other is the proportion of examples requiring more complex corrections of three or more tokens, occasionally with reordering.

most two tokens, without reordering. An example is:

MR: *answer river loc_2 stateid state_name*
prediction: *answer loc_2 stateid state_name*

where the gold MR can be recovered by inserting *river* in the second position. More complex errors require correcting three or more tokens, and can also require reordering of the output. Table 3 reports statistics of our analysis. In general, we found that errors on monotonic examples are of the simpler category in much higher proportion than for non-monotonic: across languages, non-monotonic sequences require much more complex corrections involving three or more tokens as well as considerable reordering.

Another interesting finding is that, despite BART and our LSTM-based seq2seq model achieve similar results in English (see Table 2), the LSTM-based model makes more complex mistakes, particularly in the monotonic case. For these examples, the vast majority of the errors for BART were one-token, and we found that most of these were minor mistakes such as predicting the token *loc_2* instead of *loc_1*. The predictions of the LSTM-based model are more dissimilar to the gold MR.

4 Related Work

Several grammar formalisms have been proposed for semantic parsing, including categorical grammars (Steedman, 1996, 2000; Zettlemoyer and Collins, 2005; Clark and Curran, 2003; Zettlemoyer and Collins, 2007; Kwiatkowksi et al., 2010; Kwiatkowski et al., 2011) and synchronous context free grammars (Wong and Mooney, 2006). Both approaches model alignments explicitly and they are induced from data. There have also been attempts to derive a more general formalism to unify the different grammar based approaches to semantic parsing (Jones et al., 2011).

More recently, neural seq2seq models were proposed for semantic parsing in Dong and Lapata (2016); Jia and Liang (2016); Iyer et al. (2017). The seq2seq approach aims to relax the reliance upon high-quality lexicons, i.e. domain-specific word alignments. Most seq2seq systems implement an attention mechanism such as those proposed by Bahdanau et al. (2015); Luong et al. (2015); Xu et al. (2015), which can be seen as a strategy to learn soft alignments (Dong and Lapata, 2016).

Recently there has been an interest in testing the generalization abilities of neural semantic parsers, which resulted in the creation of several new benchmarks (Bastings et al., 2018; Lake and Baroni, 2018; Loula et al., 2018; Ruis et al., 2020; Keysers et al., 2020; Kim and Linzen, 2020) on which recent work has shown improved performance by introducing more alignment bias in the models either explicitly (Liu et al., 2021), or implicitly (Wang et al., 2021).

5 Conclusion

In this paper we introduced the GEO-ALIGNED dataset that offers an evaluation framework for testing the performance of semantic parsers over examples of varying alignment complexity. Our experiments have shown that seq2seq neural parsers perform significantly better over simpler monotonic alignments, suggesting that they have an implicit bias. We hope that GEO-ALIGNED can be used by other researchers to further test alignment biases.

Acknowledgments

The authors would like to thank the reviewers as well as the other members of the INTERACT group at Universitat Politècnica de Catalunya for their helpful feedback and suggestions. This work is supported by the European Research Council (ERC) under the European Union's Horizon 2020 research and innovation program (grant agreement No.853459).

References

Dzmitry Bahdanau, Kyunghyun Cho, and Yoshua Bengio. 2015. Neural machine translation by jointly learning to align and translate. In *3rd International Conference on Learning Representations, ICLR 2015, San Diego, CA, USA, May 7-9, 2015, Conference Track Proceedings*.

Jasmijn Bastings, Marco Baroni, Jason Weston, Kyunghyun Cho, and Douwe Kiela. 2018. Jump to better conclusions: SCAN both left and right. In *Proceedings of the 2018 EMNLP Workshop BlackboxNLP: Analyzing and Interpreting Neural Networks for NLP*, pages 47–55, Brussels, Belgium. Association for Computational Linguistics.

Stephen Clark and James Curran. 2003. Log-linear models for wide-coverage CCG parsing. In *Proceedings of the 2003 Conference on Empirical Methods in Natural Language Processing*, pages 97–104.

Jacob Cohen. 1960. A coefficient of agreement for nominal scales. *Educational and Psychological Measurement*, 20(1):37–46.

Li Dong and Mirella Lapata. 2016. Language to logical form with neural attention. In *Proceedings of the 54th Annual Meeting of the Association for Computational Linguistics (Volume 1: Long Papers)*, pages 33–43, Berlin, Germany. Association for Computational Linguistics.

Alessandra Giordani and Alessandro Moschitti. 2013. Automatic generation and reranking of sql-derived answers to nl questions. In *Trustworthy Eternal Systems via Evolving Software, Data and Knowledge*, pages 59–76, Berlin, Heidelberg. Springer Berlin Heidelberg.

Sepp Hochreiter and Jürgen Schmidhuber. 1997. Long short-term memory. *Neural computation*, 9:1735–80.

Srinivasan Iyer, Ioannis Konstas, Alvin Cheung, Jayant Krishnamurthy, and Luke Zettlemoyer. 2017. Learning a neural semantic parser from user feedback. In *Proceedings of the 55th Annual Meeting of the Association for Computational Linguistics (Volume 1: Long Papers)*, pages 963–973, Vancouver, Canada. Association for Computational Linguistics.

Robin Jia and Percy Liang. 2016. Data recombination for neural semantic parsing. In *Proceedings of the 54th Annual Meeting of the Association for Computational Linguistics (Volume 1: Long Papers)*, pages 12–22, Berlin, Germany. Association for Computational Linguistics.

Bevan Jones, Mark Johnson, and Sharon Goldwater. 2011. Formalizing semantic parsing with tree transducers. In *Proceedings of the Australasian Language Technology Association Workshop 2011*, pages 19–28, Canberra, Australia.

Bevan Jones, Mark Johnson, and Sharon Goldwater. 2012. Semantic parsing with Bayesian tree transducers. In *Proceedings of the 50th Annual Meeting of the Association for Computational Linguistics (Volume 1: Long Papers)*, pages 488–496, Jeju Island, Korea. Association for Computational Linguistics.

Rohit Kate, Yuk Wong, and Raymond Mooney. 2005. Learning to transform natural to formal languages. volume 3, pages 1062–1068.

Daniel Keysers, Nathanael Schärli, Nathan Scales, Hylke Buisman, Daniel Furrer, Sergii Kashubin, Nikola Momchev, Danila Sinopalnikov, Lukasz Stafiniak, Tibor Tihon, Dmitry Tsarkov, Xiao Wang, Marc van Zee, and Olivier Bousquet. 2020. Measuring compositional generalization: A comprehensive method on realistic data. In *International Conference on Learning Representations*.

Najoung Kim and Tal Linzen. 2020. COGS: A compositional generalization challenge based on semantic interpretation. In *Proceedings of the 2020 Conference on Empirical Methods in Natural Language Processing (EMNLP)*, pages 9087–9105, Online. Association for Computational Linguistics.

Tom Kwiatkowksi, Luke Zettlemoyer, Sharon Goldwater, and Mark Steedman. 2010. Inducing probabilistic CCG grammars from logical form with higher-order unification. In *Proceedings of the 2010 Conference on Empirical Methods in Natural Language Processing*, pages 1223–1233, Cambridge, MA. Association for Computational Linguistics.

Tom Kwiatkowski, Luke Zettlemoyer, Sharon Goldwater, and Mark Steedman. 2011. Lexical generalization in CCG grammar induction for semantic parsing. In *Proceedings of the 2011 Conference on Empirical Methods in Natural Language Processing*, pages 1512–1523, Edinburgh, Scotland, UK. Association for Computational Linguistics.

Brenden Lake and Marco Baroni. 2018. Generalization without systematicity: On the compositional skills of sequence-to-sequence recurrent networks. pages 2873–2882. PMLR.

Mike Lewis, Yinhan Liu, Naman Goyal, Marjan Ghazvininejad, Abdelrahman Mohamed, Omer Levy, Veselin Stoyanov, and Luke Zettlemoyer. 2020. BART: Denoising sequence-to-sequence pre-training for natural language generation, translation, and comprehension. In *Proceedings of the 58th Annual Meeting of the Association for Computational Linguistics*, pages 7871–7880, Online. Association for Computational Linguistics.

Chenyao Liu, Shengnan An, Zeqi Lin, Qian Liu, Bei Chen, Jian-Guang Lou, Lijie Wen, Nanning Zheng, and Dongmei Zhang. 2021. Learning algebraic recombination for compositional generalization. In *Findings of the Association for Computational Linguistics: ACL-IJCNLP 2021*, pages 1129–1144, Online. Association for Computational Linguistics.

Qian Liu, Shengnan An, Jian-Guang Lou, Bei Chen, Zeqi Lin, Yan Gao, Bin Zhou, Nanning Zheng, and Dongmei Zhang. 2020. Compositional generalization by learning analytical expressions. In *NeurIPS*.

João Loula, Marco Baroni, and Brenden Lake. 2018. Rearranging the familiar: Testing compositional generalization in recurrent networks. In *Proceedings of the 2018 EMNLP Workshop BlackboxNLP: Analyzing and Interpreting Neural Networks for NLP*, pages 108–114, Brussels, Belgium. Association for Computational Linguistics.

Wei Lu, Hwee Tou Ng, Wee Sun Lee, and Luke S. Zettlemoyer. 2008. A generative model for parsing natural language to meaning representations. In *Proceedings of the 2008 Conference on Empirical Methods in Natural Language Processing*, pages 783–792, Honolulu, Hawaii. Association for Computational Linguistics.

Thang Luong, Hieu Pham, and Christopher D. Manning. 2015. Effective approaches to attention-based neural machine translation. In *Proceedings of the 2015 Conference on Empirical Methods in Natural Language Processing*, pages 1412–1421, Lisbon, Portugal. Association for Computational Linguistics.

Ana-Maria Popescu, Oren Etzioni, and Henry Kautz. 2003. Towards a theory of natural language interfaces to databases. In *Proceedings of the 8th International Conference on Intelligent User Interfaces*, IUI '03, page 149–157, New York, NY, USA. Association for Computing Machinery.

Laura Ruis, Jacob Andreas, Marco Baroni, Diane Bouchacourt, and Brenden M Lake. 2020. A benchmark for systematic generalization in grounded language understanding. *Advances in neural information processing systems*, 33:19861–19872.

M. Schuster and K.K. Paliwal. 1997. Bidirectional recurrent neural networks. *IEEE Transactions on Signal Processing*, 45(11):2673–2681.

Mark Steedman. 1996. *Surface structure and interpretation*. MIT press.

Mark Steedman. 2000. *The syntactic process*. MIT press.

Mark Steedman. 2020. A formal universal of natural language grammar. *Language*, 96:618–660.

Bailin Wang, Mirella Lapata, and Ivan Titov. 2021. Structured reordering for modeling latent alignments in sequence transduction. In *Advances in Neural Information Processing Systems*.

Thomas Wolf, Lysandre Debut, Victor Sanh, Julien Chaumond, Clement Delangue, Anthony Moi, Pierric Cistac, Tim Rault, Rémi Louf, Morgan Funtowicz, Joe Davison, Sam Shleifer, Patrick von Platen, Clara Ma, Yacine Jernite, Julien Plu, Canwen Xu, Teven Le Scao, Sylvain Gugger, Mariama Drame, Quentin Lhoest, and Alexander M. Rush. 2020. Transformers: State-of-the-art natural language processing. In *Proceedings of the 2020 Conference on Empirical Methods in Natural Language Processing: System Demonstrations*, pages 38–45, Online. Association for Computational Linguistics.

Yuk Wah Wong and Raymond Mooney. 2006. Learning for semantic parsing with statistical machine translation. In *Proceedings of the Human Language Technology Conference of the NAACL, Main Conference*, pages 439–446, New York City, USA. Association for Computational Linguistics.

Dekai Wu. 2010. Alignment. In Nitin Indurkhya and Fred Damerau, editors, *Handbook of Natural Language Processing*. Chapman Hall/CRC.

Kelvin Xu, Jimmy Lei Ba, Ryan Kiros, Kyunghyun Cho, Aaron Courville, Ruslan Salakhutdinov, Richard S. Zemel, and Yoshua Bengio. 2015. Show, attend and tell: Neural image caption generation with visual attention. In *Proceedings of the 32nd International Conference on International Conference on Machine Learning - Volume 37*, ICML, page 2048–2057. JMLR.org.

John M. Zelle and Raymond J. Mooney. 1996. Learning to parse database queries using inductive logic programming. In *Proceedings of the Thirteenth National Conference on Artificial Intelligence - Volume 2*, AAAI'96, page 1050–1055. AAAI Press.

Luke Zettlemoyer and Michael Collins. 2007. Online learning of relaxed CCG grammars for parsing to logical form. In *Proceedings of the 2007 Joint Conference on Empirical Methods in Natural Language Processing and Computational Natural Language Learning (EMNLP-CoNLL)*, pages 678–687, Prague, Czech Republic. Association for Computational Linguistics.

Luke S. Zettlemoyer and Michael Collins. 2005. Learning to map sentences to logical form: Structured classification with probabilistic categorial grammars. In *Proceedings of the 21st Conference on Uncertainty in Artificial Intelligence*, UAI, page 658–666, Arlington, Virginia, USA. AUAI Press.

A Implementation and training details

We based our LSTM-based seq2seq model on Bahdanau et al. (2015). We use a one-layer bidirectional LSTM for our encoder and a one-layer unidirectional LSTM for our decoder. At training we minimize the cross entropy loss between the predictions and the ground-truth MR sequences. We use a batch size of 32, Adam optimizer and learning rate of 0.001. We manually tune the hyperparameters, and train for 100 epochs on one NVIDIA TESLA V100 16GB GPU.

For BART, we used the pre-trained BART-base model provided by the HuggingFace transformers library (Wolf et al., 2020). We fine-tune for 100 epochs with a learning rate of 0.00001 on one NVIDIA TESLA V100 16GB GPU. Fine-tuning took approximately 1h30mins.

Improved Induction of Narrative Chains via Cross-Document Relations

Andrew Blair-Stanek
University of Maryland
Carey School of Law
ablair-stanek@law.umaryland.edu

Benjamin Van Durme
Department of Computer Science
Johns Hopkins University
vandurme@cs.jhu.edu

Abstract

The standard approach for inducing narrative chains considers statistics gathered per individual document. We consider whether statistics gathered using cross-document relations can lead to improved chain induction. Our study is motivated by legal narratives, where cases typically cite thematically similar cases. We consider four novel variations on pointwise mutual information (PMI), each accounting for cross-document relations in a different way. One proposed PMI variation performs 58% better relative to standard PMI on recall@50 and induces qualitatively better narrative chains.

1 Introduction

Narrative chains are sets of events centered around a common protagonist. They can be induced from corpora using various unsupervised methods, many using pointwise mutual information (PMI) between events. To our knowledge, no prior work has used the information available in relations between documents in a corpus when inducing narrative chains.

To illustrate the potential for improved narrative chain induction based on document relations, we develop four novel variants of pointwise mutual information (PMI) that assume a directed graph structure between documents (i.e. relations that are edges). We test these[1] on a corpus of all U.S. federal court cases, which has a readily accessible relation between documents: citation. One case will cite prior cases as precedent in explaining its decision. We find that one of our four variants of PMI performs particularly well in the standard event cloze evaluation (Chambers and Jurafsky, 2008) and in inducing meaningful narrative chains.

2 Background

Unsupervised *narrative chain* induction from a corpus was introduced by Chambers and Jurafsky (2008), inspired by the notion of *scripts* owing to Schank and Abelson (1977). Coreference chains were extracted over the Gigaword corpus (Graff, 2002) to extract event chains with the same protagonist. A syntactic parser identified each *event* in which the protagonist was involved, defined as the combination of a verb and dependency relation, such as (convict, obj). They then calculated the pointwise mutual information (PMI) (Church and Hanks, 1989, 1990) for each combination of two events and used this PMI to do agglomerative clustering to induce narrative chains. We follow the basic approach of Chambers and Jurafsky (2008), with the major extension that we take relations between the documents into account for the first time.

There have been numerous improvements on the Chambers and Jurafsky (2008) approach, including using language modeling approaches (Rudinger et al., 2015), neural networks (Pichotta and Mooney, 2016; Weber et al., 2018), and graphs where events are the vertices (Li et al., 2018, 2021). None of these improvements has considered relations between documents in the corpus.

3 Alternative Measures

Much of the narrative chain induction literature, following Chambers and Jurafsky (2008), has used PMI. Specifically, for any given coreference chain C anywhere in the corpus, the standard PMI of two events e_1 and e_2 is defined by,

$$pmi_{standard}(e_1, e_2) = \log \frac{P(e_1 \in C \wedge e_2 \in C)}{P(e_1 \in C)P(e_2 \in C)}$$

PMI provides a measure of how often e_1 and e_2 actually occur together, as compared to what we would expect if they were independent. If they were independent, then:

$$P(e_1 \in C \wedge e_2 \in C) = P(e_1 \in C)P(e_2 \in C)$$

Note that the definition of $pmi_{standard}$ has the equation above's left hand side in the numerator and right hand side in the denominator.

[1] Code is at https://github.com/BlairStanek/cross-doc

Proceedings of the 11th Joint Conference on Lexical and Computational Semantics, pages 208 - 212
July 14-15, 2022

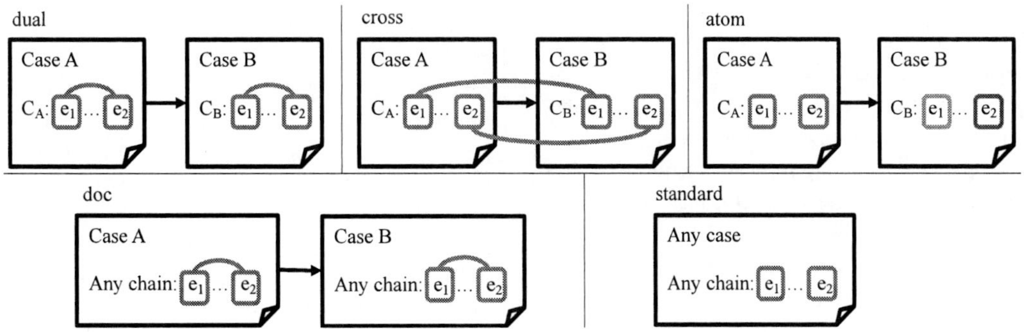

Figure 1: Illustration of events considered in the denominator of each PMI variant. Case A cites case B.

Given some relation between the documents making up the corpus, e.g. case citations, we consider four different ways to define an extension of PMI. One is document-by-document, and three are chain-by-chain.

To develop the three chain-by-chain measures, we define A and B to be documents with a relation (e.g. case A cites case B), and define C_A to be a chain of events in document A, and C_B to be a chain of events in document B. Thus, assuming independence between all occurrences of e_1 and e_2, we can derive four equivalent expressions:

$$\begin{aligned}&P(e_1 \in C_A \wedge e_2 \in C_A \wedge e_1 \in C_B \wedge e_2 \in C_B)\\ =&P(e_1 \in C_A \wedge e_2 \in C_A)P(e_1 \in C_B \wedge e_2 \in C_B)\\ =&P(e_1 \in C_A \wedge e_1 \in C_B)P(e_2 \in C_A \wedge e_2 \in C_B)\\ =&P(e_1 \in C_A)P(e_2 \in C_A)\cdot\\ &\quad P(e_1 \in C_B)P(e_2 \in C_B)\end{aligned}$$

These are the probabilities that, if you randomly select a chain C_A and a chain C_B where case A cites case B, that these chains have these events. For example, if you've randomly selected C_A and C_B, then $P(e_1 \in C_A)$ is the probability that the event e_1 appears in C_A.

By taking the first expression above as the numerator and using the last three expressions above as the denominators, we get three different extensions of PMI:

$$pmi_{dual}(e_1, e_2) = \log \frac{P(e_1, e_2 \in C_A \wedge e_1, e_2 \in C_B)}{P(e_1, e_2 \in C_A)P(e_1, e_2 \in C_B)}$$

$$pmi_{cross}(e_1, e_2) = \log \frac{P(e_1, e_2 \in C_A \wedge e_1, e_2 \in C_B)}{P(e_1 \in C_A, C_B)P(e_2 \in C_A, C_B)}$$

$$pmi_{atom}(e_1, e_2) = \log \frac{P(e_1, e_2 \in C_A \wedge e_1, e_2 \in C_B)}{P(e_1 \in C_A)P(e_2 \in C_A)P(e_1 \in C_B)P(e_2 \in C_B)}$$

A fourth approach can come from considering an analogous measure that works document-by-document, rather than chain-by-chain. Given related documents A and B (e.g. case A cites case B), if we assume that occurrences of e_1 and e_2 are independent, then the following must be true:

$$\begin{aligned}&P(\exists C_A : e_1, e_2 \in C_A \wedge \exists C_B : e_1, e_2 \in C_B)\\ =&P(\exists C_A : e_1, e_2 \in C_A)P(\exists C_B : e_1, e_2 \in C_B)\end{aligned}$$

This expression, unlike the chain-by-chain expression, cannot be further factored into two other alternatives. Why? There can be (and typically are) multiple chains in each document. Within a document, there may exist no chains with both e_1 and e_2, even though there exists a chain with e_1 and another chain with e_2.

We can get the fourth extension of PMI by dividing the two sides of the equation directly above:

$$pmi_{doc}(e_1, e_2) = \log \frac{P(\exists C_A\colon e_1,e_2 \in C_A \wedge \exists C_B\colon e_1,e_2 \in C_B)}{P(\exists C_A\colon e_1,e_2 \in C_A)P(\exists C_B\colon e_1,e_2 \in C_B)}$$

4 Experimental Setup

4.1 Dataset

We used all U.S. federal court cases since 1970 that have at least 800 total characters and that either cite to or are cited by another U.S. federal court case. All text came from the Caselaw Access Project (CAP). Cases with under 800 characters and cases neither cited to or by other federal were summary dispositions or procedural rulings that lacked meaningful description of the underlying facts of the case. The resulting corpus had 965,467 cases. (Each case is exactly one document.)

4.2 Coreference

Following Chambers and Jurafsky (2008) and subsequent literature, we extract all coreference chains from each document in the corpus. Since court decisions may be quite long (often exceeding 100,000 characters), we use the efficient long-coreference methodology of Xia et al. (2020). We hand-annotated coreference on 35 randomly selected cases (with average length of 3,518 words per case) aiming to fine-tune that model.[2] We only hand-annotated 35 cases since annotating a long document for coreference takes substantial human effort. We found that Xia et al. (2020)'s original model achieved 0.931 F1 on those 35 cases. Unfortunately, fine-tuning on splits of these 35 cases, with a variety of hyperparameters, uniformly reduced performance below this baseline.

So, we proceeded with (Xia et al., 2020)'s original model on all 965,467 cases, which took approximately 4100 hours of Quadro RTX GPU processing time. The coreference spans are available to download,[3] and we will share the spans plus tokens with those with researcher approval from the Caselaw Access Project.

4.3 Parsing and Chain Extraction

We use Stanford CoreNLP (Manning et al., 2020) for syntactic parsing, including POS tagging, lemmatization, and dependency parsing. We then use PredPatt (White et al., 2016) to extract predicates and arguments from the dependency parse. If an argument matches one of the entities identified during coreference, we consider the event as a 2-tuple of the predicate's lemma and the dependency type (e.g. (convict, obj)). Although the predicate is often a verb, it need not be, unlike in Chambers and Jurafsky (2008), which restricted predicates to being verbs. We retained all chains of length 2 or more; most cases had multiple chains. We do not follow Chambers and Jurafsky (2008) in attempting partial temporal ordering of events. Thus, each chain is an unordered set of events that shares the same co-referring entity.

Using these chains, we calculated all four of our proposed PMI variations that rely on the relations between documents (i.e., citations between cases). We also calculated $pmi_{standard}$, which does not rely on the relations. All these training calculations were by CPU and ran on the entire corpus, except for some cases held out for testing. So, the calculations were run on 955,810 cases, between which there were 10,606,964 citation relations, containing a total of 27,166,457 chains and 24,364,877,760 combinations of chain C_A from case A and chain C_B from case B, where case A cites case B. The complete set of event chains from each case are available for download.[4]

Measure	R@1	R@5	R@50	MRR
$\text{pmi}_{standard}$	1.7%	4.9%	15.9%	0.037
pmi_{dual}	0.4%	1.2%	6.1%	0.011
pmi_{cross}	**2.1%**	**6.6%**	**25.2%**	**0.050**
pmi_{atom}	1.4%	4.5%	19.0%	0.036
pmi_{doc}	0.4%	1.2%	6.3%	0.012

Table 1: Cloze Performance on test set of 27,324 held-out chains, measured by Recall@1, Recall@5, Recall@50, and Mean Reciprocal Rank.

5 Results and Discussion

5.1 Quantitative evaluation

We measure the effectiveness of the different measures of PMI using the event cloze task, following Chambers and Jurafsky (2008), where we randomly remove an event from each test chain and use the PMI measures to predict what event should fill that. For test, we used 0.3 percent of the corpus (2783 cases) that had been held back and not used to calculate any of the PMI measures, either as a citing case or cited case. We used all chains with 3 or more events, which resulted in 27,324 chains used for the cloze test, each with one event randomly removed. (We used chains with 3 or more events because, when removing one event for cloze, that leaves chains with 2 or more events.) Each possible event that might complete the cloze is evaluated as the sum of the PMIs with the other events in the chain (i.e. other than the one removed). We measure performance in several ways: the percentage of chains where the correct event is the top prediction (recall@1); within the top 5 predictions (recall@5); within the top 50 predictions (recall@50); and, finally, mean reciprocal rank (MRR).

Looking at Table 1, we see that two of our four PMI variants substantially underperform standard PMI: pmi_{doc} and pmi_{dual}. It is worth noting that the former is just a document-by-document version

[2] The full 35 annotations are at https://doi.org/10.7281/T1/QVAHMD

[3] https://doi.org/10.7281/T1/QVAHMD

[4] https://doi.org/10.7281/T1/QVAHMD

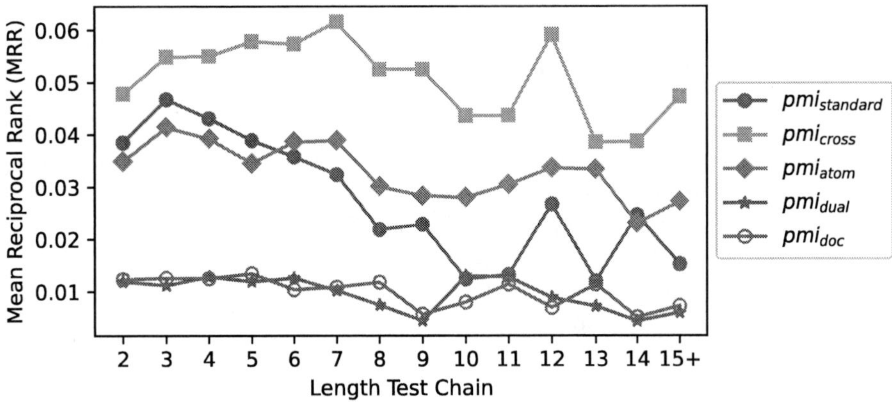

Figure 2: Performance of the five types of PMI, measured by mean reciprocal rank, by length of the test chain. For example, a test chain of length 2 originally had 3 events, one of which is removed for cloze prediction, and the reported performance is how well that PMI measure predicts the actual removed event.

of the latter. Both compare the frequency of both events e_1 and e_2 in both a cited and citing case to the frequency of both events in cases by themselves. We hypothesize that the decision of a court to cite a previous decision is noisy and unpredictable, so that even when both an earlier case and a later case have a chain with both e_1 and e_2, the decision of the judge authoring the later case to cite the earlier case is noisy.

By contrast, pmi_{cross} normalizes out the noisiness of the decision of whether to cite or not. Its denominator uses the probability that e_1 is in both C_A and C_B multiplied by the probability that e_2 is in both C_A and C_B. By definition, these probabilities already take into account the decision of the author of the later case A to cite the earlier case B. We observe that pmi_{cross} substantially outperforms the standard $pmi_{standard}$ that has been the foundation for most narrative chain induction work, achieving a recall@50 of 25.2% (versus 15.9%, a 58% relative improvement) and a mean reciprocal rank (MRR) of 0.050 (versus 0.037).

Note that the cloze test used for this evaluation runs entirely on chains within a single case, not relying in any way on citation relations between cases. Yet our newly introduced pmi_{cross}, which is calculated using the citation relations, outperforms $pmi_{standard}$, which is calculated solely on chains within single cases and does not use the relations.

To determine whether these trends in performance are attributable to chains of a particular length, in Figure 2 we graph all five variations of PMI by chain length. We see that pmi_{cross} outperforms all other measures, including $pmi_{standard}$ for all chain lengths.

5.2 Qualitative evaluation

High-quality narrative chains should correspond to sensible groupings of events actually encountered. A U.S.-trained lawyer reviewed a sample of chains from both and found that the narrative chains induced using pmi_{cross} and agglomerative clustering are qualitatively better than those induced in the same way but using $pmi_{standard}$. To do agglomerative clustering, we build a cluster around every set of two events that appears in any chain, and we repeatedly add the event with the highest sum of PMIs with the existing events, until we reach a desired maximum set size (we used 6). These sets are the narrative chains. We use dynamic programming to avoid duplication, and we rank the final clusters by the total sum of PMIs between all elements. Here are two 6-event-long example narrative chains induced using pmi_{cross} that were not induced using $pmi_{standard}$. One relates to a criminal defendant and the other relates to a trademark being found generic and thus invalid (as happened to Kleenex's trademark):

(have, nsubj)	(trademark, nsubj)
(commit, nsubj)	(mark, nsubj)
(perpetrate, nsubj)	(term, nsubj)
(plead, nsubj)	(use, nsubj:pass)
(sentence, obj)	(descriptive, nsubj)
(serve, nsubj)	(generic, nsubj)

6 Conclusion

We have explored four new measures of PMI that can take advantage of relationships between documents in corpora. Applying them to the corpus of federal cases, we find that one such measure, pmi_{cross} shows substantial improvement over standard PMI. Future work may consider the use of these new PMI measures on other corpora where the documents may have relationships that can be characterized as directed edges, including hyperlinks and references.[5]

We focused on a PMI-based approach to inducing narrative chains owing to its familiarity within the community. Based on these results demonstrating the benefits of utilizing document-to-document relations, future work can consider extensions such as using temporal relations, causality, and neural modeling.

Acknowledgements

The authors would like to thank Patrick Xia, Nils Holzenberger, Rachel Rudinger, Anton Belyy, Noah Weber, and the anonymous reviewers.

References

Caselaw access project. `https://case.law`. Accessed: 2020.

Nathanael Chambers and Dan Jurafsky. 2008. Unsupervised learning of narrative event chains. In *Proceedings of the Association of Computational Linguistics*, pages 789–797.

Kenneth Church and Patrick Hanks. 1989. Word association norms, mutual information, and lexicography. In *ACL 27th Annual Meeting*, pages 76–83.

Kenneth Church and Patrick Hanks. 1990. Word association norms, mutual information, and lexicography. *Computational linguistics*, 16(1):22–29.

David Graff. 2002. English gigaword. *Linguistic Data Consortium.*

Manling Li, Sha Li, Zhenhailong Wang, Lifu Huang, Kyunghyun Cho, Heng Ji, Jiawei Han, and Clare Voss. 2021. The future is not one-dimensional: Complex event schema induction by graph modeling for event prediction. In *Proceedings of the 2021 Conference on Empirical Methods in Natural Language Processing*, pages 5203–5215.

Zhongyang Li, Xiao Ding, and Ting Liu. 2018. Constructing narrative event evolutionary graph for script event prediction. In *Proceedings of the Twenty-Seventh International Joint Conference on Artificial Intelligence (IJCAI-18)*, pages 4201–4207.

Christopher Manning, Mihai Surdeanu, John Bauer, Jenny Finkel, Steven J. Bethard, and David McClosky. 2020. The Stanford CoreNLP Natural Language Processing Toolkit. In *Proceedings of the 52nd Annual Meeting of the Association for Computational Linguistics: System Demonstrations*, pages 55–60.

Karl Pichotta and Raymond J. Mooney. 2016. Learning statistical scripts with LSTM recurrent neural networks. In *Proceedings of the Thirtieth AAAI Conference on Artificial Intelligence*, pages 2800–2806.

Rachel Rudinger, Pushpendre Rastogi, Francis Ferraro, and Benjamin Van Durme. 2015. Script induction as language modeling. In *In Proceedings of the 2015 Conference on Empirical Methods in Natural Language Processing*, pages 1681–1686.

Roger C. Schank and Robert P. Abelson. 1977. *Scripts, plans, goals and understanding: An inquiry into human knowledge structures.*

Noah Weber, Leena Shekhar, Niranjan Balasubramanian, and Nathanael Chambers. 2018. Hierarchical quantized representations for script generation. In *Proceedings of the 2018 Conference on Empirical Methods in Natural Language Processing*, pages 3783–3792.

Aaron Steven White, Drew Reisinger, Keisuke Sakaguchi, Tim Vieira, Sheng Zhang, Rachel Rudinger, Kyle Rawlins, and Benjamin Van Durme. 2016. Universal decompositional semantics on Universal Dependencies. In *Proceedings of the 2016 Conference on Empirical Methods in Natural Language Processing*, pages 1713–1723.

Patrick Xia, João Sedoc, and Benjamin Van Durme. 2020. Incremental neural coreference resolution in constant memory. In *Proceedings of the 2020 Conference on Empirical Methods in Natural Language Processing*, pages 8617–8624.

[5]Our new PMI measures can trivially be extended to relationships that are undirected edges or even weighted edges.

DRS Parsing as Sequence Labeling

Minxing Shen
Heinrich Heine University Düsseldorf
Universitätsstraße 1
40225 Düsseldorf, Germany
minxing.shen@hhu.de

Kilian Evang
Heinrich Heine University Düsseldorf
Universitätsstraße 1
40225 Düsseldorf, Germany
kilian.evang@hhu.de

Abstract

We present the first fully trainable semantic parser for English, German, Italian, and Dutch discourse representation structures (DRSs) that is competitive in accuracy with recent sequence-to-sequence models and at the same time *compositional* in the sense that the output maps each token to one of a finite set of meaning *fragments*, and the meaning of the utterance is a function of the meanings of its parts. We argue that this property makes the system more transparent and more useful for human-in-the-loop annotation. We achieve this simply by casting DRS parsing as a sequence labeling task, where tokens are labeled with both fragments (lists of abstracted clauses with relative referent indices indicating unification) and *symbols* like word senses or names. We give a comprehensive error analysis that highlights areas for future work.[1]

1 Introduction

Semantic parsing is the task of mapping natural-language sentences to symbolic representations of their meaning. Although most current natural language understanding (NLU) applications are handled by end-to-end systems that solve specific tasks (such as machine translation, conversation, or sentiment analysis) without intermediate symbolic meaning representations, semantic parsing continues to attract research interest for good reasons: first, next-generation NLU systems may become more accurate and certainly more easily explainable and debuggable by combining symbolic representations with end-to-end techniques. Second, symbolic meaning representations are amenable to symbolic reasoning, which may be instrumental in enabling, e.g., digital assistants to solve more complex tasks. Third, better and more transparent computational models of text-meaning mapping can be a useful tool for semantics, i.e., to understand how natural-language semantics works.

In recent years, most work on annotating natural-language text with comprehensive, broad-coverage meaning representations has been performed in three frameworks: Abstract Meaning Representations (Banarescu et al., 2013), Universal Cognitive Conceptual Annotation (Abend and Rappoport, 2013), and Discourse Representation Structures (Abzianidze et al., 2017). Accurate parsers exist for all three (e.g., Lindemann et al., 2020; Oepen et al., 2020; van Noord et al., 2020). Each formalism has its specific strength: AMRs go very far in abstracting away from surface variation in how a certain meaning is expressed, UCCA has a clear mapping between form and meaning and a modular architecture, and DRSs ground natural language meaning in first-order logic, by explicitly representing the scopes of negation, quantification, disjunction, etc. In this paper, we focus on parsing to DRSs.

State-of-the-art DRS parsers follow the encoder-decoder paradigm pioneered for machine translation by Sutskever et al. (2014): the input sequence is encoded by a neural network into a vector, then another network predicts the output sequence (or in this case: output DRS) from that vector. Rather than improve upon the accuracy of such parsers on standard benchmarks, our aim in this paper is to achieve some of their benefits (ability to learn from examples, high accuracy, low computational complexity, robustness to atypical input, utilization of off-the-shelf language models, conceptual simplicity) while also having a degree of *compositionality*, traditionally a property of grammar-based systems. Specifically, our system learns to assign each token of an utterance one of a finite set of abstract meaning *fragments* that are deterministically combined to give the meaning of the whole utterance. While our system may not fulfill all criteria of compositionality according to some definitions, it can

[1]Our system is available at https://github.com/ShenMinX/DRS-parser

Proceedings of the 11th Joint Conference on Lexical and Computational Semantics, pages 213 - 225
July 14-15, 2022 ©2022 Association for Computational Linguistics

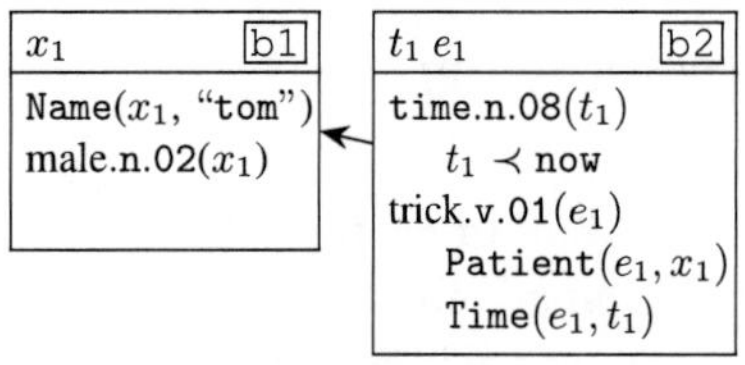

Figure 1: DRS for the sentence "Tom was tricked" in box notation

```
b1 REF x1                    % Tom [0...3]
b1 Name x1 "tom"             % Tom [0...3]
b1 PRESUPPOSITION b2          % Tom [0..3]
b1 male "n.02" x1             % Tom [0..3]
b2 REF t1                    % was [4...7]
b2 TPR t1 "now"              % was [4...7]
b2 Time e1 t1                % was [4...7]
b2 time "n.08" t1            % was [4...7]
b2 REF e1               % tricked [8...15]
b2 Patient e1 x1        % tricked [8...15]
b1 trick "v.01" e1      % tricked [8...15]
                             % . [15...16]
```

Figure 2: DRS for the sentence "Tom was tricked" in clause notation

arguably reap some of compositionality's benefits, which make it suitable for use in semi-automatic annotation workflows. We discuss this further in Section 5.

Previous work has introduced trainable compositional semantic parsers for AMR (Lindemann et al., 2020) and DRS (Evang, 2019; Bladier et al., 2021). In this paper, we improve upon the latter parser using a novel way to encode anchored DRSs as sequences, and thereby cast DRS parsing simply as a sequence labeling task (§2). We use a standard transformer-based model to learn this task, followed by post-processing to ensure well-formed DRSs (§3). We use training data from the Parallel Meaning Bank (§4). The accuracy of our model approaches the state of the art with the additional benefit of being, to a degree, compositional (§5). We give an error analysis in §6 and conclude in §7.

2 Encoding Anchored DRSs as Sequences

Gómez-Rodríguez and Vilares (2018); Strzyz et al. (2019); Vilares et al. (2020) encode syntax trees as token labels to cast syntactic parsing as a sequence labeling task. We apply a similar method to DRS parsing. We will use a simplified example from the Parallel Meaning Bank (PMB; Abzianidze et al., 2017) for exposition.

Figure 1 shows the DRS for the sentence "Tom was tricked" in *box notation*. It consists of two sub-DRSs or *boxes*, `b1` and `b2`. `b1` introduces an entity named "Tom" `x1`. `b2` introduces a "tricking" event `e1` (an event of type `trick.v.01` in the WordNet ontology, Fellbaum (2000)) whose Patient role is filled by `x1`. Because "Tom" is a definite NP, it introduces a *presupposition*: `b2` presupposes `b1`. The event is in the past, i.e., its Time role is filled by a time entity (an entity of type `time.n.08` in WordNet) `t1` which precedes the time `"now"`.

Figure 2 shows the same DRS in *clause notation*. Here, a DRS is a set of clauses. A clause consists of a *box label* indicating which box the clause is part of, a *predicate* such as a word sense, a semantic role, or a discourse relation, and one or two *arguments*, which may be *referents* such as `e1` or `x1`, or *constants* such as `"hearer"`, `"now"`, or `"+"`.

Our sequence-labeling method assumes training DRSs to be *anchored*, that is, each clause must be aligned to one (or more) input token. Thanks to the grammar-based annotation method of the PMB, this is approximately the case, as can be seen in the clause representation. We thus encode the DRS as a sequence of labels, one for each token, where each label consists of zero or more clauses, as row (1) of Figure 3 shows. We call these labels *fragments*. Although labels are complex because they can consist of multiple clauses, our sequence labeling model treats them as atomic.

In prediction tasks, it is important that label predictions generalize to unseen data. In contrast to this, the numeric part of referent labels in clauses are not meaningful and depend on the number of referents that were introduced before in the same sentence, so they would generalize poorly. Thus, in row (2), we change the referents to be *relative*, inspired by Bos (2021): referents that have not occurred before get the index `0` and referents that have occurred get a negative index, indicating how long ago the same referent last occurred (counting back among all occurrences of referents of the same type).

To further reduce proliferation of different fragments, we also experiment with factorizing fragments into fragments proper and *integration labels*. In this factorization, the first backreference of every type in a fragment always has index `-1`, and a separately predicted integration label specifies how much to subtract from that to get to the actual index. This can be seen in row (3), where the first `b` label for the word *was* has index `-1` instead of `-2`, and

	Tom	was	tricked
(1)	b1 REF x1 b1 Name x1 "tom" b1 PRESUPPOSITION b2 b1 male "n.02" x1	b2 REF t1 b2 TPR t1 "now" b2 Time e1 t1 b2 time "n.08" t1	b2 REF e1 b2 Patient e1 x1 b2 trick "v.01" e1
(2)	b0 REF x0 b-1 Name x-1 "tom" b-1 PRESUPPOSITION b0 b-2 male "n.02" x-1	b-2 REF t0 b-1 TPR t-1 "now" b-1 Time e-1 t-1 b-1 time "n.08" t-1	b-1 REF e-1 b-1 Patient e-1 x-1 b-1 trick "v.01" e-1
(3)	b0 REF x0 b-1 Name x-1 "DUMMY" b-1 PRESUPPOSITION b0 b-2 male "n.02" x-1	b-1 REF t0 b-1 TPR t-1 "now" b-1 Time e-1 t-1 b-1 time "n.08" t-1	b-1 REF e-1 b-1 Patient e-1 x-1 b-1 DUMMY "v.00" e-1
	[b0 e0 n0 p0 s0 t0 x0] tom	[b-1 e0 n0 p0 s0 t0 x0] -	[b0 e0 n0 p0 s0 t0 x0] trick "v.01"

(0) is the sentence row.

Figure 3: Sequence encoding of anchored DRSs. From top to bottom: (0) the sentence, (1) basic sequence encoding, (2) relative sequence encoding, (3) factored sequence encoding with separate integration and symbol labels.

the integration label `[b-1 e0 n0 p0 s0 t0 x0]` indicates that 1 should be subtracted from that to get to the actual relative index. This allows *was* in our example to have the same fragment as in *Someone was tricked*, where the subject does not introduce a presupposition and the actual index is thus `-1` rather than `-2` because there is one less box intervening.[2]

Another important factorization concerns large-class and open-class symbols, *viz.* (content-word) word senses, names, numbers, and time expressions. We follow Evang (2019) in replacing these with dummy expressions in the fragments and predicting them separately, as explained below in Section 3. We also follow them in heuristically changing the representation of first and second person pronouns, which introduce `"speaker"` and `"hearer"` constants instead of discourse referents in the PMB, for more consistent representation of predicates.

3 Parsing Model

Our parsing model consists of a standard transformer sequence labeling model, followed by post-processing to assemble the predicted labels into a DRS.

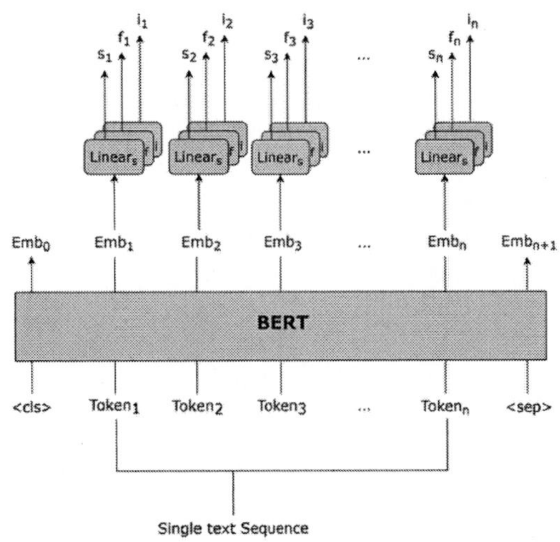

Figure 4: Neural model

[2]As pointed out by a reviewer, an even better factorization of fragments could potentially be achieved by indexing not with respect to linear position but with respect to the syntactic head word. This would require introducing a dependency parsing component. We leave this for future work.

Sequence Labeling Transformer Model Our model is schematically depicted in Figure 4. It takes an input sequence of tokens $X = w_1 \ldots w_n$ and produces aligned output sequences Y_s, Y_f, Y_i, which are word senses, fragments, and integration labels. Our model simply consists of a pre-trained BERT model (Devlin et al., 2019) and three linear classifiers. Each classifier can be seen as a sub-system of the semantic parser that produces one of the three labels (word sense, fragment, and integration label).

Each input token must further be tokenized into *wordpieces* before they can be fed into the BERT model. To obtain a single representation for a token that consists of N wordpieces and thus produces N embedding vectors, we experiment with two commonly used strategies: taking only the first wordpiece, or averaging the embeddings of all N wordpieces.

Post-processing After the neural model predicts a fragment and a word sense for each token, we assemble these predictions into a complete clause list by choosing unique new names for discourse referents with index `0` and unifying other discourse referents with them according to their relative indices. We also replace `DUMMY` strings in clauses by the predicted word senses and by symbols for names, cardinalities, and date/time expressions, which are predicted from the tokens by a rule-based system similar to that of Evang (2019). For example, for the proper name *Tom* it predicts the symbol `"tom"`, for the numeral *two* it predicts `"2"`, and for the time expression *five o'clock*, it predicts `"17:00"`. Special clauses like `b1 "speaker" x1` and `b1 "hearer" x1` are removed and the corresponding referent (`x1` in the example) replaced by the symbols `"speaker"` and `"hearer"`. Finally, we use a set of postprocessing rules similar to that of van Noord et al. (2020) to ensure the validity of the resulting DRS: if there is a loop in the subordination relation among boxes, an arbitrary box in the loop is chosen, and all its clauses are removed to break the loop (cf. Figure 9 in the Appendix). Furthermore, a `REF` clause is introduced for each referent that is now used but not introduced by a `REF` clause, in the box where it first occurs. Finally, connectedness of all boxes is ensured by introducing `CONTINUATION` relations between top-level unconnected boxes.

	gold	silver	bronze	total
English	8 403	97 958	146 371	252 372
German	1 979	5 250	121 111	128 340
Italian	1 062	2 772	64 305	68 139
Dutch	1 012	1 301	21 550	23 863

Table 1: Numbers of DRSs in the PMB 3.0.0

4 Experimental Setup

Data and Splits We train and evaluate our models on the Parallel Meaning Bank (PMB; Abzianidze et al., 2017), version 3.0.0. This sembank contains sentences annotated with anchored DRSs in four languages (English, German, Italian, Dutch) and three annotation statuses: *gold* DRSs have been fully corrected by human annotators, *silver* ones have been partially corrected, and *bronze* ones are the unchecked outputs of rule-based pre-annotation. Table 1 gives an overview. We use the standard split into training, development, and test data suggested in the PMB release. Note that for Italian and Dutch, the number of gold DRSs is very small and they are only used for development and testing, leaving only bronze and silver data for training.

PLMs and Hyperparameters The backbone of our PyTorch (Paszke et al., 2019) implementation is the *Transformer* and *WordpieceTokenizer* classes offered by Hugging Face (Wolf et al., 2019). We use pre-trained BERT models provided on `huggingface.co`: `bert-base-cased`, `dbmz/bert-base-german-cased`, `dbmz/bert-base-italian-cased`, and `Geotrend/BERT-base-nl-cased` (Abdaoui et al., 2020), keeping their default configuration. The only hyperparameters we choose ourselves are the batch size (24), the learning rate, and the number of epochs. We used the Adam optimizer to train all the parameters in our model including the pretrained BERT. To ensure stability and avoid overfitting, we used a linear scheduler with no warm-up step, which gradually reduces the learning rate from 0.0015 to 0 for each training iteration. During preliminary experiments on the development set, we found that training loss barely changed after five epochs.

BERT has 12 layers, each of which has a 768-dimensional output embedding per wordpiece. There is some mixed information in the literature as to which layer's output is most suitable for seman-

Parameters	114 M
Training time	12 mins
Word senses	5 864
Fragments w/ integration labels	1 864
Fragments w/o integration labels	2 694
Integration labels	100

Table 2: Initial model statistics for English

all concepts	0.7584
nominal	0.8217
verbal	0.6173
adjectival	0.5861
adverbs	0.5977

Table 3: Word sense f-scores in the initial model for English

tic parsing tasks. According to Chronis and Erk (2020), the middle layer is most transferable for downstream semantic tasks, while van Noord et al. (2020) claim that the last layer provides the best results for their DRS parser, so we experimented with both.

Evaluation We evaluate the performance of our parser using Counter (van Noord et al., 2018a), an extension of the Smatch evaluation metric (Cai and Knight, 2013). Counter approximates an optimal mapping between the referents in the gold DRS and the predicted DRS using hill-climbing, then outputs recall, precision, and f-score for the predicted clauses compared to the gold clauses.

5 Results and Discussion

Integration Labels We trained an initial model on the English gold training data, for which we give some statistics in Table 2. As can be seen, factoring fragments leads to 100 distinct integration labels and reduces the number of distinct fragments from 2 694 to 1 864. We found however that the factorization does not necessarily help the model, as the integration labels are extremely unbalanced. In fact, 80.1% of tokens in the training data have the "empty" integration label `[b0 e0 n0 p0 s0 t0 x0]`. In a direct comparison, we found that factoring out integration labels improves the prediction accuracy on the fragments by 3%. However, since prediction of integration labels is not perfect, the overall Counter f-score is not improved significantly (the difference in f-score is smaller than 0.01%). We nevertheless conduct all further experiments with integration labels enabled.

Word Senses The next label we take a closer look at is the word senses. Table 3 shows the f-score of our model's sense predictions, as reported by Counter, overall and broken down into nominal, verbal, adjectival, and adverbial word senses. The accuracy is much higher for nouns than for verbs,

Layer Wordpiece	7 initial	7 mean	12 mean
sense acc.	0.8663	0.8670	0.8648
fragment acc.	0.8630	0.8659	0.8651
integration acc.	0.9461	0.9475	0.9436
Counter f1	0.7873	0.7882	0.7836

Table 4: Choice of BERT output layer and wordpiece embeddings

which reflects the fact that the former are less polysemous than the latter according to WordNet statistics.[3] Another possible reason is that many nominal senses do not stem from predictions of the word sense layer but from "function" senses that appear in many fragments, such as `time "n.08"` in the fragment for *was* in Figure 3. The lower scores for adjectival and adverbial can be explained with data sparsity, for there only 1 593 adjectives and 210 adverbs in the gold data. For comparison, the number of nouns and verbs are 20 192 and 6 108.

Choice of BERT Output Layer and Wordpiece Embeddings We were interested in how the choice of BERT output layers and word piece embeddings impacts performance of our model. Hence, we did the following experiments with our base model, shown in Table 4. First, we use BERT's middle (7th) output layer, using the embedding of the initial word piece for each word as input to the classifiers. Second, we used the middle layer, but with the mean vector of all word pieces (this is the method we used in all previous experiments). Third, we used the mean value of the final (12th) BERT output layer, which helped van Noord et al. (2020) build their best model, yet according to Chronis and Erk (2020) contains too much "information residual", hence is more suitable for syntactical tasks. To minimize the effect of

[3]`https://wordnet.princeton.edu/documentation/wnstats7wn`, retrieved 2022-03-11

	g	g+s	g+s+b
# senses	5 864	42 147	60 740
# fragments	1 864	20 170	27 949
# integrations	100	2 901	4 121
Counter f1	0.7896	0.8554	0.8640

Table 5: Training on silver and bronze data

Model	dev	test
Bladier et al. (2021)	81.4	81.4
van Noord et al. (2018b)	84.3	84.9
van Noord et al. (2019)	86.8	87.7
van Noord et al. (2020) (base)	87.6	88.5
van Noord et al. (2020) (best)	**88.4**	**89.3**
Pro Boxer	88.2	88.9
this work	86.4	88.4

Table 6: Comparison of our English parser with prior art (Counter f-scores on PMB 3.0.0)

random errors, we did five trials on each of these embedding approaches and averaged the results. Although the differences are rather small, the mean vector of the middle layer seems to provide the best scores across the board. Therefore, we stuck to this setting for subsequent experiments.

Bronze and Silver Training Apart from the small gold set whose quality is guaranteed by human annotators, PMB 3.0.0 also contains silver and bronze data with partial or no manual checking of the annotations. Their lower quality is compensated for by quantity. Liu et al. (2019) report a large improvement for their DRS parser when first training on the bronze and silver data, then "fine-tuning" on gold data. Since we are using a Transformer model like them, we expected this technique could also boost our parser's performance. Thus, we tested our model with 5 epochs training on silver and bronze followed by 5 epochs on gold. The results are shown in Table 5. They confirm that more data means better results even when the data is not perfect. Although the bigger training set also increases the number of classes for all three labels more than 10-fold, the model seems to handle it just fine. The only downside is the longer training time: as the silver and bronze sets for English are, respectively, 21 and 25 times larger than the gold one, the time consumption jumps from a few minutes to more than 10 hours.

Final Model for English We compare our final best model for English to previous work, shown in Table 6. Note that Bladier et al. (2021) is an improved version of Evang (2019)'s transition-based DRS parser. The models presented by van Noord et al. (2018b, 2019, 2020) are all character-wise sequence-to-sequence models. No results on the same data are available for the encoder-decoder model of Liu et al. (2019); however, on PMB 2.2.0 its difference in Counter f-score with van Noord et al. (2019) was less than 1% on the dev and test set. The "base" model of van Noord et al. (2020) is the character-wise sequence-to-sequence parser of van Noord et al. (2019) with the addition of BERT embeddings, and their "best" model encodes the character embedding and the BERT embedding separately before feeding their concatenated vector into the decoder, which achieved state-of-the-art results. Worth noting is their claim that it's best to keep BERT parameters "frozen", which we did not find to be the case for our model: in preliminary experimentation, finetuning BERT parameters with our model outperformed a corresponding frozen model by 20% in Counter f-score.

We also compare with the semi-rule-based system used for pre-annotating the Parallel Meaning Bank (Abzianidze et al., 2017). Van Noord et al. (2020) call this system "Pro Boxer". In a sense, Pro Boxer is closest in approach to ours because it makes use of neural taggers for making token-level tagging predictions. It differs from ours and all other systems however in that it is not fully trainable from examples; the translation from tags to DRSs is done via hand-crafted rules. Moreover, it relies on a CCG parser that creates explicit syntactic representation which is perhaps more complexity than needed. As van Noord et al. also point out, the comparison with Pro Boxer is not quite fair because it is the system that produced the PMB pre-annotations and thus profits from anchoring bias.

The results in Table 6 show that our best model beats all available previous scores on the English PMB 3.0.0 test set except for Pro Boxer and van Noord et al. (2020) and is also very competitive on the dev set. Its difference with the state-of-the-art model on the test set is within 1%. Compared with the best previous fully trainable *compositional* model in Bladier et al. (2021), our model improves performance by a large margin.

	en-dev	en-test	de-dev	de-test	it-dev	it-test	nl-dev	nl-test
van Noord et al. (2020)	88.4	89.3	82.4	82.0	80.0	80.5	71.8	71.2
our system	86.4	88.4	79.2	78.3	79.5	80.4	72.5	72.1

Table 7: Comparison of our German, Dutch, and Italian models with prior art (Counter f-scores on PMB 3.0.0)

Results for German, Italian, and Dutch Although most DRS parsers to date have only been evaluated on English, the PMB also contains data in German, Italian, and Dutch. We trained our best model on the German (gold, silver, bronze), Italian (silver, bronze), and Dutch (silver, bronze) data and compared the results with the current state of the art in van Noord et al. (2020), shown in Table 7. The performance of both models is aligned with the amount of data available for each language, and also the proportion of manually corrected (gold) data. Another source of variation (and possible reason for the large gap in accuracy between the two parsers for German) is the choice of pretrained BERT model. For consistency, we only used the cased models that are available in the Hugging Face library, and if possible from the same source.

Compositionality and Its Benefits Is our semantic parser compositional? Bender et al. (2015) provide a definition of compositionality in meaning systems, which we summarize as follows: (1) there is a finite set of atomic word-meaning pairings, (2) there is a finite number of rules combining constituent-meaning pairings into larger constituent-meaning pairings, and any non-atomic constituent-meaning pairing is a function of the constituent-meaning pairings from which it is created and of the rule that creates it, (3) meaning representations are not changed destructively. They argue that compositional aspects of meaning such as predicate-argument structure should be processed by compositional systems, whereas non-compositional aspects such as anaphora or word senses should be handled by different mechanisms. Our parser largely follows these recommendations: ad (1), the fragments that represent abstract word meanings are drawn from a finite set, learned from the training data, while non-compositional word senses, names, etc. are handled by separate mechanisms. Ad (2), our system does away with the notion of constituent by not using syntactic structure, but it is trivial to express the mechanism that combines the word meanings into an utterance meaning in terms of a single rule that iteratively combines adjacent words into larger structures, fulfilling this criterion as well. Ad (3), our combining rule amounts to unifying discourse referents which is perhaps not strictly non-destructive, as it involves renaming them. However, unification can also be expressed in terms of adding variable bindings or combining graphs, so this criterion should be considered fulfilled too. Of course, the post-processing heuristics that are occasionally needed to obtain valid DRSs do not fit into a compositional framework. Furthermore, we do not currently have any dedicated mechanisms to handle partially compositional or non-compositional layers of meaning such as scope or anaphora.

Why care about compositionality in semantic parsing? If the goal of semantic parsing is not merely to automatically obtain a representation of the meaning of an utterance but also to understand why the parser produced that answer, i.e., an explainable and transparent system, compositionality can help. In particular, in the output of our parser, every token is mapped to one of a finite number of meaning fragments (unlike a sequence-to-sequence system where a single token can in principle give rise to an unbounded number of output symbols), every clause belongs to one of these fragments (unlike a sequence-to-sequence system where the output is not usually anchored), and there is a straightforward rule that combines fragments into utterance meanings (unlike sequence-to-sequence systems where the interactions between tokens are opaque). This type of transparency is especially important in human-in-the-loop annotation, where parsers produce an initial annotation and annotators correct them. To do this efficiently and consistenly, annotators need to pinpoint where an error arises, and word-meaning pairings with a finite number of meanings seem a good handle on that. Bender et al. (2015) make a similar argument about grammar-based sembanking, pointing out the consistency, comprehensiveness, and scalability that compositionality afford.

The fact that the accuracy of our compositional DRS parser now almost reaches that of the best

Phenomenon	with	without
NP coordination (2 conjuncts)	85.6	86.1
NP coordination (3 conjuncts)	54.1	87.5
Temporal expression	82.5	86.6
Cardinality	83.9	86.7
Named entity	86.1	86.7
Universal quantification	77.6	86.8
Presupposition	87.5	82.4
Rhetorical relation	84.1	86.5

Table 8: DRS clauses anchored to the conjunction *and* in the phrase *Lungs, heart, veins, arteries, and capillaries*

Table 9: Average f-scores for DRSs with and without certain phenomena

```
...
b1 Sub x1 x2 % and [30...33]
b1 Sub x1 x3 % and [30...33]
b1 Sub x1 x4 % and [30...33]
b1 Sub x1 x5 % and [30...33]
b1 Sub x1 x6 % and [30...33]
...
```

Figure 5: DRS clauses anchored to the conjunction *and* in the phrase *Lungs, heart, veins, arteries, and capillaries*

sequence-to-sequence ones is a big step ahead towards transparent DRS parsing. It is also worth noting that our sequence encoding scheme is equally applicable to incremental parsers, which potentailly afford a greater degree of psycholinguistic plausibility. In addition, the multi-task architecture of our approach is modular and allows for arbitrary additional sequence labeling tasks and factorizations.

6 Error Analysis

We were interested in which semantic phenomena present particular challenges to our parser and thus performed an error analysis of the output of our best model on the English development data, shown in Table 9. Each of the listed phenomena is identified by the presence of a particular type of clause in the gold DRS, such as a Sub relation for coordination, a Quantity relation for quantities, etc. For each phenomenon, we give the f-score for sentences with it vs. sentences without it.

While NP coordination with two conjuncts seems to be handled well, with three conjuncts, accuracy drops dramatically. This can partially be explained by poor generalization of conjunction fragments across different numbers of conjuncts, see, e.g., Figure 5. A realignment step similar to the one we use for first and second person pronouns could help here. Temporal expressions, cardinalities, and named entities all involve the prediction of open-class strings independently of the neural model. Considering that these strings typically only affect a single clause, the underperformance of our parser on sentences involving them is not small, thus improving the predictions—perhaps replacing rules with specialized neural transcoders—could be a worthwhile area for future work. Universal quantification (expressed using the CONSEQUENCE relation in DRSs) also correlates with significant difficulties, perhaps due to the diversity of lexical triggers (*one, everybody, both, everything, all, always...*) and associated fragments. Rhetorical relations present a difficulty because they are often not aligned to a token, therefore not seen in training by our parser. Presupposition on the other hand is correlated with higher scores, presumably because the vast majority of sentences contains at least one definite expression.

To gain a better understanding of common error types, we did an exploratory manual analysis, randomly sampling 100 DRSs produced by our best model on the English development set. Thanks to the compositional model structure, we could easily replicate the PMB-style word-clause alignment in the output, which makes these analyses much easier. The examples we refer to can be found in the Appendix.

In the sample, the most common errors we found were incorrect word senses, for which 36% of the sample DRSs had at least one instance. The second is semantic roles and discourse relations (30%). Despite our intention to separate them into two different sub-tasks, in our sample, these two error types often co-occur (cf. Appendix, Figure 6). In fact, in our sample, we could not find a single case where the predicted word sense of a verb and the predicted semantic roles are not compatible with each other. We hypothesize that correlations between both are learned well by the underlying BERT model, which informs both the fragment classifier and the word sense classifier. In a sense, word sense errors could be expected to be much more frequent than semantic role errors, because word senses form a larger class than verbal fragments. It could be that our model tends to produce internally "consistent" meanings (with matching senses and roles) even at the price of predicting incorrect roles, for which it is penalized, since Counter does not reward consistency but only correctness. We leave a closer investigation of this hypothesis to future work.

Compared to verbs, noun fragments have less variation, thus we generally observe fewer errors with them. However, there is a noun-related error that consistently occurs in our sample, *viz.* failure to recognize demonyms as such and assign them the corresponding analysis, which involves a presupposed country (cf. Appendix, Figure 7).

Our parser also consistently fails to recognize generic *you* as opposed to deictic *you* (cf. Appendix, Figure 8), which points to the importance of discourse context for understanding the (speaker) meaning of even a single word, and perhaps to something that all current DRS parsers lack: an explicit distinction between sentence meaning and speaker meaning (cf. Bender et al., 2015).

Besides the very large class of word senses, there is also the completely open classes of symbols: names, cardinalities, and times. Our parser predicts them from the corresponding tokens using rule-based heuristics, which we have only implemented for English for now. Simply copying the token often gives the correct symbol, which is partly why we only saw a 1% difference for them in the previous evaluation and why other languages still have acceptable f-scores (the other reason being that Counter arguably underpenalizes incorrect symbols). Of course, things can also go wrong (cf. Appendix, Figure 7).

Finally, we look at fragment predictions with incorrect discourse referent indices, which lead to incorrectly unified discourse referents in the output. The tendency in our sample seems to be that things here go right most of the time, but when they go wrong, they go very wrong, leading to DRSs that are not just incorrect but *invalid* and can thus not be scored by Counter. One way for a DRS to be invalid is to have a loop in its subordination relation, e.g., when two boxes presuppose each other. The way our repair heuristics fix this is to completely delete one of the boxes, and then fix unintroduced referents by introducing new `REF` clauses, and fix a nonconnected subordination relation by introducing `CONTINUATION` relations between boxes (cf. Appendix, Figure 9). Although a bit crude and drastic, these fixing heuristics seem to hurt f-score less than one might expect, for they mainly affect DRSs that were quite wrong to begin with.

7 Conclusions

We have presented the first fully trainable DRS parser that is both competitive with the state of the art and compositional. Unlike sequence-to-sequence models it provides an explicit mapping between tokens and clauses, and fixed fragments ensure consistent analyses. Unlike traditional pipelines, it does not make use of explicit syntactic representations or λ-expressions but uses a simple sequence factorization, and wraps up much of the complexity in a general-purpose BERT model. We argue that these characteristics make our model especially suitable for interactive annotation with humans in the loop, but is also good enough for other applications. Beyond producing more and better data, our error analysis suggests that the next frontier in DRS parsing will involve better modeling of discourse context, and perhaps an explicit separation of sentence meaning and speaker meaning.

Acknowledgments

We would like to thank the three anonymous reviewers for insightful comments. We also thank Laura Kallmeyer for her support. The second author's work on this paper was carried out as part of the research project TreeGraSP, funded by a Consolidator Grant of the European Research Council (ERC).

References

Amine Abdaoui, Camille Pradel, and Grégoire Sigel. 2020. Load what you need: Smaller versions of mutililingual BERT. In *Proceedings of SustaiNLP: Workshop on Simple and Efficient Natural Language Processing*, pages 119–123, Online. Association for Computational Linguistics.

Omri Abend and Ari Rappoport. 2013. UCCA: A semantics-based grammatical annotation scheme. In *Proceedings of the 10th International Conference on Computational Semantics (IWCS 2013) – Long Papers*, pages 1–12, Potsdam, Germany. Association for Computational Linguistics.

Lasha Abzianidze, Johannes Bjerva, Kilian Evang, Hessel Haagsma, Rik van Noord, Pierre Ludmann, Duc-Duy Nguyen, and Johan Bos. 2017. The Parallel Meaning Bank: Towards a multilingual corpus of translations annotated with compositional meaning representations. In *Proceedings of the 15th Conference of the European Chapter of the Association for Computational Linguistics: Volume 2, Short Papers*, pages 242–247, Valencia, Spain. Association for Computational Linguistics.

Laura Banarescu, Claire Bonial, Shu Cai, Madalina Georgescu, Kira Griffitt, Ulf Hermjakob, Kevin Knight, Philipp Koehn, Martha Palmer, and Nathan Schneider. 2013. Abstract Meaning Representation for sembanking. In *Proceedings of the 7th Linguistic Annotation Workshop and Interoperability with Discourse*, pages 178–186, Sofia, Bulgaria. Association for Computational Linguistics.

Emily M. Bender, Dan Flickinger, Stephan Oepen, Woodley Packard, and Ann Copestake. 2015. Layers of interpretation: On grammar and compositionality. In *Proceedings of the 11th International Conference on Computational Semantics*, pages 239–249, London, UK. Association for Computational Linguistics.

Tatiana Bladier, Gosse Minnema, Rik van Noord, and Kilian Evang. 2021. Improving DRS parsing with separately predicted semantic roles. In *Proceedings of the Workshop on Computing Semantics with Types, Frames and Related Structures*.

Johan Bos. 2021. Variable-free discourse representation structures. `https://semanticsarchive.net/Archive/jQzMzJlY/`, accessed 2022-02-25.

Shu Cai and Kevin Knight. 2013. Smatch: an evaluation metric for semantic feature structures. In *Proceedings of the 51st Annual Meeting of the Association for Computational Linguistics (Volume 2: Short Papers)*, pages 748–752, Sofia, Bulgaria. Association for Computational Linguistics.

Gabriella Chronis and Katrin Erk. 2020. When is a bishop not like a rook? when it's like a rabbi! multi-prototype BERT embeddings for estimating semantic relationships. In *Proceedings of the 24th Conference on Computational Natural Language Learning*, pages 227–244, Online. Association for Computational Linguistics.

Jacob Devlin, Ming-Wei Chang, Kenton Lee, and Kristina Toutanova. 2019. BERT: Pre-training of deep bidirectional transformers for language understanding. In *Proceedings of the 2019 Conference of the North American Chapter of the Association for Computational Linguistics: Human Language Technologies, Volume 1 (Long and Short Papers)*, pages 4171–4186, Minneapolis, Minnesota. Association for Computational Linguistics.

Kilian Evang. 2019. Transition-based DRS parsing using stack-LSTMs. In *Proceedings of the IWCS Shared Task on Semantic Parsing*, Gothenburg, Sweden. Association for Computational Linguistics.

Christiane D. Fellbaum. 2000. Wordnet: an electronic lexical database. *Language*, 76:706.

Carlos Gómez-Rodríguez and David Vilares. 2018. Constituent parsing as sequence labeling. In *Proceedings of the 2018 Conference on Empirical Methods in Natural Language Processing*, pages 1314–1324, Brussels, Belgium. Association for Computational Linguistics.

Matthias Lindemann, Jonas Groschwitz, and Alexander Koller. 2020. Fast semantic parsing with well-typedness guarantees. In *Proceedings of the 2020 Conference on Empirical Methods in Natural Language Processing (EMNLP)*, pages 3929–3951, Online. Association for Computational Linguistics.

Jiangming Liu, Shay B. Cohen, and Mirella Lapata. 2019. Discourse representation parsing for sentences and documents. In *Proceedings of the 57th Annual Meeting of the Association for Computational Linguistics*, pages 6248–6262, Florence, Italy. Association for Computational Linguistics.

Stephan Oepen, Omri Abend, Lasha Abzianidze, Johan Bos, Jan Hajic, Daniel Hershcovich, Bin Li, Tim O'Gorman, Nianwen Xue, and Daniel Zeman. 2020. MRP 2020: The second shared task on cross-framework and cross-lingual meaning representation parsing. In *Proceedings of the CoNLL 2020 Shared Task: Cross-Framework Meaning Representation Parsing*, pages 1–22, Online. Association for Computational Linguistics.

Adam Paszke, Sam Gross, Francisco Massa, Adam Lerer, James Bradbury, Gregory Chanan, Trevor Killeen, Zeming Lin, Natalia Gimelshein, Luca Antiga, Alban Desmaison, Andreas Kopf, Edward Yang, Zachary DeVito, Martin Raison, Alykhan Tejani, Sasank Chilamkurthy, Benoit Steiner, Lu Fang, Junjie Bai, and Soumith Chintala. 2019. Pytorch: An imperative style, high-performance deep learning library. In *Advances in Neural Information Processing Systems*, volume 32. Curran Associates, Inc.

Michalina Strzyz, David Vilares, and Carlos Gómez-Rodríguez. 2019. Viable dependency parsing as sequence labeling. In *Proceedings of the 2019 Conference of the North American Chapter of the Association for Computational Linguistics: Human Language Technologies, Volume 1 (Long and Short Papers)*, pages 717–723, Minneapolis, Minnesota. Association for Computational Linguistics.

Ilya Sutskever, Oriol Vinyals, and Quoc V Le. 2014. Sequence to sequence learning with neural networks. In *Advances in Neural Information Processing Systems*, volume 27. Curran Associates, Inc.

Rik van Noord, Lasha Abzianidze, Hessel Haagsma, and Johan Bos. 2018a. Evaluating scoped meaning representations. In *Proceedings of the Eleventh International Conference on Language Resources and Evaluation (LREC 2018)*, Miyazaki, Japan. European Language Resources Association (ELRA).

Rik van Noord, Lasha Abzianidze, Antonio Toral, and Johan Bos. 2018b. Exploring neural methods for parsing discourse representation structures. *Transactions of the Association for Computational Linguistics*, 6:619–633.

Rik van Noord, Antonio Toral, and Johan Bos. 2019. Linguistic information in neural semantic parsing with multiple encoders. In *Proceedings of the 13th International Conference on Computational Semantics*

- *Short Papers*, pages 24–31, Gothenburg, Sweden. Association for Computational Linguistics.

Rik van Noord, Antonio Toral, and Johan Bos. 2020. Character-level representations improve DRS-based semantic parsing even in the age of BERT. In *Proceedings of the 2020 Conference on Empirical Methods in Natural Language Processing (EMNLP)*, pages 4587–4603, Online. Association for Computational Linguistics.

David Vilares, Michalina Strzyz, Anders Søgaard, and Carlos Gómez-Rodríguez. 2020. Parsing as pretraining. pages 9114–9121.

Thomas Wolf, Lysandre Debut, Victor Sanh, Julien Chaumond, Clement Delangue, Anthony Moi, Pierric Cistac, Tim Rault, Rémi Louf, Morgan Funtowicz, and Jamie Brew. 2019. Huggingface's transformers: State-of-the-art natural language processing. *CoRR*, abs/1910.03771.

A Examples from Error Analysis

Gold (dev):
"Look out !"

b1 REF e1	% Look [0...4]
b1 Experiencer e1 "hearer"	% Look [0...4]
b1 look_out "v.01" e1	% Look [0...4]
	% out [5...8]
	% ! [8...9]

Prediction:
"Look out !"

b1 look "v.01" e1	% Look
b1 Agent e1 "hearer"	% Look
b1 REF e1	% Look

Figure 6: Gold and predicted DRS for the sentence "Look out!" Both the word sense and the semantic role were predicted incorrectly.

a. Gold (dev):
"He 's Argentinian."

b1 REF x1	% He [0...2]
b1 PRESUPPOSITION b2	% He [0...2]
b1 male "n.02" x1	% He [0...2]
b2 REF t1	% 's [2...4]
b2 EQU t1 "now"	% 's [2...4]
b2 Time e1 t1	% 's [2...4]
b2 time "n.08" t1	% 's [2...4]
b2 REF e1	% Argentinian [5...16]
b2 Source e1 x2	% Argentinian [5...16]
b2 Theme e1 x1	% Argentinian [5...16]
b2 be "v.03" e1	% Argentinian [5...16]
b3 REF x2	% Argentinian [5...16]
b3 Name x2 "argentina"	% Argentinian [5...16]
b3 PRESUPPOSITION b2	% Argentinian [5...16]
b3 country "n.02" x2	% Argentinian [5...16]
	% . [16...17]

b. Prediction (original dev):
"He 's Argentinian."

b1 male "n.02" x1	% He
b1 PRESUPPOSITION b2	% He
b1 REF x1	% He
b2 time "n.08" t1	% 's
b2 Time e1 t1	% 's
b2 EQU t1 "now"	% 's
b2 REF t1	% 's
b2 person "n.01" x1	% Argentinian
b2 location "n.01" x2	% Argentinian
b2 REF x1	% Argentinian
b2 Source x1 x2	% Argentinian
b2 Name x2 "argentinian"	% Argentinian
b2 REF x2	% Argentinian
b2 REF e1	% Argentinian

Figure 7: Gold and predicted DRS for the sentence "He's Argentinian". Our parser failed to choose the correct fragment and symbol for the demonym "Argentinian".

Gold (dev):
"You can buy ø stamps at any post~office."

b4 CONDITION b5	%
b2 CONDITION b3	% You [0...3]
b3 REF x1	% You [0...3]
b3 CONSEQUENCE b4	% You [0...3]
b3 person "n.01" x1	% You [0...3]
b1 POSSIBILITY b2	% can [4...7]
b4 REF e1	% buy [8...11]
b4 Agent e1 x1	% buy [8...11]
b4 Theme e1 x2	% buy [8...11]
b4 buy "v.01" e1	% buy [8...11]
b4 REF x2	% stamps [12...18]
b4 stamp "n.04" x2	% stamps [12...18]
b6 Location e1 x3	% at [19...21]
b5 REF x3	% any [22...25]
b5 CONSEQUENCE b6	% any [22...25]
b5 post_office "n.01" x3	% post~office [26...37]
	% . [37...38]

Prediction:
"You can buy stamps at any post~office."

b1 POSSIBILITY b2	% can
b2 buy "v.01" e1	% buy
b2 Agent e1 "hearer"	% buy
b2 REF e1	% buy
b2 Theme e1 x1	% buy
b2 stamp "n.04" x1	% stamps
b2 REF x1	% stamps
b2 Location e1 x2	% at
b2 REF x2	% any
b2 post_office "n.01" x2	% post~office

Figure 8: Gold and predicted DRS for the sentence "You can buy stamps at any post office". Our parser did not recognize "you" as generic as opposed to deictic.

1. Gold (dev):
" Tom is ø Mary 's stepson."

```
b1 REF x1                      % Tom [0...3]
b1 Name x1 "tom"               % Tom [0...3]
b1 PRESUPPOSITION b4           % Tom [0...3]
b1 male "n.02" x1              % Tom [0...3]
b4 REF e1                      % is [4...6]
b4 REF t1                      % is [4...6]
b4 Co-Theme e1 x3              % is [4...6]
b4 EQU t1 "now"                % is [4...6]
b4 Theme e1 x1                 % is [4...6]
b4 Time e1 t1                  % is [4...6]
b4 be "v.02" e1                % is [4...6]
b4 time "n.08" t1              % is [4...6]
b2 REF x2                      % Mary [7...11]
b2 Name x2 "mary"              % Mary [7...11]
b2 PRESUPPOSITION b3           % Mary [7...11]
b2 female "n.02" x2            % Mary [7...11]
b3 REF x3                      % 's [11...13]
b3 Of x4 x2                    % 's [11...13]
b3 REF x4                      % stepson [14...21]
b3 PRESUPPOSITION b4           % stepson [14...21]
b3 Role x3 x4                  % stepson [14...21]
b3 person "n.01" x3            % stepson [14...21]
b3 stepson "n.01" x4           % stepson [14...21]
                               % . [21...22]
```

2. Prediction (Loop):
"Tom is Mary 's stepson."

```
b1 male "n.02" x1                 % Tom
b1 PRESUPPOSITION b2              % Tom
b1 Name x1 "tom"                  % Tom
b1 REF x1                         % Tom
b2 time "n.08" t1                 % is
b2 be "v.02" e1                   % is
b2 REF e1                         % is
b2 Time e1 t1                     % is
b2 Theme e1 x1                    % is
b2 Co-Theme e1 x2                 % is
b2 EQU t1 "now"                   % is
b2 REF t1                         % is
b3 female "n.02" x3               % Mary
b3 PRESUPPOSITION b4              % Mary
b3 Name x3 "mary"                 % Mary
b3 REF x3                         % 's
b4 PRESUPPOSITION b2              % stepson
b4 REF x2                         % stepson
b4 User x2 x3                     % stepson
b4 person "n.01" x1               % stepson
b4 driver's_license "n.01" x2     % stepson
b4 PRESUPPOSITION b3              % stepson
b4 Role x1 x2                     % stepson
b4 REF x1                         % stepson
```

3. Prediction (Disconnects):
"Tom is Mary 's stepson."

```
b1 male "n.02" x1                 % Tom
b1 PRESUPPOSITION b2              % Tom
b1 Name x1 "tom"                  % Tom
b1 REF x1                         % Tom
b2 time "n.08" t1                 % is
b2 be "v.02" e1                   % is
b2 REF e1                         % is
b2 Time e1 t1                     % is
b2 Theme e1 x1                    % is
b2 Co-Theme e1 x2                 % is
b2 EQU t1 "now"                   % is
b2 REF t1                         % is
b3 female "n.02" x3               % Mary
b3 PRESUPPOSITION b4              % Mary
b3 Name x3 "mary"                 % Mary
b3 REF x3                         % 's
b2 REF x2
```

4. Prediction (Postprocessing fixed):
"Tom is Mary 's stepson."

```
b1 male "n.02" x1                 % Tom
b1 PRESUPPOSITION b2              % Tom
b1 Name x1 "tom"                  % Tom
b1 REF x1                         % Tom
b2 time "n.08" t1                 % is
b2 be "v.02" e1                   % is
b2 REF e1                         % is
b2 Time e1 t1                     % is
b2 Theme e1 x1                    % is
b2 Co-Theme e1 x2                 % is
b2 EQU t1 "now"                   % is
b2 REF t1                         % is
b3 female "n.02" x3               % Mary
b3 PRESUPPOSITION b4              % Mary
b3 Name x3 "mary"                 % Mary
b3 REF x3                         % 's
b2 REF x2
b2 CONTNUATION b3
```

Figure 9: Gold, predicted, and fixed DRSs for the sentence "Tom is Mary's stepson". The initial prediction is invalid because boxes `b3` and `b4` presuppose each other. This is fixed by completely deleting `b4`, which leaves an unintroduced referent `x2` and two unconnected boxes `b2` and `b3` behind. These errors are fixed, respectively, by introducing a `REF` clause for `x2` where it first occurs (in `b2`) and introducing a `CONTINUATION` relation between `x2` and `x3`.

How Does Data Corruption Affect Natural Language Understanding Models? A Study on GLUE Datasets

Aarne Talman[*§] **Marianna Apidianaki**[◇]
Stergios Chatzikyriakidis[†‡§] **Jörg Tiedemann**[*]

[*]Department of Digital Humanities, University of Helsinki
{name.surname}@helsinki.fi
[◇]Department of Computer and Information Science, University of Pennsylvania
marapi@seas.upenn.edu
[†]Department of Philology, University of Crete
stergios.chatzikyriakidis@uoc.gr
[‡]Centre of Linguistic Theory and Studies in Probability, FLoV, University of Gothenburg
[§]Basement AI

Abstract

A central question in natural language understanding (NLU) research is whether high performance demonstrates the models' strong reasoning capabilities. We present an extensive series of controlled experiments where pre-trained language models are exposed to data that have undergone specific corruption transformations. These involve removing instances of specific word classes and often lead to non-sensical sentences. Our results show that performance remains high on most GLUE tasks when the models are fine-tuned or tested on corrupted data, suggesting that they leverage other cues for prediction even in non-sensical contexts. Our proposed data transformations can be used to assess the extent to which a specific dataset constitutes a proper testbed for evaluating models' language understanding capabilities.

1 Introduction

The super-human performance of recent Transformer-based pre-trained language models (Devlin et al., 2019; Liu et al., 2019) on natural language understanding (NLU) tasks has raised scepticism regarding the quality of the benchmarks used for evaluation (Wang et al., 2018, 2019). There is increasing evidence that these datasets contain annotation artefacts and other statistical irregularities that can be leveraged by machine learning models to perform the tasks (Gururangan et al., 2018; Poliak et al., 2018b; Tsuchiya, 2018; Glockner et al., 2018; Talman and Chatzikyriakidis, 2019; Pham et al., 2020; Talman et al., 2021). These studies have so far largely focused on the natural language inference (NLI) and textual entailment tasks. The scope of our work is wider, in the sense that we address all but one NLU tasks comprised in the GLUE benchmark, specifically: linguistic acceptability (COLA), paraphrasing (MRPC and QQP), sentiment prediction (SST-2), and semantic textual similarity (STS-B).

	Sentence 1	Sentence 2
paraphrase	*~~Easynews~~ ~~Inc.~~ was subpoenaed late last ~~week~~ by the ~~FBI~~, which was seeking ~~account~~ ~~information~~ related to the ~~uploading~~ of the ~~virus~~ to the ~~ISP's~~ ~~Usenet~~ ~~news~~ ~~group~~ ~~server~~.*	*~~Easynews~~ ~~Inc.~~ said ~~Monday~~ that it was co-operating with the ~~FBI~~ in trying to locate the ~~person~~ who uploaded the ~~virus~~ to a ~~Usenet~~ ~~news~~ ~~group~~ hosted by the ~~ISP~~.*
non-paraphrase	*~~Arison~~ said ~~Mann~~ may have been one of the ~~pioneers~~ of the ~~world~~ ~~music~~ ~~movement~~ and he had a deep ~~love~~ of Brazilian ~~music~~.*	*~~Arison~~ said ~~Mann~~ was a ~~pioneer~~ of the ~~world~~ ~~music~~ ~~movement~~ – well before the ~~term~~ was coined – and he had a deep ~~love~~ of Brazilian ~~music~~.*

Table 1: Example sentence pairs from the corrupted MRPC training dataset where all instances of nouns have been removed.

We present a series of experiments where the datasets used for model training and evaluation undergo a number of corruption transformations, which involve removing specific word classes from the data. We remove words pertaining to a specific class (e.g., nouns, verbs), instead of random words, to see the relative importance of word classes for the NLU tasks. For instance, verbs arguably play a significant role in sentence level semantics and removing them is expected to have a bigger impact on the GLUE scores, compared to say determiners.

The transformations seriously affect the quality of the sentences found in the datasets, making them in many cases unintelligible (cf. examples in Table 1); a decrease in performance for mod-

Proceedings of the 11th Joint Conference on Lexical and Computational Semantics, pages 226 - 233
July 14-15, 2022

	Task	Baseline	Metric
COLA	The Corpus of Linguistic Acceptability (Warstadt et al., 2018)	64.05	Matthew's correlation
MNLI-M	Multi-Genre Natural Language Inference (Williams et al., 2018)	87.89	accuracy
MRPC	Microsoft Research Paraphrase Corpus (Dolan and Brockett, 2005)	88.73	accuracy
QNLI	Question Natural Language Inference (Rajpurkar et al., 2016)	92.64	accuracy
QQP	Quora Question Pairs	91.32	accuracy
RTE	Recognizing Textual Entailment (Dagan et al., 2006)	70.04	accuracy
SST-2	The Stanford Sentiment Treebank (Socher et al., 2013)	94.61	accuracy
STS-B	Semantic Textual Similarity Benchmark (Cer et al., 2017)	90.08	Pearson correlation

Table 2: Baseline results obtained for different GLUE tasks with RoBERTa-base and the relevant metric.

els fine-tuned on these corrupted datasets would, thus, be expected. High performance would, instead, indicate that the models rely on lexical cues that remain after corruption, and possibly on other dataset artefacts, to perform a task without necessarily understanding the meaning of the processed utterances.

Our results show that performance after the corruptions remains high for most GLUE tasks, suggesting that the models leverage other cues for prediction even in non-sensical contexts.

2 Related Work

Annotation artefacts and statistical biases in NLI datasets are easily leveraged by the models and can guide prediction (Lai and Hockenmaier, 2014; Marelli et al., 2014; Poliak et al., 2018a; Gururangan et al., 2018). Examples include explicit negation being indicative of contradiction, and generic nouns suggesting entailment. Artefacts are also present in other types of datasets, for example in the ROC Story dataset where models can provide story endings without looking at the actual stories (Schwartz et al., 2017; Cai et al., 2017). Several works have proposed more challenging and cleaner NLI datasets where artefacts have been removed (McCoy et al., 2019). An efficient way to do this is using adversarial filtering (Nie et al., 2020; Zellers et al., 2018). The superior quality of the resulting NLI datasets is confirmed by Talman et al. (2021) in a series of experiments where it is shown that data corruption affects these higher quality datasets to a greater extent than previous datasets.

This work follows the same experimental direction where text perturbations serve to explore the sensitivity of language models to specific phenomena (Futrell et al., 2019; Ettinger, 2020; Taktasheva et al., 2021; Dankers et al., 2021). It has been shown, for example, that shuffling word order causes significant performance drops on a wide range of QA tasks (Si et al., 2019; Sugawara et al., 2019), but that state-of-the-art NLU models are not sensitive to word order (Pham et al., 2020; Sinha et al., 2021). Syntax-based perturbations have also been studied in relation to robustness and faithfulness of machine translation models (Parthasarathi et al., 2021).

We add to this line of research by applying data corruption transformations that involve removing entire word classes (Talman et al., 2021) to all but one GLUE tasks.[1] We interpret high performance of models fine-tuned and/or tested on corrupted datasets as an indication of the presence of lexical cues, and possibly artefacts, guiding prediction, since the meaning of the corrupted utterances is often hard to recover.

3 Datasets and Corruptions

In our experiments, we address eight tasks included in the General Language Understanding Evaluation (GLUE) benchmark for the English language (Wang et al., 2018): CoLa, MNLI, MRPC, QNLI, QQP, RTE, SST-2, STS-B. Following Talman et al. (2021), we corrupt the training and development sets available for these tasks by removing words of specific word classes.[2] We use the development sets for evaluation, since annotated test data have not been made publicly available.[3] We create three configurations for each task: (a) CORRUPT-TRAIN: fine-tuning on the corrupted training set, evaluation on the original development set; (b) CORRUPT-TEST: fine-tuning on the original training set, evaluation on the corrupted test set; (c) CORRUPT-TRAIN AND TEST: training and evaluation on corrupted data. The corruption procedure

[1] We exclude WNLI as its development dataset was designed to be adversarial (Wang et al., 2018) and hence the corruptions do not have any impact on this dataset when evaluating with the development set.

[2] We annotate the original texts with universal part of speech (POS) tags using the NLTK library (https://www.nltk.org/) and the averaged perceptron tagger.

[3] For MNLI, we use the matched development set (Williams et al., 2018).

Data	CORRUPT-TRAIN	Δ	CORRUPT-TEST	Δ	CORRUPT-TRAIN AND TEST	Δ
COLA-NOUN	39.72	-24.34	17.75	-46.30	34.33	-29.73
MNLI-M-NOUN	85.64	-2.24	72.85	-15.04	77.46	-10.42
MRPC-NOUN	86.27	-2.45	82.35	-6.37	80.15	-8.58
QNLI-NOUN	89.13	-3.51	71.02	-21.62	82.02	-10.62
QQP-NOUN	86.69	-4.63	72.57	-18.75	84.17	-7.16
RTE-NOUN	47.29	-22.74	53.79	-16.25	47.29	-22.74
SST-2-NOUN	94.04	-0.57	87.27	-7.34	88.76	-5.85
STS-B-NOUN	81.67	-8.41	56.12	-33.96	63.52	-26.56
COLA-VERB	23.26	-40.79	4.30	-59.75	20.22	-43.83
MNLI-M-VERB	86.95	-0.94	77.61	-10.28	80.32	-7.57
MRPC-VERB	85.54	-3.19	85.54	-3.19	85.05	-3.68
QNLI-VERB	92.00	-0.64	87.41	-5.24	90.15	-2.49
QQP-VERB	89.49	-1.84	86.01	-5.31	89.05	-2.27
RTE-VERB	65.34	-4.69	65.70	-4.33	65.34	-4.69
SST-2-VERB	93.69	-0.92	89.33	-5.28	89.56	-5.05
STS-B-VERB	87.63	-2.46	85.54	-4.54	86.22	-3.86

Table 3: Example results for the RoBERTa-`base` model fine-tuned on CORRUPT-TRAIN and tested on the original evaluation set (columns 2 and 3); fine-tuned on the original data and tested on CORRUPT-TEST; fine-tuned on CORRUPT-TRAIN and tested on CORRUPT-TEST (columns 6 and 7). Δ is the difference to the baseline scores obtained by RoBERTa-`base` on the original dataset, given in Table 2.

involves removing all instances of a specific word class from the corresponding dataset (ADJ, ADV, CONJ, DET, NOUN, NUM, PRON, VERB). We label the corrupted datasets by indicating the class of the words that have been removed (e.g., COLA-NOUN, QNLI-VERB). Given the possible combinations of tasks, datasets and corruptions, we end up with 192 setups for our experiments.

Note that the resulting sentence fragments do not constitute propositions. Although not ideal, this is not necessarily problematic for tasks such as sentiment analysis. For inference, the assumption that the task can only be performed at the propositional level is a strong claim, especially given that examples which are not propositions are abundant in existing benchmarks such as MNLI (e.g., examples extracted from dialogue).

4 Models

We fine-tune the pre-trained RoBERTa-`base` model (Liu et al., 2019) from the Huggingface Transformers library (Wolf et al., 2020a) in each of our 192 configurations. We use the same fine-tuning and evaluation set up for all the experiments. We retrieve the GLUE datasets using the Huggingface Datasets library (Wolf et al., 2020b). We fine-tune the models for 3 epochs, using a batch size of 32 and a learning rate of 0.00002.

5 Results

The baseline results using the original (non-corrupted) datasets are shown in Table 2. Given the large number of configurations, we only report the exact evaluation results for the -NOUN and -VERB settings in Table 3, as these content word

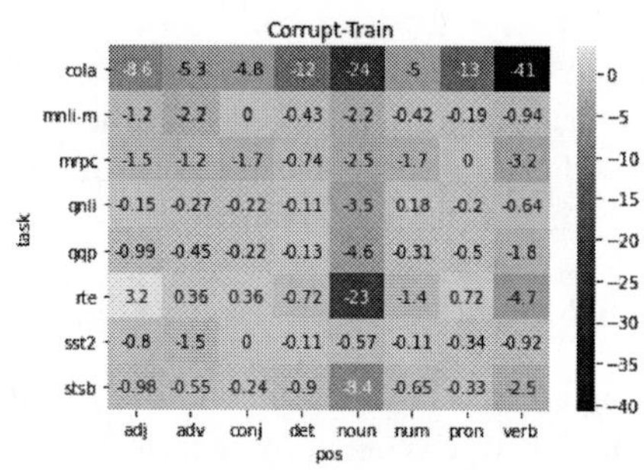

Figure 1: Impact of specific data corruptions in the CORRUPT-TRAIN setting. The columns correspond to the removed word class and the rows to the GLUE tasks.

classes arguably contribute a lot to the meaning of utterances. For the remaining configurations, we visualise the effect of the corruptions using heatmaps that show the difference in performance compared to the baseline results (Figures 1 to 3).

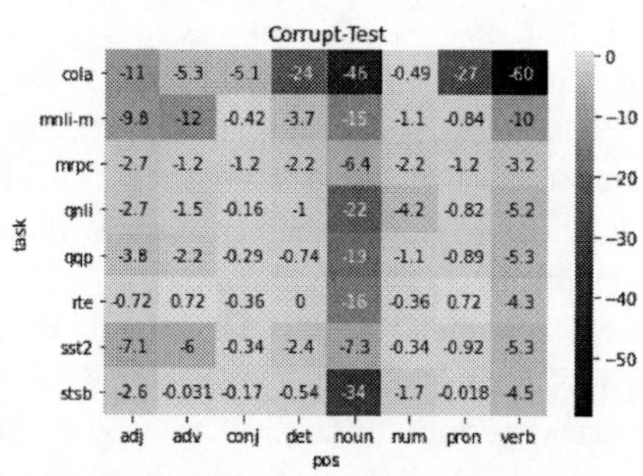

Figure 2: Impact of specific data corruptions in the CORRUPT-TEST setting for each task.

Our results for the -NOUN and -VERB corruptions in CORRUPT-TRAIN (Table 3), and for all

Original Sentences	CORRUPT-TEST-NOUN	CORRUPT-TEST-ADJ	Labels	Gold label
An unclassifiably awful study in self - and audience-abuse.	*an unclassifiably awful in - and.*	*an unclassifiably study in self - and audience-abuse.*	positive	negative
It proves quite compelling as an intense, brooding character study.	*it proves quite compelling as an intense, brooding.*	*it proves quite as an, brooding character study.*	positive	positive

Table 4: Labels assigned by NRCLex to sentences from the SST-2 CORRUPT-TEST-NOUN/-ADJ datasets.

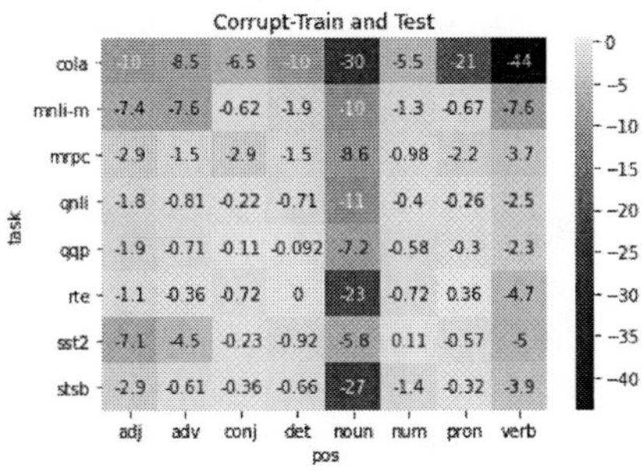

Figure 3: Impact of specific data corruptions in the CORRUPT-TRAIN AND TEST setting for each task.

configurations in Figure 1, show a notable decrease in performance on COLA and RTE, especially when nouns are removed. The impact on MNLI-M and QNLI datasets is small, confirming previous findings regarding the presence of annotation artefacts and lexical cues that can guide model prediction. Our results suggest that this is the case also in other GLUE datasets, such as MRPC and SST-2, where the models still manage to perform fairly well compared to the baseline when fine-tuned on corrupted data.

Our CORRUPT-TEST results in Table 3 and in Figure 2 show that removing nouns from the data used for evaluation has a much larger impact across tasks, compared to CORRUPT-TRAIN. The biggest drop in performance is observed on COLA, MNLI-M and STS-B. However, accuracy on MRPC and SST-2 is still very high, suggesting that good performance does not require sentence-level understanding but can be achieved by relying on lexical cues present in the data. In the CORRUPT-TRAIN AND TEST setting (Table 3 and Figure 3), we observe the biggest drop in performance on COLA, MNLI-M and STS-B, and a lower impact on QNLI, QQP and SST-2.

6 Discussion and Analysis

6.1 Lexical Cues

Our results show that model performance in many tasks is marginally affected by the imposed corruptions which, however, in many cases alter the meaning of utterances. We conduct additional analyses aimed at identifying the lexical cues that remain after corruption and can guide model prediction. We focus on MRPC (Microsoft Research Paraphrase Corpus) and SST-2 (Stanford Sentiment Treebank), where the impact of CORRUPT-TEST transformations was the smallest.

Word class	Dataset	Accuracy
NOUN	CORRUPT-TEST	14.7%
NOUN	original	34.1%
VERB	CORRUPT-TEST	31.1%
VERB	original	66.4%

Table 5: Accuracy of RoBERTa-BASE in predicting a masked word in the MRPC development set.

MRPC addresses the paraphrase relationship between sentence pairs. We explore the semantic similarity of the information that remains after corruption. Our assumption is that if a sentence pair (from which nouns or verbs have been removed) still contains synonyms or longer paraphrases, this can guide the model towards detecting a similarity or entailment relationship. For this analysis, we use the unigram paraphrases in the L (large) package of PPDB 2.0 (Pavlick et al., 2015). We find that in the CORRUPT-TEST-NOUN MRPC dataset, 76% of the sentence pairs for which the model made correct predictions still include a lexical paraphrase.

SST-2 involves detecting the sentiment expressed in individual sentences. We use the NRCLex tool[4] to measure the sentiment expressed by lexical cues in the CORRUPT-TEST sentences for which model predictions are correct. Given that sentiment can be expressed in a text by words pertaining to different grammatical categories, we explore whether lexical cues indicating the polarity of the text still remain after removing instances of a specific word class. In Table 4, we show the labels predicted by NRCLex for corrupted test sentences, where the nouns and adjectives have been dropped. We observe that even if sentences become non-sensical

[4]NRCLex is based on the expanded version of the NRC Word-Emotion Association Lexicon (Mohammad and Turney, 2010, 2013). We only use the 'positive' and 'negative' keys.

after corruption, it is still possible to detect the (positive or negative) polarity of the sentences from the remaining words. Relying on these lexical cues, RoBERTa often manages to predict the correct sentiment. Specifically, according to the NRCLex predictions, the correct sentiment is still present in 383 out of 761 corrupted sentences where RoBERTa made correct predictions in the CORRUPT-TEST-NOUN setting. If both nouns and adjectives are removed (CORRUPT-TEST-NOUN-ADJ), NRCLex detects that the correct sentiment is still present in 125 out of the 672 examples that were correctly predicted by RoBERTa.

6.2 Can RoBERTa Guess the Missing Tokens?

As RoBERTa has been pre-trained using a Masked Word Prediction task, it is reasonable to ask if high model performance with our corrupted datasets could be due to the model's ability to "fill in the gaps" and predict the missing words. To test this, in each sentence of the MRCP development set, we replace the first token that is aimed by a specific corruption procedure (-NOUN/VERB) with the [MASK] token. We do this in the original sentence (by removing only the first noun/verb instance) and in the corrupted sentence (where all other nouns/verbs are missing). For example, from the first sentence in Table 4, we generate two cloze-task queries in the -NOUN setting:

(a) An unclassifiably awful [MASK] in self - and audience-abuse.

(b) An unclassifiably awful [MASK] in - and.

We use these queries to test RoBERTa's token prediction capability. As shown in Table 5, it is easier to predict the masked token in the original sentences, but the model is still able to make correct predictions in the corrupted sentences. This could partly explain the high performance observed for MRPC in the corrupted setting (cf. Section 5).

7 Conclusion

We apply a set of controllable corruption transformations to the datasets of NLU tasks in the GLUE benchmark, and study their impact on model performance. The proposed transformations are generic enough to be applicable to other NLU tasks, and can enrich the available artillery for dataset quality assessment in terms of how efficiently they trigger and test the language understanding capabilities of the models. Our results indicate that understanding the meaning of utterances is not required for high performance in most GLUE tasks. This finding suggests caution in interpreting leaderboard results and in the conclusions that can be drawn regarding the language understanding capabilities of the models. We make our code available[5] in order to promote the application of these tests to other NLU datasets, and to favour the development of benchmarks addressing the actual capability of the models to reason about language.

Acknowledgments

During the course of this project, Marianna Apidianaki and Jörg Tiedemann were supported by the FoTran project, funded by the European Research Council (ERC) under the European Union's Horizon 2020 research and innovation programme (grant agreement no. 771113). Stergios Chatzikyriakidis is supported by grant 2014-39 from the Swedish Research Council, which funds the Centre for Linguistic Theory and Studies in Probability (CLASP) in the Department of Philosophy, Linguistics, and Theory of Science at the University of Gothenburg. We thank the reviewers for their thoughtful comments and valuable suggestions.

References

Zheng Cai, Lifu Tu, and Kevin Gimpel. 2017. Pay Attention to the Ending: Strong Neural Baselines for the ROC Story Cloze Task. In *Proceedings of the 55th Annual Meeting of the Association for Computational Linguistics (Volume 2: Short Papers)*, pages 616–622, Vancouver, Canada. Association for Computational Linguistics.

Daniel Cer, Mona Diab, Eneko Agirre, Iñigo Lopez-Gazpio, and Lucia Specia. 2017. SemEval-2017 Task 1: Semantic Textual Similarity Multilingual and Crosslingual Focused Evaluation. In *Proceedings of the 11th International Workshop on Semantic Evaluation (SemEval-2017)*, pages 1–14, Vancouver, Canada. Association for Computational Linguistics.

Ido Dagan, Oren Glickman, and Bernardo Magnini. 2006. The PASCAL recognising textual entailment challenge. In *Machine learning challenges. evaluating predictive uncertainty, visual object classification, and recognising tectual entailment*, pages 177–190. Springer.

[5]`https://github.com/Helsinki-NLP/nlu-dataset-diagnostics`

Verna Dankers, Elia Bruni, and Dieuwke Hupkes. 2021. The paradox of the compositionality of natural language: a neural machine translation case study. *arXiv preprint arXiv:2108.05885*.

Jacob Devlin, Ming-Wei Chang, Kenton Lee, and Kristina Toutanova. 2019. BERT: Pre-training of Deep Bidirectional Transformers for Language Understanding. In *Proceedings of ACL*, pages 4171–4186, Minneapolis, Minnesota. Association for Computational Linguistics.

William B. Dolan and Chris Brockett. 2005. Automatically Constructing a Corpus of Sentential Paraphrases. In *Proceedings of the Third International Workshop on Paraphrasing (IWP2005)*.

Allyson Ettinger. 2020. What BERT is not: Lessons from a new suite of psycholinguistic diagnostics for language models. *Transactions of the Association for Computational Linguistics*, 8:34–48.

Richard Futrell, Ethan Wilcox, Takashi Morita, Peng Qian, Miguel Ballesteros, and Roger Levy. 2019. Neural language models as psycholinguistic subjects: Representations of syntactic state. In *Proceedings of the 2019 Conference of the North American Chapter of the Association for Computational Linguistics: Human Language Technologies, Volume 1 (Long and Short Papers)*, pages 32–42, Minneapolis, Minnesota. Association for Computational Linguistics.

Max Glockner, Vered Shwartz, and Yoav Goldberg. 2018. Breaking NLI Systems with Sentences that Require Simple Lexical Inferences. In *Proceedings of the 56th Annual Meeting of the Association for Computational Linguistics (Volume 2: Short Papers)*, pages 650–655, Melbourne, Australia. Association for Computational Linguistics.

Suchin Gururangan, Swabha Swayamdipta, Omer Levy, Roy Schwartz, Samuel Bowman, and Noah A. Smith. 2018. Annotation artifacts in natural language inference data. In *Proceedings of the 2018 Conference of the North American Chapter of the Association for Computational Linguistics: Human Language Technologies, Volume 2 (Short Papers)*, pages 107–112, New Orleans, Louisiana. Association for Computational Linguistics.

Alice Lai and Julia Hockenmaier. 2014. Illinois-LH: A Denotational and Distributional Approach to Semantics. In *Proceedings of the 8th International Workshop on Semantic Evaluation (SemEval 2014)*, pages 329–334, Dublin, Ireland.

Yinhan Liu, Myle Ott, Naman Goyal, Jingfei Du, Mandar Joshi, Danqi Chen, Omer Levy, Mike Lewis, Luke Zettlemoyer, and Veselin Stoyanov. 2019. RoBERTa: A Robustly Optimized BERT Pretraining Approach. *arXiv preprint arXiv:1907.11692*.

Marco Marelli, Stefano Menini, Marco Baroni, Luisa Bentivogli, Raffaella Bernardi, and Roberto Zamparelli. 2014. A SICK cure for the evaluation of compositional distributional semantic models. In *Proceedings of the Ninth International Conference on Language Resources and Evaluation (LREC'14)*, pages 216–223, Reykjavik, Iceland. European Language Resources Association (ELRA).

Tom McCoy, Ellie Pavlick, and Tal Linzen. 2019. Right for the wrong reasons: Diagnosing syntactic heuristics in natural language inference. In *Proceedings of the 57th Annual Meeting of the Association for Computational Linguistics*, pages 3428–3448, Florence, Italy. Association for Computational Linguistics.

Saif Mohammad and Peter Turney. 2010. Emotions Evoked by Common Words and Phrases: Using Mechanical Turk to Create an Emotion Lexicon. In *Proceedings of the NAACL HLT 2010 Workshop on Computational Approaches to Analysis and Generation of Emotion in Text*, pages 26–34, Los Angeles, CA. Association for Computational Linguistics.

Saif M. Mohammad and Peter D. Turney. 2013. Crowdsourcing a Word–Emotion Association Lexicon. *Computational Intelligence*, 29.

Yixin Nie, Adina Williams, Emily Dinan, Mohit Bansal, Jason Weston, and Douwe Kiela. 2020. Adversarial NLI: A new benchmark for natural language understanding. In *Proceedings of the 58th Annual Meeting of the Association for Computational Linguistics*, pages 4885–4901, Online. Association for Computational Linguistics.

Prasanna Parthasarathi, Koustuv Sinha, Joelle Pineau, and Adina Williams. 2021. Sometimes We Want Ungrammatical Translations. In *Findings of the Association for Computational Linguistics: EMNLP 2021*, pages 3205–3227, Punta Cana, Dominican Republic. Association for Computational Linguistics.

Ellie Pavlick, Pushpendre Rastogi, Juri Ganitkevitch, Benjamin Van Durme, and Chris Callison-Burch. 2015. PPDB 2.0: Better paraphrase ranking, fine-grained entailment relations, word embeddings, and style classification. In *Proceedings of the 53rd Annual Meeting of the Association for Computational Linguistics and the 7th International Joint Conference on Natural Language Processing (Volume 2: Short Papers)*, pages 425–430, Beijing, China. Association for Computational Linguistics.

Thang M. Pham, Trung Bui, Long Mai, and Anh Nguyen. 2020. Out of Order: How important is the sequential order of words in a sentence in Natural Language Understanding tasks? *arXiv preprint arXiv:2012.15180*.

Adam Poliak, Aparajita Haldar, Rachel Rudinger, J. Edward Hu, Ellie Pavlick, Aaron Steven White, and Benjamin Van Durme. 2018a. Collecting Diverse Natural Language Inference Problems for Sentence Representation Evaluation. In *Proceedings of the 2018 Conference on Empirical Methods in Natural Language Processing*, pages 67–81, Brussels, Belgium. Association for Computational Linguistics.

Adam Poliak, Jason Naradowsky, Aparajita Haldar, Rachel Rudinger, and Benjamin Van Durme. 2018b. Hypothesis Only Baselines in Natural Language Inference. In *Proceedings of the Seventh Joint Conference on Lexical and Computational Semantics*, pages 180–191, New Orleans, Louisiana. Association for Computational Linguistics.

Pranav Rajpurkar, Jian Zhang, Konstantin Lopyrev, and Percy Liang. 2016. SQuAD: 100,000+ Questions for Machine Comprehension of Text. In *Proceedings of the 2016 Conference on Empirical Methods in Natural Language Processing*, pages 2383–2392, Austin, Texas. Association for Computational Linguistics.

Roy Schwartz, Maarten Sap, Ioannis Konstas, Leila Zilles, Yejin Choi, and Noah A. Smith. 2017. The Effect of Different Writing Tasks on Linguistic Style: A Case Study of the ROC Story Cloze Task. In *Proceedings of the 21st Conference on Computational Natural Language Learning (CoNLL 2017)*, pages 15–25, Vancouver, Canada. Association for Computational Linguistics.

Chenglei Si, Shuohang Wang, Min-Yen Kan, and Jing Jiang. 2019. What does BERT learn from multiple-choice reading comprehension datasets? *arXiv preprint arXiv:1910.12391*.

Koustuv Sinha, Robin Jia, Dieuwke Hupkes, Joelle Pineau, Adina Williams, and Douwe Kiela. 2021. Masked Language Modeling and the Distributional Hypothesis: Order Word Matters Pre-training for Little. *arXiv preprint arXiv:2104.06644*.

Richard Socher, Alex Perelygin, Jean Wu, Jason Chuang, Christopher D. Manning, Andrew Ng, and Christopher Potts. 2013. Recursive Deep Models for Semantic Compositionality Over a Sentiment Treebank. In *Proceedings of the 2013 Conference on Empirical Methods in Natural Language Processing*, pages 1631–1642, Seattle, Washington, USA. Association for Computational Linguistics.

Saku Sugawara, Pontus Stenetorp, Kentaro Inui, and Akiko Aizawa. 2019. Assessing the Benchmarking Capacity of Machine Reading Comprehension Datasets. *arXiv preprint arXiv:1911.09241*.

Ekaterina Taktasheva, Vladislav Mikhailov, and Ekaterina Artemova. 2021. Shaking Syntactic Trees on the Sesame Street: Multilingual Probing with Controllable Perturbations. In *Proceedings of the 1st Workshop on Multilingual Representation Learning*, pages 191–210, Punta Cana, Dominican Republic. Association for Computational Linguistics.

Aarne Talman, Marianna Apidianaki, Stergios Chatzikyriakidis, and Jörg Tiedemann. 2021. NLI Data Sanity Check: Assessing the Effect of Data Corruption on Model Performance. In *Proceedings of the 23rd Nordic Conference on Computational Linguistics (NoDaLiDa)*, pages 276–287, Reykjavik, Iceland (Online). Linköping University Electronic Press, Sweden.

Aarne Talman and Stergios Chatzikyriakidis. 2019. Testing the Generalization Power of Neural Network Models across NLI Benchmarks. In *Proceedings of the 2019 ACL Workshop BlackboxNLP: Analyzing and Interpreting Neural Networks for NLP*, pages 85–94, Florence, Italy. Association for Computational Linguistics.

Masatoshi Tsuchiya. 2018. Performance Impact Caused by Hidden Bias of Training Data for Recognizing Textual Entailment. In *Proceedings of the Eleventh International Conference on Language Resources and Evaluation (LREC 2018)*, Miyazaki, Japan. European Language Resources Association (ELRA).

Alex Wang, Yada Pruksachatkun, Nikita Nangia, Amanpreet Singh, Julian Michael, Felix Hill, Omer Levy, and Samuel Bowman. 2019. SuperGLUE: A Stickier Benchmark for General-Purpose Language Understanding Systems. In *Advances in Neural Information Processing Systems*, volume 32. Curran Associates, Inc.

Alex Wang, Amanpreet Singh, Julian Michael, Felix Hill, Omer Levy, and Samuel Bowman. 2018. GLUE: A Multi-Task Benchmark and Analysis Platform for Natural Language Understanding. In *Proceedings of BlackboxNLP: Analyzing and Interpreting Neural Networks for NLP*, pages 353–355, Brussels, Belgium.

Alex Warstadt, Amanpreet Singh, and Samuel R Bowman. 2018. Neural Network Acceptability Judgments. *arXiv preprint arXiv:1805.12471*.

Adina Williams, Nikita Nangia, and Samuel Bowman. 2018. A Broad-Coverage Challenge Corpus for Sentence Understanding through Inference. In *Proceedings of the 2018 Conference of the North American Chapter of the Association for Computational Linguistics: Human Language Technologies, Volume 1 (Long Papers)*, pages 1112–1122, New Orleans, Louisiana. Association for Computational Linguistics.

Thomas Wolf, Lysandre Debut, Victor Sanh, Julien Chaumond, Clement Delangue, Anthony Moi, Pierric Cistac, Tim Rault, Remi Louf, Morgan Funtowicz, Joe Davison, Sam Shleifer, Patrick von Platen, Clara Ma, Yacine Jernite, Julien Plu, Canwen Xu, Teven Le Scao, Sylvain Gugger, Mariama Drame, Quentin Lhoest, and Alexander Rush. 2020a. Transformers: State-of-the-art natural language processing. In *Proceedings of the 2020 Conference on Empirical Methods in Natural Language Processing: System Demonstrations*, pages 38–45, Online. Association for Computational Linguistics.

Thomas Wolf, Quentin Lhoest, Patrick von Platen, Yacine Jernite, Mariama Drame, Julien Plu, Julien Chaumond, Clement Delangue, Clara Ma, Abhishek Thakur, Suraj Patil, Joe Davison, Teven Le Scao, Victor Sanh, Canwen Xu, Nicolas Patry, Angie McMillan-Major, Simon Brandeis, Sylvain Gugger,

François Lagunas, Lysandre Debut, Morgan Funtowicz, Anthony Moi, Sasha Rush, Philipp Schmidd, Pierric Cistac, Victor Muštar, Jeff Boudier, and Anna Tordjmann. 2020b. Datasets. *GitHub. Note: https://github.com/huggingface/datasets*, 1.

Rowan Zellers, Yonatan Bisk, Roy Schwartz, and Yejin Choi. 2018. SWAG: A large-scale adversarial dataset for grounded commonsense inference. In *Proceedings of the 2018 Conference on Empirical Methods in Natural Language Processing*, pages 93–104, Brussels, Belgium. Association for Computational Linguistics.

Leveraging Three Types of Embeddings from Masked Language Models in Idiom Token Classification

Ryosuke Takahashi* **Ryohei Sasano** **Koichi Takeda**
Graduate School of Informatics, Nagoya University
ryosuke.takahashi.cs@gmail.com,
{sasano,takedasu}@i.nagoya-u.ac.jp

Abstract

Many linguistic expressions have idiomatic and literal interpretations, and the automatic distinction of these two interpretations has been studied for decades. Recent research has shown that contextualized word embeddings derived from masked language models (MLMs) can give promising results for idiom token classification. This indicates that contextualized word embedding alone contains information about whether the word is being used in a literal sense or not. However, we believe that more types of information can be derived from MLMs and that leveraging such information can improve idiom token classification. In this paper, we leverage three types of embeddings from MLMs; uncontextualized token embeddings and masked token embeddings in addition to the standard contextualized word embeddings and show that the newly added embeddings significantly improve idiom token classification for both English and Japanese datasets.

1 Introduction

Potentially idiomatic phrases are often used both in the idiomatic and literal sense. For example, "blew whistle" in (1) is used in the literal sense, whereas that in (2) is used in the idiomatic sense, that is, the meaning of the phrase has shifted and in this case it means *accuse*. Deciding whether each occurrence of a potentially idiomatic phrase is a literal or idiomatic usage is an essential process for text understanding. We call this processing *idiom token classification* following Salton et al. (2016).

(1) The referee blew the whistle to end the match.

(2) I blew the whistle on government corruption.

Recently, contextualized word embeddings have been shown to be useful for word sense disambiguation (Hadiwinoto et al., 2019). Furthermore, Shwartz and Dagan (2019) showed that the contextualized embeddings including BERT (Devlin et al., 2019) are useful for recognizing meaning shift of words in idioms. However, they only used contextualized embeddings, even though comparing them with the standard embeddings of the target word can be beneficial for precise detection of meaning shifts. Thus, in this paper, we propose a method to improved a BERT-based idiom token classifier by leveraging uncontextualized word embeddings.

Specifically, we use the token embedding of BERT, which is the uncontextualized embedding that is input to BERT and the same vector as is used for the prediction in the task of masked language model. Our assumption can be explained using (1) and (2) as follows: since "whistle" in (2) is used as a part of an idiomatic phrase, its contextualized embedding differs more from the uncontextualized embedding of "whistle" than in the case of (1).

Furthermore, we also leverage the masked token embedding of the target word in BERT, which is generated when the target phrase constituents are masked. This embedding can be considered to represent the meaning inferred from its context, and we assume that if the target phrase is used in the literal sense, as in (1), the output embedding will not significantly differ from the original embedding and thus the differences between the BERT embeddings without masking and those with masking are expected to be small.

2 Task and Baseline

2.1 Datasets and Settings

We focus on the idiom token classification of phrases consisting of verb-noun pairs in English and Japanese. As the English dataset, we use the VNC-Tokens dataset[1] (Cook et al., 2008). This dataset consists of 2,984 sentences containing 53 different potentially idiomatic verb-noun pairs in

*Ryosuke Takahashi is currently at SB Technology Corp.

[1] https://people.eng.unimelb.edu.au/paulcook/English_VNC_Cook.zip

Proceedings of the 11th Joint Conference on Lexical and Computational Semantics, pages 234 - 239
July 14-15, 2022 ©2022 Association for Computational Linguistics

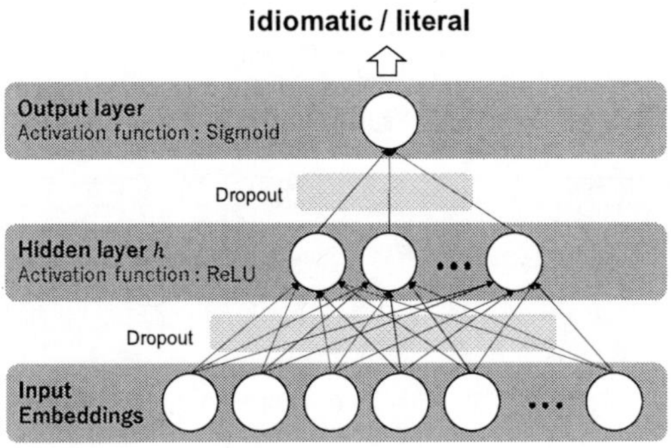

Figure 1: The *Embed-Encode-Predict* model.

English, where each sentence is labeled with "I" (idiomatic), "L" (literal), or "Q" (unknown). We use 28 out of the 53 idioms that have similar numbers of idiomatic and literal occurrences and only those sentences labeled as "I" or "L" following Salton et al. (2016).

As the Japanese dataset, we use the OpenMWE Corpus[2] (Hashimoto and Kawahara, 2008). This dataset consists of 102,846 sentences containing 146 different potentially idiomatic verb-noun pairs in Japanese, where each sentence is labeled with "I" (idiomatic) or "L" (literal). We use 90 out of the 146 idioms for which more than 50 examples for both idiomatic and literal usages are available following Hashimoto and Kawahara (2008).

In this study, we adopt the zero-shot setting because we are interested in detecting meaning shifts of words that are not included in the training data. Specifically, we employ the one-versus-rest scheme with the fully zero-shot setting. That is, we build a classifier for each phrase, which is trained on the phrases that contain neither the verb nor the noun that makes up the target phrase. For example, when building a classifier for *blew whistle*, we exclude phrases whose verb is *blew* or whose noun is *whistle* from the training data. We take one fifth of each training dataset as development data.

2.2 Baseline Systems

As the baseline system, we adopted a minimal *Embed-Encode-Predict* model (Shwartz and Dagan, 2019) that uses only contextualized embeddings of the constituent words of the target phrase as input. The reason for adopting a relatively simple model as a baseline is that the purpose of this study is to confirm the effectiveness of the newly

Models	English	Japanese
Majority Baseline	0.672	0.629
Salton et al. (2016)	0.780	-
Hashimoto and Kawahara (2008)	-	0.740
BERT[$\boldsymbol{v}_{\mathrm{V}}$]	0.829	0.816
BERT[$\boldsymbol{v}_{\mathrm{N}}$]	0.836	0.821
BERT[$\boldsymbol{v}_{\mathrm{V}}; \boldsymbol{v}_{\mathrm{N}}$]	**0.840**	**0.823**

Table 1: Macro-averaged accuracy for baseline systems.

added embeddings. Figure 1 shows the outline of the model, which consists of an input layer, a hidden layer, and an output layer. The output layer predicts whether the input phrase is idiomatic or literal. The size of the hidden layer is half of the input embedding size in all models in the paper. We applied dropout on the input embeddings and hidden layer. The dropout rates are both 50%.

As the input, we used $[\boldsymbol{v}_{\mathrm{V}}; \boldsymbol{v}_{\mathrm{N}}]$, a concatenation of the contextualized embeddings of the verb and noun that comprise the target phrase. We used the pre-trained models `BERT-Base, Uncased`[3] for English and `BERT-Base, WWE`[4] for Japanese. Both models have 12 layers and 768 hidden dimensions per token. Japanese sentences were tokenized by Juman++[5] in advance. We used the development data to determine the number of training epochs and to determine which BERT hidden layer to use as the input embeddings of the *Embed-Encode-Predict* model. We refer to this model as BERT[$\boldsymbol{v}_{\mathrm{V}}; \boldsymbol{v}_{\mathrm{N}}$]. In addition, we developed models that only leverages one of the contextualized embeddings $\boldsymbol{v}_{\mathrm{V}}$ and $\boldsymbol{v}_{\mathrm{N}}$ to confirm the importance of each embedding. We refer to them as BERT[$\boldsymbol{v}_{\mathrm{V}}$] and BERT[$\boldsymbol{v}_{\mathrm{N}}$], respectively.

For reference, we also implemented support vector machine (SVM) based models with the features used in previous work. For English, we employed Salton et al. (2016)'s model that leveraged Skip-Thought Vectors (Kiros et al., 2015) as features. For Japanese, we implemented the features used by Hashimoto and Kawahara (2008), consisting of POS, lemma, token n-gram, hypernym, domain, voice, negativity, modality, adjacency, and adnominal information.

Table 1 lists the macro-averaged accuracy for each baseline model with the accuracy of the majority baseline. Each accuracy is the average of 5 runs with different random seeds. For both English

[2] http://openmwe.sourceforge.jp/Idiom/corpus/OpenMWE-Corpus-0.02.tar.bz2

[3] https://storage.googleapis.com/bert_models/2018_10_18/uncased_L-12_H-768_A-12.zip

[4] http://nlp.ist.i.kyoto-u.ac.jp/nl-resource/JapaneseBertPretrainedModel/Japanese_L-12_H-768_A-12_E-30_BPE_WWM.zip

[5] https://github.com/ku-nlp/jumanpp

and Japanese dataset, BERT[$v_V; v_N$] achieved the highest accuracy, which demonstrates that BERT embeddings are useful for idiom token classification even in a zero-shot setting and supposedly capture the general characteristic of idiomaticity. We measured the statistical significance between BERT[$v_V; v_N$] and the other models with an approximate randomization test (Chinchor, 1992) with 99,999 iterations and significance level $\alpha = 0.05$ after Bonferroni correction. We found significant differences against the Majority Baseline and Salton et al. (2016) with respect to English and against Majority Baseline and Hashimoto and Kawahara (2008) with respect to Japanese.

3 Leveraging Additional Embeddings

The relatively high performance of BERT[$v_V; v_N$] in a zero-shot setting indicates that the standard BERT embeddings contain information about how much the meaning differs from the standard meaning of the words that comprise the phrase. However, the performance of idiom token classification can be improved by explicitly incorporating the standard meaning of the constituent words and the meaning inferred from its context.

3.1 Additional embeddings

We add two types of embeddings to BERT[$v_V;v_N$]: uncontextualized token embeddings and masked token embeddings of the phrase constituents.

Uncontextualized token embeddings We use the token embedding of BERT, which is the uncontextualized embedding that is input to BERT and the same vector as is used for the prediction in the task of masked language model in BERT. This embedding can be considered to represent the standard meaning of the word and thus if the target phrase is used in the literal sense, the BERT embeddings, which are contextualized, should be similar to the token embeddings. We refer to the uncontextualized token embeddings of a verb and a noun as v_{V_t} and v_{N_t}, respectively.

Masked token embeddings We use the hidden layer of BERT when the target token is replaced with a special token `[MASK]`. This embedding can be considered to represent the meaning inferred from its context. If the target phrase is used in the literal sense, the differences between the BERT embeddings without masking and those with masking are expected to be small. We refer to the masked

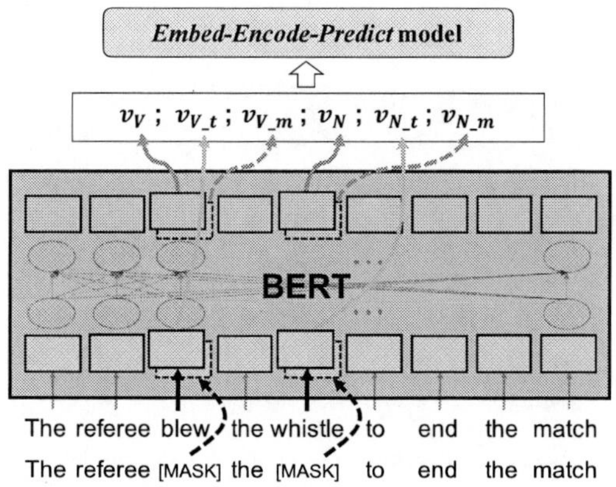

Figure 2: Overview of the proposed model.

Embeddings	English	Japanese
$v_V; v_N$	0.840	0.823
$v_V; v_{V\_t}; v_N; v_{N\_t}$	0.859	0.842
$v_V; v_{V\_m}; v_N; v_{N\_m}$	0.852	0.829
$v_V; v_{V\_t}; v_{V\_m}; v_N; v_{N\_t}; v_{N\_m}$	**0.865**	**0.847**

Table 2: Macro-averaged accuracy for different combinations of input embeddings.

token embeddings of a verb and a noun as v_{V_m} and v_{N_m}, respectively.

Figure 2 shows the overview of the proposed model. When a sentence containing the target phrase is given, a *masked sentence*, in which the verb and noun that comprise the phrase are masked, is generated and input to the BERT in addition to the original sentence. Then, v_V, v_{V_t}, v_{V_m}, v_N, v_{N_t}, and v_{N_m} are extracted and their concatenation is input to the *Embed-Encode-Predict* model.

3.2 Experiments and analysis

We performed the idiom token classification experiments with the additional embeddings. Table 2 lists the macro-averaged accuracy for different combinations of input embeddings. We can confirm that leveraging uncontextualized token embeddings and masked token embeddings in addition to the standard BERT embeddings is beneficial for idiom token classification. The statistical significance test shows that the difference between the accuracy of BERT[$v_V; v_{V\_t}; v_{V\_m}; v_N; v_{N\_t}; v_{N\_m}$] and that of BERT[$v_V; v_N$] are significant for both English and Japanese datasets. The accuracy of BERT[$v_V; v_{V\_t}; v_N; v_{N\_t}$] was slightly better than that of BERT[$v_V; v_{V\_m}; v_N; v_{N\_m}$]. We can say that the difference between the standard BERT embeddings and the uncontextualized token embed-

Usage	English		Japanese	
	v vs. v_t	v vs. v_m	v vs. v_t	v vs. v_m
Literal	**0.157**	**0.593**	**0.197**	**0.545**
Idiomatic	0.122	0.517	0.166	0.428

Table 3: Means of the cosine similarities of standard BERT embeddings (v) against uncontextualized token embeddings (v_t) and masked token embeddings (v_m) for literal and idiomatic cases, respectively.

dings should be a good indicator of idiomaticity.

We assumed that when the target phrase is used in the literal sense, the uncontextualized token embeddings and the masked token embeddings tend to be similar to the standard BERT embeddings. To verify this assumption, we calculated the means of their cosine similarities for the literal and idiomatic cases, respectively. Table 3 lists the means of the cosine similarities. For English dataset, the mean of the cosine similarities between the uncontextualized token embeddings and standard BERT embeddings for the literal cases was 0.157, which was larger than that for the idiomatic cases, 0.122. Similarly, the mean of the cosine similarities between the masked token embeddings and standard BERT embeddings for the literal cases was 0.593, which was larger than that for the idiomatic cases, 0.517. The same trend can be observed for the Japanese dataset. It has been confirmed that all the differences are statistically significant. These results support our assumption.

4 Related Work

Several researchers have tackled the task of idiom token classification. Hashimoto and Kawahara (2008) is one of the earliest works. They created a Japanese annotated data for idiom token classification and proposed an SVM-based model with a set of features that commonly used for WSD. Fazly et al. (2009) proposed statistical measures that quantify the degree of lexical, syntactic, and overall fixedness of a verb noun combination. Sporleder and Li (2009) proposed a model for unsupervised idiom token classification based on the observation that literally used expressions typically exhibit cohesive ties with the surrounding discourse, while idiomatic expressions do not.

Li and Sporleder (2010) explored various features, such as global lexical context, discourse cohesion, syntactic structure, and local lexical features. They reported that global lexical context and discourse cohesion were most effective for idiom token classification. Peng et al. (2014) treated idiom token identification as a problem of outlier detection. They extracted topics from paragraphs containing idioms and from paragraphs containing literals by using Latent Dirichlet Allocation (LDA).

A broad range of neural network-based models have been proposed in recent years. Gharbieh et al. (2016) obtained phrase representations by averaging skip-gram (Mikolov et al., 2013) vectors of words that appear around the target phrase and applied them to idiom token classification. Salton et al. (2016) constructed an SVM-based classifier using the distributed representation of sentences generated by the Skip-Thought model (Kiros et al., 2015). King and Cook (2018) improved the performance of word embedding-based methods by incorporating syntactic and lexical patterns of idiomatic expressions.

More recently, methods using contextualized word embeddings such as ELMo (Peters et al., 2018) and BERT (Devlin et al., 2019) have been proposed. Shwartz and Dagan (2019) showed that the contextualized embeddings of constituent words were useful for recognizing meaning shifts of phrases. Hashempour and Villavicencio (2020) and Kurfalı and Östling (2020) worked on the idiom token classification task using BERT embeddings and reported that the BERT-based model achieved high accuracy in a phrase-specific setting. Garcia et al. (2021) proposed probing measures to examine how accurately idiomaticity in noun compounds is captured in vector space models and concluded that idiomaticity is not yet accurately represented by contextualized word embeddings.

Studies that used multiple types of embeddings in BERT, similar to our method, include the work by Zhang et al. (2020) and Yamada et al. (2021). Zhang et al. used the weighted sum of the input embedding and the mask embedding for spelling error correction whereas Yamada et al. used the weighted sum of the input embedding and the mask embedding for semantic frame induction.

5 Conclusion

We demonstrate that leveraging uncontextualized token embeddings and masked token embeddings in addition to the standard contextualized word embeddings significantly improve idiom token classification in a zero-shot setting. We also show that the results of investigating the similarities of these embeddings for each of the literal and idiomatic cases support our assumption that the uncontextualized token embeddings and the masked token embeddings tend to be similar to the standard BERT embeddings when the target phrase is used in the literal meaning. One of the advantages of the proposed method is that it does not require training a new model because it extracts and uses embeddings with different properties from the same language model. We believe that the three types of embedding introduced in this study can be applied to other natural language tasks.

Acknowledgements

This work was supported by JSPS KAKENHI Grant Numbers 21K12012.

References

Nancy Chinchor. 1992. The statistical significance of the MUC-4 results. In *Proceedings of the 4th Message Understanding Conference (MUC)*, pages 30–50.

Paul Cook, Afsaneh Fazly, and Suzanne Stevenson. 2008. The VNC-tokens dataset. In *Proceedings of the LREC Workshop on Towards a Shared Task for Multiword Expressions (MWE)*, pages 19–22.

Jacob Devlin, Ming-Wei Chang, Kenton Lee, and Kristina Toutanova. 2019. BERT: Pre-training of deep bidirectional transformers for language understanding. In *Proceedings of the 2019 Conference of the North American Chapter of the Association for Computational Linguistics: Human Language Technologies (NAACL-HLT)*, pages 4171–4186.

Afsaneh Fazly, Paul Cook, and Suzanne Stevenson. 2009. Unsupervised type and token identification of idiomatic expressions. *Computational Linguistics*, 35(1):61–103.

Marcos Garcia, Tiago Kramer Vieira, Carolina Scarton, Marco Idiart, and Aline Villavicencio. 2021. Probing for idiomaticity in vector space models. In *Proceedings of the 16th Conference of the European Chapter of the Association for Computational Linguistics (EACL)*, pages 3551–3564.

Waseem Gharbieh, Virendra Bhavsar, and Paul Cook. 2016. A word embedding approach to identifying verb-noun idiomatic combinations. In *Proceedings of the 12th Workshop on Multiword Expressions (MWE)*, pages 112–118.

Christian Hadiwinoto, Hwee Tou Ng, and Wee Chung Gan. 2019. Improved word sense disambiguation using pre-trained contextualized word representations. In *Proceedings of the 2019 Conference on Empirical Methods in Natural Language Processing and the 9th International Joint Conference on Natural Language Processing (EMNLP-IJCNLP)*, pages 5297–5306.

Reyhaneh Hashempour and Aline Villavicencio. 2020. Leveraging contextual embeddings and idiom principle for detecting idiomaticity in potentially idiomatic expressions. In *Proceedings of the Workshop on the Cognitive Aspects of the Lexicon (CogALex)*, pages 72–80.

Chikara Hashimoto and Daisuke Kawahara. 2008. Construction of an idiom corpus and its application to idiom identification based on WSD incorporating idiom-specific features. In *Proceedings of the 2008 Conference on Empirical Methods in Natural Language Processing (EMNLP)*, pages 992–1001.

Milton King and Paul Cook. 2018. Leveraging distributed representations and lexico-syntactic fixedness for token-level prediction of the idiomaticity of English verb-noun combinations. In *Proceedings of the 56th Annual Meeting of the Association for Computational Linguistics (ACL)*, pages 345–350.

Ryan Kiros, Yukun Zhu, Russ R Salakhutdinov, Richard Zemel, Raquel Urtasun, Antonio Torralba, and Sanja Fidler. 2015. Skip-thought vectors. In *Proceedings of Advances in Neural Information Processing Systems 28 (NIPS)*, pages 3294–3302.

Murathan Kurfalı and Robert Östling. 2020. Disambiguation of potentially idiomatic expressions with contextual embeddings. In *Proceedings of the Joint Workshop on Multiword Expressions and Electronic Lexicons (MWE)*, pages 85–94.

Linlin Li and Caroline Sporleder. 2010. Linguistic cues for distinguishing literal and non-literal usages. In *Proceedings of the 23rd International Conference on Computational Linguistics (COLING)*, pages 683–691.

Tomas Mikolov, Ilya Sutskever, Kai Chen, Greg Corrado, and Jeffrey Dean. 2013. Distributed representations of words and phrases and their compositionality. In *Proceedings of the 26th International Conference on Neural Information Processing Systems (NIPS)*, pages 3111–3119.

Jing Peng, Anna Feldman, and Ekaterina Vylomova. 2014. Classifying idiomatic and literal expressions using topic models and intensity of emotions. In *Proceedings of the 2014 Conference on Empirical Methods in Natural Language Processing (EMNLP)*, pages 2019–2027.

Matthew Peters, Mark Neumann, Mohit Iyyer, Matt Gardner, Christopher Clark, Kenton Lee, and Luke Zettlemoyer. 2018. Deep contextualized word representations. In *Proceedings of the 2018 Conference of the North American Chapter of the Association for Computational Linguistics: Human Language Technologies (NAACL-HLT)*, pages 2227–2237.

Giancarlo Salton, Robert Ross, and John Kelleher. 2016. Idiom token classification using sentential distributed semantics. In *Proceedings of the 54th Annual Meeting of the Association for Computational Linguistics (ACL)*, pages 194–204.

Vered Shwartz and Ido Dagan. 2019. Still a pain in the neck: Evaluating text representations on lexical composition. *Transactions of the Association for Computational Linguistics*, 7:403–419.

Caroline Sporleder and Linlin Li. 2009. Unsupervised recognition of literal and non-literal use of idiomatic expressions. In *Proceedings of the 12th Conference of the European Chapter of the Association for Computational Linguistics (EACL)*, pages 754–762.

Kosuke Yamada, Ryohei Sasano, and Koichi Takeda. 2021. Semantic frame induction using masked word embeddings and two-step clustering. In *Proceedings of the 59th Annual Meeting of the Association for Computational Linguistics and the 11th International Joint Conference on Natural Language Processing (ACL-IJCNLP)*, pages 811–816.

Shaohua Zhang, Haoran Huang, Jicong Liu, and Hang Li. 2020. Spelling error correction with soft-masked BERT. In *Proceedings of the 58th Annual Meeting of the Association for Computational Linguistics (ACL)*, pages 882–890.

"What makes a question inquisitive?" A Study on Type-Controlled Inquisitive Question Generation

Lingyu Gao*[1], Debanjan Ghosh[2], and Kevin Gimpel[1]
[1]Toyota Technological Institute at Chicago
[2]Educational Testing Service
{lygao, kgimpel}@ttic.edu,
dghosh@ets.org

Abstract

We propose a type-controlled framework for inquisitive question generation. We annotate an inquisitive question dataset with question types, train question type classifiers, and fine-tune models for type-controlled question generation. Empirical results demonstrate that we can generate a variety of questions that adhere to specific types while drawing from the source texts. We also investigate strategies for selecting a single question from a generated set, considering both an informative vs. inquisitive question classifier and a pairwise ranker trained from a small set of expert annotations. Question selection using the pairwise ranker yields strong results in automatic and manual evaluation. Our human evaluation assesses multiple aspects of the generated questions, finding that the ranker chooses questions with the best syntax (4.59), semantics (4.37), and inquisitiveness (3.92) on a scale of 1-5, even rivaling the performance of human-written questions.

Context	...The plan places an indicated value on the real estate operation, Santa Fe Pacific Realty Corp., of $ 2 billion.
Source sentence	Santa Fe Pacific directors are expected to **review** the plan at a meeting today, according to people familiar with the transaction.
BASE	What kind of meeting?
SPAN	How will the directors review the plan?
Explanation	Why are they reviewing the plan?
Background	Is it expected to review the plan today?
Elaboration	What will the review entail?
Instantiation	Which directors are expected to review the plan?
Definition	what is that?
Forward	What are the directors expected to review?
Informative	Who are Santa Fe Pacific directors expected to review?

Table 1: Examples of generated questions given the article context and source sentence (with span in **bold**).

1 Introduction

Recently, interest has grown in the task of automatic question generation (AQG) from text (Sun et al., 2018; Kumar and Black, 2020). AQG is useful in building conversational AI systems (Bordes et al., 2017; Gao et al., 2019), generating synthetic examples for QA (Alberti et al., 2019; Dong et al., 2019; Sultan et al., 2020), and educational applications, such as intelligent tutoring and instructional games (Chen et al., 2018; Flor and Riordan, 2018). In the majority of such studies, AQG focuses on generating factual questions that tend to ask about specific information in the text (i.e., "who did what to whom") (Du et al., 2017).

Instead of asking factual questions with answers already present in the text, Ko et al. (2020) argued that human readers instinctively ask questions that are curiosity-driven, answer-agnostic, and seek a high-level understanding of the document being read. They released a dataset of such curiosity-driven questions (henceforth INQUISITIVE; for details, see Section 2). The objective of our work is to generate deeper, inquisitive questions based on the INQUISITIVE dataset.

Our motivations for generating inquisitive questions are two-fold. Educators can obtain *diverse* questions for a specific source text when designing quizzes or choosing questions to test students' reading comprehension ability. They can focus into different aspects of the context (e.g., questioning the background information or asking to elaborate a fact) for diverse question generation (Cho et al., 2019; Wang et al., 2020; Sultan et al., 2020). Likewise, students can also be assisted in knowledge acquisition and building reasoning skills by practising over a large number of diverse questions (Cao and Wang, 2021).

Though our initial efforts are similar to Ko et al. (2020), we found this to be insufficient as it does not leverage the inherent diversity of question types

* Partially done as part of an internship at Educational Testing Service.

Proceedings of the 11th Joint Conference on Lexical and Computational Semantics, pages 240 - 257
July 14-15, 2022 ©2022 Association for Computational Linguistics

in the dataset. Ko et al. (2020) concatenated the context, source sentence, and the question to learn a language model for question generation using GPT-2 (Radford et al., 2019). On the contrary, we first annotated 1550 questions from the training partition of the INQUISITIVE dataset to identify the question types, such as questions requesting background information, asking about the cause of an event, asking for details on underspecified facts, etc. (see Section 2.2 for details). We finetune a RoBERTa-large model (Liu et al., 2019) to predict the question types on the rest of the dataset. We then use the question types in a controlled generation framework based on BART (Lewis et al., 2020) to generate type-specific inquisitive questions.

Consider the example in Table 1. The BASE model is BART finetuned on INQUISITIVE to generate questions from the context and source sentence. The SPAN model additionally uses the span, a part of the source sentence the annotators are curious about. We then show six questions of specific types (e.g., Explanation, ..., Forward) generated by our type-controlled finetuned BART model. In comparison, the informative question is generated by finetuning on SQuAD (Rajpurkar et al., 2016), a popular dataset for generating factual questions. The informative question asks for surface-level information ("who are Santa Fe Pacific directors expected to review?") whereas the inquisitive questions ask for deeper information (e.g., "why are they reviewing the plan?"), such as the reason for the directors' actions.

As mentioned earlier, our motivations for generating diverse inquisitive questions are to provide educational tools and resources. However, there are also cases where an educator or student may prefer only a single high-quality question for a span or a ranked list of questions. We investigate two strategies for automatic question selection/ranking for this latter scenario. The first strategy ranks questions using an inquisitive vs. informative question classifier, where questions from SQuAD are used as informative questions. In the second strategy, we collect expert annotations of partial rankings for a subset of generated questions, and then train a pairwise ranker to select the best question (denoted as TYPE_r). In automatic evaluation, we find that TYPE_r yields questions that have reasonably strong match to references while also being novel relative to the training set (Section 4.1). We report a large-scale human evaluation via Mechanical Turk and demonstrate that questions generated from the same TYPE_r model have the best syntax (4.59), semantics (4.37), and inquisitiveness (3.92) on a scale of 1-5 (Section 4.2). We make the annotations, code, and the MTurk judgements from our research publicly available.[1]

2 Data

We will now describe the annotation of questions with question types, which is one of the main contributions of our work. We describe the annotation process in detail in Section 2.2. But first, we briefly introduce the INQUISITIVE dataset.

Human annotators created the inquisitive questions while reading the initial part (i.e., five sentences) of news articles from the WSJ portion of the Penn Treebank (Marcus et al., 1993) or Associated Press articles from the TIPSTER corpus (Harman and Liberman, 1993).[2] Annotators first highlighted a span within the sentence that they were curious about and then wrote a maximum of three questions. Next, a separate set of annotators validated the questions and excluded unqualified questions (around 5%).

An instance in INQUISITIVE has the following components: a **source sentence**, the sentence the annotator read when asking the question, **context** that includes all the sentences before the source sentence in the same article, a **span** within the source sentence the annotators were most curious about, and finally, the **question** the annotator wrote. INQUISITIVE is split into *training* (15,897 instances), *test* (1,885 instances), and *dev* (1,984 instances).

2.1 Question Type Annotation

In the USA, K-12 standards describe what students should understand and be able to do by the end of each grade.[3] The guidelines state that even in very early grades students should understand how individuals and events evolve and interact in a text. The *hows* and *whys* of the text (i.e., inquisitive questions) come naturally to us (Ko et al., 2020).

Ko et al. (2020) evaluated the question types over a small set of 120 questions and identified a few question types that appear frequently and address various *how* and *why* questions.[4] Although they

[1] `https://github.com/EducationalTestingService/inquisitive-questions`

[2] They also use Newsela (Xu et al., 2015) but it was not publicly released.

[3] `http://www.corestandards.org`

[4] The evaluation is not available in the released dataset.

Question Type (# samples)	Example	
	[*context*] [*source sentence* with span in **bold**]	Question
Explanation (443)	[...unraveling of the on-again, off-again UAL buy-out slammed the stock market.][Now, stock prices seem to be in a general **retreat.**]	Why are the stock prices retreating?
Elaboration (364)	[...Beth Capper has gone without food ...][It's not drugs or alcohol or even baby formula that has **put her in such a bind.**]	What has put her in this bind?
Background (407)	[...John R. Stevens, ..., was named senior executive vice president...][He **will continue** to report to Donald Pardus, ...]	How long has he been reporting to Donald Pardus?
Definition (114)	[Oh, that terrible Mr. Ortega.][Just when American liberalism had pulled the **arms plug** on the Contras ...]	What is the arms plug?
Instantiation (159)	[...in their office, Rajiv Maheswaran and Yu-Han Chang can catch a glimpse of Staples Center ...][Whiteboards inside their office are filled with **algorithms** in shades of red, blue and green.]	what kind of algorithms?
Forward-looking (31)	[The federal government would not actually shut down. Agents would still patrol ...][Mail carriers would **still deliver mail.**]	Would it arrive on time?
Other (32)	[...the entire neighborhood can fall victim.] [At this stage some people just **"walk away"** from homes...]	Why is it quoted?

Table 2: Annotated question type distributions and salient examples of each question type. Context and source sentences are presented where the spans in source sentences are bold. More examples are in the Appendix.

presented a fully data-driven approach without any theoretical underpinnings we notice such curiosity driven questions – such as asking for background information, elaborating details, and why one action led to another – are linked to Rhetorical Structure Theory (RST) (Mann and Thompson, 1988). In RST, relations such as *background, elaboration,* and *cause* provide a systematic way to analyze the text and understand the discourse relations among segments of the text. Likewise, the questions generated in this work inquire about the background or causal information and those are close to the rhetorical relations in the text. For our annotation, we use the same set of question types as Ko et al. (2020), which are described below:

- **Explanation**: Questions signaled by the interrogative "why" as well as its paraphrases such as "what is the reason". These questions are often asked to explain why something happened or identify its cause ("why did he choose to speak to the press?").
- **Elaboration**: Questions that seek more details about concepts, entities, relations, or events expressed in the text, e.g., "what are some details about this performance?"
- **Background**: Questions that seek more information about the context of the story or seek clarification about something described in the text ("how much loan was guaranteed?").
- **Definition**: Questions that ask for the meaning of a specific term ("what does hubris mean?").
- **Instantiation**: Questions that ask about a specific instance (e.g., "what is the name of the newspaper?") or a set of instances (e.g., "who are these other cable partners?").
- **Forward-looking**: Questions that ask about future events, e.g., "would it arrive on time?"
- **Other**: Other types of questions, e.g., inference questions ("how many women were found?") that ask to deduce information from the source, or that ask something irrelevant ("Does seaweed look like cotton candy?")

Three expert annotators who are experienced at annotation tasks initially annotated 50 questions with the types above. Pairwise κ's between annotators were 0.570, 0.572, and 0.872 (moderate and substantial agreement). The annotators exchanged notes and decided on final annotation guidelines. In the next round, each annotator independently annotated 500 random questions from the training partition of INQUISITIVE, thus producing a total set of 1,550 annotated questions. We used majority vote for the first 50 questions. Table 2 presents the question type distribution with salient examples.

Table 3 shows the most common leading unigrams for each question type in our annotated

Explanation	Elaboration	Background	Definition	Instantiation	Forward-looking	Other
why (396)	what (164)	what (108)	what (95)	what (62)	what (9)	why (5)
what (28)	how (135)	how (91)	does (5)	which (50)	how (8)	does (5)
is (5)	is (11)	is (40)	how (3)	who (36)	will (3)	is (4)
how (4)	where (6)	who (34)	who (2)	in (3)	would (2)	what (3)
if (3)	in (5)	where (18)	definition (2)	at (2)	did (2)	of (2)

Table 3: Most common leading unigrams in annotated questions (lowercased) for each type (counts in parentheses).

data.[5] Although WH question words such as "why", "when", "who", etc. have been used to generate a variety of question types before (Zhou et al., 2019), they cannot fully express the semantic content of questions (Cao and Wang, 2021). Likewise, we observe there is no one-to-one relationship between WH words and question types. Each type encompasses multiple question words. Some types, like Explanation and Definition, have a single dominant leading unigram, while others have two or three. The word "what" is the most common leading unigram for five question types.

2.2 Question Type Prediction

We aim to generate a question that follows a particular question type as control code. However, to do so, we must first determine the question types in the entire INQUISITIVE dataset. To this end, we finetune RoBERTa-large as a multi-class classifier on the annotated set of 1,550 questions and use the classifier to predict the question types of the remaining questions in INQUISITIVE. As input, we concatenate the context, source sentence, span, and question, using the "[SEP]" token as delimiter.[6] We use 1,400 examples for training and the remaining 150 as the validation set (also used for early stopping)[7], on which we reach an accuracy of 73.3%.

3 Methods

In this section, we present our computational approaches for question generation. The input x is a sequence of tokens $x = \langle x_1, ..., x_n \rangle$, which may consist of one or more sentences. The output is a question q that consists of sequence of tokens, i.e., $q = \langle q_1, ..., q_m \rangle$. Using the standard autoregressive sequence-to-sequence architecture (Sutskever et al., 2014) we model $P_\theta(q \mid x)$ as follows:

$$P_\theta(q \mid x) = \prod_i P_\theta(q_i \mid q_1, \ldots, q_{i-1}, x) \quad (1)$$

We use the pretrained BART model (Lewis et al., 2020), a transformer (Vaswani et al., 2017) composed of a bidirectional encoder and an autoregressive decoder. In our simplest setup (called BASE), we concatenate the source sentence and the context. The next setting also concatenates the span; we refer to it as SPAN. Each element (e.g., context, span) is separated with the special token "[SEP]".

3.1 Controlled Generation

Our next set of models use the question types as control codes to guide question generation. Controlled generation models (Kikuchi et al., 2016; Hu et al., 2017; Ficler and Goldberg, 2017; Tsai et al., 2021) condition on a control code c in addition to the input x to model the distribution of $P_\theta(q \mid x, c)$. Similar to Eq. (1), we can write,

$$P_\theta(q \mid x, c) = \prod_i P_\theta(q_i \mid q_1, \ldots, q_{i-1}, x, c) \quad (2)$$

Text generation conditioned on such control codes, such as sentiment control of movie reviews, style for chatbots, diverse story continuations, etc., have been used effectively in recent research (Tu et al., 2019; Krause et al., 2021; Roller et al., 2021). We use the same idea for question generation by conditioning on the question type c as identified in Section 2.2. We simply concatenate the question type as an additional token and finetune BART. Using the example from Table 1, the input to BART with the question type Explanation would be:
The plan places ...2 billion [SEP] Santa Fe ...transaction [SEP] review [SEP] Explanation

Inference. We specify the question type to generate specific questions. Top-k sampling with $k = 5$ is used to generate questions, where the questions are constrained to be from 5 to 30 tokens, with a length penalty 2.0 (Ott et al., 2019). The length

[5] See appendix for bigrams.

[6] We use a special token "NO_CONTEXT" if the source sentence is the first sentence in the article.

[7] We keep the distribution of question types in train and dev set roughly the same, and the majority question type (Explanation) is about 29% of the total data.

penalty is an exponential penalty on the length, where a penalty > 1 favors longer generations.

For each test instance, we generate a question for all question types except "Other".[8] Table 1 shows examples of generated questions.

3.2 Automatic Question Type Selection

As stated in the Introduction section, besides being able to generate a variety of questions based on a single span, another motivation of this work is to identify a single high-quality question or to rank the list of the questions. In case of controlled generation, one challenge is determining what control code to use at inference time when a single output is desired. We explore two ways to choose a single question from the six generated for each input.

Informative vs. inquisitive question classifier. We consider using a binary question classifier (RoBERTa-large with default parameters) to classify whether a question is from INQUISITIVE or SQuAD. We view SQuAD questions as more "informative" than inquisitive so we hope for this classifier to capture what it means for a question to be inquisitive. We train on the training questions in INQUISITIVE and an equal number of questions drawn from SQuAD.[9] At inference time, given one generated question for each type, we choose the one that maximizes the classifier's probability of being inquisitive. Our hypothesis is that an inquisitive/informative classifier can serve as a scoring function for selecting the best candidate from a set of inquisitive questions. For the example in Table 1 the classifier chose the Definition question "what is that?" with the highest inquisitiveness probability. Below we refer to this method as TYPE_s, where the "s" indicates that the SQuAD dataset is used.

Pairwise ranking classifier with expert annotations. In this setup, we collect a small set of question ranking annotations and train a pairwise ranking classifier (Liu et al., 2009) to select the best question. First, we randomly select 300 instances from the 1,885-instance test set from INQUISITIVE. Next, two expert annotators (each with extensive annotation experience) independently ranked each of the six generated questions per instance. The annotators' task was to rank the questions according to their inquisitiveness and relevance to the context, source, and span. The annotators judged all six questions for each instance and identified at least three questions (rank 1-3) as the best where the rest of the questions were deemed to be of lower quality. In some cases, the annotators even ranked top-five questions (rank 1-5). Precision@1, 2, 3 ranks are 0.70, 0.88, and 0.95 respectively (i.e., in 70% cases one annotator's top-1 selection was found in the other annotator's top-3 selection).[10]

We then approximate the learning-to-rank problem (Joachims et al., 2007; Liu et al., 2009) with a classification problem, i.e., by training a binary classifier to determine whether one question is better than another. For a single input, let Q, q_{rel}, and q_{nrel} represent the total set of generated questions, relevant questions, and irrelevant questions, respectively. In our pairwise ranking setup, the training instances are the combination of (a) a question q_i from q_{rel} and a question q_j from q_{nrel}, and (b) two questions q_i and q_j from q_{rel} if and only if the two questions are separated by ≥ 2 ranks. Algorithm 1 in the appendix details the procedure.

In addition to the two questions q_i and q_j, we also use the source sentence as another input. During training, for each instance from (a) and (b) above, we create two training examples of the form *source* + "[SEP]" + q_i + "[SEP]" + q_j and *source* + "[SEP]" + q_j + "[SEP]" + q_i. If the first question in the sequence has a better rank we label the instance as positive, otherwise negative. This way we have 2,867 examples; we use 2,581 for training and the rest for validation. We finetune a RoBERTa-large model as a binary classifier with default hyperparameters, attaining a validation accuracy of 76.2%.

For each test instance, similar to the training setup, for each generated question pair q_i, q_j we form a pair of examples. Given that we have six question types, we create altogether thirty examples and classify them using the RoBERTa-large classifier. We return the question that is preferred the largest number of times.[11] Given the example in Table 1 this model selects the Explanation question, i.e., "Why are they reviewing the plan?" Below we refer to this method as TYPE_r, where the "r" represents the use of the ranker described above.

[8] We made this choice because "Other" includes many subtypes, e.g., inference questions and comparisons, giving us only a few examples per type. We leave this to future work.

[9] We also attempted to include the source sentences. However, given the differences between the two datasets (WSJ/AP for INQUISITIVE vs. Wikipedia for SQuAD), this caused the classifier to focus more on the source sentences than the questions.

[10] Please refer to Table 9 in the Appendix section for examples.

[11] In case of ties, we use the classifier scores as the tie breaker.

4 Experiments

For all models, we use BART-large with the same settings. For training, we use the Adam optimizer (Kingma and Ba, 2015) with learning rate 3e-5, weight decay 0.01, clip norm 0.1, dropout 0.1, 15 epochs in total, warm-up updates 500, use cross entropy loss with label smoothing ($\alpha = 0.1$), and set the maximum number of tokens per batch to 1024. More details of the experimental setup are given in the Appendix (Section A.1).

We evaluate the following five settings:

- BASE: uncontrolled generation using the context and source sentence as input
- SPAN: uncontrolled generation using the context, source sentence, and span as input
- TYPE$_s$: type-controlled generation with type selection via informative vs. inquisitive classifier
- TYPE$_r$: type-controlled generation with type selection via pairwise ranking classifier
- TYPE$_o$: type-controlled generation with question type of reference question

Since the TYPE methods use question types, in order to compare those methods to others, we need a way to automatically select a single generated question. For TYPE$_o$, we run our question type classifier on a human-written reference question and use the predicted type. Thus, TYPE$_o$ is an oracle method (hence the mnemonic "o" in its name) since it assumes access to a reference question. For TYPE$_s$ and TYPE$_r$ we use the classifiers described in Section 3.2. All TYPE methods use the context, source sentence, and span as input, like SPAN.

4.1 Automatic Evaluation

Since inquisitive question generation is an open-ended task, a high-quality generated question may not overlap with the gold question. However, automatic metrics that measure the overlap between generations and gold questions could still be useful diagnostics for characterizing models.

Table 4 presents several automatic metrics: BLEU (Papineni et al., 2002), METEOR (Denkowski and Lavie, 2014), ROUGE-L (Lin, 2004), BERTScore (Zhang et al., 2020), perplexity under GPT2-XL (Radford et al., 2019), and the entropy (averaged over questions) of the RoBERTa-large question type classifier applied to the generated question.[12] Although INQUISITIVE contains a test set of 1,885 instances (see Section 2), we used only 1,585 instances as our test set because we chose the remaining (random) 300 instances to build our pairwise ranking classifier (Section 3.2).

For BLEU, METEOR, ROUGE-L, and BERTScore, the oracle model TYPE$_o$ achieves the highest scores, presumably because this model generates questions that are similar to the reference types. We notice, TYPE$_r$, and SPAN have similar scores, with TYPE$_r$ being slightly ahead for BLEU and METEOR. In the case of TYPE$_s$, the low scores across metrics can be attributed to the fact that the inquisitive vs. informative classifier prefers question types that are unique to the INQUISITIVE dataset, such as Definition and Instantiation questions. These types are not appropriate for all spans and in many cases are quite different from the reference questions.

We also find that TYPE$_r$ has the lowest GPT2 perplexity, indicating that the ranker is favoring highly probable questions according to a general-purpose language model. A lower perplexity is likely indicative of greater fluency, a point we will return to in our human evaluations. Likewise, the lowest entropy of TYPE$_r$ implies that its questions can be classified with high confidence by our question type classifier. In contrast, TYPE$_s$ shows higher entropy, i.e., its questions are more difficult to classify. The entropy of the human-generated questions is higher than nearly all of our models, indicating that the human questions are also harder to classify than model outputs.

The last three columns of Table 4 show the metrics designed by Ko et al. (2020), namely *Train-n*, *Article-n*, and *Span*. These metrics measure the extent of copying from the source materials into the generated questions, i.e., % of n-grams in the generated questions that appear in the training questions (*Train-n*) and the context/source sentence (*Article-n*). For brevity, we only report *Train-2* and *Article-2*. *Span* measures the % of words in the annotated span present in the generated questions.

Among our models, TYPE$_r$ attains the lowest value of the *Train-2* metric, which is also closest to the HUMAN value. Aside from TYPE$_s$, the other models have higher *Article-2* than HUMAN, meaning that the generated questions have a higher % of n-grams that appear in the source sentence or the context. TYPE$_r$ has the highest value for the *Span* metric, indicating that the ranker prefers questions that use words from the span. SPAN is second high-

[12] We reported the average scores of 5 runs with different random seeds.

Model	%BLEU	%METEOR	%ROUGE-L	%F$_{BERT}$	GPT2 ppl	Entropy	Train-2	Article-2	Span
HUMAN	-	-	-	-	272	0.777	0.467	0.126	0.354
BASE	4.3	11.8	27.4	39.6	119	0.699	0.518	0.186	0.184
SPAN	8.5	17.5	36.1	47.6	148	0.726	0.505	0.182	0.452
TYPE$_s$	5.7	13.6	30.9	41.6	219	0.823	0.530	0.090	0.346
TYPE$_r$	8.6	18.3	35.3	47.4	89	0.612	0.473	0.195	0.542
TYPE$_o$	9.7	19.5	39.1	50.1	154	0.751	0.488	0.149	0.475

Table 4: Automatic metrics on our test set for our models as well as the reference questions (HUMAN).

Model	Syntax	Semantics	Relevancy	Inquisitive
BASE	4.30	4.11	4.16	3.71
SPAN	4.30	4.17	4.32	3.75
TYPE$_s$	4.02	3.50	3.51	3.14
TYPE$_r$	4.59	4.37	4.27	3.92
TYPE$_o$	4.33	4.10	4.09	3.78
HUMAN	4.36	4.41	4.33	3.98

Table 5: Results of human evaluation. The HUMAN row shows judgments for reference questions from the INQUISITIVE dataset.

1	is it the aha?
2	how much has inflation?
3	nativity happens for buddha?
4	When he decide?
5	how much has inflation?

Table 6: Examples of gold questions from INQUISITIVE dataset that are judged as ungrammatical by the Turkers.

est and BASE, which does not use the annotated span, has the lowest value.

In the Appendix, we also report an automatic evaluation of controllability, finding that certain question types (Explanation, Definition, and Instantiation) can be generated with high precision, while others (Elaboration, Background, and Forward-looking) are more easily confused.

4.2 Human Evaluation

In this section, we report the results from a human evaluation we have conducted to assess a variety of subjective aspects of the generated questions, namely the *syntax*, *semantics*, *relevancy*, and the degree of *inquisitiveness*.

We collected annotations using the crowdsourcing platform Amazon Mechanical Turk (MTurk). We randomly selected 500 test instances. For each, we asked three annotators the following four questions to measure quality along four aspects:

1. Does the question seem syntactically correct?
2. Does the question make sense (semantically)?
3. Does the question seem relevant to the source?
4. Does the question show inquisitiveness to learn more about the topic?

The annotators were given the following three options to choose from: *yes*, *somewhat*, and *no*. Each human intelligence task (HIT) contained five instances to judge and we paid $2 per HIT.

Table 5 presents the average of the human judgments, where the answers *yes*, *somewhat*, and *no* are converted to scores 5, 3, and 1, respectively. In all four aspects, we notice several scores are over 4. For the *inquisitiveness* aspect, the TYPE$_r$ model achieves the highest score among all models. This score is higher than the oracle model (TYPE$_o$) showing the usefulness of the ranker to generate inquisitive questions. Likewise, TYPE$_r$ achieves the highest average score for *semantics*, showing that its questions are semantically meaningful almost all the time. We also note that both TYPE$_r$ and SPAN are competitive in *relevancy*. Finally, for *syntax*, each model (aside from TYPE$_s$) was rated close to 4.5. Although transformers usually produce fluent output (Yates et al., 2021), TYPE$_r$ scored higher than the human generated gold questions on *syntax*, which warrants further investigation.

We manually analyzed all the questions from TYPE$_r$ and HUMAN where the majority of annotators rated 1 for *syntax*, and we found out there are 14 and 33 such questions, respectively, explaining why TYPE$_r$ scored higher. This also explains why the perplexity of HUMAN is high in Table 4. In Table 6 we provide a few examples from the HUMAN set that were deemed grammatically incorrect. Table 14 in the Appendix contains examples of grammatical errors from all models.

If we compute a simple average over all the aspects for each model, TYPE$_r$ scores the highest, slightly better than HUMAN, and the SPAN model is second. The SPAN model is trained on the INQUISITIVE dataset so it has the freedom of generating inquisitive questions. However, what separates

Source	Model	Question	Syn.	Sem.	Rel.	Inq.
... The State Security court said it was ordering the seizure of Kemal's book, ..., because it **provokes "hatred and enmity"** on the basis of differences ...	BASE	What is the reason for the seizure?	4.3	3.7	4.3	4.3
	SPAN	How does the author's book provoke hatred and enmity?	5.0	5.0	5.0	5.0
	TYPE$_s$	what is hatred?	4.3	4.3	2.3	1.7
	TYPE$_r$	How can a book provoke hatred and enmity?	5.0	5.0	5.0	3.0
	TYPE$_o$	How did it provocate the book and what did the author write in the book?	5.0	2.3	3.0	2.3
	HUMAN	How does the book provoke "hatred and enmity"?	4.3	5.0	4.3	3.7
Olin Corp. said **third-quarter** net income rose 26 % on the strength of its chemical business.	BASE	Why were they on the strength of their chemical business?	1.0	1.0	3.0	3.0
	SPAN	what happened to the second quarter?	3.7	3.7	4.3	3.0
	TYPE$_s$	What was the quarter?	4.3	4.3	4.3	4.3
	TYPE$_r$	Why was third-quarter net income up 26 %?	5.0	5.0	4.3	4.3
	TYPE$_o$	What year did the third-quarter consist of?	5.0	5.0	4.3	5.0
	HUMAN	What happened to the net income in the first and second quarter?	3.7	5.0	5.0	5.0
... most significant change in surgical training since the early 1900s, they are working with **local medical device companies** to develop new generations of software ...	BASE	How are medical device companies working with the University of Minnesota??	5.0	5.0	5.0	4.3
	SPAN	Which local medical device companies?	2.3	3.0	4.3	3.0
	TYPE$_s$	who are the local medical device companies?	4.3	3.7	2.3	2.3
	TYPE$_r$	Why are they working with local medical device companies?	5.0	5.0	5.0	5.0
	TYPE$_o$	Who are the local medical device companies?	5.0	3.7	4.3	5.0
	HUMAN	Which medical device companies are being worked with?	2.3	3.7	5.0	5.0

Table 7: Examples of generated questions from different models. Syn., Sem., Rel., Inq. represent Syntax, Semantics, Relevancy and Inquisitiveness, respectively. For brevity the context is not shown. Spans are bold.

SPAN from TYPE$_r$ is, for the latter, we have the ability to control the generation with specific question types and also select the *best* question for the same source sentence. We also notice that the generations from TYPE$_s$ scored lowest across all four aspects. The TYPE$_s$ model often selects Definition/Instantiation question types that are unsuitable for the source sentence and the span, which is why the annotations score low for this type of question.

Table 7 shows several examples from our models along with average human ratings for all four aspects. We highlight three salient observations here. First, in general, TYPE$_r$ has high scores across all aspects for all examples. Second, the Turkers have treated the aspects independently as we have requested. Even if they rated the HUMAN annotations 2.3 and 3.7 for *syntax* and *semantics* for the last example, they have given high ratings for the other two aspects. Third, interestingly, "what is hatred?", a very generic question, scored high on *syntax* and *semantics* (TYPE$_s$ model for the first example) but low on the other two aspects due to its lack of *relevancy* and *inquisitiveness*.

Finally, we note that for the first example in Table 7, the SPAN and HUMAN questions are extremely similar, but their ratings differ for three out of the four attributes. This example illustrates the variability of human judgments for this task, which suggests that more annotations may be needed to increase confidence in our results.

5 Related Work

In recent years, automatic question generation has attracted many NLP researchers, perhaps due to its versatility, e.g., question generation for conversational AI (Bordes et al., 2017; Gao et al., 2019), synthetic examples for QA tasks (Alberti et al., 2019; Olney et al., 2012; Sultan et al., 2020), clarifications on information-seeking conversation (Aliannejadi et al., 2019), and knowledge evaluation and educational application areas (Mitkov and Ha, 2003; Brown et al., 2005; Chen et al., 2009; Stasaski et al., 2021), which is specifically related to our use cases.

In earlier work, methods such as transforming declarative sentences into questions (Heilman and Smith, 2010) or using semantic roles (Flor and Riordan, 2018) were popular. However, recently sequence-to-sequence architectures (Du et al., 2017; FitzGerald et al., 2018) and pretrained models (Cao and Wang, 2021) are more often used. Similar to Ko et al. (2020), our work is related to answer-agnostic question generation. We focus on exploiting question type information for generating deeper questions. Although related work in the answer-unaware setting exists (Nakanishi et al., 2019), they mostly focus on identifying question-worthy text for generation (Scialom and Staiano,

2020; Wang et al., 2019) from factual (Rajpurkar et al., 2016), conversational (Choi et al., 2018), or social media platforms (Fan et al., 2019), different from the WSJ/AP news dataset used in our work.

We are building on past work on controllable generation, generating text that reflects specific characteristics of control variables. In some earlier work, embedding vectors of the control variables were fed into the model for controlling the output (Kikuchi et al., 2016; Fan et al., 2018; Tu et al., 2019). However, our approach resembles recent efforts where the control variable is concatenated to the main input using some separator (Keskar et al., 2019; Schiller et al., 2021). Methods such as PPLM are useful for similar guided controllable generations (Dathathri et al., 2020); however, PPLM requires gradient descent at inference time, while our question type selection approach is highly scalable and efficient.

We consider controllable question generation based on specific question types, noting that different question templates or ontologies have been studied for question generation. For example, a Wikipedia-driven ontology is used for generation (Labutov et al., 2015), or contextualized questions are generated for any semantic role (Pyatkin et al., 2021). Likewise, Pascual et al. (2021) proposed guided generation focusing on including specific keywords (e.g., "wh" words for questions), while we showed in Table 3 that "wh" words do not have a 1-to-1 relationship with question types.

Our work is closer to that of Cao and Wang (2021), who proposed a question type ontology (based on cognitive science) inspired by manually constructed templates (Olney et al., 2012). On the contrary, we chose a dataset that focuses on inquisitive questions only and chose our question types accordingly, while they used a dataset with a broader set of questions. In addition, instead of predicting the text span ("focus" in (Cao and Wang, 2021)) we directly use the annotated span in our research. Finally, we focused on post-processing the generations to identify the best question (or rank them) related to the source content.

6 Conclusions and Future Work

We proposed a type-controlled framework that generates inquisitive questions given a source sentence, annotated span, and a longer context. We annotated a set of question types related to curiosity driven questions and demonstrated that our framework can generate a variety of questions from a single input. We also developed an effective method (TYPE_r) to select a single question using a pairwise ranker trained on a small set of ranking annotations. Our generations, especially from TYPE_r, show high novelty. The human evaluation demonstrates that questions generated from TYPE_r rival human-written questions on all four aspects of quality.

Future work could include annotating a larger partition of the INQUISITIVE dataset while exploring finer-grained analysis of question types (e.g., sub-categories of elaboration questions). We are also interested in employing a framework to generate questions and identify the span jointly.

Acknowledgments

The authors would like to thank Yuan Wang and Hillary Molloy for annotations, Mengxuan Zhao and Rob Bobkoskie for the MTurk experiments, and Swapna Somasundaran for helpful comments and suggestions.

7 Ethical Considerations

We leverage the freely available open access question dataset INQUISITIVE for annotation and model training. Though we have not exhaustively checked the source dataset manually, given they are sourced from the WSJ partition of the Penn Treebank and Associated Press articles from the TIPSTER corpus, we consider them relatively safe and do not find any objectionable content.

Training is done using large pretrained models that have been shown to have bias. Although the generated questions do not appear biased, they may hallucinate content, which is a common problem for neural generation models.

Finally, we obtained institutional review board permission to conduct MTurk based data collection.

References

Chris Alberti, Daniel Andor, Emily Pitler, Jacob Devlin, and Michael Collins. 2019. Synthetic QA corpora generation with roundtrip consistency. In *Proceedings of the 57th Annual Meeting of the Association for Computational Linguistics*, pages 6168–6173, Florence, Italy. Association for Computational Linguistics.

Mohammad Aliannejadi, Hamed Zamani, Fabio Crestani, and W. Bruce Croft. 2019. Asking clarifying questions in open-domain information-seeking conversations. In *Proceedings of the 42nd International ACM SIGIR Conference on Research and Development in Information Retrieval, SIGIR 2019, Paris, France, July 21-25, 2019*, pages 475–484. ACM.

Antoine Bordes, Y-Lan Boureau, and Jason Weston. 2017. Learning end-to-end goal-oriented dialog. In *5th International Conference on Learning Representations, ICLR 2017, Toulon, France, April 24-26, 2017, Conference Track Proceedings*. OpenReview.net.

Jonathan Brown, Gwen Frishkoff, and Maxine Eskenazi. 2005. Automatic question generation for vocabulary assessment. In *Proceedings of Human Language Technology Conference and Conference on Empirical Methods in Natural Language Processing*, pages 819–826, Vancouver, British Columbia, Canada. Association for Computational Linguistics.

Shuyang Cao and Lu Wang. 2021. Controllable open-ended question generation with a new question type ontology. In *Proceedings of the 59th Annual Meeting of the Association for Computational Linguistics and the 11th International Joint Conference on Natural Language Processing (Volume 1: Long Papers)*, pages 6424–6439, Online. Association for Computational Linguistics.

Guanliang Chen, Jie Yang, Claudia Hauff, and Geert-Jan Houben. 2018. LearningQ: A large-scale dataset for educational question generation. In *Proceedings of International Conference on Web and Social Media (ICWSM)*.

Wei Chen, Gregory Aist, and Jack Mostow. 2009. Generating questions automatically from informational text.

Jaemin Cho, Minjoon Seo, and Hannaneh Hajishirzi. 2019. Mixture content selection for diverse sequence generation. In *Proceedings of the 2019 Conference on Empirical Methods in Natural Language Processing and the 9th International Joint Conference on Natural Language Processing (EMNLP-IJCNLP)*, pages 3121–3131, Hong Kong, China. Association for Computational Linguistics.

Eunsol Choi, He He, Mohit Iyyer, Mark Yatskar, Wen-tau Yih, Yejin Choi, Percy Liang, and Luke Zettlemoyer. 2018. QuAC: Question answering in context. In *Proceedings of the 2018 Conference on Empirical Methods in Natural Language Processing*, pages 2174–2184, Brussels, Belgium. Association for Computational Linguistics.

Sumanth Dathathri, Andrea Madotto, Janice Lan, Jane Hung, Eric Frank, Piero Molino, Jason Yosinski, and Rosanne Liu. 2020. Plug and play language models: A simple approach to controlled text generation. In *8th International Conference on Learning Representations, ICLR 2020, Addis Ababa, Ethiopia, April 26-30, 2020*. OpenReview.net.

Michael Denkowski and Alon Lavie. 2014. Meteor universal: Language specific translation evaluation for any target language. In *Proceedings of the Ninth Workshop on Statistical Machine Translation*, pages 376–380, Baltimore, Maryland, USA. Association for Computational Linguistics.

Li Dong, Nan Yang, Wenhui Wang, Furu Wei, Xiaodong Liu, Yu Wang, Jianfeng Gao, Ming Zhou, and Hsiao-Wuen Hon. 2019. Unified language model pre-training for natural language understanding and generation. In *Advances in Neural Information Processing Systems*, volume 32. Curran Associates, Inc.

Xinya Du, Junru Shao, and Claire Cardie. 2017. Learning to ask: Neural question generation for reading comprehension. In *Proceedings of the 55th Annual Meeting of the Association for Computational Linguistics (Volume 1: Long Papers)*, pages 1342–1352, Vancouver, Canada. Association for Computational Linguistics.

Angela Fan, David Grangier, and Michael Auli. 2018. Controllable abstractive summarization. In *Proceedings of the 2nd Workshop on Neural Machine Translation and Generation*, pages 45–54, Melbourne, Australia. Association for Computational Linguistics.

Angela Fan, Yacine Jernite, Ethan Perez, David Grangier, Jason Weston, and Michael Auli. 2019. ELI5: Long form question answering. In *Proceedings of the 57th Annual Meeting of the Association for Computational Linguistics*, pages 3558–3567, Florence, Italy. Association for Computational Linguistics.

Jessica Ficler and Yoav Goldberg. 2017. Controlling linguistic style aspects in neural language generation. In *Proceedings of the Workshop on Stylistic Variation*, pages 94–104, Copenhagen, Denmark. Association for Computational Linguistics.

Nicholas FitzGerald, Julian Michael, Luheng He, and Luke Zettlemoyer. 2018. Large-scale QA-SRL parsing. In *Proceedings of the 56th Annual Meeting of the Association for Computational Linguistics (Volume 1: Long Papers)*, pages 2051–2060, Melbourne, Australia. Association for Computational Linguistics.

Michael Flor and Brian Riordan. 2018. A semantic role-based approach to open-domain automatic question generation. In *Proceedings of the Thirteenth Workshop on Innovative Use of NLP for Building Educational Applications*, pages 254–263, New Orleans, Louisiana. Association for Computational Linguistics.

Yifan Gao, Piji Li, Irwin King, and Michael R. Lyu. 2019. Interconnected question generation with coreference alignment and conversation flow modeling. In *Proceedings of the 57th Annual Meeting of the Association for Computational Linguistics*, pages 4853–4862, Florence, Italy. Association for Computational Linguistics.

Donna Harman and Mark Liberman. 1993. TIPSTER complete LDC93T3A. web download. Philadelphia: Linguistic Data Consortium.

Michael Heilman and Noah A. Smith. 2010. Good question! statistical ranking for question generation. In *Human Language Technologies: The 2010 Annual Conference of the North American Chapter of the Association for Computational Linguistics*, pages 609–617, Los Angeles, California. Association for Computational Linguistics.

Zhiting Hu, Zichao Yang, Xiaodan Liang, Ruslan Salakhutdinov, and Eric P. Xing. 2017. Toward controlled generation of text. In *Proceedings of the 34th International Conference on Machine Learning, ICML 2017, Sydney, NSW, Australia, 6-11 August 2017*, volume 70 of *Proceedings of Machine Learning Research*, pages 1587–1596. PMLR.

Thorsten Joachims, Hang Li, Tie-Yan Liu, and ChengXiang Zhai. 2007. Learning to rank for information retrieval (LR4IR 2007). *SIGIR Forum*, 41(2):58–62.

Nitish Shirish Keskar, Bryan McCann, Lav R. Varshney, Caiming Xiong, and Richard Socher. 2019. CTRL: A conditional transformer language model for controllable generation. *CoRR*, abs/1909.05858.

Yuta Kikuchi, Graham Neubig, Ryohei Sasano, Hiroya Takamura, and Manabu Okumura. 2016. Controlling output length in neural encoder-decoders. In *Proceedings of the 2016 Conference on Empirical Methods in Natural Language Processing*, pages 1328–1338, Austin, Texas. Association for Computational Linguistics.

Diederik P. Kingma and Jimmy Ba. 2015. Adam: A method for stochastic optimization. In *3rd International Conference on Learning Representations, ICLR 2015, San Diego, CA, USA, May 7-9, 2015, Conference Track Proceedings*.

Wei-Jen Ko, Te-Yuan Chen, Yiyan Huang, Greg Durrett, and Junyi Jessy Li. 2020. Inquisitive question generation for high level text comprehension. In *Proceedings of the 2020 Conference on Empirical Methods in Natural Language Processing, EMNLP 2020, Online, November 16-20, 2020*, pages 6544–6555. Association for Computational Linguistics.

Ben Krause, Akhilesh Deepak Gotmare, Bryan McCann, Nitish Shirish Keskar, Shafiq Joty, Richard Socher, and Nazneen Fatema Rajani. 2021. GeDi: Generative discriminator guided sequence generation. In *Findings of the Association for Computational Linguistics: EMNLP 2021*, pages 4929–4952, Punta Cana, Dominican Republic. Association for Computational Linguistics.

Vaibhav Kumar and Alan W. Black. 2020. Clarq: A large-scale and diverse dataset for clarification question generation. In *Proceedings of the 58th Annual Meeting of the Association for Computational Linguistics, ACL 2020, Online, July 5-10, 2020*, pages 7296–7301. Association for Computational Linguistics.

Igor Labutov, Sumit Basu, and Lucy Vanderwende. 2015. Deep questions without deep understanding. In *Proceedings of the 53rd Annual Meeting of the Association for Computational Linguistics and the 7th International Joint Conference on Natural Language Processing (Volume 1: Long Papers)*, pages 889–898, Beijing, China. Association for Computational Linguistics.

Mike Lewis, Yinhan Liu, Naman Goyal, Marjan Ghazvininejad, Abdelrahman Mohamed, Omer Levy, Veselin Stoyanov, and Luke Zettlemoyer. 2020. BART: Denoising sequence-to-sequence pre-training for natural language generation, translation, and comprehension. In *Proceedings of the 58th Annual Meeting of the Association for Computational Linguistics*, pages 7871–7880, Online. Association for Computational Linguistics.

Chin-Yew Lin. 2004. ROUGE: A package for automatic evaluation of summaries. In *Text Summarization Branches Out*, pages 74–81, Barcelona, Spain. Association for Computational Linguistics.

Tie-Yan Liu et al. 2009. Learning to rank for information retrieval. *Foundations and Trends® in Information Retrieval*, 3(3):225–331.

Yinhan Liu, Myle Ott, Naman Goyal, Jingfei Du, Mandar Joshi, Danqi Chen, Omer Levy, Mike Lewis, Luke Zettlemoyer, and Veselin Stoyanov. 2019. Roberta: A robustly optimized BERT pretraining approach. *CoRR*, abs/1907.11692.

William C Mann and Sandra A Thompson. 1988. Rhetorical structure theory: Toward a functional theory of text organization. *Text-interdisciplinary Journal for the Study of Discourse*, 8(3):243–281.

Mitchell P. Marcus, Beatrice Santorini, and Mary Ann Marcinkiewicz. 1993. Building a large annotated corpus of English: The Penn Treebank. *Computational Linguistics*, 19(2):313–330.

Ruslan Mitkov and Le An Ha. 2003. Computer-aided generation of multiple-choice tests. In *Proceedings of the HLT-NAACL 03 Workshop on Building Educational Applications Using Natural Language Processing*, pages 17–22.

Mao Nakanishi, Tetsunori Kobayashi, and Yoshihiko Hayashi. 2019. Towards answer-unaware conversational question generation. In *Proceedings of the 2nd Workshop on Machine Reading for Question Answering*, pages 63–71, Hong Kong, China. Association for Computational Linguistics.

Andrew McGregor Olney, Arthur C. Graesser, and Natalie K. Person. 2012. Question generation from concept maps. *Dialogue Discourse*, 3(2):75–99.

Myle Ott, Sergey Edunov, Alexei Baevski, Angela Fan, Sam Gross, Nathan Ng, David Grangier, and Michael Auli. 2019. fairseq: A fast, extensible toolkit for sequence modeling. In *Proceedings of the 2019 Conference of the North American Chapter of the Association for Computational Linguistics (Demonstrations)*, pages 48–53, Minneapolis, Minnesota. Association for Computational Linguistics.

Kishore Papineni, Salim Roukos, Todd Ward, and Wei-Jing Zhu. 2002. Bleu: a method for automatic evaluation of machine translation. In *Proceedings of the 40th Annual Meeting of the Association for Computational Linguistics*, pages 311–318, Philadelphia, Pennsylvania, USA. Association for Computational Linguistics.

Damian Pascual, Beni Egressy, Clara Meister, Ryan Cotterell, and Roger Wattenhofer. 2021. A plug-and-play method for controlled text generation. In *Findings of the Association for Computational Linguistics: EMNLP 2021*, pages 3973–3997, Punta Cana, Dominican Republic. Association for Computational Linguistics.

Valentina Pyatkin, Paul Roit, Julian Michael, Yoav Goldberg, Reut Tsarfaty, and Ido Dagan. 2021. Asking it all: Generating contextualized questions for any semantic role. In *Proceedings of the 2021 Conference on Empirical Methods in Natural Language Processing*, pages 1429–1441, Online and Punta Cana, Dominican Republic. Association for Computational Linguistics.

Alec Radford, Jeff Wu, Rewon Child, David Luan, Dario Amodei, and Ilya Sutskever. 2019. Language models are unsupervised multitask learners.

Pranav Rajpurkar, Jian Zhang, Konstantin Lopyrev, and Percy Liang. 2016. SQuAD: 100,000+ questions for machine comprehension of text. In *Proceedings of the 2016 Conference on Empirical Methods in Natural Language Processing*, pages 2383–2392, Austin, Texas. Association for Computational Linguistics.

Stephen Roller, Emily Dinan, Naman Goyal, Da Ju, Mary Williamson, Yinhan Liu, Jing Xu, Myle Ott, Eric Michael Smith, Y-Lan Boureau, and Jason Weston. 2021. Recipes for building an open-domain chatbot. In *Proceedings of the 16th Conference of the European Chapter of the Association for Computational Linguistics: Main Volume, EACL 2021, Online, April 19 - 23, 2021*, pages 300–325. Association for Computational Linguistics.

Benjamin Schiller, Johannes Daxenberger, and Iryna Gurevych. 2021. Aspect-controlled neural argument generation. In *Proceedings of the 2021 Conference of the North American Chapter of the Association for Computational Linguistics: Human Language Technologies*, pages 380–396, Online. Association for Computational Linguistics.

Thomas Scialom and Jacopo Staiano. 2020. Ask to learn: A study on curiosity-driven question generation. In *Proceedings of the 28th International Conference on Computational Linguistics*, pages 2224–2235, Barcelona, Spain (Online). International Committee on Computational Linguistics.

Katherine Stasaski, Manav Rathod, Tony Tu, Yunfang Xiao, and Marti A. Hearst. 2021. Automatically generating cause-and-effect questions from passages. In *Proceedings of the 16th Workshop on Innovative Use of NLP for Building Educational Applications*, pages 158–170, Online. Association for Computational Linguistics.

Md Arafat Sultan, Shubham Chandel, Ramón Fernandez Astudillo, and Vittorio Castelli. 2020. On the importance of diversity in question generation for QA. In *Proceedings of the 58th Annual Meeting of the Association for Computational Linguistics*, pages 5651–5656, Online. Association for Computational Linguistics.

Xingwu Sun, Jing Liu, Yajuan Lyu, Wei He, Yanjun Ma, and Shi Wang. 2018. Answer-focused and position-aware neural question generation. In *Proceedings of the 2018 Conference on Empirical Methods in Natural Language Processing*, pages 3930–3939, Brussels, Belgium. Association for Computational Linguistics.

Ilya Sutskever, Oriol Vinyals, and Quoc V. Le. 2014. Sequence to sequence learning with neural networks. In *Advances in Neural Information Processing Systems 27: Annual Conference on Neural Information Processing Systems 2014, December 8-13 2014, Montreal, Quebec, Canada*, pages 3104–3112.

Alicia Y. Tsai, Shereen Oraby, Vittorio Perera, Jiun-Yu Kao, Yuheng Du, Anjali Narayan-Chen, Tagyoung Chung, and Dilek Hakkani-Tür. 2021. Style control for schema-guided natural language generation. *CoRR*, abs/2109.12211.

Lifu Tu, Xiaoan Ding, Dong Yu, and Kevin Gimpel. 2019. Generating diverse story continuations with controllable semantics. In *Proceedings of the 3rd Workshop on Neural Generation and Translation*, pages 44–58, Hong Kong. Association for Computational Linguistics.

Ashish Vaswani, Noam Shazeer, Niki Parmar, Jakob Uszkoreit, Llion Jones, Aidan N. Gomez, Lukasz Kaiser, and Illia Polosukhin. 2017. Attention is all you need. In *Advances in Neural Information Processing Systems 30: Annual Conference on Neural Information Processing Systems 2017, December 4-9, 2017, Long Beach, CA, USA*, pages 5998–6008.

Siyuan Wang, Zhongyu Wei, Zhihao Fan, Yang Liu, and Xuanjing Huang. 2019. A multi-agent communication framework for question-worthy phrase extraction and question generation. In *The Thirty-Third AAAI Conference on Artificial Intelligence, AAAI 2019, The Thirty-First Innovative Applications of Artificial Intelligence Conference, IAAI 2019, The Ninth AAAI Symposium on Educational Advances in Artificial*

Intelligence, EAAI 2019, Honolulu, Hawaii, USA, January 27 - February 1, 2019, pages 7168–7175. AAAI Press.

Zhen Wang, Siwei Rao, Jie Zhang, Zhen Qin, Guangjian Tian, and Jun Wang. 2020. Diversify question generation with continuous content selectors and question type modeling. In *Findings of the Association for Computational Linguistics: EMNLP 2020*, pages 2134–2143, Online. Association for Computational Linguistics.

Wei Xu, Chris Callison-Burch, and Courtney Napoles. 2015. Problems in current text simplification research: New data can help. *Trans. Assoc. Comput. Linguistics*, 3:283–297.

Andrew Yates, Rodrigo Nogueira, and Jimmy Lin. 2021. Pretrained transformers for text ranking: BERT and beyond. In *Proceedings of the 2021 Conference of the North American Chapter of the Association for Computational Linguistics: Human Language Technologies: Tutorials*, pages 1–4, Online. Association for Computational Linguistics.

Tianyi Zhang, Varsha Kishore, Felix Wu, Kilian Q. Weinberger, and Yoav Artzi. 2020. Bertscore: Evaluating text generation with BERT. In *8th International Conference on Learning Representations, ICLR 2020, Addis Ababa, Ethiopia, April 26-30, 2020*. OpenReview.net.

Wenjie Zhou, Minghua Zhang, and Yunfang Wu. 2019. Question-type driven question generation. In *Proceedings of the 2019 Conference on Empirical Methods in Natural Language Processing and the 9th International Joint Conference on Natural Language Processing (EMNLP-IJCNLP)*, pages 6032–6037, Hong Kong, China. Association for Computational Linguistics.

A Appendix

A.1 Experimental Setup

For BASE, SPAN, TYPE$_s$, TYPE$_r$, and TYPE$_o$, we use BART-large with the same settings. We train 15 epochs in total, using cross entropy loss (label smoothing with $\alpha = 0.1$), and set the maximum number of tokens per batch as 1024. There's a normalization layer after the embedding layer, and the embedding matrices for encoder input, decoder input, and decoder output are tied. For training, we use the Adam optimizer (Kingma and Ba, 2015) with learning rate 3e-5, weight decay 0.01, clip norm 0.1, dropout 0.1, and warm-up updates 500.

For the question type classifier, we finetune RoBERTa-large for 15 epochs with batch size 8. We use Adam with learning rate 1e-5, weight decay 0.1, dropout 0.1, and warm-up updates 157. We use the same settings for the inquisitive vs. informative classifier and pairwise ranking classifier except some hyperparameters. For the inquisitive vs. informative classifier, we train for 10 epochs with batch size 32 and warm-up updates set to 300. For the pairwise ranking classifier, we train for 20 epochs with warm-up updates set to 387. Under this setting, we compute all warm-up updates with $6\% N_{tr} N_{epo} / N_{bsz}$, where N_{tr} is the training set size, N_{epo} is the number of training epochs, and N_{bsz} is the batch size.

A.2 Leading Bigrams for Question Types

Table 8 shows the most common leading bigrams for each question type in our annotated data. We observe that for Background questions that start with "what", the bigrams are more scattered with multiple combinations, and "how is/are/was/were/do" etc. appear more often in Elaboration than in Background questions.

A.3 Data Selection for Pairwise Ranking Classifier

Annotators may make the same or completely different choices, and two examples of annotator's ranking choices are shown in Table 9.

Algorithm 1 shows how training data is produced for the pairwise ranking classifier. The training instances are the combination of (a) a question q_i from q_{rel} and a question q_j from q_{nrel} and (line 2-6 in Algorithm 1) (b) two questions q_i and q_j from q_{rel} if and only if the two questions are separated by ≥2 ranks (line 8-16 in Algorithm 1).

Algorithm 1 Data selection for pairwise ranker

Input: $Q = \{q_{rel}, q_{nrel}\}$, where Q is the total set of generated questions for an instance, q_{rel} is the set of relevant questions where $q_{rel} = \{(r_1, q_1), \cdots, (r_n, q_n)\}$, q_{nrel} is the set of non-relevant questions, and r_j is the rank for question q_j.

```
   ▷ Find relevant vs. non-relevant
1: for q_j ∈ q_rel do
2:     for q_k ∈ q_nrel do
3:         yield (q_j, q_k)
4:     end for
5: end for
6:
   ▷ Find questions with rank difference ≥ 2
7: for j = 1, ··· , n do
8:     k ← j + 2
9:     while k ≤ n do
10:        if r_k − r_j ≥ 2 then
11:            yield (q_j, q_k)
12:        end if
13:        k ← k + 1
14:    end while
15: end for
```

A.4 Controllability Evaluation

We generate test set questions with six question types except "Other", and then classify the generations with our question type classifier. The test accuracy is shown in Table 10, with confusion matrix shown in Figure 1. As the largest number in each row/column is along the diagonal (aside from forward-looking questions, which the classifier never predicts in this set), the model and classifier are in alignment a significant fraction of the time. We also observe that Explanation is doing well in both precision and recall, Elaboration and Background are tricky to discriminate from each other, and Definition and Instantiation are being classified with high precision though not with very high recall. When the model is asked to generate a forward-looking question, the classifier labels it as Elaboration or Background in most cases. This is likely because there are very few forward-looking questions in the training data.

A.5 Additional Results

All results in Table 11 and Table 12 are averaged over 5 different runs with standard deviations.

Table 11 reports BLEU scores for 1/2/3/4-grams.

Explanation	Elaboration	Background	Definition	Instantiation	Forward-looking	Other
why is(87)	what is(39)	who is(20)	what is(53)	what are(24)	how will(5)	why is(4)
why did(75)	what are(31)	how long(19)	what are(17)	who are(16)	what will(2)	does this(3)
why was(51)	how did(27)	what was(17)	what does(15)	who is(8)	when will(2)	is it(2)
why are(50)	what does(17)	how did(16)	what do(6)	what other(5)	will the(2)	of which(2)
why were(24)	how is(12)	what is(14)	how is(2)	what kind(5)	what would(2)	yes what(1)
why would(21)	how do(12)	is that(10)	definition of(2)	what types(4)	what is(2)	what year(1)
why do(19)	how would(9)	how much(10)	is that(1)	which other(4)	what are(1)	does seaweed(1)
why does(18)	how are(9)	what are(9)	what 's(1)	what were(3)	how is(1)	does taxing(1)
why has(9)	how does(9)	is this(9)	does n't(1)	what sort(3)	were they(1)	what was(1)
what caused(7)	how many(8)	how many(8)	does note(1)	which companies(3)	is the(1)	this sounds(1)
what is(7)	what was(7)	is it(7)	does opportunities(1)	which year(3)	did they(1)	they must(1)
why will(7)	what kind(7)	are they(7)	i would(1)	what is(3)	how does(1)	there is(1)
is there(4)	how was(7)	where is(7)	does this(1)	which monday(2)	was their(1)	who is(1)
what makes(4)	what would(6)	how was(6)	what was(1)	what type(2)	did it(1)	what brass(1)
why have(3)	how much(6)	what did(6)	it means(1)	which officials(2)	so that(1)	should they(1)
what was(3)	how will(5)	how does(5)	who were(1)	in which(2)	how would(1)	which year(1)
why should(3)	how long(5)	where did(5)	what comprises(1)	who were(2)	what happened(1)	how many(1)
what were(2)	what makes(5)	what do(5)	thrift industry(1)	which countries(2)	would there(1)	is this(1)
why only(2)	how were(4)	why did(5)	how do(1)	which scientists(2)	would it(1)	is he(1)
why could(2)	in what(4)	when did(5)	who are(1)	which states(2)	will it(1)	which dollar(1)

Table 8: Most common leading bigrams in annotated questions (lowercased) for each type (counts shown in parentheses).

[*context*][*source* with span in **bold**]	[NO_CONTEXT][MILWAUKEE-The electric barrier on the **Chicago Sanitary and Ship Canal** that is considered the last line of defense to stop an Asian carp invasion of Lake Michigan has a problem : Fish can swim through it.]	[LOS ANGELES-Little-known fact : When it comes to extracting oxygen from the air we breathe, we humans are just OK. Birds are more efficient breathers than we are. So are alligators and, according to a new study, monitor lizards, and probably most dinosaurs were as well.][Humans are what are called **tidal breathers**.]
Definition	What is Chicago Sanitary and Ship Canal?	what is a tidal breather?
Background	where is that?	Are they considered \"tidal breathers\"?
Instantiation	Which section of the canal?	Who are these people?
Explanation	Why is this a problem?	Why are humans tidal breathers?
Forward	where is this?	How did they come up with this term?
Elaboration	What is the name of the canal?	Are they not?
Annotator A	1. Forward 2. Explanation 3. Background	1. Definition 2. Explanation 3. Forward
Annotator B	1. Definition 2. Instantiation 3. Elaboration	1. Definition 2. Explanation 3. Forward

Table 9: Examples of different ranking choices of expert annotators.

Question Type	% Acc
Explanation	97.82
Elaboration	65.84
Background	48.91
Definition	54.85
Instantiation	50.23
Forward-looking	0.

Table 10: Test accuracy for question type prediction for model generation of different question types.

While BASE always scores lowest and TYPE$_o$ is always highest, SPAN is second-highest for BLEU-1, BLUE-2 and BLEU-3[13], and beat by TYPE$_r$ for BLEU-4.

Table 12 reports all the metric scores that are specifically implemented by Ko et al. (2020). We see that TYPE$_r$ has lowest scores for *Train-n*. For *Article-n*, the model order is changed when n is varied, e.g., BASE is higher than TYPE$_r$ on *Article-1* but lower on *Article-2* and *Article-3*. Nevertheless, TYPE$_s$ is always lower than HUMAN on *Article-n*, and other models are always higher than scores of HUMAN.

A.6 Additional Examples

Table 13 lists more annotated examples for each question type, and Table 14 includes examples (gold and generated questions by our models) that are judged ungrammatical by annotators.

[13]The difference between SPAN and TYPE$_r$ is too small in BLEU-3 to be shown in the table.

Model	%BLEU-1	%BLEU-2	%BLEU-3	%BLEU-4	%METEOR	%ROUGE-L	$\%F_{\text{BERT}}$	GPT2 ppl	Entropy
BASE	26.9±0.2	12.0±0.3	6.8±0.2	4.3±0.2	11.8±0.3	27.4±0.3	39.6±0.5	119±25	0.699±0.015
SPAN	35.1±0.9	19.4±0.5	12.4±0.4	8.5±0.4	17.5±0.7	36.1±0.5	47.6±0.4	148±10	0.726±0.062
TYPE_s	28.9±1.1	14.6±0.7	8.7±0.6	5.7±0.5	13.6±0.5	30.9±0.3	41.6±0.5	219±18	0.823±0.024
TYPE_r	33.4±1.4	18.9±1.0	12.4±0.8	8.6±0.6	18.3±0.4	35.3±0.7	47.4±0.8	89±7	0.612±0.025
TYPE_o	37.7±1.0	21.6±0.8	14.0±0.8	9.7±0.8	19.5±0.4	39.1±0.4	50.1±0.5	154±18	0.751±0.008

Table 11: Automatic metrics on our test set for our models.

	Train-2	Train-3	Train-4	Article-1	Article-2	Article-3	Span
Human	0.467	0.203	0.059	0.386	0.126	0.064	0.354
BASE	0.518±0.018	0.267±0.019	0.097±0.009	0.469±0.020	0.186±0.020	0.104±0.018	0.184±0.007
SPAN	0.505±0.015	0.246±0.020	0.079±0.012	0.455±0.025	0.182±0.022	0.101±0.019	0.452±0.029
TYPE_s	0.530±0.006	0.288±0.012	0.102±0.012	0.315±0.015	0.090±0.010	0.041±0.006	0.346±0.023
TYPE_r	0.473±0.013	0.218±0.015	0.068±0.010	0.445±0.018	0.195±0.016	0.112±0.013	0.542±0.030
TYPE_o	0.488±0.011	0.233±0.012	0.073±0.004	0.401±0.020	0.149±0.016	0.078±0.012	0.475±0.024

Table 12: Metric scores from Ko et al. (2020) that measure the extent of copying content from the training partition, articles, and spans in the source sentences to the generated questions. All scores are reported on our test set.

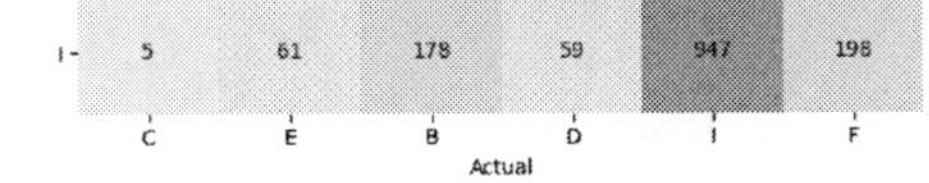

Figure 1: Heatmap showing confusion matrix for type controllability evaluation. The "Actual" type is the desired type passed as control code to the model, and the "Predicted" type is the output of running the question type classifier on the generated question. C: Explanation (causal), E: Elaboration, B: Background, D: Definition, I: Instantiation, F: Forward-looking.

Question Type (# samples)	Example	
	[*context*] [*source* with span in **bold**]	Question
Explanation (443)	[...Osip Nikiforov is recording Chopin's Etude Op. 10, No. 1, without capturing any of its sound.] [**Instead,** a sensor-equipped piano is recording the "data" of his performance ....]	Why is there a sensor-equipped piano recording data of his performance?
Elaboration (364)	[NO_CONTEXT][Miami Shores, Fla., tech **consultant** Rudo Boothe, age 33, attributes his professional success ....]	For what company?
	[NO_CONTEXT][The Agriculture Department says Americans seem to be eating a bit more each year but are **choosier** about what's on the menu.]	what are they choosing?
	[One of Ronald Reagan's attributes as President was that he rarely gave his blessing to the claptrap ....] [In fact, he liberated the U.S. from one of the world's most **corrupt** organizations – UNESCO.]	How is UNESCO corrupt?
Background (407)	[NO_CONTEXT][...a young man and his mentor practice bull-fighting techniques under the **light** of an atrium.]	Are they practicing at night?
Definition (114)	[NO_CONTEXT][LOS ANGELES - The booming illegal international wildlife trade forced **conservationists** to do the unthinkable Tuesday ....]	Who were the conservationists?
	[People start their own businesses for many reasons. But a chance to fill out sales - tax records is rarely one of them.] [Red tape is the **bugaboo** of small business.]	what is a bugaboo?
Instantiation (159)	[The Bush administration's nomination of Clarence Thomas to a seat on the federal appeals court here received a blow this week ...] [People familiar with the Senate Judiciary Committee, ..., said some **liberal members** of the panel are likely to question the ABA rating in hearings on the matter.]	Which liberal members are likely to question the ABA ratings?
Forward-looking (31)	[Bethlehem Steel Corp. has agreed in principle to form a joint venture with the world's second-largest steelmaker ....] [The entire division employs about **850 workers**.]	How will they need to increase or decrease staff?
Other (32)	[...there's one easy way to make a July beach vacation even better than expected: Add seaweed ...] [...his back covered in what looked like strands of **chartreuse cotton candy,** the 7-year-old Beijing boy was having the time of his life Sunday ...]	Does seaweed look like cotton candy?

Table 13: Annotated question type distributions and salient examples of each question type. Context and source sentences are presented where the spans in source sentences are bold.

HUMAN	why would it do that? is it the aha? in which year? WHAT COUTRIES RECIEVED LOANS? What specifically are the unhappy about with the direction?
BASE	What goal does everyone have? What happened that they didn't agree? What kind of violence? what are these signs? What was Andrew Coltart doing at 69?
SPAN	Why weren't the details unavailable? Why is there a hard time posting an upset over Germany? What is their goal in common? Which lawmakers and others arguing? How did they inflating the stock price?
TYPE$_s$	which meetings? What meetings? What are the details about this other than that? What details? What goal? What goal? what were they? what prefecture?
TYPE$_r$	Who are the Serbs from Croatia and Bosnian Muslims opposed to the Bosnian government? Why would NATO take in Poland, Hungary and others asMembers? How does Dominican authorities know the whereabouts of the banker and two Dominicans? How does a report about AIDS come to a conclusion? Why is this symbol of America?
TYPE$_o$	How many peacekeepers? How was anreement to conceal the agreement made? Did these talks involve a lot of talks? How long has the explosion been taking place? What are terms and syndicate manager?

Table 14: Examples of gold questions from INQUISITIVE and questions generated by models that are judged as ungrammatical by annotators.

Pretraining on Interactions for Learning Grounded Affordance Representations

Jack Merullo
jack_merullo@brown.edu

Dylan Ebert
dylan_ebert@brown.edu

Carsten Eickhoff
carsten@brown.edu

Ellie Pavlick
ellie_pavlick@brown.edu

Abstract

Lexical semantics and cognitive science point to *affordances* (i.e. the actions that objects support) as critical for understanding and representing nouns and verbs. However, study of these semantic features has not yet been integrated with the "foundation" models that currently dominate language representation research. We hypothesize that predictive modeling of object state over time will result in representations that encode object affordance information "for free". We train a neural network to predict objects' trajectories in a simulated interaction and show that our network's latent representations differentiate between both observed and unobserved affordances. We find that models trained using 3D simulations from our SPATIAL dataset outperform conventional 2D computer vision models trained on a similar task, and, on initial inspection, that differences between concepts correspond to expected features (e.g., *roll* entails *rotation*). Our results suggest a way in which modern deep learning approaches to grounded language learning can be integrated with traditional formal semantic notions of lexical representations.

Figure 1: We investigate whether observing interactions with an object in a 3D environment encodes information about their affordances and whether this generalizes in the zero shot setting to unseen object types

1 Introduction

Much of natural language semantics concerns events and their participants–i.e., verbs and the nouns with which they compose. Evidence from cognitive science (Borghi and Riggio, 2009; Mazzuca et al., 2021) and neuroscience (Sakreida et al., 2013) suggests that grounding such words in perception is an essential part of linguistic processing, in particular suggesting that humans represent nouns in terms of their *affordances* (Gibson, 1977), i.e., the interactions which they support. Affordance-based representations have been argued to form the basis of formal accounts of compositional syntax and semantics (Steedman, 2002). As such, prior work in formal semantics has sought to build grounded lexical semantic representations in terms of objects and their interactions in 3D space. For example, Pustejovsky and Krishnaswamy (2014) and Siskind (2001) represent verbs like *roll* as a set of entailed positional and rotational changes specified in formal logic, and Pustejovsky and Krishnaswamy (2018) argue that nouns imply (latent) events–e.g., that *cups* generally *hold* things–which should be encoded as TELIC values within the noun's formal structure.

Such work provides a compelling story of grounded semantics, but has not yet been connected to the types of large scale neural network models that currently dominate NLP. Thus, in this work, we ask whether such semantic representations emerge naturally as a consequence of self-supervised predictive modeling. Our motivation stems from the success of predictive language modeling at encoding syntactic structure. That is, if neural language models trained to predict text sequences learn to encode desirable grammatical structures (Kim and Smolensky, 2021; Tenney et al., 2018), perhaps similar models trained to predict event sequences will learn to encode desirable semantic structures. To test this intuition, we investigate whether a transformer (Vaswani et al., 2017) trained to predict the

Proceedings of the 11th Joint Conference on Lexical and Computational Semantics, pages 258 - 277
July 14-15, 2022 ©2022 Association for Computational Linguistics

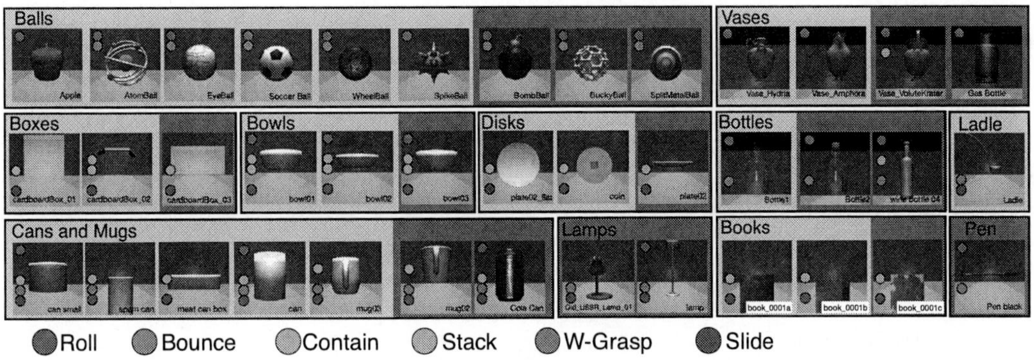

Figure 2: Objects uses for train (light gray) and test (dark gray). Colored dots indicate which affordances each object has.

future state of an object given perceptual information about its appearance and interactions will latently encode affordance information of the type thought to be central to lexical semantic representations. In sum:

- We present a first proof-of-concept neural model that learns to encode the concept of affordance without any explicit supervision.
- We demonstrate empirically that 3D spatial representations (simulations) substantially outperform 2D pixel representations in learning the desired semantic features.
- We release the `SPATIAL` dataset of 9.5K simulated object interactions and accompanying videos, and an additional 200K simulations without videos to support further research in this area.[1]

Overall, our findings suggest a process by which grounded lexical representations–of the type discussed by Pustejovsky and Krishnaswamy (2014) and Siskind (2001)–could potentially arise organically. That is, grounded interactions and observations, without explicit language supervision, can give rise to the types of conceptual representations to which nouns and verbs are assumed to ground. We interpret this as corroborative of traditional feature-based lexical semantic analyses and as a promising mechanism of which modern "foundation" model (Bommasani et al., 2021) approaches to language and concept learning can take advantage.

[1]`https://github.com/jmerullo/affordances`

2 Experimental Setup

2.1 Objects and Affordances in SPATIAL

To collect a set of affordances to use in our study, we begin with lists of affordances and associated objects that have been compiled by previous work on affordance learning: Aroca-Ouellette et al. (2021) provides on a small list of concrete actions for evaluating physical reasoning in large language models; Myers et al. (2015) provides a small list for training computer vision models to recognize which parts of objects afford certain actions; Chao et al. (2015) use crowdworkers[2] to judge noun-verb pairs and includes over 900 verbs that are both abstract and concrete in nature. We then filter this list down to only a subset of concrete actions that include objects which exist in the Unity asset store, since we use Unity simulated environments to build our training and evaluation data (§2.4). This results in a list of six affordances (`roll`, `slide`, `stack`, `contain`, `wrap-grasp`, `bounce`) which are used to assign binary labels to each of 39 objects from 11 object categories (Figure 2; see also Appendix A).

2.2 Representation Learning

We hypothesize that predictive modeling of object state will result in implicit representations of affordance and event concepts, similarly to how predictive language modeling results in implicit representations of syntactic and semantic types. Thus, for representation learning, we use a sequence-modeling task defined in the visual and/or spatial world. Specifically, given a sequence of frames

[2]In the case of Chao et al. (2015), we use a score ≥ 4 as positive label, as they do in their paper.

depicting an object's trajectory, our models' objective is to predict the next several timesteps of the object's trajectory as closely as possible. We consider several variants of this objective, primarily differing in how the represent they frames (e.g., as 2D visual vs. 3D spatial features). These models are described in detail in Section 3.

2.3 Evaluation Task

We are interested in evaluating which variants of the above representation learning objective result in readily-accessible representations of affordance and event concepts. To do this, we train probing classifiers (Belinkov and Glass, 2019) on top of the latent representations that result from the representation learning phase. That is, we freeze the weights of our pretrained models and feed the intermediate representation for a given input from the encoder into a single linear-layer trained to classify whether the observed object has the affordance. We train a separate classifier probe for each affordance.

We construct train and test splits by holding out a fraction of the objects from each category. In some cases, the held-out objects are very similar to what has been seen in training (e.g., slightly different dimensions of boxes) and in other cases, the objects are visually very distinct (e.g., a wine bottle vs. a gas tank as instances of objects which afford both `roll` and `contain`). Figure 2 shows our objects, affordances, and train-test splits.

2.4 `SPATIAL` Environment and Data Collection

The `SPATIAL` dataset consists of simulations of interactions with a variety of 3D objects in the Unity game engine[3]. Our data is collected in a flat empty room using the Unity physics engine on the above-described 39 objects. For each sequence, an object is instantiated at rest on the ground. A random impulse force–either a 'push' flat along the ground, or a 'throw' into the air–is exerted on the object. We only exert a single impulse on an object per sequence. The sequence ends when the object stops moving or after 4 seconds elapse.

We record the coordinates of the object in 3D space at a rate of 60 frames per second. Specifically, each sequence is defined by the coordinates describing the object's 3D position in space $P = \{p_1, ..., p_t\}$ for t timesteps. Since we care about capturing the manner in which the object travels and rotates through space, p_i contains 9 distinct 3D points around the object: 8 corners around an imaginary bounding box and the center point of that bounding box (see Appendix A for a visual aid). Simultaneously we collect videos of each interaction from a camera looking down at a 60 degree angle towards the object that we will use to train our 2D vision based model. Each image in the videos is collected at a resolution of 384x216 pixels. We filter videos where the object leaves the frame. Overall, this process results in 2,376 training sequences and 9,283 evaluation sequences. Due to computational constraints, we decided to focus on collecting as many evaluation examples as possible to make comparison to spatial models easier and more accurate. It may be the case that adding more data creates stronger representations, but even with this smaller training set, we see high test time performance on the visual dynamics task. All our data are publicly available at `https://github.com/jmerullo/affordances`.

2.5 Assumptions and Limitations

This work serves as initial investigation of our hypothesis about representation learning for affordances (§2.2). We use simple simulations which involve only a single object. Thus, we expect that our setup makes some affordances (`roll, slide, bounce`) more readily available than others (`contain, stack, w-grasp`). For example, our models likely will observe objects rolling during pretraining, but will never observe objects being stacked on top of one another. However, during evaluation, we will assess how well the model's internal representations encode both types of affordances. This is intended. Our hypothesis is that, to a large extent, these affordances are a function of the relationship between the shape[4] of the objects and the physics of how those objects behave in our simulation. For example, we expect that long, thin `grasp`-able objects will display different trajectories than will wide, round objects

[3] `https://unity.com/`

[4] In fact, Gibson (1977)'s original theory of affordances defined them to be purely-perceptual, without even depending on internal processing and representation. We do not endorse this view in general; we are enthusiastic about future work which involves richer internal processing (e.g., interaction and planning) during pretraining. See Şahin et al. (2007) for a review of the various definitions and interpretations of the term that have been used in different fields and Mota (2021) for an argument that affordances are not solely perceptual. That said, this basic-perception approach is helpful starting point for understanding the relationship between pretraining and affordance representations.

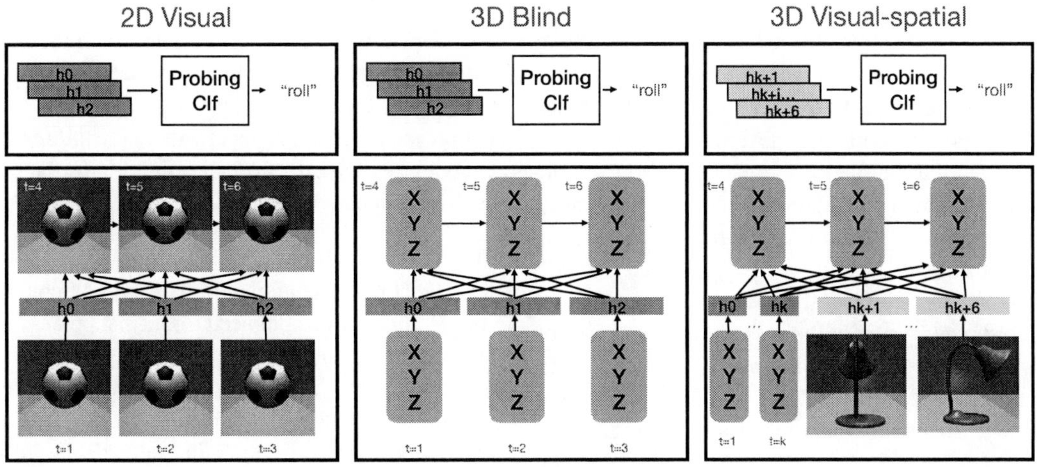

Figure 3: Model architectures. The model receives either images, 3D coordinates or both to make predictions. For the 3D models, the transformer encoder encodes the input sequence (and multiview images, if applicable) and the decoder predicts the rest of the sequence. For the 2D model (`RPIN`), a convolutional network extracts object-centric features (h_i) and interaction reasoning is performed over each to predict the next time steps.

that cannot be grasped. Thus, we expect that a model trained to predict object trajectories can encode differences that map onto affordances such as `grasp` or `contain`, even without observing those actions *per se*. Given initial promising results (§4), we are excited about future work which extends the simulation to include richer multi-object and agent-object interactions, which likely would enable learning of more complex semantic concepts.

3 Models

We consider two primary variants of the representation learning task described in Section 2.2 which differ in how they represent the world state–i.e., using 2D visual data (§3.1) vs. using 3D visual-spatial data (§3.2). To provide additional insights into performance differences, we also consider two ablations in the 3D model (§3.2.2), one that removes visual information and one that further removes pretraining altogether. These models are summarized in Figure 3.

3.1 2D Visual Model

We first consider a standard computer-vision (CV) approach for our defined representation learning objective. For this, we use a Region Proposal Interaction Network (`RPIN`) proposed in Qi et al. (2021). We choose to use `RPIN` because it was designed to solve a task very similar to ours–i.e., object tracking over time–and has access to object representations via bounding boxes provided as supervision during training. Using a model with access to explicit object representations ensures that we are not unfairly handicapping the CV approach (by requiring it to learn the concept of objects from scratch) but rather are analyzing the relative benefits of a 2D CV approach vs. a 3D spatial data approach for latently encoding semantic event and affordance concepts.

We train the model with similar settings to those Qi et al. (2021) used to train on the Simulated Billiards dataset, but with some small differences. For example, we subsample our frames to be coarser-grained to encourage learning of longer-range dependencies. Exact details and explanations of other parameter differences can be found in Appendix B.

To probe object representations for affordance properties, we take the average of the hidden representations–i.e., the model's representations just prior to predicting explicit bounding box coordinates on the screen.

3.2 3D Visual-spatial Model

3.2.1 Full Model

Recent work has argued that models based directly on 3D game engine data are more cognitively plausible for modeling verb semantics (Ebert and Pavlick, 2020). In this spirit, we consider a model that learns to encode the objects visual appearance jointly with predicting the objects' behavior in 3D space. Specifically, our model is trained with both an object loss and a trajectory loss as follows.

To model the 3D trajectory, the model encodes a sequence P containing positions $\{p_1, p_2, ..., p_t\}$. As described in Section 2, each position p_i contains 9 distinct points corresponding to the object center and the 8 corners of the rectangular bounding box encapsulating the object. We use a single linear layer to project the 27D (9 3D points) input coordinate vectors to the embedding dimension of a transformer (Vaswani et al., 2017). The transformer is then fed the first $t-k$ timesteps where $k \geq 1$. We treat k as a hyperparameter, and find that a value of $k = 8$ or $k = 16$ tends to work the best. Our model is trained to minimize the Mean Squared Error (MSE) computed against the true future location of the object, summed over all of the predicted points.

To model the object appearance, we give the model access to a static view of the object at rest. We use ResNet-34 (He et al., 2016) to encode the object's *multiview*–i.e., images of the object's six faces, one from each side of the object–denoted as I, and pass these as additional inputs to the model, separated by a SEP token. The transformer encoder encodes the sequence P and I together, and the transformer decoder predicts the object's next several positions in space. To encourage the model to connect the sequence and image representations, we randomly (50% of the time) replace the object in I with an object with different affordances and add an auxiliary loss in which the model must classify whether the object was perturbed. We add a linear binary classification layer on top of a CLS token to perform this task, and add the cross entropy loss of this objective to our MSE loss for the trajectory objective.

The hidden representation we use for probing experiments is the average pooled transformer encoder output of the multiview tokens only.

3.2.2 Ablation Models

To better understand which aspects of the above model matter most, we also train and evaluate two ablated variants.

Without Visual Information (3D Blind). Our 3D Blind model is like the above, but contains no multiview tokens or associated loss. That is, the model is trained only on the 3D positional data, using an MSE loss to predict the future location of the object. For probing, we average the transformer encoder outputs across all timesteps and feed the single averaged emebedding into the probing classifier. This model provides insight into how well the physical behavior alone, with *no visual inputs*, encodes key features for determining affordances, such as shape and material.

Without Pretraining (No-Training). Gibson believed that understanding affordances only required raw perception, without need for mental processing. Given how saliently actions like rolling and sliding are encoded in 3D coordinates (Figure 6), it is reasonable to ask how much benefit our pretraining objective provides for encoding affordance information. To test this, we evaluate a model that is identical to the 3D Blind model, but contains only randomly initialized encoder weights (i.e., which are never set via pretraining). If the pretraining task encodes affordance structure the way we hypothesize, the randomly initialized model should perform much worse than the trained 3D Blind variant. We refer to this model simply as the No-Training model.

4 Results

Figure 4 shows our primary results. Overall, the 3D Visual-spatial model substantially outperforms the 2D Vision-only model across all affordances, often by a large margin (4–11 percentage points). We also see, perhaps unexpectedly, that the 3D pretrained representations encode information about affordances even when the associated actions are not explicitly observed. For example, the model differentiates objects that can `stack` and objects that can `contain` other objects from those that cannot, even though the model has not directly observed objects being stacked or serving as containers during training. This result points to the richness of the physical information that is required to perform the pretraining task of next-state prediction.[5]

Looking more closely at the ablated variants of the 3D model, we see that most of the gains are from the 3D input representation itself. That

[5]We note that, unintuitively, `stack` and `contain` probes generally outperform `slide` probes. One reason may be because our data are labeled by object rather than by individual interaction. For example, although an object *typically* slides, it's not hard to imagine scenarios where a cardboard box might roll over. This is not the case for affordances like `stack` and `contain`. In the rolling cardboard box example, the sharp edges of the box and the distinct way it rolls is still indicative of the object being stackable.

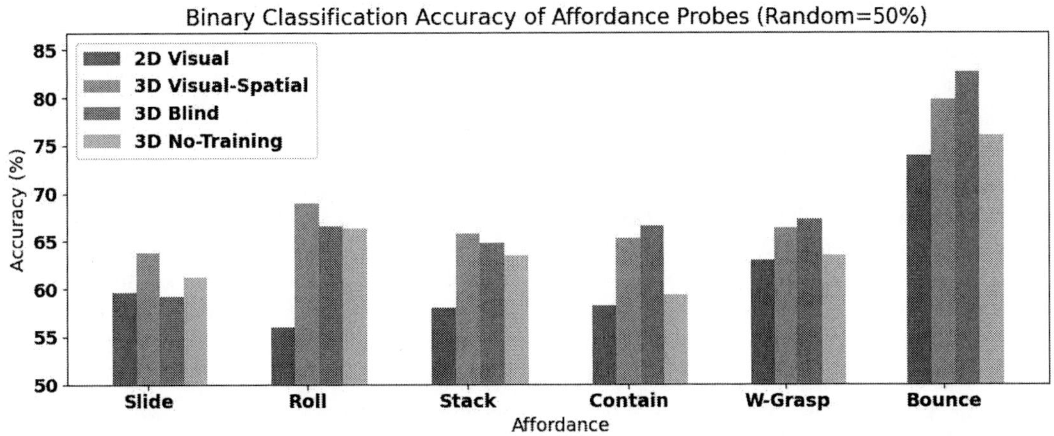

Figure 4: Results for predicting affordances of objects given frozen hidden states of 2D and 3D sequence prediction models. Test sets are balance so that random guess achieves 50%. 3D models (even ablated variants) outperform the 2D computer vision models across the board.

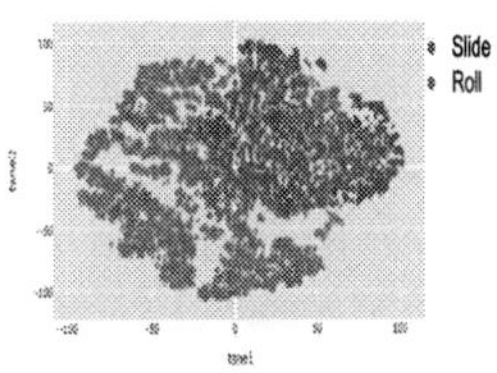

(a) 3D Blind model

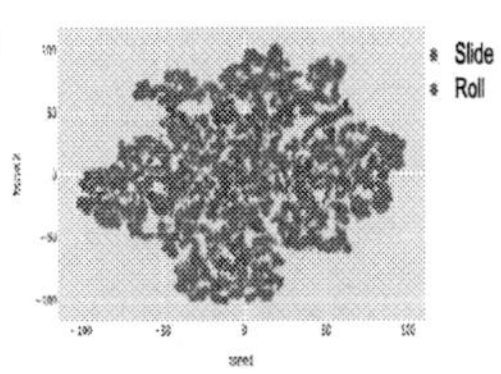

(b) 3D Visual-spatial model

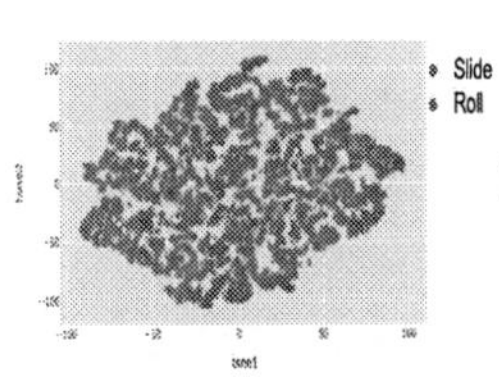

(c) 3D No-Training

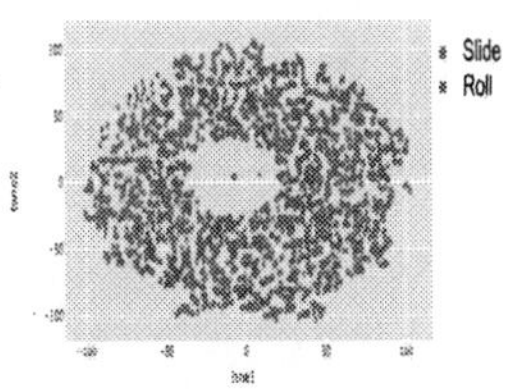

(d) 2D Computer-Vision model (RPIN).

Figure 5: t-SNE projections of model representations of sliding (red) vs. rolling (blue) objects.

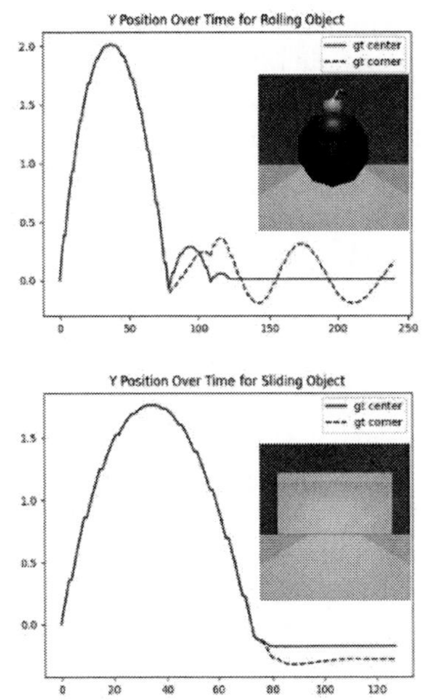

Figure 6: Visualization showing how 3D coordinate data clearly distinguishes a rolling object from a sliding one, making it easier for a model to learn the difference between the two.

is, the 3D No-Training model–which does not include visual information and does not even include pretraining–outperforms the CV baseline in all cases, and often substantially. Pretraining on top of the 3D inputs often (but not always) yields performance gains. Pretraining with visual information does not provide a clear benefit over pretraining on the spatial data alone–i.e., visual information leads to performance gains on three affordances (`slide`, `roll`, and `stack`) and losses on the other three (`contain`, `w-grasp`, and `bounce`).

5 Qualitative Analysis

In order to better understand the nature of the affordance-learning problem, we run a series of qualitative analyses on the trained models. We focus our analysis on the pair of affordances `roll` vs. `slide`. These are verbs have received significant attention in prior literature (Pustejovsky and Krishnaswamy, 2014; Levin, 1993) since they exemplify the types of manner distinctions that we would like lexical semantic representations to encode.

We first compare the 2D video vs. 3D simulation variants of our pretraining objective. Figure 5 shows a t-SNE projection of the sequence representations from all four models, labeled based on if the object affords rolling or sliding. We find that object representations from the 3D Blind model cluster strongly according to the distinction between these two concepts. The trend is notably not apparent in the No-Training model. Figure 6 demonstrates why spatial data pretraining may encourage this split. In the example shown, we take two thrown objects from our dataset–one round and one not round–and track the height of the center point of the object and one of the corners of the object bounding box. When they hit the ground the center point stays relatively constant as it moves across the floor in both, but in the rolling action, the corner point moves up and down as it rotates around the center point. Since this is so distinguishable given the input representation, the model is better able to differentiate these concepts.

It may be that the next state prediction task facilitates learning the slide vs. roll distinction in the 3D Blind setting. However, the same pattern is not present in the 3D Visual-spatial model (which also predicts next state). One possibility is that the presence of visual information competes with the 3D information, and as a result the joint space does not encode this distinction as well as the 3D space alone. Designing more sophisticated models that incorporate visual and spatial information and preserve the desirable features of both is an interesting area for future work.

5.1 Counterfactual Perturbations

An important aspect of lexical semantics is determining the *entailments* of a word–e.g., what about an observation allows it to be described truthfully as `roll`? Thus, in asking whether affordances are learned from next-state-prediction pretraining, it is important to understand not just whether the model can differentiate the concepts, but whether it differentiates them for the "right" reasons.

We investigate this using counterfactual perturbations of the inputs as a way of doing feature attribution, similar in spirit to prior work in NLP (Huang et al., 2020) and CV (Goyal et al., 2019). Specifically, we create a controlled dataset in which, for each of 10 interactions, we generate 20 minimal-pairs which differ from their originals by a single parameter of the underlying physics simulation. The parameters we perturb are {`mass, force velocity, starting x position, starting z position, shape, angular rotation`}. For example, given an instance of a lamp rolling across the floor, we would generate one minimally-paired example in which we only change the mass of the lamp, and another the same as the original except it does not exhibit any angular rotation, and so forth for each of the parameters of interest. More implementation details are given in Appendix C.

We use our pretrained `slide` probe to classify the representations from each sequence as either rolling or sliding, and compare the effect of each perturbation on the model's belief about the affordance label. Figure 7 shows the resulting belief changes for several of the perturbed parameters. We see that changing the angular rotation of an otherwise identical sequence has the greatest effect on whether an instance is deemed to afford `rolling`. This is an encouraging result, as it aligns well with standard lexical semantic analyses: i.e., generally, `roll` is assumed to entail rotation in the direction of the translation.

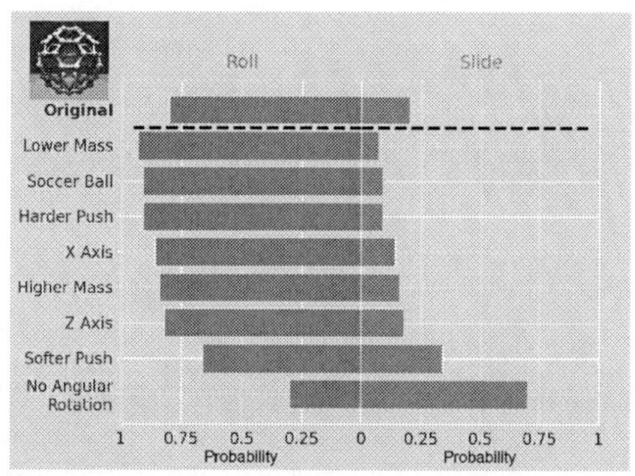

Figure 7: Change in predicted probability of the encoding of a round object affording `slide` after generating the interaction again with one feature changed (See Appendix C for a visualization)

However, our analysis also reveals that the models rely on some spurious features which, ideally, would not be part of the lexical semantic representation. For example, the 3D blind model is affected by the travel distance the object. If we increased the mass or decreased the force applied to a rolling object, such that it only moved a small distance or rotated a small number of times, the model was less inclined to label the instance as rolling; though this was usually not by enough to have the undesirable effect of flipping the prediction. Intuitively this makes sense given the model's training data: rolling objects tend to travel a greater distance than sliding objects. An interesting direction for future work is to investigate how changes in pretraining or data distribution influence which features are encoded as "entailments", i.e., key distinguishing features of a concept's representation.

6 Related Work

6.1 Lexical Semantics and Cognitive Science

In formal semantics, there has been significant support for the idea that motor trajectories and affordances should form the basis of lexical semantic representations (Pustejovsky and Krishnaswamy, 2014; Siskind, 2001; Steedman, 2002). Such work builds on the idea in cognitive science that simulation lies at the heart of cognitive and linguistic processing (Feldman, 2008; Bergen et al., 2007; Bergen, 2012). For example, Borghi and Riggio (2009) argue that language comprehension involves mental simulation resulting in a "motor prototype" which encodes stable affordances and affects processing speed for identifying objects. Cosentino et al. (2017) point to such simulation as a factor in determining surprisal of affordances depending on linguistic context. Similar arguments have been made based on evidence from fMRI data (Sakreida et al., 2013) as well as processing in patients with brain lesions (Taylor et al., 2017). It is worth noting that there is debate on the general nature of affordances in humans. For instance, Mota (2021) argues that affordances are not solely perceptual. We view our work as being compatible with this more general view of affordances, in which direct perception plays a role, but not the only role, in concept formation.

6.2 Affordances in Language Technology

The idea of affordances has been incorporated into work on robotics (Şahin et al., 2007; Zech et al., 2017). Kalkan et al. (2014); Ugur et al. (2009) build a model of affordances based on (object, action, effect) tuples, but focus only on start and end state, and do not encode anything about manner. Relatedly, Nguyen et al. (2020) connects images of objects to language queries describing their uses.

Affordances are also well studied for text understanding tasks. McGregor and Jezek (2019) discuss the importance of affordances in disambiguating meaning of sentences such as "we finished the wine". Other neural net based approaches for affordance learning have relied on curated datasets with explicit affordance labels for each object (Chao et al., 2015; Do et al., 2018). Sometimes, affordance datasets leverage multimodal settings such as images (Myers et al., 2015), or 3D models and environments (Suglia et al., 2021; Mandikal and Grauman, 2021; Nagarajan and Grauman, 2020), but require annotations for every object. In contrast, our model learns affordances in an unsupervised manner, and unlike Fulda et al. (2017), Loureiro and Jorge (2018), McGregor and Lim (2018), and Persiani and Hellström (2019) which extract affordance structure automatically from word embeddings alone, our model learns from interacting with objects in a 3D space, grounding its representations to cause-and-effect pairs of physical forces and object motion.

6.3 Physical Commonsense Reasoning

There has been success in building deep learning networks that reason about object physics by learning to predict their trajectories. These can be broken up into either predicting points in 3D space given object locations (like our approach, e.g. Mrowca et al. (2018), Byravan and Fox (2017), Battaglia et al. (2016), Fragkiadaki et al. (2016), Ye et al. (2018), Rempe et al. (2020)) or inferring future bounding box locations of objects in videos (Weng et al., 2006; Do et al., 2018; Qi et al., 2021; Ding et al., 2021). Both approaches have been successful in encoding complex visual and physical features of objects. We focus on training with 3D simulations, but also test a visual dynamics model (Qi et al., 2021) to compare the affordance information that is encoded from spatial vs. visual data.

More broadly, we contribute to a line of work on building non-linguistic representations of lexical concepts (Bisk et al., 2019). Explicit attempts at grounding to the physical world ground language in 2D images or videos (i.e., pixels) (Hahn et al., 2019; Groth et al., 2018), despite the fact that recent work suggests that text and video pretraining offers no boost to lexical semantic understanding (Yun et al., 2021). Such efforts motivate the creation of large datasets such as Krishna et al. (2016), Yatskar et al. (2016), and Gupta and Malik (2015), which require in-depth human provided annotations that provide a limited list of semantic roles of objects.

Our approach is most directly related to prior

work that learns in interactive, 3D settings (Thomason et al., 2016; Ebert and Pavlick, 2020). Especially related are Nagarajan and Grauman (2020) and Zellers et al. (2021). However, their models do not directly ground to the physical phenomena (e.g., entailed positional changes). Instead, they use a symbolic vocabulary of object state changes, whereas our model learns from unlabeled interactions.

7 Conclusion

We propose an unsupervised pretraining method for learning representations of object affordances from observations of interactions in a 3D environment. We show that 3D trajectory data is a strong signal for grounding such concepts and performs better than a standard computer vision approach for learning the desired concepts. Moreover, we show through counterfactual analyses that the learned representations can encode the desired entailments–e.g., that `roll` entails axial rotation.

Our work contributes to an existing line of work that seeks to develop lexical semantic representations of nouns and verbs that are grounded in physical simulations. We advance this agenda by offering a way in which modern "foundation model" approaches to visual and linguistic processing can in fact be corroborative of traditional feature-based approaches to formal lexical semantics. Our results suggest a promising direction for future work, in which pretraining objectives can be augmented to include richer notions of embodiment (e.g., planning, agent-agent interaction) and consequently encoder richer lexical semantic structure (e.g., presuppositions, transitivity).

Acknowledgments

This research is supported in part by DARPA via the GAILA program (HR00111990064). The views and conclusions contained herein are those of the authors and should not be interpreted as necessarily representing the official policies, either expressed or implied, of DARPA or the U.S. Government. Thanks to Chen Sun, Roman Feiman, members of the Language Understanding and Representation (LUNAR) Lab and AI Lab at Brown, and the reviewers for their help and feedback on this work.

References

Stéphane Aroca-Ouellette, Cory Paik, Alessandro Roncone, and Katharina Kann. 2021. PROST: Physical reasoning about objects through space and time. In *Findings of the Association for Computational Linguistics: ACL-IJCNLP 2021*, pages 4597–4608, Online. Association for Computational Linguistics.

Peter Battaglia, Razvan Pascanu, Matthew Lai, Danilo Jimenez Rezende, and koray kavukcuoglu. 2016. Interaction networks for learning about objects, relations and physics. In *Advances in Neural Information Processing Systems*, volume 29. Curran Associates, Inc.

Yonatan Belinkov and James Glass. 2019. Analysis methods in neural language processing: A survey. *Transactions of the Association for Computational Linguistics*, 7:49–72.

Benjamin K Bergen. 2012. *Louder than words: The new science of how the mind makes meaning*. Basic Books.

Benjamin K Bergen, Shane Lindsay, Teenie Matlock, and Srini Narayanan. 2007. Spatial and linguistic aspects of visual imagery in sentence comprehension. *Cognitive science*, 31(5):733–764.

Yonatan Bisk, Jan Buys, Karl Pichotta, and Yejin Choi. 2019. Benchmarking hierarchical script knowledge. In *Proceedings of the 2019 Conference of the North American Chapter of the Association for Computational Linguistics: Human Language Technologies, Volume 1 (Long and Short Papers)*, pages 4077–4085, Minneapolis, Minnesota. Association for Computational Linguistics.

Rishi Bommasani, Drew A. Hudson, Ehsan Adeli, Russ Altman, Simran Arora, Sydney von Arx, Michael S. Bernstein, Jeannette Bohg, Antoine Bosselut, Emma Brunskill, Erik Brynjolfsson, Shyamal Buch, Dallas Card, Rodrigo Castellon, Niladri S. Chatterji, Annie S. Chen, Kathleen Creel, Jared Quincy Davis, Dorottya Demszky, Chris Donahue, Moussa Doumbouya, Esin Durmus, Stefano Ermon, John Etchemendy, Kawin Ethayarajh, Li Fei-Fei, Chelsea Finn, Trevor Gale, Lauren Gillespie, Karan Goel, Noah D. Goodman, Shelby Grossman, Neel Guha, Tatsunori Hashimoto, Peter Henderson, John Hewitt, Daniel E. Ho, Jenny Hong, Kyle Hsu, Jing Huang, Thomas Icard, Saahil Jain, Dan Jurafsky, Pratyusha Kalluri, Siddharth Karamcheti, Geoff Keeling, Fereshte Khani, Omar Khattab, Pang Wei Koh, Mark S. Krass, Ranjay Krishna, Rohith Kuditipudi, and et al. 2021. On the opportunities and risks of foundation models. *CoRR*, abs/2108.07258.

Anna M Borghi and Lucia Riggio. 2009. Sentence comprehension and simulation of object temporary, canonical and stable affordances. *Brain Research*, 1253:117–128.

Arunkumar Byravan and Dieter Fox. 2017. SE3-nets: Learning rigid body motion using deep neural networks. In *2017 IEEE International Conference on Robotics and Automation (ICRA)*, pages 173–180.

Yu-Wei Chao, Zhan Wang, Rada Mihalcea, and Jia Deng. 2015. Mining semantic affordances of visual object categories. In *2015 IEEE Conference on Computer Vision and Pattern Recognition (CVPR)*, pages 4259–4267.

Erica Cosentino, Giosuè Baggio, Jarmo Kontinen, and Markus Werning. 2017. The time-course of sentence meaning composition. n400 effects of the interaction between context-induced and lexically stored affordances. *Frontiers in Psychology*, 8.

David Ding, Felix Hill, Adam Santoro, Malcolm Reynolds, and Matt Botvinick. 2021. Attention over learned object embeddings enables complex visual reasoning. In *Advances in Neural Information Processing Systems*, volume 34, pages 9112–9124. Curran Associates, Inc.

Thanh-Toan Do, Anh Nguyen, and Ian Reid. 2018. Affordancenet: An end-to-end deep learning approach for object affordance detection. In *2018 IEEE International Conference on Robotics and Automation (ICRA)*, pages 5882–5889.

Dylan Ebert and Ellie Pavlick. 2020. A visuospatial dataset for naturalistic verb learning. In *Proceedings of the Ninth Joint Conference on Lexical and Computational Semantics*, pages 143–153.

Jerome Feldman. 2008. *From molecule to metaphor: A neural theory of language*. MIT press.

Katerina Fragkiadaki, Pulkit Agrawal, Sergey Levine, and Jitendra Malik. 2016. Learning Visual Predictive Models of Physics for Playing Billiards. *arXiv:1511.07404 [cs]*. ArXiv: 1511.07404.

Nancy Fulda, Daniel Ricks, Ben Murdoch, and David Wingate. 2017. What can you do with a rock? affordance extraction via word embeddings. In *Proceedings of the Twenty-Sixth International Joint Conference on Artificial Intelligence, IJCAI-17*, pages 1039–1045.

James J Gibson. 1977. The theory of affordances. *Hilldale, USA*, 1(2):67–82.

Yash Goyal, Ziyan Wu, Jan Ernst, Dhruv Batra, Devi Parikh, and Stefan Lee. 2019. Counterfactual visual explanations. In *International Conference on Machine Learning*, pages 2376–2384. PMLR.

Oliver Groth, Fabian B. Fuchs, Ingmar Posner, and Andrea Vedaldi. 2018. Shapestacks: Learning vision-based physical intuition for generalised object stacking. In *The European Conference on Computer Vision (ECCV)*.

Saurabh Gupta and Jitendra Malik. 2015. Visual semantic role labeling. *arXiv preprint arXiv:1505.04474*.

Meera Hahn, Andrew Silva, and James M. Rehg. 2019. Action2Vec: A Crossmodal Embedding Approach to Action Learning. *arXiv:1901.00484 [cs]*. ArXiv: 1901.00484 version: 1.

Kaiming He, Xiangyu Zhang, Shaoqing Ren, and Jian Sun. 2016. Deep residual learning for image recognition. In *2016 IEEE Conference on Computer Vision and Pattern Recognition (CVPR)*, pages 770–778.

Po-Sen Huang, Huan Zhang, Ray Jiang, Robert Stanforth, Johannes Welbl, Jack Rae, Vishal Maini, Dani Yogatama, and Pushmeet Kohli. 2020. Reducing sentiment bias in language models via counterfactual evaluation. In *Findings of the Association for Computational Linguistics: EMNLP 2020*, pages 65–83, Online. Association for Computational Linguistics.

Sinan Kalkan, Nilgün Dag, Onur Yürüten, Anna M Borghi, and Erol Şahin. 2014. Verb concepts from affordances. *Interaction Studies*, 15(1):1–37.

Najoung Kim and Paul Smolensky. 2021. Testing for grammatical category abstraction in neural language models. *Proceedings of the Society for Computation in Linguistics*, 4(1):467–470.

Ranjay Krishna, Yuke Zhu, Oliver Groth, Justin Johnson, Kenji Hata, Joshua Kravitz, Stephanie Chen, Yannis Kalantidis, Li-Jia Li, David A Shamma, Michael Bernstein, and Li Fei-Fei. 2016. Visual genome: Connecting language and vision using crowdsourced dense image annotations.

Beth Levin. 1993. *English verb classes and alternations: A preliminary investigation*. University of Chicago press.

Daniel Loureiro and Alípio Jorge. 2018. Affordance extraction and inference based on semantic role labeling. In *Proceedings of the First Workshop on Fact Extraction and VERification (FEVER)*, pages 91–96, Brussels, Belgium. Association for Computational Linguistics.

Priyanka Mandikal and Kristen Grauman. 2021. Learning dexterous grasping with object-centric visual affordances. In *ICRA*.

Claudia Mazzuca, Chiara Fini, Arthur Henri Michalland, Ilenia Falcinelli, Federico Da Rold, Luca Tummolini, and Anna M. Borghi. 2021. From affordances to abstract words: The flexibility of sensorimotor grounding. *Brain Sciences*, 11(10).

Stephen McGregor and Elisabetta Jezek. 2019. A distributional model of affordances in semantic type coercion. In *Proceedings of the 13th International Conference on Computational Semantics - Short Papers*, pages 1–7, Gothenburg, Sweden. Association for Computational Linguistics.

Stephen McGregor and KyungTae Lim. 2018. Affordances in grounded language learning. In *Proceedings of the Eight Workshop on Cognitive Aspects of Computational Language Learning and Processing*, pages 41–46, Melbourne. Association for Computational Linguistics.

Sergio Mota. 2021. Dispensing with the theory (and philosophy) of affordances. *Theory & Psychology*, 31(4):533–551.

Damian Mrowca, Chengxu Zhuang, Elias Wang, Nick Haber, Li Fei-Fei, Joshua B. Tenenbaum, and Daniel Yamins. 2018. Flexible neural representation for physics prediction. In *NeurIPS*.

Austin Myers, Ching L. Teo, Cornelia Fermüller, and Yiannis Aloimonos. 2015. Affordance detection of tool parts from geometric features. In *2015 IEEE International Conference on Robotics and Automation (ICRA)*, pages 1374–1381.

Tushar Nagarajan and Kristen Grauman. 2020. Learning affordance landscapes for interaction exploration in 3d environments. In *NeurIPS*.

Thao Nguyen, Nakul Gopalan, Roma Patel, Matthew Corsaro, Ellie Pavlick, and Stefanie Tellex. 2020. Robot Object Retrieval with Contextual Natural Language Queries. In *Proceedings of Robotics: Science and Systems*, Corvalis, Oregon, USA.

Michele Persiani and Thomas Hellström. 2019. Unsupervised inference of object affordance from text corpora. In *Proceedings of the 22nd Nordic Conference on Computational Linguistics*, pages 115–120, Turku, Finland. Linköping University Electronic Press.

James Pustejovsky and Nikhil Krishnaswamy. 2014. Generating simulations of motion events from verbal descriptions. In *Proceedings of the Third Joint Conference on Lexical and Computational Semantics (*SEM 2014)*, pages 99–109, Dublin, Ireland. Association for Computational Linguistics and Dublin City University.

James Pustejovsky and Nikhil Krishnaswamy. 2018. Every object tells a story. In *Proceedings of the Workshop Events and Stories in the News 2018*, pages 1–6, Santa Fe, New Mexico, U.S.A. Association for Computational Linguistics.

Haozhi Qi, Xiaolong Wang, Deepak Pathak, Yi Ma, and Jitendra Malik. 2021. Learning long-term visual dynamics with region proposal interaction networks. In *ICLR*.

Davis Rempe, Srinath Sridhar, He Wang, and Leonidas J. Guibas. 2020. Predicting the physical dynamics of unseen 3d objects. *Proceedings of the Winter Conference on Applications of Computer Vision (WACV)*.

Katrin Sakreida, Claudia Scorolli, Mareike M Menz, Stefan Heim, Anna M Borghi, and Ferdinand Binkofski. 2013. Are abstract action words embodied? an fmri investigation at the interface between language and motor cognition. *Frontiers in human neuroscience*, 7:125.

Jeffrey Mark Siskind. 2001. Grounding the lexical semantics of verbs in visual perception using force dynamics and event logic. *Journal of artificial intelligence research*, 15:31–90.

Mark Steedman. 2002. Plans, affordances, and combinatory grammar. *Linguistics and Philosophy*, 25(5):723–753.

Alessandro Suglia, Qiaozi Gao, Jesse Thomason, Govind Thattai, and Gaurav S. Sukhatme. 2021. Embodied BERT: A transformer model for embodied, language-guided visual task completion. *CoRR*, abs/2108.04927.

Lawrence J. Taylor, Carys Evans, Joanna Greer, Carl Senior, Kenny R. Coventry, and Magdalena Ietswaart. 2017. Dissociation between semantic representations for motion and action verbs: Evidence from patients with left hemisphere lesions. *Frontiers in Human Neuroscience*, 11.

Ian Tenney, Patrick Xia, Berlin Chen, Alex Wang, Adam Poliak, R Thomas McCoy, Najoung Kim, Benjamin Van Durme, Samuel R Bowman, Dipanjan Das, et al. 2018. What do you learn from context? probing for sentence structure in contextualized word representations. In *International Conference on Learning Representations*.

Jesse Thomason, Jivko Sinapov, Maxwell Svetlik, Peter Stone, and Raymond J. Mooney. 2016. Learning multi-modal grounded linguistic semantics by playing "i spy". In *Proceedings of the 25th International Joint Conference on Artificial Intelligence (IJCAI-16)*, pages 3477–3483, New York City.

Emre Ugur, Erol Sahin, and Erhan Oztop. 2009. Predicting future object states using learned affordances. In *2009 24th International Symposium on Computer and Information Sciences*, pages 415–419. IEEE.

Ashish Vaswani, Noam Shazeer, Niki Parmar, Jakob Uszkoreit, Llion Jones, Aidan N Gomez, Ł ukasz Kaiser, and Illia Polosukhin. 2017. Attention is all you need. In *Advances in Neural Information Processing Systems*, volume 30. Curran Associates, Inc.

Shiuh-Ku Weng, Chung-Ming Kuo, and Shu-Kang Tu. 2006. Video object tracking using adaptive Kalman filter. *Journal of Visual Communication and Image Representation*, 17(6):1190–1208.

Mark Yatskar, Luke Zettlemoyer, and Ali Farhadi. 2016. Situation recognition: Visual semantic role labeling for image understanding. *2016 IEEE Conference on Computer Vision and Pattern Recognition (CVPR)*, pages 5534–5542.

Tian Ye, Xiaolong Wang, James Davidson, and Abhinav Gupta. 2018. Interpretable intuitive physics model. In *ECCV*.

Tian Yun, Chen Sun, and Ellie Pavlick. 2021. Does vision-and-language pretraining improve lexical grounding? In *Findings of EMNLP*.

Philipp Zech, Simon Haller, Safoura Rezapour Lakani, Barry Ridge, Emre Ugur, and Justus Piater. 2017. Computational models of affordance in robotics: a taxonomy and systematic classification. *Adaptive Behavior*, 25(5):235–271.

Rowan Zellers, Ari Holtzman, Matthew E. Peters, R. Mottaghi, Aniruddha Kembhavi, Ali Farhadi, and Yejin Choi. 2021. PIGLeT: Language Grounding Through Neuro-Symbolic Interaction in a 3D World. In *ACL/IJCNLP*.

Erol Şahin, Maya Çakmak, Mehmet R. Doğar, Emre Uğur, and Göktürk Üçoluk. 2007. To afford or not to afford: A new formalization of affordances toward affordance-based robot control. *Adaptive Behavior*, 15(4):447–472.

A Appendix A

Figure 8: Example of an interaction from SPATIAL. The model predicts the position of the soccer ball at future timesteps. To do that, it must encode some knowledge that soccer balls bounce and roll. As input, our model takes 9 3D points: the eight corners of the box surrounding the ball, plus the center point.

A.1 Spatial Model Training Details

For both of the 3D spatial data models, we train with an encoder-decoder transformer with one encoder and one decoder layer with one attention head. We found that changing the number of attention heads did not affect performance noticeably in either direction. We use a batch size of 64 and a transformer embedding dimension of 100. We use a feed-forward dimension of 200. We initialize with a learning rate of 1e-4. The models were trained to predict the next $k = 8 - 16$ frames and we did not see a large benefit in training to predict longer sequences. We trained the models for 400 epochs although we notcied the ablated 3D Blind model tended to converge at or before 100 epochs across our experiments.

The beginning of the sequence, which was up to four seconds minus the k prediction frames, was fed into the transformer encoder which encoded representations of dimension e. We averaged these output embeddings as input in our probing experiments. The e embeddings were fed into the decoder network, which then predicts the next k frames. We believe that training with longer sequences would be more beneficial for training a decoder-only model, which we would like to explore in future work. In preliminary experiments, we tested whether masking a proportion of frames in the encoder would be beneficial for the representation learning task. We saw a slight decrease in performance, and so did not perform a thorough analysis on the effect of masking.

A.2 t-SNE Configuration

We report a t-SNE of representations derived from our 3D Blind model and the 2D Visual model. The parameters for creating each t-SNE was similar but varied in a few ways: **Common Hyperparameters:** learning rate: 200, iterations: 1000, stopping threshold of gradient norm: 1e-7 **3D Blind t-SNE specifics:** perplexity: 30, initialized randomly **2D Visual specifics:** perplexity: 5, initialized with PCA. We found that random initialization was inconsistent in that it would sometimes cause small clouds of dense points to appear as their own clusters.

B Appendix B

B.1 RPIN Training details

We use a learning rate of 1e-3 with a batch size of 50 and train for a maximum of 20M iterations with 40,000 warmup iterations. Training data is augmented with random horizontal flips. Unlike in Qi et al. (2021) we don't use vertical flips because our videos contain objects falling due to gravity. One important difference is that at training time the model predicts 10 frames in the future, and at test time predicts 20 (as opposed to 20 and 40 respectively in Simulated Billiards). Within one video, our interactions seem more complex than one sequence in the Simulated Billiards dataset, so we introduced this difference to create more training examples.

C Appendix C

C.1 Counterfactual Perturbations Setup

We start with a base set of 10 sequences: 5 with a sliding object (cardboardBox_03) and 5 with a rolling object (BuckyBall). We then create 20 minimal-edit perturbations to create a final set of 200 sequences. We perturb the following features one at a time: {mass, force velocity, starting x position, starting z position, shape, angular rotation}. For most features, we generate 4 perturbations. For example, the x and z positions are altered by {-2m, -1m, +1m, +2m} where 'm' is the Unity meter. All objects start with 1.14 units of mass and similar to the starting position variable, is altered by $1.14 + (i \times .1)$ where i is in the set {-2, -1, 1, 2}. For the shape parameter, we only change the 3D model used to generate the base sequence.

For the sliding videos, we use `plate02` and `book_0001c`. For the rolling videos we use `BombBall` and `modified Soccer Ball`. Note that we modify the `Soccer Ball` model that is in the train set, but modify the mass (1.14) and size of the model so that it is technically an unseen object. We chose to do this because we wanted to use a more plain spherical object, which was not an option for the remaining test objects. Angular rotation either perturbs the sequence by freezing the rotation along all axes (in the case of objects that normally roll) or replacing the physics collider with a sphere (causing the object to roll – in the case of objects that tend to slide instead of roll). Figure 11 shows additional perturbations and a sliding object example of the counterfactual analysis.

Object	Test set?	Slide	Roll	Stack	Contain	W-Grasp	Bounce
BombBall	✓		✓				✓
EyeBall			✓				✓
SpikeBall			✓				
Vase_Amphora			✓				
Vase_Hydria			✓				
Vase_VoluteKrater	✓		✓		✓		
book_0001a		✓		✓			
book_0001b		✓		✓			
book_0001c	✓	✓		✓			
bowl01		✓	✓	✓	✓		
cardboardBox_01		✓		✓			
cardboardBox_02		✓		✓	✓		
cardboardBox_03	✓	✓		✓			
Cola Can		✓	✓	✓		✓	
Pen black	✓		✓			✓	
Gas Bottle	✓		✓				
Soccer Ball			✓				✓
can small		✓	✓	✓		✓	
can	✓	✓	✓	✓		✓	
meat can box		✓		✓			
spam can		✓		✓		✓	
AtomBall			✓				✓
Bottle2	✓		✓			✓	
plate02	✓	✓		✓			
plate02_flat		✓		✓			
Bottle1			✓			✓	
WheelBall			✓				✓
wine bottle 04	✓		✓		✓	✓	
coin	✓	✓		✓			
BuckyBall	✓		✓				✓
SplitMetalBall	✓		✓				✓
bowl02		✓	✓	✓	✓		
bowl03	✓	✓	✓	✓	✓		
mug02		✓			✓	✓	
mug03	✓	✓			✓	✓	
Old_USSR_Lamp_01	✓	✓				✓	
lamp	✓	✓	✓			✓	
Ladle		✓				✓	
Apple			✓				

Table 1: All objects in the dataset and their associated affordances

Binary Classification Accuracy of Affordance Probes (Random=50%)									
	N examples	3D Blind		3D Visual-Spatial		2D Visual		No-Training	
Affordance		Acc. (%)	F1	Acc. (%)	F1	Acc. (%)	F1	Acc. (%)	F1
Slide	1715	59.2	62	**63.7**	67	59.6	62	61.2	64
Roll	1258	66.5	66	**69.0**	70	56.0	58	66.3	66
Stack	1307	64.7	65	**65.7**	63	58.0	58	63.4	63
Contain	1510	**66.5**	68	65.2	67	58.2	63	59.3	64
W-Grasp	1652	**67.2**	68	66.3	0.68	62.9	61	63.4	64
Bounce	276	**82.6**	83	79.7	79	73.9	76.	76.0	75

Table 2: Results from probing experiments on RPIN compared to the unity models trained on the same amount of data. Because data was limited, we partition the data so that there is an even number of positive and negative examples in the test set for each affordance. Interaction based pretraining outperforms visual dynamics in all categories

Affordance	Number of Objects	Percentage of objects (%)
Slide	22	56.41
Roll	23	58.97
Stack	17	43.59
Contain	8	20.51
Wrap-grasp	13	33.33
Bounce	7	17.95

Table 3: Each affordance we are interested in learning and the number and percentage of objects out of the 39 have a positive label for that affordance.

RPIN Model validation loss in the $t \in [T_{train}, 2 \times T_{train}]$ setting	
Model	Loss (MSE)
SimB (Qi et al., 2021)	25.77
SimB (our results)	15.53
Unity Videos	20.98

Table 4: Each affordance we are interested in learning and the number and percentage of objects out of the 39 have a positive label for that affordance.

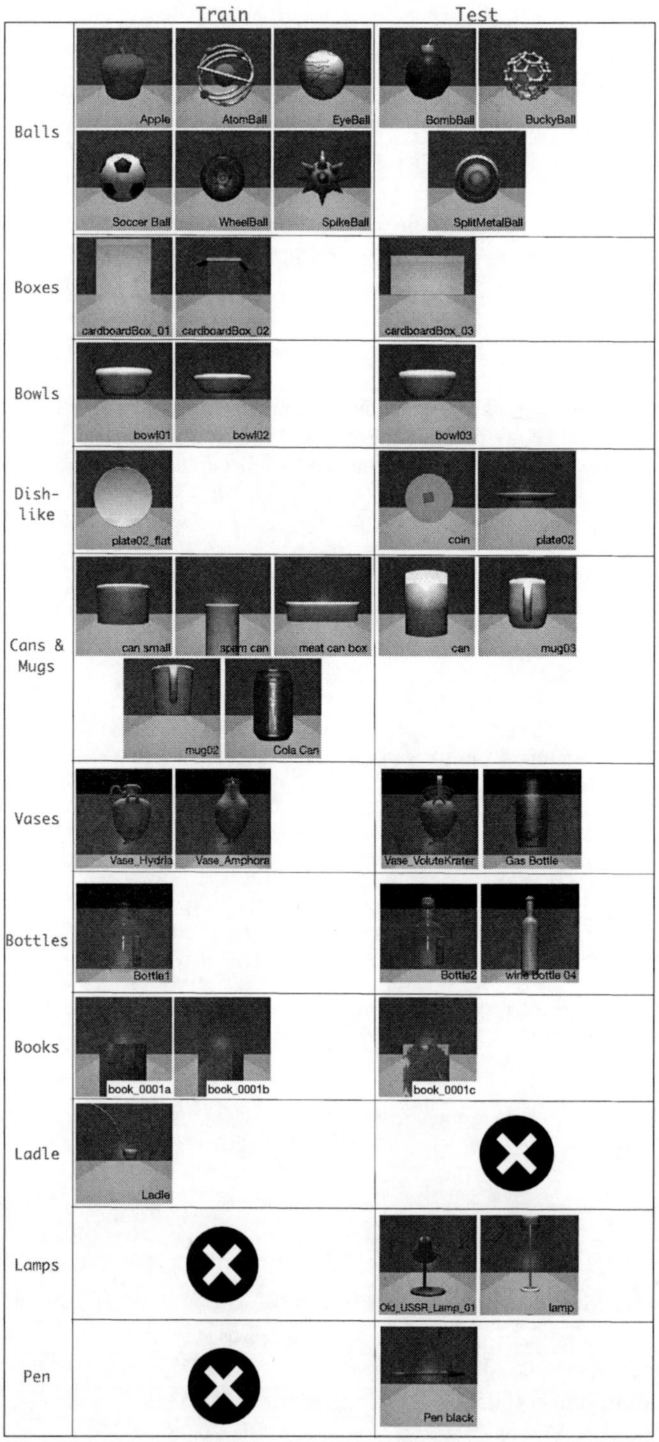

Figure 9: All objects that were used in training and testing. Some objects in the test set are visually similar to their training analogues, but differ in size and mass.

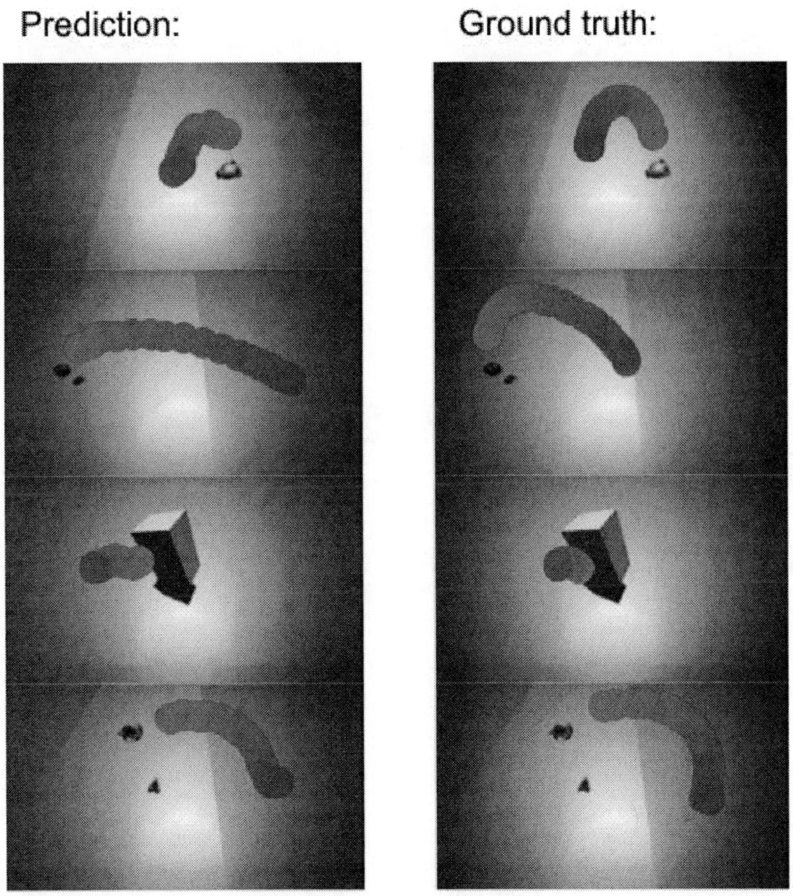

Figure 10: Results from the training of the RPIN visual dynamics model on videos of our Unity dataset interactions. Red circles show the predictions of the following center points of the bounding boxes of the object given the start of the interaction

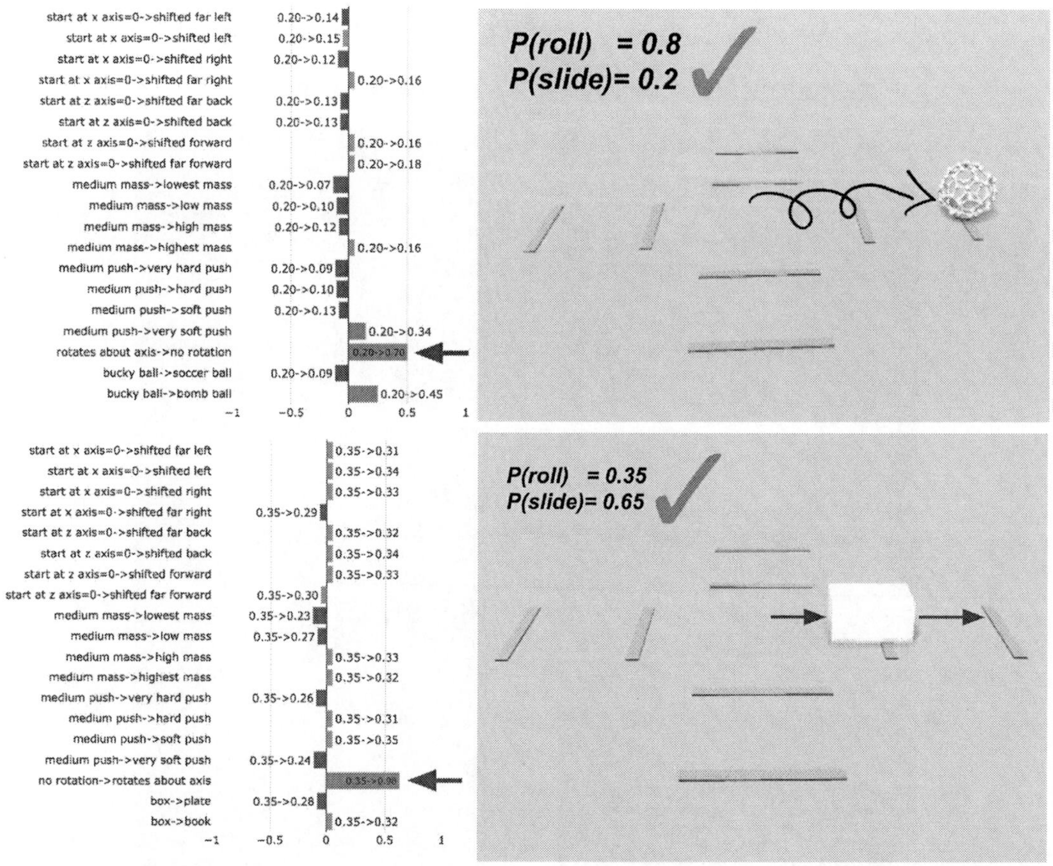

Figure 11: Two examples from the counterfactual analysis that show robustness to changing spurious features. The table in the top example displays the changes in probability in predicting the object as sliding. Conversely, the bottom example table shows the change in probability of predicting the object as rolling. Arrows in the left table indicate where the perturbation *does* affect the label of the action (either by making the object able or unable to roll). In both cases, the probe correctly flips its prediction on the encoding. The sequence prediction model appears to be sensitive to certain features such as distance traveled. For example, changing the object from the "bucky ball" to the "bomb ball" decreases the model's confidence that the object rolling (though, the probe still correctly assigns a majority of the probability to `roll`). However, in this perturbation, the bomb ball gets stuck on its 'cap' (Figure 9) and only completes one rotation.

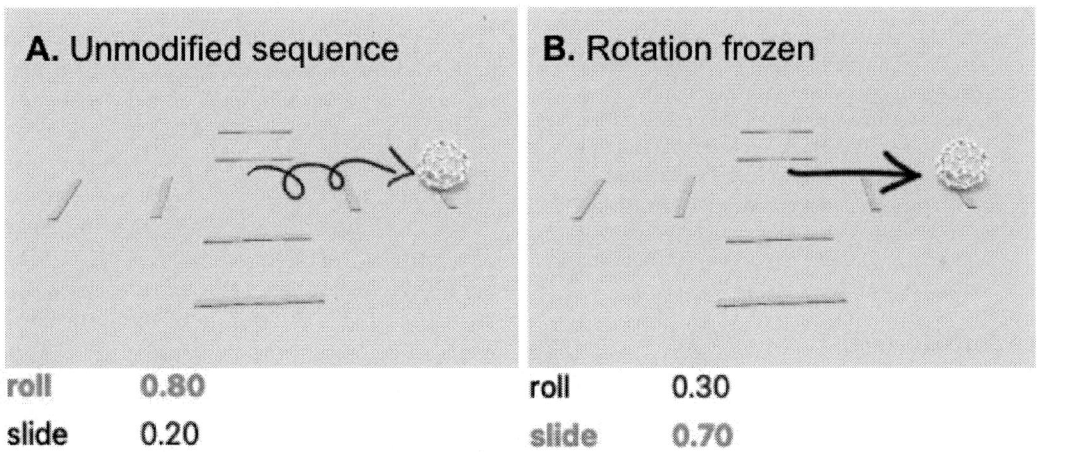

Figure 12: Left: a sequence generated with normal physics. Right: rotation locked, with all other physical properties of the interaction the same. Freezing the rotation such that the object slides causes the model to encode the action as a `slide` rather than a `roll`

PropBank Comes of Age—Larger, Smarter, and more Diverse

Sameer Pradhan[1,2], Julia Bonn[3], Skatje Myers[3], Kathryn Conger[3]. Tim O'Gorman[4], James Gung[5], Martha Palmer[3]

[1]University of Pennsylvania, Philadelphia, PA, 19104, [2]`cemantix.org`
[3]University of Colorado, Boulder, CO 80303,
[4]Thorn, MI (`thorn.org`), [5]Amazon AI, New York City, NY
`pradhan@cemantix.org`, `martha.palmer@colorado.edu`

Abstract

This paper describes the evolution of the PropBank approach to semantic role labeling over the last two decades. During this time the PropBank frame files have been expanded to include non-verbal predicates such as adjectives, prepositions and multi-word expressions. The number of domains, genres and languages that have been PropBanked has also expanded greatly, creating an opportunity for much more challenging and robust testing of the generalization capabilities of PropBank semantic role labeling systems. We also describe the substantial effort that has gone into ensuring the consistency and reliability of the various annotated datasets and resources, to better support the training and evaluation of such systems.

1 Introduction

Twenty years ago traditional statistical machine learning techniques were holding sway and successful stochastic syntactic parsing was on the rise. The availability of accurate syntactic parses opened the door to richer, deeper representations. The second Human Language Technology conference included a presentation on *Adding Predicate Argument Structure to the Penn Treebank* and the Proposition Bank (PropBank) was born (Kingsbury and Palmer, 2002). Over the next few years, with the able guidance of a steering committee consisting of Ralph Weischedel, Mitch Marcus, Doug Appelt, Mark Villain and Ralph Grishman, the annotation guidelines and the annotation continued to grow, with the end result of over 110,000 predicate argument structures pointing directly to syntactic nodes in the phrase structure syntax trees of the roughly 50,000 sentences of the Penn Treebank. The annotation of these structures was guided by a set of approximately 3300 Frame Files that provided a verb specific set of semantic roles as the arguments for each verb. The substantial size of the data set and the consistency of the annotation gave rise to a flurry of popular semantic role labeling systems and semantic role labeling shared tasks (Carreras and Màrquez, 2005; Surdeanu et al., 2008) that continue to this day. The Penn Treebank is entirely composed of Wall Street Journal articles, and annotation of additional data taken from the more diverse English genres of the Brown corpus allowed for out of domain testing, with predictable dismal results. Since that time, DARPA and NSF have funded substantial additional PropBank annotation, focusing on additional domains and genres for English, as well as additional languages such as Chinese, Arabic, Hindi and Urdu. The deep learning revolution has not abated the interest in semantic role labeling performance, and the incorporation of PropBank Frame files into the Abstract Meaning Representation (AMR) Editor (Banarescu et al., 2013), to guide the labeling of the AMR nested predicate argument structures, ensures its longevity. This paper details the new genres, domains and datasets that are now available, as well as the expansion of the original PropBank verb Frame Files to adjectival and nominal forms. Today PropBank has a prominent web presence[1] and plans to evolve and cater to the growing, global, distributed, diverse community by means of a GitHub organization[2]. Github supports the infrastructure for streamlining contributions and resolving issues that are bound to arise in the future. Multiple versions of stable annotations are made available to the community for promoting open, reproducible research[3]. Different versions of the frame lexicon can be viewed and searched online in a human friendly format[4].

We start by reviewing the framework and assumptions for the original PropBank and detail

[1]`http://propbank.org`

[2]`http://github.com/propbank`

[3]Many diverse sources and subcorpora are covered by the sum total of all annotations. Access to various data slices is governed by the data and privacy restrictions on the underlying source. A bulk of the data is accessible free of charge for research use upon completion of relevant data use paperwork. The details can be found on the main website.

[4]`http://propbank.org/v3.4.0/frames`

Proceedings of the 11th Joint Conference on Lexical and Computational Semantics, pages 278 - 288
July 14-15, 2022

the changes that have been made as it matured in Section 2. Section 3 describes the additional new domains and genres that are covered in subsequent annotation efforts. In Section 4 we provide novel baseline results on these new corpora to stimulate additional research in the robustness and portability of semantic role labeling. Finally we summarize our contributions in Section 5.

2 The Proposition Bank, Then and Now

PropBank (Kingsbury and Palmer, 2002; Palmer et al., 2005a) is a paradigm for the development of corpora annotated with predicate argument structures. In its original form, these predicate arguments structures were applied to the syntactic scaffolding provided by the Penn Treebank. While creating a global inventory of semantic roles was traditionally viewed as too difficult, PropBank sidestepped the issue by using an "individual thematic roles" approach (Dowty, 1991) in which roles are custom-defined within each (coarse-grained) sense of a predicate. The decision as to what constitutes a semantic role and the use of Penn Treebank as the syntactic scaffolding for the annotation contributed to high inter-annotator agreement, which led to higher performing machine learning models and fueled interest in the task. PropBank has been instrumental in creating a subfield of NLP called Semantic Role Labeling (SRL). The following three subsections describe the evolution of PropBank in terms of the kind of predicates that were annotated, the changes seen in the data structures as paradigm matured, and the genre of data annotated over the past two decades.

2.1 Frames—Predicate Rolesets and Arguments

The core of the PropBank paradigm consists of an annotation schema and a lexical inventory collectively referred to as the **Frames**. Frames are a set of files that house "rolesets", which are predicate argument structures associated with coarse-grained senses for eventualities. Within a roleset, roles that are considered semantically and/or syntactically core are bundled together as predicate-specific numbered arguments[5]. In annotation, all rolesets across all predicates share a larger pool of "adjunct" arguments such as ARGM-LOC for location, ARGM-TMP for temporal, ARGM-GOL for goals and beneficiaries, etc. These three-letter ARGM tags cover generalized thematic role information that is more specific than argument numbers but more categorical than custom role definitions, and so the pool of ARGMs has become the basis for a set of *function tags* that are now applied to roles. The list of function tags includes PAG (proto-agent) and PPT (proto-patient), taken from Dowty (1991); the list of function tags continues to grow along with PropBank's expansion into more domain-specific corpora. Each role in every roleset comes with an argument number, a custom definition, and a function tag as described in Figure 1.

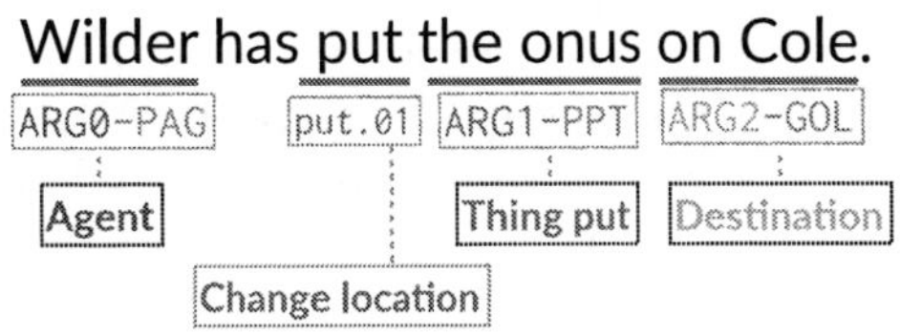

Figure 1: In this example, the verb predicate `put` invokes the *change of location* roleset `put.01` in which the proto-agent (PAG) is the numbered argument ARG0 getting assigned a value ARG0-PAG; *Thing put*, is the proto-patient (PPT), getting value ARG1-PPT; and *the destination* being a goal (GOL) getting the value ARG2-GOL.

The Frames are not in themselves organized according to any kind of semantic hierarchy; rolesets are grouped inside frame files according to polysemy and etymological closeness and nothing more (e.g. the `leave` frame file includes rolesets for multiple `leave` and `left` predicates). However, each roleset potentially includes links with other lexical resources such as VerbNet (Schuler, 2005), FrameNet (Baker et al., 1998), etc., as well as to word senses in WordNet (Fellbaum, 2010) and therefore to those in OntoNotes (Weischedel et al., 2011; Pradhan et al., 2013). This collectively forms a rich, interconnected, high coverage, semantic network.

Over time, the significance of the lexicon of predicate frames has risen to the level where it is *not just an artifact of PropBank*, but has become a resource in its own right, forming the backbone of various meaning representations such as AMR, Uniform Meaning Representation (UMR) (Gysel et al., 2021), etc.

[5]We use the term "argument" when referring to the general notion of arguments of a predicate; and the terms "role" and "rolesets" when we are referring to the vocabulary of roles assigned to each argument of a predicate in the lexicon of (mostly lemma specific) frames.

2.2 Coverage—Genres and Languages

The original PropBank comprised a single news genre, as represented by the WSJ. Over time more genres and languages were PropBanked. At first a small subset of the Brown corpus was annotated to test the generalizability of machine learning models. Subsequently, as part of the OntoNotes project, it covered more genres and was adapted to two other languages—Chinese (Palmer et al., 2005b) and Arabic. The OntoNotes genres include broadcast news, broadcast conversations, web text (blogs, newsgroups), telephone conversations (Godfrey et al., 1992; Taylor, 1996), and a pivot corpus of New and Old Testament text.

The methodology has been adapted to Korean (Palmer et al., 2006), Hindi/Urdu (Bhatt et al., 2009), Finnish (Haverinen et al., 2013), Turkish (Sahin, 2016), Persian (Mirzaei and Moloodi, 2016), Russian (Moeller et al., 2020), and Brazilian Portuguese (Duran and Aluísio, 2011).

PropBank was further extended to additional languages by the Universal PropBanks (Akbik et al., 2015; Jindal et al., 2022). Some of these were automatically generated by projecting English SRL annotation onto parallel text in seven languages and further refining them through filtering and bootstrapping.

2.3 Evolution of the Data Structure

The first version of the PropBank was annotated on top of constituent trees of the Penn Treebank. As a result, with a few exceptions, the PropBank semantic role labels represent nodes in a constituent parse tree. As PropBank grew, it uncovered areas in the Treebank guidelines that conflicted with the PropBank semantic interpretation choices. This led to an effort to synchronize the two resources, creating an improved version of each (Babko-Malaya et al., 2006). Initial machine learning approaches converted the annotation into a series of text spans (Carreras and Màrquez, 2005) and relied heavily on a syntactic parser for good performance (Pradhan et al., 2005). The period starting around 2007 saw a significant rise in the use of dependency representation of parses. International evaluations of dependency parse based semantic role labeling were originally organized by automatically mapping the constituent tree semantic roles to dependency trees (Surdeanu et al., 2008). In the last decade, thanks in part to a combination of the advent of deep learning and the maturity of the guidelines and existing models, PropBank annotations have been freed from the syntactic scaffolding provided by the Treebank. The more recent PropBank annotations are performed on flat text[6]. The core lexicon for PropBank which are the frame files follow an XML specification which has evolved through several iterations over the years. All annotations have been updated to match the latest version of the specification.

2.3.1 Why XML and not JSON?

Contrary to popular notion, JSON is NOT universally better than XML[7]. In fact, as this three part series of articles[8,9,10] highlights, as of now, XML schema[11] is still the most versatile form of defining and validating declarative data specifications and constraints when compared to its JSON counterpart—JSON Schema. We are currently in the process of moving away from a somewhat restrictive DTD specification to a full-fledged XML schema. We could consider migrating to the JSD(x) which uses a JSON schema definition language (JSD) modeled closely with XML Schema language and guarantees a one-to-one mapping between the two[12]

2.4 Frames—Updated Specification

2.4.1 Synchronizing with AMR

The first release of PropBank only covered verbal predicates. Nominal forms in the Penn Treebank were handled by the NomBank project at NYU (Meyers et al., 2004). During the OntoNotes project, the PropBank Frame Files were expanded to include eventive nominals such as NomBank nominalizations, which had already been based on the original verb frame files, as well as light verb constructions (Hwang et al., 2010). By 2012, in support of the Abstract Meaning Representation (AMR) project, PropBank introduced other non-verbal predicates including additional noun

[6]More details regarding the evolution of annotation file formats can be found in the documentation available on the PropBank website.

[7]This subsection added to address a reviewer concern.

[8]`https://www.toptal.com/web/json-vs-xml-part-1`

[9]`https://www.toptal.com/web/json-vs-xml-part-2`

[10]`https://www.toptal.com/web/json-vs-xml-part-3`

[11]Two expressive XML schema languages are in widespread use—XML Schema (with a capital S) and RELAX NG.

[12]The combination JSD and JSDx—shortened as JSD(x)—is a self-describing schema where the language JSD(x) is expressed in JSD(x) itself and allows declarative specification of structural and functional constraints equivalent to XML schema. Moving from XML schema to JSONx should be quite straight-forward when the supporting infrastructure reaches a reasonable level of maturity.

forms, adjectives, and certain multi-word expressions. AMR's aim was to abstract away from syntactic specificity and annotate semantic argument structures for eventualities regardless of their part of speech. Initially, new predicate types were added as distinct rolesets–for example, `fear-n.01` (noun) and `afraid-j.01` (adjective) were modeled after `fear-v.01` (verb), sharing its semantics and argument structure but operating independently (Bonial et al., 2014, 2012, 2017). While the new additions more than tripled the range of what was annotatable, they also introduced a certain amount of redundancy into the lexical inventory, and so the entire lexicon was put through an extensive overhaul to unify etymologically-related rolesets, increasing the similarity to FrameNet frames. The 2017 post-unification release introduced a new roleset structure in which multiple predicates (aliases) could be included in a single roleset (e.g. `fear.01`, with aliases `fear-v`, `fear-n`, and `afraid-j`) (O'Gorman et al., 2018). It also introduced new varieties of complex multi-word predicates including multi-word expressions (MWEs)—fully noncompositional idioms like `jump_the_shark` as well as semi-decompositional expressions like `have_in_mind`—and predicating prepositional phrases like `in_love`.

In the five years since the post-unification release, PropBank's lexical inventory has been recruited for an increasingly broad range of domain-specific annotation projects across PropBank and AMR. With each of these projects comes a unique set of annotation needs that have broadened the scope of the lexical inventory. For example, the Spatial AMR annotation project expands the PropBank lexicon and AMR annotation schema to allow for grounded annotation of multimodal spatial corpora (Bonn et al., 2020; Narayan-Chen et al., 2019). The particular needs of the project meant expanding the rolesets to allow non-eventuality predicate types, like prepositional relations and their etymologically-related adverbial counterparts (e.g. spatial direction terms like `back`, `left`. While not eventualities, such expressions still benefit from the sense disambiguation and essential role clustering that come with roleset treatment. Because grounded annotation of directed spatial expressions requires tracking the linguistic frame of reference of each instance, these spatial rolesets are also the first in the PropBank lexicon to introduce numbered arguments for roles that are essential yet almost never explicitly realized.

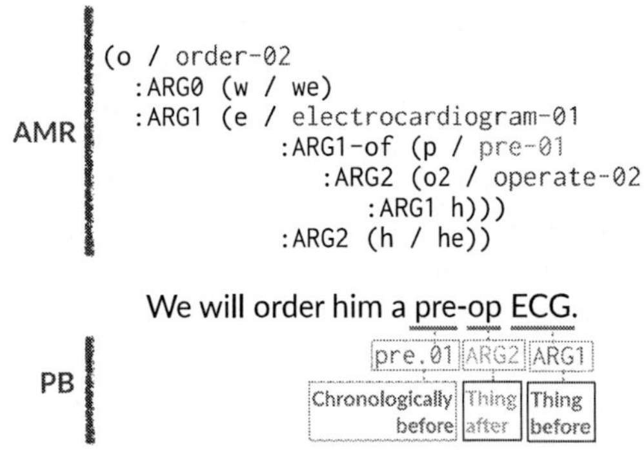

Figure 2: This example shows how the frame lexicon is shared between two representations—Abstract Meaning Representation (AMR) and PropBank (PB) in the clinical domain. The predicate `pre` invokes the *Chronologically before* roleset `pre.01`, where, the *Thing before* is assigned the role ARG1 and the *Thing after* is assigned the role ARG2. Note that the AMR shows the arguments of three additional predicate rolesets: i) `order-02`; ii) `electrocardiogram-01`; and iii) `operate-02`, which correspond to what PropBank would annotate as predicates for the tokens having the surface forms "order", "ECG," and "op" respectively.

The THYME project is another domain-specific AMR annotation project that has required significant, specialized expansion of the lexical inventory. The THYME colon cancer corpus consists of cancer-related clinical-narrative documents that have been annotated in such a way as to provide temporal-relation extraction of clinical events (Albright et al., 2013; Styler et al., 2014; Wright-Bettner et al., 2019). The corpus contains highly specialized medical terminology rarely seen in the general domain: surgical procedures, anatomical parts, diseases, disorders, symptomatology, etc. One of the great challenges of this project has been to determine which of these types to treat as unnamed (decomposable) entities, which to treat as named entities, and which to treat with rolesets. The emphasis on temporal relations in THYME reveals that concepts that would not formerly have been considered eventive enough to qualify for roleset treatment do in fact function as eventulaties in medical corpora, with complex argument structures that need to be tracked even when implicit. THYME is also responsible for adding PropBank's first affix rolesets for temporally-indicative prefixes like `pre-` and `post-`, which, for temporal relation purposes, need to be annotated separately from their stem events. An example[13] of this is shown in Figure 2.

[13]There is a slight notational difference between AMR us-

With the needs of domain-specific annotation projects pulling further and further from the center of the original framing guidelines, PropBank has been overdue for an update that emphasizes flexibility for domain-of-use. While the inventory continues to exist as a single cohesive whole, we have added structures into the files that allow users to extract rolesets that are associated with domain-specific projects. For general domain rolesets, we have also made it easier to identify ways in which the roleset may be applied differently from one project to another, including usage tags as well as expanded examples that showcase differences in annotation strategies for different projects. Rolesets may now include aliases from any of the following parts of speech as required by a project: verb (`v`), noun (`n`), adjective (`j`), LVC[14] (`l`), MWE (`m`), preposition (`p`), adverb (`r`), and affix (`f`). There may now also be aliases (`argaliases`) associated with numbered arguments (e.g., ARG0 of `teach.01` may have an `argalias` of `teacher`). The next section describes how these changes are manifest in the Frames' `xml` files..

2.4.2 Enriched Contents

This latest PropBank 3.4.0 release[15] uses an enriched `xml` specification which provides some additional features and allows for better validation and disambiguation.

Lexlink Tags We aim to provide mappings between PropBank and other lexical resources within the frame files themselves, when available. The `<lexlinks>` tag provides correspondences between a given roleset and equivalents in VerbNet, FrameNet, or OntoNotes senses. The `<rolelinks>` tag additionally provides mappings between specific roles and these external resources.

For example, `sing.01` includes `<lexlink>` tags linking the roleset to both `manner_speaking-37.3` and `sound_emission-43.2` in VerbNet 3.4. The `<rolelink>` tags on the ARG1 specify that it is the equivalent of *topic* and *theme* for those two VerbNet classes, respectively.

Usage Tags The updated version also now includes `<usage>` tags to specify whether they were included during the development of a particular version of a resource. Many rolesets were constructed only for use with AMRs (`*-91`), and some only for a particular project, such as Spatial AMRs. Table 1 lists the various values and the corpora they correspond with. Within the repository, we provide a utility script that can reduce the XML files down to only the rolesets included in a specified resource/version.

Example Tags The `<example>` tags within the frame files have had a major overhaul. In order to accommodate AMRs, these tags now use `<propbank>` to contain the PropBank annotations for an example sentence and `<amr>` to contain the AMR graph. Additionally, the `<amr>` tag may specify the version of AMR, as AMR projects may annotate the same text in different ways.

Example sentence text now comes with the expectation of being tokenized. The `<arg>` and `<rel>` tags previously only required specification of the text that should be annotated, but this allowed for ambiguous interpretations. If an argument was a word that showed up multiple times in the sentence, there was no way to clarify which instance was the correct argument. The improved format requires the specification of start/end indices for annotated spans. Not only does this prevent ambiguity, it also allows for machine reading/validation of the examples created by human annotators, such as ensuring that arguments do not overlap.

Additionally, `<arg>` tags within the examples now use a single `type` attribute to specify the role, such as ARG0 or ARGM-MNR. This primarily serves to improve readability of the XML compared to the previous `f` and `n` attributes used to specify the same information.

One of the most significant changes to the examples is transforming them to a syntax-agnostic format. Previously, examples in the frame files used a variety of syntactic notation to aid annotators using the constituent-parse-based Jubilee tool with the expectation of a regimen of post-processing. Arguments were frequently noted to be a syntactic trace, such as `*trace*`. We have eliminated these by either resolving them to their true text span or removing the argument entirely if it is only implied but not present in the text. Converting the examples to this more generalized format greatly improves readability and adaptability for new projects or annotation schemes that don't depend on phrase structure parses.

MWE tags Multi-word expressions that receive mappings between literal and figurative meanings

ing a hyphen instead of a period separating the lemma and the roleset.

[14]Light Verb Construction

[15]Henceforth we are going to follow the SemVer (semantic versioning) scheme: `https://semver.org/`

Resource	Version	Description
PropBank	3.4.0	Latest release
PropBank	Flickr 1.0	Flickr captions dataset
PropBank	3.1	Unification release (ON, BOLT, LORELEI) English Web Treebank (EWT)
PropBank	2.1.5	OntoNotes v5.0 (ON)
PropBank	1.0	Proposition Bank I
AMR	2019	General-purpose AMR rolesets
AMR	THYME 1.0	THYME colon cancer corpus
AMR	Spatial 1.0	Minecraft Dialogue Corpus

Table 1: Resource/version combinations present in the <usage> tags.

have changed format as well. In the previous release, an <mwe> tag inside the <aliases> tag housed elements describing the <tokens> involved in the expression, and a <mappings> tag that was sister to <aliases> housed the source to target semantic mappings. The new version renames <mwe> as <mwp-descriptions>, places the <tokens> inside a new element called <syntaxdesc>, and pulls the <mappings> in so that all MWE-related information is contained in one place in the file.

2.4.3 Quality control

The format overhaul required significant examination of the current data. Through a combination of conservative automated processes and extensive manual correction, the new release offers consistency that previously was unavailable and impractical. Subsequent releases will benefit from both these corrections and a format more compatible with future machine validation. We are in the process of updating the way the proposition layer is serialized. The original version was a file with a `prop` extension which contained one predicate argument structure per line, and where the predicate and arguments were identified using pointers to node(s) in the Treebank parse of the sentence containing the predicate. The new serialization will no longer be so tightly coupled with the nodes in the parse tree[16].

The new release updates examples to current PropBank guidelines. Outdated SLC and RCL roles have been updated to use the current R- argument convention. In the sentence "The acre of ground *that* adjoins our property.", the relativizer *that* used to be annotated with ARGM-SLC, which was linked to the span *the acre of ground* (tagged as ARG1 of predicate *adjoins*). This was an artifact of the strong alignment of PropBank role (spans) to nodes in the syntactic parse tree and required an additional processing step. The annotation for the relativizer is now tagged as R-ARG1. Examples that used ARGA were too sparse and infrequent and have been updated and that role has been eliminated.

As part of validating the frame examples, we've corrected numerous cases caused by human error, such as examples missing a <rel> tag, the specified argument text not corresponding with the sentence text, or multiples of the same numbered argument.

Within the repository, we provide a script to perform a validation check on a directory of frame files. This includes not only checking the XML format according to the DTD, but other common sense checks, such as that example arguments' indices correspond correctly with the example text, that arguments don't overlap, and ensuring the same numbered argument isn't present multiple times.

2.4.4 Available Tools

We previously named two scripts to help users work with the frame files: one that provides validation checks and another that can pare the XML files down to only rolesets included in a particular resource. These scripts are available on the git repository.

Additionally, we provide a script that can be used to generate a user-friendly website based on this new format of XML files. The website provides searchability based on roleset ID or alias, allowing annotators to navigate the frames faster and more easily than before. Visible rolesets can be filtered according to the projects specified in the <usage> tags.

[16] Although it is very likely that the span will align with a node in the parse tree of a given sentence.

3 Fresh Corpora—New Domains and Genres

Several diverse corpora have been PropBanked and are now available on our GitHub site.

OntoNotes The first major expansion to the original WSJ PropBank was OntoNotes[17], described above.

BOLT The BOLT corpus (Garland et al., 2012; Song et al., 2014) was treebanked and PropBanked as part of the DARPA BOLT project. It is composed of 628,000 tokens of informal text, divided into SMS and text chat data (SMS), online discussion forums(DF), and translations of informal Arabic and Chinese data in English (CTS).

English Web Text The third corpus, the English Web Treebank (Bies et al., 2012), is 250k tokens of web text covering weblogs, newsgroups, emails, reviews and online question-answer pairs, and was funded by Google.

These three corpora not only provide three different genres, but each contains a wide range of subcorpora. One simple illustration of this within-corpus variety can be witnessed in the fact that the conversational speech in OntoNotes and in BOLT range from 7-10 words per sentence, whereas the OntoNotes weblog and BOLT discussion forums have an average sentence length of 20 words. One can see that each corpus contains very reduced, conversational examples such as the SMS, Emails, or the OntoNotes telephone conversation data. Similarly, each contains long, syntactically complex data—with data such as the BOLT Discussion Forum data differing from traditional newswire, not in complexity, but in editing and syntactic coherence.

3.1 Additional Diversification

Brown The original CoNLL-2005 task evaluated upon a small set of less than a thousand annotations. This corpus was augmented with additional annotation of some 15,000 verb predicates since the original CoNLL-2005 shared task. This larger dataset had preliminary analyses in (Pradhan et al., 2008), but was not released publicly. The updated version of this new corpus will be part of this collection. As one can see from Table 2, this annotation is entirely upon verbs, and therefore only measures verbal out-of-domain ability of models. Moreover, it should be noted that the Brown corpus—well-edited fiction texts released before 1961—depicts a very specific kind of out-of-domain test, and should likely be viewed as reflecting only one kind of out-of-domain performance.

LORELEI The English Reflex Core from DARPA LORELEI (Strassel and Tracey, 2016) consists of newswire text, a phrasebook, and an elicitation corpus. Approximately 100k English tokens (24k predicates) were manually treebanked and annotated with SRL. These sentences were also translated into twenty-four other languages to provide a parallel corpus for multi-lingual research.

Flickr-8k consists of image captions of the Flickr-8k corpus (Hodosh et al., 2013). The first large-scale PropBank project mapped to dependency trees involved the addition of SRL labels to Flickr image captions. 5147 image captions were double annotated and adjudicated. A first pass of annotation was completed on flat, unparsed sentences, followed by mappings to dependency parses.

ClearEarth The ClearEarth (Duerr et al., 2015, 2016) project aimed to port NLP tools to the earth sciences. This project produced annotated SRL corpora in several domains: sea ice blogs/news, sea ice academic journal articles, educational wiki on ecology (77k tokens), and earthquake (40k tokens). Both of these corpora will be released in the near future. Portions of the THYME corpus featured as data for TempEval shared tasks (Bethard et al., 2017). THYME corpus will be available soon on hNLP[18]

4 New Benchmarks

4.1 Evaluation Setup

The current, most common benchmarks for SRL comprise the OntoNotes v5.0 corpus (Pradhan et al., 2013; Weischedel et al., 2011) and a much smaller subset of the Brown corpus (and also the original WSJ subset with verb specific, and legacy annotations based on the first release of PropBank 1.0). These additional subcorpora, updated to match the revised, unified annotation guidelines and with a more generalized view of the concept of a *predicate* (i.e., including nouns and adjectives), can now supplant the common benchmarks for evaluations and provide a better view of the generalization capabilities of the latest SRL models.

[17] https://ontonotes.org

[18] https://healthnlp.hms.harvard.edu/center

Corpora	Genre	Predicate Type			
		Verbs (V)	Nouns (N)	(Light V)	Adj.
OntoNotes (ON)	NW, BN, BC, WB, TC, PT	349,352	40,163	(2,215)	750
English Web TB (EWT)	WB, QS	44,736	9,453	(732)	3,305
BOLT	CTS, SMS, DF	132,642	18,839	(1,973)	10,957
BROWN	FICTION, LETTERS, ETC.	15,646	0	(0)	0
LORELEI	WB	18,871	4,089	(196)	780
Flickr-8k	IMAGE CAPTIONS	5,897	551	(91)	51
ClearEarth	EARTH SCIENCES	10,070	5713	(8)	468
SHARP (hNLP)	CLINICAL NOTES	27,667	15,807	(22)	0
THYME (hNLP)	CLINICAL NOTES	49,649	17,906	(89)	756

Table 2: Core Corpora Annotated with PropBank rolesets for general English. Light verbs are annotated using nominal frames (Hwang et al., 2010) and therefore a subset of the nominal predicates.
Legends: NW: Newswire; BN: Broadcast News; BC: Broadcast Conversation; TC, CTS: Telephone Conversations; SMS: Text Messages; DF: Discussion forums; WB: Miscellaneous webdata; TB: Treebank

4.2 Choice of Tagger

We provide preliminary results on the performance of a state of the art, deep learning based tagger (Li et al., 2020) trained on the OntoNotes training data (Pradhan et al., 2013) which does not rely on an explicit syntactic structure. For the purposes of generating a baseline, neither did we retrain the model nor updated the constraints—rolesets, and other constraints—it uses during its structural tuning process.

4.3 Experiment Partitions

We reused all experimental partitions that were previously identified and used by other researchers. The two main examples of these are the CoNLL-2012 partitions[19] for the OntoNotes corpus and the Universal Dependencies (UD) partitions of the EWT and the Brown partitions that conform to the CoNLL-2005 evaluation and the experiments reported by Pradhan et al. (2008). We created new partitions for the BOLT data with an aim at stratification of the various sources and genres. All these partitions are explicitly available with the data and we plan to further ease their use by creating subdirectories within the git repository similar to the CoNLL-2012 partitions.

4.4 Recreating the Setup

As mentioned earlier, all the annotations will be available for download on the PropBank GitHub organization. All the annotations, except for the clinical notes and the earth sciences data will be made available as skeleton files exactly as in the case of the CoNLL-2012 release. Most of the underlying source text cannot be re-distributed owing to various copyright restrictions and needs to be obtained from LDC. The source text is present as part of the relevant corpora releases from LDC. The final evaluation data files can be created using the scripts provided on the git repository to populate the skeleton files with the words from the corpora releases by specifying the location of the downloaded corpora in the appropriate configuration files. Further details will be available in the documentation with the released corpora.

This mode of corpus distribution, though somewhat complex, has the advantage of making updated annotations available to the research community without having to make a separate release through LDC, which is not an instantaneous process. The underlying source text is not expected to change. It is well known that manually annotated data can never be perfect. There are always some errors that are found when the corpus is used by many researchers. Updating corpora too frequently to fix data errors has a negative effect of somewhat destabilizing the benchmarks and potentially obfuscating the interpretation of results. As a rule of thumb, releasing a new version of a corpus after a reasonable period of time (at least several years) allows the data to be cleaned of the inconsistencies[20]. This approach also allows a better workflow for incorporating corrections into the annotations when identified by the community via established

[19] https://github.com/ontonotes/conll-formatted-ontonotes-5.0

[20] This trend could be changing as better tools and evaluation infrastcutures become widely available.

software engineering best practices such as pull requests.

4.5 Regarding Conversational Data

One aspect of conversational data is the presence of noise in the form of restarts, repairs, disfluencies, non-speech words (laugh, cough, etc.). The Treebank annotations label conversational disfluencies and repairs with a specific EDITED phrase label, "He went (EDITED to) , to the store". The release in CoNLL-2012 removed those phrases from the surface strings for two main reasons: i) so that one could train upon the cleaned "He went to the store" instead; and ii) the coreference annotation ignored such cases anyway. The unified PropBank release follows the same approach for consistency. Though, given the reduced or eliminated reliance on parse structure for tagging semantic roles, it would be interesting to see if these artifacts can be learned and ignored by the deep learning models.

4.6 Experimental Results

The baseline results on the test partitions of four corpora are shown in Table 3 below. We use the CoNLL-2012 test set which is derived from the OntoNotes v5.0 corpus for evaluation and on which the semantic role labeling system has been trained. Note that there are two versions of the OntoNotes data. The second one uses the version of PropBank frame files that is consistent with the AMR frames. Notice that the inclusion of additional predicative parts of speech and more diverse genres increases the difficulty of the task significantly.

	Trained on OntoNotes v5.0 CoNLL-2012)
Test Set	F_1
ON (v5.0/CoNLL-2012)	86.7
ON (PB v3.4.0)	83.2
BOLT	80.1
EWT	80.5
BROWN	77.3

Table 3: Baseline performance on four main corpora annotated with PropBank v3.4.0 rolesets for English. The results include performance across all parts of speech. Follow latest updates and analysis at `https://leaderboard.propbank.org`

5 Summary and Discussion

This paper summarized the last twenty years of development and evolution of an approach to semantic role labeling called PropBanking. We've outlined the methods for converting PropBank to a unified form, and the advantages provided by that unified form and by the larger size of the PropBank corpora now available. The result is a set of consistently annotated corpora representing diverse genres and domains, all relying on a general set of English Frame Files. Where domain specific frame files are used, they are clearly marked. Tools are now available to view the frame files as a whole or as domain-specific subsets on an easily accessible web site. Similarly annotated corpora in several other languages are also available.

These new datasets offer opportunities for additional testing and evaluation that can advance the ability of SRL systems to generalize to new application areas and to new languages. We suggest that testing against the combination of OntoNotes, English Web Treebank, and BOLT corpora presented here can provide a more challenging SRL evaluation, requiring systems to better handle diverse domains and genres and non-verbal predicates.

In the coming year we look forward to toasting both PropBank on its 21st birthday and the winning systems of new SRL evaluation tasks.

References

Alan Akbik, Laura Chiticariu, Marina Danilevsky, Yunyao Li, Shivakumar Vaithyanathan, and Huaiyu Zhu. 2015. Generating high quality Proposition Banks for multilingual semantic role labeling. In *Proceedings of the 53rd Annual Meeting of the ACL and the 7th International Joint Conference on NLP*, pages 397–407, Beijing, China.

Daniel Albright, Arrick Lanfranchi, Anwen Fredriksen, William F Styler IV, Colin Warner, Jena D Hwang, Jinho D Choi, Dmitriy Dligach, Rodney D Nielsen, James Martin, et al. 2013. Towards comprehensive syntactic and semantic annotations of the clinical narrative. *Journal of the American Medical Informatics Association*, 20(5):922–930.

Olga Babko-Malaya, Ann Bies, Ann Taylor, Szu-ting Yi, Martha Palmer, Mitch Marcus, Seth Kulick, and Libin Shen. 2006. Issues in synchronizing the english treebank and propbank. In *Proceedings of the Workshop on Frontiers in Linguistically Annotated Corpora 2006*, pages 70–77.

Collin F. Baker, Charles J. Fillmore, and John B. Lowe. 1998. The Berkeley FrameNet project. In *Proceedings of the 17th International Conference on Compu-*

tational Linguistics (COLING/ACL-98), pages 86–90, Montreal.

Laura Banarescu, Claire Bonial, Shu Cai, Madalina Georgescu, Kira Griffitt, Ulf Hermjakob, Kevin Knight, Philipp Koehn, Martha Palmer, and Nathan Schneider. 2013. Abstract meaning representation for sembanking. In *Proceedings of the 7th Linguistic Annotation Workshop and Interoperability with Discourse*.

Steven Bethard, Guergana Savova, Martha Palmer, and James Pustejovsky. 2017. SemEval-2017 task 12: Clinical TempEval. In *Proceedings of the 11th International Workshop on Semantic Evaluation (SemEval-2017)*, pages 565–572, Vancouver, Canada. Association for Computational Linguistics.

Rajesh Bhatt, Bhuvana Narasimhan, Martha Palmer, Owen Rambow, Dipti Misra Sharma, and Fei Xia. 2009. A multi-representational and multi-layered Treebank for Hindi/Urdu. In *Proceedings of the Third Linguistic Annotation Workshop*, pages 186–189. Association for Computational Linguistics.

Ann Bies, Justin Mott, Colin Warner, and Seth Kulick. 2012. English Web Treebank (LDC2012T13). *Linguistic Data Consortium, Philadelphia, PA*.

Claire Bonial, Julia Bonn, Kathryn Conger, Jena Hwang, and Martha Palmer. 2014. PropBank: Semantics of New Predicate Types. In *LREC*, pages 3013–3019.

Claire Bonial, Julia Bonn, Kathryn Conger, and Jena D. Hwang. 2012. English propbank annotation guidelines.

Claire Bonial, Kathryn Conger, Jena D Hwang, Aous Mansouri, Yahya Aseri, Julia Bonn, Timothy O'Gorman, and Martha Palmer. 2017. Current directions in English and Arabic PropBank. In *Handbook of Linguistic Annotation*, pages 737–769. Springer.

Julia Bonn, Martha Palmer, Zheng Cai, and Kristin Wright-Bettner. 2020. Spatial AMR: Expanded spatial annotation in the context of a grounded Minecraft corpus. In *Proceedings of The 12th Language Resources and Evaluation Conference*, pages 4883–4892, Marseille, France. European Language Resources Association.

Xavier Carreras and Lluís Màrquez. 2005. Introduction to the CoNLL-2005 shared task: Semantic role labeling. In *Proceedings of the Ninth Conference on Computational Natural Language Learning*, pages 152–164. Association for Computational Linguistics.

David Dowty. 1991. Thematic proto-roles and argument selection. *language*, pages 547–619.

R Duerr, A Thessen, CJ Jenkins, M Palmer, S Myers, and S Ramdeen. 2016. The ClearEarth Project: Preliminary findings from experiments in applying the CLEARTK NLP pipeline and annotation tools developed for biomedicine to the earth sciences. In *AGU Fall Meeting Abstracts*.

Ruth Duerr, Skatje Myers, Martha Palmer, Chris J Jenkins, Anne Thessen, and James Martin. 2015. Natural language processing and machine learning (nlp/ml): Applying advances in biomedicine to the earth sciences. In *AGU Fall Meeting Abstracts*, volume 2015, pages IN51A–1784.

Magali Sanches Duran and Sandra Maria Aluísio. 2011. Propbank-br: a brazilian portuguese corpus annotated with semantic role labels. In *Proceedings of the 8th Symposium in Information and Human Language Technology, Cuiabá/MT, Brazil*.

Christiane Fellbaum. 2010. WordNet. In *Theory and applications of ontology: computer applications*, pages 231–243. Springer.

Jennifer Garland, Stephanie Strassel, Safa Ismael, Zhiyi Song, and Haejoong Lee. 2012. Linguistic resources for genre-independent language technologies: user-generated content in BOLT. In *Workshop Programme*, page 34.

John J Godfrey, Edward C Holliman, and Jane McDaniel. 1992. Switchboard: Telephone speech corpus for research and development. In *Acoustics, Speech, and Signal Processing, 1992. ICASSP-92., 1992 IEEE International Conference on*, volume 1, pages 517–520. IEEE.

Jens Van Gysel, Meagan Vigus, Jayeol Chun, Kenneth Lai, Sarah Moeller, Jiarui Yao, Timothy J. O'Gorman, Andrew Cowell, W. Bruce Croft, Chu-Ren Huang, Jan Hajic, James H. Martin, Stephan Oepen, Martha Palmer, James Pustejovsky, Rosa Vallejos, and Nianwen Xue. 2021. Designing a uniform meaning representation for natural language processing. *Künstliche Intell.*, 35:343–360.

Katri Haverinen, Veronika Laippala, Samuel Kohonen, Anna Missilä, Jenna Nyblom, Stina Ojala, Timo Viljanen, Tapio Salakoski, and Filip Ginter. 2013. Towards a dependency-based PropBank of general Finnish. In *Proceedings of the 19th Nordic Conference of Computational Linguistics (NODALIDA 2013); May 22-24; 2013; Oslo University; Norway. NEALT Proceedings Series 16*, 085, pages 41–57. Linköping University Electronic Press.

Micah Hodosh, Peter Young, and Julia Hockenmaier. 2013. Framing image description as a ranking task: Data, models and evaluation metrics. *Journal of Artificial Intelligence Research*, 47:853–899.

Jena D Hwang, Archna Bhatia, Clare Bonial, Aous Mansouri, Ashwini Vaidya, Nianwen Xue, and Martha Palmer. 2010. PropBank annotation of multilingual light verb constructions. In *Proceedings of the Fourth Linguistic Annotation Workshop*, pages 82–90. Association for Computational Linguistics.

Ishan Jindal, Alexandre Rademaker, Michał Ulewicz, Huyen Nguyen, Ha Linh, Khoi-Nguyen Tran, Huaiyu Zhu, and Yunyao Li. 2022. Universal proposition bank 2.0. Marseille, France.

Paul Kingsbury and Martha Palmer. 2002. From Treebank to PropBank. In *LREC*, pages 1989–1993.

Tao Li, Parth Anand Jawale, Martha Palmer, and Vivek Srikumar. 2020. Structured tuning for semantic role labeling. In *Proceedings of the 58th Annual Meeting of the Association for Computational Linguistics*, pages 8402–8412, Online.

Adam Meyers, Ruth Reeves, Catherine Macleod, Rachel Szekely, Veronika Zielinska, Brian Young, and Ralph Grishman. 2004. The NomBank project: An interim report. In *HLT-NAACL 2004 workshop: Frontiers in corpus annotation*, volume 24, page 31.

Azadeh Mirzaei and Amirsaeid Moloodi. 2016. Persian Proposition Bank. In *Proceedings of the Tenth International Conference on Language Resources and Evaluation (LREC'16)*, pages 3828–3835, Portorož, Slovenia.

Sarah Moeller, Irina Wagner, Martha Palmer, Kathryn Conger, and Skatje Myers. 2020. The Russian PropBank. In *Proceedings of the 12th Language Resources and Evaluation Conference*, pages 5995–6002.

Anjali Narayan-Chen, Prashant Jayannavar, and Julia Hockenmaier. 2019. Collaborative dialogue in Minecraft. In *Proceedings of the 57th Annual Meeting of the Association for Computational Linguistics*, pages 5405–5415, Florence, Italy.

Tim O'Gorman, Sameer Pradhan, Martha Palmer, Julia Bonn, Kathryn Conger, and James Gung. 2018. The New Propbank: Aligning Propbank with AMR through POS Unification. In *Proceedings of the Eleventh International Conference on Language Resources and Evaluation (LREC 2018)*, Miyazaki, Japan.

Martha Palmer, Daniel Gildea, and Paul Kingsbury. 2005a. The Proposition Bank: An annotated corpus of semantic roles. *Computational linguistics*, 31(1):71–106.

Martha Palmer, Shijong Ryu, Jinyoung Choi, Sinwon Yoon, and Yeongmi Jeon. 2006. Korean PropBank. *LDC Catalog No.: LDC2006T03 ISBN*, pages 1-58563.

Martha Palmer, Nianwen Xue, Olga Babko-Malaya, Jinying Chen, and Benjamin Snyder. 2005b. A parallel Proposition Bank II for Chinese and English. In *Proceedings of the Workshop on Frontiers in Corpus Annotations II: Pie in the Sky*, pages 61–67. Association for Computational Linguistics.

Sameer Pradhan, Kadri Hacioglu, Valerie Krugler, Wayne Ward, James Martin, and Dan Jurafsky. 2005. Support vector learning for semantic argument classification. *Machine Learning Journal*, 60(1):11–39.

Sameer Pradhan, Alessandro Moschitti, Nianwen Xue, Hwee Tou Ng, Anders Björkelund, Olga Uryupina, Yuchen Zhang, and Zhi Zhong. 2013. Towards robust linguistic analysis using OntoNotes. In *Proceedings of the Seventeenth Conference on Computational Natural Language Learning*, pages 143–152, Sofia, Bulgaria.

Sameer S Pradhan, Wayne Ward, and James H Martin. 2008. Towards robust semantic role labeling. *Computational linguistics*, 34(2):289–310.

GG Sahin. 2016. Verb sense annotation for Turkish PropBank via crowdsourcing. In *Proceedings of 17th international conference on intelligent text processing and computational linguistics. CICLING.*

Karin Kipper Schuler. 2005. *VerbNet: A broad-coverage, comprehensive verb lexicon*. University of Pennsylvania.

Zhiyi Song, Stephanie Strassel, Haejoong Lee, Kevin Walker, Jonathan Wright, Jennifer Garland, Dana Fore, Brian Gainor, Preston Cabe, Thomas Thomas, et al. 2014. Collecting natural SMS and chat conversations in multiple languages: The BOLT phase 2 corpus. In *LREC*, pages 1699–1704.

Stephanie Strassel and Jennifer Tracey. 2016. Lorelei language packs: Data, tools, and resources for technology development in low resource languages. In *LREC*.

William F Styler, Steven Bethard, Sean Finan, Martha Palmer, Sameer Pradhan, Piet C De Groen, Brad Erickson, Timothy Miller, Chen Lin, Guergana Savova, et al. 2014. Temporal annotation in the clinical domain. *Transactions of the association for computational linguistics*, 2:143–154.

Mihai Surdeanu, Richard Johansson, Adam Meyers, Lluís Màrquez, and Joakim Nivre. 2008. The CoNLL-2008 shared task on joint parsing of syntactic and semantic dependencies. In *Proceedings of the Twelfth Conference on Computational Natural Language Learning*, pages 159–177.

Ann Taylor. 1996. Bracketing Switchboard: an addendum to the Treebank II bracketing guidelines. *Linguistic Data Consortium.*

Ralph Weischedel, Eduard Hovy, Mitchell Marcus, Martha Palmer, Robert Belvin, Sameer Pradhan, Lance Ramshaw, and Nianwen Xue. 2011. OntoNotes: A large training corpus for enhanced processing. In Joseph Olive, Caitlin Christianson, and John McCary, editors, *Handbook of Natural Language Processing and Machine Translation: DARPA Global Autonomous Language Exploitation*. Springer.

Kristin Wright-Bettner, Martha Palmer, Guergana Savova, Piet de Groen, and Timothy Miller. 2019. Cross-document coreference: An approach to capturing coreference without context. In *Proceedings of the Tenth International Workshop on Health Text Mining and Information Analysis (LOUHI 2019)*, pages 1–10, Hong Kong. Association for Computational Linguistics.

Speech acts and Communicative Intentions for Urgency Detection

Enzo Laurenti[1] **Nils Bourgon**[2] **Farah Benamara**[2]
[1]IJN, CNRS/ENS/EHESS, PSL University
firstname.lastname@ens.fr

Alda Mari[1] **Véronique Moriceau**[2] **Camille Courgeon**[1]
[2] IRIT, Université de Toulouse, CNRS, Toulouse INP, UT3
firstname.lastname@irit.fr

Abstract

Recognizing speech acts (SA) is crucial for capturing meaning beyond what is said, making communicative intentions particularly relevant to identify urgent messages. This paper attempts to measure for the first time the impact of SA on urgency detection during crises, in tweets. We propose a new dataset annotated for both urgency and SA, and develop several deep learning architectures to inject SA into urgency detection while ensuring models generalisability. Our results show that taking speech acts into account in tweet analysis improves information type detection in an out-of-type configuration where models are evaluated in unseen event types during training. These results are encouraging and constitute a first step towards SA-aware disaster management in social media.

1 Introduction

Discovered by (Austin, 1962) and extensively promoted by (Searle, 1975), speech acts (henceforth SA) have been the object of extensive discussion in the philosophical and the linguistic literature (Sadock, 2004; Portner, 2018). According to the Austinian initial view, SA are to achieve action rather than conveying information. When uttering *I now pronounce you man and wife*, the priest accomplishes the action of marrying rather than just stating a proposition. Beyond these prototypical cases, the literature has quickly broaden the understanding of the notion of SA as a special type of linguistic object that encompasses questions, orders and assertions and transcends propositional content revealing communicative intentions on the part of the speaker (Bach and Harnish, 1979; Portner, 2018; Giannakidou and Mari, 2021).

Because recognizing speakers' intentions is crucial for capturing meaning beyond what is said (Noveck, 2018), SA have given rise to an extensive body of work in the computational linguistics literature where various approaches have been proposed to detect them in both synchronous (e.g., meeting, phone) (Stolcke et al., 2000; Keizer et al., 2002) as well as asynchronous dialogues (e.g., emails, tweet threads) (Carvalho and Cohen, 2005; Joty and Mohiuddin, 2018; Bracewell et al., 2012). SA have shown to be an important step in many down stream NLP applications such as strategic action prediction (Cadilhac et al., 2013), dialogue summarization (Goo and Chen, 2018) and conversational systems (Higashinaka et al., 2014). In this paper, we attempt to measure for the first time the role of SA on urgency detection in tweets, focusing on natural disasters (hurricanes, storms, floods, etc.).

SA are particularly relevant to identify urgent messages, i.e. those that raise situational awareness over a crisis (including human/material damages, security instructions, etc.), providing therefore actionable information that will help to set priorities for the human teams and decide appropriate rescue actions. By tweeting, speakers seek to achieve impact via enhancing a chain of reactions. They do not necessarily seek to merely express themselves. The greater the number of re-tweets and replies the greater the impact. Therefore, tweets are not only public, but they are also interactive. They mostly aim to make interlocutors react (perlocutionary level) by different linguistic means (illocutionary level), in view of achieving a purpose (on perlocutionary / illocutionary, see (Austin, 1962; Searle, 1975)). We illustrate this in the following examples[1] where speaking subjects perform qualitatively very different language acts depending on the situation they find themselves in. In the tweet (1a), the writer publicly expresses an explicit commitment to provide help after the Irma hurricane tragedy, using an explicit action verb ("*to help*") which is under the scope of an explicit attitude verb ("*want*"), thus aiming to obtain a reply on what to do to provide help. (1b) on the other hand ex-

[1]These are examples taken from our French corpus translated into English.

Proceedings of the 11th Joint Conference on Lexical and Computational Semantics, pages 289 - 298

presses an intention to complain about the absence of assistance without using any explicit intent keywords and thus raise awareness and attention on the part of the people in charge of assistance.

(1) #Irma Hurricane: "I want to go there to help."

(2) Irma hurricane: where is disaster assistance one month later?

When annotating tweets posted during a crisis (like earthquakes, bombing, attacks) according to different taxonomies of SA, state of the art corpus-based studies observe a majority of *statements*, essentially supplemented by *suggestions* and *comments* – in contrast, the topics dealing with e.g. celebrities are essentially made up of *comments* (Zhang et al., 2011; Vosoughi, 2015; Elmadany et al., 2018a; Saha et al., 2020). These results have however been obtained after manual annotations, the focus being rather on SA classification of topic oriented tweets. The next step now is to show to what extent these observations are still valid from a computational point of view. Our contribution is threefold and consists in:

1. **A new dataset of 6,669 tweets in French annotated for both urgency and SA** for disaster events of various types that occurred in France;[2]

2. **A set of deep learning experiments to inject SA information into urgency detection** using monotask and multitask architectures. We investigate the role of communicative intentions in three classification settings: relatedness (i.e., useful vs. non useful for emergency responders), urgency detection (i.e., non useful vs. urgent vs. non urgent), and information type following a predefined taxonomy of six actionable categories;

3. **An evaluation of the proposed classifiers** while measuring their ability to generalize over new events. Our results show that SA are helpful for filtering out urgent from non urgent messages. This is particularly salient for information type detection in an out-of-type configuration where models are evaluated in unseen event types during training. These results are encouraging and constitute a first step towards SA-aware disaster management in social media.

   beating several SA agnostic state of the art baselines.

This paper is organized as follows. We first provide related work on NLP-based approaches to crisis management as well as SA in social media. We then describe our data, the annotation procedure and the results of the annotation campaign. We detail the experiments we carried out on injecting SA in urgency detection in Section 4 and discuss our results in Section 5. We end the paper by some perspectives for future work.

2 Related Work

2.1 Crisis Datasets

The literature on emergencies detection has been growing fast in the recent years and several datasets (mainly tweets) have been proposed to account for crisis related phenomena.[3] Messages are annotated according to relevant categories that are deemed to fit the information needs of various stakeholders like humanitarian organizations, local police and firefighters. Well-known dimensions include relatedness (also known as usefulness or informativeness) to identify whether the message content is useful (Jensen, 2012), situation awareness (also known as urgency, criticality or priority) to filter out on-topic relevant (e.g., immediate post-impact help) vs. on-topic irrelevant information (e.g. supports and solicitations for donations) (Imran et al., 2013; McCreadie et al., 2019; Sarioglu Kayi et al., 2020; Kozlowski et al., 2020), and eyewitness types to identify direct and indirect eyewitnesses (Zahra et al., 2020). For most of the existing datasets, annotations usually apply at the text level. Some studies propose to additionally annotate images within the tweets (see for example (Alam et al., 2018)).

The question of how speakers convey emergency at the sentence level has nonetheless been only tangentially addressed in a literature that has considered the correlation between specific speech acts and specific topics, without overtly addressing what the speech act shape of urgent messages is (see below).

[2]The dataset will be made available to the research community.

[3]See `https://crisisnlp.qcri.org/` for an overview.

2.2 Speech Acts in Social Media

Some amount of attention has been indeed devoted to understanding how speech acts (as used on Twitter) vary qualitatively according to the *topic* discussed. In this line of questioning, SA have been studied as filters for new topics.

Zhang et al. (2011) in particular, resort to a Searlian typology of SA that distinguishes between assertive statements (description of the world), expressive comments (expression of a mental state of the speaker), interrogative questions and imperative suggestions. Concerning the question of emergency, Zhang et al. (2011) showed that the SA's distribution on Twitter in the context of a natural disaster (e.g. earthquake in Japan) is distinctive: it is essentially composed by statements, associated to comments and suggestions / orders. In this context new information or ideas on how to (re)act are indeed expected and assertions are the most suitable to this aim. By contrast, discussion over a celebrity will mostly generate comments and almost no order or suggestion. Indeed, in this context, subjectivity matters more than immediate action. The same conclusions have been drawn by Vosoughi (2015); Vosoughi and Roy (2016) when distinguishing the *topic* discussed in the tweets, from the *type* of topic (*Entity-oriented*–celebrities, *Event-oriented topics*–bombing events, or *Long-standing topics*–cooking). Their corpus study shows that there is a greater similarity of distribution of SA between *entity-oriented* and *event-oriented*, with a majority of assertions and expressions.

In this same perspective of topic identification, Elmadany et al. (2018b) classify 21,000 tweets in Arabic according to their topic type and distinguish events (for example, in our case, natural disasters), entities (especially people) and various issues such as travel or cooking. Each tweet is associated to a pair of speech act/sentiment according to the following classification: Assertions, Recommendations, Expressions and Requests, and among Sentiments, the standard Positive, Negative, Mixed and Neutral categories. Their study makes emerge a salient association between assertions and people/events and neutrality on the one hand and an association between expressivity long-standing topics and negativity on the other.

Our classification of speech acts relies on the fourfold distinction between asserting, ordering, asking and expressing a subjective view (cf. *infra*, section 3.2 for the definitions and specifications of these categories). The novelty of our work lies in exploring communicative intentions in the context of urgency detection, an enterprise which, to our best knowledge, has never been undertaken. This paper fills this gap by crossing the urgency classification and the SA classification in order to elucidate the interactions between speaker's attitudes and urgency categories (and their associated actions).

3 Dataset

Since our focus is on crises that occur in metropolitan France and its overseas departments, we rely on the only available corpus of French tweets by (Kozlowski et al., 2020)[4] composed of about 12k tweets collected using dedicated keywords about ecological crises that occurred in France from 2016 to 2019 and posted 24h before, during (48h) and 72h after the crisis: 2 floods that occurred in Aude and Corsica regions, 10 storms–Béryl, Berguitta, Fionn, Eleanor, Bruno, Egon, Ulrika, Susanna, Fakir and Ana, and 2 hurricanes–Irma and Harvey, and 1 sudden crisis (Marseille building collapse). It is important to note that in this dataset, some crises occurred in the same time period which implies that some messages that were scraped for some crises actually belonged to other (they were annotated as NOT USEFUL in this case, as they are not related to the targeted crisis, see below).

3.1 Urgency Annotation Layer

In this dataset, each tweet is annotated according to its relatedness, urgency and six information type categories, namely HUMAN DAMAGES and MATERIAL DAMAGES which concern missing, injured, displaced and dead people or any damaged infrastructure that was caused by a crisis, WARNING-ADVICE that gives security instructions, tips to limit the damage or weather reports, SUPPORT messages to the victims, CRITICS messages that denounce the lack of effectiveness of rescue services, and OTHER messages that do not have an immediate impact on actionability but contribute to raising situational awareness. The first three types are subcategories of urgent messages while the last three are subcategories of non urgent messages. The dataset comes with additional metadata including: number of likes and retweets of the tweet, and number of likes, followers, following of the user.

[4] https://github.com/DiegoKoz/french_ecological_crisis

The collection is extremely imbalanced with 11.24% useful but NOT URGENT, 16.74% URGENT and 72.02% NOT USEFUL messages, which is in line with the proportions reported in other crisis corpora. A subset of this dataset composed of $6,669$ tweets have been selected for SA annotations, so that almost all URGENT (2,080) and NON URGENT (1,401) messages have been annotated. Only 3,188 NOT USEFUL tweets have been selected in order to reduce the size of this class but keep it majoritary. Note that pre-existing urgency tags and metadata information have been removed to prevent annotators from getting biased by specific urgency-SA pairs.

3.2 Speech Act Annotation Layer

Our classification of SA elaborates on the fundational Austinian and later Searlian distinction by (i) relying on propositional content and lexical clues such as modals (*should*, *must*, *can*, ...), evaluative adjectives, attitude verbs (*think*, *believe*, *want*, *hope* ...); (ii) introducing the category 'subjectives', which reshuffles some of the earlier classifications ('wishes', for instance are 'subjectives' rather than 'jussives' in our classification (e.g. (Condoravdi and Lauer, 2012)); (iii) considering presuppositional content as well (see (Mari, 2016) on French).

We distinguish four categories which are mutually exclusive and define tweets as wholes, at a holistic level, as follows:

(1) JUSSIVES, as defined by (Zanuttini et al., 2012), enhance commitment to take action, as in (3). In our classification we distinguish: *commissives* (i.e. the speaker commits himself or herself), *exhortatives* (i.e. the speaker commits some relevant individuals), *orders* (i.e. the speaker commits the addressee, in the case of authority relations), and *open-options* (i.e. the speaker describes the existence of a possibility).

(3) #Inondation Si vous êtes en zone inondable, découvrez comment préparer un kit de survie
(#Flooding If you are in an area at risk of flooding, discover how to prepare a survival kit).

(2) ASSERTIVES. Assertions are considered to convey objective truth (as opposed to subjective truth (Giannakidou and Mari, 2021)). With assertives, the speaker is committed toward the truthfulness of the proposition that is being uttered ((Portner, 2018) a.o.) and require their interlocutor to update the common ground (Ginzburg, 2012).

(4) Inondations dans l'Aude : la région débloque 25M€, le président Macron sur place lundi
(Flooding in Aude: the region unlocks 25M€, the president Macron on the spot on Monday).

(3) INTERROGATIVES. This category is dedicated to a variety of questions including both those that require an informative answer and those that, besides triggering an answer, reveal bias and expectations on the part of the speaker (see (Ladd, 1981)).

(5) Salut Chelsea, comment ça va, la tempête, par chez vous?
(Hi Chelsea, how is the storm at your place?).

(4) SUBJECTIVES. Finally, with subjectives, the speaker shares a mental state that can be either a personal evaluation or preference (see among many others (Lasersohn, 2005)) or an expressive state (an emotion or a feeling). The interlocutor is asked to update the common ground not just with the content of the evaluation but with the evaluation itself (see (Simons, 2007), and for recent discussion on French (Mari and Portner, 2021)). In our classification, 'wishes', for instance are 'subjectives' rather than 'jussives' as they do not trigger any committment to act so to make the content of the wish true.

(6) Grosse pensée à ma Laure qui est en Martinique avec l'ouragan
(My thoughts are with my Laure, who is in Martinique with the hurricane.)

Finally, **OTHERS** is added to the classification, for uncertain or unclassifiable cases, as in (7).

(7) Simulation #3D d'une #inondation à Issy-les-Moulineaux merci à @Ubick3D pour le prêt #ortho3D #InterAtlas
(3D simulation of a flood in Issy-les-Moulineaux thanks to @Ubick3D for the loan #ortho3D #InterAtlas).

The final dataset is therefore composed of 6,669 tweets. Here is a representative example of a tweet in our dataset, along with its corresponding annotation: Relatedness=USEFUL, Urgency=URGENT, Information type=HUMAN DAMAGE, SA=ASSERTIVE:

(8) #irma st martin: nouveau bilan provisoire avec 8 morts et 21 blessés à St. Martin (#irma st martin: new provisional death toll of 8 dead and 21 injured in St. Martin)

3.3 Results of the Annotation Campaign

We hired two native French speaking annotators, both master's degree students in Linguistics in order to annotate tweets. We performed a two-step annotation where an intermediate analysis of agreement and disagreement between the annotators was carried out. 448 tweets have been annotated in the first step by both annotators so that the inter-annotator agreement could be computed (Cohen's Kappa=0.62). Most cases of disagreement come from the difficulty of disentangling SUBJECTIVES from ASSERTIVES, in particular when attitudes and modal expressions are used such as *believe*, *think that*, etc. Indeed, both the subjective expressions (*think*, *believe*, or even more complex modal-tense-aspect combinations such as *fallait*, which translates as 'should have been' with an additional implicature of preference in (9)) or their content can be targeted, according to their contextual relevance. This delicate distinction is often resolved in different manners by annotators.

(9) Et maintenant il n'y a presque plus de fumée... Il fallait arrêter le trafic ce matin et pas au milieu de la journée.
(And now there is almost no more smoke... Traffic should have been stopped this morning and not in the middle of the day).

Table 1 details the frequency of SA tags when paired with the original urgency annotations. The final distribution of annotated tweets is 59.8%, 22.3%, 10%, 4.5% and 3.3% for ASSERTIVE, SUBJECTIVE, JUSSIVE, OTHER and INTERROGATIVE respectively. Concerning the two most frequent SA (ASSERTIVE and SUBJECTIVE), two observations emerge: (1) Among URGENT messages (resp. NON URGENT), 86.6% (resp. 48.7%) are ASSERTIVE; and (2) Only 5% of URGENT messages are SUBJECTIVE while 29% of NON URGENT messages are. Similarly, we observe that 7% of JUSSIVE are URGENT vs. 14% NON URGENT. All these frequencies are statistically significant using the $\chi 2$ test ($\chi 2 = 1, 1011.62,\ df = 8, p < 0.01$). When measuring the dependency strength between urgency and SA categories using the Cramer's V, we get ($V = .28,\ df = 2$) which confirms the statistical correlation between these two classifications.

	URG	NON URG	NON USEF	TOTAL
ASSERT.	1,802	682	1,506	**3,990**
JUSS.	145	203	321	**669**
SUBJ.	106	406	976	**1,488**
INTERR.	20	58	145	**223**
OTHER	7	52	240	**299**
Total	**2,080**	**1,401**	**3,188**	**6,669**

Table 1: Urgency- SA annotation pairs statistics.

Table 2 further details the SA distribution for each crisis. We can see that ASSERTIVE messages are the most frequent ones regardless of the crisis. Another interesting finding concerns the distribution of SA in sudden crisis. Indeed, SA frequencies are relatively similar in natural disaster crisis (flood, storms and hurricane) with about 60% of ASSERTIVE and 20% of SUBJECTIVE. However in the Marseille building collapse, we observe a higher proportion of SUBJECTIVE (35% vs. 49% for ASSERTIVE) showing that people tend to express fewer messages of warning-advice but many critics denouncing the lack of effectiveness of government social action.

4 Speech Acts for Urgency Detection

We propose several models to automatically classify a tweet according to its relatedness (binary classification–REL), urgency (three classes–URG) and information type categories (multiclass–INF) while injecting SA information into the learning process. Our models have been compared to SA-agnostic baselines while analyzing the impact of SA on generalization to new disaster events which is important for this application, since disasters can vary widely with respect to both their specific properties as well as their types. Although SA detection is an important preliminary step, this is however out of the scope of this paper. Note that a baseline CamemBERT model (Martin et al., 2019) fine-tuned to predict the five SA tags achieves a macro F-score of 0.686 with a precision of 0.690 and recall of 0.701. Improvement of these results is left for future work.

		ASSERTIVE	SUBJECTIVE	JUSSIVE	INTERROGATIVE
Flood	Aude	718 (71.37%)	184 (18.29%)	84 (8.35%)	20 (1.99%)
	Corse	248 (63.75%)	73 (18.77%)	45 (11.57%)	23 (5.91%)
	Other Flood	631 (64.65%)	180 (18.44%)	137 (14.04%)	28 (2.87%)
	Total	1,597 (67.36%)	437 (18.43%)	266 (11.22%)	71 (2.99%)
Storms	Beryl	174 (59.18%)	87 (19.59%)	22 (7.48%)	11 (3.74%)
	Bruno	201 (61.47%)	94 (28.75%)	17 (5.20%)	15 (4.59%)
	Susanna	230 (61.66%)	92 (24.66%)	45 (12.06%)	6 (1.61%)
	Ulrika	170 (60.71%)	60 (21.43%)	43 (15.36%)	7 (2.5%)
	Berguitta	189 (60.77%)	73 (23.47%)	35 (11.25%)	14 (4.5%)
	Fionn Corse	238 (69.79%)	69 (20.23%)	28 (8.21%)	6 (1.76%)
	Egon	185 (58.92%)	95 (30.25%)	24 (7.64%)	10 (3.18%)
	Eleanor	208 (67.10%)	69 (22.26%)	26 (8.39%)	7 (2.26%)
	Total	1,595 (62.55%)	639 (25.06%)	240 (9.41%)	76 (2.98%)
Hurricane	Harvey	168 (58.74%)	59 (20.63%)	36 (12.59%)	23 (8.04%)
	Irma	487 (55.72%)	251 (28.78%)	100 (11.44%)	36 (4.12%)
	Total	655 (56.47%)	310 (26.72%)	136 (11.72%)	59 (5.09%)
Collapse	Marseille	143 (49.48%)	102 (35.39%)	27 (9.34%)	17 (5.88%)

Table 2: SA distribution for each crisis.

4.1 SA-agnostic Models

SA-aware models have been compared to Kozlowski et al. (2020), the only existing work in French that has shown to outperform state of the art on urgency detection. Kozlowski et al. (2020) models rely on a language adaptation version of FlauBERT base cased model (Le et al., 2020), initially trained on a general domain, and fine-tuned for the crisis domain using a set of French unlabeled dataset of 358,834 tweets. Our baselines are:

– **FlauBERT$_{\textbf{tuned}}$**. This is the original tuned version of FlauBert trained on our dataset with a cross-entropy loss. We newly add **FlauBERT$_{\textbf{tuned}}$**^{wl}, a variant that uses the weighted loss instead to handle class imbalance.[5] The results obtained with this variant model being more productive, the weighted loss has been used in all the following models.

–**ML**^{3}. FlauBERT$_{\text{tuned}}$^{wl} is trained in a multitask fashion by learning simultaneously the three urgency tasks, namely relatedness, urgency classification, and information type. The classifiers share and update the same low layers of FlauBERT$_{\text{tuned}}$^{wl} except the final task-specific classification layer.

These baselines have been boosted by adding tweet meta data, as given by the dataset, as they have been shown to be quite informative in urgency detection (Truong et al., 2014; Kozlowski et al., 2020; Neppalli et al., 2018). This leads to two extra-models: **FlauBERT$_{\textbf{tuned}}$**^{wl}**+Meta** and **ML**^{3}**+Meta**.

[5]We also experimented with focal loss (Lin et al., 2017) but the results were lower.

4.2 SA-aware Models

SA are incorporated into FlauBERT models in two ways. First, rely on SA gold annotations as additional extra-features. We experimented with several ways to inject SA among which representing SA as numerical values (0 for ASSERTIVE, 1 for SUBJECTIVE, etc.), inserting SA tags at the end of the tweet using a specific marker (e.g., $< Assertif >$ for ASSERTIVE tweets), representing SA as one hot vector, and finally consider each SA tag as a unique binary feature to model its presence or absence. The last option was the most productive and is used in four models: **FlauBERT$_{\textbf{tuned}}$**^{wl}**+SA**, **FlauBERT$_{\textbf{tuned}}$**^{wl}**+SA+Meta**, **ML**^{3}**+SA**, and **ML**^{3}**+SA+Meta**.

The previous configuration is an ideal case where urgency detection benefits from gold SA which may not be available for unseen/new disaster events. We therefore designed a more realistic scenario where SA detection is considered as an auxiliary task. This is a multitask learning approach that jointly learns urgency detection with SA classification as a secondary task. Two models are newly proposed:

–**ML**^{2}: It corresponds to FlauBERT$_{\text{tuned}}$^{wl} trained to perform SA together with one urgency task (i.e., two tasks among REL+SA, URG+SA or INF+SA). This configuration aims to investigate what are the tasks that may benefit the most from injecting SA information among relatedness, urgency and information type.

–**ML**^{4}: FlauBERT$_{\text{tuned}}$^{wl} learns SA together with the three urgency tasks. This is a four task configuration that corresponds to SA+REL+URG+INF.

These two models are further augmented with tweet meta features, resulting in two other models: **ML^2+Meta** and **ML^4+Meta**.

4.3 Experimental Settings

Following the general trends in evaluating urgency detection during disaster events, we designed two evaluation protocols:

- **[OE]** *out-of-event* by testing on unseen events for which no manually annotated data is available during training. To ensure a fair comparison with (Kozlowski et al., 2020), we used the same test sets composed of crises Eleanor and Bruno. This choice is also motivated by the fact that these two crises did not show the mentioned overlap with other crises and hence there was no information leak from one event to another (cf. Section 3);
- **[OT]** *out-of-type* by training on a pool of events related to different types of crises and testing on a particular different type. We used the building collapse as a test set. While the hurricanes and floods are known with anticipation, a building collapse is a sudden event with pretty different distributions in terms of urgency categories, making the [OT] configuration more challenging.

During the experiments, all the five SA tags have been taken into account for urgency detection. [6]

5 Results

5.1 Out-of-event and Out-of-type Detection

The results of [OE] and [OT] configurations in terms of macro-F1 scores are given in Table 3. It shows that SA-enhanced models beat SA agnostic ones for urgency and information type detection in both the [OE] and [OT] evaluation settings. In [OE], ML^3+SA+Meta improves over the FlauBERT$_{\text{tuned}}{}^{wl}$ and FlauBERT$_{\text{tuned}}{}^{wl}$+Meta baselines and this is more salient for information type classification. The same observations hold for [OT] where SA boost the scores when injected both as extra-features and as an auxiliary task. Another interesting finding is that joint learning of SA and urgency tags (i.e., ML^2) achieves results comparable to those obtained in the ideal case, i.e. when incorporating gold SA annotations as extra-features. Also, when coupling SA with tweet meta features, the results improve in most experiments, confirming the importance of extra-linguistic information for urgency detection. On the other hand, when compared to the best baseline, SA injection into relatedness detection achieves similar scores in [OE] while they decrease in [OT]. This was however expected as the relatedness baseline classifiers perform relatively well (F-score=0.849 and F-score=0.856 for [OE] and [OT] respectively). This can be explained by the same proportions of SA we observed in each of the USEFUL and NOT USEFUL class where ASSERTIVE messages are a majority followed by SUBJECTIVE ones (see Table 2).

When looking into the scores per class for urgency detection in [OE] (see Table 4), we observe that SA are the most helpful for predicting URGENT messages with an important boost up to (+3%) for NON URGENT tweets. A boost is observed in [OT] where SA injection improves by +1.2% over the SA-agnostic best model. Regarding the ability of the models to filter-out irrelevant messages, we observe that the results with SA are stable in [OE] (with an F-score=0.887) while they increased in [OT]. It is interesting to note that the results obtained in real scenario via multitask learning models (i.e., ML^2 and ML^4) achieve good results compared to the models that rely on SA gold annotations. More importantly, multitask models outperform SA-agnostic baselines which show the importance of SA for fine-grained urgency detection in social media.

Concerning information type classification, Table 5[7] shows that the SA-aware model in the [OE] setting is able to predict MATERIAL DAMAGES, NOT USEFUL as well as OTHER non urgent messages (related to animals, messages that aim to provide additional information via external links via URLs, photos or videos, and prevention messages that provide general-purpose safety instructions upstream of crisis). When testing on a particular different event (i.e., a sudden event like the building collapse in Marseille), the [OT] configuration shows an improvement on MATERIAL DAMAGES and WARNING ADVICE. Finally, it is also interesting to note that major improvements concern the

[6] We tried several groupings of SA tags among which ASSERTIVE vs. not ASSERTIVE, (ASSERTIVE+SUBJECTIVE) vs. (INTERROGATIVE+JUSSIVE+OTHER) to measure what are the SA combinations that contribute the most to the task at hand. Our results show that all SA are relevant.

[7] The two events used for testing do not have any CRITICS messages.

		OUT-OF-EVENT			OUT-OF-TYPE		
		REL	URG	INF	REL	URG	INF
SA-agnostic‡	FlauBERT$_{\text{tuned}}$	0.846	0.681	0.537	0.838	0.709	0.459
	FlauBERT$_{\text{tuned}}^{wl}$	0.847	0.688	0.646	0.842	0.714	0.476
	FlauBERT$_{\text{tuned}}^{wl}$+Meta	0.837	0.698	0.545	**0.856**	0.707	0.512
	ML^3	0.842	0.654	0.604	0.838	0.704	0.487
	ML^3+Meta	**0.849**	0.679	0.635	0.844	0.689	0.441
SA-aware as extra-features	FlauBERT$_{\text{tuned}}^{wl}$+SA	**0.849**	0.680	0.550	0.844	**0.725**	**0.515**
	ML^3+SA	**0.849**	0.693	0.612	0.839	**0.720**	**0.521**
	ML^3+SA+Meta	0.844	**0.708**	**0.660**	0.848	0.704	0.503
SA-aware as an auxiliary task	ML^2	0.841	**0.703**	**0.651**	0.845	0.708	**0.533**
	ML^2+Meta	0.841	0.693	**0.654**	0.834	0.688	**0.531**
	ML^4	0.847	0.697	**0.660**	0.835	0.684	**0.521**
	ML^4+Meta	0.842	0.689	0.640	0.816	0.703	0.433

Table 3: Urgency detection results in terms of Macro F1-score. ‡: SA agnostic strong baselines. Bold font: Outperforming models over the baselines.

	NOT USF.	URG	NOT URG.
OUT-OF-EVENT SA-agnostic			
FlauBERT$_{\text{tuned}}^{wl}$+Meta	**0.877**	0.847	0.370
ML^3+Meta	**0.877**	**0.851**	0.308
OUT-OF-EVENT SA-aware			
ML^2	**0.877**	0.839	**0.392**
ML^3+SA+Meta	0.873	**0.851**	**0.400**
ML^4	0.876	**0.856**	0.357
OUT-OF-TYPE SA-agnostic			
FlauBERT$_{\text{tuned}}^{wl}$	0.891	**0.722**	0.531
OUT-OF-TYPE SA-aware			
FlauBert$_{\text{tuned}}^{wl}$+SA	**0.918**	0.714	**0.543**
ML^2	**0.900**	0.713	0.513

Table 4: Impact of SA injection for urgency classification per class in terms of macro F1-scores.

classes with the less number of instances in the test set.

To test whether these improvements are type-of-event dependent, we split the dataset into 4 main groups of events: floods (F), storms (S), hurricanes (H) and collapse (C). We then evaluate our [OT] models by calculating the mean of the F1-scores for the following experiments : (1) train on (F, S, H) and test on (C); and (2) train on (F, S, C) and test on (H).[8] We obtain average F1-scores of 0.587 and 0.601 for information type multiclass classification for FlauBERT^{wl}+SA and ML^2 models respectively which represents an improvement up to 2.3% and 3.7% over FlauBERT^{wl}+Meta, our best performing baseline.

5.2 Error Analysis

A manual error analysis for ML^2, the best model in a real scenario, shows that misclassifications for urgency are not due to SA error prediction: indeed, 82% of urgent misclassified instances have a correct SA prediction for [OE] (resp. 84% for [OT]). Errors for [OE] are mainly non-useful tweets (71%), such as *Be careful, a storm is a bad omen for next year* classified as urgent probably because of the phrase *be careful.* Among misclassified urgent instances, 38.4% are tweets conveying several information type categories, for example *LIVE - Two apartment buildings collapse in downtown Marseille - A third one threatens to collapse - At least two light injuries* which contains both information about HUMAN DAMAGES (prediction) and a MATERIAL DAMAGES (annotation).

[8] Training on (S, H, C) (resp. (F, H, C)) and testing on (F) (resp. (S)) is not possible since the training sets are too small.

6 Conclusion

This paper newly addresses the role of speech acts in urgency detection in tweets. In particular, we propose a dataset of French tweets about urgent situations and create models that utilize speech acts to classify the tweets. We also analyze the generalization of the models over new urgent events. Our results are encouraging and demonstrate that SA improve urgency detection. This is more salient for out-of-type evaluation setting, where the SA-aware approach has shown to have a good generalisation power in fine-grained classification.

This work could be very useful to government workers who need to respond to natural disasters and to decide how to deploy possibly limited resources. As future work, we plan to explore a finer-grained SA taxonomy on urgency detection.

Acknowledgment

This work has been supported by the INTACT project funded by the AAP CNRS - INHESJ 2022 and the FIESPI grant with the French Interior Min-

Best models	NOT USF.	HUM. DAM.	MAT. DAM.	WAR. ADV.	SUP.	CRI.	OTH.
OUT-OF-EVENT SA-agnostic							
FlauBERT^{wl}	0.855	**0.746**	0.638	0.843	**0.545**	–	0.246
OUT-OF-EVENT SA-aware							
ML^{4}	**0.886**	0.721	**0.656**	0.844	0.500	–	**0.356**
OUT-OF-TYPE SA agnostic							
FlauBERT^{wl}+Meta	**0.899**	**0.759**	0.432	0.000	**0.917**	**0.326**	**0.250**
OUT-OF-TYPE SA aware							
ML^{2}	0.895	0.737	**0.500**	**0.308**	0.783	0.323	0.188

Table 5: Impact of SA injection for information type classification per class in terms of macro F1-scores.

istry. Alda Mari gratefully acknowledges ANR-17-EURE-0017 FrontCog. The research of Farah Benamara and Véronique Moriceau is also partially supported by DesCartes: the National Research Foundation, Prime Minister's Office, Singapore under its Campus for Research Excellence and Technological Enterprise (CREATE) program.

References

Firoj Alam, Ferda Ofli, and Muhammad Imran. 2018. CrisisMMD: Multimodal Twitter Datasets from Natural Disasters. *arXiv:1805.00713 [cs]*.

John Langshaw Austin. 1962. *How to do things with words*. Oxford University Press.

Kent Bach and Robert M Harnish. 1979. *Linguistic communication and speech acts*. MIT Press.

David Bracewell, Marc Tomlinson, and Hui Wang. 2012. Identification of social acts in dialogue. In *Proceedings of COLING 2012*, pages 375–390, Mumbai, India. The COLING 2012 Organizing Committee.

Anaïs Cadilhac, Nicholas Asher, Farah Benamara, and Alex Lascarides. 2013. Grounding strategic conversation: Using negotiation dialogues to predict trades in a win-lose game. In *Proceedings of the 2013 Conference on Empirical Methods in Natural Language Processing*, pages 357–368, Seattle, Washington, USA. Association for Computational Linguistics.

Vitor R. Carvalho and William W. Cohen. 2005. On the collective classification of email "speech acts". In *Proceedings of the 28th Annual International ACM SIGIR Conference on Research and Development in Information Retrieval*, SIGIR '05, page 345–352, New York, NY, USA. Association for Computing Machinery.

Cleo Condoravdi and Sven Lauer. 2012. Imperatives: Meaning and illocutionary force. *Empirical issues in syntax and semantics*, 9:37–58.

AbdelRahim Elmadany, Hamdy Mubarak, and Walid Magdy. 2018a. Arsas: An arabic speech-act and sentiment corpus of tweets. In *Proceedings of the Eleventh International Conference on Language Resources and Evaluation (LREC 2018)*, Paris, France. European Language Resources Association (ELRA).

AbdelRahim Elmadany, Hamdy Mubarak, and Walid Magdy. 2018b. Arsas: An arabic speech-act and sentiment corpus of tweets. *OSACT*, 3:20.

Anastasia Giannakidou and Alda Mari. 2021. *Truth and veridicality in grammar and thought: Mood, modality, and propositional attitudes*. University of Chicago Press.

Jonathan Ginzburg. 2012. *The interactive stance*. Oxford University Press.

Chih-Wen Goo and Yun-Nung Chen. 2018. Abstractive dialogue summarization with sentence-gated modeling optimized by dialogue acts. In *Proceedings of 7th IEEE Workshop on Spoken Language Technology*.

Ryuichiro Higashinaka, Kenji Imamura, Toyomi Meguro, Chiaki Miyazaki, Nozomi Kobayashi, Hiroaki Sugiyama, Toru Hirano, Toshiro Makino, and Yoshihiro Matsuo. 2014. Towards an open-domain conversational system fully based on natural language processing. In *Proceedings of COLING 2014, the 25th International Conference on Computational Linguistics: Technical Papers*, pages 928–939, Dublin, Ireland. Dublin City University and Association for Computational Linguistics.

Muhammad Imran, Shady Mamoon Elbassuoni, Carlos Castillo, Fernando Diaz, and Patrick Meier. 2013. Extracting information nuggets from disaster-related messages in social media. *Proc. of ISCRAM, Baden-Baden, Germany*.

Gunilla Elleholm Jensen. 2012. Key criteria for information quality in the use of online social media for emergency management in New Zealand. Master's thesis.

Shafiq Joty and Tasnim Mohiuddin. 2018. Modeling speech acts in asynchronous conversations: A neural-CRF approach. *Computational Linguistics*, 44(4):859–894.

Simon Keizer, Rieks op den Akker, and Anton Nijholt. 2002. Dialogue act recognition with Bayesian networks for Dutch dialogues. In *Proceedings of the Third SIGdial Workshop on Discourse and Dialogue*, pages 88–94, Philadelphia, Pennsylvania, USA. Association for Computational Linguistics.

Diego Kozlowski, Elisa Lannelongue, Frédéric Saudemont, Farah Benamara, Alda Mari, Véronique

Moriceau, and Abdelmoumene Boumadane. 2020. A three-level classification of french tweets in ecological crises. *Information Processing & Management*, 57(5):102284.

D. Robert Ladd. 1981. A First Look at the Semantics and Pragmatics of Negative Questions and Tag Questions. In *Seventeenth Regional Meeting of the Chicago Linguistic Society (CLS) 17*.

Peter Lasersohn. 2005. Context dependence, disagreement, and predicates of personal taste. *Linguistics and philosophy*, 28(6):643–686.

Hang Le, Loïc Vial, Jibril Frej, Vincent Segonne, Maximin Coavoux, Benjamin Lecouteux, Alexandre Allauzen, Benoit Crabbé, Laurent Besacier, and Didier Schwab. 2020. FlauBERT: Unsupervised language model pre-training for French. In *Proceedings of the 12th Language Resources and Evaluation Conference*, pages 2479–2490, Marseille, France. European Language Resources Association.

Tsung-Yi Lin, Priya Goyal, Ross Girshick, Kaiming He, and Piotr Dollár. 2017. Focal loss for dense object detection. In *Proceedings of the IEEE international conference on computer vision*, pages 2980–2988.

Alda Mari. 2016. Assertability conditions of epistemic (and fictional) attitudes and mood variation. In *Semantics and Linguistic Theory*, volume 26, pages 61–81.

Alda Mari and Paul Portner. 2021. Mood variation with belief predicates: Modal comparison and the raisability of questions. *Glossa: a journal of general linguistics*, 40(1).

Louis Martin, Benjamin Muller, Pedro Javier Ortiz Suárez, Yoann Dupont, Laurent Romary, Éric Villemonte de la Clergerie, Djamé Seddah, and Benoît Sagot. 2019. CamemBERT: a Tasty French Language Model. *arXiv e-prints*, page arXiv:1911.03894.

Richard McCreadie, Cody Buntain, and Ian Soboroff. 2019. TREC incident streams: Finding actionable information on social media. In *Proceedings of the 16th International Conference on Information Systems for Crisis Response and Management, València, Spain, May 19-22, 2019*. ISCRAM Association.

Venkata Kishore Neppalli, Cornelia Caragea, and Doina Caragea. 2018. Deep Neural Networks versus Naive Bayes Classifiers for Identifying Informative Tweets during Disasters. In *Proceedings of the 15th International Conference on Information Systems for Crisis Response and Management*, ISCRAM'2018.

Ira Noveck. 2018. *Experimental pragmatics: The making of a cognitive science*. Cambridge University Press.

Paul Portner. 2018. *Mood*. Oxford University Press.

Jerrold Sadock. 2004. 3 speech acts. *The handbook of pragmatics*, page 53.

Tulika Saha, Aditya Prakash Patra, Sriparna Saha, and Pushpak Bhattacharyya. 2020. A transformer based approach for identification of tweet acts. In *2020 International Joint Conference on Neural Networks (IJCNN)*, pages 1–8. IEEE.

Efsun Sarioglu Kayi, Linyong Nan, Bohan Qu, Mona Diab, and Kathleen McKeown. 2020. Detecting urgency status of crisis tweets: A transfer learning approach for low resource languages. In *Proceedings of the 28th International Conference on Computational Linguistics*, pages 4693–4703, Barcelona, Spain (Online). International Committee on Computational Linguistics.

John R Searle. 1975. Indirect speech acts. In *Speech acts*, pages 59–82. Brill.

Mandy Simons. 2007. Observations on embedding verbs, evidentiality, and presupposition. *Lingua*, 117(6):1034–1056.

Andreas Stolcke, Klaus Ries, Noah Coccaro, Elizabeth Shriberg, Rebecca Bates, Daniel Jurafsky, Paul Taylor, Rachel Martin, Carol Van Ess-Dykema, and Marie Meteer. 2000. Dialogue act modeling for automatic tagging and recognition of conversational speech. *Computational Linguistics*, 26(3):339–374.

Brandon Truong, Cornelia Caragea, Anna Squicciarini, and Andrea H. Tapia. 2014. Identifying valuable information from Twitter during natural disasters. In *Proceedings of the ASIST Annual Meeting*, volume 51, pages 1–4. 51.

Soroush Vosoughi. 2015. *Automatic detection and verification of rumors on Twitter*. Thesis, Massachusetts Institute of Technology.

Soroush Vosoughi and Deb Roy. 2016. Tweet acts: A speech act classifier for twitter. *Proceedings of the Tenth International AAAI Conference on Web and Social Media (ICWSM 2016)*.

Kiran Zahra, Muhammad Imran, and Frank O Ostermann. 2020. Automatic identification of eyewitness messages on twitter during disasters. *Information Processing & Management*, 57(1):102–107.

Raffaella Zanuttini, Miok Pak, and Paul Portner. 2012. A syntactic analysis of interpretive restrictions on imperative, promissive, and exhortative subjects. *Natural Language & Linguistic Theory*, 30(4):1231–1274.

Renxian Zhang, Dehong Gao, and Wenjie Li. 2011. What are tweeters doing: Recognizing speech acts in twitter. In *Workshops at the Twenty-Fifth AAAI Conference on Artificial Intelligence*.

What *Drives* the Use of Metaphorical Language? Negative Insights from Abstractness, Affect, Discourse Coherence and Contextualized Word Representations

Prisca Piccirilli and Sabine Schulte im Walde
Institute for Natural Language Processing, University of Stuttgart, Germany
{prisca.piccirilli,schulte}@ims.uni-stuttgart.de

Abstract

Given a specific discourse, which discourse properties trigger the use of metaphorical language, rather than using literal alternatives? For example, what drives people to say *grasp the meaning* rather than *understand the meaning* within a specific context? Many NLP approaches to metaphorical language rely on cognitive and (psycho-)linguistic insights and have successfully defined models of discourse coherence, abstractness and affect. In this work, we build five simple models relying on established cognitive and linguistic properties – frequency, abstractness, affect, discourse coherence and contextualized word representations – to predict the use of a metaphorical vs. synonymous literal expression in context. By comparing the models' outputs to human judgments, our study indicates that our selected properties are not sufficient to systematically explain metaphorical vs. literal language choices.

1 Introduction

Metaphors are "not just nice", but represent a "necessary" element of everyday thought and communication (Ortony, 1975; Lakoff and Johnson, 1980; van den Broek, 1981; Schäffner, 2004, i.a.), and are ubiquitous in natural language text corpora (Gedigian et al., 2006; Shutova and Teufel, 2010; Steen et al., 2010, i.a.). From the perspective of natural language processing (NLP), automatic approaches to metaphor processing are therefore important for any task that requires natural language understanding, and NLP has been concerned with the detection (Köper and Schulte im Walde, 2016; Alnafesah et al., 2020; Ehren et al., 2020; Dankers et al., 2020, i.a.), the interpretation (Shutova, 2010; Bizzoni and Lappin, 2018; Mao et al., 2018, i.a.) and, the generation (Stowe et al., 2021; Zhou et al., 2021) of metaphors.[1]

As to our knowledge, however, no study so far has raised the question of WHY a metaphorical expression is used within a specific discourse, rather than an equally plausible literal alternative. For example, consider the discourse in table 1, where both the metaphorical expression *grasp the meaning* and its synonymous literal alternative *understand the meaning* seem equally acceptable (Piccirilli and Schulte im Walde, 2021, 2022). What are the factors priming for one use or the other? Are there cues within the discourse which influence the selection of one usage over the other? To which extent can computational approaches based on discourse properties model human behavior regarding the choice between synonymous metaphorical vs. literal language usage?

According to psycholinguistics and computational linguistics research, the processing of words is a function of their **frequency of occurrence** in the language (van Jaarsveld and Rattink, 1988; Wittmann et al., 2017, i.a.). Is the choice between a metaphorical and a literal expression therefore just an effect of frequency? In contrast, conceptual metaphor theory establishes metaphorical language as a figurative device for transferring knowledge from a concrete domain to a more abstract domain (Lakoff and Johnson, 1980), and the hypothesis that metaphorical usages correlate with the **abstractness of the context** has been supported in numerous NLP studies on automatic metaphor identification (Turney et al., 2011; Tsvetkov et al., 2013; Köper and Schulte im Walde, 2016; Alnafesah et al., 2020; Hall Maudslay et al., 2020). **Affect** has also been explored with regard to metaphoricity. Not only has metaphorical language been found to carry a stronger emotional load than literal language (Blanchette and Dunbar, 2001; Crawford, 2009), but metaphorical words and sentences are also judged to be "more emotionally engaging" than their synonymous literal paraphrases (Citron and Goldberg, 2014; Mohammad et al., 2016), and

[1] See Tong et al. (2021) for a systematic, comprehensive review and discussion of the most recent metaphor processing systems and datasets.

Proceedings of the 11th Joint Conference on Lexical and Computational Semantics, pages 299 - 310
July 14-15, 2022 ©2022 Association for Computational Linguistics

This wasn't just a play on words, rather it was a demand that they should 'maintain a consistency between their words and their actions'. But I agree, that still does not absolve them from the need to speak truth to power. In our times when people spend so much time with TV and the internet, do they have the interest and time to read poetry? Many people believe that it is difficult to read poetry. Can everyone [*grasp / understand the meaning*] of a good poem, or is a skill necessary?

Table 1: Example of a discourse from the dataset introduced by Piccirilli and Schulte im Walde (2021). Both the literal expression *understand meaning* and its metaphorical counterpart *grasp meaning* seem equally acceptable in the discourse.

informing NLP models with **emotion** features has proven useful for metaphor detection (Gargett and Barnden, 2015; Köper and Schulte im Walde, 2018; Dankers et al., 2019). When analyzing metaphorical discourse features (Glucksberg, 1989; Steen, 2004) and the interactions of **discourse coherence** with the contextual salience of metaphorical vs. literal expressions (Inhoff et al., 1984; Gibbs, 1989; Giora, 1997; Giora and Fein, 1999; Gibbs, 2002; Kövecses, 2009), findings are directly connected with the theory of discourse cohesion, i.e., the principle that discourse should be a "group of collocated, structured, and coherent sentences" (Halliday and Hasan, 1976; Jurafsky and Martin, 2019). Models relying on the coherence of lexical semantic discourse structures have therefore been successful in identifying metaphors (Sporleder and Li, 2009; Bogdanova, 2010; Mesgar and Strube, 2016; Dankers et al., 2020). From a yet different perspective, Transformer-based pretrained language models (T-PLMs) (Vaswani et al., 2017), pre-trained on the language modeling task, are able to predict masked items in context and produce **contextual embeddings** accounting for both left and right contexts, and resulting in word representations that are dynamically informed by the surrounding words.

The rich previous interdisciplinary research on figurative language seems to agree on tight interactions between metaphorical language detection and properties of the respective discourses, i.e., **cognitive aspects** (abstractness and affect), **discourse coherence** and **contextual properties**. Do these discourse properties indeed trigger the use of a metaphorical vs. its synonymous counterpart? We address this question by exploring five simple discourse-based models inspired by the above-mentioned properties, namely frequency, abstractness, affect, discourse coherence and contextualized word representations. We approach the question within two studies. First, we explore discourse features of metaphorical usages occurring in natural language by applying the cognitive and linguistically-inspired models to existing discourses from the English corpus *ukWaC* (Baroni et al., 2009). Then, we zoom into the models' predictions and evaluate them against human preferences (i.e., annotations) for metaphorical vs. literal language within the same discourses. By modeling the prediction for synonymous metaphorical vs. literal expressions motivated by the above discourse perspectives, we gain insight into human behavior for metaphorical vs. literal languages choices.

2 Dataset

Research on figurative language has produced impressive resources on the metaphoricity of lexical items. However, these resources have limitations regarding the specific task we are addressing in this work: (i) the context in which words are metaphorically used is not large enough, providing human judgments only on the *word-level* (Steen et al., 2010) or on the *sentence-level* (Stefanowitsch, 2008; Shutova and Teufel, 2010; Mohammad et al., 2016), (ii) the target words or expressions are *ambiguous*, i.e., they may have both a metaphorical and a literal sense (Tsvetkov et al., 2013; Mohler et al., 2016), (iii) they are *extended* metaphors (Gibbs, 2006; Martin, 2008), (iv) the paraphrases to metaphorically-used words are automatically generated and no manual annotations were provided to evaluate the outputs (Bollegala and Shutova, 2013; Bizzoni and Lappin, 2018, i.a.).

We therefore use our recently released dataset specifically designed to investigate the choice of metaphorical vs. literal expressions in context (Piccirilli and Schulte im Walde, 2021, 2022). It contains a total of 1,000 discourses of five to six sentences (98 words on average), in which the final sentence of each discourse contains either a metaphorical expression or its literal alternative from a pair of synonymous subject–verb (SV) or verb–object (VO) expressions. Table 1 presents an example for the VO pair *grasp/understand meaning*. The overall 50 pairs of English expressions were selected from Shutova (2010) and Mohammad et al. (2016), and for each of the pairs, we extracted 20 discourses from the *ukWaC* (Baroni et al., 2009), 10 of which containing the metaphorical usage (e.g., *grasp*) and

10 of which containing the literal paraphrase (e.g., *understand*). To gain insight into human preferences between the selected pairs of metaphorical vs. literal expressions, we also collected crowdsourced human judgments for these 1,000 discourses, asking annotators to choose which expression they favored given the preceding discourse. This dataset is therefore optimal for the task at hand, as it provides (i) synonymous metaphorical vs. literal expressions, (ii) at the *discourse-level*, (iii) manually annotated. In the present work, we make use of the 1,000 discourses containing the original expressions in the *ukWaC* and the annotators' choices for metaphorical vs. literal usages within a subset of 287 discourses, where 70% or more annotators agreed on the preference (metaphorical or literal).

3 Models and Experimental Setup

3.1 Prediction models

We approach the task of predicting the use of metaphorical vs. literal expressions as a *prompting task*: given an input prompt[2], the models predict whether the missing span should be the metaphorical or the literal expression. We apply five models relying on discourse properties, where each model approaches the task from a different perspective, to give us insight on which discourse features influence the metaphorical vs. literal selection.

Frequency approach When given the choice between a metaphorical expression and its synonymous counterpart, do we tend to favor the most frequent usage? **Baseline (Freq.):** Our baseline relies on the occurrences of the SV and OV tuples in the original *ukWaC* corpus: the model receives the prefix prompt as input, and always outputs the most frequent expression of the pair.

Cognitively-inspired approaches The cognitive interaction between abstractness/affect and metaphorical language raises the question: to which extent (i) a more abstract discourse and (ii) a more emotionally-loaded discourse favor a metaphorical usage? **Abstractness (Abstr.):** We measure the abstractness of a discourse preceding the target expression within four settings, based on the norms from Brysbaert et al. (2014). We assign abstractness scores to *all* words (Abstr.all), only *nouns* (Abstr.n), only *verbs* (Abstr.v) or only *adjectives* (Abstr.adj). We then obtain an overall rating of abstractness for each discourse by computing the median of the respective lexical items' abstractness scores. For each setting, we use as threshold the abstractness median of the respective part-of-speech class, and the model predicts the metaphorical expression if the overall abstractness score of the discourse is below that threshold (i.e., more abstract/less concrete), and the literal counterpart if above (i.e., less abstract/more concrete). **Emotionality (Emo.):** We build a model predicting the target expression based on the emotionality of the preceding discourse, which we represent using the English emotion lexicon from Buechel et al. (2020). Each lexical item from the preceding discourse is assigned an emotionality score, and the median represents the overall emotionality score of the discourse. Appendix A.1 provides details on the emotionality score.

Discourse coherence approach Is the choice of an expression from a synonymous pair driven by the semantic relatedness between the components of that expression and the lexical items in the surrounding context? We adapt the **Lexical Coherence Graph (LCG)** introduced by Mesgar and Strube (2016) to measure the semantic relatedness between the words in the preceding context and the target expression contained in the final discourse sentence: we compute the cosine scores for the two components in the SV/VO expressions (i.e., the verb and its argument) and each word in the preceding discourse, relying on contextualized BERT embeddings (Devlin et al., 2019). The output is a graph connecting the preceding context to both the metaphorical expression and its synonymous alternative; edge weights are represented by the average of the respecting cosine values. The expression – metaphorical or literal – with the maximum weight (i.e., the largest average cosine score) is selected. Appendix A.2 provides details on the LCG score.

Contextualized discourse properties How do contextualized word representations prime for the use of a metaphorical vs. literal preference? Our question triggers a *cloze-task* style (Taylor, 1953) and applies the **Pre-trained Language Model BERT** (Devlin et al., 2019) in a zero-shot manner. We give a *cloze prompt* as input to the model, as in table 1: we mask the target expression, and the model selects the most probable answer amongst the two candidates (metaphorical or literal). We experiment with both $\text{BERT}_{\text{base}}$ and $\text{BERT}_{\text{large}}$.

[2]The input prompt is a *prefix prompt* for all models except for BERT, whose input is a *cloze prompt*.

3.2 Experimental Setup

We compare our models' predictions against two gold standards. We first evaluate the models' outputs against the 1,000 discourses collected from *ukWaC*, containing the balanced *originally*-used metaphorical or literal expressions (**Orig. Data**) to investigate which discourse aspects (abstractness, emotionality, coherence, word representations) might have primed the metaphorical vs. literal selection. We expect the model predictions to provide insight into the features that influenced the *original* speakers' preferences. We then zoom into the *annotated* version of the same data (**Anno. Data**), for which participants were asked which expression, metaphorical or literal, they favored in the given 287 discourses (cf. Section 2). We analyze whether (dis-)agreements between humans are also reflected in the models' predictions.

4 Results and Analyses

We first analyze the models' predictions with regard to metaphorical vs. literal usages in the *originally*-extracted data (**Orig. Data**), to address the question: do cognitive and linguistically-inspired models reflect metaphorical language usage encountered in natural language corpora? The first column of figure 1 presents the accuracy score of each model with regard to Orig. Data. All models reach around 50% of accuracy; however, they behave very differently regarding their individual predictions.[3] Figure 1 presents the percentages of overlapping output decisions between our five models, revealing interesting insights: we observe 77% overlapping predictions between the PLMs with the frequency baseline, suggesting that the majority of PLM predictions is frequency-driven, which is not the case for most abstractness settings and emotionality. Emotionality itself correlates with abstractness in all settings but the one where we consider only adjectives, which is surprising as adjectives tend to carry a lot of emotions (Mohammad and Turney, 2010; Bostan and Klinger, 2019). The overlap between LCG and BERT reaches 62%, whereas its correlations with abstractness and emotionality are rather low, suggesting that decisions based on abstractness and emotionality are different to those based on word representations and semantic relatedness. At first sight, our different perspectives seem rather complementary, which is yet to be verified in future studies.

[3]Appendix B.1 presents further prediction differences.

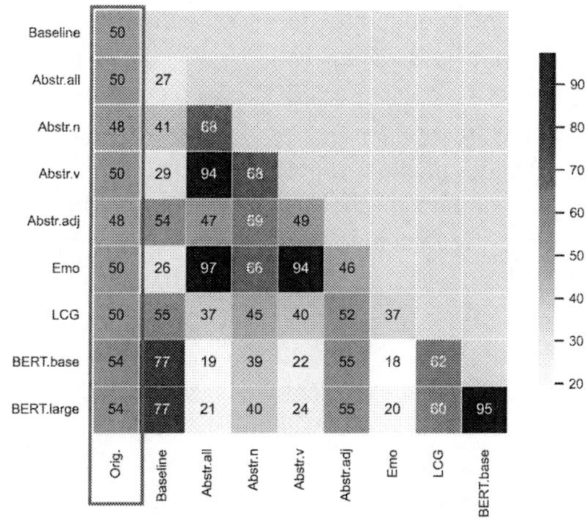

Figure 1: Accuracy scores of each model with regard to the original data (1st column in red) and percentages of overlapping output decisions between models.

Overall, none of our models seems to reliably predict what is observed in natural language data. We thus cannot derive what might have triggered the original speakers to favor a metaphorical or literal expression over the other.

We then compare our models' predictions to human behavior: are the proportions of metaphorical vs. literal predictions from our models similar to human perceptions (**Anno. Data**)? Figure 2 presents the proportions of the metaphorical expressions predicted by four of the models in relation to the proportions of metaphorical usages favored by the human judges.[4] If humans and models were making similar decisions, all data points, each representing the proportion of metaphorical uses for a pair of expressions, would be on the regression line. We make different observations depending on the model in question. As far as frequency is concerned, the model predicts either the metaphorical or the literal expression (100% or 0% respectively, in the graph). Many literal expressions that are favored by participants (low x-axis %) seem to correlate with their higher occurrences in natural language corpora, e.g., *make* vs. *throw remark* (VO). However, humans also favor many metaphorical expressions which are less frequently used, e.g., *stir* vs. *cause excitement* (VO) and inversely, a few metaphorical expressions which are more frequent than their literal counterparts are not necessarily favored by people, e.g., *poison* vs. *corrupt mind* (VO). Thus, frequency does not seem to be a systematic factor for metaphorical/literal choices. Regard-

[4]Appendix B.2 shows the graphs for all models.

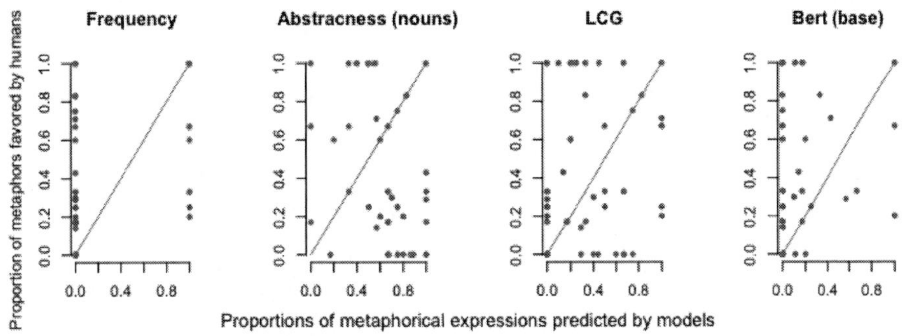

Figure 2: Proportions of predicted metaphorical expressions for each model, with regard to the proportions of these metaphorical expressions favored by annotators. Appendix B.2 shows the graphs for all models.

ing abstractness, many expressions fall perfectly on the regression line, e.g., *twist vs. misinterpret word* (VO), *story grab vs. intrigue* (SV), suggesting at first some interactions between the expression preferences and the abstractness of the respective discourses. However, the numerous metaphorical expressions that are predicted by the model (80%+) but not by humans, e.g., *taste* vs. *experience freedom* (VO), *factor shape* vs. *determine* (SV) do not confirm that hypothesis. Concerning the LCG, the picture is less clear. Many literal expressions are favored by both the model and humans, e.g., *color* vs. *affect judgement* (VO), but many metaphorical usages are preferred by humans when the model predicts the literal ones, e.g., *breathe* vs. *instill life* (VO). Therefore, metaphorical vs. literal coherence does not seem either to be a determining factor for metaphorical vs. literal preference, respectively, which does not support the context-salience hypothesis, where one would expect a metaphorical expression to be favored following a metaphorical discourse, and ditto for a literal expression/literal discourse (Kövecses, 2009). Finally, the overall low metaphorical predictions by the PLM are expressions for which humans provide high metaphorical proportions, such as *abuse* vs. *drink alcohol* (VO). This suggests a potential lack of metaphorical language representation, in line with our observation concerning abstractness and emotionality.

5 Discussion and Future Work

Previous research has provided evidence for interactions between metaphorical language and discourse properties, namely frequency, abstractness, affect, discourse coherence and contextualized word representations, on the *word-* and *sentence-level*. In this work, we took a step further: we looked at the task of predicting the use of a metaphorical vs. synonymous literal expression and built models based on the above-mentioned features on the *discourse-level*. Our findings show that these discourse properties do not seem to be indicative of metaphorical usage.

We propose several directions for future work. First of all, we considered discourses of around five sentences, but the decision on the context window might have an impact on the findings. Further work exploring the optimal size of preceding context would be interesting. Another promising direction might analyze PLMs' attention mechanisms (Tenney et al., 2019; Clark et al., 2019) on the presented task, and also explore the extent to which modifying the attention of such models, i.e., fine-tuning (Peters et al., 2019; Zhao and Bethard, 2020), improves their performance to mimic human preferences for metaphorical vs. literal usages. Finally, we have looked at five features; needless to say that exploring further discourse properties is necessary, such as co-reference, complexity, aptness, creativity, prototypicality, and the influence of genre and specific domains (e.g., religious/scientific texts).

6 Conclusion

We suggested five simple models to investigate WHY humans choose to use a metaphorical expression in a specific discourse. Regardless of the perspectives, our work demonstrates that a range of previously suggested salient discourse properties do not seem to influence preferences on the choice between synonymous metaphorical vs. literal expressions. Our findings thus ask for a more nuanced approach to metaphorical language choices in NLP.

Acknowledgements

We thank the anonymous reviewers for their useful and quality feedback. This research was supported by the DFG Research Grant SCHU 2580/4-1 *Multimodal Dimensions and Computational Applications of Abstractness*.

References

Ghadi Alnafesah, Harish Tayyar Madabushi, and Mark Lee. 2020. Augmenting Neural Metaphor Detection with Concreteness. In *Proceedings of the Second Workshop on Figurative Language Processing*, pages 204–210, Online. Association for Computational Linguistics.

Marco Baroni, Silvia Bernardini, Adriano Ferraresi, and Eros Zanchetta. 2009. The WaCky Wide Web: A Collection of Very Large Linguistically Processed Web-Crawled Corpora. *Language Resources and Evaluation*, 43(3):209–226.

Yuri Bizzoni and Shalom Lappin. 2018. Predicting Human Metaphor Paraphrase Judgments with Deep Neural Networks. In *Proceedings of the Workshop on Figurative Language Processing*, pages 45–55, New Orleans, Louisiana. Association for Computational Linguistics.

Isabelle Blanchette and Kevin Dunbar. 2001. Analogy Use in Naturalistic Settings: The Influence of Audience, Emotion, and Goals. *Memory & Cognition*, 29(5):730–735.

Daria Bogdanova. 2010. A Framework for Figurative Language Detection Based on Sense Differentiation. In *Proceedings of 2010 Conference the Association for Computational Linguistics: Student Research Workshop*, pages 67–72, Uppsala, Sweden. Association for Computational Linguistics.

Danushka Bollegala and Ekaterina Shutova. 2013. Metaphor Interpretation Using Paraphrases Extracted from the Web. *PLOS ONE*, 8(9):1–10.

Laura Ana Maria Bostan and Roman Klinger. 2019. Exploring Fine-Tuned Embeddings that Model Intensifiers for Emotion Analysis. In *Proceedings of the Tenth Workshop on Computational Approaches to Subjectivity, Sentiment and Social Media Analysis*, pages 25–34, Minneapolis, USA. Association for Computational Linguistics.

Marc Brysbaert, Amy Beth Warriner, and Victor Kuperman. 2014. Concreteness Ratings for 40 Thousand Generally Known English Word Lemmas. *Behavior Research Methods*, 64(3):904–911.

Sven Buechel and Udo Hahn. 2018a. Emotion Representation Mapping for Automatic Lexicon Construction (Mostly) Performs on Human Level. In *Proceedings of the 27th International Conference on Computational Linguistics*, pages 2892–2904, Santa Fe, New Mexico, USA. Association for Computational Linguistics.

Sven Buechel and Udo Hahn. 2018b. Word Emotion Induction for Multiple Languages as a Deep Multi-Task Learning Problem. In *Proceedings of the 2018 Conference of the North American Chapter of the Association for Computational Linguistics: Human Language Technologies, Volume 1 (Long Papers)*, pages 1907–1918, New Orleans, Louisiana. Association for Computational Linguistics.

Sven Buechel, Susanna Rücker, and Udo Hahn. 2020. Learning and Evaluating Emotion Lexicons for 91 Languages. In *Proceedings of the 58th Annual Meeting of the Association for Computational Linguistics*, pages 1202–1217, Online. Association for Computational Linguistics.

Francesca M.M. Citron and Adele E. Goldberg. 2014. Metaphorical Sentences Are More Emotionally Engaging Than Their Literal Counterparts. *Journal of cognitive neuroscience*, 26(11):2585–2595.

Kevin Clark, Urvashi Khandelwal, Omer Levy, and Christopher D. Manning. 2019. What Does BERT Look at? An Analysis of BERT's Attention. In *Proceedings of the 57th Annual Meeting of the Association for Computational Linguistics: Workshop BlackboxNLP: Analyzing and Interpreting Neural Networks for NLP*, pages 276–286, Florence, Italy. Association for Computational Linguistics.

L. Elizabeth Crawford. 2009. Conceptual Metaphors of Affect. *Emotion review*, 1(2):129–139.

Verna Dankers, Karan Malhotra, Gaurav Kudva, Volodymyr Medentsiy, and Ekaterina Shutova. 2020. Being Neighbourly: Neural Metaphor Identification in Discourse. In *Proceedings of the Second Workshop on Figurative Language Processing*, pages 227–234, Online. Association for Computational Linguistics.

Verna Dankers, Marek Rei, Martha Lewis, and Ekaterina Shutova. 2019. Modelling the Interplay of Metaphor and Emotion through Multitask Learning. In *Proceedings of the 2019 Conference on Empirical Methods in Natural Language Processing and the 9th International Joint Conference on Natural Language Processing*, pages 2218–2229, Hong Kong, China. Association for Computational Linguistics.

Jacob Devlin, Ming-Wei Chang, Kenton Lee, and Kristina Toutanova. 2019. BERT: Pre-training of Deep Bidirectional Transformers for Language Understanding. In *Proceedings of the 2019 Conference of the North American Chapter of the Association for Computational Linguistics: Human Language Technologies*, pages 4171–4186, Minneapolis, Minnesota. Association for Computational Linguistics.

Rafael Ehren, Timm Lichte, Laura Kallmeyer, and Jakub Waszczuk. 2020. Supervised Disambiguation of German Verbal Idioms with a BiLSTM Architecture. In *Proceedings of the Second Workshop on*

Figurative Language Processing, pages 211–220, Online. Association for Computational Linguistics.

Paul Ekman. 1992. An Argument for Basic Emotions. *Cognition and Emotion*, 6(3-4):169–200.

Andrew Gargett and John Barnden. 2015. Modeling the Interaction Between Sensory and Affective Meanings for Detecting Metaphor. In *Proceedings of the Third Workshop on Metaphor in NLP*, pages 21–30, Denver, Colorado. Association for Computational Linguistics.

Matt Gedigian, John Bryant, Srini Narayanan, and Branimir Ciric. 2006. Catching Metaphors. In *Proceedings of the Third Workshop on Scalable Natural Language Understanding*, pages 41–48, New York City, New York. Association for Computational Linguistics.

Raymond W. Gibbs. 1989. Understanding and Literal Meaning. *Cognitive Science*, 13(2):243–251.

Raymond W. Gibbs. 2002. A New Look at Literal Meaning in Understanding What Is Said and Implicated. *Journal of Pragmatics*, 34(4):457–486.

Raymond W. Gibbs. 2006. Metaphor Interpretation as Embodied Simulation. *Mind & Language*, 21(3):434–458.

Rachel Giora. 1997. Understanding Figurative and Literal Language: The Graded Salience Hypothesis. *Cognitive Linguistics*, 8(3):183–206.

Rachel Giora and Ofer Fein. 1999. On Understanding Familiar and Less-Familiar Figurative Language. *Journal of Pragmatics*, 31(12):1601–1618.

Sam Glucksberg. 1989. Metaphors in Conversation: How Are They Understood? Why Are They Used? *Metaphor and Symbolic Activity*, 4(3):125–143.

Rowan Hall Maudslay, Tiago Pimentel, Ryan Cotterell, and Simone Teufel. 2020. Metaphor Detection using Context and Concreteness. In *Proceedings of the Second Workshop on Figurative Language Processing*, pages 221–226, Online. Association for Computational Linguistics.

Michael A.K. Halliday and Ruqaiya Hasan. 1976. *Cohesion in English*. Longman.

Albrecht Werner Inhoff, Susan D. Lima, and Patrick J. Carroll. 1984. Contextual Effects on Metaphor Comprehension in Reading. *Memory and Cognition*, 12(6):558–567.

Daniel Jurafsky and James H. Martin. 2019. *Speech and Language Processing: An Introduction to Natural Language Processing, Computational Linguistics, and Speech Recognition*, 3rd edition. Prentice Hall, USA.

Maximilian Köper and Sabine Schulte im Walde. 2016. Distinguishing Literal and Non-Literal Usage of German Particle Verbs. In *Proceedings of the Conference of the North American Chapter of the Association for Computational Linguistics: Human Language Technologies*, pages 353–362, San Diego, CA, USA. Association for Computational Linguistics.

Maximilian Köper and Sabine Schulte im Walde. 2018. Analogies in Complex Verb Meaning Shifts: the Effect of Affect in Semantic Similarity Models. In *Proceedings of the 2018 Conference of the North American Chapter of the Association for Computational Linguistics: Human Language Technologies, Volume 2 (Short Papers)*, pages 150–156, New Orleans, Louisiana. Association for Computational Linguistics.

Zoltán Kövecses. 2009. The Effect of Context on the Use of Metaphor in Discourse. *Ibérica: Revista de la Asociación Europea de Lenguas para Fines Específicos.*, 17(17):11–23.

George Lakoff and Mark Johnson. 1980. *Metaphors We Live By*. University of Chicago Press, Chicago.

Rui Mao, Chenghua Lin, and Frank Guerin. 2018. Word Embedding and WordNet Based Metaphor Identification and Interpretation. In *Proceedings of the 56th Annual Meeting of the Association for Computational Linguistics (Volume 1: Long Papers)*, pages 1222–1231, Melbourne, Australia. Association for Computational Linguistics.

James H. Martin. 2008. A Corpus-based Analysis of Context Effects on Metaphor Comprehension. In A. Stefanowitsch and S. Th. Gries, editors, *Corpus-Based Approaches to Metaphor and Metonymy*, pages 214–236. De Gruyter Mouton.

Mohsen Mesgar and Michael Strube. 2016. Lexical Coherence Graph Modeling Using Word Embeddings. In *Proceedings of the 2016 Conference of the North American Chapter of the Association for Computational Linguistics: Human Language Technologies*, pages 1414–1423, San Diego, California. Association for Computational Linguistics.

Saif Mohammad, Ekaterina Shutova, and Peter Turney. 2016. Metaphor as a Medium for Emotion: An Empirical Study. In *Proceedings of the Fifth Joint Conference on Lexical and Computational Semantics*, pages 23–33, Berlin, Germany. Association for Computational Linguistics.

Saif Mohammad and Peter Turney. 2010. Emotions Evoked by Common Words and Phrases: Using Mechanical Turk to Create an Emotion Lexicon. In *Proceedings of the 2010 Conference of the North American Chapter of the Association for Computational Linguistics: Human Language Technologies: Workshop on Computational Approaches to Analysis and Generation of Emotion in Text*, pages 26–34, Los Angeles, CA. Association for Computational Linguistics.

Michael Mohler, Mary Brunson, Bryan Rink, and Marc Tomlinson. 2016. Introducing the LCC Metaphor Datasets. In *Proceedings of the Tenth International Conference on Language Resources and Evaluation*, pages 4221–4227, Portorož, Slovenia. European Language Resources Association.

Andrew Ortony. 1975. Why Metaphors Are Necessary and Not Just Nice. *Educational Theory*, 25(1):45–53.

Matthew E. Peters, Sebastian Ruder, and Noah A. Smith. 2019. To Tune or Not to Tune? Adapting Pretrained Representations to Diverse Tasks. In *Proceedings of the 4th Workshop on Representation Learning for NLP*, pages 7–14, Florence, Italy. Association for Computational Linguistics.

Prisca Piccirilli and Sabine Schulte im Walde. 2021. Synonymous Pairs of Metaphorical and Literal Expressions in Context: An Empirical Study and Dataset *to tackle* or *to address the question*. In *Proceedings of the Workshop DiscAnn*, Tübingen, Germany.

Prisca Piccirilli and Sabine Schulte im Walde. 2022. Features of Perceived Metaphoricity on the Discourse Level: Abstractness and Emotionality. In *Proceedings of the 13th Conference on Language Resources and Evaluation*, Marseille, France. European Language Resources Association. To appear.

Christina Schäffner. 2004. Metaphor and Translation: Some Implications of a Cognitive Approach. *Journal of Pragmatics*, 36(7):1253–1269.

Ekaterina Shutova. 2010. Automatic Metaphor Interpretation as a Paraphrasing Task. In *Human Language Technologies: The 2010 Annual Conference of the North American Chapter of the Association for Computational Linguistics*, pages 1029–1037, Los Angeles, California. Association for Computational Linguistics.

Ekaterina Shutova and Simone Teufel. 2010. Metaphor Corpus Annotated for Source - Target Domain Mappings. In *Proceedings of the Seventh International Conference on Language Resources and Evaluation*, Valletta, Malta. European Language Resources Association.

Caroline Sporleder and Linlin Li. 2009. Unsupervised Recognition of Literal and Non-Literal Use of Idiomatic Expressions. In *Proceedings of the 12th Conference of the European Chapter of the Association for Computational Linguistics*, pages 754–762, Athens, Greece. Association for Computational Linguistics.

Gerard J. Steen. 2004. Can Discourse Properties of Metaphor Affect Metaphor Recognition? *Journal of Pragmatics*, 36(7):1295–1313.

Gerard J. Steen, Aletta G. Dorst, J. Berenike Herrmann, Anna A. Kaal, Tina Krennmayr, and Tryntje Pasma. 2010. *A Method for Linguistic Metaphor Identification. From MIP to MIPVU.* John Benjamins.

Anatol Stefanowitsch. 2008. *Words and Their Metaphors: A Corpus-Based Approach*, pages 63–105. De Gruyter Mouton.

Kevin Stowe, Nils Beck, and Iryna Gurevych. 2021. Exploring Metaphoric Paraphrase Generation. In *Proceedings of the 25th Conference on Computational Natural Language Learning*, pages 323–336, Online. Association for Computational Linguistics.

Wilson L. Taylor. 1953. "Cloze Procedure": A New Tool for Measuring Readability. *Journalism quarterly*, 30(4):415–433.

Ian Tenney, Dipanjan Das, and Ellie Pavlick. 2019. BERT Rediscovers the Classical NLP Pipeline. In *Proceedings of the 57th Annual Meeting of the Association for Computational Linguistics*, pages 4593–4601, Florence, Italy. Association for Computational Linguistics.

Xiaoyu Tong, Ekaterina Shutova, and Martha Lewis. 2021. Recent Advances in Neural Metaphor Processing: A Linguistic, Cognitive and Social Perspective. In *Proceedings of the 2021 Conference of the North American Chapter of the Association for Computational Linguistics: Human Language Technologies*, pages 4673–4686, Online. Association for Computational Linguistics.

Yulia Tsvetkov, Elena Mukomel, and Anatole Gershman. 2013. Cross-Lingual Metaphor Detection Using Common Semantic Features. In *Proceedings of the First Workshop on Metaphor in NLP*, pages 45–51, Atlanta, Georgia. Association for Computational Linguistics.

Peter Turney, Yair Neuman, Dan Assaf, and Yohai Cohen. 2011. Literal and Metaphorical Sense Identification through Concrete and Abstract Context. In *Proceedings of the 2011 Conference on Empirical Methods in Natural Language Processing*, pages 680–690, Edinburgh, Scotland, UK. Association for Computational Linguistics.

Raymond van den Broek. 1981. The Limits of Translatability Exemplified by Metaphor Translation. *Poetics Today*, 1(4):73–87.

Henk J. van Jaarsveld and Gilbert E. Rattink. 1988. Frequency Effects in the Processing of Lexicalized and Novel Nominal Compounds. *Journal of Psycholinguistic Research*, 17:447–473.

Ashish Vaswani, Noam Shazeer, Niki Parmar, Jakob Uszkoreit, Llion Jones, Aidan N. Gomez, Lukasz Kaiser, and Illia Polosukhin. 2017. Attention Is All You Need. In *ADvances in Neural Information Processing Systems*, pages 5998–6008.

Amy Beth Warriner, Victor Kuperman, and Marc Brysbaert. 2013. Norms of Valence, Arousal, and Dominance for 13,915 English Lemmas. *Behavior Research Methods*, 45(4):1191–1207.

Moritz Wittmann, Maximilian Köper, and Sabine Schulte im Walde. 2017. Exploring Soft-Clustering for German (Particle) Verbs across Frequency Ranges. In *Proceedings of the 12th International Conference on Computational Semantics*, Montpellier, France.

Yiyun Zhao and Steven Bethard. 2020. How does BERT's attention change when you fine-tune? An analysis methodology and a case study in negation scope. In *Proceedings of the 58th Annual Meeting of the Association for Computational Linguistics*, pages 4729–4747, Online. Association for Computational Linguistics.

Jianing Zhou, Hongyu Gong, and Suma Bhat. 2021. PIE: A Parallel Idiomatic Expression Corpus for Idiomatic Sentence Generation and Paraphrasing. In *Proceedings of the 17th Workshop on Multiword Expressions (MWE 2021)*, pages 33–48, Online. Association for Computational Linguistics.

A Models

A.1 Emotionality

Buechel et al. (2020) presented a new methodology to automatically generate lexicons for 91 languages comprising eight emotional variables: *Valence, Arousal, Dominance* (VAD) as well as the five basic emotions *Joy, Anger, Surprise, Fear, Surprise* (BE5) (Ekman, 1992). As a source dataset, they used the English emotion lexicon from Warriner et al. (2013), comprising about 14K entries in VAD format collected via crowdsourcing. They applied the BE5 ratings from Buechel and Hahn (2018a) to convert the VAD ratings. Via their monolingual state-of-the-art multi-task feed-forward network (Buechel and Hahn, 2018b), they projected ratings on these eight variables, resulting in an English lexicon containing 2M word type entries with very high correlation with human judgments (around 90% for each variable).

We are interested in the emotionality of lexical items, i.e., the emotional load that a term conveys, rather than the actual emotion a term refers to. We therefore use the BE5 ratings of the English lexicon for our study. Out of the five scores that a term receives – one for each emotion, we assume that its highest score is reflective of the "emotional load" of that term, i.e., how much emotion it conveys. For example, the lexical item "truth" obtained the scores 2.24, 1.46, 1.4, 1.49, 1.46 for Joy, Anger, Sadness, Fear and Surprise, respectively. In our experiments, the term "truth" is therefore attributed the score of 2.24 as its emotional load.

A.2 Lexical Coherence Graph

Following Mesgar and Strube (2016), we measure the semantic relatedness between words represented by their word embeddings, computing the cosine score between the two words of the expression (SV or VO) with each word of the preceding discourse. Consider v_a, v_b, v_c, the word vectors for word a in the preceding discourse A, word b in the metaphorical expression B_m contained in the last sentence B and word c in the literal expression C_l contained in the last sentence C, respectively. The cosine scores $\cos(v_a, v_b)$ and $\cos(v_a, v_c)$ between the two word vectors is a measure of semantic connectivity of the two words. The range of $\cos(v_a, v_b)$ and $\cos(v_a, v_c)$ is between $[-1, +1]$, showing how well the two words are semantically correlated. Figure 4 shows how relatedness is measured, and figure 5 shows the output of the graph.

B Results

B.1 Evaluation: Predictions vs. Original Data

Figure 3 presents the percentages of metaphorical expressions predicted by each model. As mentioned in section 4, the accuracy scores of all models reach around 50%, but they actually behave very differently with regard to performances for metaphorical vs. literal predictions. Remember that the originally-collected discourses are perfectly balanced (cf. Section 2), where half of the discourses contains metaphorical expressions and the other half contains literal expressions from synonymous pairs. As expected, the frequency baseline therefore reaches 50% of accuracy. We note however that the literal usage of the pairs is the most frequent in the *ukWaC* corpus (37/50 pairs), which leads the model to predict the literal counterpart in 74% of the cases. The abstractness and emotionality models mostly select for the metaphorical usages (up to 100% for Emo.), as the discourses are considered more abstract and more emotionally-loaded based on the respective norms. This suggests that original speakers did not perceive the degree of abstractness and emotionality of the discourse as triggers to favor one usage over the other. This aligns with the findings in Piccirilli and Schulte im Walde (2022), who analyzed the relationship between the abstractness and emotionality of the preceding discourses with human preferences for metaphorical vs. literal expressions. The LCG model favors the literal expressions as well (62%), while both $\text{BERT}_{\text{base}}$ and $\text{BERT}_{\text{large}}$ predominantly predict the literal expressions (81.80% and 80.10%, respectively.).

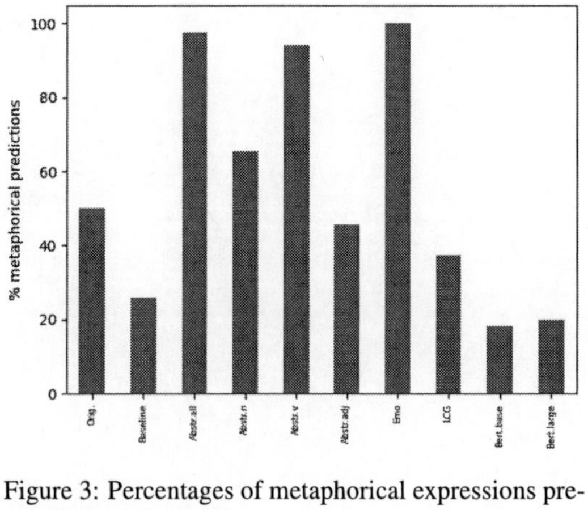

Figure 3: Percentages of metaphorical expressions predicted by each model.

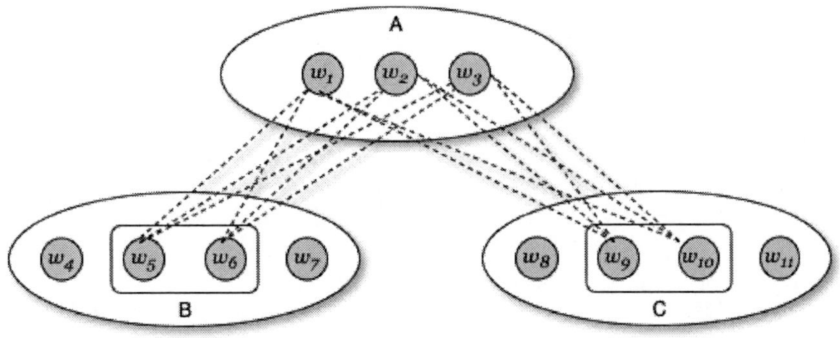

Figure 4: Discourse *A* with three words $\{w_1, w_2, w_3\}$ and sentences *B* and *C* with four words, where $\{w_5, w_6\}$ are the two words composing the metaphorical expression, and $\{w_9, w_{10}\}$ are composing the literal paraphrase. Depending on the expression input (SV or VO), the respective subject or object is identical in $\{w_5, w_6\}$ and $\{w_9, w_{10}\}$, as only the verb is used either as a metaphorical or a literal variant. The semantic relatedness between each word in $\{w_5, w_6\}$ and in $\{w_9, w_{10}\}$ is computed with each word in *A*.

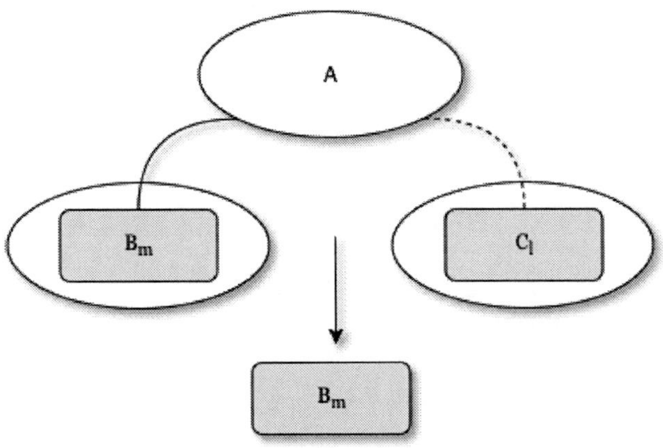

Figure 5: The word relation with the maximum weight (here B_m as indicated by the plain line) represents a stronger connection with the preceding discourse *A*.

B.2 Evaluation: Predictions vs. Annotated Data

Figure 6 presents an overview of the proportion of expressions that are predicted metaphorically by the models with regard to the preferences of the same expressions by human annotators.

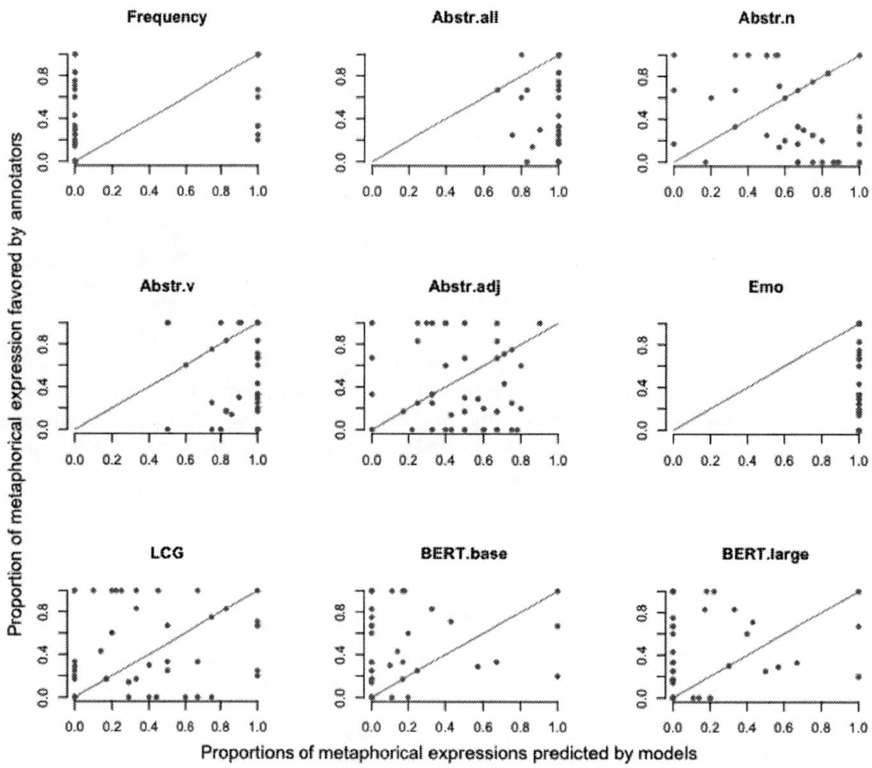

Figure 6: Proportions of the metaphorical expressions predicted by the models with regard to the proportions of these usages to be favored by the participants.

Unsupervised Reinforcement Adaptation for Class-Imbalanced Text Classification

Yuexin Wu
University of Memphis
ywu10@memphis.edu

Xiaolei Huang
University of Memphis
xiaolei.huang@memphis.edu

Abstract

Class-imbalance naturally exists when train and test models in different domains. Unsupervised domain adaptation (UDA) augment model performance with only accessible annotations from the source domain and unlabeled data from the target domain. However, existing state-of-the-art UDA models learn domain-invariant representations and evaluate primarily on class-balanced data across domains. In this work, we propose an unsupervised domain adaptation approach via reinforcement learning that jointly leverages feature variants and imbalanced labels across domains. We experiment with the text classification task for its easily accessible datasets and compare the proposed method with five baselines. Experiments on three datasets prove that our proposed method can effectively learn robust domain-invariant representations and successfully adapt text classifiers on imbalanced classes over domains. The code is available at https://github.com/woqingdoua/ImbalanceClass

1 Introduction

Unsupervised domain adaptation (UDA) is to find a shared feature space that is predictive across target and source domains (Ramponi and Plank, 2020). The shared space, *domain-independent* feature set, allows transferring of trained text classifiers from the source domain to the target domain. Methods to find the space have two major directions, pivot feature (Blitzer et al., 2006; Daumé III, 2007; Ziser and Reichart, 2018; Ben-David et al., 2020a) and adversarial learning (Ganin and Lempitsky, 2015; Chen et al., 2020b; Du et al., 2020). The pivot-based method selects a subset of shared features, called pivots, which learn important cross-domain information to represent shared feature space. Adversarial learning approaches the shared feature space by reducing document features' capability to distinguish source and target domains. The common method to achieve this is Gradient Reversal Layer (GRL) (Ganin and Lempitsky, 2015) aiming to reduce domain-specific patterns. However, the UDA approaches primarily focus on feature shifts ($p(X_{source})! = P(X_{target})$) while ignore possible class shifts ($p(Y_{source})! = p(Y_{target})$) across domains.

Class-imbalance naturally exists in data when label distributions across domains (Cui et al., 2017; Cheng et al., 2020) are different. Under the class-imbalanced scenario, the label distribution is imbalanced across domains, and the label distributions in source and target domains are not the same. Given the widely used Amazon data (Ni et al., 2019) as an example, the Book reviews may have more positive reviews than negative reviews, and the Kitchen may have a lower ratio of negative reviews. However, evaluating unsupervised domain adaptation under the class-imbalanced scenario is under-examined than the ideal scenario of the class-balanced benchmark. A wide evaluation benchmark of UDA for text classifiers is extracted from the Amazon review (Blitzer et al., 2006). The data has the same balanced-class distributions for both source and target domains. Such a well-balanced label distribution may make existing UDA models inapplicable to the real-world scenario, where class distributions can shift across domains.

In this study, we proposed an *unsupervised reinforcement adaptation model* (URAM) for text classifiers under the UDA setting that only labeled source data and unlabeled target data are available. Specifically, we propose a neural mask mechanism to generate domain-dependent and -independent feature representations and a reward policy using a critic value network (Konda and Tsitsiklis, 2000) (CRN) to learn optimal domain-independent representations. The reward policy optimizes the URAM via three joint reward factors, label, domain, and domain distance. While the label reward aims to encourage text classification models on domain-independent features to predict correct document

Proceedings of the 11th Joint Conference on Lexical and Computational Semantics, pages 311 - 322
July 14-15, 2022 ©2022 Association for Computational Linguistics

classes, the domain and domain distance rewards reduce domain variations of domain-dependent feature representations between source and target domains. We compare our reinforcement adaptation model with five baselines and experiment on four class-imbalanced data with both binary and non-binary labels. The results using the F1-score demonstrate the effectiveness of our reinforcement learning model that outperforms the baselines by 3.13 on average. The main contributions of this paper are as follows:

- We propose a reinforcement learning model for unsupervised domain adaptation that jointly leverages cross-domain variations and classification performance.
- We experiment UDA approaches on the class-imbalanced scenario that label distributions are different across domains. The class-imbalanced scenario is under-explored among the UDA models .
- We conduct an extensive ablation analysis that demonstrates how the reinforcement model can coherently combines both pivot and adversarial directions of unsupervised domain adaptation.

2 Background

This section briefly recaps the concepts of unsupervised domain adaptation (UDA) and reinforcement learning.

2.1 UDA for Class-Imbalanced Data

UDA assumes a labeled dataset with $\mathcal{D}_S = \{(x_s^i, y_s^i)\}_{i=1}^{n_s}$ from source domain and a unlabeled data $\mathcal{D}_T = \left\{x_t^j\right\}_{j=1}^{n_t}$ from target domain, data distributions of the two domains are different, $p(x_s) \neq p(x_t)$, and the two domains share the same number of *unique* annotations. UDA is to find a common feature space aligning source and target domains so that $f(p(x_s)) \approx p(x_t)$ However, class-imbalanced data naturally exist in UDA tasks that may cause inefficient knowledge transfer (Ramponi and Plank, 2020). We assume both data and labels are not equally distributed in this work.

2.2 Reinforcement Learning

Actor-Critic (Konda and Tsitsiklis, 2000) is an reinforcement learning algorithm that combines Actor and Critic networks. Critic, a value network (denote as V_{θ_c}), estimates rewards at state s_t and is optimized by state difference error as follows

$$\mathcal{L}(\theta_c) = \left\|V_{\theta_c}(s_t) - r(\mathrm{s}_t, a_t) - V_{\theta_c}(\mathrm{s}_{t+1})\right\|^2 \quad (1)$$

where $r(s_t, a_t)$ is a target reward and tells us the reward for taking action a in state s. The actor is a policy function that gives us the probability of taking action a in the state s. The actor decides which action should be taken, and the critic evaluates how good the action is and how it should adjust. The learning of the actor (θ_a) is based on policy gradient approach as the following

$$\mathcal{L}^A(\theta_a) = \sum_t \log \pi_{\theta_a}(a_t, s_t)\, A(s_t, a_t) \quad (2)$$

, where $A(s_t, a_t) = r(s_t, a_t) + \gamma V(s_{t+1}) - V(s_t)$. γ is a decay factor that discounts rewards backward over steps. To encourage the actor to explore more actions, the algorithm adds an entropy penalty,

$$\mathcal{L}^S(\theta_a) = -\sum_a \pi_\theta(a \mid s) \log \pi_{\theta_a}(a \mid s) \quad (3)$$

The overall objective is as following,

$$\mathcal{L} = \min\{\mathcal{L}(\theta_c) - (\mathcal{L}^A(\theta_a) + \mathcal{L}^s(\theta_a))\} \quad (4)$$

3 Unsupervised Reinforcement Adaptation Model

In this section, we present details of the Unsupervised Reinforcement Adaptation Model (URAM) in Figure 1. The URAM trains classifiers on the labeled data from the source domain and unlabeled data from the target domain. The model contains three major modules: 1) a base model; 2) adversarial learning; 3) reinforcement learning.

3.1 Based Model

Our based model consists of an encoder and a classifier. The encoder extracts features from input documents, and the classifier predicts document labels. The based model takes a regular in-domain training method with n_s labeled samples from the source domain

$$\min_{\theta_e, \theta_{cla}} \sum_i^{n_s} (\mathcal{L}(C(E(x_s^i, \theta_e), \theta_{cla}), y_s^i) \quad (5)$$

, where θ_e, θ_{cla} are the parameters of the encoder and classifier respectively. $\mathcal{L}(\cdot)$ is the cross-entropy loss.

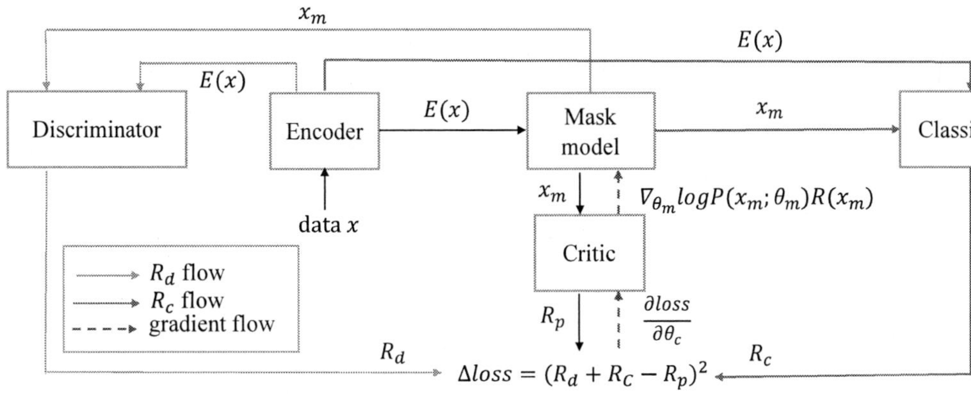

Figure 1: Illustration of URAM learning process. The yellow route is the R_d prediction progress, measuring by the confusion of the discriminator for x_m and $E(X)$. The blue route calculates the R_d by the consistency of the classifier for x_m and $E(X)$. The overall reward is made by R_d and R_c. The critic updates parameters by minimizing the mean square between the ground truth reward ($R_d + R_c$) and the predictive reward (R_c). The mask model learns from the policy gradient.

3.2 Adversarial Learning

We propose an adversarial learning using a mask strategy to learn domain-independent representations, which are transferable across domains. Domain adversarial learning (Ganin and Lempitsky, 2015) learns domain-independent features by reduce domain predictability of text classifiers, which is a common adversarial strategy in the UDA (Ramponi and Plank, 2020). The domain adversarial learning deploys a discriminator (θ_d) to predict domains by minimizing the classification error:

$$\min_{\theta_d}(\mathcal{L}(D(E(X_s), \theta_d), \mathbb{1}) + \mathcal{L}(D(E(X_t), \theta_d), \mathbb{0})). \quad (6)$$

However, the uncertainty is a major issue that can lead to uncontrollable learning process (Long et al., 2018; Ramponi and Plank, 2020) and easily fail to yield domain-independent representations.

Therefore, we propose a *mask model* to extract domain-independent features. Intuitively, if the discriminator uses the generated features from the mask model and fails to recognize domains of input data, then this indicates the features generated by the mask model are domain-independent. Therefore, our first goal is to maximize the loss of the discriminator as the following formulation:

$$R_d = \max_{\theta_m}(\mathcal{L}(D(x_m^s, \theta_m), \theta_d), \mathbb{1}) + \mathcal{L}(D(x_m^t, \theta_m), \theta_d), \mathbb{0})) \quad (7)$$

where $x_m^s = M(E(X_s)) * E(X_s)$ and $x_m^t = M(E(X_t)) * E(X_t)$. The mask model generates domain-independent representations by learning how to transform domain-dependent features and capture common knowledge cross domains.

The second objective of the mask model is for class-imbalanced distributions between source and target domains. Misclassifications occur when there is a class distribution discrepancy between training and test domains. The optimal domain adaptation is in the second stage of Fig. 2, however the class-imbalance may lead to misalignment in the third stage. As shown in the Fig. 2, while UDA models align feature spaces between source and target domains, misalignment may happen in label spaces especially when majority classes are different across domains. To reduce label distribution discrepancy, we propose an invariable prediction reward to jointly incorporate feature and label variants. Intuitively, we expect the classifier can make similar predictions by the original and masked features while reducing its dependence on domain-dependent patterns. Therefore, our goal is to make a consistent prediction between $C(E(X))$ and $C(M(E(X)))$. We follow the work (Saito et al., 2018b) and employ L1-distance to measure the representation discrepancy loss between $C(E(X))$ and $C(M(E(X)))$ as the following:

$$R_c = min(\mathcal{L}_{dis}(|C(M(E(X))) - C(E(X))|)) \quad (8)$$

, where R_c measures cross-domain variations.

3.3 Actor-Critic Learning

To reduce the uncertainty of extracting domain-independent representations by the mask model,

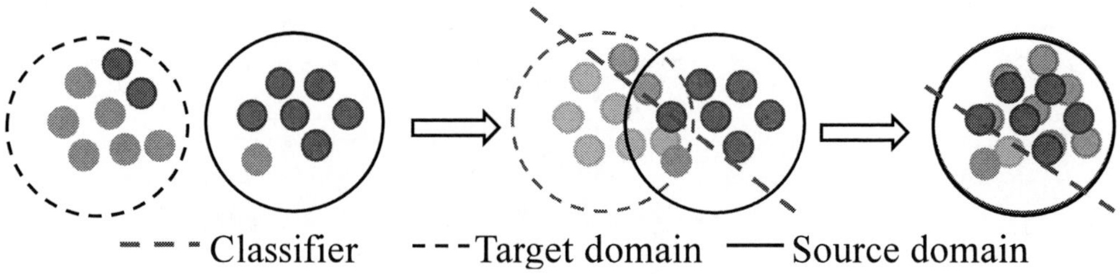

Figure 2: Illustration of alignment process for the class-imbalanced data.

we adopt the policy gradient via the actor-critic algorithm (Konda and Tsitsiklis, 2000) to explore the optimal solution.

First, we introduce a value estimation network, critic. The critic helps to estimate an action's reward by giving a state. Our critic is a 2-layer feed-forward network f with the input of $M(E(X))$ and $E(X)$, the predictive reward R_p is formulated as follow:

$$R_p = f(M(E(X)) * E(X)). \tag{9}$$

The loss function is the difference between of realistic reward $(R_d + R_c)$ and the predictive reward (R_p) from the critic as the following,

$$\mathcal{L}(\theta_c) = \left(R_d + R_c - R_p\right)^2 \tag{10}$$

The critic is trained with Adam on a mean squared error $\mathcal{L}(\theta_c)$.

The mask model generates a mask matrix $\mathcal{M}_a$ and is an actor model by a fully connected neural network and a sigmoid unit. It accepts inputs from the encoder and calculates a masked probability of each features $\mathcal{M}_p$. Then we adopt Bernoulli sampling and obtain a logical matrix $\mathcal{M}_a$. The elements in $\mathcal{M}_a$ belongs to $\{0, 1\}$. We denote the output of the mask model as $x_m = \mathcal{M}_a * E(x)$. The mask model's training objective is to maximum the total reward R_d and R_c defined in e.q. 7 and e.q. 8

$$J(\mathcal{M}_a \mid E(X)) = \mathbb{E}_{\mathcal{M}_a \sim \pi(\mathcal{M}_p \mid E(X))}\{R_d - R_c + R_{reg}\}, \tag{11}$$

, where π is a policy function and R_{reg} is a regularization term, controlling the number of masked features. We set $R_{reg} = (\sum \mathcal{M}_a)$. Since the mask model only make one action to transfer the state $M(E(X))$ from $E(X)$, we do not need to consider the future reward and the decay factor γ in e.q. 2 is zero. Thus, we can obtain the following optimization by combining with the e.q. 2 and e.q. 3,

$$\mathcal{L}(\theta_m) = -\log \pi_{\theta_m}(a, s)\, A(s, a) + \pi_{\theta_m}(a \mid s) \log \pi_{\theta_m}(a \mid s) \tag{12}$$

, where $A(s, a) = R_d + R_c - R_p$. We update θ_m by minimizing $\mathcal{L}(\theta_m)$.

Algorithm 1 Optimization Process of Our Model.

Input: The source data $D_s = (X_s, Y_s)$ and target data $D_t = (X_t)$, maximum iteration I;

Output: The network parameter $\theta_e, \theta_{cla}, \theta_d, \theta_m, \theta_c$;

```
for i = 1; i < I; i++ do
    Samples a batch from D_s and D_t;
    Update θ_e, θ_cla via e.q.(5);
    Update θ_d via e.q.(6)
    Update θ_m, θ_c via section (3.3)
end for
return θ_e, θ_cla, θ_d, θ_m, θ_c;
```

3.4 Training Procedure

Our training procedure includes three steps: 1) **step A** trains the encoder and classifier as e.q. 5; 2) **step B** trains the discriminator by e.q. 6; 3) **step C** training the mask model by the reinforcement learning. We summarize the optimization process in Algorithm 1.

4 Experiment

4.1 Datasets

We assembled four datasets, three online reviews and one Twitter data. The reviews are binary labels, and the Twitter data has 11 unique labels. We summarize data statistics in Table 2.

Amazon, Yelp, and IMDB Review are standard data sources for evaluating UDA models (Ramponi and Plank, 2020). We retrieved the **Yelp** and **IMDB** reviews[1] from torchtext and top four product gen-

[1] https://pytorch.org/text/stable/datasets.html

Method	MeToo - Davidson	Davidson-MeToo	Book-Kitchen	Kitchen-Book	Yelp-IMDB	IMDB-Yelp
			LSTM			
DANN	45.00	23.17	83.33	93.55	45.16	61.79
MCD	40.25	23.61	83.85	94.17	48.27	61.54
JUMBOT	46.94	23.26	81.79	93.66	42.57	56.78
ALDA	38.20	23.31	84.14	93.88	42.30	52.46
URAM	47.06	24.00	85.09	94.49	50.58	62.50
			BERT			
DANN	78.20	23.50	73.23	69.64	54.36	43.44
MCD	79.51	23.39	74.33	69.54	43.67	42.37
JUMBOT	73.74	23.23	80.57	75.00	53.37	43.08
ALDA	77.26	24.42	77.21	70.54	47.01	39.84
URAM	81.93	27.09	86.24	76.97	57.70	45.16

Table 1: Cross-domain performance of UDA models using F1 score. Each UDA model testifies over two popular neural feature extractor, LSTM and BERT. We list extensive evaluations in the Appendix.

	Docs	Tokens	pos/neg
M-MeToo	4480	13.86	-
M-Davidson	4480	19.13	-
A-Book	2000	25.65	0.65
A-Kitchen	2000	29.73	4.78
Yelp	2000	231.57	0.26
IMDB	2000	146.01	0.67

Table 2: Data statistics summary of Morality and three review data, Amazon, Yelp and IMDB. We include multi-label distributions of the Morality data in appendix, Table 7.

res of Amazon reviews (Ni et al., 2019), including Books (B), DVDs (D), Electronics (E) and Kitchen (K). We treat the four Amazon genres, Yelp, and IMDB as domains. Following the standard benchmark (Blitzer et al., 2006) for the UDA evaluations, we randomly select 2000 samples from each domain, while label distributions are not the same cross domains. We name cross-domain evaluations by the source-target format. For example, Books-Kitchen means that Books is the source data and Kitchen is the target data.

MFTC (Hoover et al., 2020) is a multi-label classification Twitter data with 35,108 tweets. These tweets are drawn from seven different discourse domains with moral sentiment across seven social movements, including MeToo, Black Lives Matter (BLM), Sandy, Davidson, Baltimore, All Lives Matter (ALM), and US Presidential Election (Election). We treat social movements as domains. These domains share the same set of 11 moral sentiment types: Subversion, Authority, Cheating, Fairness, Harm, Care, Betrayal, Loyalty, Purity, Degradation, Non-moral. The rates of each of the virtues and vices vary substantially across the domain. For example, only approximately 2% of the ALM data were labeled as degradation while approximately 14% of the Sandy data were labeled as degradation.

We conduct an exploratory analysis of *domain shifts* in data and labels. The analysis follows the name format as source-target. We use KL-divergence of the class distribution to measure the category-wise distribution and Euclidean distance to measure the domain-wise distribution. The domain-wise discrepancy refers to the euclidean distance of the encoder's output between the training and test sets. The category-wise is the KL-divergence of labels' distribution between the training and test sets. We extract feature vectors using LSTMs trained over the domains. We show cross-domain discrepancy in Table 3. We can find that the multi-label Twitter data has more variations in both domain and label distributions.

4.2 Baselines

We compare our models with four recent methods.

- DANN (Ganin and Lempitsky, 2015) maps source and target domains to a common subspace through shared parameters. This approach introduces a gradient reversal layer to confuse domain prediction to improve classification robustness across domains with the adversarial train.

- MCD (Saito et al., 2018a) proposes to maximize the discrepancy between two classifiers' outputs to detect target samples that are far from the support of the source. Then, A feature generator learns to generate target features near the support to minimize the discrep-

Table 3: Summary of domain shifts in data (domain-wise) and label (category-wise) distributions.

discrepancy	MeToo-Davidson	Davidson-MeToo	Book-Kitchen	Kitchen-Book	Yelp-IMDB	IMDB-Yelp
domain-wise	10889	661	15986	11680	1.523	1.692
category-wise	0.1197	0.1933	2.0×10^{-4}	1.0×10^{-4}	0.044	0.050

ancy.

- JUMBOT (Fatras et al., 2021) proposes a new formulation of the mini-batch optimal transport strategy coupled with an unbalanced optimal transport program to calculate optimal transport distance.
- ALDA (Chen et al., 2020b) constructs a new loss function by introducing a confusion matrix. The confusion matrix reduces the gap and aligns the feature distributions in an adversarial manner.

4.3 Implementation Details

In this study, we evaluate the UDA methods using two standard neural models as feature extractors, LSTM (Hochreiter and Schmidhuber, 1997) and BERT (Devlin et al., 2019). For the LSTM-based encoder, we use pre-trained word vectors GloVe (Pennington et al., 2014) by torchtext [2] to train word embedding. The learning rate is set to 1×10^{-3} and batch size set to 64. We utilize a Bidirectional LSTM as our encoder and set the LSTM hidden number as 256. For the BERT-based encoder, we load the pre-trained BERT model (`bert-base-uncased`) from the transformer toolkit (Wolf et al., 2020). We set the learning rate as 1×10^{-5} and batch size as 16.

In all the above experiments, we used Adam (Kingma and Ba, 2015) to optimize our model and maximum iteration set to 50 in all experiments. We run each experiment five times and average F1 as the final performance.

4.4 Result

Table 4: The domain-wise discrepancy based on domain adaptation methods.

	DANN	MCD	JUMBOT	ALDA	URAM
MeToo - Davidson	3.937	5.806	0.072	7.902	0.401
Davidson-MeToo	0.016	10.862	0.121	0.016	0.044
Book-Kitchen	0.950	1.651	0.046	3.922	0.233
Kitchen-Book	0.649	1.749	0.073	2.984	0.196
Yelp-IMDB	3.376	3.029	0.492	8.106	0.586
IMDB-Yelp	2.951	6.184	0.733	31.469	0.665

In this section, we present model performance on the cross-domain adaptation task and conduct an ablation analysis to examine the effects of the two reward factors, R_d and R_c. We include extensive evaluation results in the appendix (Section B).

Overall Performance. The table 1 reports the overall performance. Our method achieves the best result in the datasets with a significant discrepancy both in domain and category. We obtain a significant improvement on Amazon datasets, Book-Kitchen (1.12%-17.7%) and Kitchen-Book (2.62%-10.68%), respectively. Amazon datasets follow the traditional assumption that different domains have significant feature discrepancies but have similar label distributions. Our improvement on Amazon datasets verifies our model effectiveness of learning transferable knowledge. On the other hand, our method also can release the category discrepancy problem. As shown in the table 1, our method outperforms existing methods remarkably on the MFTC dataset (Metoo-Davidson) with the significant discrepancy in domain and category since we can align the distribution both in-text features and labels. We notice some latest methods fail to compete with DANN. We infer the reasons behind this are that some methods do not consider category discrepancy. For example, the performance of ALDA is lower than DANN on Metoo-Davidson since ALDA tries to align category discrepancy by narrowing domain discrepancy, which causes negative knowledge transfer. The other reason is due to poor robustness. Some methods may ascribe samples' feature discrepancy to domain discrepancy, and aligning these sample's specific features lead to a lower distinguished ability among different samples (e.g., ALDA on Yelp-IMDB). All methods have similar performance on Davidson-Metoo since Davidson datasets have an extreme label distribution. Most samples focus on the same category, which causes models not to access enough samples to learn the features in other classes.

Convergence Investigation The convergence curves of our model and baselines are respectively depicted in Fig. (3). We conduct a convergence experiment on Book-Kitchen datasets based on LSTM to verify the training stability during knowl-

[2]https://pytorch.org/text/stable/index.html

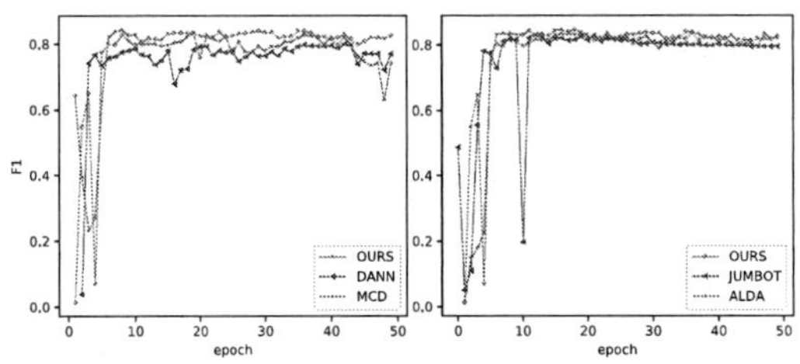

Figure 3: The convergence comparison between our model and baselines on Book-Kitchen.

edge transfer. This task focuses on evaluating the ability to align domain-wise discrepancy since the feature's center of Book and Kitchen have a remarkable difference (up to 15986), but their categories are similar. Specifically, we observe that our model significantly outperforms DANN and MCD during training. DANN has relatively low stability since it only aligns different domain features without considering task-specific features. Compared with ALDA, our model achieves similar stability. Our model can achieve efficient convergence after iterating 15 epochs, which proves our model's robustness.

Knowledge Transfer. We measure the feature center distance between the training set in the source data and the test set in the target data to evaluate models' ability to transfer knowledge. Generally, the domain-wise discrepancy is significantly narrowed after applying domain adaptation methods. Our model achieves relatively significant improvements, but there are some exceptions. For example, ALDA has a lower domain-wise discrepancy on Davidson-MeToo than ours. However, ALDA's performance is unsatisfactory, especially when the datasets have similar domains (e.g., Yelp-IMDB and IMDB-Yelp). A similar situation also happens on DANN and MCD. These methods enlarge domain-wise discrepancy when the domains have similar feature distribution. Compared with JUMBOT, our model has a slightly large domain-wise discrepancy. However, our model is more efficient on knowledge transfer when the domain has huge category-wise discrepancies. For example, the distance of our model is .0438 on Davidson-MeToo, while the corresponding figure is .1207 on JUMBOT.

4.5 Ablation Analysis

In this subsection, we investigate the importance of different rewards in reinforcement learning by conducting variant experiments, as shown in the Table 5.

$-R_c$ means we delete reward R_c in our R_{adv}. R_c is a unsupervised reward. Instead of aligning features, R_c aims to search subspace features, ensuing the consistent prediction between completed features $E(X)$ and sub-spaced features $M(E(X))$. This method is efficient since removing R_c is significantly detrimental to cross-domain performance. Especially, we find that R_c plays a more critical role Book-Kitchen and Kitchen-Book tasks by comparing the R_d since removing R_c lower the performance than R_d.

R_d is proposed to align domain features by fooling the discriminator. $-R_d$ means we do not need to train the discriminator and R_{adv} only combines with R_c and R_{reg}. $-R_d$ achieves a better performance than our completed model on Book-Kitchen. We infer the reason behind this is because R_d only focuses on feature shift rather than considering the discrepancy among different classes, which causes class-specific features to be weakened, and the model fails to distinguish the boundaries of other classes. However, removing R_d decreases the performance in most of the situations, which proves feature shift is efficient in domain adaptation.

Generally, R_d and R_c work together to guide critical knowledge transfer and removing any one of them significantly degrades the performance. Which reward dominates an improvement depends on the datasets' property. When the domains have significant discrepancy both in features and label distribution, R_d and R_c work in an adversarial way to ensure shifting features as well as keeping class-specific features.

5 Related work

Unsupervised Domain Adaptation for text classification has several major types of approaches, pivot features (Blitzer et al., 2006; Daumé III, 2007; Ziser and Reichart, 2018; Ben-David et al., 2020b), instance weighting (Jiang and Zhai, 2007; Wang et al., 2019; Gong et al., 2020), and domain adversaries (Ganin and Lempitsky, 2015; Qu et al., 2019; Du et al., 2020). A recent survey (Ramponi and Plank, 2020) shows that the most widespread methods for neural UDA are based on the use of domain adversaries, which reduces the discrepancy between the source and target distributions by reversing gradient updates for domain prediction networks. Our study follows the same track to obtain domain-invariant representations, however, there

Table 5: Ablation studies of our model on LSTM

Method	MeToo - Davidson	Davidson-MeToo	Book-Kitchen	Kitchen-Book	Yelp-IMDB	IMDB-Yelp
$-R_d$	31.97	23.14	86.09	84.15	43.28	61.40
$-R_c$	35.84	23.19	84.51	80.87	43.71	60.87
URAM	47.06	24.00	85.09	94.49	50.58	62.50

are two major differences than the existing UDA for text classifiers: 1) a mask model to distill domain-invariant features, 2) and a reinforcement learning approach to optimize the adversarial network. While existing UDA models have not explicitly incorporate domain shifts in label distributions, our proposed URAM jointly models domain variants in both data and label shifts.

Reinforcement Learning With the robustness in learning sophisticated policies, recent works introduce Reinforcement learning (RL) into the unsupervised domain adaptation task (Chen et al., 2020a; Dong et al., 2020; Zhang et al., 2021). DARL (Chen et al., 2020a) employs deep Q-learning in partial domain adaptation. The DARL framework designs a reward for the agent-based on how relevant the selected source instances are to the target domain. With the action-value function optimizer, DARL can automatically select source instances in the shared classes for circumventing negative transfer as well as to simultaneously learn transferable features between domains by reducing the domain shift. However, DARL does not generalize to unsupervised domain adaptation. Highly relying on the rich labels in the source domain will cause failure when insufficient labels are in the target domain. To address this problem, Zhang et al. develop a new reward across both source and target domains. This reward can guide the agent to learn the best policy and select the closest feature pair for both domains. However, rarely study has deployed the reinforcement UDA into the class-imbalanced text classification. To our best knowledge, we are the first work introducing RL for the UDA under the class-imbalanced text classification.

Imbalanced-class Increasing works study the class-imbalanced domain adaptation (Tan et al., 2020; Lee et al., 2020; Bose et al., 2021; Li et al., 2020). COAL (Tan et al., 2020) deals with feature shift and label shift in a unified way. With the idea of prototype-based conditional distribution alignment and class-balanced self-training, COAL tackles feature shift in the context of label shift. However, present works only focus on computer vision, and the imbalanced class domain adaptation in NLP is unexplored. The other similar works is category-level feature alignment (Qu et al., 2019; Luo et al., 2019; Li et al., 2021, 2019; Yang et al., 2020). These works usually focus on domain shifts and propose domain-level aligned strategies while ignoring the local category-level distributions, reducing cross-domain text classifiers' effectiveness. A popular strategy for category-level alignment is aligning the same class features among different domains respectively by resorting to pseudo labels (Dong et al., 2020; Yang et al., 2020).

6 Conclusion

In this study, we have proposed an unsupervised reinforcement adaptation model (URAM) for the novel cross-domain adaptation challenge where the source and target domains are class-imbalanced. We demonstrate the effectiveness of our reinforcement approach with the other four state-of-art baselines on the task of text classification. The URAM learns domain-independent representations by leveraging three reward factors, label, domain, and domain distance, which coherently combines pivot and adversarial approaches in UDA. Extensive experiments and ablation analysis show that the URAM can obtain robust domain-invariant representations and effectively adapt text classifiers over both domains and imbalanced data.

6.1 Limitation and Future Work

Our work opens several future directions on the limitations of this study. First, class-imbalanced data naturally exist in NLP tasks, such as discourse inference (Spangher et al., 2021), text generation (Nishino et al., 2020), and question answering (Li et al., 2020). Our next step will examine the effectiveness of our model over the NLP tasks. Second, we only validate the URAM on English datasets, and additional multilingual settings will be verified in future work, such as multilingual text classification (Schwenk and Li, 2018).

7 Acknowledgement

The authors thank reviewers for their valuable comments. The work is partially supported by an internal award from the University of Memphis.

References

Eyal Ben-David, Carmel Rabinovitz, and Roi Reichart. 2020a. PERL: Pivot-based Domain Adaptation for Pre-trained Deep Contextualized Embedding Models. *Transactions of the Association for Computational Linguistics*, 8:504–521.

Eyal Ben-David, Carmel Rabinovitz, and Roi Reichart. 2020b. PERL: Pivot-based domain adaptation for pre-trained deep contextualized embedding models. *Transactions of the Association for Computational Linguistics*, 8:504–521.

John Blitzer, Ryan McDonald, and Fernando Pereira. 2006. Domain adaptation with structural correspondence learning. In *Proceedings of the 2006 Conference on Empirical Methods in Natural Language Processing*, pages 120–128, Sydney, Australia. Association for Computational Linguistics.

Tulika Bose, Irina Illina, and Dominique Fohr. 2021. Unsupervised domain adaptation in cross-corpora abusive language detection. In *Proceedings of the Ninth International Workshop on Natural Language Processing for Social Media*, pages 113–122, Online. Association for Computational Linguistics.

Jin Chen, Xinxiao Wu, Lixin Duan, and Shenghua Gao. 2020a. Domain adversarial reinforcement learning for partial domain adaptation. *IEEE Transactions on Neural Networks and Learning Systems*, pages 1–15.

Minghao Chen, Shuai Zhao, Haifeng Liu, and Deng Cai. 2020b. Adversarial-learned loss for domain adaptation. In *Proceedings of the AAAI Conference on Artificial Intelligence*, volume 34, pages 3521–3528.

Lu Cheng, Ruocheng Guo, K Selçuk Candan, and Huan Liu. 2020. Representation learning for imbalanced cross-domain classification. In *Proceedings of the 2020 SIAM international conference on data mining*, pages 478–486. SIAM.

Xia Cui, Frans Coenen, and Danushka Bollegala. 2017. Effect of data imbalance on unsupervised domain adaptation of part-of-speech tagging and pivot selection strategies. In *First International Workshop on Learning with Imbalanced Domains: Theory and Applications*, pages 103–115. PMLR.

Hal Daumé III. 2007. Frustratingly easy domain adaptation. In *Proceedings of the 45th Annual Meeting of the Association of Computational Linguistics*, pages 256–263.

Jacob Devlin, Ming-Wei Chang, Kenton Lee, and Kristina Toutanova. 2019. BERT: Pre-training of deep bidirectional transformers for language understanding. In *Proceedings of the 2019 Conference of the North American Chapter of the Association for Computational Linguistics: Human Language Technologies, Volume 1 (Long and Short Papers)*, pages 4171–4186, Minneapolis, Minnesota. Association for Computational Linguistics.

Jiahua Dong, Yang Cong, Gan Sun, Yuyang Liu, and Xiaowei Xu. 2020. Cscl: Critical semantic-consistent learning for unsupervised domain adaptation. In *Computer Vision – ECCV 2020*, pages 745–762, Cham. Springer International Publishing.

Chunning Du, Haifeng Sun, Jingyu Wang, Qi Qi, and Jianxin Liao. 2020. Adversarial and domain-aware BERT for cross-domain sentiment analysis. In *Proceedings of the 58th Annual Meeting of the Association for Computational Linguistics*, pages 4019–4028, Online. Association for Computational Linguistics.

Kilian Fatras, Thibault Séjourné, Nicolas Courty, and Rémi Flamary. 2021. Unbalanced minibatch optimal transport; applications to domain adaptation. *CoRR*, abs/2103.03606.

Yaroslav Ganin and Victor Lempitsky. 2015. Unsupervised domain adaptation by backpropagation. In *Proceedings of the 32nd International Conference on International Conference on Machine Learning - Volume 37*, ICML'15, page 1180–1189. JMLR.org.

Chenggong Gong, Jianfei Yu, and Rui Xia. 2020. Unified feature and instance based domain adaptation for aspect-based sentiment analysis. In *Proceedings of the 2020 Conference on Empirical Methods in Natural Language Processing (EMNLP)*, pages 7035–7045, Online. Association for Computational Linguistics.

Sepp Hochreiter and Jürgen Schmidhuber. 1997. Long short-term memory. *Neural Comput.*, 9(8):1735–1780.

Joe Hoover, Gwenyth Portillo-Wightman, Leigh Yeh, Shreya Havaldar, Aida Mostafazadeh Davani, Ying Lin, Brendan Kennedy, Mohammad Atari, Zahra Kamel, Madelyn Mendlen, Gabriela Moreno, Christina Park, Tingyee E. Chang, Jenna Chin, Christian Leong, Jun Yen Leung, Arineh Mirinjian, and Morteza Dehghani. 2020. Moral foundations twitter corpus: A collection of 35k tweets annotated for moral sentiment. *Social Psychological and Personality Science*, 11(8):1057–1071.

Jing Jiang and ChengXiang Zhai. 2007. Instance weighting for domain adaptation in NLP. In *Proceedings of the 45th Annual Meeting of the Association of Computational Linguistics*, pages 264–271, Prague, Czech Republic. Association for Computational Linguistics.

Diederik P. Kingma and Jimmy Ba. 2015. Adam: A method for stochastic optimization. In *3rd International Conference on Learning Representations, ICLR 2015, San Diego, CA, USA, May 7-9, 2015, Conference Track Proceedings*.

Vijay Konda and John Tsitsiklis. 2000. Actor-critic algorithms. In *Advances in Neural Information Processing Systems*, volume 12. MIT Press.

Suhyeon Lee, Junhyuk Hyun, Hongje Seong, and Euntai Kim. 2020. Unsupervised domain adaptation for semantic segmentation by content transfer. *CoRR*, abs/2012.12545.

Lusi Li, Haibo He, Jie Li, and Guang Yang. 2019. Adversarial domain adaptation via category transfer. In *2019 International Joint Conference on Neural Networks (IJCNN)*, pages 1–8.

Shuai Li, Jianqiang Huang, Xiansheng Hua, and Lei Zhang. 2021. Category dictionary guided unsupervised domain adaptation for object detection. In *AAAI*.

Xiaoya Li, Xiaofei Sun, Yuxian Meng, Junjun Liang, Fei Wu, and Jiwei Li. 2020. Dice loss for data-imbalanced NLP tasks. In *Proceedings of the 58th Annual Meeting of the Association for Computational Linguistics*, pages 465–476, Online. Association for Computational Linguistics.

Mingsheng Long, ZHANGJIE CAO, Jianmin Wang, and Michael I Jordan. 2018. Conditional adversarial domain adaptation. In *Advances in Neural Information Processing Systems*, volume 31, page 11. Curran Associates, Inc.

Yawei Luo, Liang Zheng, Tao Guan, Junqing Yu, and Yi Yang. 2019. Taking a closer look at domain shift: Category-level adversaries for semantics consistent domain adaptation. In *2019 IEEE/CVF Conference on Computer Vision and Pattern Recognition (CVPR)*, pages 2502–2511.

Jianmo Ni, Jiacheng Li, and Julian McAuley. 2019. Justifying recommendations using distantly-labeled reviews and fine-grained aspects. In *Proceedings of the 2019 Conference on Empirical Methods in Natural Language Processing and the 9th International Joint Conference on Natural Language Processing (EMNLP-IJCNLP)*, pages 188–197, Hong Kong, China. Association for Computational Linguistics.

Toru Nishino, Ryota Ozaki, Yohei Momoki, Tomoki Taniguchi, Ryuji Kano, Norihisa Nakano, Yuki Tagawa, Motoki Taniguchi, Tomoko Ohkuma, and Keigo Nakamura. 2020. Reinforcement learning with imbalanced dataset for data-to-text medical report generation. In *Findings of the Association for Computational Linguistics: EMNLP 2020*, pages 2223–2236, Online. Association for Computational Linguistics.

Jeffrey Pennington, Richard Socher, and Christopher D. Manning. 2014. Glove: Global vectors for word representation. In *Empirical Methods in Natural Language Processing (EMNLP)*, pages 1532–1543.

Xiaoye Qu, Zhikang Zou, Yu Cheng, Yang Yang, and Pan Zhou. 2019. Adversarial category alignment network for cross-domain sentiment classification. In *Proceedings of the 2019 Conference of the North American Chapter of the Association for Computational Linguistics: Human Language Technologies, Volume 1 (Long and Short Papers)*, pages 2496–2508, Minneapolis, Minnesota. Association for Computational Linguistics.

Alan Ramponi and Barbara Plank. 2020. Neural unsupervised domain adaptation in NLP—A survey. In *Proceedings of the 28th International Conference on Computational Linguistics*, pages 6838–6855, Barcelona, Spain (Online). International Committee on Computational Linguistics.

Kuniaki Saito, Kohei Watanabe, Y. Ushiku, and Tatsuya Harada. 2018a. Maximum classifier discrepancy for unsupervised domain adaptation. *2018 IEEE/CVF Conference on Computer Vision and Pattern Recognition*, pages 3723–3732.

Kuniaki Saito, Kohei Watanabe, Yoshitaka Ushiku, and Tatsuya Harada. 2018b. Maximum classifier discrepancy for unsupervised domain adaptation. In *2018 IEEE/CVF Conference on Computer Vision and Pattern Recognition*, pages 3723–3732.

Holger Schwenk and Xian Li. 2018. A corpus for multilingual document classification in eight languages. In *Proceedings of the Eleventh International Conference on Language Resources and Evaluation (LREC 2018)*, Miyazaki, Japan. European Language Resources Association (ELRA).

Alexander Spangher, Jonathan May, Sz-Rung Shiang, and Lingjia Deng. 2021. Multitask semi-supervised learning for class-imbalanced discourse classification. In *Proceedings of the 2021 Conference on Empirical Methods in Natural Language Processing*, pages 498–517, Online and Punta Cana, Dominican Republic. Association for Computational Linguistics.

Shuhan Tan, Xingchao Peng, and Kate Saenko. 2020. Class-imbalanced domain adaptation: An empirical odyssey. In *Computer Vision – ECCV 2020 Workshops*, pages 585–602, Cham. Springer International Publishing.

Zhi Wang, Wei Bi, Yan Wang, and Xiaojiang Liu. 2019. Better fine-tuning via instance weighting for text classification. In *Proceedings of the Thirty-Third AAAI Conference on Artificial Intelligence and Thirty-First Innovative Applications of Artificial Intelligence Conference and Ninth AAAI Symposium on Educational Advances in Artificial Intelligence*, AAAI'19/IAAI'19/EAAI'19. AAAI Press.

Thomas Wolf, Lysandre Debut, Victor Sanh, Julien Chaumond, Clement Delangue, Anthony Moi, Pierric Cistac, Tim Rault, Remi Louf, Morgan Funtowicz, Joe Davison, Sam Shleifer, Patrick von Platen, Clara Ma, Yacine Jernite, Julien Plu, Canwen Xu, Teven Le Scao, Sylvain Gugger, Mariama Drame, Quentin Lhoest, and Alexander Rush. 2020. Transformers: State-of-the-art natural language processing. In *Proceedings of the 2020 Conference on Empirical Methods in Natural Language Processing: System Demonstrations*, pages 38–45, Online. Association for Computational Linguistics.

Guanglei Yang, Haifeng Xia, Mingli Ding, and Zhengming Ding. 2020. Bi-directional generation for unsupervised domain adaptation. In *Proceedings of the AAAI Conference on Artificial Intelligence*, volume 34, pages 6615–6622.

Youshan Zhang, Hui Ye, and Brian D. Davison. 2021. Adversarial reinforcement learning for unsupervised domain adaptation. In *2021 IEEE Winter Conference on Applications of Computer Vision (WACV)*, pages 635–644.

Yftah Ziser and Roi Reichart. 2018. Pivot based language modeling for improved neural domain adaptation. In *Proceedings of the 2018 Conference of the North American Chapter of the Association for Computational Linguistics: Human Language Technologies, Volume 1 (Long Papers)*, pages 1241–1251, New Orleans, Louisiana. Association for Computational Linguistics.

A Additional Data Statistics

In this section, we summarize additional data and label statistics in Table 6 and 7.

	Docs	Tokens	pos/neg
D-DVD	2000	30.51	2.52
E-Electronic	2000	27.65	2.26

Table 6: Stats of the Amazon review data. We present the average number of tokens and the imbalanced-class ratio.

B Cross-domain Evaluations

dataset	Non-moral	Degradation	Harm	Fairness	Subversion	Care	Cheating	Purity	Betrayal	Authority	Loyalty
MeToo	21.40	15,30	6.86	6.30	14.70	3.40	11.00	2.98	5.83	6.93	5.29
BLM	23.59	4.23	19.36	8.58	5.74	5.93	13.84	2.76	2.71	5.40	7.83
Sandy	13.68	1.94	1.69	3.82	9.63	21.30	9.80	1.45	3.12	9.46	8.86
Davidson	92.13	1.34	2.76	0.08	0.14	0.18	1.24	0.10	0.82	0.40	0.82
Baltimore	54.93	0.55	4.86	2.60	5.34	3.26	9.38	0.69	11.18	0.40	6.83
ALM	20.98	3.18	19.15	13.42	2.37	11.88	13.16	2.11	1.04	6.36	6.36
Election	47.70	2.13	9.09	8.66	2.55	6.15	9.59	6.32	1.98	2.61	3.20

Table 7: Label distributions of the multi-class morality dataset (Hoover et al., 2020)

No-adapt	MeToo	BLM	Sandy	Davidson	Baltimore	ALM	Election
MeToo	47.16	18.09	6.28	35.61	29.58	14.61	16.95
BLM	16.23	76.32	17.22	26.27	25.28	16.16	26.40
Sandy	8.81	14.46	58.50	19.27	7.49	15.68	9.04
Davidson	23.12	31.98	8.09	99.17	66.96	24.93	58.49
Baltimore	23.32	32.42	10.07	99.17	66.54	25.00	59.09
ALM	12.11	17.60	14.27	24.88	25.12	43.71	20.33
Election	23.18	32.59	15.24	99.11	66.57	24.95	58.87
DANN	MeToo	BLM	Sandy	Davidson	Baltimore	ALM	Election
MeToo	40.03	17.98	9.74	45.00	20.65	13.69	24.30
BLM	16.33	75.40	15.48	35.68	22.94	17.82	24.39
Sandy	8.37	14.55	56.84	6.78	6.47	14.65	9.34
Davidson	23.17	31.98	8.17	99.17	66.96	24.93	58.49
Baltimore	23.17	32.42	9.82	99.17	66.24	24.95	59.03
ALM	12.63	16.78	14.93	19.18	20.87	60.88	17.26
Election	23.14	32.57	14.23	99.17	66.57	24.93	64.01
ALDA	MeToo	BLM	Sandy	Davidson	Baltimore	ALM	Election
MeToo	21.50	25.89	14.17	38.21	1.12	9.84	58.75
BLM	14.82	56.82	13.97	51.90	39.98	16.53	23.39
Sandy	23.36	14.23	34.84	33.81	6.01	22.06	28.03
Davidson	23.31	31.99	26.59	99.17	66.96	32.31	58.49
Baltimore	23.03	31.63	8.77	42.12	65.33	25.50	28.77
ALM	22.43	14.83	5.94	31.16	58.96	38.50	37.35
Election	25.44	39.70	19.16	98.32	66.54	23.17	58.87

MCD	MeToo	BLM	Sandy	Davidson	Baltimore	ALM	Election
MeToo	48.14	25.86	13.77	40.25	38.86	22.81	32.41
BLM	16.48	78.42	17.27	29.17	55.27	23.40	34.51
Sandy	24.37	16.68	60.17	15.74	32.50	16.52	12.58
Davidson	23.62	31.99	13.94	99.17	66.96	25.73	58.49
Baltimore	23.12	32.44	14.80	99.17	66.21	24.93	59.09
ALM	16.88	23.37	15.48	37.11	34.33	63.18	25.22
Election	23.12	32.53	14.10	99.17	66.54	24.93	63.91
JUMBOT	MeToo	BLM	Sandy	Davidson	Baltimore	ALM	Election
MeToo	43.12	28.32	10.47	46.94	42.33	21.08	36.11
BLM	24.37	72.57	16.02	52.20	48.92	32.18	48.91
Sandy	19.34	33.17	57.60	10.86	41.23	30.86	39.59
Davidson	23.26	32.99	8.35	99.17	66.96	26.64	58.49
Baltimore	23.48	32.66	12.16	99.17	66.18	25.03	59.09
ALM	23.30	39.82	17.04	66.60	61.70	42.01	46.50
Election	23.12	32.49	15.20	99.17	66.42	24.93	60.41
URAM	MeToo	BLM	Sandy	Davidson	Baltimore	ALM	Election
MeToo	45.54	19.34	10.48	47.07	38.14	16.97	34.80
BLM	16.03	79.12	15.86	50.31	30.57	18.56	26.74
Sandy	9.28	14.65	60.44	10.50	10.28	15.28	8.86
Davidson	24.00	32.53	11.59	99.17	66.96	25.02	58.49
Baltimore	23.10	28.57	12.09	98.96	63.52	24.93	53.43
ALM	12.58	16.51	15.70	34.43	27.88	63.11	17.29
Election	22.54	31.92	12.38	99.06	58.10	24.88	65.23

Table 8: Cross-domain performance evaluation over the Morality dataset (Hoover et al., 2020) using F1. Each subtable presents results of one UDA model.

	book-dvd	dvd-book	book-eletronic	eletronic-book	kitchen-eletronic	eletronic-kitchen	dvd-kitchen	kitchen-dvd	dvd-eletroic	eletronic-dvd
DANN	83.16	94.00	86.87	92.15	95.24	91.21	94.24	94.29	94.63	92.57
MCD	84.39	94.34	85.06	93.36	94.08	91.61	94.14	94.99	94.22	92.54
JUMBOT	82.27	91.51	77.34	84.83	92.91	85.58	92.49	94.01	91.64	92.23
ALDA	84.49	93.52	84.14	94.49	93.93	92.39	92.70	94.21	94.00	90.91
URAM	86.56	94.58	87.90	93.51	94.96	92.87	94.81	95.15	95.03	93.02

Table 9: Cross-domain performance evaluation over the Amazon review dataset (Blitzer et al., 2006).

Event Causality Identification via Generation of Important Context Words

Hieu Man[1], **Minh Van Nguyen**[2], **and Thien Huu Nguyen**[2]
[1] VinAI Research, Vietnam
[2] Dept. of Computer and Information Science, University of Oregon, Eugene, OR, USA
v.hieumdt@vinai.io,
{minhnv,thien}@cs.uoregon.edu

Abstract

An important problem of Information Extraction involves Event Causality Identification (ECI) that seeks to identify causal relation between pairs of event mentions. Prior models for ECI have mainly solved the problem using the classification framework that does not explore prediction/generation of important context words from input sentences for causal recognition. In this work, we consider the words along the dependency path between the two event mentions in the dependency tree as the important context words for ECI. We introduce dependency path generation as a complementary task for ECI, which can be solved jointly with causal label prediction to improve the performance. To facilitate the multi-task learning, we cast ECI into a generation problem that aims to generate both causal relation and dependency path words from input sentence. In addition, we propose to use the REINFORCE algorithm to train our generative model where novel reward functions are designed to capture both causal prediction accuracy and generation quality. The experiments on two benchmark datasets demonstrate state-of-the-art performance of the proposed model for ECI.

1 Introduction

In Information Extraction (IE), Event Causality Identification (ECI) aims to predict causal relation between a pair of events mentioned in text. For instance, in the sentence "*Massive fires cause major damages in the downtown area.*", an ECI system needs to realize the causal relation between the two events triggered by "*fires*" and "*damages*" (called event mentions), i.e., "*fires*" $\xrightarrow{\text{cause}}$ "*damages*". ECI is an important problem with many applications in NLP (Hashimoto, 2019; Berant et al., 2014).

Compared to the feature-based methods (Do et al., 2011; Ning et al., 2018), recent deep learning models have demonstrated their state-of-the-art performance for ECI (Kadowaki et al., 2019; Liu et al., 2020; Zuo et al., 2021). As such, prior work has mainly treated ECI as a classification problem where the only output from the models is a label to indicate causal or non-causal relation between input events. A major issue with this classification formulation is that current ECI models do not output important contexts for causal prediction of two event mentions. In this work, important contexts refer to the words in the input sentence that are critical to reveal the causal relation between two given event mentions (e.g., the words "*caused*" and "*by*" in our example). This limitation of current ECI models is undesirable as we expect that including important context words as a part of the outputs for ECI models can improve the training signals for the models. In particular, motivated by relation exaction models in IE (Zhang et al., 2018), we use the words along the dependency path between the two event mentions in the dependency tree to represent important context words for ECI. Our intuition is that dependency path generation is a related/complementary task for causal label prediction in ECI, and training a model to jointly generate causal labels and dependency path words (i.e., multi-task learning) can boost the performance.

A potential challenge with this idea involves the varying number of dependency path words where the generation of a context word or causal label might need to condition on previously generated ones (e.g., dependencies at the output level). As the result, such dependencies make it difficult to extend existing classification-based ECI models to perform multi-task learning with important context prediction. To address this issue, we propose to solve ECI via a new generative formulation: given a pair of event mentions in an input sentence, our ECI model aims to simultaneously generate causal label and the dependency path words between the two event mentions. In our model, causal label and dependency path words are combined into a single output sequence that will be generated by a

Proceedings of the 11th Joint Conference on Lexical and Computational Semantics, pages 323 - 330
July 14-15, 2022 ©2022 Association for Computational Linguistics

generative model from the input sentences in an autoregressive fashion, thus facilitating the encoding of dependencies between output words in our multi-task learning idea. Finally, to solve the resulting sequence-to-sequence problem for ECI, we leverage the generative pre-trained language model T5 (Raffel et al., 2020). To our knowledge, this is the first work to use generative models to solve ECI. The generation of dependency paths for relation extraction problems is also novel in IE.

Following prior work that reformulates NLP tasks into generative problems (Paolini et al., 2021; Zhang et al., 2021), we can train the generative model for ECI by maximizing the likelihood of the golden output sequences. However, this approach suffers from a potential mismatch between the used optimization objective (i.e., the likelihood) and the targeted performance measure (e.g., the accuracy for event causal prediction). In addition, as the words along the dependency paths might outnumber the causal label in the output sequence, likelihood maximization training will downgrade the importance of causal labels as a training signal in our multi-task learning framework for ECI. To this end, we propose to train our generative model for ECI using the policy-gradient method REINFORCE (Williams, 1992) that allows us to directly treat the targeted performance measure as the reward to train the generative model. Our training reward will contain separate terms for the accuracy of the predicted causal labels and the similarity of the generated and golden output sequences to allow an emphasis on the ECI performance for training. We also present a new auxiliary reward that encourages the similarity between predicted and input sentences with respect to the causal prediction ability to enrich the training signals. Finally, we conduct experiments on two benchmark datasets, demonstrating advantages of the proposed model with state-of-the-art performance for ECI.

2 Model

Given a sentence W and two event mentions e_s and e_t in W, ECI aims to predict whether e_s and e_t are involved in a causal relation in W. In this work, we depart from the traditional classification formulation (Tran and Nguyen, 2021) to a generative approach for ECI. Our generative model follows the sequence-to-sequence setting where the input sequence should capture the input sentence W along with the two event mentions e_s and e_t. In contrast, the output sentence will include the causal label and the dependency path between e_s and e_t in the dependency tree of W to achieve multi-task learning with important context word generation. To this end, the input I for our generative ECI model is obtained by combining W and a prompt $P(e_s, e_t)$ to specify the two input event mentions and the goal of ECI, i.e., $I = W : P(e_s, e_t)$. In this work, we use a simple template for $P(e_s, e_t)$ in the form of "*Is there a causal relation between e_s and e_t?*". As such, the output sequence O is then formed using the concatenation: $O = l, D(e_s, e_t)$ (called golden output). Here, l is either "*Yes*" or "*No*" to indicate the existence of a causal relation between e_s and e_t (i.e., causal label) while $D(e_s, e_t)$ represents the dependency path between e_s and e_t in W. In our example, the input and output sequences are:

I: Massive fires cause major damages in the downtown area: Is there a causal relation between fires and damages?

O: Yes, fires cause damages

Given the transformed input-output pair (I, O) for every example in the training data of ECI, we adopt the pre-trained tranformer-based language model T5 (Raffel et al., 2020) to solve the resulting sequence-to-sequence problem. In particular, we train T5 on the transformed input-output pairs (I, O) from ECI training data. At inference time, given an input sentence and two event mentions, we use the trained T5 model to generate the output sequence (with greedy decoding) from which the causal label can be extracted from the first token (i.e., l in O) to serve as the prediction.

Training: As presented in the introduction, to employ label accuracy as the direct training signal, we propose to leverage the REINFORCE algorithm (Williams, 1992) to train our T5 model for ECI where label accuracy will be used to form the reward function. In addition, the flexibility of REINFORCE allows us to include the similarity between the predicted output sequence, denoted by C, from T5 and the golden output O and input I as terms in the reward function to train our generative model. As such, we propose the following information for the reward function $R(C)$ for REINFORCE:

• **Performance-based Reward** $R^{per}(C)$: We compute this reward based on the accuracy of the causal label p in the generated sequence C (i.e., the first token of either "*Yes*" or "*No*"). In particular, $R^{per}(C) = 1$ if p is consistent with the provided relation between e_s and e_t in W, and 0 otherwise.

• **Output-based Reward** $R^{out}(C)$: This reward aims to encourage the similarity between the generated sequence C and the golden output sequence O to train the generative model T5. As such, we employ the ROUGE-2 measure (Lin, 2004) between C and O for this reward term: $R^{gold}(C)$ = ROGUE-2(C, O)[1].

• **Input-based Reward** $R^{in}(C)$: Our goal is to generate the dependency path between e_s and e_t for multi-task learning for ECI. Given that the dependency path is expected to contain important contexts in W to reveal the causal relation and the input I is customized for the causal prediction purpose, we argue that the input and output sequences I and O should have similar meanings. Based on that intuition, we introduce a novel reward term $R^{in}(C)$ to promote the similarity between the generated sequence C from T5 and the input sequence I. In particular, we first send C and I (prepended with the special tokens </s>) to the encoder of T5. The vectors for </s> in the last transformer layer for C and I are then used for their representation vectors $V(C)$ and $V(I)$ respectively. Finally, the reward $R^{in}(C)$ is computed via the representation similarity, i.e., $R^{in}(C) = cosine(V(C), V(I))$.

Consequently, the overall reward function $R(C)$ to train our T5 model for ECI is: $R(C) = \alpha_{per} R^{per}(C) + \alpha_{out} R^{out}(C) + \alpha_{in} R^{in}(C)$ (α_{per}, α_{out}, and α_{in} are trade-off parameters). In this way, we can explicitly make sure that label accuracy (i.e., our main performance goal) is well represented and not dominated by the generation rewards in the training. Let $P(C|I)$ be the distribution over generated sequences that T5 induces. In our model, REINFORCE trains T5 by minimizing the negative expected reward $R(C)$ over the possible choices of C from T5: $\mathcal{L} = -\mathbb{E}_{C' \sim P(C'|I)}[R(C')]$. Using policy gradient and one roll-out sample with the generated sequence C, the gradient of $\mathcal{L}$ can be estimated for training via: $\nabla \mathcal{L} = -(R(C) - b) \nabla \log P(C|I)$ where b is a baseline to reduce variance. Here, we obtain the baseline b via: $b = \frac{1}{|B|} \sum_{q=1}^{|B|} R(C^q)$, where $|B|$ is the mini-batch size and C^q is the generated sequence for the q-th sample.

Finally, before REINFORCE training, we first bootstrap T5 by training it over the transformed pairs (I, O) with maximum likelihood objective. This helps constrain the large action space with text generation to improve the learning for REINFORCE (Ranzato et al., 2016; Paulus et al., 2018).

[1]We have tried BLUE, METEROR, and other variants of ROUGE; however, ROUGE-2 leads to the best performance.

3 Experiments

Datasets and Hyperparameters: We evaluate our proposed generative model, called **GenECI**, on two benchmark English datasets for ECI, i.e., EventStoryLine and Causal-TimeBank. Proposed by (Caselli and Vossen, 2017), EventStoryLine (i.e., version 0.9) involves 258 documents, 22 topics, 4316 sentences, 5334 event mentions, and 1770 of 7805 event mention pairs with causal relation in a sentence. Following the same data split in previous work (Tran and Nguyen, 2021; Zuo et al., 2021), we utilize the last two topics in EventStoryLine for the development data while the remaining 20 topics are used for 5-fold cross-validation evaluation. For Causal-TimeBank (Mirza, 2014a), there are 184 documents, 6813 event mentions, and 318 of 7608 event mention pairs annotated with causal relation. Using the same setting and data split as previous work (Liu et al., 2020; Zuo et al., 2021), we perform 10-fold cross-validation evaluation.

We tune the hyperparameters for GenECI on the development data of EventStoryLine; the chosen parameters are employed to train the models for both EventStoryLine and Causal-TimeBank. The selected hyperparameters from our tuning process involve: $5e$-5 for the learning rate with the Adam optimizer; 32 for the mini-batch size; and 1.0, 0.5 and 0.1 for the trade-off-parameters α_{per}, α_{out} and α_{in} (respectively) in the overall reward function $R(C)$. Finally, we use the base version of T5 (Raffel et al., 2020) for the generative model in this work.

Comparison: We compare our model with the state-of-the-art (SOTA) models for ECI. For EventStoryLine, we consider the following baselines: (1) **LSTM** (Gao et al., 2019) adopted from (Cheng and Miyao, 2017); (2) **Seq** (Gao et al., 2019) adopted from (Choubey and Huang, 2017) for ECI; and (3) **LR+** and **LIP** (Gao et al., 2019): document structure-based models for ECI. For Causal-TimeBank, we evaluate **RB**: a rule-based system in (Mirza, 2014b), and **ML**: a feature-based model for ECI in (Mirza, 2014a). For both datasets, we also compare with the following BERT-based models for ECI: (i) **BERT**: a BERT-based baseline in (Zuo et al., 2021); (ii) **KnowDis** (Zuo et al., 2020): a model with distant supervision; (iii) **Know** (Liu et al., 2020): a model with ConceptNet; (iv) **RichGCN** (Tran and Nguyen, 2021): a graph convolutional network with rich information, and (v) **LearnDA** (Zuo et al., 2021): a data augmentation method. **RichGCN** has the best reported performance on EventStoryLine while **LearnDA** is the current SOTA model for Causal-TimeBank. Finally, we also report the performance of **T5 Classify** that is similar to the classification-based model **BERT** (Zuo et al., 2021), but replaces the BERT encoder with the encoder from T5.

Model	EventStoryLine			Causal-TimeBank		
	P	R	F1	P	R	F1
LSTM	34.0	41.5	37.4	-	-	-
Seq	32.7	44.9	37.8	-	-	-
LR+	37.0	45.2	40.7	-	-	-
LIP	37.4	55.8	44.7	-	-	-
RB	-	-	-	36.8	12.3	18.4
ML	-	-	-	67.3	22.6	33.9
BERT	36.1	56.0	43.9	38.5	43.9	41.0
KnowDis	39.7	66.5	49.7	42.3	60.5	49.8
Know	41.9	62.5	50.1	36.6	55.6	44.1
RichGCN	49.2	63.0	55.2	39.7	56.5	46.7
LearnDA	42.2	69.8	52.6	41.9	68.0	51.9
T5 Classify	39.1	69.5	47.7	39.1	67.7	48.3
GenECI (ours)	59.5	57.1	**58.8**	60.1	53.3	**56.5**

Table 1: Model performance on two datasets.

Table 1 presents the performance of the models on two datasets. The most important observation is that GenECI significantly outperforms ($p < 0.01$) the baseline models with substantial gaps on both datasets (e.g., 3.6% better than the second best model RichGCN on EventStoryLine using F1 score). Compared to "*T5 Classify*" that uses the same encoder as GenECI, it is clear that the generation-based approach with T5 is more beneficial for ECI than the classification-based method. In addition, we note that the baseline models for ECI often need external knowledge resources (e.g., ConceptNet) or additional training data (e.g., via data augmentation) to improve the performance. Our generative model does not require such resources to achieve the best performance.

Line	Model	P	R	F1
1	**GenECI** (full)	59.5	57.1	**58.8**
2	GenECI - $R^{per}(C)$	59.8	49.3	53.4
3	GenECI - $R^{out}(C)$	50.3	59.8	56.9
4	GenECI - $R^{in}(C)$	49.5	60.9	56.1
5	GenECI - ML pre-training	49.1	62.4	57.3
6	GenECI - dep path	57.0	53.9	55.4
7	Only ML training	60.0	53.5	55.7
8	Only ML training with no dep path	56.5	45.6	50.1

Table 2: Ablation study.

Ablation Study: This section studies the contribution of each designed component for GenECI. In particular, the major components in GenECI involve the dependency path generation, the REINFORCE training with different reward terms, and the maximum likelihood (ML) pre-training. Table 2 shows the performance of the ablated models on the test set of EventStoryLine when the components are eliminated from GenECI. As can be seen from lines 2, 3, 4, and 5, the proposed reward functions $R^{per}(C)$, $R^{out}(C)$, $R^{in}(C)$ and the ML pre-training are all important to produce best performance for GenECI. In line 6, we exclude the dependency paths from the output sequences O (i.e., O only contains the causal label), which essentially amounts to not using multi-task learning with dependency path generation for GenECI. This also leads to the exclusion of the reward terms $R^{out}(C)$ and $R^{in}(C)$ from $R(C)$. It is clear from the table that the performance of GenECI suffers significantly due to the dependency path removal, verifying the effectiveness of multi-task learning with dependency paths for ECI. Next, in lines 7 and 8, we present the performance of T5 when it is only trained with the ML objective. As the performance of ML training is substantially worse, it suggests that REINFORCE training with the designed rewards is more effective for generative ECI.

Input Sentence	GenECI	ML Train
Iranian rescue workers handed out blankets, food and water Monday to survivors of a powerful ***earthquake*** *on a Gulf island that killed 10 people and forced villagers to* ***spend*** *the night in tents.*	Yes, earthquake killed forced spend	No, earthquake survivors handed forced spend
Power was ***restored*** *to the afflicted villages on the Gulf island of Qeshm after a blackout caused by the* ***quake****, which struck on Sunday with a force of about 6.0 on the Richter scale.*	No, restored blackout caused quake	Yes, restored caused quake

Table 3: Examples with successful generation of causal labels from GenECI and incorrect generation of causal labels from ML Training. Event mentions are highlighted. ML Training generates incorrect dependency paths that include irrelevant/noisy words (e.g., "*survivors*" and "*handed*" in the first example) or miss important context words (e.g., "*blackout*" in the second example). Such missing or irrelevant information suggests inability to encode important context for successful causal label prediction.

Analysis: To better understand the operation of GenECI, we analyze the examples in EventStoryLine that are successfully predicted by GenECI, but cannot be recognized correctly by the ML training model (i.e., only training T5 with maximum likelihood objective). Our main finding from the analysis is that GenECI can generate correct dependency paths between two given event mentions that demonstrates the ability to learn necessary context for successful prediction. In contrast, ML training tends to produce incorrect dependency paths (i.e., including irrelevant words or missing important words), thus showing limited representation learning ability and leading to causal prediction failure. Table 3 presents two examples to demonstrate the effectiveness of GenECI and reveal issues for ML Training.

4 Related Work

In the early methods, ECI has been mostly approached by feature-based models (Beamer and Girju, 2009; Do et al., 2011; Riaz and Girju, 2014; Hidey and McKeown, 2016; Ning et al., 2018; Hashimoto, 2019; Gao et al., 2019). Recently, ECI has been further solved by deep learning models (Gao et al., 2019) where external knowledge and additional training data are leveraged to improve the performance (Liu et al., 2020; Zuo et al., 2020, 2021; Tran and Nguyen, 2021). We are different from such prior work as we are the first to model ECI via a generative model.

Using generative models for traditional classification-based problems has also been explored recently, e.g., for named entity recognition (Athiwaratkun et al., 2020; Yan et al., 2021), sentiment analysis (Zhang et al., 2021), and event extraction (Lu et al., 2021). However, none of such prior work considers generative models for ECI. Finally, we also note related work on extracting other types of relations between event triggers, including temporal relation (Ning et al., 2017; Leeuwenberg and Moens, 2017; Ning et al., 2018b; Tran Phu et al., 2021), subevent relation (Glavaš et al., 2014; Araki et al., 2014; Aldawsari and Finlayson, 2019; Man et al., 2022), and coreference relation (Nguyen et al., 2016; Choubey and Huang, 2018; Huang et al., 2019; Choubey et al., 2020; Phung et al., 2021; Minh Tran et al., 2021).

5 Conclusion

We introduce a novel model for ECI that solves the problem via a generation framework with the T5 model. Our model explores multi-task learning that jointly generates the dependency paths between two event mentions for ECI. We also introduce a training procedure based on REINFORCE and novel reward functions, which leads to the SOTA performance for ECI. In the future, we plan to extend the model to other relation extraction tasks.

Acknowledgement

This research has been supported by the Army Research Office (ARO) grant W911NF-21-1-0112 and the NSF grant CNS-1747798 to the IUCRC Center for Big Learning. This research is also based upon work supported by the Office of the Director of National Intelligence (ODNI), Intelligence Advanced Research Projects Activity (IARPA), via IARPA Contract No. 2019-19051600006 under the Better Extraction from Text Towards Enhanced Retrieval (BETTER) Program. The views and conclusions contained herein are those of the authors and should not be interpreted as necessarily representing the official policies, either expressed or implied, of ARO, ODNI, IARPA, the Department of Defense, or the U.S. Government. The U.S. Government is authorized to reproduce and distribute reprints for governmental purposes notwithstanding any copyright annotation therein. This document does not contain technology or technical data controlled under either the U.S. International Traffic in Arms Regulations or the U.S. Export Administration Regulations.

References

Mohammed Aldawsari and Mark Finlayson. 2019. Detecting subevents using discourse and narrative features. In *Proceedings of the 57th Annual Meeting of the Association for Computational Linguistics (ACL)*.

Jun Araki, Zhengzhong Liu, Eduard Hovy, and Teruko Mitamura. 2014. Detecting subevent structure for event coreference resolution. In *Proceedings of the Ninth International Conference on Language Resources and Evaluation (LREC)*.

Ben Athiwaratkun, Cicero Nogueira dos Santos, Jason Krone, and Bing Xiang. 2020. Augmented natural language for generative sequence labeling. In *Proceedings of the 2020 Conference on Empirical Methods in Natural Language Processing (EMNLP)*.

Brandon Beamer and Roxana Girju. 2009. Using a bigram event model to predict causal potential. In *CICLing*.

Jonathan Berant, Vivek Srikumar, Pei-Chun Chen, Abby Vander Linden, Brittany Harding, Brad Huang, Peter

Clark, and Christopher D. Manning. 2014. Modeling biological processes for reading comprehension. In *Proceedings of the 2014 Conference on Empirical Methods in Natural Language Processing (EMNLP)*, pages 1499–1510, Doha, Qatar. Association for Computational Linguistics.

Tommaso Caselli and Piek Vossen. 2017. The event StoryLine corpus: A new benchmark for causal and temporal relation extraction. In *Proceedings of the Events and Stories in the News Workshop*, pages 77–86, Vancouver, Canada. Association for Computational Linguistics.

Fei Cheng and Yusuke Miyao. 2017. Classifying temporal relations by bidirectional LSTM over dependency paths. In *Proceedings of the 55th Annual Meeting of the Association for Computational Linguistics (Volume 2: Short Papers)*, pages 1–6, Vancouver, Canada. Association for Computational Linguistics.

Prafulla Kumar Choubey and Ruihong Huang. 2017. A sequential model for classifying temporal relations between intra-sentence events. In *Proceedings of the 2017 Conference on Empirical Methods in Natural Language Processing*, pages 1796–1802, Copenhagen, Denmark. Association for Computational Linguistics.

Prafulla Kumar Choubey and Ruihong Huang. 2018. Improving event coreference resolution by modeling correlations between event coreference chains and document topic structures. In *Proceedings of the 56th Annual Meeting of the Association for Computational Linguistics (ACL)*.

Prafulla Kumar Choubey, Aaron Lee, Ruihong Huang, and Lu Wang. 2020. Discourse as a function of event: Profiling discourse structure in news articles around the main event. In *Proceedings of the 58th Annual Meeting of the Association for Computational Linguistics*, pages 5374–5386, Online. Association for Computational Linguistics.

Quang Do, Yee Seng Chan, and Dan Roth. 2011. Minimally supervised event causality identification. In *Proceedings of the 2011 Conference on Empirical Methods in Natural Language Processing*, pages 294–303, Edinburgh, Scotland, UK. Association for Computational Linguistics.

Lei Gao, Prafulla Kumar Choubey, and Ruihong Huang. 2019. Modeling document-level causal structures for event causal relation identification. In *Proceedings of the 2019 Conference of the North American Chapter of the Association for Computational Linguistics: Human Language Technologies, Volume 1 (Long and Short Papers)*, pages 1808–1817, Minneapolis, Minnesota. Association for Computational Linguistics.

Goran Glavaš, Jan Šnajder, Marie-Francine Moens, and Parisa Kordjamshidi. 2014. HiEve: A corpus for extracting event hierarchies from news stories. In *Proceedings of the Ninth International Conference on Language Resources and Evaluation (LREC)*.

Chikara Hashimoto. 2019. Weakly supervised multilingual causality extraction from Wikipedia. In *Proceedings of the 2019 Conference on Empirical Methods in Natural Language Processing and the 9th International Joint Conference on Natural Language Processing (EMNLP-IJCNLP)*, pages 2988–2999, Hong Kong, China. Association for Computational Linguistics.

Christopher Hidey and Kathy McKeown. 2016. Identifying causal relations using parallel Wikipedia articles. In *Proceedings of the 54th Annual Meeting of the Association for Computational Linguistics (Volume 1: Long Papers)*, pages 1424–1433, Berlin, Germany. Association for Computational Linguistics.

Yin Jou Huang, Jing Lu, Sadao Kurohashi, and Vincent Ng. 2019. Improving event coreference resolution by learning argument compatibility from unlabeled data. In *Proceedings of the 2019 Conference of the North American Chapter of the Association for Computational Linguistics: Human Language Technologies (NAACL-HLT)*.

Kazuma Kadowaki, Ryu Iida, Kentaro Torisawa, Jong-Hoon Oh, and Julien Kloetzer. 2019. Event causality recognition exploiting multiple annotators' judgments and background knowledge. In *Proceedings of the 2019 Conference on Empirical Methods in Natural Language Processing and the 9th International Joint Conference on Natural Language Processing (EMNLP-IJCNLP)*, pages 5816–5822, Hong Kong, China. Association for Computational Linguistics.

Artuur Leeuwenberg and Marie-Francine Moens. 2017. Structured learning for temporal relation extraction from clinical records. In *Proceedings of the Conference of the European Chapter of the Association for Computational Linguistics (EACL)*.

Chin-Yew Lin. 2004. ROUGE: A package for automatic evaluation of summaries. In *Text Summarization Branches Out*.

Jian Liu, Yubo Chen, and Jun Zhao. 2020. Knowledge enhanced event causality identification with mention masking generalizations. In *Proceedings of the Twenty-Ninth International Joint Conference on Artificial Intelligence, IJCAI-20*, pages 3608–3614. International Joint Conferences on Artificial Intelligence Organization.

Yaojie Lu, Hongyu Lin, Jin Xu, Xianpei Han, Jialong Tang, Annan Li, Le Sun, Meng Liao, and Shaoyi Chen. 2021. Text2Event: Controllable sequence-to-structure generation for end-to-end event extraction. In *Proceedings of the 59th Annual Meeting of the Association for Computational Linguistics and the 11th International Joint Conference on Natural Language Processing (ACL)*.

Hieu Man, Nghia Trung Ngo, Linh Van Ngo, and Thien Huu Nguyen. 2022. Selecting optimal context sentences for event-event relation extraction. In *Proceedings of the Conference on the Advancement of Artificial Intelligence (AAAI)*.

Hieu Minh Tran, Duy Phung, and Thien Huu Nguyen. 2021. Exploiting document structures and cluster consistencies for event coreference resolution. In *Proceedings of the 59th Annual Meeting of the Association for Computational Linguistics and the 11th International Joint Conference on Natural Language Processing (Volume 1: Long Papers)*, pages 4840–4850, Online. Association for Computational Linguistics.

Paramita Mirza. 2014a. Extracting temporal and causal relations between events. In *Proceedings of the ACL 2014 Student Research Workshop*, pages 10–17, Baltimore, Maryland, USA. Association for Computational Linguistics.

Paramita Mirza. 2014b. Fbk-hlt-time: a complete italian temporal processing system for eventi-evalita 2014. In *EVALITA*.

Thien Huu Nguyen, , Adam Meyers, and Ralph Grishman. 2016. New york university 2016 system for kbp event nugget: A deep learning approach. In *Proceedings of the Text Analysis Conference (TAC)*.

Qiang Ning, Zhili Feng, and Dan Roth. 2017. A structured learning approach to temporal relation extraction. In *Proceedings of the Conference on Empirical Methods in Natural Language Processing (EMNLP)*.

Qiang Ning, Zhili Feng, Hao Wu, and Dan Roth. 2018. Joint reasoning for temporal and causal relations. In *Proceedings of the 56th Annual Meeting of the Association for Computational Linguistics (Volume 1: Long Papers)*, pages 2278–2288, Melbourne, Australia. Association for Computational Linguistics.

Qiang Ning, Ben Zhou, Zhili Feng, Haoruo Peng, and Dan Roth. 2018b. CogCompTime: A tool for understanding time in natural language. In *Proceedings of the 2018 Conference on Empirical Methods in Natural Language Processing: System Demonstrations (EMNLP)*.

Giovanni Paolini, Ben Athiwaratkun, Jason Krone, Jie Ma, Alessandro Achille, Rishita Anubhai, Cicero dos Santos Nogueira, Bing Xiang, and Stefano Soatto. 2021. Structured prediction as translation between augmented natural languages. In *Proceedings of the 9th International Conference on Learning Representations (ICLR)*.

Romain Paulus, Caiming Xiong, and Richard Socher. 2018. A deep reinforced model for abstractive summarization. In *Proceedings of the International Conference on Learning Representations (ICLR)*.

Duy Phung, Tuan Ngo Nguyen, and Thien Huu Nguyen. 2021. Hierarchical graph convolutional networks for jointly resolving cross-document coreference of entity and event mentions. In *Proceedings of the Fifteenth Workshop on Graph-Based Methods for Natural Language Processing (TextGraphs-15)*, pages 32–41, Mexico City, Mexico. Association for Computational Linguistics.

Colin Raffel, Noam Shazeer, Adam Roberts, Katherine Lee, Sharan Narang, Michael Matena, Yanqi Zhou, Wei Li, and Peter J. Liu. 2020. Exploring the Limits of Transfer Learning with a Unified Text-to-Text Transformer. In *Journal of Machine Learning Research*.

Marc'Aurelio Ranzato, Sumit Chopra, Michael Auli, and Wojciech Zaremba. 2016. Sequence level training with recurrent neural networks. In *Proceedings of the International Conference on Learning Representations (ICLR)*.

Mehwish Riaz and Roxana Girju. 2014. In-depth exploitation of noun and verb semantics to identify causation in verb-noun pairs. In *SIGDIAL*.

Minh Phu Tran and Thien Huu Nguyen. 2021. Graph convolutional networks for event causality identification with rich document-level structures. In *Proceedings of the 2021 Conference of the North American Chapter of the Association for Computational Linguistics: Human Language Technologies*, pages 3480–3490, Online. Association for Computational Linguistics.

Minh Tran Phu, Minh Van Nguyen, and Thien Huu Nguyen. 2021. Fine-grained temporal relation extraction with ordered-neuron LSTM and graph convolutional networks. In *Proceedings of the Seventh Workshop on Noisy User-generated Text (W-NUT 2021)*, pages 35–45, Online. Association for Computational Linguistics.

Ronald J. Williams. 1992. Simple statistical gradient-following algorithms for connectionist reinforcement learning. In *Kluwer Academic*.

Hang Yan, Tao Gui, Junqi Dai, Qipeng Guo, Zheng Zhang, and Xipeng Qiu. 2021. A unified generative framework for various NER subtasks. In *Proceedings of the 59th Annual Meeting of the Association for Computational Linguistics and the 11th International Joint Conference on Natural Language Processing (ACL)*.

Wenxuan Zhang, Xin Li, Yang Deng, Lidong Bing, and Wai Lam. 2021. Towards generative aspect-based sentiment analysis. In *Proceedings of the 59th Annual Meeting of the Association for Computational Linguistics and the 11th International Joint Conference on Natural Language Processing (ACL)*.

Yuhao Zhang, Peng Qi, and Christopher D. Manning. 2018. Graph convolution over pruned dependency trees improves relation extraction. In *Proceedings of the 2018 Conference on Empirical Methods in Natural Language Processing*, pages 2205–2215, Brussels, Belgium. Association for Computational Linguistics.

Xinyu Zuo, Pengfei Cao, Yubo Chen, Kang Liu, Jun Zhao, Weihua Peng, and Yuguang Chen. 2021. LearnDA: Learnable knowledge-guided data augmentation for event causality identification. In *Proceedings of the 59th Annual Meeting of the Association for*

Computational Linguistics and the 11th International Joint Conference on Natural Language Processing (Volume 1: Long Papers), pages 3558–3571, Online. Association for Computational Linguistics.

Xinyu Zuo, Yubo Chen, Kang Liu, and Jun Zhao. 2020. KnowDis: Knowledge enhanced data augmentation for event causality detection via distant supervision. In *Proceedings of the 28th International Conference on Computational Linguistics*, pages 1544–1550, Barcelona, Spain (Online). International Committee on Computational Linguistics.

Capturing the Content of a Document through Complex Event Identification

Zheng Qi, Elior Sulem, Haoyu Wang, Xiaodong Yu, Dan Roth
Department of Computer and Information Science, University of Pennsylvania
{issacqzh, eliors, why16gzl, xdyu, danroth}@seas.upenn.edu

Abstract

Granular events, instantiated in a document by predicates, can usually be grouped into more general events, called *complex events*. Together, they capture the major content of the document. Recent work grouped granular events by defining event regions, filtering out sentences that are irrelevant to the main content. However, this approach assumes that a given complex event is always described in consecutive sentences, which does not always hold in practice. In this paper, we introduce the task of complex event identification. We address this task as a pipeline, first predicting whether two granular events mentioned in the text belong to the same complex event, independently of their position in the text, and then using this to cluster them into complex events. Due to the difficulty of predicting whether two granular events belong to the same complex event in isolation, we propose a context-augmented representation learning approach CONTEXTRL that adds additional context to better model the pairwise relation between granular events. We show that our approach outperforms strong baselines on the complex event identification task and further present a promising case study exploring the effectiveness of using complex events as input for document-level argument extraction.[1].

Five protesters were *(e2:killed)* when they were *(e3:attacked)* by an armed group. The armed group *(e5:attacked)* the demonstrators who have for days been staging their *(e7:protest)* against the military government. Many protesters are supporters of an ultraconservative Islamist candidate in *(e8:elections)* who was expelled from the election *(e10:race)* when it was *(e11:discovered)* that his mother held dual Egyptian-U.S citizenship. The *(e13:attack)* on Wednesday *(e14:wounded)* at least 50 protesters, and the attackers *(e15:used)* stones, sticks and Molotov cocktails.

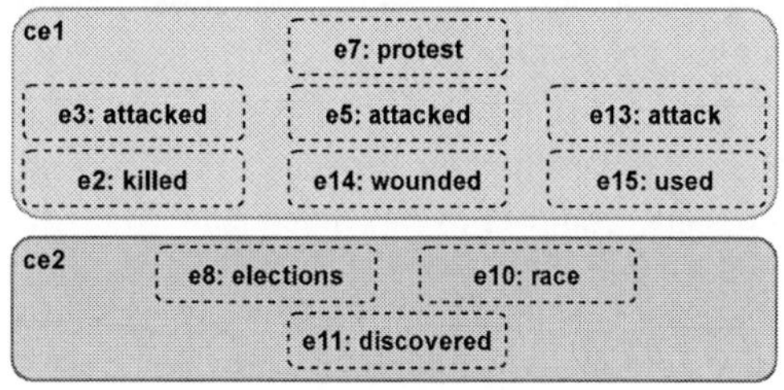

Figure 1: An example of complex events (ce1 and ce2) described in the document. For clarity, not all event mentions are shown in the figure.

1 Introduction

Event extraction aims to identify event predicates and arguments from text and then identify their types and roles respectively, helping humans to easily understand the events. It has attracted considerable interest in the last few years (Chen et al., 2015; Nguyen et al., 2016; Sha et al., 2018; Lin et al., 2020; Ebner et al., 2020; Chen et al., 2020b; Li et al., 2021) due to the vast amounts of unstructured text available in domains like e-commerce, healthcare and industry. However, considering each granular event instantiated in the document by a predicate in isolation is not sufficient for understanding the entire context of the document. Since granular events can be grouped into more general events, called *complex events*, we suggest using them to capture the major content of the document.

A document could contain any number of complex events where each complex event contains more than one granular event. For example, Figure 1 represents 10 granular events appearing in a document. One can group the granular events into two complex events as follows: (i) **ce1** (in green) that includes the granular events related to a protest, (ii) **ce2** (in red) that includes granular events that, taken together, describe elections. These two complex events represent the major two events that the text describes.

Recently, Chen et al. (2020a) used the notion of event regions, a byproduct of document-level argument extraction, by filtering out sentences that are irrelevant to the main content and then parti-

[1]The data and code are available at http://cogcomp.org/page/publication_view/978

Proceedings of the 11th Joint Conference on Lexical and Computational Semantics, pages 331 - 340
July 14-15, 2022 ©2022 Association for Computational Linguistics

tioning the text into several parts. Therefore, event regions are defined as consecutive sentences that include relevant arguments. However, compared to the complex event that groups related granular events together, the event region fails to capture the following two scenarios: (i) sentences that include granular events in the same complex event (e.g. the first and the last sentences in Figure 1) are separated by sentences that include granular events in another complex event; (ii) two granular events belonging to different complex events may appear in the same sentence.

Therefore, in this paper, we introduce the task of complex event identification which aims to group granular events instantiated by predicates into complex events, independently from the position of the predicates in the text. For example, in Figure 1, $e2$ and $e13$ belong to the same complex event (**ce1**) while $e8$ belongs to **ce2**.

To perform complex event identification, we first (i) predict whether two granular events belong to the same complex event, independently of their positions in the document, and then (ii) cluster them into complex events based on the pairwise relation predicted from step (i).

However, only considering the joint representations of two granular events is not sufficient to model the pairwise relation. For example, in Figure 1, it is difficult to infer that "demonstrators have for days been staging their *protest* against the government" ($e7$) and "the attackers *used* stones, sticks and Molotov cocktails" ($e15$) belong to the same complex event until we know that "The armed group *attacked* the demonstrators" ($e5$). Moreover, since both "demonstrators have for days been staging their *protest* against the government" ($e7$) and "Many protesters are supporters of a candidate in *elections*" ($e8$) mention some information about the protest, they might be considered to be in the same complex event. However, after reading more parts of the document, we know that $e8$ belong to the election complex event (**ce2**), which occurs before the protest complex event (**ce1**) containing $e7$.

Hence, we propose a context-augmented representation learning approach CONTEXTRL that adds additional context to model the pairwise complex event relation. Specifically, we compute the attention distribution of other granular events in the document based on the joint representation of two granular events and select the one with the highest score as the context event. Regarding two granular events as a single entity, if they belong to the same complex event, the system would add a granular event in the same complex event, to improve the expressiveness of their relatedness; if they are not in the same complex event, then the system would add an additional granular event to make them more distinguishable, relative to this context event.

Since there is not a dataset tailored to the task of complex event identification, we derive the complex event annotation from the HiEve dataset (Glavaš et al., 2014) that focuses on event-event relations. We show that our proposed approach outperforms strong baselines.

Moreover, since related granular events are grouped into the same complex event, the scope of the complex event is supposed to include all the information required for the prediction of the arguments of its granular events. Hence, we conduct a case study on the WIKIEVENTS dataset (Li et al., 2021) to explore the effectiveness of using complex events as the input for the document-level argument extraction task. We show that, when enough granular events are annotated, using complex events as input filters out noisy and irrelevant information, motivating the model to only focus on the related granular events.

The major contributions of this paper can be summarized as follows:

1. We introduce the complex event identification task that allows one to group related granular events, independently from the position of the predicates in the text, into complex events that, together, capture the major content of the document.

2. We present a context-augmented representation learning approach CONTEXTRL tailored to this task, showing that this approach outperforms strong baselines on the complex event annotation derived from the HiEve dataset. We also analyze the effect of the context event.

3. We conduct an exploratory case study on the WIKIEVENTS dataset, showing that using complex events as the input for document-level argument extraction allows the system to only consider relevant sentences and is a promising approach for this task.

2 Related Work

Event Extraction In the last few years, most of the work on event extraction focuses on the sentence level (Chen et al., 2015; Nguyen et al., 2016; Sha et al., 2018; Lin et al., 2020). Experiments are usually performed on the ACE dataset (Walker et al., 2006). In that setting, events correspond to predicates and event extraction consists in (i) identifying the predicates in the sentence (Trigger Identification); (ii) classifying them according to a predefined ontology (Trigger Classification); (iii) identifying the arguments (Argument Identification); (iv) identifying the role of the argument relative to the predicate (Argument Classification).

However, since arguments are usually scattered across sentences, recent works (Ebner et al., 2020; Chen et al., 2020b; Li et al., 2021) extended the argument extraction components (iii) and (iv) to the document level, trying to capture arguments that are not in the same sentence as the predicate. Li et al. (2021) introduced the WIKIEVENTS dataset, going beyond the RAMS dataset (Ebner et al., 2020) by annotating several granular events per document. However, this approach does not address complex events and focuses on argument roles relative to granular events. In Section 4.6, we explore the effectiveness of using complex event as input for document-level argument extraction, experimenting on the WIKIEVENTS dataset.

Event Regions Chen et al. (2020a) addressed document-level argument extraction as well but they also obtain as byproducts event regions, defined as adjacent sentences that include relevant arguments. Complex events differ conceptually from event regions in two main points: (i) sentences that contain predicates of granular events in the same complex event can be separated in the text by sentences that include predicates of granular events in other complex events. (ii) the context of complex events may be overlapping as granular events in different complex events may share the same sentence.

Event-Event Relations Event-event relations include coreference and subevent relations. Event coreference (Lee et al., 2017; Barhom et al., 2019; Yu et al., 2022) allows one to group granular events referring to the same granular event while a subevent relation (Aldawsari and Finlayson, 2019; Wang et al., 2020) indicates that one granular event is a parent or child of another granular event. However, the notion of complex events is broader than both of them: (i) granular events in the same complex event also have other relations than subevent relations, such as temporal and causal relations; (ii) granular events in the same complex event can have different content. For example, $e3$: "attacked" and $e14$: "wounded" in Figure 1 are in the same complex event although they are not coreferred.

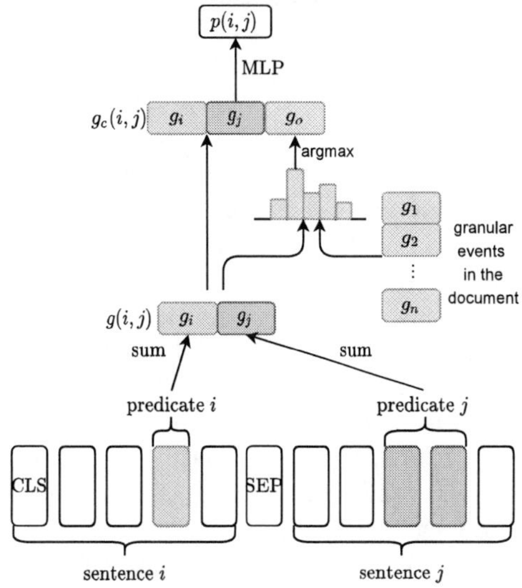

Figure 2: CONTEXTRL framework. g_i,g_j are contextualized representations of predicate i and j respectively. $g(i, j)$ denotes the concatenation of two granular event representations and g_o denotes the context event representation. $g_c(i, j)$ denotes the concatenation of $g(i, j)$ and g_o. $p(i, j)$ denotes the probability of belonging to the same complex event.

3 Method

In this section, we present our context-augmented learning approach CONTEXTRL. We address the complex event identification task as a pipeline, first predicting whether two granular events belong to the same complex event, independently of their position in the text, and then grouping them into complex events based on pairwise predictions. We first introduce our pairwise complex event relation extraction model in Section 3.1 and then introduce the granular event clustering step in Section 3.2.

3.1 Context-Augmented Pairwise Complex Event Relation Extraction

Our context-augmented model takes two sentences that contain predicates and the representations of other granular events (context event candidates) in the document as input, outputting a score indicating how likely two granular events belong to the same complex event. Since it is time-consuming and computationally expensive to encode all other granular events every time, we propose an efficient and effective way to obtain the representations of some granular events except the two granular events without further computation and regard them as context event candidates. During training and evaluation, with a batch size of n, we obtain representations of $2n$ granular events and use $2(n-1)$ granular events except the two granular events as context event candidates. To make sure these $2(n-1)$ granular events are in the same document as the two granular events, we only shuffle pairs within each document instead of shuffling across documents. We show its effectiveness in Section 4.5.

Given two granular events i and j, as shown in Figure 2, we first concatenate the sentences where their predicates appear using *[CLS]* and *[SEP]* and then encode the sequence using RoBERTa (Liu et al., 2019) to learn a contextualized representation for each token in the sequence. The concatenation of two sentences allows each token to learn the context from both sentences. Since granular events are instantiated by predicates, which are consecutive spans within the sentence, we sum up representations of tokens in the predicates element-wisely to obtain the predicate representations g_i and g_j.

Next, to select the context event, we first use the concatenation of two granular event representations $g(i,j)$ and the representations of other granular events in the document s to compute the attention distribution $\alpha(i,j)$ as follows:

$$e_k(i,j) = v^{\mathsf{T}}\tanh(W_g g(i,j) + W_s s_k + b_e)$$
$$\alpha(i,j) = \text{Softmax}(e(i,j))$$

where v, W_g, W_s are learnable matrix, b_e is a bias vector, s_k is the representation of k_{th} granular event and $e(i,j)$ is attention scores.

Then we select the granular event with the highest attention score as the context event and concatenate its representation g_o with the representations of two granular events to obtain the context-augmented representation $g_c(i,j)$ as follows:

$$o = \text{argmax}(\alpha(i,j))$$
$$g_c(i,j) = [g_i; g_j; g_o]$$

We also manually set an attention distribution threshold to guarantee that there is a granular event highly related to the two granular events. If the highest attention score is lower than the threshold, we mask the context event with 0.

Finally, we forward the context-augmented representation $g_c(i,j)$ into a linear layer to output the probability of belonging to the same complex event as follows:

$$p(i,j) = \text{Softmax}(W_c g_c(i,j) + b_c)$$

where W_c and b_c are a learnable weight matrix and a bias vector respectively.

3.2 Granular Event Clustering

After obtaining the pairwise complex event relation for each pair of granular events in the document, similar to the clustering step of previous work on the event coreference task (Choubey and Huang, 2017; Kenyon-Dean et al., 2018; Barhom et al., 2019; Cattan et al., 2020), we cluster them into complex events using agglomerative clustering. We define the distance between two granular events as the likelihood of not belonging to the same complex event. Agglomerative clustering merges event clusters until no cluster pairs have a linkage distance lower than the threshold, where the linkage distance is defined as the average distance of all the event pairs across two clusters.

In addition, we assume the scope of the complex event is the set of sentences that contain granular event predicates. Since a sentence may contain multiple predicates, the overlapping of scope between complex events is allowed by nature, which also contrasts with the event region definition shown in Section 2.

4 Experiments and Results

We conduct experiments on the complex event identification task, using our context-augmented representation learning approach CONTEXTRL to first extract pairwise relations and then group granular events into complex events through agglomerative clustering. We further present a promising case study on the WIKIEVENTS dataset (Li et al., 2021), showing the effectiveness of using only complex events as input for document-level argument extraction in Section 4.6.

	# Doc.	# Pairs	# CE	# Events/ CE
Train	60	38124	121	7.01
Dev	20	13810	44	6.93
Test	20	16227	54	7.07

Table 1: Statistics for the HiEve dataset and the complex event annotation derived from the HiEve dataset. CE denotes complex event.

4.1 Dataset

Since there is not a dataset tailored to the complex event identification task, we derive the complex event annotation from HiEve dataset (Glavaš et al., 2014) that annotates subevent and coreference relations. For each document, we first build an undirected acyclic graph where vertices are granular events connected by subevent relations (i.e., two events have either Parent-Child or Child-Parent relation) as edges, and then regard granular events in the same graph as belonging to the same complex event. We summarize the data statistics in Table 1. Note that the replication of this work on other texts requires the annotation of subevent relations with the constraint of not having two parents for the same subevent, unless they are co-referred, as in HiEve. Then, complex events can be derived from the annotation, as described here. We plan to explore the direct annotation of complex events in future work, which requires the compilation of fine-grained guidelines.

4.2 Baselines and Evaluation Metrics

We compare our model with three baselines. The first baseline is a Sequence Classification model (SC) plus the clustering step, where the Sequence Classification model encodes concatenated sentences using RoBERTa (Liu et al., 2019) and forwards the contextualized *[CLS]* token to a linear layer to compute the probability of belonging to the same complex event.

The second baseline is a strong predicate representation learning model (PRL) plus the clustering step, which replaces the contextualized *[CLS]* token with the concatenation of two predicate representations. The difference from our proposed model is that it does not use the context event.

Furthermore, since our complex event annotation is derived from the HiEve dataset that annotates subevent and coreference relations, we also compare our model with Wang et al. (2020), a SOTA joint constrained learning framework for extracting subevent, coreference and temporal relations, plus the clustering step. Since the HiEve dataset does not have temporal annotation, we only use its constraints related to subevent and coreference relations.

In terms of the clustering step, we use agglomerative clustering for the first two baselines that directly identify complex events. However, for the third baseline that extracts subevent relations to build complex events, since not all pairs of granular events in the same complex event have a subevent relation, using the probability of having subevent relations as distance would hinder such pairs from being grouped together. Thus, we follow the same graph-based clustering method as in Section 4.1.

In addition, we note that the method of Chen et al. (2020a) for event regions is not comparable with our method for complex event identification for the following reasons:

- The complex event and event region definitions are conceptually different, as the latter does not group granular events instantiated by predicates but rather partitions the document into segments, based on arguments.

- In the complex event annotation derived from the HiEve dataset, the proportion of complex events with consecutive sentences is only 91/219 = 41.6%, hindering Chen et al. (2020a)'s method from achieving competitive performance.

- Current datasets do not include gold data allowing such a comparison. Specifically, the HiEve dataset does not include argument annotation while the datasets CFEED and MUC-4 used in Chen et al. (2020a) do not annotate granular events.

Since both complex event identification and coreference resolution build clusters of granular events, we use coreference evaluation metrics [2] for evaluation, including MUC (Vilain et al., 1995), B^3 (Bagga and Baldwin, 1998), $CEAF_e$ (Luo, 2005) and BLANC (Recasens and Hovy, 2011), and report the results in Table 2. We also report CoNLL F_1 which is the average of MUC, B^3 and $CEAF_e$.

In addition, we report intermediary performances. For the pairwise complex event relation extraction task, the precision, recall and F_1 scores are reported in Table 3. For the subevent relation extraction task, we use the same evaluation setting as Wang et al. (2020), testing the model using 20% of the documents. The macro average precision, recall and F_1 scores of Parent-Child and Child-Parent relations are also reported in Table 3. Note that Wang et al. (2020) only kept 40% negative NoRel examples of the test set during evaluation while we evaluate on the entire test set.

[2]https://github.com/conll/reference-coreference-scorers

Model	MUC	B^3	$CEAF_e$	BLANC	CoNLL F_1
Using Subevent Relations for Complex Event Identification					
Wang et al. (Baseline)	72.68	60.38	55.39	47.22	62.82
Direct Complex Event Identification					
SC (Baseline)	51.69	59.94	43.34	48.9	51.66
PRL (Strong Baseline)	76.97	80.51	80.57	74.06	79.35
CONTEXTRL (Ours)	77.21	81.99	81.72	77.08	80.31

Table 2: Complex event identification performance on the complex event annotation derived from the HiEve. The columns correspond to different evaluation metrics. CoNLL F_1 is the average of MUC, B^3 and $CEAF_e$. We present our approach with 3 baselines. Wang et al. extracts subevent relations and then builds complex events by grouping granular events in the same acyclic graph to the same complex event. The last three models directly identify pairwise complex event relations and then cluster granular events into complex events through agglomerative clustering.

4.3 Experimental Setup

We encode the concatenated sequence using RoBERTa-large (Liu et al., 2019) to obtain 1024 dimensional token representations. Since the clustering step requires the pairwise prediction probability for each pair of granular events within the document, we set the max sequence length to 140 so that all pairs in the development set could fit in. The model contains 358.5M parameters in total. We use AdamW (Loshchilov and Hutter, 2017) to optimize the parameters, with a learning rate of 1e-6. For each setting, we train 12 epochs with a batch size of 16, and each epoch takes about 25 minutes. The attention distribution threshold of 0.047 is set based on the performance of the development set. The agglomerative clustering threshold for each setting is finetuned on the development set. We run all experiments on TITAN Xp GPU of size 12 GB.

Model	Precision	Recall	F_1
Subevent Relation Extraction			
Wang et al.	15.88	60.81	25.03
Pairwise Complex Event Relation Extraction			
SC	44.65	13.70	20.96
PRL	56.39	62.19	59.15
CONTEXTRL	55.75	64.85	59.96

Table 3: Subevent relation extraction performance on HiEve and Pairwise complex event relation extraction performance on the complex event annotation derived from the HiEve dataset. For Wang et al., we report the macro average scores of Precision, Recall and F_1. SC denotes the Sequence Classification model. PRL denotes the predicate representation learning model.

4.4 Complex Event Identification Results

In Table 2, we report evaluation metric scores for our approach and baselines. Our context-augmented representation learning approach CONTEXTRL outperforms all baselines, with a CoNLL F_1 score of 80.31. Besides, since it outperforms the SOTA subevent relation extraction model by a large margin, it motivates the study of complex event identification as an independent task.

We also show an example of complex events in the document predicted by CONTEXTRL in Figure 3. Granular events in green belong to a complex event describing the recent filing while granular events in red belong to another complex event describing the crime. These two complex events are interleaved in the document.

4.5 Context Event Analysis

As shown in Table 3, CONTEXTRL outperforms both baselines on the pairwise complex event relation extraction task. It achieves a F_1 score of 59.96, which is 0.81 higher than the strong baseline PRL. Compared with PRL, CONTEXTRL has a much higher recall which indicates it has fewer false negatives and more true positives. However, more true positives but a slightly lower precision indicates it contains more false positives. We discuss the reasons in the following paragraphs.

Effectiveness of Using Other Granular Events in the Batch as Context Event Candidates As shown in Table 4, in the test set, there are 2256 pairs of granular events belonging to the same complex event (positive pairs) and 13971 pairs of granular events not belonging to the same complex event (negative pairs). Of all positive pairs, 2238 (99.2%)

Complex Event Prediction

A new lawyer for OJ Simpson has filed a new attempt to gain his release from prison, alleging he was so badly *(e4: represented)* by lawyers in his *(e6: trial)* that he deserves a retrial. A 94-page document *(e7: filed)* in Court faults the *(e8: trial)* performance of attorneys Galanter and Grasso. It says he wanted to recover from sports memorabilia dealers family photos and personal mementoes *(e10: stolen)* from him. Simpson was convicted of charges including *(e14: kidnapping)* and armed *(e15: robbery)* in a hotel room crammed with two memorabilia dealers and a middle man, Simpson later *(e16: convicted)* of *(e17: felonies)*. Simpson, 64, was *(e18: sentenced)* to nine to 33 years behind bars. The *(e19: filing)* is a common next-step appeals strategy to blame trial and initial appeals attorneys for a defendant's conviction. Almost all grounds that lawyer *(e21: cited)* in the document fault Mr Galanter and Mr Grasso. Mr Grasso said "I'm behind OJ and I hope this *(e25: petition)* helps him get out of prison".

Figure 3: An example showing the prediction of complex events described in a document from the HiEve development set. Granular events in green belong to one complex event while granular events in red belong to another complex event. For clarity, not all event mentions are shown in the figure.

have at least one context event candidate that belongs to the same complex event as the pair of granular events, providing the opportunity of using an additional context event in the same complex event to improve the expressiveness of their relatedness. Of all negative pairs, 9440 (67.57%) have at least one context event candidate that belongs to the same complex event as one of the granular events in the pair. Of the rest of 4531 negative pairs, 4038 (89.12%) have both granular events that are not in any complex event. Such statistics indicate that negative pairs could select an additional context event from diversified candidates to make the pair of granular events distinguishable, relative to this context event.

Use Context Event in Positive Examples As we can see in Table 4, of all 2238 positive pairs that contain at least one context event candidate belonging to the same complex event as the pair of granular events, 655 mask the context event and the prediction accuracy is 64.12%. Of the rest of 1583 positive pairs, 942 use an additional context event that belongs to the same complex event as the pair of granular events, achieving an accuracy of 66.03%, while 641 pairs use other context events, having an accuracy of 64.12%. Therefore, adding an additional context event that belongs to the same complex improves the accuracy, which is equivalent to the number of true positives, and adding a context event not in the same complex event for positive pairs does no harm to the prediction.

Positive Pairs			
Same CE	Real Context	Mask	Total
Yes	1583 (1033)	655 (420)	2238
No	12 (6)	6 (3)	18
Total	1595	661	2256
Negative Pairs			
Same CE	Real Context	Mask	Total
Yes	5989 (5261)	3451 (3063)	9440
No	2700 (2670)	1831 (1816)	4531
Total	8689	5282	13971

Table 4: Analysis of the Pairwise complex event relation extraction performance of CONTEXTRL on complex event annotation. Real Context and Mask denote whether the pair uses a non-masked context event or not. Same CE (Yes or No) denotes whether the batch contains a context event candidate that belongs to the same Complex Event as one (for negative pairs) or two (for positive pairs) of the granular events in the pair. Number in parenthesis denotes the number of pairs predicted correctly.

Use Context Event in Negative Examples As shown in Table 4, of all 13971 negative pairs, 5282 mask the context event and the prediction accuracy is 92.37%. Of the rest of 8689 pairs, 2559 use a context event that belongs to the same complex event as one of the granular events in the pair, achieving an accuracy of 84.16%, while 6130 pairs use other context events, having an accuracy of 94.27%. Therefore, adding a context event in the same complex event as one of the granular events in a negative pair motivates the model to identify them to belong to the same complex event, increasing the number of false positives. Besides, since the model regards two granular events that describe different things as a single entity when computing the attention distribution, it is likely to select a context event not related to any of them in isolation, thus predicting the pair as negative with a great chance.

4.6 Complex Event as the Input of Document-level Argument Extraction

Since arguments are usually scattered across sentences, recent works on Argument Extrac-

	Train	Dev	Test
# Event types	49	35	34
# Arg types	57	32	44
# Docs	206	20	20
# Sentences	5262	378	492
# Events	3241	345	365

Table 5: Statistics for WIKIEVENTS dataset.

tion (Ebner et al., 2020; Chen et al., 2020b; Li et al., 2021) move from the sentence-level to the document-level (i.e., extracting the arguments from the whole document rather than a single sentence). However, the document not only has many noisy and irrelevant entities that prevent the model from extracting the arguments correctly, but also is too long to fit into a transformer-based model which limits the max sequence length.

Since granular events in the same complex event usually describe the same general content and they are unrelated to the granular events in other complex events, we assume the complex event should contain all the information required for the prediction of the arguments of its granular events.

Therefore, we conduct a case study on the WIKIEVENTS dataset to investigate the effectiveness of using complex events as input for document-level argument extraction. If the granular event belongs to a complex event, we use the sentences that contain granular event predicates in the same complex event as input; If the granular event does not belong to any complex event, we still use the entire document as input. We summarize the data statistics in Table 5.

Since WIKIEVENTS dataset does not have complex event annotation, we directly use our model CONTEXTRL trained on the complex event annotation derived from the HiEve dataset to group granular events in each document into complex events. Since the average number of annotated events per sentence in the test set is only 0.74, only using annotated granular events is not sufficient to build complex events. Therefore, we leverage an off-the-shelf verbal and nominal SRL system[3] to extract more granular events from documents. Consequently, 260/365 granular events belong to a complex event and using complex events as input reduces the average word count from 787.90 to 539.25.

After training the argument extraction model proposed in Li et al. (2021), we evaluate it on the test set with complex events as input and compare the performance with using the whole document as input. When using the whole document as input, the argument identification and classification head word F_1 scores are 71.21 and 66.55 respectively while using the complex event as input results in F_1 scores of 71.07 and 66.25 respectively. We could see that the model still achieves fairly close performance with much shorter inputs. Moreover, note that the complex event identification system is not trained on the WIKIEVENTS dataset, thus directly using the pre-trained model to identify complex events may also result in low performance.

We further show an "attack" granular event from the document, which has the largest improvement on the argument identification, in Figure 4. Using the complex event as input motivates the model to focus on the "attack" granular event, whereas using the whole document as input adds much irrelevant information (i.e. what is included in the interviews), distracting the model from the "attack" event and thus extracting incorrect arguments. Such difference in input and performance demonstrates the effectiveness of using complex events as the input for document-level argument extraction.

Complex Event as the Context
Osama bin Laden is charged to have had a role in the October 2000 attack on the USS Cole in the Yemeni port of Aden. This report features reporting by a Pulitzer-Prize-nominated team of New York Times reporters.
Whole Document as the Context
photo © 2001 corbis images all rights reserved web site copyright 1995-2014 WGBH educational foundation Hunting Bin Laden Osama bin Laden is charged to have had a role in the October 2000 attack on the USS Cole in the Yemeni port of Aden. This report features reporting by a Pulitzer-Prize-nominated team of New York Times reporters. Tracing the trail of evidence linking bin Laden to terrorist attacks, this report includes interviews with Times reporters. They discuss the terrorist attacks linked to bin Laden's complex network of terrorists, outline the elements of his international organization and details of its alliances and tactics.

Figure 4: An example showing the difference between using the complex event as the input and using the whole document as the input of document-level argument extraction. The predicate "attack" is in blue. Arguments in green are correctly extracted; arguments in red are missed; arguments in orange are extracted incorrectly.

[3]https://github.com/CogComp/SRL-English

5 Conclusion

In this work, we introduce the task of complex event identification and present a context-augmented approach CONTEXTRL tailored to this task. We show that our approach outperforms strong baselines on the annotation derived from the HiEve dataset and analyze positive effects of the context event. We further show the potential usefulness of using complex events as input for document-level argument extraction. For future work, we plan to directly annotate complex events from scratch with fine-grained guidelines. We also seek to extend our approach towards an end-to-end system with granular event extraction.

Acknowledgements

We thank the members of the Cognitive Computation Group for their insightful feedback ad well as the reviewers of the paper for their useful suggestions. This work was supported by Contracts FA8750-19-2-1004 and FA8750-19-2-0201 with the US Defense Advanced Research Projects Agency (DARPA). Approved for Public Release, Distribution Unlimited. This research is also based upon work supported in part by the Office of the Director of National Intelligence (ODNI), Intelligence Advanced Research Projects Activity (IARPA), via IARPA Contract No. 2019-19051600006 under the BETTER Program. The views and conclusions contained herein are those of the authors and should not be interpreted as necessarily representing the official policies, either expressed or implied, of ODNI, IARPA, the Department of Defense, or the U.S. Government. The U.S. Government is authorized to reproduce and distribute reprints for governmental purposes notwithstanding any copyright annotation therein.

References

Mohammed Aldawsari and Mark Finlayson. 2019. Detecting subevents using discourse and narrative features. In *ACL*, pages 4780–4790.

Amit Bagga and Breck Baldwin. 1998. Algorithms for scoring coreference chains. In *The first international conference on language resources and evaluation workshop on linguistics coreference*, volume 1, pages 563–566. Citeseer.

Shany Barhom, Vered Shwartz, Alon Eirew, Michael Bugert, Nils Reimers, and Ido Dagan. 2019. Revisiting joint modeling of cross-document entity and event coreference resolution. In *ACL*, pages 4179–4189.

Arie Cattan, Alon Eirew, Gabriel Stanovsky, Mandar Joshi, and Ido Dagan. 2020. Streamlining cross-document coreference resolution: Evaluation and modeling. *arXiv preprint arXiv:2009.11032*.

Pei Chen, Hang Yang, Kang Liu, Ruihong Huang, Yubo Chen, Taifeng Wang, and Jun Zhao. 2020a. Reconstructing event regions for event extraction via graph attention networks. In *AACL*, pages 811–820.

Yubo Chen, Liheng Xu, Kang Liu, Daojian Zeng, and Jun Zhao. 2015. Event extraction via dynamic multi-pooling convolutional neural networks. In *ACL*, pages 167–176.

Yunmo Chen, Tongfei Chen, and Benjamin Van Durme. 2020b. Joint modeling of arguments for event understanding. In *Proceedings of the First Workshop on Computational Approaches to Discourse*, pages 96–101.

Prafulla Kumar Choubey and Ruihong Huang. 2017. Event coreference resolution by iteratively unfolding inter-dependencies among events. In *EMNLP*, pages 2124–2133.

Seth Ebner, Patrick Xia, Ryan Culkin, Kyle Rawlins, and Benjamin Van Durme. 2020. Multi-sentence argument linking. In *ACL*, pages 8057–8077. Association for Computational Linguistics.

Goran Glavaš, Jan Šnajder, Marie-Francine Moens, and Parisa Kordjamshidi. 2014. HiEve: A corpus for extracting event hierarchies from news stories. In *LREC*, pages 3678–3683.

Kian Kenyon-Dean, Jackie Chi Kit Cheung, and Doina Precup. 2018. Resolving event coreference with supervised representation learning and clustering-oriented regularization. In *Proc. of the Joint Conference on Lexical and Computational Semantics*, pages 1–10.

Kenton Lee, Luheng He, Mike Lewis, and Luke Zettlemoyer. 2017. End-to-end neural coreference resolution. In *EMNLP*, pages 188–197.

Sha Li, Heng Ji, and Jiawei Han. 2021. Document-level event argument extraction by conditional generation. In *NAACL-HLT*, pages 894–908. Association for Computational Linguistics.

Ying Lin, Heng Ji, Fei Huang, and Lingfei Wu. 2020. A joint neural model for information extraction with global features. In *EMNLP-IJCNLP*, pages 7999–8009.

Yinhan Liu, Myle Ott, Naman Goyal, Jingfei Du, Mandar Joshi, Danqi Chen, Omer Levy, Mike Lewis, Luke Zettlemoyer, and Veselin Stoyanov. 2019. Roberta: A robustly optimized bert pretraining approach. ArXiv preprint arXiv:1907.11692.

Ilya Loshchilov and Frank Hutter. 2017. Decoupled weight decay regularization. In *ICLR*.

Xiaoqiang Luo. 2005. On coreference resolution performance metrics. In *EMNLP*, pages 25–32.

Thien Huu Nguyen, Kyunghyun Cho, and Ralph Grishman. 2016. Joint event extraction via recurrent neural networks. In *ACL*, pages 300–309.

Marta Recasens and Eduard Hovy. 2011. Blanc: Implementing the rand index for coreference evaluation. *Natural Language Engineering*, 17(4):485–510.

Lei Sha, Feng Qian, Baobao Chang, and Zhifang Sui. 2018. Jointly extracting event triggers and arguments by dependency-bridge rnn and tensor-based argument interaction. In *AAAI*.

Marc Vilain, John D Burger, John Aberdeen, Dennis Connolly, and Lynette Hirschman. 1995. A model-theoretic coreference scoring scheme. In *Sixth Message Understanding Conference (MUC-6): Proceedings of a Conference Held in Columbia, Maryland, November 6-8, 1995*.

Christopher Walker, Stephanie Strassel, Julie Medero, and Kazuaki Maeda. 2006. Ace 2005 multilingual training corpus ldc2006t06, 2006. *URL https://catalog. ldc. upenn. edu/LDC2006T06*.

Haoyu Wang, Muhao Chen, Hongming Zhang, and Dan Roth. 2020. Joint Constrained Learning for Event-Event Relation Extraction. In *Proc. of the Conference on Empirical Methods in Natural Language Processing (EMNLP)*.

Xiaodong Yu, Wenpeng Yin, and Dan Roth. 2022. Paired representation learning for event and entity coreference. In *Proc. of the Joint Conference on Lexical and Computational Semantics*.

Online Coreference Resolution for Dialogue Processing: Improving Mention-Linking on Real-Time Conversations

Liyan Xu **Jinho D. Choi**
Department of Computer Science
Emory University, Atlanta, USA
{liyan.xu,jinho.choi}@emory.edu

Abstract

This paper suggests a direction of coreference resolution for online decoding on actively generated input such as dialogue, where the model accepts an utterance and its past context, then finds mentions in the current utterance as well as their referents, upon each dialogue turn. A baseline and four incremental-updated models adapted from the mention-linking paradigm are proposed for this new setting, which address different aspects including the singletons, speaker-grounded encoding and cross-turn mention contextualization. Our approach is assessed on three datasets: *Friends*, *OntoNotes*, and *BOLT*. Results show that each aspect brings out steady improvement, and our best models outperform the baseline by over 10%, presenting an effective system for this setting. Further analysis highlights the task characteristics, such as the significance of addressing the mention recall.

1 Introduction

It has been made practical recently to apply coreference resolution to assist a broad scope of NLP tasks (Peng et al., 2017; Sahu et al., 2019; Gao et al., 2019), especially with the advent of neural end-to-end decoding and contextualized encoding (Lee et al., 2017, 2018; Joshi et al., 2019, 2020; Wu et al., 2020). However, it is quite limited to use existing coreference models in real-time dialogue processing systems, as most of them are not trained to handle an online decoding environment. In the dialogue domain, recent efforts have focused on ellipsis recovery and query rewriting (Quan et al., 2019; Tseng et al., 2021); in this work, we target to address a new perspective specifically for the online decoding, where the model sequentially accepts utterances in a dialogue and spits out valid mentions as well as their referent links for each latest utterance turn upon arrival, to be consumed by the downstream dialogue processing (Figure 1).

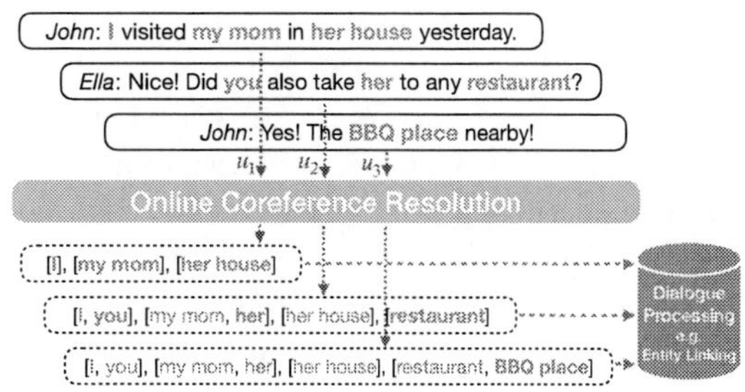

Figure 1: Illustration of the online setting. Predictions upon each turn are made immediately and ready for consumption by downstream applications. New mentions at each turn are marked by boldface in orange.

More formally, let u_i be the current (i'th) utterance in a dialogue $(u_1, .., u_i, ..)$; $\mathcal{M}_i$ be the mentions in u_i; $\mathcal{M}^{i-1}$ be the mentions from previously predicted clusters till u_{i-1}. The objective upon i'th turn is to: (1) identify $\mathcal{M}_i$ (2) identify conference links among $\mathcal{M}_i$, as well as from $\mathcal{M}_i$ to $\mathcal{M}^{i-1}$. We do not allow updates on $\mathcal{M}_i$ later, since that would be equivalent to general coreference resolution; in this work, we specifically target this underexplored online scenario under this setting, which requires accurate predictions upon each turn that could be directly consumed by downstream applications.

Several quasi-online coreference models have been proposed that maintain and update referents sequentially (Clark and Manning, 2015, 2016; Liu et al., 2019; Toshniwal et al., 2020; Xia et al., 2020). However, these models differ from our real online setting in two ways. First, only the latest utterance and its past sequence are visible in our setting, so that decisions need to be made without knowing the unseen future. Second, the decision of whether a span should be extracted or linked to others needs to be made immediately at each utterance turn, while quasi-online models can maintain an internal pool of candidates and make one final prediction after the entire document is processed.

For this task, we first introduce our baseline adapted from the classic mention-linking (ML) ap-

Proceedings of the 11th Joint Conference on Lexical and Computational Semantics, pages 341 - 347
July 14-15, 2022 ©2022 Association for Computational Linguistics

proach (Wiseman et al., 2015; Lee et al., 2017), and then propose four models where each one does an incremental update upon the previous model and addresses a specific perspective of this task, including the online inference, singletons, speaker-grounded encoding, and mention contextualization across utterance turns. For our approach, we do not use models that maintain explicit entities, because: (1) it has been shown that higher-order features from entity representation provide negative to marginal positive impact over ML counterparts despite their complexities (Xu and Choi, 2020; Xia et al., 2020; Toshniwal et al., 2020); (2) ML models are "stateless" so that they do not need to maintain decision states for previous mentions, which makes it more adaptable to applications in practice.

All models are evaluated on three datasets to test the generalizability of our approach, and the best model obtains over 10% improvement over the baseline on all datasets. Results and further analysis suggest that each aforementioned aspect can bring out steady improvement under the online setting, and highlight the singleton recovery to be the most critical component.

2 Approach

End-to-End Resolution Our model backbone is based on the end-to-end coreference resolution (Lee et al., 2018) with a Transformers encoder (Joshi et al., 2020). It scores every span for being a mention, and extracts top spans as mention candidates. Pairwise scoring is then performed among all candidates to determine the coreference links. Details of the model architecture can be referred by the paper from Lee et al. (2018), and we denote the original **c**oreference loss as $\mathcal{L}_c$.

Baseline (BL) We first present our baseline that takes the end-to-end model and trains in the exact same non-online way as prior work, but adapts the decoding to fit in our online inference setting.

Let u_i be the i'th utterance in the dialogue, and $|u_i|$ be its length (number of tokens). During online decoding upon u_i, this model takes an utterance sequence with past context as input, denoted by $\mathcal{U}_k^i = (u_k, .., u_i)$; $k \in [1, i)$ is dynamically determined by $\sum_{j=k}^{i} |u_j| \leq \Upsilon$ where Υ is the max number of tokens that the encoder accepts. Different from Lee et al. (2018), the mention candidates now consist of two parts: (1) the extracted top candidates solely from u_i, denoted as $\mathcal{X}_i$; (2) mentions from previously predicted clusters from $\mathcal{U}_k^{i-1}$, denoted as $\mathcal{M}_k^{i-1}$. Thereby the final candidate set $\mathcal{X}$ can be denoted as $\mathcal{X}_i \cup \mathcal{M}_k^{i-1}$. The same pairwise scoring as prior work is then performed on all candidates $\mathcal{X}$. Since we do not modify previous decisions in our setting, we keep coreference links among $\mathcal{X}_i$, or from $\mathcal{X}_i$ to $\mathcal{M}_k^{i-1}$, but not among $\mathcal{M}_k^{i-1}$. The predicted clusters after u_i will be updated in the same way by picking the referent antecedents according to coreference links.

Singleton Recovery (SR) SR is built upon BL to address the singleton problem. In BL, after processing each utterance sequence $\mathcal{U}_k^i$, the model filters out mention candidates from $\mathcal{X}_i$ that are not referent to any other candidates, according to the mention-linking paradigm. However, it results on losing non-anaphoric mentions that do not have referents in u_i, and yields a critical issue for online inference because mentions in u_i that are currently singletons but potentially will find referents in later utterances can get discarded too early.

To address this issue, we adopt a simple strategy similar to (Xu and Choi, 2021) that preserves any candidates whose mention scores are larger than a threshold of 0, denoted as $s_m > 0$, and creates a singleton cluster for each of which have not yet found any referent (intermediate singletons). However, as many annotation schemes do not require annotating singletons, e.g. CoNLL 2012, we may not have "true" gold labels covering every valid mentions, similar to the "misguidance of unlabeled entities" problem in named entity recognition (NER) (Li et al., 2021). Let Ψ_m^+ be the set of s_m of gold candidates according to the annotation, and Ψ_m^- be the set of s_m of other candidates that may also contain certain valid mentions (singletons). We mitigate the false negative issue of unlabeled mentions by applying dynamic negative sampling on Ψ_m^-, denoted as Φ_m^-, where $|\Psi_m^+| \approx |\Phi_m^-|$. Binary cross-entropy (BCE) loss is then used for this optimization to aid the threshold requirement:

$$\mathcal{L}_m = \text{BCE}(\Psi_m^+, \Phi_m^-) \quad (1)$$

$$\mathcal{L} = \alpha_c \cdot \mathcal{L}_c + \alpha_m \cdot \mathcal{L}_m \quad (2)$$

The final loss $\mathcal{L}$ is estimated by the weighted sum of $\mathcal{L}_m$ and $\mathcal{L}_c$ using the hyperparameters α_c and α_m.

Online Resolution (OR) OR is designed specifically for online inference on dialogues. Distinguished from BL that takes the whole document as input in training, OR takes $\mathcal{U}_k^i$ as input for both training and decoding, closing the gap. To capture subtle nuances from different speakers in the dialogue, we collect speaker names within each dialogue and assign a special token of position-based ID to each speaker (e.g. $\texttt{S}_1$, $\texttt{S}_2$) based on speaking orders, which is then prepended to its corresponding utterance (Wu et al., 2020). We also add `[SEP]` before u_i to signal the latest utterance. The following sequence is used as input for `OR`:

$$\{\texttt{S}_k\}^\frown u_k^\frown \cdots ^\frown \{\texttt{[SEP]}\}^\frown \{\texttt{S}_i\}^\frown u_i \quad (3)$$

During training upon the i'th turn, gold mentions in $\mathcal{U}_k^{i-1}$ are used as $\mathcal{M}_k^{i-1}$; the losses $\mathcal{L}_m$ and $\mathcal{L}_c$ are estimated only on candidates from u_i. Gradient accumulation is applied across multiple utterance turns, and we warm-start `OR` by initializing from the parameters of `SR`, followed by the online training described above. The decoding step for `OR` is kept the same as `BL` and `SR`.

Speaker-Grounding (`SG`) `SG` adds a speaker-grounding subtask upon `OR`, which is to facilitate the encoding of multi-speaker interaction which is an important aspect in dialogues. In `OR`, although each input token is conditioned on speaker tokens as in Eq (3), it is not obvious to the model that each token is from which speaker, which can be a barrier to learn the speaker interaction. To explicitly regularize the speaker encoding, we add a subtask to predict whether two candidates are from the same speaker based on their embeddings: the model gives a same-speaker score s_s such that pairs from the same speaker have $s_s > 0$ and others $s_s \leq 0$, forcing the semantic representation to fuse the speaker interaction. Let Ψ_s^+ be the set of s_s of pairs from the same speaker; Ψ_s^- be the set of s_s of other pairs. We optimize s_s by `BCE`, adding the loss in addition to $\mathcal{L}_c$ and $\mathcal{L}_m$:

$$s_s(x,y) = w_s \cdot [g_x \oplus g_y \oplus (g_x \circ g_y) \oplus (g_x - g_y)]$$

$$\mathcal{L}_s = \texttt{BCE}(\Psi_s^+, \Psi_s^-) \quad (4)$$

$$\mathcal{L} = \alpha_c \cdot \mathcal{L}_c + \alpha_m \cdot \mathcal{L}_m + \alpha_s \cdot \mathcal{L}_s \quad (5)$$

g_x/g_y denotes the representation of a candidate and w_s is the scoring parameter. $\oplus$ denotes concatenation and $\circ$ is the element-wise multiplication. We also apply negative sampling to keep $|\Psi_s^+| \approx |\Psi_s^-|$.

Span-Level Self-Attention (`SA`) `SA` is also added upon `OR` to achieve candidate contextualization. For each input $\mathcal{U}_k^i$, the representation of all candidates $\mathcal{X}$ is contextualized on the token-level because of Transformers' encoding. However, $\mathcal{M}_k^{i-1}$ is not used until the pairwise scoring. Therefore, $\mathcal{X}_i$ is not explicitly conditioned on the previously extracted mentions ($\mathcal{M}_k^{i-1}$) on the span-level. To capture the dependency among all mention candidates across utterances, we pass $\mathcal{X}$ to a scaled dot-product self-attention layer (Vaswani et al., 2017) before the pairwise scoring:

$$G' = \text{softmax}(\frac{(GW_q)(GW_k)^T}{\sqrt{d}})(GW_v), \quad (6)$$

where $G \in \mathbb{R}^{|\mathcal{X}| \times d}$ is the embedding matrix of all candidates, d is the embedding size, W_q, W_k, W_v are the parameters. G' is the new candidate-aware embedding matrix, which provides enhanced candidate representation for the pairwise scoring.

3 Experiments

Datasets All models are experimented on the following three datasets. *Friends* contains transcripts from the TV show in which personal mentions are annotated for entity linking. Each scene is considered an independent dialogue where utterances and speaker IDs are provided. We adapt the data split suggested by Zhou and Choi (2018). *Onto-Conv* consists of documents in three genres selected from OntoNotes 5.0: broadcasting and telephone conversations, and web text including discussion forums. We adapt the data split provided by Pradhan et al. (2012) and treat each document as a dialogue and every sentence as an utterance. *BOLT* follows the same annotation guideline as OntoNotes although documents are from discussion forums, SNS chats, and telephone conversations (Li et al., 2016). Since this is the first work using *BOLT* for this task, we create a new data split for future replicability (see A.1). Out of these three datasets, only *Friends* provides annotation of singletons.

The numbers of documents in the training, development, and test set of *Friends*, *Onto-Conv*, *BOLT* are provided in Table 2, along with the averaged numbers of speakers, entity clusters and utterances per document of each dataset. More details regarding the datasets are provided in Appendix A.1.

Settings Our implementation are based on the PyTorch coreference models from Xu and Choi (2020), and SpanBERT$_{\text{BASE}}$ is adopted as the encoder. The implementation and trained models

	Friends				*Onto-Conv*				*BOLT*			
	MUC	B^3	$CEAF_{\phi_4}$	Avg F1	MUC	B^3	$CEAF_{\phi_4}$	Avg F1	MUC	B^3	$CEAF_{\phi_4}$	Avg F1
BL	81.9	62.2	54.5	66.2 ($\pm$ 0.7)	70.5	54.8	43.9	56.4 ($\pm$ 0.2)	73.3	61.2	51.1	61.9 ($\pm$ 0.3)
SR	85.5	68.3	61.7	71.8 ($\pm$ 0.5)	77.5	63.2	55.2	65.2 ($\pm$ 0.6)	79.6	71.8	61.7	71.0 ($\pm$ 0.4)
OR	85.8	71.9	65.7	74.5 ($\pm$ 0.5)	78.0	63.6	55.6	65.7 ($\pm$ 0.3)	79.5	72.0	63.2	71.5 ($\pm$ 0.3)
+SG	85.7	73.6	67.0	75.3 ($\pm$ 0.4)	78.1	**64.3**	56.5	66.3 ($\pm$ 0.3)	**79.9**	72.3	63.4	71.8 ($\pm$ 0.3)
+SG+SA	**86.4**	**73.7**	**68.2**	**76.1** ($\pm$ 0.1)	**78.9**	**64.3**	**56.9**	**66.8** ($\pm$ 0.1)	**79.9**	**72.7**	**64.1**	**72.3** ($\pm$ 0.2)

Table 1: Results of all models in Section 2 on the evaluation sets of *Friends*, *Onto-Conv*, and *BOLT* datasets. MUC, B^3, and $CEAF_{\phi_4}$ show the F1 scores of the corresponding metrics, and their macro-average score (Avg F1) is used as the main evaluation metric. All scores presented here are the averaged scores over 3 repeated experiments; the standard deviations of Avg F1 scores are provided in the parentheses.

	TRN	DEV	TST	NS	NC	NU
F	987	122	192	3.7	4.6	18.7
O	566	100	95	2.4	16.2	49.5
B	943	117	117	2.9	9.2	18.1

Table 2: Statistics of the dataset *Friends* (F), *Onto-Conv* (O), *BOLT* (B). TRN, DEV, TST are the numbers of documents in the training, development, and test set of each dataset. NS, NC, NU are the averaged numbers of speakers, entity clusters, utterances per document of each dataset.

have been partially integrated with the open source project ELIT[1] (He et al., 2021).

During inference, all predicted clusters are collected and merged accordingly across utterances, and get evaluated by comparing them to the ground truth (all gold non-singleton clusters) at the end of each dialogue, in the same way as the CoNLL'12 shared task protocol. Detailed experimental settings are provided in Appendix A.2.

Results Table 1 describes the performance of all models on the test sets in the three datasets. These results are averaged across 3 repeated experiments; Avg-F1 is used as the main evaluation metric. Each proposed model gives steady improvement, and the best result is achieved by the OR+SG+SA model, surpassing the BL model on all datasets by significant margins of $\approx$10%. Among these models, singleton recovery contributes the most upon BL, demonstrating that albeit simple and intuitive, the training and inference of intermediate singletons is essential in online coreference resolution.

3.1 Analysis on Online Inference

To identify how model predictions are affected by online inference, all mentions in the predicted clusters are examined against the gold clusters. Table 3 shows the results of mention precision and recall from the four experimental settings.

	Friends		*Onto-Conv*		*BOLT*	
	P	R	P	R	P	R
N:BL	92.0	92.5	88.1	**83.6**	85.2	**82.8**
O:BL	**92.5**	85.3	**92.1**	60.6	**89.0**	64.8
O:SR	**92.5**	**93.2**	89.4	78.8	87.4	78.3
O:SR-	**92.5**	92.5	90.4	74.8	88.4	76.7

Table 3: The **P**recision and **R**ecall of all mentions in the predicted clusters on the test sets in the three datasets. N is **N**on-online inference as in CoNLL'12 shared task, O is **O**nline inference as in this work. SR- is the **S**ingleton **R**ecovery (SR) model without applying negative sampling on the mention loss in training.

Following observations are drawn by this analysis: **(1)** Comparing N:BL and O:BL, online inference indeed leads to a large drop on the mention recall as expected, without as much increase on precision, due to the omission of intermediate singletons. **(2)** Comparing O:BL and O:SR, singleton recovery (SR) significantly improves the mention recall (8% for *Friends* and 13+% for others) without sacrificing much precision. However, notice that the recall of O:SR for *Friends* is even higher than that of non-online inference (N:BL), but the recall for *Onto-Conv* and *BOLT* is still 4+% lower than that of N:BL. This is due to the fact that *Friends* does have singletons annotated while the other two do not. Thus, O:SR for *Friends* does not suffer from the "misguidance of unlabeled entities" problem. **(3)** Comparing O:SR and O:SR-, it illustrates the positive impact of applying negative sampling on mentions to alleviate the false-negative issue of unlabeled mentions, which improves recall while maintaining similar precision for online inference.

3.2 Analysis on Utterance Interaction

As we aim to build a robust online resolution model in the dialogue domain, understanding of individual

[1] https://github.com/emorynlp/elit

speakers is important especially in multi-party interaction. In comparison to the binary indicator used in BL and SR that can handle only up to two speakers, adding the subtask for speaker-grounded encoding is shown to perform better for multi-speaker dialogues: the improvement of OR+SG over SR is 3.5% F1 for *Friends*, but around 1% F1 for the other two. Our statistics show that 43% dialogues in *Friends* have at least 4 speakers, while being only 15% and 24% for the other two, suggesting that the multi-speaker environment indeed benefits more from the new speaker encoding scheme.

In addition, the percentages of pronouns in the gold mentions are 80.3%, 53.5%, and 63.5% in *Friends*, *Onto-Conv*, and *BOLT* respectively, which also highlights the importance of a better encoding scheme to handle a large portion of pronouns present in dialogue. Thus, we suggest to employ a more advanced dialogue encoding that utilizes the speaker interaction clues as one of the future research direction for this online-decoding task.

4 Conclusion

This paper presents a new coreference resolution direction that aims towards an online decoding setting for dialogue processing. A baseline and four incremental-updated models are proposed and evaluated on three datasets of the dialogue domain, and the best-performing model shows significant improvement over the baseline by ≈10% F1. Further analysis suggests the importance of mention recall and speaker encoding, which could serve as the next future directions of this online setting.

References

Kevin Clark and Christopher D. Manning. 2015. Entity-centric coreference resolution with model stacking. In *Proceedings of the 53rd Annual Meeting of the Association for Computational Linguistics and the 7th International Joint Conference on Natural Language Processing (Volume 1: Long Papers)*, pages 1405–1415, Beijing, China. Association for Computational Linguistics.

Kevin Clark and Christopher D. Manning. 2016. Improving coreference resolution by learning entity-level distributed representations. In *Proceedings of the 54th Annual Meeting of the Association for Computational Linguistics (Volume 1: Long Papers)*, pages 643–653, Berlin, Germany. Association for Computational Linguistics.

Yifan Gao, Piji Li, Irwin King, and Michael R. Lyu. 2019. Interconnected question generation with coreference alignment and conversation flow modeling. In *Proceedings of the 57th Annual Meeting of the Association for Computational Linguistics*, pages 4853–4862, Florence, Italy. Association for Computational Linguistics.

Han He, Liyan Xu, and Jinho D. Choi. 2021. Elit: Emory language and information toolkit.

Mandar Joshi, Danqi Chen, Yinhan Liu, Daniel S. Weld, Luke Zettlemoyer, and Omer Levy. 2020. Spanbert: Improving pre-training by representing and predicting spans. *Transactions of the Association for Computational Linguistics*, 8:64–77.

Mandar Joshi, Omer Levy, Luke Zettlemoyer, and Daniel Weld. 2019. BERT for coreference resolution: Baselines and analysis. In *Proceedings of the 2019 Conference on Empirical Methods in Natural Language Processing and the 9th International Joint Conference on Natural Language Processing (EMNLP-IJCNLP)*, pages 5803–5808, Hong Kong, China. Association for Computational Linguistics.

Kenton Lee, Luheng He, Mike Lewis, and Luke Zettlemoyer. 2017. End-to-end neural coreference resolution. In *Proceedings of the 2017 Conference on Empirical Methods in Natural Language Processing*, pages 188–197, Copenhagen, Denmark. Association for Computational Linguistics.

Kenton Lee, Luheng He, and Luke Zettlemoyer. 2018. Higher-order coreference resolution with coarse-to-fine inference. In *Proceedings of the 2018 Conference of the North American Chapter of the Association for Computational Linguistics: Human Language Technologies, Volume 2 (Short Papers)*, pages 687–692, New Orleans, Louisiana. Association for Computational Linguistics.

Xuansong Li, Martha Palmer, Nianwen Xue, Lance Ramshaw, Mohamed Maamouri, Ann Bies, Kathryn Conger, Stephen Grimes, and Stephanie Strassel. 2016. Large multi-lingual, multi-level and multi-genre annotation corpus. In *Proceedings of the Tenth International Conference on Language Resources and Evaluation (LREC'16)*, pages 906–913, Portorož, Slovenia. European Language Resources Association (ELRA).

Yangming Li, lemao liu, and Shuming Shi. 2021. Empirical analysis of unlabeled entity problem in named entity recognition. In *International Conference on Learning Representations*.

Fei Liu, Luke Zettlemoyer, and Jacob Eisenstein. 2019. The referential reader: A recurrent entity network for anaphora resolution. In *Proceedings of the 57th Annual Meeting of the Association for Computational Linguistics*, pages 5918–5925, Florence, Italy. Association for Computational Linguistics.

Nanyun Peng, Hoifung Poon, Chris Quirk, Kristina Toutanova, and Wen-tau Yih. 2017. Cross-sentence n-ary relation extraction with graph LSTMs. *Transactions of the Association for Computational Linguistics*, 5:101–115.

Sameer Pradhan, Alessandro Moschitti, Nianwen Xue, Olga Uryupina, and Yuchen Zhang. 2012. CoNLL-2012 shared task: Modeling multilingual unrestricted coreference in OntoNotes. In *Joint Conference on EMNLP and CoNLL - Shared Task*, pages 1–40, Jeju Island, Korea. Association for Computational Linguistics.

Jun Quan, Deyi Xiong, Bonnie Webber, and Changjian Hu. 2019. GECOR: An end-to-end generative ellipsis and co-reference resolution model for task-oriented dialogue. In *Proceedings of the 2019 Conference on Empirical Methods in Natural Language Processing and the 9th International Joint Conference on Natural Language Processing (EMNLP-IJCNLP)*, pages 4547–4557, Hong Kong, China. Association for Computational Linguistics.

Sunil Kumar Sahu, Fenia Christopoulou, Makoto Miwa, and Sophia Ananiadou. 2019. Inter-sentence relation extraction with document-level graph convolutional neural network. In *Proceedings of the 57th Annual Meeting of the Association for Computational Linguistics*, pages 4309–4316, Florence, Italy. Association for Computational Linguistics.

Shubham Toshniwal, Sam Wiseman, Allyson Ettinger, Karen Livescu, and Kevin Gimpel. 2020. Learning to Ignore: Long Document Coreference with Bounded Memory Neural Networks. In *Proceedings of the 2020 Conference on Empirical Methods in Natural Language Processing (EMNLP)*, pages 8519–8526, Online. Association for Computational Linguistics.

Bo-Hsiang Tseng, Shruti Bhargava, Jiarui Lu, Joel Ruben Antony Moniz, Dhivya Piraviperumal, Lin Li, and Hong Yu. 2021. CREAD: Combined resolution of ellipses and anaphora in dialogues. In *Proceedings of the 2021 Conference of the North American Chapter of the Association for Computational Linguistics: Human Language Technologies*, pages 3390–3406, Online. Association for Computational Linguistics.

Ashish Vaswani, Noam Shazeer, Niki Parmar, Jakob Uszkoreit, Llion Jones, Aidan N Gomez, Ł ukasz Kaiser, and Illia Polosukhin. 2017. Attention is all you need. In *Advances in Neural Information Processing Systems*, volume 30, pages 5998–6008. Curran Associates, Inc.

Sam Wiseman, Alexander M. Rush, Stuart Shieber, and Jason Weston. 2015. Learning anaphoricity and antecedent ranking features for coreference resolution. In *Proceedings of the 53rd Annual Meeting of the Association for Computational Linguistics and the 7th International Joint Conference on Natural Language Processing (Volume 1: Long Papers)*, pages 1416–1426, Beijing, China. Association for Computational Linguistics.

Wei Wu, Fei Wang, Arianna Yuan, Fei Wu, and Jiwei Li. 2020. CorefQA: Coreference resolution as query-based span prediction. In *Proceedings of the 58th Annual Meeting of the Association for Computational Linguistics*, pages 6953–6963, Online. Association for Computational Linguistics.

Patrick Xia, João Sedoc, and Benjamin Van Durme. 2020. Incremental neural coreference resolution in constant memory. In *Proceedings of the 2020 Conference on Empirical Methods in Natural Language Processing (EMNLP)*, pages 8617–8624, Online. Association for Computational Linguistics.

Liyan Xu and Jinho D. Choi. 2020. Revealing the myth of higher-order inference in coreference resolution. In *Proceedings of the 2020 Conference on Empirical Methods in Natural Language Processing (EMNLP)*, pages 8527–8533, Online. Association for Computational Linguistics.

Liyan Xu and Jinho D. Choi. 2021. Adapted end-to-end coreference resolution system for anaphoric identities in dialogues. In *Proceedings of the CODI-CRAC 2021 Shared Task on Anaphora, Bridging, and Discourse Deixis in Dialogue*, pages 55–62, Punta Cana, Dominican Republic. Association for Computational Linguistics.

Ethan Zhou and Jinho D. Choi. 2018. They exist! introducing plural mentions to coreference resolution and entity linking. In *Proceedings of the 27th International Conference on Computational Linguistics*, pages 24–34, Santa Fe, New Mexico, USA. Association for Computational Linguistics.

A Appendix

A.1 Dataset

The annotation in *Friends* includes plural links where a mention can belong to more than one entity clusters. We discard those mentions with plural links in our experiments and leave them as future work. All remaining mentions for *Friends* are personal mentions.

BOLT does not come with a predefined train/dev/test split. We use a random split of 80%, 10%, 10% of documents in each genre for the train/dev/test split. In addition, we only use genres "en" and "sm" in *BOLT*, as other genres currently do not have user IDs provided and only constitute less than 5% documents of entire dataset. The details of our split are provided in `https://github.com/lxucs/online-bolt`.

A.2 Implementation

For training on entire dialogue contexts as document input (`BL` and `SR`), we follow the similar hyperparameter settings as Joshi et al. (2019, 2020); Xu and Choi (2020), where long documents are split into independent segments with the maximum sequence length of 384 for $\text{SpanBERT}_{\text{BASE}}$. We employ the learning rate of 2×10^{-5} for BERT parameters and 2×10^{-4} for task parameters with the dropout rate as 0.3. Maximum span length is set to 6 for *Friends* and 25 for *Onto-Conv* and *BOLT*. In the coarse pruning stage, we keep a maximum number of antecedents as 20 for *Friends* and 50 for *Onto-Conv* and *BOLT*.

For online training and inference on the utterance sequence input (`OR`, `+SG`, `+SA`), we use one BERT segment so that the length of current utterance with past context does not exceed 384 tokens in our experiments. Gradient accumulation of 16 steps is applied during online training. We use the same learning rates and training epochs, similar as training on document input. Our best model has $\alpha_c = 1, \alpha_m = 0.1, \alpha_s = 0.1$ for the multi-task learning.

All experiments are conducted on NVIDIA TITAN RTX GPUs with 24GB memory. Training on document input takes around 3 hours and training on online input takes around 8-12 hours. All proposed methods have similar inference time, as they follow similar architecture and all operate on the online inference for prediction.

Author Index

Association for Computational Linguistics
209 N. Eighth Street
Stroudsburg, Pennsylvania 18360

ISBN 978-1-7138-5641-2

9 781713 856412

CURRAN ASSOCIATES INC.
proceedings.com